WASHINGTON NOW

A Cass Canfield BOOK

Other Kiplinger books

Boom and Inflation Ahead, 1958

Washington Is Like That, 1942

W. M. Kiplinger
  with Austin H. Kiplinger

WASHINGTON

Harper & Row, Publishers

NOW by Austin H. Kiplinger
with Knight A. Kiplinger

New York, Evanston, San Francisco, London

FIRST EDITION

Designed by C. Linda Dingler

Library of Congress Cataloging in Publication Data

Kiplinger, Austin H   1918–
    Washington now.

    (A Cass Canfield book)
    Includes index.
    1. United States—Politics and government—
1945–   2. Washington, D.C.—Description—1951–
I. Kiplinger, Knight A., joint author.   II. Title.
JK271.K46   1975   320.9′73′0924   74–15835
ISBN 0-06-012397-4

75 76 77 78 79 10 9 8 7 6 5 4 3 2 1

CONTENTS

ACKNOWLEDGMENTS   vii

1. PLACE OF POWER AND POLITICS   1
2. THE PRESIDENT   10
3. THE WHITE HOUSE   20
4. SOME IMPORTANT PEOPLE   28
5. NIXON'S WATERGATE   61
6. A DAY IN THE LIFE OF WASHINGTON   69
7. THE CAPITAL IN THE MAKING   80
8. THE CITY AND ITS PEOPLE   91
9. THE SOCIAL SCENE   109
10. GOVERNMENT WORKERS GALORE   124
11. CONGRESS   137
12. THE PRACTICE OF POLITICS   155
13. COURTS AND JUSTICE   167
14. CORRUPTION OVER THE YEARS   177
15. LAWYERS, LAWYERS, LAWYERS   190
16. LOBBIES AT WORK   203
17. THE PENTAGON AT PEACE   216
18. THE MAKING OF FOREIGN POLICY   229
19. AMBASSADORS ON THE JOB   243
20. THE NEWS CORPS   257
21. WOMEN IN WASHINGTON   273
22. CONSUMER CAPITAL   288
23. THE BLACK PRESENCE   299

24. EQUAL OPPORTUNITY   320

25. MANAGING THE ECONOMY   333

26. DOING BUSINESS WITH THE GOVERNMENT   348

27. WHERE YOUR TAXES GO   354

28. WHAT YOUR GOVERNMENT KNOWS ABOUT YOU   361

29. LABOR HEADQUARTERS   375

30. ASSOCIATIONS FOR ALL   390

31. THE EDUCATION VINEYARDS   398

32. SCIENCE AND THINK TANKS   411

33. REGULATING BUSINESS   421

34. GOVERNMENT AND ENERGY   433

35. FOOD, FARMERS, AND THE GROCERY BILL   439

36. MONTHLY CHECKS FOR MILLIONS   450

37. MONITORING THE ENVIRONMENT   456

38. GOVERNMENT AND HEALTH   470

39. HOUSING HELPER   482

40. BATTLEGROUND OF TRANSPORTATION   494

41. THE POSTAL SERVICE   505

42. PATRON OF THE ARTS   513

43. IMPORTED WEALTH
       (AND SOME HOME GROWN)   524

44. SEEING THE SIGHTS   536

45. CAPITAL OF THE FUTURE   548

     INDEX   553

ACKNOWLEDGMENTS

This book was begun at the same time Snoopy began writing his. I am happy to say we finished first, although it has taken nearly three years. Before that, *Washington Now* had a record of thirty years of gestation (which is more than even an elephant requires). It really began in 1942 with the publication of *Washington Is Like That,* authored by my father, W. M. Kiplinger. I was his collaborator on the project, but the spiritual genie behind it was Cass Canfield, then as now one of the great editorial catalysts in the publishing world. It was his idea that updated versions be published from time to time—a plan which, though sound enough, was blocked by World War II and by various editorial exigencies in ensuing years.

Finally in 1972, I agreed to write a new book about Washington. As things turned out, the book's time-in-work spanned the era of Watergate, the resignation of a Vice President and a President, the succession of a new President, and the formation of two new Congresses. Anything that lasts that long in Washington undergoes considerable change, and this book is no exception. During its preparation the U.S. economy roared into double-digit inflation, then skidded into recession. To cope with all the facets of this changing scene, I have had to have help, and I have called for it wherever I could find special expertise.

To the staff of the *Kiplinger Letters* and *Changing Times* magazine, I extend thanks for a continuing stream of information, judgment, and criticism.

I offer special thanks to:

Cass Canfield for his wise counsel (and his persistence in keeping our feet to the fire).

Kitty Benedict of Harper & Row for her coordination and constant prodding.

Emilie Mayer, my administrative assistant, who suffered through the whole effort from original outline to final proofs.

Elma Dotter, who checked the copy for factual accuracy (but if some errors did slip through the fault is mine).

Mort Singer, executive editor of the *Kiplinger Letters,* for his editorial guidance.

George Kennedy, senior editor of the *Letters,* for his copy help.

For invaluable assistance on background facts and editing, thanks to: Bill Senior, Dick Golden, Dale Taft, John Harms, Sid Levy, Alva Fitch, Len Fried, Jack Kiesner, Milt Christie, Steve Ivins, Bob Harvey, Charles Cerami, Sid Sulkin, Arnold Barach, Jack Hazard, Charles Schaeffer, Ted Miller, and Mamie Hardy.

A number of "old Washington hands" provided me with factual memoranda on parts of the subject. For this I extend my appreciation to: Winzola McLendon, Lealon Martin, Fannie Granton, Julius Duscha, Mary Clay Berry,

John Cramer, Lloyd Norman, Michael Frome, Theodor Schuchat, Paul Hencke, S. J. Micciche, and Arch Parsons.

To my wife Gogo and my son Todd I apologize for any irascibility that can be charged to the writing of this book.

And with highest professional respect, I thank Knight Kiplinger, my son and collaborator, a talented reporter and writer who, I hope, has enjoyed this experience as much as I have enjoyed working with him.

AUSTIN H. KIPLINGER

Washington, D.C.
April, 1975

1 PLACE OF POWER AND POLITICS

Washington, for better or worse, is an integral part of your life.

As a city, Washington is synthetic—created expressly to be a nation's capital and only recently acquiring the finer amenities of life. It is synthetic in another way, too, for it is a synthesis of what America has poured into it. It is a place of accommodation, where ideals and ambitions collide and merge into laws and programs for 213 million Americans, from the cradle to the grave.

Washington is neither as good as some wish it to be nor as bad as many believe it is. It could be better and probably will be. It could be worse, and there will be times when it is. Good, bad, and in between, Washington affects what you do and what you may not do, how well you live, how warm your house will be in winter, how cool in summer, and how you will get to your office, school, or shopping center.

Whatever happens elsewhere in the country has its effect on Washington, and is affected by it. Washington responds to droughts in the corn belt and floods in Mississippi. It vibrates to riots in the cities, strikes in the coal country, and mortgage interest rates. Washington hears from Henry Kissinger as he travels in the Middle East, and it hears from the voters as they cast their ballots in the Middle West. It gets graded by the people who pay the bills, and so it is concerned with prosperity and depression, with bank failures and airline mergers, with conservation, preservation, grocery bills, and gasoline supply.

Washington is a great sluiceway for money. Not much of the money stays in Washington, but more than $300 billion gets taken in and paid out every year. It collects payroll taxes (in) and sends social security checks (out). It takes corporation taxes (in) and pays for defense procurement (out). It deals with gasoline taxes (in) and makes transit grants (out). It levies import duties (in) and dispenses research grants (out).

Washington, in fact, has something for everyone. Like a giant prescription counter, it can dispense a concoction for every symptom, though some of its critics have suspected for years that its prescriptions may not always be the right medicine for the ailment (and some of them may be definitely "contra-indicated").

Some of what Washington has, you may not like—like taxes. Some of what it has, like social security payments, take a lifetime to collect. And nearly everything it does has impact, so you have to pay attention to it. In Washington the United States finds out what it thinks. Not that Washington "thinks," because Washington doesn't really do much original thinking. The thinking is more likely to be done around the country—in homes, schools, and churches, in union halls and chambers of commerce, in stores, offices, laboratories, and bars.

Washington does not always do the leading, either. It often follows. In some ways, Washington is like a space satellite relay station absorbing what is sent to it and bouncing back a reflection of what it receives.

Washington often seems to be talking when it is, in fact, listening and reacting to what it has heard. Even when a loser complains that Washington is not sensitive to his views, or the new legislation is not to his liking, the chances are that the sensitive antennae of Washington operatives have been accurately tuned to the signals from elsewhere and have rebroadcast a sympathetic response.

In Washington there is no greater security than knowing you are in solid with the people back home, and if you're not, you may end up back home where you started. Back home is where the votes are. Back home is where the strength comes from, where the power really lies.

Washington is where the power gets put together, where the diversity of America is translated into policy. The many pieces of power—from New York and Illinois, from California and Texas, from New Hampshire, Ohio, Tennessee, or South Carolina—are like parts of a jigsaw puzzle. When you see the final picture, you may not like it, but more often than not, it is an accurate picture of American life.

Washington is a city of superlatives, providing one of the world's greatest collections of "mosts" and "more thans."

Washington ranks first among the big cities of the world in the number of telephones per capita. It has the highest per capita number of lawyers, journalists, and party caterers (and also psychiatrists). It ranks first in the nation in per capita liquor sales. It has the highest average level of education of any large city in the nation, and two of its suburban counties (Montgomery in Maryland and Fairfax in Virginia) rank first and second in per capita median incomes.

Something else you should note about Washington: it has an astonishing ability to absorb or cushion national conflict, then transform the episode into national policy. If it cannot concoct a policy to suit the situation, Washington can blunt the issue, smother it in talk, or stifle it with procrastination. It has done this for years with such issues as national health insurance, environmental controls, and national energy policy—keeping the matters muted but alive until circumstances and public opinion were finally ready for action. It did this with civil rights, until in the 1960s the question became an issue whose time had arrived.

Washington used the same delaying tactics on relations between business and labor until finally, in the midst of the depression 1930s, Congress resolved the bloody battles between unions and employers with passage of the Wagner Act, and a few years later it reshaped its earlier handiwork with the Taft-Hartley law.

Again in 1973 and 1974, Washington demonstrated its capacity to wrestle with an agonizing and divisive issue by public dissection of the scandal called Watergate. Through two long and painful years, the Washington apparatus ground through a series of charges and countercharges, investigations, indictments, hearings, trials, and impeachment proceedings. In the end, it produced a consensus which brought the resignation of Richard Nixon, even without the panoply of a Senate trial. More than a hundred years earlier, another President, Andrew Johnson, had stood firm and been acquitted. In both cases, the nation accepted the verdict that had been rendered—however untidily—in the chambers, corridors, and committee rooms of Washington.

You hear people ask, "What does Washington think?" Well, it thinks a lot of different things, all at the same time.

It thinks taxes are too high—and too low.

It thinks there should be more legislation—and less.

It thinks there are too many tax "loopholes"—or that these aren't loopholes at all, only "incentives."

It believes in the poor and the rich and the young and the old.

It likes subsidies, and it abhors them.

It believes in federal aid to education and in local initiative.

It believes in more welfare and less.

The ultimate result of this mishmash and variety is a stream of laws and regulations (with a heavy by-product of paper, for Washington is one of the nation's biggest producers of waste paper).

Washington's output of laws covers almost everything under the sun, from food and fuel to wild horses; from taxes to trucks and from trade to mortgage interest rates.

Make your own list. You can do it by looking around the room, and you will find a law or regulation affecting every object in it, except the ideas expressed in the Holy Bible, the Torah, or the Koran, each of which the government is forbidden to touch, by virtue of the separation of church and state.

Most of all, the laws that emanate from Washington create—or reflect—the tone and climate of our lives: in our work, our leisure, and ultimately our survival. The rules and regulations reflect not only what we think but also what we feel, what we want to be and what we think we ought to be, and above all, what we actually are.

Washington is a rare collection of people. It includes such specimens as the President and his Cabinet, members of Congress, judges of the courts, Pentagon brass and enlisted personnel, government workers, representatives of labor, business, and the arts, agents of the Izaak Walton League, foot doctors, and the National Organization for Women. There are also ambassadors, representing other governments. There are the wealthy transplants from other parts of the country who came here to see and be seen. (They are not recluses, for there is no point in coming to Washington to be a recluse.) There are journalists and lawyers and experts on financial disintermediation. There are economists and lobbyists, as well as a horde of sightseers. There are old cynics and young idealists. There are blacks, whites, and American Indians, who get along together pretty well most of the time.

Washington is located midway between North and South, and definitely in "the East," about six hours' jet flying time from London and Paris, both of which are closer than the fiftieth state of the U.S.—Hawaii. Washington's location was set by compromise in the early days of the Republic, and it has been a symbol of compromise ever since.

Most other large world capitals (with the exception of Ottawa, Brasilia, and Canberra) were already ancient and natural cities when they became capitals. They already had their temper and style and way of life. But in Washington, these have been created within less than two hundred years. Not until 1800 did the President have a permanent house to live in, and even then

Abigail Adams complained that it was drafty and gloomy when she hung out her laundry in the East Room. But Washington grew slowly. People came in small numbers in the early days, and many of them left as soon as they could. The politics of the nation changed slowly also. And even in recent years, the "new politics" ends up being much like the "old politics," despite the advertising gloss applied now and then by campaign managers.

Yet within the past forty years, Washington's influence on the lives of people has intensified. Bernard Baruch, in presenting his public papers to Princeton University in 1964, observed: "The role of government and its relationship to the individual has been changed so radically that today government is involved in almost every aspect of our lives." The observation was by no means original, but, at age ninety-three, he had been around to see it all happen. Out of the depths of the depression of the 1930s, Washington rose in strength. During the Roosevelt New Deal, it fashioned a central government out of a collection of local and regional interests. Seventy years after the Civil War had kept the nation from flying apart, Washington at last cemented it together. And then, with World War II, Washington was turned into an international capital, the defense center of the Western democratic world. Allied liaison and lend-lease were blended in Washington, and out of them came postwar reconstruction, also headquartered in the U.S. capital. The International Monetary Fund and the World Bank set up shop. Washington was riding tall in the international saddle, as yet undisturbed by dollar gaps, dollar gluts, or Mideast oil embargoes.

All this brought changes in the appearance of Washington and its pace. From a culturally provincial federal district of 800,000 people (with a thin fringe of suburbia), it has grown into a metropolitan area of about 3 million. Surrounding suburbs became citified, and former countryside became suburbs in the manner of other big cities around the world.

The changes in size brought a new life style, culturally embellished by a Kennedy Center, an Arena Stage, new art galleries, concerts in the parks, little theaters, small studios, and hippie-style saloons. Now there are swinger joints and posh restaurants and new private clubs. There are also robberies, muggings, and break-ins—other evidence of contemporary big-city life.

As the nation prepares for the two hundredth anniversary of U.S. independence, Washington's Bicentennial Commission tries valiantly to pull its diverse elements together into a cohesive program reflecting civic pride, purpose, historic appreciation, and a commitment to continued improvement. The white community and the black community (still quite aloof from each other) spar for leadership. Washington does not stir in the hearts of its citizens the same hometown spirit that motivates the citizens of such cities as Philadelphia, Chicago, Cincinnati, or San Francisco. Though Washington has its Board of Trade, composed of local businessmen who hope to devise a formula to give the city added strength, the nation's capital remains blasé toward most of their importunings.

Behind the changing life styles, the business of governing goes on—with confrontations between White House and Congress, collisions between opposing lobbies, friction between legislative blocs, consisting of northern liberals, southern conservatives, and moderate middle Americans. In the end, it often turns out that the "new Washington," like the new cleanser, isn't any more effective than the old Fels Naphtha, but one way or another, it turns out its product of policies and programs.

The laws and policies that bear the dateline "Washington" don't really originate in Washington. They are born inside the thousands of groups and interests and organizations around the country. The ideas get sent to Washington through the associations that represent these groups. Every year, more such associations move their headquarters to the capital, because this is where their contacts are. Look in the Washington telephone book, under "ASSOCIA- TIONS." There you will find "AAA" (the American Automobile Association). Read on and you will find the AARP (American Association of Retired Persons) and ASCAP (American Society of Composers, Authors and Pub- lishers). A little bit farther, you will come to American Association of School Administrators. Later you graduate into "American Associations of . . ." and "Associations for . . ."

Associations for what? For Jesuit colleges, for cultural interchange, for children with learning disabilities; for third-class mail users, tobacco manufac- turers, and cinema laboratories; for governing boards, Indian affairs, physical training, and thousands of other interests. Seven pages and thirty solid columns later, you will arrive at the final listings: "Zero Population Growth" and "Zionist Organization."

These are working parts of the governmental system. They headquarter in the capital city of Washington because they are part of the gear system which transmits needs and interests into final legislation. They are called "interest groups," and they are considered insidious or selfish if they represent some- body else. Yet without them, Congress could not function. Recently, two Senate members scolded an association for not giving them a positive program for enactment. "We know we have to do something and we agree with your position, but we don't know enough about the details to draft a plan. Tell us what you want."

And then there are the lawyers. Washington is made to order for lawyers, and lawyers are made to order for Washington. It's a perfect marriage. There are lawyers who regulate and lawyers who persuade the regulators. Lawyers who write rules and lawyers who interpret the rules (and other lawyers who oppose the rules). Lawyers for industry, for labor, for consumers, lawyers for causes (with a fee), and lawyers for causes (without a fee). Lawyers who litigate, lawyers who negotiate, and lawyers who mediate. Lawyers, lawyers, lawyers. If anyone ever succeeded in following the advice of Dick the Butcher to Jack Cade—"The first thing we do, let's kill all the lawyers"—Washington would hardly know what to do with itself. But such a fate is not likely, since Washington is a creature of law, and the lawyers have ample resources for defending themselves.

Another thing: almost nobody ever leaves Washington. Defeated congress- men? They may drop out of sight, but most of them stay around to practice law, to lobby, or to get appointed to the Tariff Commission, the Court of Claims, or some little-known agency or advisory board. Newspaper obituaries contain biographies of men and women who were prominent in public affairs forty or fifty years ago and lived quietly in Washington long after: such colorful personalities as former Senator Burton K. Wheeler of Montana, former Senator Henry Fountain Ashurst of Arizona, and Gerald P. Nye, a onetime isolationist senator from North Dakota. And such stately dowagers as Mrs. Edith Bolling Galt Wilson, the widow of President Woodrow Wilson, who, with the famous Colonel Edward House, informally ran the affairs of state while her husband lay ill in the White House. Recently, when a Connecticut Avenue apartment building was converted into a condominium, an enterprising local real estate editor reported that the building's tenants included a granddaughter of Ulysses S. Grant, Princess Julia Grant Cantacuzene, now ninety-eight years old, who was born in the White House and married a Russian nobleman in 1899. Another tenant was Mrs. Nellie Tayloe Ross, who had been elected governor of Wyoming in 1924 and was appointed by Franklin D. Roosevelt to be Director of the Mint in 1933. (Mrs. Ross elected to buy one of the condominiums.)

A few former White House staffers and Cabinet members leave town to return to private business in Los Angeles (as H. R. "Bob" Haldeman did before going on trial for Watergate) or to join the faculty of the University of Texas (as Walt Rostow did after LBJ) or retire to New Hampshire (as Sherman Adams did after Ike). Some move into important jobs in major corporations (like Nicholas Katzenbach, who became general counsel of IBM, or John Connor, who became chairman of Allied Chemical). Some go back to their former company (as did David Packard after leaving the Defense Department). Or they go home to Alabama to run for the Senate (as did Winton "Red" Blount). But unless there's something pretty juicy in prospect at the other end of the line, most ex-officials stay around their old Washington haunts. Here, they feel, is where the action is. Even so nonpolitical a personage as Eva Gabor said, after a performance in Washington: "When I retire . . . I plan to live here. Everything that happens in the world happens here."

What about the government workers—the rest of the 348,000 civilian employees on the federal payroll in Washington? What about those who fill the GS-1 to GS-18 ratings, with pay and fringes that Congress is always adjusting to make them "comparable to private industry"? Don't they go back to their old town when they retire? No, not many of them leave Washington either, even when they are "riffed" (which is government jargon for "reduced in force," laid off on account of budget reductions). Somehow they find another job, either related to their former work or a job in a private company or an industry that wants to maintain liaison with the government. When "the wife and kids" get settled in, it's hard to move, and unlike the corporate executives who become vagabond travelers from post to post, Washington government workers usually stay put.

Foreign diplomats, however, do rotate (except for Ambassador Guillermo Sevilla-Sacasa of Nicaragua, who recently passed his thirty-second year in Washington and tenaciously holds on to the title of "Dean of the Diplomatic Corps"). Others serve their term in this capital city, then move on to Rome or Copenhagen, or go home to be premier, foreign minister, or chancellor of the exchequer. A diplomatic post in Washington is often a stepping stone to a higher post at home.

Among the more permanent Washingtonians (except for fifth-generation "cave dwellers") are the economic experts at the International Monetary

Fund and the World Bank. Year after year they occupy their sumptuous quarters at 19th and H Streets N.W., enjoying some of the best cuisine in town (in their private dining room), walking on some of the most beautiful Oriental rugs outside their conference room, and relaxing at their own private country club in nearby Maryland (called Bretton Woods). They keep their heads down but their eyes and ears open, and on any given day they know more about what's going on in the world than almost anyone else in Washington.

Washington notables have very few heroes, at least among themselves. Celebrities and famous names are so plentiful that they cancel each other out. No one can hold center stage very long. Only the President upstages everybody else—with his entourage of Secret Service agents, advance men, and administrative planners, who assure that the President's entrance is impressive (replete with the Army, Navy, Marine, or Air Force Band playing ruffles and flourishes followed by "Hail to the Chief").

But many Cabinet officers can slip quietly in and out of a party or down a sidewalk without creating much stir. Senators, except for a current TV celebrity, can go almost unnoticed, for most Washington political figures are known by name but not by face. Only Henry Kissinger and Senator Edward M. Kennedy (D-Mass.) create a big flurry when they enter a restaurant or social gathering.

With 535 members of the House and Senate, plus Cabinet officers, Supreme Court Justices, numerous foreign ambassadors, and other VIPs—both foreign and domestic—the Washington celebrity list is so long that it effectively stifles any "ohs" and "ahs." There is always some guest at dinner who will blandly ask Senator John Pastore of Rhode Island whether he is a Republican or a Democrat. The chances are that the most identifiable figures on a Washington street will be Mayor Walter Washington, Redskins' running back Larry Brown, or one of his teammates, quarterback Sonny Jurgensen or Billy Kilmer. These are the faces that are recognized, and these are people who get asked for their autographs.

More recognizable than the face is the license plate. Personalized D.C. plates bearing the initials "GC" signal the arrival of Gwen Cafritz, the widow of a wealthy Washington real estate developer who has made her mark as a hostess. "DLK" marks the limousine of David Lloyd Kreeger, wealthy insurance executive and chairman of the National Symphony Board. The initials "BB" belong to Betty Beale, a society columnist for the Washington *Star*. Until recently the initials "MM" signaled the car belonging to Maryland McCormick, widow of Colonel Robert R. McCormick, late publisher of the Chicago *Tribune*. Some prominent members of Congress, however, prefer not to personalize their license plates, since they may take their car to addresses where they would rather not be recognized.

License-plate watching in Washington is a sport something like bird watching. A Wyoming license plate bearing the legend 5 GALE on a convertible driving toward the Maryland suburb of Kenwood Park indicates that Senator Gale McGee is on his way home. (He used to have U S Senator 1—telling the license-plate watcher that McGee is the senior senator from his state, having served in the Senate longer than his Republican colleague, Clifford Hansen.)

A District of Columbia license plate bearing the number "1" tells you that it is Mayor Washington's car. Other numbers up to 10 belong to members and former members of the City Council. In years past, the White House was assigned a series of numbers ranging upward from 100, but today the numbers on White House limousines are standard-looking and are recognized only by insiders or those who take the trouble to commit them to memory.

On the whole, Washington is a city for people who are still on the make. Nobody really ever completely "arrives." In years past, it was assumed that a second-term President was on safe ground, but Presidents Johnson and Nixon found that even they could not assume smooth sailing. For nearly everyone in Washington, there is a possible higher rung—one more level to attain, a better appointment, a more prestigious post, a more powerful job.

And that's what makes the wheels go round, keeps people working, keeps them politicking and lobbying, keeps the blood flowing in the nation's capital year after year, election after election, law upon law, appointment after appointment.

In Washington, every action has an opposite (though not necessarily equal) reaction. It is a hallmark of the scene, and inherent in the democratic process. It is also why Washington reflects the moods and wants of voters, and since these are not consistent, Washington is not consistent. You can see it in Congress when opposing members who plan to be out of town get together and agree to "pair" their votes, so both will be recorded but on opposite sides of an issue (like the husband and wife who agree to stay home rather than cancel each other out at the polls). You see it in congressional hearings where investigative committees have their majority and minority counsels. You see it in hearings before the Federal Trade Commission, or the U.S. District Court, or the Supreme Court, when every proposition has its opposing representation.

This point-counterpoint of contradicting views is one of the things that characterizes the capital city of the world's most powerful democracy. While many people speak sneeringly of "compromise" and "accommodation," the methods which they represent are the methods of democracy. Workable solutions are the end product. John F. Kennedy practiced "pragmatic idealism." Lyndon Johnson considered it the art of the "do-able." The evangelists of pure doctrine may shudder at this as heresy, but such is the way of Washington.

And it works. Not always well, but better than most people think and better than many other neater, crisper, more ordered governmental patterns that are described in textbooks. It works because it suits the people it serves, and because, despite the occasional stoppages in the pipelines of public opinion, people *do* make themselves heard—in elections, peace marches, poverty encampments, pray-ins, letter-writing campaigns, and visits to their congressmen, or by collaring their duly elected representatives on the street at home during the Labor Day recess.

Washington was concocted for the purposes of government. For years it was a soggy southern town, maligned by historians, by world travelers, and by many who had to live in it. Most of them fled in summertime to enjoy a pleasanter life where there were cooler breezes, brighter lights, theater and music, and something else going on besides politics. But gradually Washington has grown into a metropolis. Gradually it has become cosmopolitan, livable, an amiable place for people as well as politics. Out of its years of cultural drought—when it could claim only a struggling symphony orchestra, no resident ballet or opera, and only a single stream of theater, it evolved into a livelier milieu for the arts. From what one observer called "a dismal collection of scattered private homes and a few government buildings," it became a metropolitan center for more than 3 million people, and the capital of the most powerful democratic nation in the world.

For all its newness, its inconsistencies, its pockets of naïveté and corruption, and its patterns of compromise, it is Washington, a city with impact on people's lives—a city you may not love but cannot ignore.

Winston Churchill is credited with having said that democracy is a very inefficient form of government and is only preferable to any of its alternatives.

He might have been talking about Washington.

2 THE PRESIDENT

On August 9, 1974, when Gerald R. Ford became the thirty-eighth President of the United States, his reputation with the U.S. public was a mixture of "average American," "nice guy," "open," "friendly," "level-headed," and "unexciting."

No one described him as "brilliant," "charismatic," "forceful," "aggressive," or "dynamic." Yet within the first months of his administration, he made two moves which were forceful, if not popular. He pardoned Richard Nixon, and he nominated Nelson Rockefeller to be Vice President. In the first act, he went against the instinctive feelings of a majority of the voting public. In the second, he alienated the conservative wing of his own party. In these acts, he demonstrated a basic tenet of his political career: Follow your own judgment, even if it doesn't fit the mold that other people have prepared for you.

Though the tone of his career in Congress was generally regarded as "moderate," he voted a consistently conservative line. And though his congressional district around Grand Rapids, Michigan, contained a sizable union labor vote, he remained independent of organized labor influence. He campaigned in working-class neighborhoods, talked with labor people, then voted against many of their pet projects. It is a measure of his political acumen that he was able to get away with it.

Gerald Ford has a kind of doggedness about him that is sometimes confused with mediocrity. There was a myth in past years that Ford was somehow "not very bright," but this was a misconception of intellectual observers and political commentators who confused brightness with political fashionableness. The Ford hallmark is steadfastness, a kind of plodding determination which has nothing to do with intellectual dullness.

After all, Gerald R. Ford, of Michigan, received a baccalaureate degree from the University of Michigan and a law degree from Yale University, two institutions which are not in the habit of awarding degrees to dolts. What the earlier observers of Gerald Ford failed to understand was the difference between brainpower and style. As the Ford administration moves ahead, the confusion may continue in another form: a conflict between basic concepts of government—its proper role in the lives of its citizens. Ford, believing in a minimum of governmental direction, already has collided with his political opposition, who continue to press him for more governmental action in economic affairs.

In Congress, Ford was not an initiator. He introduced almost no legislation in his congressional career. Some colleagues (like his friend, Republican Senator Robert Griffin of Michigan) became co-sponsors of bills which became laws and bore their names (the Landrum-Griffin Act). Others became known for a single-issue campaign or a particular political posture. But Congressman Ford was content to marshal the forces, work out voting arrangements, and work his way up to be Republican leader of the House, which turned out to be his stepping stone to the office of Vice President and subsequently President of the United States.

Despite his unspectacular performance on the wider public scene, Ford did somehow attract the attention of some astute observers in Washington. Recently, a few of these earlier judgments have come to light. In 1958 a Washington editor approached one of the capital's best-informed business representatives for an appraisal of some of the rising members of the House of Representatives. The informant singled out three midwesterners who, he said, bore special watching: a young Wisconsin congressman named Melvin Laird, another Wisconsinite named John Byrnes, and a third member of the House, from Michigan, Gerald Ford. Laird subsequently became secretary of defense, Byrnes a ranking member of the powerful Ways and Means Committee, and Ford, President of the United States.

Other people noticed the Michigan congressman, too. A Washington lawyer and business executive, Bruce Sundlun, recalled his first encounter with Congressman Ford at an Aspen, Colorado, "think session" during the administration of President Kennedy. The subject, "science and society," involved a number of brilliant and well-known intellectuals, but when the meeting was over, Sundlun recalls, Ford was the one who had mastered the fundamental problems and stated the consensus that everyone, scientists and laymen alike, could subscribe to.

Ford's quality of mind is the uncomplicated approach which proceeds, without sophisticated embellishments, from point to point. And along the way, he has also acquired the reputation of being a good listener. Even the political leadership of the Black Caucus, after visiting the White House in the fall of 1974, paid tribute to his willingness to hear out the opposition case and try to assimilate the unfamiliar points of view. What this portends for the remainder of his administration is difficult now to assess, but it may, in the longer run, result in some policy decisions that are far less orthodox than his career in Congress would suggest. A President after all, is different from a congressman, even when the man himself is the same. Senator Robert Dole of Kansas, former Republican national chairman, pointed this out during a television interview in November 1974. Dole said the President would have to give up the "Boy Scout image" that he had in the public eye and would have to "toughen up a little" if he hoped to win the Presidency in 1976.

THE MAN HIMSELF

The biographical facts about Gerald Ford got the appropriate airing when he was nominated to be Vice President in October 1973 and received another burst of publicity on his succession to the Presidency in August 1974. Nothing brand new came out at either time, except that a former Washington lobbyist, Robert N. Winter-Berger, published two sensation-seeking books charging Ford with having taken $15,000 in loans and never having repaid them. The congressional committees investigating Ford's fitness for the Vice Presidency examined the record, listened to Ford's account, and concluded that Ford did, indeed, know Winter-Berger and had dealings with him during his period in the House of Representatives, but found discrepancies in Winter-Berger's story and cleared Ford of impropriety.

The other surprise to most Americans was the revelation that Ford was the son of divorced parents and that his natural father's name was Leslie King. Ford found out about it when he was a teenager in Grand Rapids, Michigan, his boyhood home. Ford's mother and father and stepfather are now dead, and Ford freely tells the story of how, one day when he was working at a Grand Rapids restaurant, his real father came in, identified himself, and asked him to step outside for a talk. Ford recalled that he was "really startled."

There is no evidence that this had any major impact on his personality or his view of life, since his mother and stepfather had brought him up in a firm and loving environment, along with three half brothers: Tom, five years younger than the President, now a legislative audit coordinator for the state of Michigan; Dick, now fifty, president of the family paint and varnish company; and the youngest brother, Jim, forty-seven, an optometrist. All the brothers are good athletes and stand between 6 feet and 6 feet 3 inches tall.

Ford was a popular student at South High School. Known then as "Junie" (for junior), he was a good student, an athlete, and a contestant for the position of president of the class of 1931. He lost the election, running on a Progressive platform, and ever after that he won as a moderate or conservative. Some of his close associates recall, however, that during his first campaign for the House of Representatives he was regarded as something of a "reform candidate" and spoke of putting new blood in the Congress. The year in which he won his seat the first time was 1948, when Harry Truman, a Democrat, was winning the Presidency over the Republican candidate, Thomas E. Dewey.

Ford went on to the University of Michigan, where he became a regular starting center on the football team and a choice for the Big-Ten All-Star Team. He was graduated from Michigan in the depression year of 1935 and the next fall entered Yale Law School. To earn his way, he also took a job coaching boxing and junior varsity football. Because he was classified as "faculty," he could take courses only in the summer. Later, the rule was relaxed, but he still needed six years to get the required course work. He received his bachelor of laws degree in 1941, graduating in the upper third of his class, even while working part-time. The class that graduated that year produced a number of prominent lawyers, and the intellectual pace was generally regarded as being pretty brisk. Again, Ford was not pronounced among the most brilliant, but his performance was steady and solid. His decision to go to Yale tells something about him, since the University of Michigan Law School itself was a distinguished one and he could have easily stayed in the Middle West.

Who's Who biographies and the sketches which appear in the *Congressional Directory* sometimes say as much about a man's view of himself as they do of the objective facts. President Nixon, for example, omitted from his *Who's Who* sketch any reference to his defeat for the Presidency in 1960 and to his unsuccessful attempt to become governor of California in 1962. President Ford's biography in *Who's Who* mentions his selection by *Sports Illustrated* to receive its Silver Anniversary All-American award in 1959. It also duly lists his selection by the U.S. Junior Chamber of Commerce as one of the nation's ten outstanding young men. This was in 1950, during his second year in Congress, and it came in a year when another Republican congressman, named Everett Dirksen, also was being declared to be one of the most promising congressmen on the Hill in Washington.

Ford was born in Omaha, Nebraska, on July 14, 1913, and was christened Leslie King, Jr. When his mother was divorced from King and subsequently remarried, he was renamed for his stepfather and became Gerald Rudolph Ford, Jr. The Fords lived in plain but comfortable circumstances in Grand Rapids. Ford was a Boy Scout and worked up to be an Eagle Scout, the highest level of scouting achievement. He attended the Episcopal church, joined the "Deke" fraternity at Michigan, and was subsequently initiated into the Masonic Fraternal Order.

During his college days, Ford recalls, he was an isolationist, but his views on foreign relations were changed by the one-world concepts of Wendell Willkie in 1940, by World War II, and later by Michigan Senator Arthur Vandenberg, who backed the internationalist reconstruction program known as the Marshall Plan. In 1940 Ford had worked for the election of Willkie as President on the Republican ticket. In 1974, he told a group of young people that Willkie's defeat taught him that he could "take part on the losing side—and even be wiped out in the polls—yet still survive."

After passing the bar exams in Michigan in 1941, he set up a law firm with Philip Buchen, now his chief legal adviser at the White House. Their practice, general in nature, was also short-lived, being interrupted by the entry of the United States into World War II. Ford was on active duty in the Navy from 1942 to 1946, reaching the rank of lieutenant commander. He saw service, first, as an athletic instructor in preflight training, and later as a ship's officer aboard the aircraft carrier *Monterey* in eight Pacific battles, from the Gilbert Islands to Leyte Gulf in the Philippines. Later he served—again with the physical education program—at the Naval Reserve Training Command at Glenview, Illinois. In 1946 he put away his naval uniform, returned to Grand Rapids, Michigan, and went back to the practice of law in a firm with which his former partner, Buchen, was then associated.

In 1948 Ford decided to make a try at public office. He won the Republican nomination and went into the election as a newcomer and a decided underdog. His campaign style was unpretentious but thorough. He recalls that some of his best votes came from dairy farmers whom he contacted before daybreak while they were in the barns milking the cows.

Ford interrupted his campaign long enough to get married to Elizabeth Bloomer, an attractive thirty-year-old divorcée who had been raised in Michigan and had studied to be a professional dancer with the Martha Graham troupe in New York. Back in Grand Rapids, she met the handsome, blond young lawyer, was courted by him, and they were married on October 15, 1948. Ford was then thirty-five years old. During their entire married life, Washington has been their principal base, and it has been in the Washington suburbs that they have raised four children: Michael, John, Steven, and Susan. As the Fords began their first full year in the White House, in January 1975, only the youngest, Susan, then seventeen years old, was living with them.

Susan continued her classes at the Holton Arms girls school in Bethesda, Maryland. Steven, taking a year off from school, was on a ranch in Montana; Jack was a senior in forestry at Utah State University; Michael was pursuing his studies toward a career in the ministry at Gordon-Conwell Theological Seminary at South Hamilton, Massachusetts.

The Fords maintained a home address in their congressional district, as do all congressmen, and for them it was 1614 Sherman Street S.E., Grand Rapids, Michigan, but they rented the house to another couple. Their own home in the years before August 1974 was at 514 Crown View Drive, a suburban community in Alexandria, Virginia, directly across the Potomac River from Washington, D.C., and about a twenty-minute drive from the Capitol where Representative Gerald Ford had his office.

FORD AS CONGRESSMAN

When Ford was nominated for the Vice Presidency in October 1973, the Twenty-Fifth Amendment to the U.S. Constitution required that he be confirmed by a majority of the Senate and the House. Both bodies referred the matter to appropriate committees for investigation, and in ensuing weeks, and until he was sworn in as Vice President on December 6, Ford's record and performance as a congressman were squarely on the griddle. The vote in the Senate committee was 9 to 0 in favor of confirmation. The vote in the House Judiciary Committee was 29 in favor, 8 opposed and one abstaining. Did the 8 opposition votes signify "something rotten in Denmark"? As it turned out, the colleagues who voted "nay" did so because they were strongly out of sympathy with his voting record and some of the positions he had taken in his twenty-five-year career in the House of Representatives.

Ford as a congressman was a strong partisan, and he did not hide his Republican party label. Further, he had instigated charges against Supreme Court Justice William O. Douglas and taken the leadership in an effort to have the Justice censured for unseemly conduct. While the campaign may have been good politics in Grand Rapids, Michigan, it did not endear him to some of his liberal colleagues. When the 8 dissenting views on his fitness to be Vice President were examined, the Douglas attack turned up in all of them. He was also criticized for his role in excluding Rep. Adam Clayton Powell (D-N.Y.) from his seat, and for voting against certain civil rights and social welfare bills. Yet even in the dissenting opinion, the "nay" voters gave him good marks for candor.

In the Senate there were similar mixed feelings from Senator William Proxmire of Wisconsin, a liberal Democrat, who had known Ford since they were at Yale (Proxmire as an undergraduate, Ford as a law student). Of the new nominee for Vice President, Proxmire said: "He is not a man of imagination or humor. However, he is a man that the country may be looking for. As I have known him, he has always appeared to be a man of integrity and character." Proxmire added, "Of course, I think he has been consistently wrong on almost every issue. But that is my viewpoint."

Other critics were even sharper. Joseph L. Rauh, Jr., a vice chairman of the liberal Americans for Democratic Action, told the Senate Rules Committee, "At a time when the nation needs a healer, the nominee is a divisive influence who has fought civil rights legislation at every turn."

In the comments of Proxmire and Rauh are the outlines of policy differences which may widen the operating gap between President Ford and the present Congress, despite the pleasantry about his candor and integrity.

The fact remains that President Ford, during his congressional days, was at the opposite pole from the Democratic majority on many issues, and if these issues arise again, there will not be a meeting of the minds. Still, conditions change political responses, and President Ford will not be as limited in his options as Congressman Ford was, either on civil rights or on economics. And it was not an accidental occurrence that Ford received support from the United Auto Workers in his selection for Vice President. Leonard Woodcock said: "I have known Gerald Ford since he first began service in Congress—as a matter of fact, I supported him in the Republican primary in 1948. I have great respect for his ability and integrity and personally support the President's recommendation that he be confirmed as Vice President."

Throughout his career in Congress, Ford has been considered "a friend of business," though he has been careful to keep his pipelines open to labor as well. Actually, in the Fifth District of Michigan, there is nothing contradictory in such a record. Among his constituents, business and labor alike, the "work ethic" is alive and well and much admired, and Grand Rapids has a large populace of blue-collar working people. Ford's life, while not marked by any severe deprivation, was certainly marked by consistent work at all steps along the way, and this attitude was fundamental to his policies on economic questions in Congress. Ford never forgot that his power derived from the people who elected him, and in his thirteen elections, he never received less than 60 percent of the vote.

Ford's progress in the Republican leadership in the House was steadily upward. He became chairman of the House Republican Conference for 1963–64, and in 1965 was elected House Minority Leader, ousting Representative Charles Halleck of Indiana. Throughout his rising prominence, however, he maintained a reputation for looking after the homefolks and always servicing the constituency whenever they needed anything in Washington.

While Ford's speaking style has never been florid, he has had plenty of exposure to radio and television, most prominently when he teamed with Senator Everett Dirksen for their weekly Republican reports from 1965 to 1968. It was then that the former "Ev and Charlie Show" (with Charlie Halleck) came to be known as the "Ev and Jerry Show," and what Ford lacked in oratorical grandiloquence was amply supplied by the honeyed tones of "Ev" Dirksen of Illinois. Ford's role was that of the "straight man"— informative, direct, and sincere. During this period, Ford worked closely with a number of men who later became his advisers and counselors at the White House: Republican Senator Charles Goodell of New York, who was once "purged" by President Nixon for opposing his policies; Melvin Laird, Republican congressman from Wisconsin; and Robert Hartmann, former Washington bureau chief of the Los Angeles *Times,* who had been a staff member of the House Republican Conference. Hartmann is now a senior Counselor to the President.

Ford, in his role as Minority Leader, actually was a national political leader to a greater degree than almost anyone else in the party. Richard Nixon was quietly building up party strength by traveling the country and getting ready to capture the presidential nomination in 1968, but simultaneously Ford was crisscrossing the country making speeches, too. David LeRoy, former Washington editor and now with the Republican Congressional Committee, estimates that Ford made approximately 200 speeches a year as Minority Leader, many of them in other parts of the country.

Clearly, the Ford forte has been party organization and the gathering of strengths from different blocs and personalities. As an instigator of legislation, his record was meager, but he has a thorough and instinctive grasp of legislative techniques, tactics, and timing. His grasp of content is adequate, but he takes much of it from others. While he has not been imaginative in proposing new plans, he digests and absorbs what others propose.

Ford served on the Warren Commission investigating the circumstances of the assassination of President Kennedy and was one of the signators of the report. To those Americans who felt—and still feel—that the crime was the work of a conspiracy, the report was unsatisfying.

Ford's attack on Justice Douglas was probably the most controversial event of his political career, and even now there is dispute as to whether it was his own idea or an "errand" for the Nixon White House. In any event, the attack was vigorous. He excoriated Douglas for his writings (which appeared, among other places, in avant-garde publication, *Evergreen Review*); for his service on the Board of the Parvin Foundation (whose donor had ownership connections with some Las Vegas gambling casinos); and for other "inflammatory" actions and writings. The Judiciary Committee of the House investigated the Ford charges, but censure proceedings never were instituted against the Justice.

On the Vietnam war, Ford supported President Lyndon Johnson, criticizing him principally for not pressing harder for victory. While Joseph Rauh criticized the Ford voting record on civil rights, Clarence Mitchell, the Washington director of the National Association for the Advancement of Colored People (NAACP), analyzed Ford's voting record on civil rights as "28 favorable, 26 against." As a congressman, Ford supported the principle of federal aid to parochial education. On crime, he was characterized as a strong "law and order" man. His record was consistently in favor of budget cutting and budget balancing, though during his tenure on the House Appropriations Committee he supported large outlays for national defense. He worked for and voted for the 1971 federal election campaign act. Like many of his Republican colleagues, he supported rigid farm supports until the principle of flexible supports became popular in recent years. He was an enthusiastic backer of the federal highway program and voted against opening the trust fund to mass transit uses. On minimum wages, his position was cautious, urging a go-slow policy on increases. On welfare, he spoke for the Nixon family assistance plan, with special emphasis on job training and work alternatives for welfare recipients.

HOW FORD WORKS

Ford, as President, has been described by his intimates as being partial to a "competitive" type of staff operation. Rather than sifting everything through a "czar" or single director, he is inclined toward naming one man as the focal point on each particular issue, and then soliciting other views. Top men on economic policy issues are Secretary of the Treasury Simon and Economic Adviser Alan Greenspan, but White House Associate L. William Seidman is the moderator and collector of other opinions (from the Council of Economic

Advisers, the Federal Reserve, and elsewhere). Commerce Secretary Rogers C. B. Morton is specified as coordinator on energy policy, but the Federal Energy Administration (FEA) and the Energy Research and Development Administration (ERDA) also have input (for more on staff operations see Chapter 3, "The White House"). Vice President Rockefeller is vice chairman of the Domestic Council and James M. Cannon is its executive director, but domestic policy advice flows into the White House from many other channels as well. It is doubtful that the staffing of the Ford Presidency will ever resemble the tight circle which surrounded President Nixon. Not only are the two men different, but so also are the issues. No longer will a domestic council and a foreign affairs adviser be able to divide the field and operate separately. Increasingly in the coming years, domestic policy will be intertwined with foreign policy—as energy supplies, food, currency problems, balance of payments, and international investment press in on domestic taxes, prices, and related issues. Ford, as a political being, will be required to pull the fields together, and in the process he undoubtedly will continue his lifelong practice of doing a lot of listening.

Ford also does a lot of reading on current topics. It is his custom to scan as many as ten newspapers every day to get a spread of opinion and news treatment of major stories. His first press secretary, Jerry terHorst, said that the ten newspapers he looked at were the Washington *Post,* the *New York Times,* the Washington *Star,* the Los Angeles *Times,* the Baltimore *Sun,* the Detroit *Free Press,* the Detroit *News,* the Grand Rapids *Press,* the *Christian Science Monitor* and the *Wall Street Journal.* Now he has the benefit of a morning news report prepared under the direction of his press secretary, Ron Nessen. The daily summary is delivered to him in the morning along with the newspapers.

After breakfast on an average working day, Ford settles into a solid routine of meetings, conferences, and public appearances. His appointments secretary has the line-up ready for him to go over with Staff Director Don Rumsfeld. A typical day may include a meeting with Secretary of State Kissinger at 9 A.M., followed by a visit with a delegation from Congress, a skull session with Counselor Bob Hartmann, some conferring with political Counselor John Marsh, a get-together with a visiting business delegation, a report from his economic coordinator, L. William Seidman, a Cabinet meeting, a news conference, and a brief break to sign a proclamation—before donning black tie and dinner jacket to receive the visiting chancellor of a European nation.

While it must sound like an exhausting routine, it is a typical day for a political leader, and, like most political leaders, Ford seems not only to thrive on the diet but actually to savor it. During the 1974 congressional campaign, he maintained a fourteen-hour day of barnstorming, often returning to the White House well after midnight.

Nowadays, Ford has had to forgo his former morning swim, since the White House swimming pool no longer exists, but he does swim on weekends during visits to the presidential retreat, Camp David, near Catoctin, Maryland, about 60 miles north of the White House. He also plays golf at Burning Tree, the all-male golf club in suburban Bethesda, Md., where his golfing companions are likely to include Melvin Laird, his close congressional friend, one or two congressmen, and perhaps William G. Whyte, a vice president of U.S. Steel and a longtime personal friend. In the winter, as time permits, he makes skiing trips to Vail, Colorado, where the family owns a condominium unit.

The Presidency gets reshaped with each new occupant of the White House. The Ford administration is building on top of foundations and precedents that have been growing for years. In the short Kennedy administration (less than three years) JFK was just putting his stamp on things when the assassination snuffed out his effort. Lyndon Johnson, while of the same political party, changed faces at the White House, and his breezy Texas manner contrasted with the clipped, somewhat understated style of John Kennedy. Still, there were similarities. Both men believed in personal exercise of power. Kennedy proved it in the Cuban missile crisis in 1962 and in his dealings with the steel industry when it insisted on raising prices. Kennedy relied on personal judgment in the Bay of Pigs venture and came a cropper. Lyndon Johnson was determined to bull it through in Vietnam and ended his term of office in virtual isolation from his party. Richard Nixon established a tight pyramid of power at the White House, concentrating authority in his Domestic Counselor, John Ehrlichman, and his Chief Presidential Assistant, H. R. (Bob) Haldeman—and concurrently relegating the Cabinet to bureaucratic exercises and occasional opportunities to lay out "options" for the White House to choose from.

Nixon's way of working was in sharp contrast with the methods employed by Dwight Eisenhower, under whom Nixon had been Vice President. Eisenhower raised the Cabinet to a position of group policymaking that was unprecedented in recent times. Secretary to the Cabinet Max Rabb was an important aide and a conduit through whom President Eisenhower could receive recommendations from his Cabinet advisers. Some observers of Washington believed at that time that the strong Cabinet system might survive to become a permanent part of presidential operations, but John F. Kennedy allowed it to languish, preferring the direct personal methods of Franklin Roosevelt and Harry Truman. It was not unusual for JFK to use the phone at almost any time of day or night for a direct call to one of his Cabinet officers (including his brother Robert, the Attorney General), and others well down the line.

The staying power of a President's style was clear during the waning months of the Nixon administration, after his trusted counselors, Haldeman and Ehrlichman, were removed and replaced by General Alexander Haig as Chief of Staff. As a gesture toward a more "open" presidential office, Nixon appointed Melvin Laird and recalled Bryce Harlow, a seasoned legislative expert and former Nixon and Eisenhower counselor, to the White House team. But the ploy made no dent in the tight top-level control. In no time flat, the system was back in shape, and squeezed into the narrow pyramid. It had to be concluded that this was the way President Nixon wanted things run, and nothing would change the way a President wants his staff to work.

The power of the Presidency is enormous, both express and implicit. Time and again, the White House patterns are automatically determined by the mental set of the President himself. Even the words that other people write for a President come out, in the end, sounding like the words of the President himself. Speechwriters get to talking like their bosses, not the other way around. Agnew's speeches were usually put together by a speechwriter, but before long they typified the turn of the Agnew tongue. President Eisenhower's speechwriter, Malcolm Moos (who subsequently became president of the University of Minnesota), turned out speeches with the circumlocutions of military expressions. Moos later confided that whenever he put in some of Eisenhower's folksy and colorful expressions, the President penciled them out, since he did not want to appear too informal in his official personality. No one doubted that the speeches of Richard Nixon were "pure Nixon" even when they were worked on by someone else. At Camp David or Key Biscayne, Nixon sketched his thoughts out on long pads of legal-size yellow paper, and the final delivery on radio and TV bore the unmistakable stamp of his own personality.

Gerald Ford's speaking style is uncomplicated and easily understood. Fashioned by his longtime associate Robert Hartmann or by speechwriter Milton Friedman, the words come out as pure Ford. In a collection of Ford speeches published in 1973, it is obvious that the Ford rhetoric, while pedestrian, is clear, direct, and easily understood. There is reason to believe that the same attributes will characterize his tenure of office as President.

3 THE WHITE HOUSE

The White House is an office and a home.

It is also a ceremonial center for entertaining foreign dignitaries and domestic visitors.

It is the working headquarters for a President who wears many hats. The President is the head of state, with some of the duties of a king or queen. He is the chief executive, like a president or chancellor elsewhere. He is the political leader of his party, corresponding to the prime minister in a parliamentary government. He is judge of the court of last resort on pardons; he is the final voice on foreign policy, and he is commander in chief of the armed forces. All these duties of the President are reflected in the organization of the White House, which provides him with a place and a staff for his work.

The White House, further, is a sentimental symbol of the American government (a role it shares with the Capitol). As a symbol it is both a building and a collection of people—a place in which the U.S. government comes to a head, manned by 1,600 men and women with extraordinary power—members of the President's working staff whose specialties range from budgeting to speechwriting, and including foreign policy, economics, defense, administration and congressional liaison.

You hear it asked what the White House "thinks." News dispatches start with: "The White House said today . . ." (as though the White House actually spoke to the nation). In a figurative sense, the White House does think, and say, and decide. Under different administrations, the White House thinks and says and decides different things in different ways. Sometimes the White House is "in disarray" (as it was in the final days of the Nixon administration). Sometimes it is in "a mood of euphoria" (as in the first days of the Ford administration). And sometimes it is "at odds with Congress" (as it is in almost *every* administration).

But at all times it is a concrete place: 1600 Pennsylvania Avenue, Washington, D.C. 20500. Telephone: 202-456-1414. The telephone number is in the government listings in the Washington directory preceded by "West Heating Plant" and followed by "Wiretapping & Electronic Surveillance, Nat'l Com . . ."

Now let's see how this remarkable office, home, and national symbol actually works.

THE WORK WING

Inside the parts of the White House that tourists never see—the offices in the West Wing—the atmosphere is quiet. Corridors are thickly carpeted. Early American prints hang on the walls. Furniture also runs to Early American—pine and maple. Offices are cramped, except for a few reserved for the President's highest aides, and even these are tiny compared to the average senator's or deputy-assistant secretary of something-or-other. No matter. It is the prestige that counts, and prestige is measured by location: the nearer to the Oval Office, the better. A White House staffer's rank is measured not simply by his title, for several others may share it, but by the location of his office. If he has a spacious suite in the Executive Office Building, he rates below another with a small room on the upper floor of the West Wing of the White House.

Reporters are kept carefully away from the working quarters of the White House. In earlier days it was relatively easy for them to see the inner denizens. A phone call arranged an appointment, and the usher sent them on their way. Nowadays, appointments are much harder to arrange. The usher does not simply open a door; he sends for a messenger who escorts the reporter to his appointment.

In the lower level of the West Wing, reached from the street by its own side door, are the White House Situation Room and the suite occupied by Henry Kissinger's national security staff. Kissinger's office (which he occupies occasionally for his work with the National Security Council) is on the upper ground level, at the northwest corner of the West Wing, and used to be the press room. It has large windows through which he occasionally can be glimpsed at his desk—when he is in town. Other offices occupy three floors of the West Wing and another bank of offices in the East Wing, separated from the President's office by the residence itself. The two working areas are connected by an enclosed walkway that runs through the lower level of the White House.

The room closest to the President's is that of his principal assistant or chief of staff. The holder of that office today is Donald Rumsfeld, who effectively manages the President's time and has access to him continuously. Rumsfeld, a former Illinois congressman, head of the OEO (Office of Economic Opportunity) and ambassador to NATO, is not necessarily the President's chief adviser, but he must know who the President will want to see and who he would rather put off. The appointments secretary works closely with Rumsfeld, from an office adjoining his.

Scattered throughout the West Wing are the offices of Robert Hartmann, senior Counselor to the President, Philip Buchen, the President's Legal Counsel, and John O. Marsh, Jr., former Virginia congressman and now Counselor to the President in charge of congressional and political affairs. In various corners of the three floors are offices of his legislative liaison, director of the OMB, the press secretary, speechwriters, and others.

While these offices are crammed tightly into the West Wing, many of the backup facilities are located next door, to the west, in the Old Executive Office Building, known as the Old EOB. Originally built in 1888 to house the Departments of State, War, and Navy, it later became the Department of State, and then was gradually converted into an adjunct to the White House. Today, many of the working papers that are said to originate from "the White House" are actually prepared by staffs that occupy the Old EOB: parts of the Office of Management and Budget (OMB), the Council of Economic Advisers (CEA), and the staffs that support the White House operation. Other White House backup staffs are located in a new Executive Office Building just to the north along 17th Street and backing onto the old Victorian houses of Lafayette Park.

HOW THE WORK GETS DONE

It sometimes appears that a President makes policy decisions by gazing out the window of the Oval Office and consulting with himself in prayerful meditation. In fact there seem to have been some instances recently (such as the pardon of President Nixon) in which President Ford apparently has employed this method. More often, however, the President's decisions are the result of a continuing round-robin of discussion, fact finding, and exchanges of views among dozens of people, all centering on the White House. The participants include members of the Cabinet, their technical deputies, trusted members of Congress, and the White House kingpins on the various subjects under review: economic policy, foreign policy, international trade, domestic affairs, etc.

If, for example, a message or speech is in the works on economic policy, it will be preceded by daily discussion within the President's Economic Policy Board, chaired by Secretary of the Treasury Simon or Deputy Chairman William Seidman in Seidman's office in the Old Executive Office Building. Before it reaches the President, the preliminary draft recommendations probably will be passed for comment to the President's Counsel, Philip Buchen, and at the same time to such others as the President's political Counselor, John O. Marsh, Jr., the chief of Legislative Liaison, Max Friedersdorf, and the President's Chief Staff Executive, Donald Rumsfeld. If it is ready for the speechwriters, the White House Staff Secretary Jerry Jones will see that it gets to Paul Theis, executive editor in the speechwriting office, for work by Milton A. Friedman or one of the other writers. At all times Counselor Robert Hartmann is in charge of the speechwriting operation and actually drafts the most important speeches himself. When scripts are in the preparation stage, an information memo might be sent to Ron Nessen, the presidential press secretary, so he would be forewarned and ready for the final draft later on.

The President himself would be involved at crucial points along the way, but much of the spadework would continue while he was busy with something else. One of the things President Ford had to adjust to after a few months in the White House was the obvious need to separate himself from more and more of the ongoing work of the Presidency, resigning himself to be a chief executive rather than the do-it-yourselfer that he had been for so many years as a legislator on Capitol Hill. Yet the astonishing thing about the final product is that it will ultimately sound like—and be—a pretty faithful reflection of what the President himself thinks and feels on the subject. Over the years, presidential staffs and advisers have found ways to blend their own thinking and that of the President into expressions, attitudes, and thought patterns which come out miraculously like those of the man who finally utters them.

KEEPING THE WHEELS TURNING

Behind the scenes, almost totally hidden from view, are 250 "support people" of the White House Office—receiving and channeling correspondence, handling telephone calls, doing secretarial work and messenger missions, doing the filing and other paperwork that is vital to the smooth functioning of any complex organization, and especially vital to a public office with the heavy responsibilities of the White House.

Presidents may come and go, but the permanent staff of the White House Office underpins the President, his Counselors, Assistants, Chiefs of Staff, Councils, and Commissions. The 250 people are members of the Civil Service, and some of them are thirty-year veterans of their jobs.

Chief of this staff is the executive clerk of the White House, Robert D. Linder, who holds a law degree from the University of Iowa and a master of business administration from Harvard. He came to his present post in April 1973 from the Office of Management and Budget, where he was a budget examiner. A well-organized and straightforward man, he has served in various capacities under Presidents Kennedy, Johnson, Nixon, and Ford. The basic flow of work, he says, remains fairly constant, but the style changes somewhat from administration to administration. President Nixon's work pattern was highly structured. President Ford's is less so.

The operating functions of the White House support staff do not include policy decisions, yet they provide some of the liaison which is preliminary to a final decision. All bills passed by Congress (between 300 and 500 a year) are delivered to the chief clerk's office from Capitol Hill. After they are receipted for and logged in, copies are prepared and sent to all the interested departments, agencies, offices, and bureaus of the Executive Department. The agencies are given five days to return their comments, pro or con, recommending that the measure be signed or vetoed. That leaves five more days for the White House specialists to add their comments before the President's ten-day period for signature expires. (If he doesn't sign or veto by the end of the ten-day period, the bill dies by what is called a "pocket veto.") When the President does sign a bill into law in Washington, the signature is personally witnessed by Chief Clerk Linder. The clerk's office keeps track of deadlines for signing, and locates the President for the necessary action before the signature time expires.

The paperwork behind all presidential nominations also flows through Linder's staff, though the selection process is handled by the Personnel Office, headed by William N. Walker. The staff must also see that all internal memos are typed and reproduced and circulated within the office to all who have a need to know.

White House mail is a particularly delicate matter, since the presidential office receives from 2 to 3 million pieces a year, and every letter has to be carefully examined and answered (either by the White House or some other agency of government). The mail is actually received at the Old Executive Office Building, the gray stone Victorian-style building just west of the White House, where it is screened for safety (to see that there are no letter bombs, etc.), then sorted for immediate action, referral, or other treatment. In the mail division are "letter writers" and correspondence specialists who may draft suggested replies. Some of the mail, of course, goes directly to the President through the President's staff secretary, Jerry Jones.

Some of the mail may be from members of Congress, some from private citizens with ideas to express, and some from sixth graders at the Birchside Elementary School who want a photograph, a note of encouragement, or information for a term paper.

The White House also receives a steady flow of telephone calls. And the operators there are among the most tactful and adroit people in the world. They must be able to handle irate, angry, and sometimes unbalanced callers with the same aplomb that they handle calls from foreign embassies and overseas heads of government. They must also be able to track down anyone the President or one of his chief advisers decides to talk to—in any part of the world. In fact, White House telephone operators must spend a good deal of time every day reading the papers, news magazines, and anything else that keeps them up to date on the whereabouts of prominent people who might be the subject of a presidential or White House staff call. The operator has to know whether the person is likely to be at home, the office, cruising in the Mediterranean, or skiing in Aspen. All White House staffers are expected to leave a string of telephone numbers if they plan to be moving around.

White House messengers, too, must know how to find people at any time of day or night—at home or elsewhere (and the elsewhere may occasionally require considerable exercise of tact, if the official happens to be on a delicate personal visit). Presidential memos and background papers are delivered throughout Washington and the suburbs or farther away in the Maryland and Virginia countryside wherever a Cabinet officer, bureau chief, or other government official may be at the time.

All this support work requires that the chief clerk's office be manned 24 hours a day, on a three-shift basis. To keep the function running requires a budget of $16,300,000 in the 1975 fiscal budget year. It goes for salaries, maintenance, telephone service, stationery, supplies, and any necessary travel for officials and staff accompanying the President on government business.

THE RESIDENCE

To keep the White House operating as a home requires eighty-five people —cooks, maids, doormen, butlers, housemen, pantry workers, carpenters, electricians, painters, plumbers, engineers, florists, and administrators. In addition, the White House has on call a number of regular part-timers who come in to help with special functions. For further backup, there are the services of outside caterers and rental agencies that may occasionally be asked to help with hurry-up affairs or overflow-size crowds. The White House can also call on young officers from the Pentagon to serve as assistant hosts and escorts for guests at special functions.

The residential staff is separate from the President's policymaking staff and from the personnel of the White House offices which occupy the West Wing of the building. Assigned to the main house, the residence staff remains in permanent service from administration to administration. General manager of this is Rex Scouten, the chief usher (a title which dates back more than sixty years to the Taft administration when the famous "Ike" Hoover was promoted to that position). Scouten came to his present job after nine years with the Secret Service at the White House and another stint with the National Park Service. He is a 1948 graduate of Michigan State University, where he majored in police administration. His service at the White House, in different capacities, has spanned the administrations of Presidents Truman, Eisenhower, Kennedy, Johnson, Nixon, and Ford.

While the residence staff consists of eighty-five people, many more than this are involved in various functions, and it is Scouten's job to coordinate everyone and everything that needs doing. The White House grounds are the responsibility of the chief usher, but this work is done by the National Park Service of the Department of the Interior. The Park Service also supplies much of the fresh foliage and flowers for social occasions and, on a less aesthetic level, handles the bookkeeping and bill paying, after the chief usher has given his O.K. (Members of the residence staff are on the payroll of the National Park Service.)

Major repairs, plus maintenance of the offices in the West Wing, are the responsibility of the General Services Administration (though if a faucet springs a leak, the plumber from the residence staff will not refuse to come). Other agencies of government get into the act at one time or another. When surveys of structural strength are required, they are conducted under the supervision of the National Bureau of Standards. The National Oceanic Survey has the responsibility of making periodic checks to see if the residence is sinking (since parts of Washington once were a prehistoric swamp). The Survey recently set three new bench marks in Lafayette Park across the way and determined, happily, that no recent settling has taken place. On furnishings and pieces of art, the chief usher collaborates with the curator of the White House, Clement Conger. And on budget, he works with the National Park Service, which actually presents the budget items to Congress under its appropriations for the National Capital Region.

Money for the household budget, official entertainment, ongoing maintenance, and lesser repairs comes from an annual appropriation by Congress earmarked for the presidential residence. For the budget year 1974–75 it totaled $1,695,000. The amount does not cover major renovations or structural changes, though it is expected to cover routine improvements, such as the recent upgrading of the electrical system. For such matters, the engineering staff does much of the work in its own shops, located below ground, under the main north portico.

Running the White House is a little like running a ship. There has to be somebody on duty whenever the President or any of his family is home. One of the three assistant ushers "has the duty" nowadays as long as the President is awake, and since President Ford is an early riser, the shifts of duty run from six in the morning until 12 midnight. A skeleton staff, of course, is on duty at all times (in case a wakeful resident—either family or guest—gets a yen for a grilled cheese sandwich at 3 A.M.).

How many people can the White House sleep? Well, there are 142 rooms of all kinds, and two floors (second and third) of bedrooms or rooms that can become bedrooms, in various configurations. In recent years the first families have not required large numbers of bedrooms, and a total of ten to fifteen guests is about as many as the present staff can remember providing for. At the time of Lynda Johnson's wedding to Chuck Robb, the Robb family were house guests, as other in-laws have been since. But the Franklin Roosevelt family used the largest number of bedrooms among all the first families in the past fifty years. President and Mrs. Ford's bedroom is on the second floor, with another bedroom adjoining. The Ford children have their rooms on the third floor.

While the chief usher and his staff implement the social and ceremonial functions, much of the planning is done by the White House social secretary and the First Lady herself. The current social secretary, Nancy Lammerding (Mrs. Nicholas Ruwe), came to her job after a tour of duty in similar work for the State Department's Office of Protocol and an earlier stint in the White House Press Office. Another close member of the First Lady's residence staff is her press secretary, Sheila Rabb Weidenfeld, a former television news-staffer with Washington's WTTG. Mrs. Weidenfeld is the daughter of Max Rabb, who was secretary to the Cabinet under President Eisenhower.

The security of the White House falls to the Secret Service, which does not like to say how many people are involved. It is clear, however, that there are many more than there used to be. The House itself is guarded by the White House Police, now a part of the Executive Protective Service, which also guards foreign embassies. Both of these units are a part of the Secret Service, the traditional guardian of the President.

RELATIONS WITH THE PRESS

In recent years, White House press relations have grown more formal than they were. During the administration of Franklin Roosevelt, a few regulars crowded around the desk of "the Boss" and listened raptly while he alternately charmed, scolded, railed, and twitted them and then dropped his big announcements with disarming informality.

This same easy atmosphere continued into the Truman days, and a friendly relationship, though more formal, existed under Eisenhower and his press secretary, Jim Hagerty, a former *New York Times* staff member. President Kennedy's press secretary, Pierre Salinger, kept on good terms with most of the reporters, as did Lyndon Johnson's press chiefs, George Reedy, Bill Moyers, and George Christian. But after the Kennedy assassination and increasingly since then, security considerations and other factors have tended to isolate the President from the press. The Nixon administration, with its deep-seated distrust of most reporters, carried the isolation to greater extremes than at any time since the days of Herbert Hoover (whose yen for protection stemmed from a very personal sense of privacy). Now, of course, the saga of President Nixon's feud with the press is a matter of history, and his former press secretary, Ron Ziegler, no longer barks at the news corps in Washington. But around the White House, some of the formal arrangements that were built up during Nixon's Presidency still exist in day-to-day press relations, even though the spirit of the Ford administration is much more open and direct with the news correspondents.

The press room now is located in an area that was the White House swimming pool, out of sight behind an embankment between the West Wing and the White House proper. Nixon had the pool floored over. The lower level, where open cubicles are inhabited by a couple-dozen reporters, was the pool itself. Upstairs, the décor is "Howard Johnson traditional," suede sofas, pewter-topped coffee tables, a scattering of captain's chairs in decorous black, and another bank of cubicles and broadcast booths. During the Watergate hearings, TV sets appeared (usually they show up only at World Series time), and the press clustered around them until time to line up in front of the blue-draped podium. At the rear of the "briefing room" four or five TV cameras stand constantly ready on a dais. Nowadays, Ron Nessen makes known in advance what level of coverage is to be allowed. Routinely, the cameras are turned on only for major announcements or when a congressional figure is on hand for a statement. Most days, sound recording is not permitted, though many reporters bring their own tape recorders, as a backstop to their written notes.

Formerly, when the press room was just off the main lobby, reporters could lounge around to see who was coming and going. Buttonholing of presidential visitors was half the fun, but this has been almost eliminated except when a cooperative guest has something he wants to say and is happy to regale the press with his comments. The new press facilities are far more plush and comfortable than most such quarters. More typical are the press facilities at Camp David: a trailer parked inside the gate, near the helipad. Reporters formerly stood out in all sorts of weather merely to witness the comings and goings of the presidential helicopter.

Press coverage of the White House operates at two levels. One is the routine attention to surface details: the daily utterances of Ron Nessen, the President's calendar, Mrs. Ford's calendar (issued by her own press staff), the President's travels and plans. Mostly, however, this sort of coverage is cut and dried.

The other level of White House coverage is where the real news is developed. This is performed by a much smaller group of specialists who cultivate staff friendships as best they can and seek to probe inside. They are not much concerned with the official announcements—which the wire services cover competently. Rather, they try to find out who is truly close to the President, what the President is saying and doing in private, how he is "bearing up" under the pressures, what policy shifts and power realignments may be on the way, and so forth.

THE PEOPLE'S HOUSE

While the White House has been home to thirty-seven Presidents and their families, it does not belong to any of them. They are merely tenants, and this is made clear whenever the moving vans back up to the side entrance to take away the personal belongings of a former occupant.

Various Presidents have made changes in the structure. Franklin D. Roosevelt built a swimming pool (with contributed funds). Dwight Eisenhower put in a putting green. John F. Kennedy ordered an area for Caroline's pony. And Richard Nixon had the swimming pool covered over to provide for the new press room.

But the most extensive changes in the house were made during the administration of Harry S Truman. It was Truman who planned and constructed the second-floor balcony, despite the objections of many architects who thought it spoiled the dignified sweep of the columns in the south portico. Nevertheless, Truman stuck to his guns, declaring that the Executive Manson had to be a congenial place for the people who live there. During his administration, the mansion was completely rebuilt when studies showed that some of the supporting structures were not sound. While the Trumans lived across the street at Blair House, the White House was gutted, steel beams were substituted for the old wooden ones, and the interior was faithfully restored to its former appearance.

Today, the White House—office, home, symbol, and ceremonial place— stands in dignified tribute to the ideals and agonies that have been a part of its history. And as it adds to that history day by day, you can still write to it by mail or call it on the telephone.

4 SOME IMPORTANT PEOPLE

Washington abounds in Big People . . . men and women who, by force of personality, education, experience—or merely official title—affect our lives in many ways, major and minor. Here are a few of them, chosen entirely from the ranks of government service. Some of them are genuinely powerful. Others of them are less influential than little-known colleagues and subordinates who actually operate the far-flung federal agencies. In any event, these are all top officeholders, which by definition makes them VIPs of some magnitude. They are as varied an assemblage as one could ever dream up. The rich variety of their lives is one of the things that accounts for the fascinating uniqueness of Washington.

THE VICE PRESIDENT

Nelson Aldrich Rockefeller, Vice President of the United States. Born in 1908 in Bar Harbor, Maine, grandson of Standard Oil billionaire John D. Rockefeller. Raised to be "socially conscious," went to progressive private school in New York City. Graduated Phi Beta Kappa from Dartmouth. Worked for family concerns, including the new Rockefeller Center (where he was reportedly a shrewd and imaginative rental agent). Long interested in Latin American affairs, came to Washington under FDR as wartime Coordinator of Inter-American Affairs. As Assistant Secretary of State, 1944–45, worked on plan for United Nations. Was Under Secretary of HEW and presidential adviser under Ike. In first try at elective office, upset incumbent Averell Harriman for New York governorship in 1958. Held that post until his resignation in 1973. As governor, supported civil rights, culture, and creation of an enormous state college system. Became more conservative toward the end of his term, endorsing stiffer narcotics penalties and highly controversial residence requirements for welfare eligibility and permitting state troopers to bring the Attica prison revolt to a fatal end. Has contended for the GOP presidential nomination every four years since 1960. Hoped to finally turn the trick in 1976, but the ascendance of Ford scotched that. Managed to remain quiet through the Watergate mess. Nomination as V.P. looked like a shoo-in until the revelations of $3 million of cash gifts to political associates over the years; payment of $900,000 in back taxes; and news of authorization of an unsavory campaign book—financed by a brother—on onetime gubernatorial foe Arthur Goldberg. Finally won Senate confirmation by a wide margin. Brought to his job an awesome support staff of advisers, consultants, aides—thinkers and doers of all sorts, covering every imaginable field of domestic and international policy. There was originally some concern that Ford could not "contain" his understudy, but it hasn't proved to be a problem. Enormous personal and family wealth. Individual worth of some $73 million, and beneficiary of another $34 million in trusts. He and his family spent some $20 million on his various political races over the years. Has given personal gifts of over $20 million to museums. Maintains five residences: thirty-two-room apartment on Fifth Avenue, New York City; house on family's 4,180-acre estate in Westchester County, New York; house on Washington's chic Foxhall Road; vacation retreat in Maine; 18,000-acre ranch in Venezuela. Collects art of all kinds (some 1,500 pieces), especially modern American and primitive African. Five grown children (one deceased) by first marriage, which ended in divorce in 1962. Two young sons by second wife, "Happy," who likes to stay out of the public eye and isn't crazy about Washington. "Rocky" is short and stocky, with craggy face and gravelly voice. Dresses nondescriptly. Limitless energy. A ready smile. Gregarious backslapper and arm-pumper. Tough, can't be pushed around. Greets everyone with a booming "Hiya, fella!" Likes to sail for relaxation. Drinks Dubonnet on the rocks and has a passion for Oreo cookies.

THE CABINET

Henry Kissinger, Secretary of State. Born in 1923 in Germany, one of two sons of middle-class Jewish family. Father a high school teacher. Played soccer, did all right in school. With rise of Nazism, assigned to all-Jewish school. Occasionally beaten by young Nazi bullies. Family fled to U.S. in 1938, via London. (Thirteen relatives who stayed behind were killed in Nazi concentration camps.) Settled in New York City, where father had to take low clerical job. The language barrier led to loneliness but he became absorbed in schoolwork and got straight As. Did especially well at math. Worked during the day in shaving brush factory, processing pig bristles, studied accounting at night, wanting nothing more than to be a successful accountant. Drafted into Army, became U.S. citizen soon thereafter. Translator and interrogator in intelligence, also taught German history to officers. Befriended by a brilliant, German-born American private (F. G. "Fritz" Kraemer, who for a number of years has been the influential plans officer for the chief of staff of the U.S. Army), was encouraged to set his sights higher than accountancy. Went to Harvard on the GI bill, accompanied by pet cocker spaniel, which he kept in his dorm room. Did spectacularly well, eventually taking PhD in government (1954). Taught at Harvard, advised the Eisenhower administration on weapons evaluation, wrote prolifically on foreign affairs (on theme of creating international order through countervailing military might among the superpowers). Was foreign affairs aide to Nelson Rockefeller, whom he backed for the GOP nomination in 1968. Selected by victorious Nixon as national security adviser, eventually dominating the Washington foreign policy process. Named Secretary of State during second Nixon term, staying on after elevation of Gerald Ford. A tireless perfectionist who drives himself and his subordinates to the limit. Excellent sense of humor, can poke fun at himself, never took seriously his media-created image of "secret swinger." Authoritarian, enormous ego. Has thick German accent (due to which he was kept off the television and radio at the start of the first Nixon administration). Plays chess, is a fanatic fan of international soccer. Short, with round face, glasses, and curly hair combed straight back from a high forehead. Likes rich foods, which balloon his physique. Gains weight from banquets on international trips, despite the frenetic pace. Married in 1949 to girl who, like himself, was a German refugee. Had a son and daughter (now teenaged). Divorced in 1964. Married in 1974 to former Rockefeller aide Nancy Maginnes, his frequent (and preferred) companion through all the nonsense with Hollywood starlets. (She accompanies him on most world trips, and they live in a rented house in Georgetown.) Kissinger is an American in his belief in trying new approaches, reaching for any goal. But he is a European in harboring no illusions that there are any final solutions to human problems.

William E. Simon, Secretary of the Treasury, former "Energy Czar." Born in 1927 in Paterson, New Jersey, into a family that had accumulated wealth in the silk-dyeing business but lost most of it in the depression. Father an insurance broker, mother died when children were young. Had a German nanny. Was altar boy and soprano in church choir. Educated at private schools, where he was popular and a member of the swimming team. After graduation, worked as a lifeguard and joined the Army infantry in 1946, spending a year in Japan. At Lafayette College (where he was his fraternity's pledgemaster), earned money at odd jobs and playing poker. Married after sophomore year, was a father by graduation in 1952. Considered a law career, but headed for Wall Street instead. Became a crack municipal bond trader. Joined Salomon Brothers in 1964, rose to partner in less than a year, eventually becoming a multimillionaire. While serving as an adviser to the government on marketing bond issues, caught the eye of then Treasury Secretary Shultz, who recruited him for Deputy Secretary in 1972. Had contributed $15,000 to Nixon reelection campaign and helped raise a fat bundle from others on Wall Street. Won several power struggles to become head of Federal Energy Office and, later, to become chief economic adviser to Nixon and Ford. Associates call him a "workaholic" who works Saturday and Sunday and lines up several telephone calls in a row. Insists on getting all the facts, then makes a decision quickly. Pragmatic, flexible, but can be stubborn. Bad temper, but not a grudge holder. Prides himself on immediate access to the President. A fiscal conservative, continues to urge lower federal spending, balanced budgets, elimination of anticompetitive regulatory policies. Once angered the Shah of Iran by referring to him as a "nut." (Later explained he was joking, meant a "nut on the subject of oil.") Tall, slender (but once weighed 200 pounds in college days). Has worn thick, horn-rimmed glasses since early childhood. Dark, straight hair is plastered down, parted, and combed back. Neat, traditional dresser. Smokes a pipe. Nicknamed "Popeye," because of glasses and penchant for creamed spinach. Outgoing, an active partygoer, when time permits. Plays tennis. Favorite words: "Nifty," "Super." During WIN ("Whip Inflation Now") campaign, was seen wearing, as a joke, a LOSE lapel pin (which stood for "Let Our Stockbrokers Eat"). Lives with wife and several of their seven children on seven-acre estate in suburban McLean, Virginia, with swimming pool and a stable for their pony. Claims he keeps the house cool to save energy. Takes a chauffeured Chevrolet to work, drives a silver Mercedes sedan at home.

James Rodney Schlesinger, Secretary of Defense. Born in New York City in 1929, the son of a thriving Austrian-Jewish accountant who had immigrated with his family as a child. The future Secretary had a governess. Was a serious young man, nicknamed "the professor." Graduated summa cum laude from Harvard in 1950, same class as Kissinger. Took master's and doctoral degrees at Harvard, in economics. Taught economics at the University of Virginia for eight years, specializing in defense analysis. Was an expert in strategic studies at Rand Corporation, 1963–69, a gadfly who challenged the physicists' assumptions about weaponry effectiveness. Came to Washington in 1969, began odyssey through several top jobs. Was military affairs expert at the Bureau of the Budget, then chairman of the Atomic Energy Commission, then on to head the CIA (where he cut the staff, pooh-poohed the old secrecy fetish, and was very unpopular with the old guard). Finally came to rest at the Pentagon in the summer of 1973. Unprecedentedly well prepared for the job. Works well with the Joint Chiefs. Considered by some observers to be a "hawk," but considers himself to be a realist—skeptical of the permanence of "détente" with the Communist powers. An intellectual, often blunt, sometimes professorial. Understated personality, but tough. Tall, slender, unkempt blondish gray hair, fair complexion. Smokes a pipe (or toys with one) constantly. Married to a former Radcliffe student, eight children. Warm, devoted father, strict disciplinarian. Hates official social functions, spends evenings with family at suburban Arlington, Virginia, home. A man of many talents. Plays harmonica and guitar. Composes and sings his own modern-day folk songs about politics, with conservative lyrics. Is a devotee of military marches. Watches birds on Theodore Roosevelt Island (has seen nearly 600 varieties in his lifetime). Goes camping with family. Devout Lutheran (converted to Christianity after college). Reads the Bible, sings loudly in church. Drinks bourbon. Follows *Peanuts* comic strip. Wears drab, rumpled clothes and drives beat-up old car. Prefers simple foods, has no interest in gourmet restaurants. Is a voracious reader.

Edward Hirsch Levi, Attorney General. Born in Chicago in 1911, the son of a rabbi and grandson of a rabbi who spoke seventeen languages and taught Semitic languages and literature at the University of Chicago. Grew up in the university neighborhood, where his father had a congregation and where he attended a well-known, progressive "laboratory school." Took his B.A. and law degrees at the University of Chicago and a doctor of laws degree at Yale. With only a few interruptions, served at the University of Chicago from 1936 until 1975, first as a law instructor, then as professor, university provost and finally as president in 1968. During World War II worked at the Justice Department as a special assistant to the Attorney General, in the war and antitrust divisions. Counsel to a House monopoly committee in 1950, leading probes into newsprint and steel industries. During the Fifties participated in a legal research project that entailed the bugging of jury rooms to eavesdrop on deliberations. (In hindsight now considers the experiment to have been well-intentioned but ill-advised.) Considered an authority on antitrust policy. Has written and edited several books on the law. While president at Chicago, taught a general humanities course to undergraduates. During a building takeover by radical students in 1969, the new president chose to ignore the sit-in, which petered out after fifteen days of inattention. Gave no amnesty to protesters, forty-two of whom were expelled and eighty-one suspended. Has served over the years on numerous academic and governmental commissions. Nominated by President Ford in January 1975 to be Attorney General, succeeding William Saxbe, who became ambassador to India. Hailed as an ideal choice to restore the stature of a demoralized Justice Department.

Basically shy and scholarly, but firm and unflappable. Witty. Slim, balding, medium build. Wears dark suits, bow ties. Tireless worker. Married at thirty-five, has three sons. Likes occasional foreign travel. Smokes a pipe or cigar, prefers bourbon and martinis. Never been active in politics, unlike most of his predecessors. Name is pronounced LEE-vee.

Stanley K. Hathaway, Secretary of the Interior. Born in Osceola, Nebraska, in 1924, into a poor farm family with six children. Mother died during his birth. When four, was sent by father to live with Wyoming relatives who grew sugar beets. Attended a one-room school. Entered University of Wyoming, left school in 1943 to join the Air Force. Served in Europe as gunner and radio operator on a B-17 bomber. Survived two crash landings, won numerous decorations. Finished college at University of Nebraska, took a law degree there. Worked his way through school, as railroad freight handler, powerline laborer, researcher for Nebraska Farm Bureau. Married, moved back to Wyoming, practiced law. Elected Goshen County Attorney in 1954, reelected in 1958. Active in GOP affairs. Elected governor in 1966. Enthusiastically promoted state's economic growth. Advocated development of shale oil, strip mining of coal, construction of jetport in the Grand Tetons National Park, and open hunting of coyotes and golden eagles (which prey on sheep). Very popular, won reelection in 1970 with 63 percent of vote. Voluntarily stepped down after second term, could have won again easily. Due to record of economic boosterism, was opposed for Interior post by every environmental lobby, ranging from Sierra Club to American Horse Protection Association. Confirmed by Senate despite controversy. Is an efficient, tough administrator. A genial man of simple tastes. Likes to hunt duck and elk, fish for trout. Five feet eleven inches tall, heavyset. Round, fleshy face, thinning black hair. Wife active in helping underprivileged children, aiding Indians in marketing handicrafts. Two daughters, one a graduate of University of Wyoming, the other a student there.

Earl Lauer Butz, Secretary of Agriculture. Born in 1909 and raised on a Noble County, Indiana, farm. Undergraduate and doctoral degree from Purdue University. Joined Purdue agricultural economics faculty in 1937, became head of department nine years later. Was Assistant Secretary of Agriculture under Eisenhower, 1954–57, when he went back to Purdue as dean of agriculture. Later moved up to dean of continuing education and vice president of the Purdue Research Foundation. Took office as Nixon's second Agriculture Secretary in 1971, after a stormy Senate confirmation fight where he was criticized for his links to big agribusiness corporations (was a director of several, including Stokely-Van Camp and Ralston Purina). A tough free market economist. Succeeded, to a large extent, in lessening government role in agriculture. Not an economic purist, willing to accommodate political and economic pressures. Hard driving. Decisive. Outspoken. Witty. Spunky. At times feisty. Loves to talk. Gets charged up by audience reaction to his speeches. Spends up to a half hour telling one-liner jokes to a crowd. Caused a ruckus when a reporter printed a joke he had told about an Italian woman who said of the Pope's anticontraception stand: "He no playa da game, he no maka da rules." Italian-Americans complained, President Ford asked for (and got) an apology from Butz. Works a ten-hour day, often longer. Spends a third of his time on the road. Very popular with most farmers. Unpopular with most consumers. Goes grocery shopping with his wife, whom he met in Washington during the Thirties on the patio of the Agriculture building during a 4-H Youth Conference prayer meeting. He has two sons, one an economist with the Rand Corporation, the other a psychologist. Swims and uses an exercycle at his Washington apartment in Southwest redevelopment area. Still owns a home in West Lafayette, Indiana, to which he plans to return. Doesn't smoke. Will take a drink or two. Swears. Repeats his jokes. Saves string, refuses to toss out old ties, hats, and wool suits. Looks like an undertaker. Talks like a revival preacher.

Rogers Clark Ballard Morton, Secretary of Commerce, head of the Energy Resources Council. Born in Louisville in 1914, into a socially prominent and wealthy Kentucky family. Descendant of explorer-soldier George Rogers Clark (and brother of former Kentucky Senator Thruston Morton). After graduating from Yale, went into family's flour and food business, Ballard and Ballard. During war rose from private to captain in the field artillery. President of family firm after the war, until it was sold in 1951 to Pillsbury, of which he became a vice president and director. Moved to Eastern Shore of the Chesapeake Bay, where he operates a cattle farm. Became active in Maryland GOP, elected to first of several terms in Congress in 1962. Was moderate to conservative in House. GOP National Chairman 1969–71. Became Secretary of Interior in 1971, shifted to Secretary of Commerce in April 1975. A tall, big man, with broad face and lots of white hair. Friendly, easygoing, likes a good time, enjoys Washington party scene. Candid, uses spicy language. Treated for cancer in 1973, now said to be in good health. Likes outdoor sports—hunting, fishing, sailing. Married, one son, one daughter.

John Thomas Dunlop, Secretary of Labor. Born in 1914 in Placerville, California, the eldest of seven children. His father, a Presbyterian minister, grew pears commercially. Taken as a small child to the Philippines, where his father became a missionary. (Now eighty-five, the Reverend Dunlop has returned to the Philippines to resume proselyting.) Lived there through high school, then came back to the States in 1931 to enroll at Marin (California) Junior College, from which he soon transferred to the University of California at Berkeley. Was on the varsity tennis team, graduated Phi Beta Kappa. After a brief stint of teaching and studying economics at Stanford and a year of study in England on a fellowship at Cambridge, began a long association with Harvard in 1938 (picking up a Berkeley doctorate the following year). Became a specialist in the economics of organized labor. While teaching at Harvard, was an incessant commuter to Washington, serving on commissions, panels and boards dealing with such things as post-World War II price stabilization, labor relations in the atomic energy industry, jurisdictional disputes between unions in the building trades, strikes in coal mining, and labor problems at missile sites. Author of several books on labor relations. Dean of the Arts and Sciences faculty at Harvard from 1970 until becoming Secretary of Labor. During student unrest at Harvard in the late Sixties, acted as hardnosed mediator between dissidents and administration. Convinced students he would not entertain any "nonnegotiable demands." Was considered for presidency of Harvard, but was nosed out for the job by his old friend (and fellow labor specialist) Derek Bok. In 1971 was appointed to head the Construction

Industry Stabilization Committee, a precursor of the broader Cost of Living Council, of which he was executive director from January 1973 through the spring of 1974. Presided over dismantling of the Nixon wage-price controls. Is very close to, and respected by, the nation's top labor leaders, especially George Meany, who praised his appointment as Labor Secretary. Despite being an academic sort, has been able to develop rapport with nonintellectual union men, often through long, late-night bull sessions, over drinks in a smoky room. Is blunt, curt, tough, immune to flattery, leery of publicity. Has a generally low regard for the press which he accuses of oversimplifying complex economic issues. Tends to lecture reporters in an autocratic (though informative) fashion. His press conferences have been dubbed the "Dunlop graduate seminars." Wants to elevate position of Labor Secretary to a level of prominence in economic planning, renewing a trend interrupted after George Shultz left the post. Married, one daughter, two sons, the eldest of whom is a professor of Russian literature at Oberlin. (Mrs. Dunlop, who works in Boston with children who have learning disabilities, has not accompanied her husband to Washington.) A compulsive worker with no hobbies, methodical, well organized, not easy with small talk. Contemplates weighty problems while listening to classical music and taking solitary walks in the countryside around his Belmont, Massachusetts, home. Doesn't care much for Washington parties, goes back to Belmont most weekends, taking work home with him. Five feet ten inches tall, medium build. Lean face, full head of gray-brown hair, glasses. Is addicted to wearing bow ties.

Caspar W. Weinberger, Secretary of Health, Education and Welfare. Born in 1917 in San Francisco. Interested in public affairs from boyhood. Read the *Congressional Record* for fun. Student body president in high shool. Graduated Phi Beta Kappa from Harvard, editor of the daily *Crimson,* then took law degree there. Entered Army during the war as a private, served on General MacArthur's intelligence staff, got out as a captain. Clerked for a federal judge, then joined corporate firm in San Francisco. Elected to state legislature in 1952, voted "most able" by press corps in 1955. Unsuccessful bid for state attorney general. Though less conservative than Reagan, campaigned for him. Appointed Reagan's finance director, made budget cuts with gusto. Started a job-jumping spree through Washington in 1970 as chairman (briefly) of the Federal Trade Commission, which he helped revitalize before moving to number two, and later number one, spot at Office of Management and Budget. Eventually landed at HEW, where his impact has been less, probably because of the amorphous sprawl of the place. Worked hard for welfare reform, saved millions of dollars by tightening welfare eligibility rules, and did some reorganizing. Called "Cap the Knife." Thinks federal budget should be balanced. Gracious, witty, amiable, energetic. Has a steel-trap mind. Six feet tall, full head of dark brown hair. Married, one son, one daughter. Once considered becoming a newspaperman. Heavy reader, used to write book reviews for San Francisco *Chronicle,* and was moderator of local TV discussion show. Lived for several years in a small, restored Capitol Hill townhouse, across from the Library of Congress Annex, then moved to an apartment at the Sheraton Park Hotel.

Carla Anderson Hills, Secretary of Housing and Urban Development. Born in 1934 in Los Angeles, the second of two children. Father a well-to-do dealer in building materials. In her youth attended private schools, played tennis, and rode five-gaited horses. Graduated with honors from Stanford University in 1955 after a "junior year abroad" at Oxford. Was a California intercollegiate tennis champion. Had decided on a legal career early in her life, so entered Yale Law School, graduating in 1958 in the top twelve percent of the class. Married Roderick M. Hills (who had taken undergraduate and law degrees at Stanford, followed by a clerkship at the U.S. Supreme Court). Taught law at UCLA, worked two years in Los Angeles as an assistant U.S. attorney. With her husband and three others founded in 1962 the Los Angeles firm of Munger, Tolles, Hills and Rickershauser, which specializes in antitrust and securities law. Co-authored books on federal civil procedures (1961) and antitrust law (1971). Former president of the National Association of Women Lawyers. Discovered by federal recruiters in 1973 when Defense Secretary Elliot Richardson tried to convince her husband to accept an assistant secretaryship at the Pentagon. Upon the recommendation of recently resigned Attorney General Richardson, Mrs. Hills was lured to Washington in early 1974 to be assistant attorney general in charge of the Civil Division (handling cases to which the government is a party, including contract claims, patents and admiralty, as well as citizen suits against government actions in everything from roadbuilding to environmental affairs). Was in charge of some 260 lawyers and thousands of cases. Considered by her colleagues and subordinates to be a skilled lawyer and tough administrator. Nominated to head HUD by President Ford in February 1975. Nomination criticized by many housing and urban affairs lobbies on grounds she lacked experience in those fields. Despite a grilling by Senate Banking, Housing and Urban Affairs Chairman William Proxmire (D-Wis.), was confirmed by the Senate by voice vote. One of the youngest people ever to hold a Cabinet post, and only the third woman. Poised, articulate, cheerful, and strong-willed. Five feet six inches tall, slender. Fine-featured face and dazzling smile, framed by a well-coiffed head of long auburn hair. Three daughters and one son (aged fourteen to five) whose photos adorn her office desk. (Husband was chairman of Los Angeles-based Republic Corporation, a $200 million conglomerate—metals, printing, and other lines—until he accepted White House post early in 1975 as assistant legal counsel to the President.) She's at the office from 7:45 A.M. to 7 P.M., and takes unfinished work home. Lives in a fashionable part of the city (adjoining Spring Valley) in an ultra-modern, $250,000 house (with tennis court, pool, and basketball hoop) built in the Thirties by the late Washington columnist Raymond Clapper. Still plays an excellent game of tennis and can beat her husband at it.

William Thaddeus Coleman, Jr., Secretary of Transportation. Born in 1920 in the Germantown neighborhood of Philadelphia. Father a nationally known social worker who ran a boys club and summer camp for poor children. Parents wanted him to be a minister or social worker, but he decided at age eleven to be a lawyer. Used to sit in on trials as a youngster. Attended the University of Pennsylvania, where he made the track and swimming teams. Served in the Army Air Corps in World War II, as a court martial defense attorney, before finishing law school. Lost only one case out of eighteen. Graduated with high honors from Harvard Law School, an editor of the law review. As a clerk to Justice Felix Frankfurter, was the first black to clerk at the Supreme Court. Practiced law in New York City, then joined a prestigious Philadelphia firm (now titled Dilworth, Paxson, Kalish, Levy and Coleman), becoming a partner in 1956. Headed its trial department, specialized in corporate, antitrust, and transportation law. Has long been a leading lawyer in the civil rights movement, having served as president of the NAACP's Legal and Educational Defense Fund. Helped write the brief in 1954 *Brown* case on school desegregation, defended "freedom riders" and sit-in demonstrators in the Sixties, handled a case that struck down laws banning interracial marriage. Though a Republican, has served on commissions under Presidents Eisenhower, Kennedy, Johnson, and Nixon (including the staff of the Warren Commission, which investigated the assassination of John Kennedy). Was a member of the U.S. delegation to the United Nations. Was a member of the federal Price Commission, during the economic controls program. Turned down an invitation from President Johnson to accept a federal judgeship, feeling he could accomplish more in private life. Urged President Nixon to resign, to spare the nation the trauma of impeachment. An Episcopalian, is married to a Quaker (whose father was a prominent New Orleans physician). Two sons and a daughter. One son and the daughter graduated from Yale Law School and are clerking for judges. Five feet seven inches tall, weighs 175 pounds and frets about his weight. Swims, plays tennis, and sails occasionally. Reads a lot, mostly biography and other nonfiction. Is a past vice president of the Philadelphia Art Museum. Full head of hair, graying around the temples, and full sideburns. Wears large, round, black-rimmed glasses. Congenial manner, is a friend of many famous men in Pennsylvania and national politics. Has a self-deprecating humor. Drinks bourbon and gin-and-tonic. A fastidious dresser, tends toward dark, three-piece suits, white shirts and rep-striped neckties. Is the second black person to hold a post in the Cabinet.

WHITE HOUSE ADVISERS

Donald Rumsfeld, Assistant to the President, with Cabinet rank. Born in 1932 in Chicago, Illinois, son of a prosperous Winnetka real estate broker. Captain of state champion high school wrestling team. Graduated from Princeton, captain of the wrestling team. Was Navy pilot and flight instructor during Korean War. Worked a few years as a House aide on Capitol Hill (while taking night classes at Georgetown University Law School, from which he did not get a degree). Then became a stockbroker in Chicago. Won first election—to a GOP House seat on the affluent North Shore of Chicago—by a landslide in 1962. Essentially pro-business, anti-big-government conservative, but supported "liberal" causes like seniority reform and public disclosure of campaign financing. Campaigned hard for Nixon before and after nomination in 1968. After victory named chief of the Office of Economic Opportunity (whose programs he had opposed in Congress). To the surprise of liberals, helped protect OEO from total dismantling by its foes in the White House. In 1971 appointed by Nixon to head the Cost of Living Council during Phase II of the economic controls. Named to be American ambassador to NATO in 1972. A friend of Ford's since House days, became an original member of the new President's "transition team" when Nixon resigned, eventually becoming unofficial "chief of staff" upon the departure of Alexander Haig. Bright, ambitious, outgoing, with movie-star good looks. Wears glasses, smokes a pipe. Politically pragmatic. Might have eye on a Senate seat some day.

Medium height, physically fit. Tennis player, skier, sometime trampoline artist. Known to his friends as "Rummy." Married to a woman he has known since high school, two daughters, one son.

Robert T. Hartmann, Counselor to the President and chief speechwriter. Born in 1917 in Rapid City, South Dakota, raised in Niagara Falls, N.Y., and California. Son of a chemist (former research director for Carborundum) who was also a prosperous patent lawyer. Had pneumonia frequently as a child. Graduated from Stanford and took off on a tour of Europe and the Far East. Joined staff of the Los Angeles *Times* as a copy boy in 1939. Served on staffs of Admirals Halsey and Nimitz in World War II. Back at the Los Angeles *Times,* worked his way up from police reporter to Washington bureau chief (becoming one of Richard Nixon's favorite journalists). When management of the *Times* became politically liberal, was demoted to overseas bureau chief for the Mediterranean and Middle East. Back in Washington, did brief stint as P.R. man for a branch of the U.N. Then had a string of jobs for Republicans on Capitol Hill, including Minority Sergeant at Arms, writer for the House Republican Conference, and finally legislative assistant, political consultant, and speechwriter for Representative Gerald Ford. Was named chief of staff when Ford became V.P., but soon dropped administrative duties, for which he was not suited. One of the President's closest advisers and confidants. Politically very savvy. Tough, abrupt, often abrasive. Writes virtually every major address the President delivers. Knows Ford's mind and shares his bedrock conservatism. Stocky, broad-shouldered, rugged features. Full head of gray-brown hair combed back. Married, grown son and daughter. Very close-knit family. At home in suburban Maryland, swims in backyard pool and plays boccie (an Italian variety of lawn bowling). Has a home in Virgin Islands, where he skin-dives and does underwater photography. Writes unpublished short stories, reportedly in the lean style of Hemingway. Likes classical music. Formerly a heavy smoker of cigarettes, now smokes a pipe. Drinks martinis and bourbon. Knowledgeable about gourmet foods and fine wines. Family is active in the Church of Christ.

Philip W. Buchen, Counsel to the President with Cabinet rank. Born in 1916 in Wisconsin. Met Gerald Ford at a party in Grand Rapids in late Thirties, when Buchen was a student at Michigan Law School and Ford was at Yale Law School. Friendship ripened into a law partnership in Grand Rapids, shortly after both graduated. Partnership was dissolved in less than a year, when Pearl Harbor intervened and Ford joined the Navy. Buchen, a boyhood polio victim who still walks with a cane, stayed behind and expanded his firm, which eventually gathered such clients as Ford Motor Company, Brunswick, and U.S. Steel. Remained one of Ford's closest friends through the years. Was member of the American delegation that negotiated an international communications satellite agreement between 1969 and 1972. When Ford became V.P., he summoned Buchen to become executive director of the Committee on the Right of Privacy, a Cabinet-level group Ford headed. Once in Washington, Buchen quietly helped Ford in the pretransition period. Didn't intend to stay. Had tickets for a return flight to Grand Rapids dated August 9, the day Nixon resigned. ("I never got to use them," he jokes today.) Criticized for his role in several sticky matters, including the pardon of Nixon, the agreement—since abrogated—giving the former President custody of the tapes, and the resignation of press secretary terHorst (who said—with no contradiction from Buchen—that Buchen misled him on some key points of information). As head of White House Counsel's office, is the President's in-house attorney. Is actually much more—Ford's confidant. Sees the President daily, sometimes several times a day. Not fully at home in the Washington pressure cooker. Politics isn't his game. White-haired, pink-complexioned, handsome. Quiet and dignified, but with an informal air. Married, with a grown son and daughter. An avid swimmer who, like Ford, regrets that the White House pool was covered over to make more room for the press. Swims when he has a chance at the indoor pool of the University Club, on 16th Street near the White House.

L. (Lewis) William Seidman, Assistant to the President for Economic Affairs. Born in 1921 in Grand Rapids, Michigan. Son of a Russian-Jewish immigrant who became a millionaire accountant. Name pronounced "SEED-mun." Was all-conference halfback in high school. Graduated Phi Beta Kappa from Dartmouth in economics, then took a law degree at Harvard and an MBA at Michigan. After Navy service in the Pacific in World War II (a Bronze Star winner) and a brief fling at teaching college math in New York City and at Michigan State University, went back home to the accounting firm founded by his father and uncle. Helped build it into a 50-office international giant (one of whose clients was the scandal-ridden Equity Funding Corporation). Be-came a millionaire. In 1962 made only attempt at electoral office: a narrow loss in the race for state auditor (encouraged by then Governor Romney and longtime friend Representative Gerald Ford). Was later economic aide to Romney and Governor Milliken and head of the Romney presidential cam-paign office in Washington. Came back to Washington to join Vice President Ford's staff. A tireless, dynamic organizer. Was instrumental in planning the 1974 "economic summit" meeting. Has helped found a new college near Grand Rapids, a TV station, a ski club, and international student exchanges. A fiscal conservative, believes government spending must be restrained. Short, muscular, pink-faced, virtually bald (and shaves what hair is left). Self-effacing manner hides an inner toughness. Probably the brightest member of Ford's "Michigan Mafia." A sports nut. Does calisthenics and jogs a mile every morning before sunrise. Sails, skis, plays tennis, goes skin diving. Used to play a lot of polo. Married (to a onetime University of Michigan beauty queen), one son and five daughters. Nonathletic hobby: making mobiles. Has home near Grand Rapids and apartment in New York City.

John O. Marsh, Jr., Counselor to the President. Born in 1926 in Winchester, Virginia. Graduated in law from Washington and Lee University. Served during World War II with the occupation infantry in Germany. Practiced law in Strasburg, Virginia, becoming town judge and member of local school board. Was a church elder and leader of adult Bible classes. Elected to the House in 1962 as a Democrat. Served four terms, voted straight conservative line, was well liked but never a mover and shaker. Decided not to run again in 1970. Practiced law briefly in Washington, then campaigned for victorious Virginia gubernatorial candidate Mills Godwin, a Nixon-backed Republican. Soon thereafter, was named an Assistant Secretary of Defense for Legislative Affairs, making him the Pentagon's chief lobbyist in the annual military budget battles on the Hill. Brought to White House by Ford as resident authority on military affairs. Helped handle Ford's relations with Congress on the Rockefeller nomination, as well as questions relating to former President Nixon's home at San Clemente, California. Is now regarded as a full-fledged Republican, but calls himself an "independent." Uncomplicated, level-headed, unflamboyant man. Pleasant good looks, with short gray hair. Mild southern twang to his voice. Married, three children. Lives quiet life with family. Calls himself a "genuine country lawyer." A lieutenant colonel in the Virginia National Guard. Physically fit, from jogging two or three miles each day around his Arlington, Virginia, neighborhood. Has a log-and-stone cabin on the Shenandoah River, used as a retreat. Proud of having qualified as a paratrooper in the National Guard after entering Congress (apparently the only congressman who could claim that distinction). Called "Jack" by most people.

James T. Lynn, Director of the Office of Management and Budget. Born in 1927 in Cleveland, raised in the suburbs. An only child. In high school, played clarinet, sang in barbershop quartet, played basketball, and was valedictorian. Brief stint in Naval Reserves in 1945–46. Majored in economics at Western Reserve, Phi Beta Kappa. On law review at Harvard. Joined prominent corporate law firm in Cleveland, became its youngest partner ever. Not politically active, but after presidential election of 1968, dropped by Nixon headquarters in New York City and asked for a job. Was installed as general counsel in Commerce Department, later Under Secretary. Helped negotiate the Soviet trade agreement of 1972. Appointed to be Secretary of Housing and Urban Development in 1972, after departure of Secretary Romney. Personally liked for his hard work and political savvy with the Hill, even if the retrenchment housing programs over which he presided were anathema to housing industry. In 1974 appointed by President Ford to head OMB, upon resignation of former OMB Director Roy Ash. Personable, candid, witty, bright, not a trace of arrogance. Medium height and build, glasses, the All-American face of a Boy Scout. Smokes cigars. Shoots pool, watches football on TV, does photography, sings to own piano accompaniment. Fishes, swims in backyard pool, plays tennis. Married (to a former director of children's radio shows), three children.

Alan Greenspan, Chairman of the Council of Economic Advisers. Born in 1926 in New York City. Son of a stockbroker, only child. Parents were divorced when he was young. Attended George Washington High School, also the alma mater of Henry Kissinger (who, being older, did not know Greenspan). Studied clarinet for one year at Juilliard. During World War II, played in a touring dance band (in which Leonard Garment, White House aide to Nixon years later, played sax). Studied economics at New York University, graduating summa cum laude, did graduate work at Columbia, got an MA from NYU. Co-founded and eventually headed Townsend-Greenspan and Co., a prosperous economic consulting firm with a long list of blue-chip corporate clients. Earned six-figure annual income, in the neighborhood of $300,000. Was economic adviser to Nixon during 1968 campaign. Several times turned down federal job offers, accepting present position only when he became convinced he could do no worse at shaping economic policy than those who preceded him. His ultraconservative economic ideas were influenced by the rugged individualism of philosopher-novelist Ayn Rand, a friend and confidante of his for more than twenty years. His anti-Keynesian, free-market ideas include—ideally—abolition of such economic mainstays as federal price supports, antitrust laws, and even the progressive income tax. He advocates lowered government spending, balanced budgets, and slower growth of the GNP. Was married some years ago for one year (to woman through whom he met Ms. Rand). Today is single. In New York, lives in posh apartment in United Nations Plaza, overlooking the East River. In Washington, can be found at the Watergate. Listens to classical music records, especially Mozart. Plays golf (not very well) at a country club in Scarsdale, New York. Quietly self-assured, witty, erudite. Dark, slicked-back wavy hair, black-rimmed glasses. Owlish face. Lean build. No fan of big Washington cocktail parties. Jogs to work each morning at 7:30 in full business attire.

Ronald Harold Nessen, Presidential Press Secretary. Born in 1934 in middle-class Shepherd Park section of Washington. Father owned a few small furniture stores and jewelry shops in the District. Ron always wanted to a broadcast journalist. As a boy, emulated radio correspondent Lowell Thomas by reading the newspaper into his own microphone, set up in the family study. After dropping out of American University (where he was a disk jockey on the student station), worked for tiny hillbilly radio stations in West Virginia and Virginia (called himself "Old Hickory"). Finished college as a history major. Reported briefly for the Montgomery County, Maryland, *Sentinel* (which, years later, was the launching pad of Watergate sleuth Bob Woodward), then on the UPI Washington bureau. Went to NBC in 1962. Covered stories at the White House, in Vietnam (where he caught a grenade fragment in the lung), Bangladesh, South America, and elsewhere. Was tenacious, but not pugnacious, reporter. Assigned to cover Vice President Ford, he grew to like the future President, and vice versa. Ford invited the Nessens to his first state dinner, and the Nessens invited the Fords to a poolside party at their home in suburban Bethesda. Named press secretary—the first ever from the electronic media—following the resignation of Jerald terHorst, after the Nixon pardon. Announced at his first press conference, "I am a Ron, but not a Ziegler." Briefings are informal, low-key. Insists on being kept fully informed, but says press secretary needn't agree with every decision President makes. Gets generally good marks from the always critical White House press corps. Slender, medium height, receding dark hair, and thick sideburns. At times exhibits self-deprecating humor, at other times a blistering temper. Divorced from first wife (with whom he had a daughter, now nearly twenty years old), is married to a pretty Korean singer whom he met and courted in Vietnam. ("Cindy" doesn't sing professionally anymore, stays at home with their young son—and dances rock-'n'-roll with the President at White House parties.) Nessen, called "Ron" professionally and by friends, used to ride a small motorbike to work, now takes a limousine. Works long hours, not much time left for anything else.

Virginia Harrington (Wright) Knauer, consumer affairs spokesman. ("Knauer" rhymes with "hour.") Born in Philadelphia in 1915, daughter of an accounting professor. Studied fine arts at University of Pennsylvania, did graduate work at the Royal Academy in Florence, Italy. Married shortly after that. Her husband, Wilhelm, was a Philadelphia corporate lawyer, now semiretired.

Followed her husband into Republican party activities in the Eisenhower campaign of 1952. Played key role in formation of GOP women's groups and became prominent in Pennsylvania party politics. In 1960, first GOP woman elected to Philadelphia City Council. Served two terms, defeated in her bid for a third. Named head of Pennsylvania Bureau of Consumer Protection, strengthened and beefed it up. Named consumer affairs adviser by President Nixon in 1969. Very visible during first Nixon administration. Much speech-making and traveling about country. Some professional consumerists felt she lacked real clout with President or Congress. Her wings clipped by Nixon aides, who transferred her office out of White House to Department of Health, Education and Welfare. Blond, blue-eyed. Stylish dresser. A bit plumpish. Has a son and a daughter. Is a portrait painter, collector of American antiques and restorer of colonial homes. A Doberman pinscher dog fancier, headed up national club for that breed. Rents an apartment in Washington. Home is a large, nineteenth-century stone house (filled with fine antiques) in northeast Philadelphia, overlooking the Delaware River.

THE TOP MILITARY MAN

George Scratchley Brown, Air Force General, Chairman of the Joint Chiefs of Staff. Born in 1918 in Montclair, New Jersey, the son of an Army officer. Graduated from West Point, where he was captain of the polo team and adjutant of his regiment. (Yearbook called him "undisputed leader of that horsey group known as the 'station wagon set.'") Flew bombers out of England, won the Distinguished Service Cross for heroism during a raid on Rumanian oil fields. Rose through top jobs, including assistant to Defense Secretary (1959–63) and assistant to Chairman of Joint Chiefs (1966–68). Commanded all air forces in Southeast Asia near end of Vietnam war. Became Air Force Chief of Staff in 1973 and Secretary Schlesinger's personal pick for Chairman in 1974. Considered one of the brightest men at the Pentagon. Came under fire in 1974 when informal remarks he made about the "Jewish influence in this country" were widely construed as anti-Semitic. President Ford rebuked him, several members of Congress demanded his resignation, but he weathered the storm. Strong-willed, decisive. Subtle sense of humor. Compact build, strong-featured face, thinning dark hair. Married to the daughter of an Army officer, three children. Lives in large house at Fort Myer, next to Arlington National Cemetery. Enjoys playing tennis, has aggressive net game. College nickname: "Brownie."

CONGRESSIONAL LEADERS

Michael J. Mansfield, Democratic Senator from Montana, Senate Majority Leader. Born in New York City in 1903 to Irish immigrant parents who took him as a small boy to live in Montana. During World War I, enlisted in the Navy at age of fourteen, later serving in the Army and Marines (including a hitch in Nanking, China, where Marines were stationed to protect American economic interests). Worked as a miner and mining engineer for several years, taking a year of study at the Montana School of Mines. With wife's encouragement, went to college at Montana State, earning bachelor's and master's degrees in history. Taught government, Latin American and Oriental history at Montana University until election in 1942, to the House, where he served five terms. Elected to the Senate in 1952. Became majority whip in 1957 and majority leader in 1961, succeeding the strong-willed Lyndon Johnson. Has served in that position longer than anyone in history. A gentle but skillful persuader, not one who cracks the whip. Respected for his fairness, honesty, and erudition. Unflappable, patient, good-humored. Quiet, almost taciturn. Lets debates in the Senate run on and on, believes a good wind clears the air. A political liberal, one of the first senators to oppose the war in Vietnam. Fights for troop reductions in Europe. Tall, slim, with a narrow face and sharp features. Smokes a pipe, drinks very little. Doesn't care for the social whirl. Married, one grown daughter. Hobby: Oriental history and customs. Called "Mike."

Hugh Scott, GOP Senator from Pennsylvania and Senate Minority Leader. Born in 1900 in Fredericksburg, Virginia. Served in Army in World War I. Graduated from Randolph Macon College and took a law degree at University of Virginia. Went to Philadelphia as an assistant D.A. and has been a Pennsylvanian ever since. Elected to the House in 1940, served eight terms (sitting out one when defeated in 1944). Navy in World War II. GOP national chairman in 1948–49. Was a leader of Ike's presidential campaign in 1952. Elected to Senate in 1958, endured close reelection race in 1964 by dissociating himself from Goldwater. Floor-managed Rockefeller's abortive bid for the 1968 presidential nomination. Succeeded Everett Dirksen as minority leader in 1969. Politically, is an adroit tightrope walker, balancing between role as presidential spokesman in the Senate and representative of his rather liberal constituents. His voting record is a confusing patchwork of liberal and conservative gestures: opposition to Nixon nomination of Clement F. Haynsworth, Jr., to the Supreme Court, but support of nomination of G. Harrold Carswell; support of Nixon's Vietnam policy, later opposition to that same policy; championing of civil rights and the ABM, etc., etc. Cultured, urbane, droll, one of the Senate's most entertaining debaters. Has the manner and appearance of an old-style British military officer ("Colonel Puff," perhaps). Tall. Jowly face. Slicked-back thin gray hair, glasses. Smokes pipes, of which he owns more than 500, ranging from utilitarian to ornately carved meerschaums. Is an expert on Chinese art, has a large and valuable collection of it, and has written two books on the subject. Married, one grown daughter and eight grandchildren.

Robert C. Byrd, Democratic Senator from West Virginia, Senate Majority Whip. Born in North Carolina in 1918. Mother died of the flu in his infancy, father abandoned him. Adopted and raised by an aunt and her husband, Titus Byrd, a poor West Virginia coal miner. Helped earn the family's living by collecting table scraps and garbage from neighbors to feed the hogs. Got high grades in school, but had to go to work after graduating from high school. Learned to cut meat and became a butcher in a grocery store, after stints pumping gas and selling vegetables. Married his grade school sweetheart, to whom he used to give candy that another boy shared with him. Studied welding and got a job as a welder in a defense factory during World War II. While working as a butcher, got elected to the state house of delegates in 1946. (Had been member of Ku Klux Klan until quitting in 1945.) Elevated to the state senate in 1950, then U.S. House in 1953 and U.S. Senate in 1959. Got law degree while in Congress, studying nights at D.C.'s American University. In Congress, started out as a firm conservative who opposed civil rights laws and railed against "welfare chiselers" in the District of Columbia. Later moved toward the political center. Less interested in the substance of legislation than in the parliamentary maneuvering that makes laws possible. A stickler for details. Does endless favors for colleagues. Dour, humorless, hardworking. Horatio Alger of the Senate. The only person who has ever dealt a political defeat to Teddy Kennedy, when in 1971, after quietly lining up the votes, he unseated the Massachusetts liberal as majority whip (assistant majority leader). Keeps to himself, seldom goes to parties. Doesn't drink. Smokes an occasional cigar. Is devout Baptist, taught Sunday School as a young man. Medium height and build, unsmiling face, full head of dark hair, neatly combed. Only hobby: playing "hillbilly" music on the fiddle. Learned to play by ear as a child, is good enough to play professionally. Has two married daughters (one of whom is married to an Iranian).

Robert P. Griffin, GOP Senator from Michigan and Senate Minority Whip. Born in Detroit in 1923, raised in Garden City and Dearborn, Michigan. Served in the infantry in Europe in World War II. Worked his way through Central Michigan University and went to University of Michigan Law School on the GI Bill. Joined a small Traverse City law firm and got into GOP politics. Elected to the House in 1956, reelected four times. During second term was architect of the Landrum-Griffin Act, considered inimical to organized labor, but has managed to win big in union areas. Was a "Young Turk," part of the group that bucked the old-guard House GOP leadership in the early Sixties. Appointed to the Senate in 1966 to fill the unexpired term of a deceased senator, elected in his own right the same year with a big win over popular ex-governor G. Mennen (Soapy) Williams. Showed an independent streak in the upper chamber, ignoring Minority Leader Everett Dirksen's directives by fighting to block nomination of Abe Fortas to be Chief Justice. Generally conservative-to-moderate voting record. Elected minority whip (assistant minority leader) in 1969. Opposed Haynsworth nomination and SST. Against busing. Eventually called for Nixon's resignation. Serious, reserved, not a glad-handing pol. Honest. Shrewd political instincts. A perfectionist, demands a lot of his staff (and commands their respect). Has a short-fused temper, but it blows over quickly. Conservative dresser, short dark hair, glasses. Married, three sons and one daughter. Lives quietly in modest home in suburban Bethesda, Maryland. Plays a little golf, fishes. Sometimes wears a small gold lapel pin of a griffin, the mythological animal with head of an eagle and body of a lion. Likes the symbolism of it.

Carl Albert, Democratic Congressman from Oklahoma, Speaker of the House. Born in 1908 in village of Bug Tussle, Oklahoma. Eldest of five children of a poor coal miner. As a boy, practiced giving speeches under a local bridge, where the resonance gave a thrilling depth to his adolescent voice. Top student, went to University of Oklahoma on a scholarship, won a varsity letter as a wrestler (at 118 pounds), worked on the side. Won a Rhodes Scholarship to Oxford. Took law degree, clerked for a government agency. Worked as an attorney and accountant for two oil companies before settling into private practice. Served in the Army during World War II, winner of the Bronze Star. Narrowly won a House seat in 1946, reelected ever since. Became protégé of powerful Speaker Sam Rayburn of Texas. Chosen majority whip in 1955 and majority leader in 1962, when John McCormack was promoted to Speaker. According to the clockwork of House seniority, was chosen by his colleagues to be Speaker when McCormack retired in 1971. Has not been a forceful Speaker, but occasionally surprises everyone by asserting himself, stubbornly and successfully. Brighter than most of his predecessors, but underestimated by the Washington press corps. Supported House procedural reforms in 1974. Politically, a liberal on domestic issues, more conservative on foreign policy. The shortest Speaker in history at 5 feet 4 inches. Full head of brownish hair, used to be red. Round face, looks a bit like Howdy Doody. Walks with swinging arms, short steps, with an alternately worried and smiling look on his face. Dresses in conservative dark suits. Second in line for the Presidency, which he hopes he will never attain. Reserved with strangers, tries to avoid reporters. Married (to a former Pentagon clerk he met while assigned there during the war), one son, one daughter. A good bridge player. Once had a drinking problem, but got it under control after he caused a well-publicized fracas outside a Washington bar. Had a heart attack in the mid-Sixties, but no trouble since. Is a hero in his hometown of McAlester, Oklahoma, where the main street has been renamed Carl Albert Parkway.

Thomas Phillip O'Neill, Jr., Democratic Congressman from Massachusetts, Majority Leader of the House. Born in Cambridge, Massachusetts, in 1912, the son of an Irish Catholic politician. Immersed in politics from childhood, rang doorbells for presidential hopeful Al Smith in 1928. Graduated from Boston College, got into real estate and insurance, making quite a bit of money from them. Elected to the state legislature in 1935, eventually becoming speaker. Elected to House seat in 1952, succeeding John F. Kennedy. Became majority whip in 1971. Elected majority leader in 1973, when Representative Hale Boggs was lost in an Alaska plane crash. In 1967 took the unexpected step of publicly opposing LBJ's Vietnam policies (said to have been influenced by the antiwar views of his children, one of whom, Thomas P. O'Neill III, is now lieutenant governor of Massachusetts). Has supported procedural reforms in the House. Liberal voting record. More at home with the old pols of his district than the college activists of Cambridge, but the latter generally support him. Knows thousands of people in his district by first name. Friendly, warm, trusted by constituents and colleagues alike. Large, corpulent man, with big nose and gray hair that hangs down on his forehead. Wears rumpled suits too large for him. Still goes by childhood nickname, "Tip" (the moniker of a well-known baseball player of that era). Married, five children. Wife lives in Cambridge; he shares bachelor apartment in Washington with longtime pal Representative Edward Boland of Massachusetts.

John Jacob Rhodes, GOP Congressman from Arizona and Minority Leader of the House. Born in 1916 in Council Grove, Kansas. Father was a retail lumber dealer and Kansas state treasurer. Graduated from Kansas State College and Harvard Law School. Served in Air Force, World War II. Settled in Mesa, Arizona, after war and opened law office. Ran for state attorney general in 1950, at urging of Barry Goldwater, and lost. Elected Arizona's first GOP House member in Eisenhower sweep in 1952, and reelected eleven times since. Headed the House Republican Policy Committee for five-plus terms. Served as convention floor manager for Goldwater's nomination in 1964. Chaired Platform Committee at 1972 GOP convention. Elected minority leader in 1973, when Gerald Ford stepped up to Vice President. A quiet, congenial conservative. Does an excellent job marshaling GOP votes and keeping President Ford posted on the prospects of administration bills in the House. Hardly a celebrity around Washington, but doesn't mind. Can often be found golfing with friends on Friday afternoons at the exclusive Burning Tree Club, of which he is a member. Definitely not a flamboyant type, but possesses low-key strength. When he speaks, in his deep baritone voice, people generally listen. Married, three sons and one daughter. Recently let his hair grow out after 18 years with a crewcut that gave him a resemblance to George Gobel. Natty dresser. Boyish good looks. Close to his family and not much on parties.

JUDGES

Warren E. Burger, Chief Justice of the Supreme Court. Born in 1907 in St. Paul, Minnesota, of Swiss-German descent, one of seven children. Father made a meager living inspecting railroad freight and as a traveling salesman of candy and patent medicine. As a boy, the future jurist picked apples and vegetables on his family's small farm outside of St. Paul. Later, living in the city, helped family make ends meet by selling newspapers, driving a truck, lifeguarding, and counseling at a summer camp. Read Horatio Alger books. In high school played sports (not unusually well), edited the paper, played cornet in the band, sat on the student court, headed the student council. Turned down a partial scholarship to Princeton because he needed more money. Went to University of Minnesota night classes while clerking at an insurance firm during the day. Continued clerking (and selling policies) while attending St. Paul College of Law (now Mitchell College of Law), from which he graduated magna cum laude. Helped manage Harold Stassen's successful gubernatorial bid in 1938. Not accepted by the military in World War II because of a spinal condition. During private practice in St. Paul, championed local Negroes and Mexican-Americans in their campaign against police brutality. Went to 1952 GOP convention as a delegate for Stassen, but ended up helping Eisenhower get nominated. Appointed assistant attorney general in charge of the Justice Department's Civil Division, where he made a name for himself as a tough, conservative prosecutor. In 1956 was appointed by Ike to the U.S. Court of Appeals for the District of Columbia, on which he became the chief spokesman for law and order. Chosen by President Nixon in 1969 to anchor a hoped-for new conservative majority on the Supreme Court. Not brilliant, got where he is through sheer determination. Handsome, with stocky build and a bad back. A full head of wavy white hair. Married, two children. Formal, deep-voiced, straight-laced. A devotee of good wine, gourmet foods, art, cultural events. Lives in a restored pre–Civil War farmhouse on six acres in suburban Arlington, Virginia. Private wine cellar stocked with hundreds of bottles. Amateur sculptor, watercolorist, and gardener. Likes shopping for antiques, which fill his home. Comes to work in a black limousine, chauffeured by an armed driver. Haughty, secretive with people he senses to be his foes, but warm and open with friends. Keeps a revolver at home. (When a Washington *Post* reporter rang his doorbell late one night for comment on a breaking story, the Chief Justice came to the door in his bathrobe, holding the gun at his side.) Very concerned about the physical comfort and appearance of the Court. Had the straight bench broken into a curve so all the justices could hear and see better. Had parts of the building brightened with new décor, including plants both real and plastic.

William O. Douglas, Associate Justice of the Supreme Court (with the longest tenure in history). Born in Minnesota in 1898, son of a poor itinerant Presbyterian preacher. Grim religious upbringing, father died when son was six. Reared by mother in Yakima, Washington. Stricken with polio when young, left small and weak. Began hiking in mountains around home to build his health. Very bright schoolboy. Served in Army in World War I. Graduated from Whitman College, then taught in high school to earn money for law school. Rode the rails east, as a hobo. Enrolled in Columbia Law School, graduated second in class. Practiced on Wall Street a while, then taught law at Columbia and Yale. Cracked down on the securities industry as member and later chairman of the SEC. (Became close to Joseph P. Kennedy, and years later took Bobby Kennedy on an international trip, during which he is credited with converting the young Kennedy—a former Joseph McCarthy aide—from right-wing extremism to humanitarianism.) Appointed to the Supreme Court in 1939, at age forty, the youngest justice since 1811. Considered by FDR for Vice Presidency in 1944, but rejected by party chieftains in favor of Senator Truman. In 1949 was thrown from a horse while riding in the mountains; broke several ribs, punctured a lung, and missed six months of work at the Court. Brilliant, arrogant, holds grudges, does not suffer fools gladly. Curt, aloof from strangers. Prolific and rapid writer of decisions that are often quotable and polemical, but not closely reasoned. Staunchest civil libertarian on the Court. In 1970, target of abortive impeachment campaign, led by then Representative Gerald Ford. Grounds: accepting a salary from a foundation funded by a questionable financier with Las Vegas casino profits, and writing an article in favor of civil disobedience for the *Evergreen Review,* a "free-spirit" publication. Lifelong environmentalist. Since 1954 has hiked along the C&O Canal in heavy boots and western hat. Helped save canal from deterioration, for preservation as park. Married and divorced three times (siring two children by first wife) before meeting and marrying present wife Cathy in 1966, when she was a pretty, blond, twenty-three-year-old part-time college student and waitress. (Today she is a pretty, blond, and bright lawyer.) Has harmonious "open marriage." Has pacemaker to regulate his heartbeat. Suffered a severe stroke in December 1974. Medium height and build, craggy face, head of shaggy, once blond (now white) hair.

William J. Brennan, Jr., Associate Justice of the Supreme Court. Born 1906 in Newark, New Jersey, one of eight children of Irish immigrant parents. Son of a man who came to America in 1890, shoveled coal in a brewery, and later became a local union leader and minor public official in Newark. As a boy, the future judge earned money delivering milk, pumping gas, and making change on trolley cars. Graduated cum laude from University of Pennsylvania. Ranked among the top ten students in his class at Harvard Law, where he studied under Felix Frankfurter. During World War II, practiced law in the Army, rising to colonel. Private practice in Newark, specializing in labor law. Served on superior and supreme courts of New Jersey. A Democrat, but in 1956, appointed to Supreme Court by Eisenhower, to fill the "Catholic seat." A persuasive spokesman for the "liberal bloc"—once a solid majority, today either a tenuous majority or minority. Used to be a fixture on the banquet circuit of Irish fraternal groups. Gregarious, salty-tongued, but becoming quieter with age. Still tells and enjoys jokes. Short, stocky. Gray hair, leprechaun face. Married, two sons and a daughter. Used to play golf.

Potter Stewart, Associate Justice of the Supreme Court. Born in 1915 in Michigan, but reared from birth in Cincinnati. Member of old, prosperous Ohio family, son of a longtime Cincinnati mayor who also served on the Ohio Supreme Court. Went from Hotchkiss boarding school to Yale, where he was chairman of the *Yale Daily News* and Phi Beta Kappa. Worked one summer as a cub reporter on a Cincinnati paper. Republican, but voted for FDR in 1936 out of respect for New Deal social welfare programs. Studied international law on fellowship at Cambridge (England). Won moot court competition and was a law review editor at Yale Law School. Practiced corporate law in New York, then went off to war as lieutenant on an oil tanker in the Atlantic and Mediterranean. Practiced law in New York and Cincinnati after the war. Elected to City Council of Cincinnati, then vice mayor. Worked in campaigns of Senator Robert Taft and Ike. Appointed federal circuit court judge in 1954. Elevated to Supreme Court in 1958. Has become more "liberal" over the years. Serious, compassionate, hard-working, good-natured. Married, two sons, one daughter. Chain smokes. Likes to fish and golf. About 6 feet tall, trim build. Member of the best country clubs of Washington and Cincinnati.

Byron R. White, Associate Justice of the Supreme Court. Born in 1917 in Fort Collins, Colorado. Son of a small-time lumber dealer who was mayor of Wellington, Colorado, a little farming town. During high school worked in sugar beet fields and on railroad. Graduated first in class of five. Graduated first again (and valedictorian) from the University of Colorado, where he waited on tables at fraternity and sorority houses, headed the student body, played basketball and baseball, led the nation in total offense as an All-American halfback, and became a Rhodes Scholar. Nicknamed "Whizzer." Led the NFL in rushing, playing with teams in Detroit and Pittsburgh. Study at Oxford interrupted by the war. Rejected by Marines for color blindness, but served in intelligence with the Navy in the Pacific (two Bronze Stars). Clerked at Supreme Court for Chief Justice Fred Vinson, practiced corporate law in Denver, 1947–60. Had become friendly with young John F. Kennedy in England before the war (when Joseph Kennedy was ambassador there), again in the Pacific during the war, and again in Washington when Kennedy was a freshman congressman after the war. Was a key organizer for Kennedy in 1960 campaign. Appointed Deputy Attorney General in 1961, active in civil rights and organized crime cases. Appointed to Supreme Court in 1962 with no prior judicial experience. Unpredictable "swing man" on Burger court, liberal on some issues, conservative on others. The sharpest, most aggressive questioner of attorneys during oral argument. Loves to play devil's advocate to probe a lawyer. Does everything with determination. Six feet tall, muscular 190 pounds. Balding head, rugged features. Skis, plays squash, takes on Court clerks in no-holds-barred basketball games. Married, one son, one daughter. Elected to National Football Hall of Fame, 1954.

Thurgood Marshall, Associate Justice of the Supreme Court. Born in Baltimore in 1908, father a country club steward and onetime Pullman porter, mother an elementary school teacher. (Great-grandfather had been brought to

Maryland from the Congo as a slave, later winning his freedom.) Worked his way through Lincoln University as a grocery clerk, baker, and dining car waiter, finding time to be on the debating team. Intended to go to dental school, but chose law instead. Graduated from Howard Law School magna cum laude, 1933. Over the following five years practiced privately in Baltimore, eventually specializing in civil rights cases. In 1935 won suit requiring the University of Maryland to admit a Negro student. At age of thirty became special counsel to the NAACP in New York City, and in 1950 assumed leadership of the Legal Defense Fund. Appeared before Supreme Court in numerous civil rights cases, winning most of them. Led the team of lawyers that won the historic *Brown* school desegregation suit in 1954. Appointed to U.S. Court of Appeals in 1961, appointed first black U.S. Solicitor General in 1965. Became first black justice on the Supreme Court in 1967. Member of the "liberal bloc." Makes decisions more from gut instincts of fairness than from scholarly analysis. Jovial, a good storyteller, especially of ribald jokes. Has been known to "put on" white people by mimicking black jive talk. Likes to play poker, is a sports fan. Tall, heavyset. In ill health at start of 1973 term, but apparently fully recovered now. Light complexion, combed-back gray hair, and thin mustache. Married (to second wife, first wife deceased), two children. Lives in suburban Falls Church, Virginia.

Harry A. Blackmun, Associate Justice of the Supreme Court. Born 1908 in Nashville, Illinois (where mother's family had a small flour mill). Grew up in Minneapolis/St. Paul, in a strict Methodist home. Father worked at number of jobs in succession, from insurance to groceries. Excellent student in high school, delivered newspapers on the side. Close childhood chum of Warren Burger (they're called the "Minnesota Twins" today). Got partial scholarship to Harvard, worked as janitor and tutor for extra money. Majored in math, graduated Phi Beta Kappa. Thought about medical school, went to Harvard Law instead. Clerked for federal judge, then became tax and estates attorney. Resident counsel for the Mayo Clinic, 1950–59. Appointed by Eisenhower to U.S. Court of Appeals, 1959. Was moderate-to-liberal on civil rights, conservative in criminal cases. Considered fair and compassionate even by judicial foes. Took seat on Supreme Court in 1970, as part of "conservative bloc." Precise, meticulous, analytical, hard-working. Appalled by Watergate. Devout Methodist, goes to church every Sunday. Doesn't drink or smoke. Married, three daughters. Works seven days a week, even before church. Reserved, soft-spoken. Slender, with lean face and high forehead. Follows sports closely, likes classical music. Gardens, reads, does acrostic puzzles.

William H. Rehnquist, Associate Justice of the Supreme Court. Born 1924. Reared in Milwaukee, Wisconsin. After interruption of three years in the Army Air Corps in World War II, graduated Phi Beta Kappa from Stanford. Picked up a master's degree from Harvard, then graduated from Stanford Law School, first in his class and an editor of the law review. At every stage of education, a brilliant, brash student who constantly challenged his instructors. Clerked at the Supreme Court for conservative Justice Robert Jackson. Practiced law in Phoenix, Arizona, 1953–69, including service as a special state prosecutor in a fraud case against state highway officials. Became an active member of the conservative wing of the state GOP, befriended by

Barry Goldwater and Richard Kleindienst. Campaigned for presidential bids of Goldwater and Nixon. Opposed a Phoenix public accommodations law in 1964, and a local school desegregation plan in 1967. Came with Kleindienst to Justice Department in 1969, as Assistant Attorney General. As head of Office of Legal Counsel, was a strong law-and-order defender and became the chief legal spokesman for the Nixon administration, defending the legality of the President's actions in everything from the Vietnam war to wiretapping rights. Nominated to the Supreme Court in 1971 and confirmed despite opposition from civil rights groups and civil libertarians. The court's youngest member, but already its most forceful voice of conservatism. Loves a good intellectual brawl in conference. Good-natured, open, personally liked by his colleagues (even ideological enemies). Dry wit. Tall, trim, looks younger than his age. Since going on Court, has let his straight brown hair grow out a bit, and sports long sideburns. Likes to sing. Married (to a woman he met in Washington when he was a law clerk and she worked at the CIA), one son and two daughters. Lives in suburban McLean, Virginia.

Lewis F. Powell, Jr., Associate Justice of the Supreme Court. Born in Suffolk, Virginia, in 1907, into a wealthy, socially prominent family with roots in colonial Virginia. Father's family owned a furniture manufacturing business, which was sold some years ago to Sperry and Hutchinson. Educated at private schools in Richmond. At Washington and Lee University, managed football team, edited the paper, presided over the student council, and graduated Phi Beta Kappa. Took law degree at W&L, then did graduate work at Harvard Law, under Felix Frankfurter. During war, a decorated intelligence officer with Army Air Corps, rising to colonel. Back home in Richmond, practiced corporate law, helped change the structure of the city's government. As president of state board of education, worked in 1959 for harmonious integration of public schools. General counsel to Colonial Williamsburg, director of numerous corporations, including Philip Morris. Elected president of the American Bar Association. Appointed by President Nixon to the Supreme Court in 1971, to augment the growing conservative contingent. Gracious, restrained, quietly charming, proper, the perfect "southern gentleman." Married, three daughters, one son. Plays tennis. Member of Society of the Cincinnati, by virtue of ancestors who served as officers in the American Revolution.

John J. Sirica, retired Chief Judge of the U.S. District Court for the District of Columbia. Born in 1904 in Waterbury, Connecticut. Italian immigrant father was a barber, mother ran a small grocery store. Family moved to Florida, Louisiana, and finally Washington, D.C., where as a boy he worked in a service station, sold newspapers, and learned to box. Entered law school directly after high school, but dropped out twice. Enrolled again, at Georgetown University Law School, and worked his way through by coaching boxing at a Knights of Columbus hall. Following a stint in Miami as a sparring partner and semipro boxer (at 148 pounds), returned to Washington and took court-appointed indigent cases. Worked as a prosecutor in the U.S. Attorney's office 1930–33, then went into private practice. In 1944 served as counsel to a congressional investigation of the Federal Communications Commission. A lifelong Republican, had campaigned for Willkie, Dewey, and Eisenhower. From 1949 until being appointed to a federal judgeship by

President Eisenhower in 1957 was a trial attorney with the prominent Republican firm of Hogan and Hartson. On the bench got the nickname "Maximum John" for his tough, often erratic courtroom manner and sentencing. Was often reversed by the U.S. Court of Appeals on procedural grounds. Soft-spoken but aggressive. Not particularly scholarly or eloquent, is guided by gut reactions. As chief judge of the District Court (through seniority), was entitled to assign himself the Watergate case, which made his name a household word. Married at forty-seven to Lucile Camalier (nearly twenty years his junior), whose family owns several leather goods and gift shops in the Washington area. Three children, ages twelve, eighteen, and twenty-one. Lives in the affluent Spring Valley neighborhood of the District, and has a beach house on the Delaware coast. Goes to bed early, gets up before sunrise. Short, wiry, looks younger than he is. Wavy black hair, bushy eyebrows, and a craggy face. Plays golf, but not very well. Resigned from the bench, as required, at the age of seventy, but followed the Watergate trial to its conclusion. Attends mass regularly. Lifelong friend of boxing great Jack Dempsey, who was best man at his wedding.

KEY AGENCY PEOPLE

Arthur F. Burns, Chairman, Board of Governors, Federal Reserve System. Born in 1904 in Austria. Father a house painter. Was ten when parents came to U.S. Wanted to be an architect. AB and MA degrees from Columbia in 1925, followed by PhD in 1934. Worked his way through college as house painter, paperhanger, theater usher, waiter, stock clerk, and furniture salesman (liked the last job best—could study when there were no customers). Taught at Rutgers 1927–44, then at Columbia. Wrote nine books as sole or co-author. Expert on business cycles. Was chairman, National Bureau of Economic Research. Came to Washington under President Eisenhower as chairman of his Council of Economic Advisers 1953–56. Befriended V.P. Nixon, who remembered and called him back as his counselor when he became President in 1969. Named to Federal Reserve in 1970. Leading fiscal conservative. Lives in the Watergate complex, owns a farm in Vermont near Dartmouth College and next door to economist Milton Friedman's. Constant pipe smoker, often uses it as a diversion to avoid quick answers to questions. Occasionally arrogant, frequently patronizing, but always ready to enlighten his listeners. Parts his thatch of white hair smack in the middle. Reads the Bible in hotel rooms. Likes lively parties, is an enthusiastic dancer. Is in the office seven days a week. Hobby: economics. Took up abstract painting recently. Married, has two grown sons, one an economics professor, the other a government lawyer.

William Egan Colby, Director of the Central Intelligence Agency. Born in 1920 in St. Paul, Minnesota, the son of an Army officer. Grew up all over the place, including a three-year period in China. Graduated from Princeton. Spent World War II with the Office of Strategic Services (OSS), with assignments behind enemy lines in France and Norway. After the war, took law degree at Columbia and practiced in New York. Came to Washington as attorney with the National Labor Relations Board. Didn't care much for practicing law. Joined CIA in 1951, spent the next seven years attached to

American embassies in Stockholm and Rome (where he worked behind the scenes to thwart the Italian Communists in parliament). In 1959 began long career of clandestine operations in Vietnam, interrupted by six years back in Washington as CIA chief for the Far East. During years in Vietnam, worked nominally as an employee of State Department and AID. In 1968 was put in charge (with rank of ambassador) of entire "pacification" program to destroy the NLF. Appointed CIA director in 1973, when James Schlesinger moved to Defense. Despite long years of "black bag" operations, has led movement to play down the CIA's interventionist side and emphasize information gathering. "The CIA's cloak-and-dagger days have ended," he says. Was the one who revealed to Congress the extent of CIA role in Chilean President Allende's downfall. After the *New York Times* exposed the CIA's covert surveillance of American citizens, he startled the intelligence community by acknowledging the program (now defunct, he says) and volunteering information about it. Dapper, trim, neatly combed hair, clear-rimmed glasses. Myopic (tried to bluff his way through the eye test for Army paratroopers by memorizing the charts). Lives unpretentiously in a Washington suburb, with wife (a Barnard student he met while at Columbia Law) and four children. Avoids Washington social life. Catholic. Works long hours. Amiable, frank, shrewd. Usually drives himself to work (unusual for someone of his rank). Soon after becoming CIA director, returned by helicopter to the Langley, Virginia, complex after a trip. Was met at the pad by a limousine to drive him to his office, 100 yards away. Said he'd rather walk, which he did, with the car following slowly behind.

Clarence M. Kelley, Director of the Federal Bureau of Investigation. Born 1911 in Kansas City, Missouri, an only child whose father was a utility company engineer. Played baseball and football as a boy. (Dreamed of being a pro baseball player, but couldn't hit a fast ball.) Took undergraduate degree from the University of Kansas, law degree from the University of Missouri. Joined FBI right out of law school, attracted by a hard-sell recruiting spiel. Worked as an agent all over the country, in jobs ranging from firearms instructor to field supervisor. Served during World War II on a Navy transport ship in the Pacific. After twenty-one years with the FBI, tapped for police chief of Kansas City. During twelve years there, rebuilt a scandal-ridden department and pioneered such modern methods as computerized crime records and helicopter patrols. In summer of 1973, appointed by Nixon to head the FBI, which had been shaken by revelations that previous director Patrick L. Gray had allowed the White House to interfere with the Bureau's investigation of Watergate. Has continued Gray's initiatives in the post-Hoover era: making the Bureau more open, recruiting minority and women agents, curtailing domestic political surveillance, and improving relations with Congress. Considered by the FBI agents as "one of their own." Candid, straightforward, low-key, modest. Good sense of humor, able to poke fun at himself. A big man: 6 feet tall, 200 pounds. Beefy face, full head of wavy gray hair, black-rimmed glasses. Likes to eat, especially chili and barbecue. Heavy cigarette smoker. Slightly hard of hearing, from his days on the firing range. Active at his church, has taught Sunday school and delivered sermons. Prolific reader, likes historical novels. Putters in the garden of his condominium in suburban Maryland. Married, two grown children. Ardent sports fan. Nicknamed "Chief" in high school, because of his resemblance to the Indian chief trademark on a popular brand of notebook.

Frank Gustav Zarb, Administrator of the Federal Energy Administration, Executive Director of the Energy Resources Council. Born in 1935 in Brooklyn, New York, the son of a Turkish immigrant who worked as a refrigerator mechanic. Attended vocational high school, preparing to become an airline mechanic. A friendly teacher urged college instead. Graduated from Hofstra College in 1957, with degree in business administration. Was active in student affairs. Elected student council president, married the council's vice president. Held down a paying job with Hofstra, while working as coordinator of student activities. After time in the Army, returned to Hofstra for an MBA in 1961. Worked briefly in the executive training program of a major oil company, even pumping gas. Went to Wall Street, specialized in "back office" administration of stock brokerage operations. Helped pull off the takeover of large, faltering Hayden Stone by the smaller firm for which he worked. Came to Washington in 1971 as an Assistant Secretary of Labor. In 1972 rejoined Hayden Stone as executive vice president and chairman of the executive committee, making $110,000 a year. Lured back to the capital by his former boss George P. Shultz, then Secretary of the Treasury. Worked at Office of Management and Budget in energy resource matters, assisted in setting up the Federal Energy Administration during the gasoline crisis of 1973–74. A skilled negotiator, helped government settle disputes with irate truck drivers and angry American Indians. Pragmatic, decisive. Was slated to become vice president of the Export-Import Bank when President Ford named him to the top post at FEA to succeed John Sawhill. Tireless worker, puts in seventy hours a week on the job, including weekends. Has basically conservative, pro-business values, but not dogmatic. Candid, breezy personality. Medium build, strong-featured face, blue eyes. Full head of dark, curly, rather unkempt hair, graying at the temples. Smokes a pipe. Little time for hobbies, but engages in do-it-yourself work around the house (like wallpapering a couple of rooms). Household in suburban McLean, Virginia, consists of wife, daughter aged fifteen, son aged twelve, and three dogs.

Russell E. Train, Administrator of the Environmental Protection Agency. Born 1920 in Jamestown, Rhode Island, the youngest of three sons. Father a rear admiral, mother from the well-established Brown family of Washington. Grew up in Washington, went to fashionable St. Albans School. Graduated cum laude from Princeton, where he debated. Served in the field artillery during the war, discharged as major. Specialized in taxes at Columbia Law School. Held successive jobs on the Hill, for Joint Committee on Internal Revenue Taxation, Ways and Means, and Treasury Department. Appointed by Eisenhower to the U.S. Tax Court in 1957. Longstanding interest in Africa. Went on big game safari in 1956, shot an elephant, and got chased up a tree by a rhino. Became a conservationist. In 1961 set up a foundation to help emerging African nations create wildlife preservation programs. Conservation took up more and more time, so resigned from court in 1965 to become president of the Conservation Foundation. Appointed by Nixon to be Under Secretary of Interior in 1969. Headed committee that drew up environmental construction standards for Alaska pipeline. First chairman of the

White House Council on Environmental Quality, 1970. Appointed head of the EPA, 1973. Strong defender of the environment, but believes in rational, balanced use of natural resources. Reserved, but good-natured. Medium build, blue eyes, sandy-red hair, ruddy complexion. Conservative dresser. Married, two daughters, two sons. "Cave dweller," member of Chevy Chase Club and Metropolitan Club (in front of which his car can be seen most days during the lunch hour). Home on expensive Woodland Drive in the District, plus a farm in Maryland on the Eastern Shore of the Chesapeake Bay.

Elmer Boyd Staats, Comptroller General (head of the General Accounting Office). Born in 1914 on a Kansas farm, one of eight children. Graduated Phi Beta Kappa from McPherson College (Kansas), where he was class president and editor of the newspaper. Took master's degree at Kansas, doctorate (in government and public administration) at Minnesota. Was a fellow at the Brookings Institution. Joined Bureau of the Budget in 1939, becoming deputy director in 1950. Served in that job under four Presidents, with short periods away (a year as research director at Marshall Field in Chicago, four years— 1953–58—with White House National Security Council, helping infuse other agencies with the Council's international policies). Appointed comptroller general by LBJ in 1966, to serve fifteen-year, nonrenewable term, with removal only by joint resolution of Congress. His agency, the GAO, is Congress's watchdog over the efficiency and honesty of all federal programs. Its reports often ruffle a lot of feathers with criticisms of program achievement and tales of wasted spending. Staats is respected as a scholarly professional, absolutely above politics. Rugged six-footer, blue-eyed, receding blond hair. An active Methodist. Married to daughter of a former GOP congressman from Pennsylvania, three children. Gardens and golfs with wife. Lives quietly in expensive Spring Valley section of the District. Is member of intellectually prestigious Cosmos Club and socially elite Chevy Chase Club.

Dixy Lee Ray, Assistant Secretary of State for Oceans and International Environmental and Scientific Affairs, former Chairman of the Atomic Energy Commission. Born in 1914 in Tacoma, Washington, one of five daughters of a commercial printer. Wasn't named anything at birth, since parents expected a son. Chose own name at sixteen, borrowing "Dixy" from her nickname "Dickens" (or "Dick") and "Lee" from a distant family link to the Lees of Virginia. As a child spent summers on an island in Puget Sound where father owned property (later to be her permanent home). Graduated Phi Beta Kappa in zoology from Mills College, where she bused dishes for tuition money. Taught science in Oakland, California, public schools. Took PhD in biological sciences at Stanford, became eminent marine biologist over two decades of teaching and research at University of Washington. Frequent consultant to the federal government. Once hosted a local TV show aimed at popularizing science. Named first woman member of the AEC in 1972, becoming chairman when James Schlesinger headed the CIA. Urged building of more nuclear power plants, pooh-poohing criticisms of people she calls "knee-jerk environmentalists." Moved to newly created position at State Department in 1974, when the AEC was merged out of existence. Short and stout. Amber eyes and close-cropped gray hair. A loner, but genial. Good sense of humor. In Washington area, lives in a small mobile home with lots of books and two dogs (a Scottish deerhound and a miniature poodle) who go everywhere with her, even to the office. Has been known to cancel public appearances when dogs were sick. Dresses in casual, colorful clothes. Reads science fiction and technical books, watches TV. Chief hobby is studying American Indian cultures. Is an honorary member of the Kwikseutanik tribe, whose crafts decorate her office. Tribe gave her name "Oo'ma," meaning "Great Lady." Never married. Likes to spend time with her numerous nieces and nephews.

Benjamin Franklin Bailar, Postmaster General. Born in Champaign, Illinois, in 1934. Father a professor of chemistry at University of Illinois, mother an occasional mathematics instructor there. Went to the University of Colorado (as did his father and grandfather), majored in geology. Two years in the Navy supply corps, followed by a master's degree from the Harvard Business School. Worked three years for the Continental Oil Company in Houston, Texas. Joined American Can Company in 1962, rising from financial analyst to vice president for international operations. Recruited for the Postal Service in 1972 by then Postmaster General Elmer (Ted) Klassen, a former president of American Can. Held posts of senior assistant postmaster general (operating as the service's chief financial officer and later as chief administrative official), deputy postmaster general, and member of the board of directors. Promoted to the top job upon the resignation of Klassen in February 1975. Probably the second youngest P.G. in history. Thinks the price of a first-class stamp is one of the country's last great bargains, and feels that most people don't realize how good their mail service really is. Cool, low-key, genial personality. Makes decisions with dispatch. Special skill is financial analysis. Not much time for hobbies any more. Used to do a lot of photography and developing in a home darkroom. Occasionally goes fly-fishing for trout, salmon, and tarpon. Owns a Ferrari sports car, but commutes each day (from suburban Bethesda, Maryland) in a regular sedan. Six feet one inch tall, husky 200 pounds. Thinning dark hair, fashionably long sideburns, plump face. Married, one daughter (11), one son (9). Goes bike riding and ice skating with the children. Called "Ben." Named after his maternal grandfather. No relation to the original Ben Franklin, who, coincidentally, was the nation's first Postmaster General.

S. (Sidney) Dillon Ripley II, Secretary of the Smithsonian Institution. Born in 1913 in New York City into a wealthy, well-bred family. Father a stockbroker, maternal grandfather a chairman of the Union Pacific Railroad. Went to Madame Montessori's school in New York City, traveled through Europe as a child. At thirteen, toured India and Tibet with family. At elite St. Paul's boarding school, was president of bird-watching club, also rowed, wrote poems, acted, and debated. Active in fencing and dramatics at Yale. Parents wanted him to study law, but he enrolled at Columbia graduate school in zoology. Didn't have enough background in sciences, so quit. Went with zoology expedition to New Guinea (on schooner manned by family friends), spent fourteen months gathering bird specimens. Began studying and teaching at Harvard, got PhD in 1943. During World War II, with OSS in Ceylon, India, and Burma, as headquarters coordinator of agents working behind enemy lines. Taught zoology and biology at Yale. Prolific writer on birds, leader of far-flung expeditions. Director of Peabody Museum of Natural History at Yale, 1959. Appointed by LBJ to head the Smithsonian, "the nation's attic," in 1964. His domain includes National Gallery of Art, Kennedy Center for the Performing Arts, National Zoological Park, Air and Space Museum, Hirshhorn Museum, and many, many other divisions. Broadly praised (but criticized by traditionalists) for making the Smithsonian more accessible to the general public through such lively innovations as jazz concerts, folk-life festivals, a neighborhood museum in predominantly black Anacostia, and a popular magazine. Tall, slender, 6 feet 3 inches, 175 pounds. Dapper, conservative dresser. Nearly bald. Married to former Mary Moncrieffe Livingston (who also served with the OSS in the Far East during the war), three daughters. Lives in townhouse on Massachusetts Avenue, along "Embassy Row." Spends time at 150-acre estate in Litchfield, Connecticut, owned by family for more than a century. Still goes on ornithology expeditions (like one to the Himalayas in 1974, on which he caught bad case of dysentery). Tried to cancel a 1974 Smithsonian lecture that was to have been given by Erica Jong, author of the sexually explicit novel *Fear of Flying*. (Faced with attempted censorship, Ms. Jong canceled the lecture herself.) Charming, supremely self-confident, occasionally autocratic. Aristocratic manner sometimes offends simpler folks.

Nancy Hanks, Chairman, National Endowment for the Arts. Born in 1927, Miami Beach, Florida, the daughter of a lawyer from Texas who was a prominent Florida utilities executive. Named after Abraham Lincoln's mother, a distant relative. Went to high school in Montclair, New Jersey, spent summers at family's mountain home in North Carolina. Studied at the University of Colorado and at Oxford (England), before graduating from Duke University, where she was a sorority girl, Phi Beta Kappa, president of the student council, and May Queen. Came to Washington in 1951 as a receptionist in the Office of Defense Mobilization, then became a staff assistant with various Washington agencies in early Fifties, during which time she worked for Nelson Rockefeller (then Under Secretary of HEW). From 1956 to 1969, was cultural aide to the Rockefeller Brothers Fund in New York City and directed numerous seminal studies on the financial state of the arts in America. Tapped for the endowment chairmanship in 1969, she was described by one senator as "the best appointment the Nixon administration has made." Through good rapport with both the White House and Congress, has been instrumental in making the federal arts budget soar. A skilled administrator and inspirational leader for her devoted staff. A strong defender of the endowment against the attacks of philistine congressmen. Works in a brightly decorated office filled with paintings, prints, and mementos. Tall, full-figured, with a wholesomely pretty face. Conservatively coiffed and a traditional dresser. Does needlepoint, plays with her black Scotty. Quietly sociable, not a fixture on the Washington party scene. Plays golf and tennis, swims, and gardens. Never married. Lives in an apartment in the Watergate complex, also maintains a house in ritzy Southampton, Long Island.

J. (John) Carter Brown, Director of the National Gallery of Art. Born in 1934 in Providence, Rhode Island, son of real estate investor John Nicholas Brown (who at birth was dubbed "The Million Dollar Baby"). Heir to a fortune dating from colonial times, based originally on international trade (including slave shipping), rum distilling, spermaceti candles, iron, and textiles. Ancestors endowed Brown University. As a boy, traveled through Europe with his parents, and at home was surrounded by fine paintings and antiques. Schooled at elite Groton and at English boarding school. Graduated Phi Beta Kappa and summa cum laude from Harvard, then took a master's degree from Harvard Business School. Studied art history in Germany, France, the Netherlands, and Italy (with renowned art scholar Bernard Berenson, whom he refers to as "B.B."). Came to the National Gallery in 1961 as assistant to then Director John Walker. Made director in 1969. Has been instrumental in improving the gallery's collection of twentieth-century art. Boosted museum attendance to record heights with such innovations as film series and exhibits of African art. Handsome, tall, slender, with a finely featured face. Dresses with understated elegance. Has a patrician bearing and dry wit. Is a yachtsman and amateur choral singer. Once gave some thought to becoming an architect or film director. Club memberships in Washington, New York, Annapolis, and Newport. Was married to Pittsburgh heiress Constance Mellon, from whom he was separated in 1974. Lives in an apartment in the Watergate complex.

THE PARTY CHAIRMEN

Robert Strauss, Chairman of the Democratic National Committee. Born in 1918 in south Texas, father a German-Jewish immigrant, mother from an old Texas Jewish family. As a boy helped in parents' modest dry goods store. During undergraduate years at University of Texas, clerked at the State Capitol. Befriended John Connally in college (and has remained close to him ever since), was a volunteer worker in LBJ's first House race in 1937. Took law degree at Texas. Was an FBI agent during World War II. After the war, helped found a law partnership in Dallas and started on the way to becoming a millionaire in law, real estate, and broadcasting (at one time or another owning radio stations in Tucson, Dallas, and Atlanta). Began his impressive career as a political fund raiser in successful Connally gubernatorial race of 1962. Was co-manager of Humphrey-Muskie race in Texas, 1968, and was made DNC treasurer in 1970, to whittle down the Humphrey debt. Resigned during McGovern candidacy to raise money for Democratic congressional candidates. After 1972 debacle, chosen by party's old guard to get it back on its feet. Distrusted by left wing of the party, including some groups of women and blacks. Married (to daughter of the publisher of a few small Texas papers), two sons, one daughter. Wavy gray hair, combed back from a high forehead, dark prominent eyebrows. Tough, aggressive, congenial, charming. Peppers his talk with ribald expressions. Addresses women as "honey," has been known to call them "broads." Perpetual sun tan. A leader of his Reform synagogue in Dallas. Three chief hobbies: betting on horses, playing poker on Saturday nights in Dallas, and making his special recipe for chili (which he has been known to force on his friends). Starts work at 6 A.M. Has a swimming pool at his Dallas home, but would rather drink martinis next to it than swim in it. Has a Lincoln Continental with a powder blue interior and a telephone. Best-known quote: "If the Democrats wanted a loser, they wouldn't have hired me." Takes no salary for party chairmanship.

Mary Louise Smith, Chairman of the Republican National Committee. Born in 1914 in Iowa, the daughter of a banker whose bank failed. Graduated from University of Iowa with major in social work administration. Married before graduation to a medical student. (They eloped and kept it a secret, and she continued to live at her sorority.) Worked her way up through the GOP ranks, from volunteer campaign worker in late Forties to posts in county, state, and regional organizations. Was Iowa GOP vice chairman in the Goldwater campaign of 1964. Active in party reform and served on platform committee at 1968 and 1972 national conventions. Delegate in 1969 to UN conference on population, and in 1973 to general session of UNESCO. Elected first woman chairman of the RNC in 1974. Calls herself a "moderate conservative," but has worked hard to attract new groups of people to the GOP. Senator Goldwater has called for her replacement by a "real proven politician." Works from 7:45 A.M. until middle of the evening. Lives at the Mayflower Hotel, where her apartment is filled with the aroma of burning incense. Likes to play bridge. A neat, trim, attractive woman with curly gray hair and electric blue eyes. Looks like Pat Nixon. Has a gracious, ladylike manner, but knows how to get her way. Wants everyone to call her "Mary Louise." Has a sandwich—American cheese with lettuce and mayonnaise—every day for lunch (also harbors a passion for peanut butter). Physician husband served two tours in Vietnam as a volunteer doctor, is a football nut who won't miss a single University of Iowa game, so doesn't get to Washington often. They have three grown children, two sons and a daughter. Mrs. Smith commutes to Des Moines home infrequently.

WORLD FINANCE LEADERS

Hendrikus Johannes Witteveen, Managing Director, International Monetary Fund. Born in 1921 in Zeist, the Netherlands. Educated at Rotterdam School of Economics. Worked in the Dutch Central Planning Office during postwar reconstruction. Lectured at his old school 1946–48 and became professor of business cycles and economics there until 1963. Meanwhile, had tried his hand at politics, winning a seat in the lower house of parliament in 1958. From 1963 through 1971 held, successively, a seat in the upper house of parliament and posts of Minister of Finance and Deputy Prime Minister. In 1972 moved into the business world, as member of the advisory board of the giant Unilever corporation. Chosen for IMF top job at a time of monetary turmoil, when several other candidates didn't want to touch it. Immediately confronted with problem of creating new credit facilities to help countries pay soaring oil costs. Politically a liberal. Very pragmatic in approach: whatever works is better than the distant ideal. Loves English and French literature, classical music. Tall, lean, baldish, smiles a lot, is shy and retiring. Looks like a professor, but talks economics in plain horse-sense language. Married, four children. Is a past vice president of the International Religious and Philosophical Sufi Movement, a small but very old pantheistic religion that stresses good works, self-effacement, humble living, and the basic oneness of all religions.

Robert Strange McNamara, President of the World Bank. Born in San Francisco in 1916, the only son of a shoe company sales manager. Asthmatic as a child, but after high school worked for a year on a freighter in the Pacific and Caribbean (and as a seamen's union organizer). Graduated Phi Beta Kappa from California at Berkeley, then took an MBA from Harvard Business School. Worked briefly as an accountant, then returned to Harvard as assistant professor of accounting (1940–43). Classified 4-F, but worked in civilian jobs at Pentagon and then as a statistical supply analyst in the Army Air Corps in England, India, and China, getting out as a decorated lieutenant colonel. After war, he and wife hospitalized with mild cases of polio. Was one of the "Quiz Kids" (later renamed "Whiz Kids"), a group of young statistical control experts from the military hired in a group by Ford Motor Company. In fourteen years (1946–60) rose from financial analyst to become first nonfamily president of the giant automaker. At Ford, helped pioneer auto safety devices and compact cars. Unlike most auto executives, lived in university town of Ann Arbor, hobnobbed with intellectuals, and supported the NAACP. Nominally a Republican, was tapped by JFK as Secretary of Defense (the youngest ever at forty-four). Shook up the Pentagon with demands of cost-effectiveness studies, made military decisions himself when the Joint Chiefs couldn't agree. Stayed on as Secretary under LBJ. Worst black eye: participation in the escalation of the Vietnam war. Appointed president of the World Bank in 1968. Respected by the Third World recipients of Bank aid. Badgers the developed nations about not giving enough to less fortunate nations. Tall, slender. Wears rimless glasses and conservative suits. Slicks back his thin dark hair and parts it almost down the center. Reads and thinks quickly. Hard-working, thoughtful, introspective (contrary to reputation of being coldly mechanical). In recent years has become more emotional, almost gloomy, perhaps sobered by the lessons of Vietnam, the deaths of his good friends the Kennedy brothers, and the magnitude of the challenges facing the developing nations. Quiet sense of humor. Married, three children. A millionaire from his years with Ford, lives on elegant Tracy Place in the Kalorama section of the District. Skis, hikes in the mountains, listens to classical music. Not a social butterfly, but seen at many of the "major" parties (where he is known as a good ballroom dancer).

LOCAL LEADERS

Walter E. Washington, Mayor of the District of Columbia. Born in 1915 in Georgia (the great-grandson of a slave), but raised from infancy in Jamestown, New York. An only child. Father a factory worker and later proprietor of a valet shop, mother a former rural schoolteacher who died when child was eight. Only black in his class in high school, where he was a football player and student leader. Graduated from Howard University in public administration and sociology. Began career with the D.C. public housing authority in 1941, became first black director of it in 1961. Studied law in night classes at Howard, graduating and joining the D.C. bar in 1948, but has never practiced. Tapped by New York Mayor Lindsay to head city's housing authority in 1966. Chosen by LBJ as appointed "mayor" of Washington in 1967. Elected first D.C. mayor in over a century in 1974 (as a Democrat). More of an administrator than theorist. Earnest but not brilliant. Middle-of-the-road, with strong support from D.C.'s white business community, black middle class, and politically potent black ministers. Believes in gradual, realistic change. Good rapport with Congress and White House (under both Democrats and GOP). Considered too conservative by many of the young, up-and-coming black leaders. Short, heavyset, with close-cropped dark hair. Smokes a pipe. Wears traditionally cut dark suits and white shirts. Nothing flashy or hip about him. A ready handshake and smile, good with crowds. Easygoing in public, a tough political infighter behind the scenes. Married to the former Bennetta Bullock, daughter of a prominent black minister. She, who has a PhD in social work from Catholic University, is a former high school princi-pal and longtime federal official in labor affairs. One daughter, who studied at Radcliffe and the Sorbonne and has a Harvard PhD. Lives in a comfortable but not elegant house in the LeDroit Park neighborhood of the District, a once elegant area (next to Howard University) that has gone downhill in recent decades. Very active social life, mostly at parties he feels he must attend (but also enjoys). Goes to all the Redskins home games. Member of several downtown clubs, including the high-brow Cosmos Club.

Walter E. Fauntroy, Congressional Delegate from the District of Columbia. Born to black parents in Washington, D.C., in 1933. Father a low-level federal employee in the Patent Office. Grew up in the decaying Shaw area of the District. Was a Cub Scout and joined activities of the YMCA and Boys' Clubs. Played sandlot football and baseball. Regularly attended the New Bethel Baptist Church, whose congregation helped raise money to send him to Virginia Union University for religious studies. Then got a scholarship to Yale Divinity School. In 1958, at age twenty-five, was chosen as minister of New Bethel. Soon became active in civil rights movement, as Washington leader of the Reverend Martin Luther King's Southern Christian Leadership Conference. Marched and worked with King in Birmingham, Selma, and throughout the South. Directed a community development organization in Shaw, and was appointed to the D.C. City Council, serving as vice chairman. During the 1968 D.C. riots that followed King's murder, raised a calming voice, in opposition to the incendiary speeches of Stokely Carmichael. Elected to be D.C.'s first nonvoting congressional delegate in 1971. Is considered radical by some whites (for example, white business establishment on the Board of Trade) but too staid by militant blacks. Works hard on House District Committee for D.C. interests, but lacks the clout of more senior members (who have the advantage of a vote). Supported George McGovern's candidacy from the start, made a televised seconding speech at the national convention. Does not have very good relations with Mayor Washington, who supported another candidate in the first delegate race. Carried the District easily, despite getting a minority of the votes in affluent white areas west of Rock Creek Park. Favors gun control legislation. Energetic, excited person-ality. Slight build, good-looking, short hair, and thin black mustache. Looks younger than he is. High-pitched voice. Sounds like a spellbinding minister when he gives a political speech. Married, one young son. Doesn't care for chitchat and parties. Doesn't drink. Wears dark suits and white shirts. Lives in a modest home west of upper 16th Street, near Rock Creek Park. No time for hobbies.

Sterling Tucker, Chairman of the D.C. Council. Born in 1923 in Akron, Ohio, the fourth of eight children in a poor black family. As a boy, sold newspapers and shined shoes. While in high school, moved with family to another house when their old one was declared a slum and razed for public housing. In college at University of Akron, worked as an office boy at Firestone, in a dress shop, and as the first Negro busboy at a ritzy restaurant that wouldn't admit blacks. (When he and friends, dressed to the nines, went there for dinner one night, they were served, but Tucker was immediately fired.) After taking master's degree in social psychology, went to work for the Akron Urban League, later moving to the Canton, Ohio, chapter. Came to Washington Urban League in 1956, active in human rights ever since. First black member of local Jaycees, 1957. Vice chairman of the 1963 mass civil rights march on Washington, national coordinator for the Poor People's March after the Reverend Martin Luther King's death, in 1968. Lectured overseas on race relations for the State Department. Appointed to City Council by Nixon in 1969, became first elected chairman (in over a century) in 1974. A fighter for home rule, minority hiring, minority contractors on subway project, consumer protection, rent control. An independent sort, gets along with black militants and the white business establishment. Conceived idea for Pride, Inc., a grass-roots black enterprise in D.C. Skilled mediator and legislator. Fined in 1959 for tax evasion, pardoned by LBJ in 1966. Trim build, looks much younger than his years. Short hair. Avid tennis player and sports fan. Married to childhood girl friend, two daughters (one attends the private Sidwell Friends School, at which her older sister teaches). Modish dresser. Suave, outgoing personality. Lives in the District on upper 16th Street. Episcopalian. Office at the District Building is decorated with African sculpture and paintings by black Americans.

5 NIXON'S WATERGATE

Post-mortems are supposed to be conducted after death has definitely been certified, and nobody can yet certify that the issues of Watergate are dead. Yet though the nation is still testing its new leadership, and many predicted results are as yet undetermined, it may be possible to sort out some of the causes and consequences of the most disruptive political scandal of the twentieth century.

A new law on political campaign funding got through Congress late in 1974 and became the major legislative product of the Watergate affair. Any further legislative harvest from Watergate will be meager. Cynics may say the reason is that the issues are too hot to handle. But the real reason may be far less sinister. It may simply be that laws now on the books are adequate, if enforced. Remember that Watergate erupted precisely because people in and around the White House broke laws:

Breaking and entering. Illegal.

Recording other people's conversations without their permission. Illegal.

Stealing documents from a private citizen's office. Illegal.

Lying to a grand jury. Illegal.

Distributing a forged letter about an opposing candidate. Illegal.

Withholding information requested by a federal court. Illegal.

Falsifying records presented to a grand jury. Illegal.

Accepting political contributions from corporations. Illegal.

Hiding campaign contributions by sending them out of the country and reimporting the cash. Illegal.

Accepting money for influencing specific public policy. Illegal.

And so on.

Thus, while few new laws have been passed, perhaps new laws really were not what was needed. What was needed was compliance with the laws we already had, or at the very least, better enforcement of those same laws.

What brought an American President to such a point that he felt forced to resign the nation's highest office? The answer starts with the man himself.

RICHARD M. NIXON

He was raised a poor boy. His was a plain family. He acquired a deep yearning for some of the things that he did not have when he was young: luxurious surroundings, financial ease, a margin of safety against vicissitudes.

He made his own way, admired others who had done the same. Note his close personal friends. Robert Abplanalp. Bebe Rebozo. C. Arnholt Smith. Donald Kendall. W. Clement Stone. Businessmen, but men who came up from relative obscurity. He was educated in law, trained in controversy, and never shied from hot spots—in the Alger Hiss case, in the southern California contests for the House and the Senate, the Vice Presidency, and the Presidency.

He liked foreign affairs because he could operate more nearly alone, cut through the welter of advice, and pull surprises.

He jumped into public life before he had time to season. When he first ran for Congress and was elected, he had worked for less than a year in the government (Office of Price Administration), had been in Naval uniform, and had just begun a private practice of law. He never had time to make much money in private life. Only during his nearly four years as a New York lawyer with Nixon, Mudge, Rose, Guthrie and Alexander did he have anything more than a government salary.

He was always an energetic and ambitious young man, ahead of himself. As Vice President, he had risen rapidly from an obscure member of Congress, suddenly finding himself in the councils with elder statesmen. He rubbed elbows with the national hero, Eisenhower, and with such old industrial warhorses as George Humphrey of Cleveland. He was the rising young talent, but always on his mettle to prove himself.

When he first became Vice President, he lived in a very small house, totally inadequate for entertaining. It was on the edge of Spring Valley, a "good address," but a cramped corner house in full view of passing traffic. Only toward the end of his Vice Presidency did he move to a more spacious house nearby, and even this put a strain on his finances.

He was always an energetic and ambitious young man, ahead of himself. As discard, and draw again. He had few deep emotional entanglements with his governmental counselors, so acted freely. He removed old friend Bob Finch as Secretary of Health, Education and Welfare when it became clear that Finch was not a tight enough administrator. He swept the White House crew out after Watergate (though this was harder). He parted company with John Mitchell, though Mitchell had been his closest professional associate. William Rogers, Secretary of State, survived the turbulence of change longer than the others, but eventually he, too, was discarded in favor of White House dominance.

This is the man who became the first person to resign the office of President of the United States.

The man's character and traits were not unknown to the American scene. His political opponents had hammered at them in every one of his campaigns . . . for the Senate in 1950 . . . for the Vice Presidency in 1952 . . . for the Presidency in 1960 . . . for governor of California in 1962 . . . and again in his second try for the Presidency in 1968. "Tricky Dick" was the unflattering phrase. "The New Nixon" was the rebuttal from his friends.

Yet some observers who were not partisans, neither friends nor enemies, did correctly judge the character and personality of Richard Nixon. W. M. Kiplinger, the original editor of the *Kiplinger Washington Letter* and a long-time observer of the Washington scene, wrote in the October 1, 1955, issue of his weekly *Letter:* "Nixon has both merits and faults. Politically he's middle of the road. He is not exactly a 'popular figure.' Not as young, not as dour as he looks. Not always clear in seeing what is principle and what is expediency."

What many people, however, did not correctly assess was Richard Nixon's dogged determination—his "stick-to-it-iveness." Others discounted his shrewd intelligence, believing him to be devious but dull. As it turned out, dullness was not his undoing, but deviousness was.

When he had removed himself from office and the Presidency was occupied by Gerald Ford, millions of average Americans (including many who were Nixon supporters) said to each other, "Isn't it nice to have a President who does his job without always looking in the mirror to check his 'image?' "

It was this image-consciousness which led Richard Nixon to surround himself with advertising men and promotion men, and which ultimately caused him to constrict his circle of advisers to those who mirrored what he apparently wanted to hear and see. One by one, most of his old political associates—men with wide political connections—were lopped off his roster of close confidants. The friends who remained were more personal than political—men such as Bebe Rebozo, Robert Abplanalp. The shrinking world of Richard Nixon occasionally opened up enough to take in such political figures as former Democrat John Connally and former Secretary of Defense Melvin Laird, but when their advice made no dent on the President, they withdrew. Being "yes men" was not their meat, and polishing up a presidential image was not their trade.

So President Nixon fell victim to the weakness of his youth: of not being "one of the boys," of hankering to be something that his personality did not permit him to be, of overreaching, of trying to compensate for a deep-seated sense of insecurity by overreacting.

Had he not set a tone of superdefense against the political enemy, had he not condoned a program of all-out attack against the Democratic party and its candidate, his second administration might well have been given above-average marks by subsequent historians. Yet, in a tragic effort to be doubly sure and absolutely safe in an area in which there are no sure and safe positions, he destroyed a performance which only two years earlier had been judged by the American people to be "satisfactory" in a Gallup poll.

On the practical side, the Watergate-Impeachment crisis had some notable consequences.

It educated millions of American voters to the meaning of the impeachment process.

It put on TV and radio, into the newspapers and newsmagazines, millions of words of debate on "high crimes and misdemeanors"—in their twentieth-century context.

It demonstrated to a generation of younger voters that their misgivings about the American political condition might be partially right, but that remedies existed and could be effective.

CRISIS MENTALITY

It must have meant something when Richard Nixon decided to title the story of his public career *Six Crises*. Other public figures, of course, have reveled in controversy and antagonism. Franklin D. Roosevelt was always at his best when confronted with a fight. Richard Nixon was willing to stand up to a fight, and rather prided himself on it. Like John Mitchell, Nixon was fond of the old adage of football coaches and scoutmasters, "When the going gets tough, the tough get going."

He was willing to hit hard and strike for the big prize. Only six years after he first ran for public office he was elected Vice President of the United States. And in all his public exploits, he never hesitated to use rough tactics. During the Alger Hiss case, he bored in relentlessly. In his contest for the Senate in 1950, he threw tough charges at Helen Gahagan Douglas. As Vice President, he toured abroad in unfriendly territory, was attacked in Venezuela, and engaged the Soviet leader, Nikita Khrushchev, in hard debate on the Russian's home ground.

To some observers, these exploits smacked of recklessness. Yet as a political operative, Nixon was one of the most careful planners on the national scene. While traveling by plane, with members of the press aboard, he would occasionally wander down the aisle and explain to them, in advance, just which strategy and which theme he would use on which audience, and why.

Richard Nixon practiced total politics. He treated it in the manner of total war. He approached a political campaign as a military general approaches a battle. Adversaries became "enemies" (as in the White House "enemies list"). He would use every known method of gaining "intelligence" (including wiretapping, planted spies, and break-ins). He employed confusion tactics to foul up the enemy (as in campaign "dirty tricks"). He staged his attacks with strategic timing. In fact, the "all-outness" of his approach to politics led him eventually to the "overkill" of Watergate.

But perhaps what distinguished Richard Nixon more than anything else was his perseverance. After he lost the contest for President in 1960, and then the election for governor of California just two years later, most political observers counted him out forever. He had lost on his own home ground. How could he ever hope to gain a national base? But Nixon didn't give up the quest.

Between 1964 and 1968 he kept plugging away. He took midnight planes to make breakfast speeches for congressional candidates—piling up "brownie points" and creating trading stock for his later bid for the nomination. He put in personal appearances in remote parts of the country unknown to most Americans, but still amassing good-will chits for later cashing. All this he did while trying to carry on a law practice from his new base of operations, New York.

Nixon had in abundance one thing that every successful political figure must have: physical, animal energy—an inexhaustible supply of adrenalin. The pace of national politics is almost incredible to the average person: day and night, week after week, away from home for months at a time, different states, different cities, different crowds. Nixon, in all his years of campaigning, made surprisingly few slips out of disorientation. He had a remarkable ability to keep his bearings, even when traveling abroad.

But conversely, he had a single-mindedness about winning which ended his tenure—a single-mindedness which put victory ahead of some other human standards of measurement. "Win at all costs," a military-type of order. And when he lost, his loss was complete. A Watergate Waterloo.

THE PRESIDENCY

For the past dozen years, the American Presidency has bestowed on its occupants personal disaster, unhappiness, or defeat. John F. Kennedy lost his life. Lyndon Johnson retired in a cloud of Vietnam bitterness. Richard Nixon resigned in the face of impeachment. Not since the retirement of Dwight

Eisenhower in 1961 has a President left office except under unhappy circumstances, whether from the inexorability of outside forces, flaws of character, or bad judgment. In the highest office recent Presidents have suffered the penalties of assassination, repudiation, and disgrace. Thomas Jefferson once described the Presidency as a position of "splendid misery." While the splendor may be debated, the misery has been incontestable.

Another trend apparent in recent years is the selection of the President out of the ranks of Congress. For nearly a hundred years—from after the Civil War until after World War II—American Presidents were drawn from among governors, generals, and noted private citizens. But since the death of Franklin Roosevelt in 1945, all Presidents except Dwight Eisenhower have been drawn from the U.S. Senate and House. As the issues with which Presidents now wrestle have become overwhelmingly national and international, the Congress has increasingly become their training ground. Yet each of the last three Presidents (and now a fourth, Gerald Ford) has had his troubles with Congress. Indeed it seems that the alienation of the President from Congress—and from his own party—contains the seeds of trouble and/or defeat. Certainly this alienation was a major contributor to the miscalculations which led the Nixon White House to the disaster of Watergate.

A calm appraisal of the Nixon Presidency will be some time in coming. Even to his friends, it was a disappointment. Nixon's performance in domestic affairs was short of his capabilities. Inflation—inherited from earlier administrations—fell to him to deal with, and the resulting policies made few political friends, either in business or in labor.

Nixon's second term never could achieve his campaign promise to "bring us together." The Nixon personality traits and qualities of temperament were too prickly to enable him to carry out the stated goal. He could do it on paper, but emotionally he avoided meeting with people who disagreed with him. He could not bring himself to work with the Black Caucus. He could not listen to the liberal wing of his own party. And as time went on, it became increasingly difficult for him even to listen to the leadership of Congress. When he had been crossed or impeded, his tendency was to turn away, to isolate himself from the irritant.

The sad fact is that two Presidents in a row fell victim to this same malady. Lyndon Johnson ended his administration in a virtual state of siege over Vietnam. Nixon's isolation stemmed from his determination to "tough it out" on Watergate.

WHY?

Millions of Americans will some day have to try to explain Watergate to their grandchildren. If it happens to you, what will you tell them? If they ask whether the individual offenses of Watergate were wholly new, you will have to admit that all of them had been committed before, at one time or another, by someone or other, somewhere or other. There had been various forms of corruption under previous administrations in Washington. There had been wiretapping in politics, political spying, violations of campaign fund raising, affairs was short of his capabilities. Inflation—inherited from earlier adminis-

But never before, you will have to say, had so many of these practices been perpetrated at the same time by the same administration at such high levels. Watergate was new in its scale and complexity. It was unique in its combination of bugging, spying, and covering up. And it was new in the spectacle of a President being caught in the middle of it all.

What will you have to say about the electronic tapes? How will you explain the recorded private conversations, the telltale records of everything that went on in the Oval Office? At this point, you may have some difficulty understanding why a President of the most powerful nation in the world would place himself in such a vulnerable position. It may be hard to explain why a public official would record himself making intimate and damaging judgments about his close advisers to other close advisers. It may escape your powers of comprehension to explain why a man who promoted a personal "goody-goody" image in public allowed himself to be recorded in private using such gamy and earthy language. It may be hard to explain why a President who placed so much store by executive privilege and administrative discretion would himself be so indiscreet as to make an audible record of his candid reactions to people, foreign nations, and public issues. About this, you may have to plead mystification, until some day when the chief participant writes his own story (from which advance publication rights and royalties will net him millions of dollars).

Other questions that you may be called upon to answer will probably include: Why did so many well-educated, upright, and substantial citizens—many of them lawyers—fall into the web of dirty tricks, deceit, and evasion?

Well, you will say, some of them had never had much experience in politics. They became intoxicated with their nearness to the center of power. They reveled in the opportunity to make decisions in the President's name.

They isolated themselves from their own political party. They were, after all, members of the Committee to Reelect the President, the CRP (or the CREEPS, as they came to be known by others in their own party). As members of the White House staff, they developed the unmistakable attitude of prima donnas. The high-riding young political operatives mesmerized by the trappings of the office came to believe that almost anything they decided to do was all right. It was "all in the game." And yet this was not an accidental aggregation of men. Richard Nixon had hand-picked them. It was his style they were emulating.

There is one thing about Richard Nixon that is "perfectly clear." He has never been a careless man. In view of this, he could not have been so careless as not to have known, or sensed, the tactics that were being used in his reelection campaign. Whatever else he has been charged with in his political career, no one has ever accused him of being "a dupe" of the people around him. Then why did Nixon choose this group of advisers?

First, because they gave absolute personal loyalty to *him,* not the office.

Second, they were smart, in a hair-trigger way.

Third, they were energetic. (You don't work White House hours without endless energy.)

Fourth, most of them were not attached to his earlier, unsuccessful campaign for President (in 1960). With just a few exceptions (such as Maurice Stans, William Rogers, Herb Klein, and Murray Chotiner), he cut the cord on his earlier allegiances. He was now going for broke, and he didn't intend to fall short of his goal.

What about his businessmen acquaintances? Friends like Don Kendall of

Pepsico, Robert Abplanalp (the inventor of the spray can valve), Bebe Rebozo, W. Clement Stone (the multimillionaire insurance man)? Businessmen, successful, "self-made." What traits and yearnings in Richard Nixon led him to them? For the answer to this, you have to look back at the younger Richard Nixon and his enormous yearning for recognition.

The irony—and not perhaps accidental—is that he achieved the recognition he sought—in extravagant proportions. Nations everywhere came to know him. His face and name were familiar in Latin America, in China, in the Soviet Union, in Europe, the Mideast, and Africa. He appeared on the cover of *Time* more often than anyone else ever has—and by such a wide margin that no one is likely to come close to his record. Between 1952, when he broke into national politics as candidate for Vice President, and August 1974, when he resigned the nation's highest office, he was pictured on *Time*'s cover thirty-nine times. Not even Franklin Roosevelt, Winston Churchill, or Douglas MacArthur approached that many cover appearances. The reason? Controversy. As though to satisfy his craving for crisis, Richard Nixon was nearly always in the middle of controversy. And the press duly recorded his every fight. While he appeared to detest or mistrust the press, it is hard to conceive of any way in which he could have achieved such world recognition without the help of the very medium he considered his nemesis.

EFFECTS OF WATERGATE

While Watergate did not bring Washington to a standstill (as some hyperzealous detractors liked to say), it certainly created a drag on many governmental functions.

The mood of malaise permeated financial markets and contributed to the uncertainties of international currencies, which are notably sensitive to psychological factors.

Watergate widened the gap between the White House and the Republican party—a gap which had been growing since Nixon dismissed Ray Bliss as chairman of the Republican National Committee in 1969, long before the President created his own reelection unit and ignored the RNC during the 1972 campaign.

Watergate accelerated the shift of many voters from the Republican to the Democratic column. It particularly caused a moving of labor voters. George Meany, president of the AFL–CIO, said that while 68 percent of union membership is Democratic, 51 percent had voted for Nixon. After Watergate, the pattern returned to normal.

In the peculiarly parochial field of Washington law practice, the Watergate Affair was a setback for many Republican-oriented firms. While Nixon's old law firm of Mudge, Rose, Guthrie and Alexander had once ridden high, wide, and handsome, after Watergate it went into a temporary eclipse. Republican "influence business" was hard hit.

While very little major new legislation was passed as a direct result of Watergate, the sensitivity to campaign laws was increased. Corporations, unions, and other fat-cat contributors became more careful about large donations. Smaller contributors became the backbone of more campaigns. And more state and local governments passed campaign disclosure laws.

In early 1975 Congress began work on several post-Watergate measures, including a proposal for a permanent federal "special prosecutor," independent of the Justice Department, to investigate charges of wrongdoing by high-level government officials.

The American Bar Association initiated studies of legal education, and its president suggested that law schools should spend more time discussing the ethics of the profession.

In the congressional elections of November 1974, the spillover from Watergate-Impeachment-Resignation-and-Pardon doubtless contributed to the Republican loss of seats in the House of Representatives and the Senate. While losses in Congress are normal for the in-party in an off-year election, the size of the setback following two years of scandal undoubtedly contained the backlash of protest voting.

Perhaps in the long run, the most permanent effect of Watergate will be a deeply felt revulsion at the abuse of great power in high places. Perhaps the most penetrating consequence will be one more push toward higher levels of public responsibility—a step-up in the continuing escalation of standards for public figures. For, contrary to popular assumptions, standards of behavior in elective office have been rising. What was considered acceptable a few years ago—in campaign contributions, in private graft, in conflicts of interest—is now *verboten*. What was once winked at as "just politics" is increasingly being rejected as "a violation of the public trust."

It is too much to say that Watergate was good for us, but it is not too much to hope that somehow, in some way, something good may come of it.

6 A DAY IN THE LIFE OF WASHINGTON

6 A.M.

The assistant chief usher of the White House comes on duty to prepare the residence staff for the start of another presidential day.

At the State Department, the communications room receives messages from Europe. (It is already 11 A.M. in London.)

The Executive Protective Service checks its shifts of special guards at three Middle East embassies where demonstrations have occurred in recent weeks.

Seafood trucks arrive at Maine Avenue and the Eastern Market with shipments of fresh fish from the Chesapeake Bay.

Newspaper carriers deliver the Washington *Post* to homes in the city and suburbs.

7 A.M.

President Ford sits down to a breakfast of toast and coffee in the family quarters on the second floor of the White House. Briefing reports and the daily newspapers are ready for his attention.

Traffic across the Potomac River bridges builds toward the two-hour climax that will last until 9 o'clock.

Postal workers start the 7 A.M. to 3:30 P.M. shift at the Main Post Office, at the corner of North Capitol Street and Massachusetts Avenue.

At the Pentagon traffic "mixing bowl," a tow truck clears away the first morning accident that blocks the middle lane of Interstate 95.

Howard University students roll out of bed to prepare for 8 o'clock classes.

The WMAL traffic helicopter is about to take to the skies over Washington. At intervals over the next two hours, it will broadcast reports of snarled traffic, accidents, and malfunctioning stoplights to motorists desiring to avoid them.

Alarm clocks continue to ring in apartments and houses throughout the city—from Brookland to Spring Valley, Burleith to Anacostia. Coffee is brewed in kitchens in Chevy Chase, Maryland, and Dale City, Virginia. A news correspondent reads the *New York Times* at the breakfast table of his cramped townhouse in "Foggy Bottom," four blocks from the State Department.

A Capitol Hill couple rise to find the back door has been forced open during the night, and the TV, table radio, and stereo are gone.

Senate Majority Leader Mike Mansfield breakfasts at the Capitol (without his breakfast companion of twenty years, Senator George Aiken of Vermont, who retired in 1974).

A meteorologist at the U.S. Weather Service in suburban Suitland, Maryland, updates his forecast for the eastern United States, using computer data from a weather satellite.

Senator William Proxmire (D-Wis.), clad in a sweatsuit, leaves his northwest Washington home for his daily jog down Connecticut Avenue and across town to the Capitol.

At the Pentagon, the National Military Command Center (second floor) assembles the top-secret daily summary of worldwide military developments (DIA-J-3) for the chairman of the Joint Chiefs of Staff. (Copies will be sent to the CIA, State Department, and White House Situation Room.)

The national desk of the Washington *Star* edits overnight AP and UPI copy for the morning edition of the afternoon paper.

Three eight-oar crews from Georgetown University and Washington-Lee High School churn the waters of the Potomac River while their coaches, in power boats, cruise alongside, shouting instructions.

An assistant secretary of transportation leaves his suburban Arlington, Virginia, home, bound for Capitol Hill, where he has a 7:30 breakfast appointment with seventeen urban congressmen to discuss mass transit funding.

Near Chain Bridge across the Potomac River, two elderly women set up folding chairs on the towpath of the old Chesapeake & Ohio Canal and cast a fishing line into the water, hoping to pull in some catfish.

In rural Charles County, Maryland (at one end of the Washington "Standard Metropolitan Statistical Area"), a farmer fuels up his tractor for a day of work cultivating his tobacco crop.

8 A.M.

Cars stream into the District along New York Avenue, Canal Road, and South Capitol Street and move bumper to bumper on 14th Street and Key Bridge. Metrobuses whisk along the "express lane" of I-95 in Virginia, carrying bureaucrats who read the morning paper standing up. A nuclear safety analyst drives from his home in Poolesville, Maryland, across the Maryland countryside to his desk at the Nuclear Regulatory Commission in Bethesda (a successor agency to the old Atomic Energy Commission).

A young Justice Department lawyer pedals to work on the bike path along the Rock Creek Parkway.

The senior watch officer ends his midnight-to-eight shift at the State Department's Operations Center, putting final touches on the morning report to the Department's executive secretary. (The executive secretary will pass the most important items on to Secretary Kissinger.)

Thirty black sixth-graders are en route by bus from their downtown homes to an underenrolled elementary school located in a "white neighborhood" west of Rock Creek Park.

A sub-Cabinet official of the Commerce Department is chauffeured to his office in a black Mercury, while he reads the *Wall Street Journal* in the back seat.

9 A.M.

Six Negro maids step off a Metrobus at the crossroads in Potomac, Maryland, to be met by the housewives for whom they will be cleaning (at $3 an hour, plus carfare).

A college registrar from Iowa, visiting Washington for a four-day convention, hurries from the Washington Hilton coffee shop to a large room in the bowels of the hotel, where he and other registrars will spend the morning discussing college enrollment trends.

On the sidewalk outside the East Gate of the White House, a family from Milwaukee lines up to await the 10 o'clock tour of the public rooms in the presidential mansion.

A contingent of businessmen from New York City steps off the Eastern air shuttle at National Airport, ready for negotiations with a federal procurement team at the General Services Administration.

Two lawyers from Chicago, carrying small suitcases for a four-day stay, catch a cab to the Food and Drug Administration, where their client's product will be the subject of a hearing.

In Union Station, several blocks from the Capitol, a delegation of Philadelphia businessmen step off the Metroliner train. They hurry to the Cannon House Office Building for a meeting with a congressman who opposes a federal dam that they want built on the Delaware River.

An aviation lawyer with Jones, Day, Reavis and Pogue makes a final check of his notes on an airline route controversy. (In an hour he'll be standing before the Civil Aeronautics Board, arguing his client's case.)

10 A.M.

Hearings begin at Special Labor Subcommittee of the House Education and Labor Committee in the Rayburn House Office Building. Chairman Frank Thompson, Jr. (D-N.J.), calls the first witness, a public employees' union official who supports a bill to give civil servants a limited right to strike.

At the "Hair and Fibers Unit" of the FBI laboratory (in the new J. Edgar Hoover Building on Pennsylvania Avenue), a technician examines evidence from the scene of an unsolved kidnapping.

A trade association executive, whose organization recently moved to Washington from New York, is on his way to his office downtown. (He is twenty minutes late, because he got lost driving through Rock Creek Park from Kensington, Maryland.)

Nine justices of the Supreme Court announce decisions to a hushed courtroom, while an irreverent crowd of reporters mills around in the press room downstairs, awaiting release of the texts.

Out-of-state autos, packed with impatient kids and harried adults, cruise along the Mall looking for a place to park for sightseeing at the Smithsonian and National Gallery of Art.

In the concert hall of the Kennedy Center, Maestro Antal Dorati, dressed in a turtleneck sweater and loose flannel shirt, steps up to the podium to conduct a rehearsal of the National Symphony Orchestra.

From his Norman-style home in Great Falls, Virginia, Redskins football coach George Allen talks on the phone to Green Bay, Wisconsin, trying to coax a veteran linebacker to Washington.

11 A.M.

At the Longworth House Office Building, a freshman congressman takes a flattering call from a senior colleague who wants him to co-sponsor an anti-busing bill. Even though he has already decided to oppose the bill, he says, respectfully, that he will give the matter some further thought.

In the West Wing of the White House, presidential press secretary Ron Nessen fields questions from the White House news corps at the midday briefing.

At the Government Printing Office on North Capitol Street, a typesetter prepares the galley proofs of an international agreement which the United States—a party to the accord—is publishing in four languages.

A street vendor, with a plastic permit pinned to his coat, sells fresh fruits and flowers at the corner of Connecticut Avenue and K Street.

President Ford receives a delegation from the Veterans of Foreign Wars, who ask him to support increased educational benefits for Vietnam veterans.

A computer programer at the Census Bureau in suburban Suitland, Maryland, prepares a special-order tabulation of "U.S. imports of estrogens, progesterones, and gonadotropic hormones." (The Los Angeles pharmaceutical firm that requested the information will pay the government $1,400 for it.)

A cab driver named Harry takes a tourist from the Capitol to the Corcoran Gallery of Art for a mere 85¢, plus tip. All the way he complains that the Washington zone system for fares ought to be replaced by meters.

At the H Street office of the Washington International Horse Show, a harried member of the staff talks on the phone with the Embassy of Canada about that country's national equestrian team, which is scheduled to compete in the show's open jumping events.

A team of black biochemists works in a laboratory at Howard University Hospital, searching for a cure for sickle-cell anemia.

Steve Ford, the President's youngest son, repairs his motorcycle on the parking lot between the White House and the Executive Office Building. (He is visiting from his ranching job out West.)

12 NOON

The Speaker of the House of Representatives bangs his gavel, calls the House to order, and the chaplain asks God's blessing on the legislative assemblage. (But the chamber is nearly empty.)

Officers at the Pentagon don sweatsuits to huff and puff along jogging trails beside the George Washington Parkway.

J. Carter Brown, director of the National Gallery of Art, examines a Rubens of disputed authenticity that a prominent collector wants to give to the gallery.

Three buses full of high school seniors from Buffalo, New York, pull up in front of Sholl's Colonial Cafeteria on Connecticut Avenue for a fast lunch before resuming their sightseeing tour.

At the World Bank dining room, the chef prepares luncheon dishes for Moslem, Buddhist, and Christian diets. The director of the International Monetary Fund hosts a distinguished American journalist at lunch in a private dining room.

Early lunchers arrive at the Sans Souci restaurant, hungry for a glimpse of Henry Kissinger (who, in fact, is in Egypt meeting with President Sadat). They settle for a glimpse of Art Buchwald.

A succession of congressmen march into "the well" at the front of the House chamber to give one-minute speeches about anything under the sun—a longstanding House tradition.

Around the marble fountain at Dupont Circle, the benches are filled with shirt-sleeved lunchers and chess players, while long-haired young men pick guitars and beat bongos on the grass nearby.

Office secretaries and stenographers catch a quick lunch before shopping at Woodward and Lothrop, Garfinckel's, and Connecticut Avenue boutiques.

The dining room at the Metropolitan Club (17th and H Streets) begins to fill with lawyers and federal officials (all male), who will talk serious business while appearing nonchalantly social.

At the Interstate Commerce Commission in the Federal Triangle, the chairman recesses a hearing on short-haul freight rates, to resume at 2:45.

1 P.M.

An Arab sheik addresses a "newsmakers' luncheon" in the ballroom of the National Press Club on the issues of oil and politics in the Middle East. (His text has already been filed on the AP wire.)

At the corner of Pennsylvania Avenue and 18th Street N.W., near the World Bank and International Monetary Fund, friends exchange greetings in German, French, Italian, and Indonesian.

A couple from California, moving soon to Washington, hunts for a new home in suburban Montgomery and Fairfax counties, finding nothing very interesting for less than $70,000.

Over lunch at the Bagatelle restaurant, an account executive with the Hill and Knowlton public relations firm suggests to a corporate client how to neutralize the bad press the company got at a recent televised Senate hearing.

The dining room of the National Lawyers Club on H Street overflows with talk of taxes, antitrust suits, rate setting, and consent decrees (but no words about divorce, murder, or real estate).

At a table in the basement cafeteria of the Health, Education and Welfare Department, middle-level bureaucrats argue over the chances of Washington's getting a new professional baseball team.

During the lunchtime recess in a House hearing on interest rate ceilings, two lawyers for the savings and loan lobby catch a bite to eat at the 116 Club, a townhouse on Schotts Court (next to the Dirksen Senate Office Building parking lot) used by lobbyists for a rendezvous on Capitol Hill.

In a rundown block of Florida Avenue, near North Capitol Street, a Negro "spiritualist" sits in her parlor to tell fortunes for $10 apiece. A neon sign, shaped like an open hand, flashes in the front window.

An old tour guide in a chauffeur's cap approaches a weary family of tourists in Lafayette Park, offering—for a fee—to show them some sights and drive them back to their motel in Rosslyn, Virginia.

2 P.M.

From his office in the Longworth House Office Building, a Massachusetts congressman phones the Congressional Research Service of the Library of Congress to ask the name of the first black U.S. senator. He needs the fact for a speech, and in five minutes he gets word that it was Hiram Revels (R-Miss.), a senator from 1870 to 1871.

A cluster of unemployed black teenagers loiter on the street corner at 7th and U Streets, wondering where the action is.

On H Street between 5th and 6th Streets, an elderly Chinese man places a call from a pagoda-roofed telephone booth—a token of Washington's small Chinatown.

In an expensive home on North Portal Drive, near the District-Maryland line, a black society matron (wife of a judge) hosts a luncheon meeting for the women's committee of an upcoming charity ball for a Negro cause.

A senior research fellow at the Brookings Institution drafts a report on legislative options for a guaranteed annual income program.

In the paneled library of his Cleveland Park home, a young political consultant talks on the phone with a senator who has retained him to manage his reelection bid.

A D.C. policewoman pulls her gun on a robbery suspect she has cornered in an alley near the New York Avenue bus terminal.

Author Larry McMurtry, sprawled in a chair at Booked Up (his rare-book shop on 31st Street in Georgetown), is reading a new novel he will review in the Washington *Post* next Monday.

3 P.M.

A Voice of America announcer, in a recording booth at the United States Information Agency, tapes a Spanish-speaking program on American jazz for audiences throughout South America.

A four-star general is called off the golf course at Burning Tree Club in suburban Bethesda, Maryland, to take a telephone call from the Pentagon. (It turns out to be a practice conference call among top military policymakers, "just to keep the channels working.")

In the Mt. Pleasant area of the District, a young white couple sands the floors of a seedy old rowhouse they are renovating. They boast to their former neighbors in Reston, Virginia, about the broad "socioeconomic mix" of their new inner-city neighborhood.

At the National Bureau of Standards in Gaithersburg, Maryland, a computer scientist is programing an experimental robot to perform simple manual tasks. Elsewhere on the NBS' multi-building research campus, a psychologist is studying films of people walking up and down typical stairways, as part of a program to reduce stairway accidents through better design. Other NBS scientists are at work on everything from lead-based paint poisoning to weights, measures, and weighing instruments for distribution to the fifty states.

Four Marine recruits take a snooze in their barracks at Quantico, Virginia, south of the District, resting up for an evening foray into the singles bars along 21st and L Streets downtown. They will wear wigs to cover their shaved heads, and their garb will be off-duty civilian, appropriately "mod."

A female hard-hatted construction worker waves a red flag to detour traffic around an excavation for a future Metro terminal (eliciting a few whistles from passing truck drivers).

In the basement of the Russell Senate Office Building, Robotype machines pound out form-letter responses to the senators' constituent mail. Complete with personalized salutations and signatures, each finished letter looks like a product of the senator's own hand.

Four well-to-do housewives from McLean, Virginia, tour the paintings of the Phillips Collection, a block off Massachusetts Avenue's Embassy Row. Between the Klees and the Ryders, they suddenly realize it is nearly 4 o'clock, and they will be engulfed in rush-hour traffic if they don't leave soon. (They decide to leave the Rothko room and Renoir's *Luncheon of the Boating Party* for another afternoon.)

An elderly senator, late for an important vote, pushes the call button next to the track of the open-car mini-subway in the basement of the Russell Senate Office Building. (A moment later he is off on a brief and breezy ride into the Capitol basement.)

At the Metro Control Center, on 5th Street next to the old Pension Building, a team of computer experts are checking programs that will synchronize schedules for Washington's new subway system.

4 P.M.

An economist at the Department of Labor's Bureau of Labor Statistics starts cleaning off her desk in preparation for catching her car pool to Annandale, Virginia.

At the Library of Congress, a violinist in a visiting string quartet practices scales on one of the Library's Stradivarius instruments, getting ready for a chamber music concert in the Coolidge Auditorium.

A prominent western senator slips into the office of the Reporter of Debates to edit some intemperate words from the transcript of a hot argument on the Senate floor earlier in the day. He pencils in a few changes and scratches out a phrase here and there, so his remarks will seem more grammatical and prudent when they appear in the *Congressional Record* the next day.

In a large home in the Shepherd Park section of northwest Washington, a twelve-year-old black child practices a Beethoven piano sonata, when he would rather be playing his Stevie Wonder records.

Two fuchsia-colored trucks from the Bethesda warehouse of Ridgewell's Caterers speed down River Road with china, silverware, and folding chairs for an embassy bash.

At the marble Supreme Court building on Capitol Hill, the justices are having a private showing of the movie *I Should Have Stood in Bed,* to determine whether it is obscene. (Justice Douglas didn't come, since he already thinks the First Amendment gives blanket protection to virtually all expression, lewd or otherwise.)

In a gymnasium at Gallaudet College (the federal school for the deaf), students put up decorations for a rock dance, at which they will move in perfect rhythm to the unheard, but palpable, beat of the bass guitar and drums.

D.C. Mayor Walter Washington steps from his limousine at a newly renovated playground in Anacostia, snips a ribbon, says a few dedicatory words, and climbs back into his car, headed for a meeting at his District Building office with local labor leaders.

5 P.M.

A Commerce Department bureaucrat, bound for home in Landover, Maryland, stops en route at a downtown discount liquor store to buy a case of gin, paying the District's famous "low, low prices."

The editorial board of the Washington *Post* holds an impromptu conference to discuss how to feature a late-breaking story of scandal involving a member of the Cabinet. They decide to play it on page one, but "below the fold."

An Alexandria, Virginia, housewife picks up her lawyer husband in front of the 16th Street office building where he works. They're headed for a quiet off-season vacation in a cottage at Bethany Beach, Delaware, on the Atlantic shore.

A wealthy Washington hostess sits down with her social secretary at her Foxhall Road mansion to rework the seating arrangement for a dinner party. (The original plan was thrown out of kilter when an ambassador's wife took sick and the Attorney General was called out of town on important business.)

A troop of Boy Scouts from Cleveland returns to motel rooms in Silver Spring, Maryland, after a foot-wearying day of touring the Smithsonian, White House, and Arlington National Cemetery.

In a plush office on Connecticut Avenue, the chief legislative counsel of a trade association puts the finishing touches on the draft of a bill which a friendly congressman has promised to introduce.

6 P.M.

Three physicists, visiting Washington for a science conference, discuss laser beams over cocktails at the Cosmos Club.

The portly and inexhaustible Ambassador of Nicaragua, Guillermo Sevilla-Sacasa, dean of the diplomatic corps, leaves his home at 3200 Ellicott Street, N.W., to attend receptions at the French Embassy, the Argentine Embassy, and the International Monetary Fund. (His limousine bears license plates DPL-1.)

Over at the National Military Command Center in the Pentagon, an officer fluent in Russian is on the "hot line" to Moscow (called MOLINK). There's no crisis. She is merely issuing a test message to her counterpart in the Soviet Union, to make sure everything is functioning properly. (On New Year's Day, the Yanks and the Russians will exchange holiday greetings over MOLINK.)

An assistant secretary of the treasury returns to his office after a long day of meetings on inflation, looks through a pile of correspondence, answers a few letters on a dictation machine, and leaves a note to his secretary to transcribe them in the morning.

Environmental Protection Administrator Russell Train drives home to Woodland Drive in the smallest official limousine in town—a fuel-saving black Comet sedan with license plates EPA-1.

7 P.M.

A couple from Wheaton, Maryland, is at the Kennedy Center, moving by escalator from parking level B to the Hall of Nations, en route to the Center's Eisenhower Theater, to see a pre-Broadway performance of a new drama.

At the Dirksen Senate Office Building, a senator reviews his notes for an after-dinner speech he will make at the Statler Hilton Hotel to a convention of farm machinery manufacturers.

An office machine salesman settles into a comfortable chair at his Falls Church, Virginia, home to watch the local news on TV.

At the Hirshhorn Museum, a woman on the night cleaning force buffs the floor of the third-level sculpture gallery, maneuvering her machine between the pedestals of a Barlach and a Lipchitz.

At the Executive Office Building, a member of the White House press monitoring staff watches the network news programs and takes notes on commentaries by Sevareid, Smith, and Brinkley relating to President Ford's war on inflation.

Two lawyers at Koteen and Burt send their secretary out for sandwiches and coffee to help them through a long night of work on a brief that must be sent to the printer in the morning.

Sitting at his typewriter in the Senate press gallery, the correspondent of a morning paper in Columbia, South Carolina, bangs out three stories that he developed during the day. When he finishes, he'll use a desk-top Xerox telecopier to transmit each page of copy to his managing editor in South Carolina.

8 P.M.

Guests arrive for a small dinner at the posh Watergate apartment of Senator Abraham Ribicoff (D-Conn.).

A group of black intellectuals—including a Federal City College instructor, a D.C. school board member, and a playwright—meet for dinner in a restored rowhouse in the Adams-Morgan neighborhood of the District. The evening is dominated by discussion of the merits and flaws of the new D.C. "home rule" structure.

With a backgammon board tucked under his arm, a thirtyish bachelor businessman arrives at the home of a Georgetown neighbor for an evening of drinks and game playing.

A queue of black moviegoers fills the sidewalk outside the Republic Theatre on U Street to see a new film featuring athlete-actor Jim Brown.

An audience of 19,000 long-haired suburban youths squeezes into the Capital Centre, the enormous sports and entertainment pavilion on the Beltway near Largo, Maryland. (For $8 a ticket they will be treated to an incisive attack on their parents' materialism and hypocrisy, rendered by a rock star who invests his seven-figure earnings in tax-sheltered apartment buildings.)

In a turn-of-the-century rowhouse on Corcoran Street, east of Dupont Circle, a group of disenchanted career women in their mid-twenties meet to eat lasagna and pick each other's brains in a women's lib "consciousness raising" session. Sitting cross-legged on the floor are a schoolteacher, a Capitol Hill legislative aide, a newspaper reporter, a stock market trainee, and two secretaries.

9 P.M.

All over the Washington area—from Northeast D.C. to Woodbridge, Virginia—people are watching television.

Erroll Garner is at the keyboard at Etcetera on M Street, and he plays a request from the audience for his own composition "Misty."

A group of Black Muslim men and women—dressed in conservative clothes—worship quietly in a 4th Street building called Muhammad's Mosque No. 4, a few doors from the office of their official newspaper, *Muhammad Speaks*.

Standing at the bar of the Guards, an elegant Georgetown singles bar, a Capitol Hill aide asks a comely legal secretary if she'd like to come over to his apartment to see slides of his recent trip to Nova Scotia.

At 1600 Pennsylvania Avenue, President Ford and the First Lady are hosting the prime minister of a powerful European ally at a white-tie-and-tails state dinner.

At the Last Colony Theater on upper Georgia Avenue N.W., actor-director

Robert Hooks leads his D.C. Black Repertory Company through a performance of an Ed Bullins play about poverty and violence in the ghetto.

10 P.M.

A few blocks east of the chic Kalorama neighborhood of Northwest Washington, calypso and reggae music fill the air of restaurants on Columbia Road, the main artery of the Washington Latin-American community. Diners at Omega and El Caribe are filling their stomachs with paella, black beans, and fried plantains. Up the street a few blocks, a Spanish movie (with no English subtitles) is on the screen at the Ontario Theater, where ten years ago suburban families waited in line to see *The Sound of Music.*

At the Linden Hill indoor tennis club in North Bethesda, Maryland, four surgeons from the Naval Medical Center take the court for their weekly hour of doubles.

In a corridor of an abandoned building near 14th and Euclid Streets N.W., a black teenaged boy lies dying from an overdose of methadone.

In the ballroom of the Shoreham Americana Hotel, 700 gowned and tuxedoed socialites dance to the music of Howard Devron's band at a charity ball to raise money to fight a crippling disease ($25 of each person's $50 ticket is tax-deductible).

Alex and Athena, the resident owls of the Smithsonian Institution, wing out over the Mall in search of field mice to bring back to their offspring, recently hatched in the west tower of the old sandstone castle.

11 P.M.

At the Pan American Union, the national day celebration of a Central American nation gets under way, as guests arrive from small dinner parties around the city. Diplomats with chests full of ribbons and medals ascend the broad marble staircase to the second-floor ballroom, where sambas, rumbas, and bossa novas are the vogue.

In the paneled drawing room of his impeccably furnished Georgetown home, a columnist pours cognac and regales his dinner guests with anecdotes about his recent tour of the People's Republic of China. Guests include a high-ranking CIA official, the ambassador of a Middle Eastern oil nation, a senator, and a fellow journalist—plus their wives.

Rock music spills out the front doors of Apple Pie and Crazy Horse, along M Street in Georgetown, where bouncers ask teenagers for proof they are eighteen years old.

On the WTOP-TV late news, sportscaster Warner Wolf bestows a raucous "boo of the week" on the pro football commissioner for an onerous ruling.

Business is booming at the bisexual discotheques (like Pier Nine, Plus One, and Lost and Found) hidden away in quiet blocks of the Southwest and Capitol Hill. "Gay" couples of both sexes sway to the music of deafening stereo systems.

12 MIDNIGHT

At the Show Palace burlesque club on downtown 11th Street, Anne ("Boom Boom") Howe struts her stuff for an audience of conventioneers and GIs. At the bar, B-girls sweet-talk men into buying them a $5 cocktail—an ounce of cheap champagne over ice.

In front of the Jordanian ambassador's residence on Connecticut Avenue near Chevy Chase Circle, a guard of the Executive Protective Service takes his station for the early morning shift. Elsewhere, EPS guards assume their shifts at the Soviet Embassy, the Israeli Embassy, the Saudi Arabian Embassy, and other "sensitive" diplomatic buildings.

Outside the Circle Theatre, on Pennsylvania Avenue at 21st Street, six George Washington University students buy tickets for the midnight showing of *The Night of the Living Dead,* while a crowd of Humphrey Bogart fans file out of the 10 o'clock showing of *To Have and Have Not.*

In Georgetown, fashionable young professionals are eating omelets at Clyde's and sipping Irish coffee at Nathan's.

In front of a modern hotel near Thomas Circle, two black hookers from 14th Street—well dressed and coiffed in bouffant blond wigs—solicit a group of out-of-town businessmen.

At the U.S. Naval Observatory, an astronomer examines the planet Mercury through the 26-inch refractor telescope.

In a subdivision of four-acre estates in Potomac Falls, Maryland, an insurance executive repairs a stirrup leather on his saddle, to be ready for fox hunting the next morning.

At the Washington *Post* headquarters on 15th Street, the second edition is being put to bed, soon to be rolling off the presses for distribution around the metropolitan area of 3 million people.

Downtown, night cleaning crews of charwomen and janitors turn off the lights in office buildings and head for home. Some of them stop on the way at the Eddie Leonard Sandwich Shop on Good Hope Road S.E., for coffee and a hamburger.

At the Washington Golf and Country Club in Arlington, Virginia, guests begin leaving a dinner-dance in honor of a corporate executive who is being transferred to his company's home office in Detroit, after a three-year stint in Washington as vice president for government relations.

1 A.M.

At the State Department's Operations Center, the associate watch officer, the INR (Intelligence and Research) officer, and a colonel from the Pentagon confer on a message (just received on the SCAT machine, coded "Flash") about a coup in a small African nation. They refer to the "E and E (emergency and evacuation) plan" for that country, in case it becomes necessary to evacuate American citizens.

At the Government Printing Office, high-speed presses are made ready for the nightly run of the *Congressional Record.* By early morning, tens of thousands of these paperbound transcripts of the previous day's Senate and House proceedings will move on conveyor belts under North Capitol Street to the City Post Office, for delivery throughout Washington and mailing to subscribers across the nation.

The floodlights illuminating the Capitol dome are shut off until sundown tomorrow.

7 THE CAPITAL IN THE MAKING

The capital of virtually every major nation in the world was a city of some commercial or military importance before it became a seat of government. Washington is an exception.

In the American Republic of 200 years ago, as in most new nations, different regions vied for superiority. The capital of the American government during the Revolution shifted with changes in political strength, but the site was always an established city. Later, when the country was floundering in the 1780s under the weak central government of the Articles of Confederation, the Congress met in five cities—New York, Princeton, Trenton, Philadelphia, and Annapolis. Everyone seemed to agree that the prestige of the new government would be improved by a permanent capital, but the thirteen states, jealous of one another, could not agree on a place for it.

Debate raged from 1783 to 1790, during which offers of land were made by such cities as Kingston, New York, and Nottingham, New Jersey, not to mention the states of Maryland, Virginia, Pennsylvania, New York, and New Jersey. The northerners wanted the capital in a Middle Atlantic or New England state. The southerners insisted on a site south of the Mason-Dixon line. In the end, the site was selected through political compromise. Thomas Jefferson delivered southern votes for Alexander Hamilton's plan for federal assumption of the states' Revolutionary War debts, and Hamilton lined up the votes of his northern colleagues for a capital carved out of Maryland and Virginia. Congress authorized President George Washington to select a particular site in the Potomac region. He chose one a few miles upriver from his plantation, Mount Vernon.

The new city was to be located within a federal reservation, to be called the District of Columbia, donated to the government by Maryland and Virginia. In its original form, the District was a perfect square, 10 miles on a side, aligned north–south in diamond fashion. The Potomac River flowed into the District from the hilly northwest, and the Eastern Branch (later to be named the Anacostia River) curved in from the northeast. The two rivers joined within the District and flowed out through its southernmost boundary point, eventually mingling with the waters of the Chesapeake Bay.

The new District came ready-made with two small, civilized towns, Georgetown, Maryland, and Alexandria, Virginia. Founded about forty years before, both towns had prospered by shipping tobacco and grain from interior plantations to the larger cities of America and Europe. The two port towns developed into amiable cities with handsome Georgian mansions and cobblestone streets, but neither city was to be the site of the new capital. The public buildings would be built near the geographic center of the District, east of Georgetown across Rock Creek and northeast of Alexandria, across the Potomac River. As conceived in a grandly ceremonial plan by Pierre L'Enfant, a French engineer who had fought in the American Revolution, the city would occupy a low-lying tidewater basin, sloping down to the Potomac and Anacostia Rivers from a semicircular escarpment to the north (defined by Boundary Street, later renamed Florida Avenue).

One small hillock above the marshy basin was selected for the site of the "President's Palace," and a much larger one to the east, Jenkins Hill, would be adorned by the "Congress House." The two structures would be linked by Pennsylvania Avenue, one of numerous broad corridors, all named for states, that crisscrossed L'Enfant's grid of city blocks. The D.C. commissioners named the new capital the City of Washington, which goes to show how much the people of that time revered their first President, who, *mirabile dictu,* was still in office and hardly ripe for the honors that traditionally come only with death or retirement.

Federal officials made the shift from Philadelphia to Washington in the spring of 1800 and found a wilderness sprinkled with a handful of public buildings and fewer than four hundred private structures, many of which were mere shacks. Not one street was paved. Livestock grazed everywhere. Pennsylvania Avenue was little more than a wide, muddy path cluttered with tree stumps. Dignitaries, both American and foreign, longed for the amenities of Boston, Philadelphia and New York. This longing became more acute some years later, in 1814, when an unchallenged British force put a torch to virtually all the public buildings in the city. Northern congressmen urged that the District be abandoned in favor of a more established city. Only after local business interests made a large reconstruction loan to the federal government did Congress vote to keep the capital in Washington. While the gutted Capitol was being repaired over the following five years, Congress convened in the "Brick Capitol," a hastily built structure that stood on the site of the present Supreme Court building. (During the Civil War, this former seat of Congress was used as a military prison.) The President's Palace was repaired, too, and the smoke-blotched sandstone walls were given a coat of bright white paint. There's a myth that the building's present name originated with the white paint, but records show it was called the White House even before the fire of 1814. (It was officially called the Executive Mansion until 1902, when, at President Theodore Roosevelt's urging, the nickname was dignified by an act of Congress.)

Thus given a new lease on its future, the City of Washington grew at a steady pace, leaving Alexandria and Georgetown far behind in population. By 1840 Washington had 23,000 residents to Alexandria's 8,500 and Georgetown's 7,300. Despite the construction of handsome public buildings and private homes designed by such architects as William Thornton, Benjamin Latrobe, George Hadfield, James Hoban, and Robert Mills, the city was still a wasteland. The streets were unpaved, pigs ran free, and the Washington Canal, which flowed along what is now the Mall, was a smelly breeding place for mosquitoes and disease.

Charles Dickens, a visitor to the District in 1842, liked Washington even less than the other American cities he toured and despaired that it would ever achieve dignity. It was a city of what he called "broad avenues that begin in nothing and lead nowhere; streets a mile long that want only houses, roads and inhabitants; public buildings that need but a public to complete." He added that "one might fancy the season over, and most of the houses gone out of town with their masters." Some Washingtonians held the hope that the city's intellectual life would be improved by the $500,000 willed to the United States by James Smithson, a little-known English scientist and bastard son of the Duke of Northumberland. Although Smithson (who had never been to America) died in 1829, it was more than twenty years before the red sandstone Tuscan turrets of the Smithsonian Institution rose on the Mall.

Both Georgetown and Alexandria, which had never really felt at home within the federal District, sought in the 1840s to secede and return to their original states. Maryland was not eager to regain its former city, but Virginia petitioned Congress for return of all of the land it had donated to the District, including Alexandria. In 1846, Congress obliged, decreasing the District by about 31 square miles to its present size of approximately 69 square miles, on the northern and eastern side of the Potomac River. Up on Capitol Hill, Congress needed more working space. The construction of new wings for the House and Senate began in 1851 and was completed by the end of the decade. The low wooden dome between the wings was replaced by the present cast-iron dome, rising 285 feet above the ground and weighing nearly 9 million pounds. Work on the dome—one of the notable engineering feats of that era—continued through the Civil War.

CIVIL WAR AND ASSASSINATION

The fact that the new national capital would be surrounded by two slave states had apparently not bothered the founding fathers in 1790. Slavery was legal within the District until 1862, and many prominent public officials owned slaves. But Washington was also a city in which free Negroes could live in safety and financial comfort, and by 1850 the population of the free black community was three times the size of the slave population. The capital city became a microcosm of growing national tension over slavery. Abolitionists were active, and Washington was an important stop on the "underground railway" of fugitive slaves working their way north. As the outbreak of war drew closer, some Washingtonians feared the government would abandon their city in favor of a safer capital farther north. Many southern sympathizers in the city hoped Washington would become the capital of a confederation of slave-owning states. Neither situation came about, of course, owing to the strength of President Lincoln and Maryland's decision, despite her southern bent, to remain in the Union and link the District with the northern states.

On several occasions during the Civil War, the Confederacy wasted opportunities to storm the lightly defended capital. Washington weathered the war only to be beset with grief at its conclusion. In a little house at 604 H Street N.W. (today a Chinese grocery store), a plot was conceived for the assassination of the President during a stage play at Ford's Theatre. Assassin John Wilkes Booth was subsequently killed in a barn in Virginia. Four of his co-conspirators—including Mary Surratt—were hanged in Washington at the federal prison (now Fort McNair) on Greenleaf Point, where the Potomac and Anacostia Rivers flow together.

In the decade after the Civil War, Washington was swept by the same commercial zeal that characterized much of America in the new industrial age. If political integrity sank to an all-time low under President Grant's unwatchful eye, the capital managed to rise to the status of a real city, complete with paved streets, a water and sewer system, street lights, public parks, and opulent mansions and embassies. Between 1860 and 1870 the population soared from 75,000 to nearly 132,000, with more than half of the increase due to the arrival of freed Negroes. The city experienced its first real estate boom, encouraged by the free-spending territorial government of "Boss" Alexander Shepherd, who was appointed governor after chairing the Board of Public Works. When one of Congress's biggest land speculators, silver-rich Senator William Stewart of Nevada, built a mansion in 1874 on Dupont Circle—eight blocks north of the White House—it was considered so far out of town that cynics dubbed it "Stewart's Folly." But by 1901 the land under Stewart's turreted castle was too valuable for a residence, and the house was demolished for an office building.

Washington's growing pains during post–Civil War reconstruction led to a change in the structure of the District government, which in previous decades consisted formally of a popularly elected mayor and city council, but which was effectively controlled by Congress. In 1871 the citizenry lost this semblance of home rule. For three years the District was governed as a territory, with a governor and council appointed by the President and a popularly elected lower body, and was represented in Congress by a nonvoting delegate. But Boss Shepherd's administration ran up a $20 million bill for public works in barely two years, and an angry Congress abolished the territorial government and set up a temporary board of commissioners. In 1878, amid fears that a popularly elected city government would be increasingly dominated by Negroes, Congress adopted the structure of a presidentially appointed board of commissioners, which remained in effect until 1974. This was modified by the creation of a "mayor" named by the President in 1967, nonvoting delegate in 1970, and an elected mayor and council in 1974.

The 1880s and 1890s were quiet years of growth in Washington, disrupted only by the mortal wounding of President Garfield in 1881 by an embittered aspirant to public office. (The shooting occurred in a railroad station that once stood on the edge of the Mall, on the site of the present National Gallery of Art.) The city was less disrupted than annoyed by the arrival in 1894 of "Coxey's Army," a few hundred men who were victims of the depression of 1893 and who thought the government should do something about their joblessness. In their mission (social relief), the fate of their leaders (twenty days in jail for walking on the Capitol grass), and the outcome of their efforts (nothing concrete), Coxey's Army set a precedent for most of the demonstrations that would make a bid for the attention of Washington (and the nation) in later decades.

BURGEONING BUREAUCRACY

The Eighties saw a very sharp increase in the ranks of the federal bureaucracy, which became a modern establishment with the adoption of a competitive examination system in 1883. The 1881 federal employment roster of 13,000 workers swelled to 20,000 by the end of the decade. In 1884 the Washington Monument was completed, giving the nation a landmark which, as much as the dome of the Capitol, symbolizes the capital to millions of Americans and foreign peoples. The monument was begun in 1848 with lofty hopes, few funds, an unstable foundation, and a design featuring an obelisk surrounded by a circular, colonnaded base. Work stopped in 1854 because of a shortage of funds and did not resume until after the Civil War. The soggy foundation was strengthened, and attempts to embellish the shaft with various revival styles of architecture were beaten back (largely on economic rather than aesthetic grounds). The starkly simple monument is a surprisingly timeless work of art to have resulted from an era of Victorian excess.

During the last three decades of the nineteenth century, the population of the District more than doubled, reaching almost 279,000 by 1900. The 69-square-mile capital had more than enough room to accommodate the migration. L'Enfant's original grid of city streets, which extended only twenty-five blocks in each direction from the Capitol, was pushed northward as real estate developers threw up block after block of neat rowhouses for the middle class. The flight to the suburbs had begun, but the "suburbs" were merely new neighborhoods within the District boundaries. The farthest reaches of the northwest section of Washington were still rural enough in 1900 to serve the needs of fox hunters from nearby Chevy Chase, Maryland.

Black Washingtonians did not fare well in the Eighties and Nineties. The political deal in 1877 that released the South from federal supervision and brought Rutherford B. Hayes to the White House was the first ominous sign that Negro rights would be restricted throughout the nation. Washington was no exception, and Jim Crow segregation of schools, public parks, theaters and hotels became the accepted way of life. The capital's black middle class—the largest and best-educated in America—turned inward, its talents lost to the city and the nation. Howard University, the Negro institution founded in 1867, continued to produce graduates whose knowledge would be largely wasted by a white society.

The arrival of the twentieth century marked Washington's first hundred years as a city. The occasion was seized as the perfect opportunity to dust off L'Enfant's plan. The Mall—which had been cluttered for a century with produce markets, a stagnant canal, a train station, and meandering roads—was started on its way to becoming a dignified ceremonial concourse. The turn of the century also brought the third presidential assassination in thirty-six years when President William McKinley was shot and mortally wounded by an anarchist in Buffalo, New York, in 1901. The tragedy elevated maverick Theodore Roosevelt to the White House, beginning fifteen years of economic reforms that would change the way the nation did business and would concentrate more regulatory power in the federal government.

WORLD WAR I

Washington has always boomed in times of national crisis, whether depression or war. With the American entry into World War I, the government expanded every conceivable bureaucracy. Temporary buildings sprouted all over the Mall, manned by wartime workers who came to the capital by the thousands. But temporary expansions of government have a way of becoming permanent. Many of the workers stayed on after the war, and some of the "temporary offices" were still in existence until after World War II. In the early 1920s, the collapse of a disillusioned President Wilson led to the "normalcy" of President Harding—and the abnormalcy of the Teapot Dome scandals, in which the Secretary of the Interior was convicted of receiving bribes for throwing federal oil lands to private companies. The end of World War I also brought tens of thousands of rural Negroes to Washington, the first wave of a migration from the South that would continue for the next three decades. Their arrival again strained the housing and labor markets, stirring racial hostility among low-income whites. In 1919 Washington erupted in several days of riots, in which gangs of whites and blacks battled each other and the police. The rioting was similar to, but less destructive than, the postwar disturbances in Chicago and East St. Louis, Illinois.

In the middle of the 1920s, the federal government conceived a construction project that would do more to change the face of Washington than any single previous effort. The project was the Federal Triangle, a mass of neo-Greek-style offices that, by the end of the depression, occupied a 70-acre wedge between Constitution and Pennsylvania Avenues, stretching from Sixth Street to Fifteenth Street N.W., a choice section of downtown Washington between the White House and the Capitol. For many years, the neighborhood had been a slum of nondescript stores, warehouses, and alley dwellings, one section of which bore the name "Murder Bay." Among other things, it contained the city's red-light district, called "Hooker's Division," in dubious honor of the Civil War general who segregated the prostitutes there and whose troops kept them in business. Where vice once flourished, Uncle Sam built offices for the bureaucrats of the Departments of Labor, Justice, and Commerce, the Federal Trade Commission, the Internal Revenue Service, the National Archives, the Post Office, and other agencies.

After a brief business slump at the end of the First World War, Washington real estate developers embarked on a decade-long spree of building offices, hotels, apartments, and rowhouses. Convention promotion brought the 1925 meeting of the Ku Klux Klan, during which 25,000 marchers paraded down Pennsylvania Avenue in white robes and hoods. The Klan rally captured the racial mood of the Twenties more accurately than another parade, three years before, in which 1,500 Negroes marched through Washington in silent protest against lynching and Jim Crow laws. On a happier note, the "City Beautiful" movement gathered steam with the construction in the Twenties of the Lincoln Memorial, and the gradual addition of large, unspoiled sections of Northwest Washington to the already massive Rock Creek Park, which had been begun in the 1890s. In the 1930s the Memorial Bridge was built across the Potomac River to the Arlington National Cemetery.

To lure lucrative trade conventions to the capital, a group of civic leaders in 1927 established the Cherry Blossom Festival. The festival celebrates each spring the blooming of the ornamental cherry trees around the Tidal Basin that were given to the nation by the city of Tokyo in appreciation of American aid after a disastrous earthquake there.

While the First World War had made Washington a true national capital, much of the capital's power was dissipated during the laissez-faire administrations of Harding, Coolidge, and Hoover. It was Wall Street, not Pennsylvania Avenue, where the big economic decisions were made. But when the bubble burst and unemployment soared, the people once again looked to Washington to save the day. Uncle Sam's first response was to cut federal expenses "until the storm blew over." When it became apparent in 1932 that the storm wasn't going to blow over, some 80,000 World War I veterans—the "bonus marchers"—camped in Washington, demanding immediate payment of future bonuses. The Senate refused, and the veterans stayed until troops led by General Douglas MacArthur (with Major Dwight D. Eisenhower in charge of six small tanks) routed them from ramshackle buildings along the Mall and drove them to tarpaper shanties on the marshy flats along the Anacostia River. As the depression grew in force, thousands of federal workers lost their jobs or took pay cuts.

NEW DEAL THIRTIES

After flirting briefly with Hoover's policy of economy in government, Franklin D. Roosevelt shifted to spending, and proposed many recovery programs. The federal bureaucracy swelled by 30,000 employees between March 1933 and the end of 1934. Into Washington streamed would-be bureaucrats, businessmen seeking a voice in formulating NRA industry codes, intellectuals offering panaceas, clerks, secretaries, journalists bent on explaining the New Deal to readers back home, and poor blacks naïvely hoping to share in the prosperity of the only boom town in America. By the middle of the Thirties, residential construction was soaring but was still outdistanced by the demand. The federal public works program completed the Federal Triangle and built such latter-day temples as the Supreme Court Building, the Longworth House Office Building, and additions to the Bureau of Engraving and Printing, the Library of Congress, and the Departments of Agriculture and Interior. This celebration of neoclassical architecture culminated with the ground breaking in 1939, and the completion three years later, of the Jefferson Memorial next to the Tidal Basin.

During the decade of the Thirties, Washington's population grew by 36 percent, while every city in America except Los Angeles suffered a decline. By 1942, federal employment in the capital had reached 276,000, up from a mere 70,000 at the start of the New Deal nine years earlier. The city overflowed into the suburbs of surrounding Maryland and Virginia. The federal government tried its hand at city planning, building the "new town" of Greenbelt, Maryland, a community for a thousand middle-income families a few miles outside Washington. Within the District, the historic preservation spirit led to the private, piecemeal restoration of Georgetown, which had drifted downhill since the turn of the century. While this restoration preserved hundreds of homes of Federal-period architecture, it also displaced most of the low-income Negroes who had once comprised nearly half of Georgetown's population.

If the New Deal made Washington the power center of the nation, the Second World War transformed it into the military capital of the Western world. The migration to Washington that had slowed slightly at the end of the Thirties was renewed by the beginning of war preparations in 1940. Just as the government was getting around to clearing the Mall of ugly temporary buildings from World War I, the order went out to construct more of them. Soon the reflecting pool between the Washington Monument and the Lincoln Memorial was flanked by low rows of frame and stucco offices. On the Virginia side of the Potomac, construction began on the largest office building in the world, the Pentagon—the five-sided home of the War Department, where more than 40,000 people worked each day at the height of World War II.

The arrival of some 5,000 new residents each month during the early war years strained the housing capacity of an already crowded city. War workers who couldn't be accommodated in new federal dormitories slept five and six to a room in the living rooms, dining rooms, and hallways of spacious old Washington homes. Hotels were filled with "dollar-a-year" men—business executives who donated their managerial skills to the defense effort.

Washington's rush-hour traffic jams became even more snarled. In the summer of 1941, plans were made for a mass march of Negroes to protest job discrimination. Plans were canceled, however, after a tense meeting between black labor leader A. Philip Randolph (head of the sleeping car porters' union) and President Roosevelt, who forged a precedent-setting executive order banning job discrimination in all defense plants and federal offices. New federal housing for war workers, however, remained segregated. The extravagance of Washington's normal social life was out of style in the wartime capital. Parties became fewer and simpler. The annual Cherry Blossom Festivals were suspended. The tone of the city was symbolized by the darkening of the flood-lit Capitol dome, which would have been too convenient a beacon for an enemy air attack. And in 1945, for the first time in Washington history, a presidential inauguration (Roosevelt's fourth) was held at the White House rather than on a monumental platform at the Capitol.

After the death of President Roosevelt and the end of World War II, President Truman grappled with inflation, labor unrest, communism in Asia and Europe, and charges of corruption and communism in his own administration. The city of Washington was still plagued by chronic problems of disease, crime, and deteriorating schools in the black slum areas—which existed in downtown sections of the Northwest, in Foggy Bottom, on Capitol Hill, in the old Southwest area, and in parts of the sprawling Northeast. Beginning in 1948, the entire Southwest, except for fewer than ten buildings (churches, schools, waterfront restaurants, and historic houses), was leveled, leaving an empty grid of streets and sidewalks. Over the next twenty-five years the area was redeveloped with modern apartments, townhouses, federal and commercial office buildings, and shopping centers. The back-alley slums of Southwest were eliminated, but most of the poor blacks who were moved out found the new housing too expensive and resettled in other parts of the city. In 1948, President Harry S Truman moved across Pennsylvania Avenue to the Blair House, where he lived for four years while the White House was being gutted and rebuilt from the basement to the rafters. It was at the Blair House in 1950 that two Puerto Rican nationalists made an attempt on the President's life.

DESEGREGATION

The Eisenhower years brought the landmark 1954 Supreme Court decision on school integration, and subsequent federal court orders opened all public accommodations in the District to blacks, several years before integration prevailed in the rest of the nation. Partly because of this, but due also to the increasing congestion of downtown Washington and the attractiveness of the outlying open spaces, Washington experienced a renewed migration of white residents and businesses toward the affluent suburbs. The heart of the downtown business district slipped into decay. Modern office buildings, most of them faceless boxes of glass and steel, were constructed along Connecticut Avenue and K Street, creating a new fashionable district. The population of the District reached its all-time high point about 1950, with some 800,000 residents. But urban renewal began to lower the density of former slum neighborhoods, and the population dropped by about 45,000 during the next twenty years. Whereas in 1950 blacks comprised about 35 percent of the population in the District of Columbia itself, the proportion rose to more than 70 percent by 1970. The surrounding suburbs remained principally white. By early 1975 the continuing decline had brought the population of the District down to approximately 720,000.

The election of John F. Kennedy in 1960 brought more than a change of political party to the White House. It also heralded a change in the tone of life in Washington. The new administration placed more emphasis on cultural achievement and historic preservation. Jackie Kennedy redid the White House in authentic Federal style. State dinners there (frequently white tie and tails, often at least black tie) became showcases for the performing arts. President Kennedy scuttled a plan to demolish the historic townhouses that surrounded Lafayette Park across from the Executive Mansion, and commissioned a new plan that saved the houses and located office space behind them.

Meanwhile, the New Frontier legislative program mandated a further expansion of the federal government. In the three years of Kennedy's administration, and under the ensuing five of President Johnson, Washington became the home of such new agencies as the Peace Corps, VISTA, the Office of Economic Opportunity, and two new Cabinet departments—Transportation, and Housing and Urban Development. The federal government pushed at the stretched seams of the downtown office district, and soon jumped the river into new business complexes in Rosslyn and Crystal City, Virginia, and in such semirural towns as Gaithersburg and Rockville, Maryland. During the Sixties, metropolitan Washington grew faster than any other major city in America. Its population doubled between 1950 and 1970, reaching about 3 million by the start of the Seventies. Attempts to put some method into the madness of suburban sprawl resulted in the development of "new towns." Reston, Virginia, was carved out of the Fairfax County countryside. Montgomery Village, Maryland, sprang up adjacent to the sleepy town of Gaithersburg. Columbia, Maryland, was positioned midway between Washington and Baltimore.

FOCAL POINT OF PROTEST

Washington, the nation's prime pressure point, felt the social strains and tragedies of the Sixties even more intensely than the rest of America. President Kennedy, assassinated in Dallas, Texas, was brought home to Arlington National Cemetery for burial. He was joined there five years later by his brother Robert, felled by a bullet in California. Citizens brought their grievances to the government's doorstep in increasing numbers. Three hundred thousand black and white Americans—the largest assemblage up to that point in Washington history—massed in 1963 around the Lincoln Memorial and heard the Reverend Martin Luther King, Jr.'s eloquent and impassioned "I Have a Dream" address. (Later even larger gatherings protested the Vietnam war.) Washington was not spared the violence that erupted in the ghettos of many American cities. After the assassination of King in 1968, a night of rioting, looting, and burning erupted in the black business district, leaving gutted buildings along 7th and 14th Streets that still stand unrepaired more than six years later. The death of King also inspired the Poor People's March on Washington, plagued by disorganization, torrents of rain on the muddy Mall, and a cold shoulder from Congress. During the Seventies there were innumerable smaller demonstrations—busloads of poverty workers protesting fund cutbacks, Vietnam Veterans Against the War, the Reverend Carl McIntire and his legions urging victory in Vietnam, crowds marching for the impeachment of President Nixon, and many, many more.

In the late Sixties and early Seventies, Washington experienced another architectural renaissance. The Mall was cleared of the last of the "tempos" and such relics as the Navy Munitions Building and the Army Museum of Pathology. Open spaces flanking the Mall were chosen as the sites for boldly modern buildings, like the cylindrical Joseph Hirshhorn Museum and Sculpture Garden, and the trapezoidal annex to the National Gallery, as well as the Air and Space Museum. The old waterfront area of Foggy Bottom became dominated by the curvilinear design of the Watergate complex and the boxy mass of the John F. Kennedy Center for the Performing Arts. The Southwest redevelopment area was capped by the L'Enfant Plaza office and hotel complex and the new home of the Department of Housing and Urban Development.

Meanwhile, the downtown business district continued to slide, but it was given a lift by the starkly modern building for the Martin Luther King Memorial Library and renovation of the historic Patent Office into the National Collection of Fine Arts and National Portrait Gallery. A site nearby was chosen for the proposed Eisenhower Civic Center, which would displace Washington's tiny Chinatown on H Street N.W. Washingtonians who had dreamed for years of the greening of Pennsylvania Avenue were less than entranced by the construction of the forbidding and massive J. Edgar Hoover Building, a solid city block of FBI offices. The congressional hierarchy, fighting hard to keep up with the growth of the Executive Branch, ordered the clearing of several more blocks of Capitol Hill for the construction of new offices and an enormous annex to the Library of Congress, to be called the James Madison Library.

MORE CHANGES TO COME

A new spirit of "adaptive use" for old buildings resulted in transforming the original Corcoran Art Gallery, a masterpiece of French Second Empire design, into the Renwick Gallery. The Union Station, a white elephant from the golden age of railroads, was slated to become the National Visitors Center. The Romanesque Revival Old Post Office Building with its Victorian tower survived to be transformed into a fitting headquarters of the National Endowment for the Arts. To give Washingtonians and the city's tourists an alternative to congested freeways and air pollution alerts, the area and federal government began building a subway system called the Metro. As it progressed, it became the most expensive federal construction project anywhere in the nation in recent years. During the construction phase, streets were excavated into deep trenches and covered with roadways of heavy wood planks, giving Washington the look of a latter-day frontier town.

Washingtonians don't seem to mind the dirt and noise of subway construction. They have become tolerant of change and accustomed to the chaos of construction, which is a constant condition in the capital city. Washington can never sit back and survey its buildings, parks, and avenues with any sense of finality. Washington is a city that is constantly rearranging and expanding, sometimes at the expense of an earlier beauty and order. "Washington will be a nice city," the tourist jokes, "if they ever get it finished." Washingtonians agree. They know that the tourist's comment is no joke at all, but an accurate observation on the character of the nation's capital.

8 THE CITY AND ITS PEOPLE

Until about 1950, Washington had a bad case of schizophrenia. Washington the Capital had long been the nerve center of the most powerful nation on earth, but Washington the City was a backwater town, considered virtually "unlivable" by cultural sophisticates. Very little music and theater, few good restaurants, almost no commercial art galleries, and not even the divertissement of a popularly elected city government. But during the past twenty-five years, Washington has grown out of its civic and cultural adolescence.

Its quality as a city is fast approaching its importance as the seat of government. Now it has resident performing arts companies. Now it has galleries, large and small. Now it has good restaurants (not just tired seafood and steak-and-chops joints). Now there is some place to go after dark besides home to watch television. Now a modern subway system is under construction. Now it has winning professional football and basketball teams, and even pro teams in hockey, soccer, and lacrosse, but no more Washington Senators baseball team to haunt the American League cellar. Most significantly, the District of Columbia has an embryonic local government, the modest beginning of home rule that has been denied the nation's capital for a century.

The fact that these developments are noteworthy is a measure of their newness. Most cities of several million people have had such normal accoutrements of urban life for decades. But Washington has not been a city of several million people very long. In 1950 the population of the whole Washington metroplitan area was about 1.5 million. Today, the metropolitan area is home to some 3.2 million people. Only New York, Los Angeles, Chicago, Philadelphia, Detroit, Boston, and San Francisco–Oakland are bigger. During the boom times of the Soaring Sixties, Washington was the fastest-growing large city in America. The District, like many other urban cores, lost population, but the Washington suburbs tripled their population, from 705,000 in 1950 to 2.1 million in 1970.

For practical purposes Washington is *not* synonymous with the District of Columbia, which is just the 69-square-mile core of a sprawling metropolitan area. Today, what most people mean when they say Washington is the whole aggregation—the demographer's Washington, the marketing analyst's Washington—and it includes the Maryland counties of Montgomery, Prince George's, and Charles (a predominantly rural area some 30 miles south of the District), plus the Virginia counties of Arlington, Fairfax, Prince William, and Loudoun (the latter two being rural areas that are fast developing into bedroom communities). Once merely tack-ons to the District, the Washington suburbs are now nearly self-sufficient in shopping, office buildings, and night life. These days, more than half of the area's labor force goes to work each morning in the suburbs rather than the District. And the District itself has a population of only 720,000 out of the more than 3 million people in the whole metropolitan area.

Because of its rapid growth over the past two decades, the Washington area has more newcomers than natives. Two out of every three Washingtonians were born and reared somewhere else, in a place that they continue to call "home" for years after their arrival in the nation's capital. The new Washingtonians bring with them the traits of the regions they left behind—particular ways of speaking, styles of living, modes of dress, and deep-seated attitudes. The personality of Washington is a mix of the nation's hundreds of personalities, and the accents of Washington's voices are the accents of all Americans. Washington's identity is a borrowed one. Many of these transplanted people band together in "state societies" to keep alive a fervent allegiance to their home state. (The members of the Maine State Society call themselves "Mainiacs," but the Texans are undoubtedly the most chauvinistic of all expatriates in Washington.)

Washington is not a city of transients stopping on their way to some place more attractive. At the top level of government, there is a coming and going every four years (or more frequently), but most area residents—apparently unable to resist the magnetism of Washington's glamor and economic security—end up spending the rest of their lives here.

HOMETOWN CELEBRITIES

Not everyone stays in Washington, though. Some leave if there is another city more hospitable to their particular talents, especially if those talents are in entertainment. Legion are the musicians and theater people who spent some time in Washington—either in their childhoods or in their early professional careers—before leaving for the lively scenes of New York and Hollywood. The list of onetime Washingtonians includes the late Duke Ellington, Kate Smith, Helen Hayes, the late Al Jolson, Arthur Godfrey, Goldie Hawn, Billy Eckstine, Shirley MacLaine and her brother Warren Beatty, Pete Seeger (whose father, Charles L. Seeger, was a pioneering folk musicologist with the federal government), Pearl Bailey, and Marvin Gaye. Washington has also been home (however briefly) to a number of greats and near-greats of rock-'n'-roll: Jorma Kaukonen and Jack Cassady of the defunct Jefferson Airplane; John Phillips and the late Cass Elliott of the disbanded Mamas and Papas; and the late Jim Morrison of the Doors. A few prominent rockers—like Fifties great Link Wray and guitar virtuoso Roy Buchanan—still spend a lot of time around Washington. Washington is always proud to claim a celebrity as a "hometown hero" and "local-boy-made-good," but the fact remains that the vast majority of these entertainers were unknown until they left Washington to make their mark. And in the welter of political activity, they seldom get much of a hometown boost when they come back.

On the other side of the coin, Washington is apparently a congenial working atmosphere for novelists. It is the adopted city of such notables as Herman Wouk (*The Caine Mutiny, Marjorie Morningstar, The Winds of War*), who lives in stylish Georgetown; James M. Cain (*The Postman Always Rings Twice*), an octogenarian resident of suburban Hyattsville, Maryland; Larry McMurtry (*The Last Picture Show* and the novel from which the movie *Hud* was adapted), who runs a rare-book shop in Georgetown; and Katherine

Anne Porter (*Pale Horse, Pale Rider; Ship of Fools*), who lives in suburban College Park, Maryland.

THE UNIQUE WASHINGTONIANS

Although Washingtonians individually resemble their fellow Americans throughout the country, as an aggregate population they are unique, displaying traits exhibited by no other clump of 3 million people in the nation (or world).

Washingtonians are overwhelmingly white-collar (68 percent), and half the entire labor force works for some level of government (about 418,000—civilian and military—for Uncle Sam and another 155,000 for local governments). Only 6 percent of the Washington labor force work in manufacturing, but there is a large blue-collar service sector. The density of white-collar employment here accounts for the District's ranking first among the major cities of the world in per capita number of telephones. (Blue-collar employees work with their hands, government bureaucrats with their mouths, usually connected to their brains.) There are more telephones than residents in the District, 123 per 100 people, a density surpassed in all the world only by tiny Vaduz, Liechtenstein, which has nearly two phones for each person.

Several occupational groups, such as journalists, caterers, and lawyers, exist in Washington in greater proportions than anywhere else in America. And Washington boasts an army of cab drivers (more per capita than any other city), but a lot of them are part-time drivers who are apparently relaxing at home when you need a cab late at night or on a rainy Saturday afternoon. And the city is awash with law enforcement personnel—not just the cops of D.C., Maryland, and Virginia, but the FBI, Treasury "T-men," and forces that protect federal parks, the Capitol, the National Zoo, embassies, the Supreme Court, and other special bailiwicks. Washington has the highest density of psychiatrists, too (perhaps because the government is generous about reimbursing its employees for psychiatric counseling). Washington also has one of the nation's highest densities of armed services personnel (70,000) and military retirees (70,000). Washington is a haven for high-ranking retired officers, many of whom begin second careers as the Washington representatives for defense contractors.

With this concentration of white-collar occupations—professional people, business executives, trade association directors, federal bureaucrats, and so on—it is not surprising that Washington has a well-educated, high-income citizenry. Washington is the best-educated large metropolitan area in the nation (at least in terms of average education attainment). One out of every four adults is a college graduate compared with one out of ten in the population at large. Washington's median family income, about $13,000 in 1970, is also the highest among the nation's million-population metropolitan areas. In the various political jurisdictions, the 1974 medians ranged from more than $12,000 in the District to over $20,000 in Fairfax County, Virginia, and Montgomery Country, Maryland, which share the national title for the highest median income among large counties. While these prosperous counties don't have the same sort of opulent estate neighborhoods that are found outside the big industrial cities, neither do they have as many large areas of poverty.

But there is plenty of poverty in the Washington area. Some 123,000 residents of the District of Columbia—about one of every six people—could be considered poor. Almost an equal number of poor people live in parts of Washington outside the District, in rundown sections of Alexandria, Virginia, Prince George's County, Maryland, and Arlington, Virginia. Most of the poor people of the Washington area are blacks, but most blacks in the Washington area are not poor. As a matter of fact nearly one-fifth of all the Negroes in the District had incomes of $15,000 and above in 1970, and 3 percent had incomes over $25,000.

As a southern border city (where slavery persisted until the middle of the Civil War), Washington has always had a large black population. However, because of the soaring population of the predominantly white suburbs, the Negro proportion of the entire metropolitan area—about 23 percent—has remained roughly the same since the turn of the century. This percentage is the highest among the nation's thirty largest urban areas. Within the District, the white minority lives mostly in the small, affluent wedge of Northwest Washington that lies west of Rock Creek Park. The rest of the whites tend to live in the redeveloped Southwest quadrant, on Capitol Hill, and in Foggy Bottom (the area near the State Department best known for the Watergate complex).

While home ownership is dominant in the wealthy Washington suburbs, the District has an unusually high proportion of renters—about 70 percent of all households. (The highest incidence of owner-occupied homes is in the predominantly black Northeast quadrant.) In the suburbs, the average price of a new home has hit more than $50,000. In the neighborhoods of Northwest Washington west of Rock Creek Park (where the average family income exceeds $24,000), it's difficult to find a house for as little as $70,000.

WASHINGTON NEIGHBORHOODS

Most of the newer Washington suburbs are indistinguishable from each other and from hundreds of other housing developments around the nation. But several older neighborhoods of the District and suburbs have particular charms and particular kinds of people who inhabit them. People who want to immerse themselves in history (and be ultrachic as well) gravitate toward the Federal period townhouses of Alexandria, Virginia, and the Georgetown section of the District. Chevy Chase Village, in Maryland, and the Cleveland Park neighborhood of D.C.—both boasting shady streets and big turn-of-the-century houses with wide verandas and umpteen bedrooms—have a special appeal to well-to-do families with lots of kids. Many of the Cleveland Park residents are politically liberal professional people who are active in District affairs, who decry the suburbs as sterile, and who send their children either to the neighborhood public schools or (more likely) to an integrated progressive private school.

Black middle-class citizens, including thousands of federal employees, have a stronghold in the Northeast quadrant of the District, in pleasant neighborhoods of modest single-family homes like Brookland, near the Catholic University campus. The wealthy suburbs of McLean, Virginia, and Potomac, Maryland, offer two-acre mini-estates to would-be country squires (while accommodating the horsey set of fox hunters and polo players with genuine estates on the fringe of suburbia). Do-it-yourself preservationists like the

Victorian rowhouses surrounding Capitol Hill. The Virginia suburbs have a special appeal to military careerists, being so near to bases like Fort Myer, Quantico, and Fort Belvoir, as well as the Pentagon. Devotees of the "new town" concept of urban development like the contemporary houses and apartments of Reston, Virginia, and the more traditional styles of Columbia and Montgomery Village, both in Maryland. Wealthy blacks—many of them doctors and lawyers—inhabit large, comfortable houses of the upper-16th Street corridor, in Shepherd Park and the elegant neighborhoods east of Rock Creek Park known as the Gold Coast and North Portal Estates. Followers of the "counterculture"—young, white, and college-educated, with a very casual life style—inhabit the Dupont Circle and Adams-Morgan areas of the District. Many middle- and upper-level bureaucrats like the modern townhouses and apartments of the Southwest redevelopment area, where they can walk to work at the Department of Transportation, the Department of Housing and Urban Development, the Department of Health, Education and Welfare, the Postal Service, and many other agencies.

THE FOREIGN PRESENCE

One of the most conspicuous differences between Washington and other American cities of several million people is the absence here of well-defined ethnic enclaves. This is due to the lack of the sort of manufacturing jobs that lured immigrants to cities like New York, Pittsburgh, and Chicago in the late nineteenth and early twentieth centuries. There is no "Little Italy" in Washington, no neighborhoods where people still speak Polish or Yiddish, or English with a thick Irish accent. Washington's "Chinatown"—a few blocks around 6th and H Streets N.W.—is a tiny section identifiable only by rows of Chinese restaurants and pagodalike decorations on street-corner telephone booths, and even these are slowly disappearing.

The only large group of foreign-born Washingtonians with a real sense of community are the Latin-Americans who live along Columbia Road in Northwest Washington. They are relatively recent arrivals to the U.S., and many of them came to the capital to fill the domestic servant shortage caused by the improving economic situation of Washington's blacks. Columbia Road boasts numerous Latin-American restaurants and grocery stores, and even a movie theater (the Ontario) that shows features in Spanish with no English subtitles. This neighborhood is the core of a Spanish-speaking population that might number as many as 100,000 people throughout the whole Washington area (a good number of whom, it is thought, would rather not be recorded in the census, because they are illegally residing here on tourist visas).

Despite the paucity of ethnic neighborhoods, there are many people of foreign birth and/or foreign parentage throughout the metropolitan area. The 1970 census recorded some 380,000 of them—well over 10 percent of the general population. Among the largest ethnic groups, after the Latin-Americans, are those from Germany (38,000), the Soviet Union (30,000), Canada (29,000), Poland (18,000), and Ireland (17,000). Scattered as these people are residentially, maintaining ethnic identity through language, diet, and traditional observances is a formidable challenge that many families eventually give up. Several thousand of the foreign-born of Washington are still citizens of their native land. They are here to serve their countries as diplomats and embassy staff, or to work for one of the international economic organizations (the World Bank, International Monetary Fund, and Inter-American Development Bank).

One physical manifestation of the ethnic variety of Washington is the astounding array of religious denominations with churches in Washington. Within a short stretch of ritzy Massachusetts Avenue (best known as Embassy Row), one can find a Moslem mosque, a Russian Orthodox church, a Greek Orthodox church (one of five in the area), and an Episcopal cathedral. Elsewhere in the city are Armenian Apostolic churches, several Buddhist temples, a Black Muslim mosque, and churches for the orthodox Christians of Serbia, Rumania, and the Ukraine.

Of course, as elsewhere, well-established churches have the largest followings in Washington. There are more than a half-million Catholics in the Washington area (nearly one-sixth of the population), including more than 75,000 Negro Catholics who help keep Washington's rate of conversion to Catholicism the highest in the nation. A focal point for all Catholics, nationally as well as locally, is the National Shrine of the Immaculate Conception, the neo-Byzantine cathedral in Northeast Washington where Luci Baines Johnson married Pat Nugent during the administration of Luci's father, President Lyndon Johnson. The Baptists are very strong, particularly among blacks, and the Methodists, Episcopalians, and Presbyterians have high membership, too. Of special significance to Episcopalians is the magnificent Washington Cathedral, whose Gothic structure—under construction since 1907—dominates the Northwest horizon from one of the highest points in the District. Jews comprise about 6 percent of the Washington area population—more than twice the percentage in the nation as a whole—and most of them live in the District and Montgomery County. Well-to-do and highly educated, they take an unusually strong role in Washington's business, cultural, and philanthropic affairs.

The active (and affluent) community of Mormons in Washington celebrated in 1974 the completion of an enormous white marble temple, towering next to the Interstate 495 Beltway in suburban Kensington, Maryland. It is the largest of the sixteen Mormon temples in the world, and twice the size of the headquarters temple in Salt Lake City. At the opposite end of the spectrum from the magnificent religious edifices of Washington are hundreds of tiny "storefront churches"—purveyors of the pentecostal experience to inner-city blacks.

Many out-of-towners, who somehow have the impression that Washington is a godless city of amoral politicians and machinelike bureaucrats, are surprised to learn of the great number of "prayer breakfasts" held each week on Capitol Hill and in the federal agencies.

Washington has never been hit as hard by recessions and depressions as the rest of the country. Higher unemployment, a little belt-tightening, yes—and a few purchases forgone—but no widespread destitution. The fact is that every major economic dislocation has led to the creation of new federal programs that have swelled the bureaucratic ranks, taken root, and remained in

Washington long after the crisis has passed. (Some cynics even contend that the city of Washington gets more help from these relief programs than do the intended beneficiaries throughout the country.) Washington is insulated from the economic hazards that plague the rest of America, and this sometimes blunts Washington's understanding of the plight of "the folks back home." During the economic downturn of 1974, federal employment in the Washington area increased by some 9,000 jobs. While the rest of the nation tried to cope with an average unemployment rate exceeding 8 percent, the Washington area in December of 1974 experienced its worst unemployment since the depression—5.2 percent, a rate with which many metropolitan areas would be delighted.

After the federal government, tourism is the biggest industry. The largest private employers in the Washington area are the hotels, restaurants, convention services firms, tour guides, and other adjuncts of tourism. Washington, the trade association capital of the nation, is full of people whose occupational mission is to promote the interests of a particular industry in negotiations with Congress and the bureaucracy. Third in total employment is the research-and-development industry (scientific and social research firms, many of which work exclusively under contract to the federal government). Probably the fastest-growing employment group in Washington is the mass of people who sell, assemble, service, program, and manage computers. The IBM Corporation alone has some 9,000 employees in the Washington area. The high level of income in Washington gives it a particularly strong retail trade, where such venerable local department stores as Woodward & Lothrop, Hecht's, Garfinckel's, and Kann's thrive alongside branches of stylish out-of-town establishments like Lord & Taylor and Saks Fifth Avenue of New York City and Neiman-Marcus of Texas.

Washington is a natural location for the publication of public affairs material, so it's not surprising that such national periodicals as *U.S. News and World Report,* the *New Republic,* the *Kiplinger Letters,* the *National Observer, Washington Monthly, Nation's Business, National Journal, Congressional Quarterly,* and *Changing Times* originate in the nation's capital. But the largest circulation periodical published in Washington has nothing to do with politics and economics. It is the eighty-seven-year-old *National Geographic,* whose 9 million readers renew their subscriptions year after year. The most startling recent success in Washington publishing is the monthly magazine *Smithsonian,* an indescribable potpourri whose editorial interests— everything from the humanities to the natural sciences—are as broad as the jurisdiction of the Smithsonian Institution itself. Launched in 1970 as a bonus for the Smithsonian Associates (anyone who gives the Institution $10 a year), the magazine now has more than 600,000 subscribers, and is the second-fastest growing magazine in America (behind the girlie magazine *Penthouse*). Besides these well-known publications, countless small-circulation trade journals and newsletters are churned out by trade associations and research organizations in Washington.

People don't generally think of Washington as a major center of corporate headquarters, but a surprising number of nationally prominent companies are based in or near the District. These include the Marriott Corporation, the Washington Post Company (owner of *Newsweek* and several broadcast stations), Allegheny Airlines, Comsat General Corporation, Fairchild Industries, Acacia Mutual Life Insurance, Government Employees Insurance Company (GEICO), Martin Marietta, Southern Railway, Quality Inns, Peoples Life Insurance, Ringling Bros. and Barnum & Bailey Circus, International Bank (a worldwide financial and industrial conglomerate), Microwave Communications, Inc. (MCI), and the retailing group of Garfinckel, Brooks Brothers, Miller and Rhoads. Also based in the Washington area are such regional giants as Peoples Drug Stores, Giant Food, Inc., Drug Fair, Woodward & Lothrop, the Hecht Company, and Dart Drug. The Washington area is also the headquarters of the world's largest dealer in used military weapons—Interarms, whose vast warehouses line the Potomac River waterfront in downtown Alexandria. Founded in 1953 by Samuel Cummings (who in recent years has lived in Monaco), Interarms makes transactions with foreign governments (of any political persuasion) for goods ranging from automatic pistols and hand grenades to tanks and jet fighter planes.

The voice of the Washington business community is the Board of Trade. Founded in 1889 by Beriah Wilkins, an Ohio banker, ex-congressman, and controlling owner of the Washington *Post,* the board in its early years was a small, exclusive organization of the city's business elite, unique in its inclusion of Negro and Jewish business leaders. Today membershp is open to any businessman in the Washington area. Since its founding, the board has worked closely with Congress and the D.C. city government to protect the interests of its business members. Activists in Washington's poorer neighborhoods have long charged that the Board of Trade, until the advent of the new elective city council, was the District's de facto policymaker, a city council in disguise. It has been pro-highway, pro-downtown parking, pro-tourism, pro-beautification, pro-commercial rezoning (and recently pro-subway, to revitalize the downtown shopping area). It was a principal opponent of home rule for the District until 1972, when it finally accepted the fact that some sort of elected local government was inevitable. The board was headed in 1974 by Woodward & Lothrop president Edwin Hoffman. The 1975 president is National Savings and Trust v.p. Joseph H. Riley, and the 1976 president will be a past president, Joseph Danzansky of Giant Food, the indefatigable searcher for a new pro baseball team for the nation's capital.

CIVIC GROUPS AND EDUCATION

The District's most prestigious civic association is the Federal City Council, a body of leaders from Washington's business, law, education, and government circles—including a few prominent black businessmen, presidents of the major local universities, D.C. Delegate Walter Fauntroy, and Senator Thomas Eagleton (D-Mo.), chairman of the Senate District Committee. The largest group of members are the Washington representatives of major national corporations, such as Ford, GM, ITT, Texaco, U.S. Steel, RCA, and Firestone, each of which pays annual dues of $1,500. Council presidents in recent years have included William P. Rogers (when he was a lawyer in private practice), Washington lawyer and former Army Secretary Stephen Ailes, and former Ambassador to Germany George McGhee. Working behind the scenes with federal and D.C. officials, the Council attempts to improve the quality of life in the District in every area from elementary education and drug prevention to low-income housing and environmental protection. Its current president is Sol Linowitz, former board chairman of Xerox and ambassador to the OAS, now a prominent international lawyer.

Washington is not the prestigious center of higher education that one might expect of the capital of the United States. In most large cities, the resident intellectual elite is dominated by the faculties of the prominent local universities. But in Washington the colleges tend to be overshadowed by such awesome public and private centers of scholarship as the Library of Congress, National Institutes of Health, Brookings Institution, Carnegie Institution, and the National Academy of Sciences.

There are, however, a lot of four-year and two-year colleges in the Washington area (more than twenty), and their combined enrollment exceeds 150,000 students—not counting an additional few thousand who take part-time courses. The institutions range in size from several hundred students to the 33,000 who attend classes at the University of Maryland's 5,450-acre campus in suburban College Park. While none of Washington's colleges ranks at the very top of U.S. higher education, several are well regarded in particular fields. For example, Georgetown University, the venerable Jesuit college, is strong in international affairs, law, and medicine; George Washington University has an up-and-coming, innovative law school; Catholic University is outstanding in music and drama; and the University of Maryland is excellent in engineering and the sciences, especially postgraduate physics. Howard University, a federally funded institution with some 10,000 students (of whom about 2,000 are foreign), has long been considered the finest predominantly black university in the nation. The nation's only college for the deaf is federally funded Gallaudet, located on a century-old campus in the Northeast quadrant of the District.

The students of Washington are not as visible, and don't have as great an impact on the style of life in the city, as the students of, say, Boston or San Francisco. While most of the colleges of the area experienced student disorder in the late Sixties, it was comparatively mild, and faded with the back-to-work mood of the Seventies. Proximity to political power is a major drawing card of the Washington area universities. Most of them have had increases in student applications in recent years, as the nation's eyes have been focused on such Washington-based crises as Vietnam and Watergate.

CAPITAL AT LEISURE

Washingtonians spend their free time in much the same way people do in other large cities. They stay home and watch TV, visit the homes of friends for drinks and dinner, dine out at a favorite restaurant, take their families to a beach on the Virginia, Maryland, or Delaware shore, play tennis at a club or public court, and play softball on one of the diamonds near the Mall. They go to the movies, see a Broadway musical at the National Theatre downtown, or take the kids to afternoon practices of the neighborhood baseball, swimming, or soccer team. Washingtonians are crazy about the Redskins, most of whose season tickets change hands only when someone dies or moves out of town. Suburban Washingtonians have a noticeable penchant for dinner theaters, those hybrid emporiums of food, drink, and musical comedy.

Washingtonians patronize all sorts of musical events: Kennedy Center concerts of the National Symphony; the amphitheater for summer music and dance at Wolf Trap Farm; rock at the 19,000-seat Capital Centre along the Beltway at Largo, Maryland; rhythm-and-blues shows at the open-air Carter Barron Amphitheatre in Rock Creek Park; and concerts of pop and country music performers at the Post Pavilion in the new town of Columbia, Maryland. For some reason, Washingtonians have a particular affection for "bluegrass," the modern reincarnation of hill-country music. On any given night, bluegrass bands are picking guitars, mandolins, and banjos to packed houses at half a dozen bars in the District and suburbs, frequented by a mélange of college students, young executives, truck drivers, and mild-mannered federal bureaucrats. Among the "country pop" and bluegrass musicians who have worked around Washington over the years are Jimmy Dean, Roy Clark, Don Reno, the Stoneman Family, George Hamilton IV, the Country Gentlemen, Patsy Cline, Billy Grammer, Bill Clifton, and the Seldom Scene. (Many country stars got their start on radio stations owned by Washington broadcaster Connie B. Gay.)

Washingtonians like their liquor, and the District is where they buy it. As a matter of fact, D.C. is ranked first nationally in per capita liquor sales. But this doesn't mean that District residents drink it all themselves. A lot of those sales are made to suburban Washingtonians, who take advantage of the District's lower liquor taxes to stock their car trunks before commuting home in the evening to Maryland and Virginia. And the per capita consumption statistic is skewed, too, by the drinking of tourists and businessmen (many of whom take cheap Washington liquor back home in their suitcases).

Washington is only a so-so town for gambling. The black poor have their numbers games, and the well-off suburbanites have their wagering pools for football games (both illegal, but prospering). People from all walks of life have parimutuel betting at the track. Maryland is the only government of the Washington area that has a sanctioned lottery. It's a success, but, like lotteries in other states, has not made a dent in the more exciting forms of parting with one's money. Playing the numbers is not only a favorite pastime of lower income black Washingtonians, it is also an enormous business enterprise, the full scope of which is only guessed at by the police detectives who try futilely to stamp it out. In 1970 a government estimate put the daily numbers handle at $1 million, and said the racket employs some 2,000 people as "runners"—agents who collect the numbers and deliver the winnings.

Washington has become, over the past fifteen years, an excellent town for avid moviegoers. Every movie that opens in New York City—domestic or foreign, big-budget or underground, pop entertainment or "art"—will eventually make it to Washington. And the American Film Institute, headquartered at the Kennedy Center, has occasionally given a new film its American premiere, in advance of commercial release. In the early Seventies, Washington experienced a brief boom in hard-core pornographic movies (such as *History of the Blue Movie* and *Teenage Fantasies*), but this was halted after a few theater raids by the U.S. attorney's men—encouraged, it was widely assumed, by a directive from the Nixon White House. Hard-core movies made a cautious return to Washington in early 1975, until the authorities seized an uncut, uncensored version of the infamous (and boring) *Deep Throat*. The cinematic offerings of Washington run the gamut of tastes. The old downtown movie palaces give the young Negro audience a steady diet of blood-and-guts films featuring black superstars. The Circle Theatre near George Washington University and the Biograph in Georgetown offer reruns of great films from years past—Bogart, the Marx brothers, "festivals" of Truffaut and Bergman, Chaplin, and such. And the new shopping center theaters in the suburbs, catering to the largest part of Washington's population, feature the current movies that are hits with the masses.

SPORTS GALORE

Washington is a very sports-minded city, supporting as great a variety of professional and amateur athletics as can be found in any city. Before the boom of the Sixties, fans had to make do with two cellar-dwellers, the Redskins football team and the Senators baseball team, both of which did battle at the old Griffith Stadium. Then the sports scene in Washington was shocked by two unaccustomed events: the hapless Senators were moved to Texas in the fall of 1971 by their non-Washingtonian owner, Minnesota trucking magnate Bob Short, and the Redskins—surprise of surprises—began winning football games with alarming frequency. The management and ownership structure of the Redskins is typical of Washington: its president is a lawyer (famous trial attorney Edward Bennett Williams), and its largest stockholder is an out-of-towner (Canada-born, California-based cable television tycoon Jack Kent Cooke, who also owns the Los Angeles Lakers basketball team). Basketball flourishes in Washington, too, via the NBA Bullets, who moved here after their owner, Washington contractor Abe Pollin, built them a new home, the Capital Centre.

Washington is a convenient place for the followers of thoroughbred and harness racing, with such tracks as Laurel, Bowie, Rosecroft, Timonium, and Pimlico within easy driving distance in Maryland, plus Charles Town and Shenandoah Downs ninety minutes away in West Virginia, and Delaware Park only a two-hour drive to the north.

Some more esoteric sports exist, if not exactly thrive, in Washington. Polo and fox hunting are practiced in the rolling countryside outside of Washington, and the Washington International Horse Show, held each fall at the D.C. Armory, now vies with the National Horse Show at Madison Square Garden (New York City) as the nation's premier show for hunters and jumpers. The Diplomats (the latest in a succession of pro soccer teams) hold forth at Robert F. Kennedy Stadium. The Maryland Arrows play box lacrosse at the Capital Centre, which is also the home of Abe Pollin's new pro hockey franchise, the NHL Capitals (whose disastrous 1974–75 inaugural season broke virtually every negative record in NHL history, although paid attendance was strong).

The area's interest in college sports focuses largely on the University of Maryland, which boasts excellent football and basketball teams, and one of the nation's best lacrosse teams. Howard University is traditionally a power in soccer, with teams composed largely of foreign students from Africa (especially Nigeria) and Latin America.

As a training ground of athletic talent, Washington follows predictable socioeconomic patterns. Its inner-city playgrounds rank with New York City as the richest reservoir of basketball talent in the nation, while well-heeled Montgomery County, Maryland, turns out more than its share of outstanding collegiate and professional tennis players, including Harold Solomon and family dynasties named Dell, McNair, Goeltz, and Delaney. Landon School, a small private school for boys in suburban Bethesda, Maryland, has won the national interscholastic tennis championship more times in recent years than any other high school. The Northern Virginia Aquatic Club in suburban Arlington, Virginia, has developed nationally prominent swimmers, their brightest star being teenage world record holder and Olympic winner Melissa Belote. On the track scene, the D.C. Striders and Sports International Track Club have produced some of the top women sprinters in the nation.

When Washingtonians want to unwind in a natural setting, they can avail themselves of the finest network of parks in the nation. Washington boasts the only National Park set in an urban area: Theodore Roosevelt Island, an unspoiled chunk of wilderness surrounded by the Potomac River, between the high-rise office buildings of Rosslyn, Virginia, and the gleaming white mass of the Kennedy Center. Rock Creek Park, which cuts through the Northwest part of the city proper, covers 1,754 acres of woods and meadow, crisscrossed with paths for bicyclists and horseback riders. The parks flanking the Mall are alive each weekend with league games of soccer, rugby, and softball. Sunday picnickers near the Lincoln Memorial can watch free games of polo between teams from the horse country of Virginia and Maryland. And all through the mild weather months, the landscaped circles and squares of downtown Washington—each one centered on a larger-than-life statue of a military hero—are crowded at noontime with office workers carrying brown-bag lunches.

CULTURE BOOM

Local highbrows, who for decades decried a philistine mood in the capital of culturally rich America, have taken heart from the arts and entertainment explosion that engulfed Washington during the Sixties. Washington began developing its own arts rather than being merely a stop on the national circuit of pre-Broadway tryouts and traveling art exhibits. The Arena Stage, Washington's renowned repertory theater-in-the-round, premiered and sent to New York the acclaimed productions *Indians, The Great White Hope, Raisin,* and *Moonchildren.* The painters of an informal group known as the Washington Color School—Morris Louis, Kenneth Noland, Gene Davis, and others—introduced the nation to the simple visual delight of pure colors. The well-established National Symphony Orchestra, once a doughty old lady, broadened its contemporary repertoire and improved its playing under Maestro Antal Dorati, who arrived in 1970. The National Ballet became one of the nation's finest classical dance companies. Choral societies, experimental theaters, and commercial art galleries flourished. The Washington cultural scene found a new geographic focus in the John F. Kennedy Center for the Performing Arts, a vast complex of concert hall, opera house, and theaters for drama and film. And Ford's Theatre, where Abraham Lincoln was assassinated, was rejuvenated as a live theater.

Washington was once known for its "cold audiences," but now the impresarios and producers of Washington revel in the responsiveness of the Washington arts audience, a unique blend of well-educated, affluent professional people, public servants, diplomats, students, and business leaders. Washingtonians will flock to every imaginative offering, from the traditional to the avant-garde (but not too far out). Washingtonians attend ballet and modern dance performances in such numbers that the capital city is now considered as voracious a dance audience as New York City.

Of course, full houses are not enough to sustain a culture boom. Every cultural organization needs wealthy backers to subsidize ticket prices. As a nonindustrial area, Washington is handicapped by not having as many large home-grown fortunes as other cities of comparable size. Many of the wealthiest people in Washington have emotional ties to other cities and give little support to the arts here. The dark clouds gathering over the Washington arts scene are financial. In 1974 the National Ballet suspended operations at the conclusion of its most successful season in terms of both critical acclaim and attendance. The Washington Theater Club went under, too, despite a merger with the black-oriented New Theatre. The Opera Society of Washington was forced by a shortage of funds to trim the number of productions in its season. Even the venerable Corcoran Gallery of Art, Washington's oldest art museum, experienced severe financial distress.

AWARE CITIZENS

While the people of Washington come here from all over America, bringing with them the characteristics of their original hometown, before long they take on the one distinctive trait of Washingtonians: a daily, matter-of-fact preoccupation with the affairs of national government. In Washington, to a great extent, national news is local news. The creation of a new federal program, or the disbanding of an existing one, might be mildly interesting to concerned citizens elsewhere in the country, but in Washington it is a gut issue—a matter of job security and paychecks to thousands of people who work in and around the federal government. Even Washingtonians who are not civil servants, journalists, lawyers, or trade association executives know more about the workings of the government than any other group of Americans. They might deny having any particular interest in national affairs, but they cannot help absorbing—unwittingly—a vast quantity of information about what's going on in the White House, on Capitol Hill, at the Supreme Court, and in the bureaucracy. The local newspaper and broadcast stations carry a larger percentage of national news than any others. The casual conversation of Washingtonians—over lunch, the dinner table, at cocktail parties —is larded with talk of people and happenings which citizens elsewhere follow only vaguely.

National news often has practical implications for Washingtonians in businesses that serve public figures. When Gerald Ford became President, a local storage company knew it would have a job to do as soon as the new President and his family were ready to move from 514 Crown View Drive in Alexandria, Virginia, to 1600 Pennsylvania Avenue in Washington, D.C.—a distance of about five miles. And in the charge account files of Lewis & Thos. Saltz, an old local clothing store, Mr. Ford's title and address were changed the day he was sworn in, just as was done for Harry S Truman when Franklin Roosevelt died and for Lyndon B. Johnson after the assassination of John F. Kennedy.

However blasé Washingtonians act about earthshaking national events, they still take a mild interest in spotting political celebrities on the sidewalks of the city, in their limousines on the way to work, or in a dark corner of the Sea Catch restaurant. Taxicab drivers like to brag about all the bigwigs they have carried around town, and Capitol Hill secretaries can be expected to swoon if Teddy Kennedy deigns to say "Hello" as he walks past in a Senate corridor. Cocktail party chitchat is kept fueled by the particular brand of Washington "people reporting" dispensed in the columns of the *Post*'s Maxine Cheshire (whose items are apt to be embarrassing to the mentioned celebrities) and the *Star*'s Betty Beale (who seldom says anything derogatory about Washington's notables). For sheer density of prominent people (if not instantly recognizable celebrities), no city in America comes close to Washington. According to Arthur M. Louis, a *Fortune* associate editor who waded through every page of *Who's Who in America,* Washington has 257 *Who's Who* entries for every 100,000 residents—more than twice the next highest density, Pittsburgh's 121 per 100,000.

Celebrity watching in Washington is facilitated by the fact that most public figures of any importance have distinctive license plates—special tags from the home state for senators and congressmen, "DPL" plates for foreign diplomats, and low-number D.C. license plates (from 1 to 1250) for VIPs of all descriptions: social, political, philanthropic, or just cronies of those in power.

THE SIZE AND SHAPE OF WASHINGTON

Comparatively speaking, Washington is an easy city to live in and around. Sure, it confronts its residents and visitors with a multitude of urban hassles, but fewer than many other large cities. Because of the limit on building height (roughly twelve stories, imposed some seventy years ago for fire-fighting rather than aesthetic considerations), Washingtonians are not humbled by dark canyons of towering office buildings. Their skyline consists only of the assorted shapes of the Capitol, the Washington Monument, and the Romanesque tower of the Old Post Office building on Pennsylvania Avenue. The low mass of office buildings, however, is fast losing the architectural variety that was once one of the most unusual traits of the Washington cityscape. The varied historic styles that used to stand shoulder to shoulder on the District's downtown streets—Federal, Greek Revival, Italianate, Romanesque, French Beaux Arts—are now giving way to uniform concrete boxes built the same number of feet from the curb and rising to the same height.

Washington's height limit is an aberration in the Big-is-Beautiful contest. In other respects the Washington physical scene is big. Its principal avenues are much wider than most city streets, adapting easily to parades. Federal office buildings, if not tall, are often massive structures occupying a whole city block. The city-block-square Rayburn House Office Building, the most pretentious federal building of recent construction (except, perhaps, the new FBI office on Pennsylvania Avenue), has corridors wide enough and tall enough for touch football games, and lavatories in virtually every office. The Pentagon, home of the Department of Defense, is the largest office building in the world, with 6.5 million square feet enclosed within its mere five stories. (The World Trade Center in New York City, standing 110 stories, has about 8.7 million square feet, but is comprised of two separate skyscrapers.)

Washington abounds in outdoor statuary, most of which is several times larger than life. The monument to Ulysses S. Grant, at the foot of Capitol Hill, is the largest equestrian statue in America, and is surpassed in all the world only by the statue of Victor Emmanuel in Rome. Monumental Washington, by the way, is "male chauvinist." Of the few outdoor statues of women, most are symbolic, not tributes to real people. (Among the exceptions are statues of Joan of Arc and Queen Isabella of Spain, hardly contemporary women.) The only statue of a modern woman is the bronze of Negro civil rights leader and educator Mary McLeod Bethune, erected in 1974 in Lincoln Park, near the Capitol. (The monument to Mrs. Bethune is also the only statue in Washington of an actual black person.)

Many of the "superlatives" that abound in Washington—things that are the biggest, most expensive, most numerous, etc.—are a direct result of the immensity of the U.S. government, whose scope of operation and budget exceeds that of any other organization on earth. Thus Washington is the home of, to mention just a few record holders, the world's largest library (the Library of Congress, with some 74 million books, pamphlets, maps, prints, and related items); what is probably the most valuable book (the Library of Congress's Gutenberg Bible); the largest black-and-white printing operation (the U.S. Government Printing Office, which prepares some 3,500 new publications each year); and the largest bank (the World Bank, whose capitalization of $25 billion is controlled by stockholder nations, the principal one being the U.S.). Some of the superlatives are less substantial, such as former President Nixon's record for mailing the world's largest number of Christmas cards—40,000 in 1969, his first Christmas in the White House. (President Ford tied the record during the 1974 Christmas season.)

GETTING AROUND TOWN

Washington is typically American in its infatuation with the automobile. The city has had congested city streets ever since the Thirties—even when a large percentage of the population relied on public streetcars and buses. There is no major commuter train line to the District from the suburbs (only a few B&O trains that pull into Union Station each morning after picking up passengers in such places as Harpers Ferry, West Virginia, and Gaithersburg and Kensington, Maryland). The bus system, once privately owned, is now under public administration. Until construction of the new subway system was finally funded a few years ago, Congress's solution to increasing congestion was to create more downtown freeways to carry more cars. Each day, all the suburban automobiles are stashed—for about $3 a car—in private parking garages and lots, which, Congress has decided (in agreement with a persuasive local parking lobby), are better for the public welfare than public parking garages. Proposals to levy a "commuter tax" on daytime parking downtown—to ease traffic, lower air pollution, and raise revenue for the D.C. government—have always met with howls of protest from the congressmen of suburban Maryland and Virginia, as well as from D.C. businessmen who fear a further loss of patronage to suburban stores. The Metro subway system will not radiate into the suburbs until the Eighties, so it will be some time before commuters will have an attractive alternative to car pools and express buses.

Washington is as well served by air transportation as any city in America. Long- and short-haul domestic flights come in and out of National Airport (on the Virginia shore of the Potomac directly across from downtown Washington), and transcontinental and overseas flights are serviced at Dulles

International Airport, the sprawling, architecturally exciting terminal 20 miles out in the Virginia countryside. Many Washingtonians also use Baltimore-Washington International Airport (formerly called Friendship International).

Contrary to popular misconception, Washington is not the Crime Capital of America. As a matter of fact, it is not even close, at least on the basis of FBI comparative statistics compiled from local police departments around the nation. (A caveat: crime statistics should not be regarded as gospel; the degree of citizen underreporting of crime varies from city to city, and local officials have been known to fudge figures both up and down, either to improve the city's public image or to justify higher police budgets.) The FBI rankings for 1973 indicate there are twenty-three metropolitan areas with larger numbers of violent crimes—murder, rape, assault, and robbery—on a per capita basis than Washington. These cities include some very large cities (such as New York, San Francisco, Detroit, New Orleans, and Miami), but also some surprises like Saginaw, Michigan, Orlando, Florida, Albuquerque, New Mexico, and Columbia, South Carolina. For murder, there are forty-nine cities with worse per capita records, including almost all of the large cities of the South, most of the ten most populous cities in the nation, and a few unlikely spots like Stockton and Santa Cruz, California, and the metropolitan areas of Lakeland/Winter Haven and Fort Lauderdale/Hollywood, Florida. Among the thirty-one cities whose 1973 statistics for rape are worse than Washington's are Denver and Pueblo, Colorado, Ann Arbor, Michigan, Santa Rosa, California, and Daytona Beach, Florida (as well as the more predictable New York, Memphis, Los Angeles, and San Francisco). Countless cities have a higher incidence of burglary per 100,000 citizens, including Yakima, Washington, Peoria, Illinois, Wichita, Kansas, and Honolulu, Hawaii. Washington's only "top ten" ranking in a violent crime is a ninth place in robbery. The District suffered 295 homicides in 1974—the most in its recorded history—but several other large cities set their own murder records, too.

While the District's downtown commercial areas are not exactly bustling each evening, neither are they deserted. As in most big cities, much of the street crime in the District is in depressed neighborhoods that few people except residents of those areas ever set foot in. The local crimes that get national attention—such as the 1973 shooting of Senator John Stennis (D-Miss.) in his affluent Northwest Washington neighborhood—are exceptions to the normal pattern of crimes committed by the poor against the poor on their own turf. Following a national trend, crime is rising at a brisk rate in the densely developed Washington suburbs, although in absolute statistics it still lags far behind the District. It gave D.C. residents some small delight to see that the Washington boom in "massage parlors"—thinly disguised pavilions of prostitution—occurred not downtown, but in the supposedly staid Virginia suburbs.

In the century from 1874 to 1974, Washingtonians who inhabited the District had almost no say in the selection of the people who governed them or the laws by which they were governed. The basic policies of the District government—and the budget behind those policies—were set by the Senate and House District Committees and the District Appropriations Subcommittees of the two chambers. Until his defeat in 1972, House District Committee Chairman John McMillan of South Carolina had successfully blocked home rule reform for more than twenty years. The only concessions secured under his reign were an elective school board (1968) and a nonvoting congressional delegate (1970). Under new liberal leadership, the District Committees drafted and pushed through Congress a very limited home rule bill, signed into law by President Nixon on Christmas Eve, 1973, providing for an elected mayor and city council. Most budgetary and legislative powers, however, are still controlled by Congress. The federal government owns about 28 percent of all the land within the District—a high percentage for an urban area. (Elsewhere in the nation, Uncle Sam's land is mostly wilderness; the government owns, for example, 45 percent of the state of California, 64 percent of Idaho, and 87 percent of Nevada.) The federal land in D.C. is not officially taxable, but Congress votes the District government an annual payment in lieu of taxes.

Deprived for so long of any opportunity to exercise their franchise, District residents became somewhat unpolitical. The high level of civil service employment has been a factor in this, too, since all federal employees are prohibited by the Hatch Act from engaging in partisan politics. When the voters of the District do turn out for a presidential or delegate race, they vote overwhelmingly Democratic. D.C.'s electoral votes, combined with Massachusetts's, were the only ones George McGovern received in 1972. This Democratic preference covers not only the District's black majority but the city's white residents as well. The highest-ranking elected officials in Washington are both black and both Democrats: Walter E. Washington, who served under Presidents Johnson and Nixon as appointed D.C. commissioner and in 1974 was elected to be the District's first mayor in a hundred years; and Delegate Walter Fauntroy, a minister who has been the city's nonvoting representative in the House since the position was created. The elected D.C. Council is also dominated by black Democrats. (Only two of the 13 D.C. Council members are white: Democrats Polly Shackleton and David A. Clarke.)

Before the 1974 election, there were no Democratic congressmen among the five representing the Washington suburbs. Today there are three. The Virginia suburbs are represented by Representative Herbert E. Harris, a former Fairfax County supervisor and lobbyist for the Australian Meat Board, and by Representative Joseph L. Fisher, a scholarly economist who scored a stunning upset over a twenty-two-year House veteran, conservative Republican Joel Broyhill. In the Maryland suburbs, Democratic Representative Gladys N. Spellman, a longtime Prince George's County Council member, was elected to a seat formerly occupied by Representative Larry Hogan, a conservative Republican member of the House Judiciary Committee who pushed for President Nixon's impeachment and later lost a bid for the GOP gubernatorial nomination in Maryland. The two Republican representatives who survived the 1974 Democratic sweep are Representative Gilbert Gude of Montgomery County, Maryland, who is a liberal, and Representative Marjorie Holt of Anne Arundel County, Maryland, a conservative and strong opponent of busing.

CAPITAL AND CITY

So you see, there's more going on in Washington than just government and politics, even if Uncle Sam is the driving force, the sugar daddy, and the very raison d'être of life in the capital. Some people expect Washington to be the chief showcase of American achievement in every category imaginable, from higher education and modern architecture to urban planning and the arts. The city's progress in these and many other areas has been astounding over the past two decades, but Washington is not—and will never be—the epitome of excellence in all things. The nation's capital is not just a collection of massive buildings for tourists to admire and photograph. It is also a real American city—living, growing, decaying, and renewing itself constantly. There are warts on its carefully made-up face. The gleaming public buildings stand not far from slum housing (though the slums are not what they used to be). The air over the city is often hazy with auto exhaust, and the waters of the Potomac run murky brown (though both situations are gradually improving). Many fine old buildings have given way to more parking lots, offices, and inner-city freeways (but today the people are developing a reverence for the styles of yesterday).

Washington belongs, in the largest sense, to all Americans—a point made frequently by congressional opponents of home rule. But Washington is more than a capital city. It is the home, the place of work, and the daily concern of more than 3 million people, the Washingtonians described in these pages. The jobs they perform every day—and the quality of their performance—affect the way you live. Many of them work directly for you, as public servants. Some of them represent your economic, personal, and group interests, as lobbyists and lawyers and association executives. Some of them—those engaged in public and private research—are looking for new ways to improve the quality of your life (or affect it in some other way). And many of them—the members of the press corps—are your eyes and ears in Washington.

Washingtonians are different from the average American in several respects—more educated, better off financially, more aware of national affairs. But they are like other Americans in the traits they have brought to Washington from their diverse backgrounds, regions, and styles of life. The people of the capital city are a blend of American influences, but the blend is unique.

There you have it: a city where everybody talks about being from somewhere else but seldom goes there. A city not northern or southern, not entirely eastern and surely not western, but some of each. A collection of people drawn to one place for the purpose of talking, writing, arguing, studying, legislating, litigating, and mitigating. A synthesis of accents, manners, and morals that originated elsewhere. A federal district, two states, and seven counties—inhabited by people who get up in the morning, go to work, and make a living. They call Washington "home," while 210 million other Americans call it "the capital." Take away the glamor of Washington and there are still clothes to be washed, meals to be cooked, movies to be seen, games to be played, and families to raise—and that, for the most part, is what goes on in Hometown Washington.

9 THE SOCIAL SCENE

The Game of Society in Washington may be played for fun or profit.

When the Arabs entertain these days (featuring Caspian caviar), the motive may be oil or Israel. When the Russians entertain (with piroshki and vodka), it may be for wheat or easier credit. The Koreans like to discuss rice, tankers, and foreign aid. And the American oil companies, over cocktails at the 1925 F Street Club, will talk about price controls and foreign taxes. A former senator may be interested in pushing a newly adopted industry; a political donor, an ambassadorship; a lawyer, his latest client. A wealthy widow may be drumming up support for the National Symphony or the Kennedy Center; and a former New Deal Democrat, a contribution to the American Civil Liberties Union. Whatever the purpose, Washington parties are seldom without an identifiable cause. Since a cause calls for persuasion, and persuasion requires someone with power to ensure success, Washington society revolves around power. And that's the *why* of it all.

What about the *who?* Well, those who garner social standing, or some social rank, in Washington are a varied lot. Some have charm, some have gentility and erudition, some have money. But the real currency for admission to the top ranks as a Washington social celebrity is *power*. The power may be real or supposed. It may be firsthand or simply access to someone who has it. But in any event, and by any description, the aura of power is the central ingredient in social acceptability. A real Washington social celebrity should have some ability to make things move, to get things done, or to influence someone else who can.

It is also a fact that Washington social prominence is a very transitory thing. Social lions and reigning hostesses can disappear with political change-overs, election defeats, and personal retirement. In this respect, Washington society is different from that of, say, Boston, Philadelphia, Richmond, or Cincinnati, where generations of gentility count more than recent political prominence. Different, too, from such cities as Houston, Los Angeles, or Chicago, where money, however new, is a fairly good passport. Or New York, where money, moxie, and an eye for chic trends can create a Social Personage. Celebrity billing in Washington society is also enhanced by recent news attention. A Henry Kissinger—just back from Peking or Teheran—is a far more valuable Washington social catch than a third-generation millionaire who lives quietly among his ancestral bric-a-brac.

Within a few months after a new political administration arrives in Washington, word of who holds the real power gets around town, and a social pecking order is gradually established. It often has little to do with such old stuffiness as who has precedence over whom at the banquet table. Any ambitious Washington hostess would much rather adorn her party with a mere

"Counselor to the President"—if the aide is a Ford intimate like Bob Hartmann or Bill Seidman—than some run-of-the-mill senator or ambassador.

While most figures of Washington society come and go with the political tides, a few wealthy and cultured people, like Mrs. Robert Low Bacon and the late Mrs. Marjorie Merriweather Post, are always "in." And, of course, Mrs. Alice Roosevelt Longworth, daughter of President Theodore Roosevelt and widow of a Speaker of the House. Above reproach (even for the outrageous comments she drops without warning), the ninety-year-old Mrs. Longworth has occupied for decades the same down-at-the-heel townhouse, now nearly covered with a tangle of vines, on Massachusetts Avenue just west of Dupont Circle. She goes out very little these days, preferring quiet evenings of poker with old friends. (A favorite card crony is a cousin of hers, retired columnist Joseph Alsop.) An evening with Mrs. Longworth as a dinner partner is a treat to be savored for years. One evening she told a dinner partner about how her father, the President, cured her ailments when she was young. He would say, "Alice, you shouldn't be sick," and so, on command, she would get well. Mrs. Longworth apparently inherited her father's spunkiness. It has been decades since she observed publicly that "Harding was not a bad man, he was just a slob," and she hasn't curbed her tongue yet.

There's an old story that any private detective worth his salt can go into a hotel room the morning after a torrid tryst, look at the rumpled bed, and tell whether it was for love or money. The same technique might be useful to an observer of the Washington social scene. At any given party, it's hard to know who is paying the bill and for what motive you happened to be invited. If the party is at an embassy, the host nation picks up the tab to win your friendship, in the hope that the resulting goodwill will some day, somehow, benefit the host. The same is true if the party is given at a big hotel by a corporation or trade association. Even a supposedly private, strictly social gathering at the Sulgrave Club, the George Town Club, the Chevy Chase Club, or the Cosmos Club might be staged for an ulterior "business" purpose. If a party is thrown "to honor the Secretary General," or "to honor Senator Jones" or "to honor Commissioner Smith of the Federal Trade Commission," you can bet the host has some particular reason for ingratiating himself to the guest of honor.

The principal pastime at Washington parties is talking. Not eating or drinking or dancing, but talking. The hotels put their party rooms inside, often in the basement, oblivious to the panoramic views, because Washingtonians get so engrossed in their talk they wouldn't even notice the view. The talk is about politics, legislation, whose influence is ascendant, and whose power is waning. The conversation is not entirely different from the talk in other cities (there's always a lot of talk about the Redskins' football fortunes or whether it's going to snow), but it is keyed more directly to the working routine. It is not relaxing chitchat. And the decibel level frequently gets so high that anyone taller than 5 feet 10 inches has to lean down to hear what his partner is saying.

GUEST LISTS AND NEWS COVERAGE

To a greater degree than in other cities, the social circles in Washington tend to overlap and interlock, like the circles of the Ballantine beer insignia. A successful Washington hostess cannot get by with a guest list of federal bigwigs alone. She needs a smattering of foreign diplomats, a few newspaper columnists or television news stars, a couple of lawyers known to wield unusual power, a famous local author or two, a handful of prominent arts patrons, several Washington corporate representatives, and maybe an Old Washington blueblood or two (although few of these so-called cave dwellers can be lured out of their Georgetown mansions for a party at which they could not identify all of the guests as fellow cave dwellers).

Society in Washington is, to a large degree, what people think it is. And most people probably think society consists of what and whom most newspapers write about on the pages marked "society" or "women." The problem is, though, that neither of Washington's two newspapers has a section marked in just that way. On the "Style" pages of the *Post* and the "Portfolio" pages of the *Star,* Washington parties have to compete for coverage with everything from theater reviews and Ann Landers to fashion and "human interest" stories about how Washingtonians cope with their daily problems. Very few of the dozen major social gatherings held on any given night in Washington receive any coverage at all in the Washington papers. Part of this stems from the fact that hostesses today plan different kinds of parties from the extravaganzas of the past. Polly Logan's dinners in her paneled Louis Seize dining room at Firenze House, even when they include twenty couples, are quieter and more personal—for close friends, houseguests, and weekend visitors—than the big productions that once sent society writers and the public gaga. It is no longer "in" to be so conspicuous, and many of the more important "small dinners" given by the Robert McNamaras, the Roger Stevenses, or the James Biddles do not make news copy the next day.

Don't expect to read in the papers about a routine society wedding or debut, a Christmas dance at the City Tavern, or a luncheon at some society matron's house to plan for a charity ball. These events might be big news on the social pages of papers back home, but in Washington a party has to have a clever "angle" to be covered by the press, or be so spectacular that it could not pass unnoticed. One of the few local debuts to make the papers was the "coming out" party (more than ten years ago, during the Twist craze) of one of Wiley T. Buchanan's daughters, for which he rented the magnificent Pan American Union building and transformed parts of it into a replica of the Peppermint Lounge in New York City. One of the few nuptial events to be chronicled in the press was the cave-dweller wedding on New Year's Eve, 1972, of Roberta Renchard to lawyer Robin Freer—a black-tie, candlelight affair at St. Matthew's Cathedral, followed by a sumptuous reception at the Renchards' Kalorama home, where a heated tent had been erected over the terrace and pool. After nearly phasing out wedding and engagement announcements altogether, the two local newspapers began the egalitarian practice of running any announcement that is sent to them, if the sender is willing to pay a small fee for the space.

The one kind of social event that gets covered automatically, with no exceptions, is a function at the White House. Any time the President gives a dinner for a visiting foreign dignitary, hosts a reception for the leadership of Congress, pins a medal on an astronaut back from space, or steps onto the South Portico to wave at children gathered on the lawn for the annual Easter Egg Roll, the party gets covered by the press. The biggest affairs are the "state dinners"—white-tie-and-tails parties with entertainment and dancing after dinner—for foreign presidents, premiers, chancellors, kings, or whoever is the highest-ranking figure in a given country.

PROTOCOL AND POLITICS

Both Washington newspapers publish, on the day after the big White House dinners, complete, fine-printed guest lists, including an identification of the guest and his home town. The list is fascinating reading, for it gives a glimpse of the people whom the President admires, likes, needs to get along with, or depends on for financial and moral support. The guest list is put together "by committee." The President selects many of the guests himself. The White House's congressional liaison staff recommends members of Congress to be invited. Traditionally, a large number of the invitees to any big White House affair are men and women who contributed handsomely to the President's campaigns. Among the most frequent guests at former President Nixon's soirées were such fat cats as Pepsico board chairman Donald Kendall, insurance magnate W. Clement Stone, aerosol valve tycoon Robert Abplanalp, Henry Ford II, Nelson Rockefeller, Hewlett-Packard board chairman and former Deputy Secretary of Defense David Packard, King Ranch owner Robert J. Kleberg, Jr., and Florida banker-developer Charles G. "Bebe" Rebozo.

And, of course, any state dinner will include a hefty dose of foreign ambassadors based in Washington full time. This group is selected by the office of Chief of Protocol Henry Catto, Jr., with a careful eye for the sensitive relations between nations, lest the guest of honor or any other foreign guest be offended by the inclusion of someone he doesn't get along with.

Nobody, but nobody, declines to accept a White House invitation, barring some unavoidable conflict (like illness, a death in the family, or a business meeting overseas).

Every administration has its own style of White House entertaining, and it usually reflects the tastes (or aspirations) of the President. The Kennedy administration went in for sophisticated cultural offerings—recitals of opera, chamber music, and ballet. President Johnson brought a down-on-the-ranch informality to the White House, featuring barbecues and folk music (while continuing, of course, the obligatory fancy dinners for heads of state). President Nixon liked well-starched formality, but chose entertainment from the mainstream of American pop music and comedy, performers like Frank Sinatra, Bob Hope, and country music stars Johnny Cash and Merle Haggard.

The Ford style of White House entertaining is the most unpretentious in years. The attire is usually tuxedos rather than white tie. (At the first big Ford dinner party, arranged on short notice, the dress was business suits and short dresses—very casual for the Executive Mansion.) The President and First Lady actually enjoy their parties rather than viewing them as a necessary chore. As longtime fans of ballroom dancing, the Fords are on the dance floor all evening. And when the band picks up the tempo, the President does too, improvising a rock-'n'-roll step that delights the crowd (and embarrasses his mod children). The guest lists are drawn from all parts of the political spectrum and include lots of old colleagues from Capitol Hill (from both parties, unlike during the Nixon era) and even pillars of the liberal press establishment. Of course, Ford doesn't yet have any presidential campaign backers that he must reward with a gala evening at the White House.

DIPLOMATIC DOINGS

For sheer numbers of parties given and numbers of guests plied with limitless food, drink, and music, even Uncle Sam takes a back seat to the diplomatic crowd. After all, there are some 125 nations represented in Washington, and most of them give their embassies a liberal entertainment expense account (which goes an especially long way with the purchase of tax-free liquor). If you drive up Massachusetts Avenue, Washington's Embassy Row, you can tell whether a diplomatic party is in progress if you see the street lined with double-parked black limousines sporting license plates like "DPL 14" or "DPL 137." The most common kind of embassy party is the enormous cocktail bash, featuring a groaning board piled with every imaginable style of canapé and meatball. These parties are relatively easy to get invited to, but legions of suave gate crashers don't even go to the trouble of begging an invitation. (The Turkish Embassy once asked 1,300 people to attend a party at their Sheridan Circle mansion; about 3,000 revelers showed up.) Formal seated dinners are another matter. There the guests are invited with the same ulterior motives and concern for compatability that go into the selection of a White House guest list.

In years past the social prestige of a given embassy was roughly equivalent to the nation's power in world affairs (and, in turn, the opulence of its building and size of its entertainment budget). The situation is more fluid today, and the social flair of a new ambassador and his wife can suddenly render a once obscure embassy very stylish.

Russian parties aren't all that lively, but it's prestigious to be invited to an affair at their tall, somber townhouse on 16th Street. The Arab nations were very chic for a while, that is, until they began putting the U.S. through the oil wringer. Moroccans and Kuwaitis have entertained caftan-clad American VIPs at lavish parties where guests lounge on cushions and eat couscous with their fingers, while belly dancers undulate nearby. (According to a Washington *Post* account of one such party, "Hubert Humphrey wandered into the Kuwait embassy's Arabic splendor like Tom Sawyer exploring a Rudolph Valentino set. . . .")

The diplomatic social whirl is a boon to Washington and a pain in the neck to the top diplomats, who don't dare miss a party lest they offend the host nation. It's easy to see why one party-weary ambassador's wife said she welcomed a bout with pneumonia, claiming that without the forced rest she "would have died." The glut of big, loud embassy parties makes some diplomats eager for a quiet, friendly dinner party at the home of a Real American Person. This situation has been seized by many a Washington hostess as an entrée into the upper echelons of society. Hostess Gwen Cafritz once confided that she started out entertaining "little attachés" and "worked my way up to the Supreme Court."

THE DISAPPEARING DOWAGER

The biggest change in Washington social life over the past ten years has been the Decline of the Hostess. For decades there had always been a handful of women who used their inherited money (or their husband's hard-earned fortune) to throw frequent large, lavish parties for everybody who was anybody in Washington. Fifty years ago there were mining heiress Evalyn Walsh McLean, who held forth at her estate Friendship (on upper Wisconsin Avenue, where a collection of red brick apartments—McLean Gardens—now stands) and Mrs. Truxtun Beale, who presided over parties in the second-floor ballroom of her historic Lafayette Park home, Decatur House (now owned by the National Trust for Historic Preservation). During World War II, despite the pall that fell over social life in the capital, Mrs. Edward T. Stotesbury—a mainstay of society from Newport to Palm Beach—continued to give large parties at the Foxhall Road mansion (now the Belgian ambassador's residence) that she rented from her former daughter-in-law, auto heiress Delphine Dodge Cromwell Baker Goode.

And so it continued through the Forties and Fifties. Washington officialdom thronged to enormous parties given by such hostesses as Mrs. Robert Low Bacon, Laura Merriam Curtis Gross, Marjorie Merriweather Post, "Cissy" Patterson and Patricia Firestone Chatham. Outdoing everyone else in the extravagance of her bashes was Perle Mesta—daughter of a Texas-Oklahoma oil man, widow of a heavy machinery tycoon, avid Democrat and ambassador to Luxembourg during the Truman administration. Only Gwen Cafritz, the wife of a successful Washington real estate developer, came close to equaling Perle's frenetic pace. For these women, giving parties was not just an occasional diversion. It was a way of life.

An indispensable role in the old business of throwing parties was played by the social secretary, the hostess' alter ego. Usually a woman of good breeding but little wealth, the social secretary would manage all the details of the parties in exchange for a small salary (augmented, of course, by the prestige of rubbing elbows with her boss's prominent friends). Many social secretaries have lived at their boss's homes, and some of them have become trusted confidantes over years of employment. The late Mrs. Post's secretary, Margaret Voight, was with her for twenty-five years and eventually became a good friend and traveling companion of the Post Toasties heiress. Polly Logan's social aide (who prefers anonymity) has been with her for eighteen years, and Sophie Fleischer spent years with Perle Mesta. Some social secretaries plan and execute everything from invitations to menu to flowers to suggesting a dress for their patroness to wear. Others merely follow their employer's instructions. "It all depends on the woman you're working for," one explains.

There are still a few spectacular parties thrown every year by Gwen Cafritz, Polly Logan, and others of their vintage, but the golden days of hostessing are gone. Many of the big hostesses of yesterday have died, are too old to keep up the pace, are bored with the whole thing, have moved out of town (as an ailing Perle Mesta did in 1974, back to Oklahoma, where she died the following year), or are simply content to attend other people's parties, where society reporters still recognize them and refer to them in print as "hostess Mrs. So-and-So" or "Washington grande dame Mrs. Such-and-Such."

The passing of the old style of hostessing is symbolized by the fate of Washington's grand private estates. In decades past, any magnificent mansion coming onto the real estate market would have been snapped up in a hurry by a wealthy man whose wife needed an opulent starting rung for the long climb up the social ladder. Today even the richest people don't relish the idea of maintaining homes whose rooms can be counted in multiples of ten, so most of the potential buyers are embassies and nonprofit institutions. Take, for example, Tregaron, the Georgian mansion and 20-acre grounds once owned by former Ambassador to Russia Joseph E. Davies. In the nearly two decades since his death, the property—located near Rock Creek Park—has been slowly deteriorating, under the tenancy of several organizations, including a Montessori school. By 1974 the Davies heirs were anxious to sell, but they were having a hard time finding a buyer. (A tentative deal with former Senator Harold E. Hughes of Iowa, who wanted to turn Tregaron into a religious center, fell through.)

For more than seven years after the death of Patricia Chatham, her Georgetown home, Prospect House, stood empty on its majestic site overlooking the Potomac River, carrying a price tag that gradually slid from $2 million to a mere $500,000. The twenty-two-room house and gardens were eventually bought (at the latter price) in 1974 by international business consultant Louise Ansberry (an heiress to the Steinman publishing and broadcasting fortune of Lancaster, Pennsylvania), who said she intended to recover much of her purchase price by selling off part of the grounds as building sites for new townhouses. Jack and Polly Logan have quietly let it be known that they would not mind parting with their Firenze House (which is located, like so many other of Washington's castles, next to Rock Creek Park), if an appropriate buyer—public or private—could be found. Even oil heir John Archbold, who divides his time between an Upperville, Virginia, farm and his Hillandale estate (northwest of Georgetown, along Glover-Archbold Park), has succumbed to the temptation to trim his city domain. In 1974 he sold eight acres to the French government for a new chancery. But Hillandale (a veritable farm, complete with grazing donkeys) still has more acreage than any other private home in the District of Columbia.

Lots of forces, not just the rising cost of labor, converged to kill the Era of the Hostess. One of these forces was Jacqueline Bouvier Kennedy. When the First Lady was Bess Truman or Mamie Eisenhower, it wasn't hard for a stylish private hostess to compete with the White House. But the old hostesses were upstaged by the glamor of Jackie Kennedy's brief reign at the White House, combined with the New Frontier style of casual, spontaneous entertaining, typified by the status-drenched ritual of getting thrown into Bobby and Ethel Kennedy's pool at Hickory Hill in McLean, Virginia. But most of all, the big hostesses were done in by the increasing size and sophistication of Washington as a city. Twenty years ago, guzzling cocktails and gulping canapés on someone's lovely terrace was probably the best show in town. Today that pastime has to compete with theater, dining out, opera, good jazz, old foreign movies, and many other things that Washingtonians have come to enjoy.

There is no new group of hostesses cast in the old mold, but there are numerous hosts and hostesses who are well known as gracious party givers in particular circles of significant Washingtonians. Among Liberal Establishment politicians and journalists, an invitation to dinner at Joseph Alsop's, Rollie and Kay Evans', Tom and Joan Braden's or Kay Graham's house is highly prized. In GOP circles, prominent hostesses include Mrs. Poe Burling; Margot Hahn, wife of lawyer and former D.C. City Council Chairman Gilbert Hahn Jr.; and Anna Chennault, widow of the late Flying Tiger ace, General Claire

Chennault. (Mrs. Chennault, who is Chinese, is a skilled lobbyist for both the Flying Tiger Line—air freight—and the Nationalist Chinese government on Taiwan.)

Those who travel in diplomatic circles look forward to dinners at the homes of former Senator (and now ambassador to East Germany) John Sherman Cooper and his wife Lorraine; diplomat David and Evangeline Bruce; lawyer Sidney and Evelyn Zlotnick; the Averell Harrimans; and former LBJ adviser Dale Miller and his wife "Scooter." Patrons of the arts see one another at dinners given by the National Gallery's Carter Brown and insurance magnate (and accomplished amateur violinist) David Lloyd Kreeger and his wife Carmen. Mrs. George Maurice Morris, the widow of a successful Washington lawyer who once headed the American Bar Association, entertains with colonial elegance at The Lindens, a 1754 mansion that (at the Morris' bidding) was dismantled in Massachusetts and reassembled on Washington's Kalorama Road in 1934.

Bill and Buffy Cafritz (he a developer and nephew of Gwen) are prominent party givers for the Washington "smart set" of young lawyers, businessmen, politicians, and scions of old wealth. So are Howard and Nadine Joynt (owners of the Georgetown restaurant Nathan's and beneficiaries of Joynt's father's success in patent law). Also active among the younger socialites are Lee and Bitsy Folger, he a partner at the brokerage house Folger, Nolan, Fleming and Douglas, she a daughter of Neil McElroy, a self-made man who worked his way to the top of Procter and Gamble and later served as Secretary of Defense under President Eisenhower. Barbara Howar, once the social darling of the LBJ Great Society, trimmed her sails after getting divorced, but made a partial comeback when her autobiographical book *Laughing All the Way* improved her financial status. More recently the luncheon-cocktail-dinner scene has been enlivened by Taz and Jan Shepard (he a retired admiral and former naval aide to President Kennedy, she the daughter of Senator John Sparkman of Alabama). When Admiral Shepard retired from naval service after commanding a fleet force in European waters, he became Washington representative of Occidental International, a venture of international financier Armand Hammer. Thereafter the Shepards made their mark with small, sparkling gatherings of diplomats, politicians, businessmen, publishers, pundits, and luminaries of the stage.

There are few notable bachelor party givers in Washington, most of the important men being too busy to bother. But some of the most sumptuous parties in recent years were held at the Woodland Drive home of former Ambassador to Switzerland True Davis, though the frequency of these fell off sharply after he was pushed out of the presidency of the National Bank of Washington by the new regime of the United Mine Workers, which owns that bank. In the pre-Watergate days, Peter Malatesta was getting a lot of press coverage with large affairs at his rented Kalorama townhouse. (A nephew of Mrs. Bob Hope, a close friend of Frank Sinatra, and a former aide to Spiro Agnew, Malatesta has a style better suited to Palm Springs than Washington, but he has remained in the capital as deputy secretary of commerce for tourism.) One of the busiest bachelor hosts is Hill and Knowlton public relations executive Steve Martindale, whose parties at his Wesley Heights home always have a definite, if veiled, business purpose. Two of Washington's most lively bachelor hosts are Ambassador Alejandro Orfila of Argentina and

Iranian Ambassador Ardeshir Zahedi (who has been known to give diamond baubles as party favors for special guests). Tongsun Park, an amiable, forty-year-old Korean bachelor who has lived around Washington for nearly twenty years, entertains at his George Town Club and at his Kalorama residence, where he has a full-time staff of four. (Park also maintains homes in Seoul, Palm Beach, and Santa Domingo.)

CATERERS ON CALL

The ideal way to entertain, no matter what the occasion, is in your own big, beautiful house, with your own perfectly trained "family retainers." While big, beautiful houses abound in Washington, full-time staffs of servants don't. That's why caterers do such a thriving business, charging around $10 per person for cocktail parties and anywhere from $25 to $50 a head for fancy dinners. The prestigious caterers are Avignone Frères (a fifty-five-year-old firm that controls a big share of the embassy business), Ridgewell's (which began in 1928 and sometimes handles twenty parties in one day), Braun's (an outfit that advertises "USDA-inspected kitchens" and a "fleet of refrigerated trucks"), Taylor's, and Lucks (specializing in smaller parties).

The "little dinner party" for eight or ten people is almost a ritual in Washington. Some of the most frequent participants in the ritual (especially journalists) may not enjoy it that much, but fear they might miss a good bit of confidential information if they stay home. The late columnist Stewart Alsop told his English bride when she arrived in Washington years ago, "You may refuse an invitation to cocktails, but never dinner, without asking me." And once when political writer Theodore H. White's wife asked him if he was having a good time at a party, he replied, "I am working."

Bachelors are as important to a Washington party as food and drink. Single women (including divorcees or widows) outnumber single men by a wide margin, and hostesses must also find dinner companions for the wives of government bigwigs whose husbands are out of town or working late at the office. It's no wonder that former White House social secretary Lucy Winchester once said, "Washington is hog heaven for bachelors." A bachelor has no trouble getting invited to parties, according to local lore, if he is "personable, intelligent, and can push a partner around the dance floor without breaking her toes." Some hostesses who do everything to lure bachelors to their parties still complain (behind the men's backs, of course) about "the parasites." One hostess says it's "appalling the way they accept free food, free parties, free sex." (Yes, sex is a popular pastime in political Washington, and the rumor mill is always buzzing with stories of the latest clandestine affairs.)

FROLICKING FOR FUNDS

Like every big city in America, Washington has charity balls galore, which seem to be oblivious to the oft-heard rumor that charity balls are dying out. There's the Symphony Ball (the most prestigious), the Corcoran Ball (the most fun, held at the Corcoran Gallery of Art, complete with rock music and freaky artists, as well as fox-trotting, tuxedoed socialites), the Hope Ball (for the international medical program Project Hope, a Washington-based charity), the Opera Ball, the Meridian House Ball, the International Ball, the Smithsonian Ball, the Wolf Trap gala, the Eye Ball (for the sight charities), and numerous others. The Travelers Aid Ball is the most imaginative, with sites ranging annually from the National Zoo, to the Laurel Race Course, to Dulles Airport, the Wax Museum, Union Station, and the D.C. National Bank (where drinks were served at the tellers' windows). While "the big bash" is out-of-fashion for private parties, it is still permissible for benefits and political fund raisers. For "the cause," anything goes.

During a campaign year, the political fund raiser is Washington's favorite indoor sport. Even though a congressman's or senator's constituents live back home in Pocatello, a good many of his friends, associates, and people who need his help (like lobbyists, corporation executives, and lawyers) live here in the capital, so it's a natural place for fund raising. These parties are usually held at the home of a famous person, to keep down the costs and to attract people who are willing to pay a $10, $20, or $100 campaign contribution to get a look at how the glamorous Mr. and Mrs. So-and-So live. When the Coalition for a Democratic Majority staged a $50-a-head fund raiser at Mrs. Dean Acheson's Georgetown home a few years ago, no more than 75 people were expected; 300 showed up. Some of the most successful GOP events are held at Marwood, the Potomac, Maryland, estate of Louise Gore, a conservative Republican former state legislator, one time U.S. ambassador, and recent candidate for governor of Maryland. (Miss Gore is also a part-owner of the Fairfax Hotel and chic Jockey Club restaurant.) One of the most energetic Democratic fund raisers is Potomac's Esther Coopersmith, whose parties have collected more than $3 million for the campaigns of more than a hundred politicians, from congressmen to Presidents. A barbecue Mrs. Coopersmith dreamed up for Wyoming Senator Gale McGee, held at Sargent Shriver's Timberlawn estate in Rockville, Maryland, was so successful that it was the prototype for the LBJ barbecues held across the nation in 1964.

THE CAVE DWELLERS

Washington has a reputation for having a transient, rootless social life, a status tree nourished every few years by a new load of fresh political soil. The reputation has some validity, but it's not the whole story. Lurking beneath the glittery surface of the political social whirl is Old Washington Society, a resident social elite as proud of its heritage and as jealous of its privacy as any city's old guard. You won't read about their parties in the newspapers, because the sort of parties they give—relatively small, quiet affairs lacking advertised names on the guest list—wouldn't make "good copy" for the social pages (not that these people want any publicity anyway). The very names and faces of these social figures aren't even known to most Washington society reporters.

The members of this resident social elite are called "cave dwellers." There are no precise qualifications, of course, but genuine cave dwellers have roots going back at least to the turn of the century, preferably into the early decades of the nineteenth century. Yet it's not enough that your family has merely *lived* in Washington that long. Your family must also have been socially respectable and materially well fixed (but not necessarily rich) over most of that time.

Some cave dwellers bear the venerable names of (or are descended from) families that were prominent landowners, international shippers, and professionals in Maryland and Virginia even before the District of Columbia was laid out. Names like Addison, Mackall, Dunlop, Contee, Peter, Clagett,

Magruder, Sasscer, Washington, Lee, Custis, Blair, and Bowie. A larger group of cave dwellers are scions of people who amassed varying amounts of money in retail businesses, banking, real estate, and publishing and the professions in the middle of the last century: families like Hagner, Carusi, Noyes, Adams, Kauffmann, Willard, Saul, Riggs, Lothrop, Luttrell, Orme, Corcoran, Glover, and Eustis.

Although true cave dwellers are descended from families who made their money and their social name in Washington, honorary status is conferred on the scions of out-of-town fortunes who arrived in the capital decades ago and have been here ever since: descendants of people like the Leiters of Chicago (whose female scions intermarried with Trains and Clagetts), the Huidekopers of western Pennsylvania, the Archbolds of New York, the Philadelphia Newbolds, Roosevelts from Oyster Bay, New York, and the late Washington architect Jules Henri de Sibour, a Paris-born, Yale-educated descendant of King Louis XI. Several children of Ricardo J. Alfaro—a former president of Panama and ambassador to the United States in the Twenties and Thirties—married socially prominent Washingtonians and became permanent members of the cave-dweller elite. The list of bona fide cave dwellers could go on and on—Sterrett, Sturtevant, Wilkins, Darlington, Rust, Semmes, Chewning, Moran, Darneille, Legare, Davidge, Browne, Flather, Hamilton, etc., etc.

There are certain predictable patterns in the lives of the cave dwellers. Many of them, like their fathers and grandfathers, are members of the "right clubs," which means the Chevy Chase Club (for the whole family), the Metropolitan Club (for him), the Sulgrave Club (for her), and the City Tavern or the 1925 F Street Club (for the two of them). About fifty Old Washington males belong to the ultraexclusive Alibi Club, housed since the 1880s in a small Victorian house at 1806 Eye Street N.W. Its members meet for Friday lunch and occasional parties in rooms cluttered with musty memorabilia and decorated with a choice collection of genteelly bawdy pictures. A good many cave dwellers—plus quite a few political bigshots and corporate representatives—are members of Burning Tree Club, the Bethesda, Maryland, retreat where women and children are not welcome and golf is the principal activity. While the Chevy Chase Club is the bastion of Washington's prominent families in law, medicine, and finance, the Columbia Country Club, also in Chevy Chase, is the stronghold of a separate but equally deep-rooted Washington elite composed of families who made their money in such fields as construction, retail business, and automobile sales.

Cave dwellers send their children to the "right schools" (to which, by virtue of family ties, their kids are admitted more easily than the children of politicians and other striving newcomers, who must contend with long waiting lists). The boys, if they are not sent off to one of the "St. Grottlesex" group of New England prep schools, are enrolled at St. Albans or Landon, possibly Episcopal or Woodberry Forest in Virginia (if the family has definite southern sympathies), or maybe Georgetown Prep (if a Catholic education is desired). The young ladies, if they are not shipped off to Miss Porter's in Farmington, Connecticut, or Foxcroft in nearby Middleburg, Virginia, are day students at Madeira, National Cathedral School, Holton-Arms, or Stone Ridge (a Catholic school). Both girls and boys may go to Sidwell Friends, a fine, somewhat progressive school, though with less snob appeal. The proper boys and girls meet weekly (reluctantly, if not downright hostilely) at dancing classes given for decades by Mrs. Lloyd Parker Shippen. For college, the children are sent either north (Ivy League, Seven Sisters, or the Bradford-Bennett-Briarcliff group) or south (Virginia, North Carolina at Chapel Hill, Washington and Lee, Sweet Briar, Hollins).

In years past, a debut was obligatory for every cave-dweller daughter, preferably a "small dance" (a euphemism for a few hundred guests) at the Sulgrave or Chevy Chase Club. All arrangements and the guest list—composed of youths who had gone to the Right Schools—were usually handled by Mrs. Kurt Hetzel, a social secretary who specializes in presenting young ladies to society. In addition to being presented individually at a dinner, tea dance, or "small dance," about twenty lucky debutantes would be invited to come out at the now defunct Washington Debutante Ball, held during the Christmas holiday in the gilded, galleried ballroom of the Mayflower Hotel on Connecticut Avenue.

But the era of debuts seems to have passed, at least for the time being. Many girls today convince their affluent parents to spend the price of a debut on something less ephemeral, like a sports car or a summer in Europe. Adult cave-dweller activities—analogous to debuts, but still prospering—are the Thursday night dinner dances held on the terrace of the Chevy Chase Club each week during the summer, and the periodic subscription dances of the Waltz Group and the Fivers, the latter being four socialites whose informal leader is Marion Oates Leiter (Mrs. Robert H.) Charles. Cave dwellers in their twenties and thirties turn out in droves for the St. Vitus Dance (which, despite its bizarre name, is not a charity ball for any illness) and the Bachelors and Spinsters Ball, both annual black-tie affairs at the Sulgrave Club.

SOME OTHER OLD WASHINGTONIANS

If you socialized entirely in cave-dweller circles, you'd probably never have the pleasure of getting to know dozens of other Old Washingtonians—many of them as cultured, well educated, wealthy, and snobbish as any cave dweller —who happen to be Jews or who happen to be Negroes. The cave dwellers and their institutions have never embraced racial or religious minorities, although some small cracks are appearing in the barrier walls here and there.

Washington, like most large American cities, has a local social set composed primarily of people descended from German and Austrian Jewish families who immigrated to America early in the nineteenth century. Most of them made their money in business, and their descendants continued to make substantial livings as doctors, lawyers, and investors. Some of the old family names are prominent today in Washington business, civic, and philanthropic circles: Hechinger, Nordlinger, Tobriner, Lansburgh, Wolf, Hahn, Luchs, Berliner, Rich, Adler, King, and Kaufmann, to name just a few. For years this group of established Washingtonians looked down their noses at the more recent (turn-of-the-century) Jewish arrivals. But the successful members of this later wave—such as the Goldmans, Wilners, Sundluns, Himmelfarbs, Gewirzes, and Cafritzes, to name a few—eventually earned their places in the best circles. The social bastion of the Jewish elite is the Woodmont Country Club, an exclusive and expensive old club whose beautiful grounds on the Rockville Pike, south of suburban Rockville, Maryland, are now surrounded by commercial development.

Washington's Negro society has roots deeper than the Jewish community, and nearly as venerable as cave-dweller society. It includes families who can trace their lineage to early black merchants, building contractors, ministers, physicians, lawyers, congressmen, and professors. Today most of them are in the professions. They graduated from Dunbar High School, which a few decades ago (before integration) offered as fine an education as any school in America. If they didn't go to Howard University, where the men were in an elite fraternity like Alpha Phi Alpha, they went away to another good Negro college, like Lincoln, Tuskegee, or Fisk.

During the days of complete segregation in Washington (extending from the 1890s into the 1950s), they kept to themselves, entertaining friends in their comfortable homes in LeDroit Park (above Florida Avenue near Howard), the Brookland section of Northeast, and in Shepherd Park, along 16th Street. In the summer many of them vacationed at Negro resorts like Highland Beach, Maryland (along the Chesapeake Bay), Oak Bluffs at Martha's Vineyard, Massachusetts, and Sag Harbor, at the tip of Long Island, New York. They all turned out for the Howard-Lincoln and Howard-Morgan State football games, and their daughters were presented to black society at debuts. Black society was a negative-image print of white society, on a less lavish scale. Social status was directly proportional to—besides wealth and family roots—the lightness of one's skin.

The movement against racial and religious barriers in America's public life has put strains on discriminatory private organizations, and Washington's clubs are no exception. There are no known Jewish members of the Chevy Chase Club, and there are no known Gentile members of Woodmont, though the directors of both clubs emphasize that there are no explicit barriers in the bylaws. Of the downtown clubs, the Cosmos Club and the Federal City Club (which rents space from the Sheraton-Carlton Hotel on 16th Street) have no religious or racial restrictions. The Federal City Club, founded in 1963 after a walkout of several prominent members (including Robert F. Kennedy) from the Metropolitan Club over racial policies, even has women members. The chief requirements of the Cosmos Club, a venerable institution once located in Dolley Madison's old house on Lafayette Park, are that you be male and have made some sort of contribution to intellectual life in America. It probably possesses more Pulitzer and Nobel prize winners (including Henry Kissinger)—not to mention lesser-known scientists, authors, artists, and historians—than any other social club in Amerca.

The Metropolitan Club, the oldest in Washington at a spry 112 years, now has at least one Negro member (the suffragan bishop of the Washington Cathedral), and no longer do black guests cause raised eyebrows. It is *the* club for cave-dwelling lawyers and bankers, and also counts among its members many of the top news media stars (such as Eric Sevareid, Joseph Alsop, James Reston, and Marquis Childs). Among its members from Jewish backgrounds are David Lloyd Kreeger, novelist Herman Wouk, *New York Times* publisher Arthur Ochs Sulzberger, and Eugene Meyer III (a Baltimore psychiatrist and son of the patrician New York financier and Washington *Post* publisher, who was himself a member of both the Metropolitan Club and Burning Tree). Virtually all of the clubs that still follow discriminatory membership practices harbor small groups of members who are quietly pushing for a change, feeling that whatever standard the club wishes to impose— be it professional achievement, social charm, wealth, or some combination of the three—should be applied without regard to the applicant's lineage. But change will be slow in coming, as long as a handful of recalcitrant members or directors can block an applicant with the blackball system.

Slightly more egalitarian than Washington's clubs is its directory of socially prominent people, officially called the "Social List of Washington, D.C.," but commonly known as the "Green Book." Within its fake-suede green covers is a listing of nearly 6,000 Washington-area families, including quite a few from such Virginia hunt country towns as Middleburg, Upperville, Warrenton, Leesburg, and The Plains. The listings include such socially vital information as the wife's maiden name (and previous married names), addresses of principal summer and winter residences, and children's names and names of the preparatory schools and colleges they are attending. There are separate sections listing members of the diplomatic corps and Congress.

The "Green Book" is chock full of cave dwellers, but unlike the little black-bound "Social Registers" published for several large American cities (including Washington), inclusions in the "Green Book" are based as much on public power as on pedigree. Any White House adviser or assistant secretary of this-or-that is included in the "Green Book," regardless of his pre-Washington social obscurity. Outside of officialdom, the book still leans most heavily toward so-called WASPs (White Anglo-Saxon Protestants). But some of Washington's prominent Jews are included, especially those who are active in the arts and in political and social circles—such as occasional Washingtonian Joseph Hirshhorn, David Lloyd Kreeger, Sidney Zlotnick, Gilbert Hahn, Jr., and Henry L. Kimelman (a Virgin Islands financier and major contributor to the presidential campaign of Senator George McGovern). Until relatively recently the only Negroes in the book were those who held important public or quasi-public positions, like Mayor Walter E. Washington and Howard University President James E. Cheek. Now there are listings for a few black professionals who circulate in both white and Negro social circles, like lawyers Hobart Taylor, Jr., Belford and Marjorie Lawson, and Dr. Winston Churchill Willoughby, a successful dentist.

The Watergate crisis posed some thorny problems for the "Green Book." According to its seventy-year-old publisher, Carolyn Hagner Shaw (herself an Old Washingtonian), the scandal brought "an upheaval in Washington officialdom unprecedented without a change in administration." Dropped from the 1974 edition, all for reasons of "unpleasant notoriety," were such one-time administration bigwigs as John Ehrlichman, Bob Haldeman, John Dean III, Jeb Magruder, and Maurice Stans. But the "Green Book's" anonymous, four-member selection board (of whom some Washingtonians doubt the very existence, except as a cover for Mrs. Shaw) did not go so far as to exclude President Nixon and then Vice President Agnew from the 1974 list. "It's my opinion that the two top men in our government are in a different category" from the aforementioned aides, Mrs. Shaw said. By 1975, however, the situation had changed. Mrs. Shaw had a convenient excuse for dropping both Nixon and Agnew when, following their resignations, each moved from the Washington area. Other grounds for being removed from the "Green Book" are a "very messy, unpleasant divorce" (although the divorced pair can be reinstated after a suitable wait, either singly or with an acceptable new spouse) and indictment for any sort of major crime. "Guilty or not," Mrs. Shaw says, "if the story comes out in the papers, the man is automatically taken out of the book."

MIX AND STIR WELL

Status in Washington comes in many sizes, shapes, and colors, often contradictory. Transient, permanent. Staid cave dwellers, charismatic politicians. The river-view homes of rich white people on Crest Lane in McLean, Virginia, the black counterparts on Colorado Avenue and Argyle Terrace in the District. Lunch at Sans Souci, a midnight snack at Clyde's. Mercedes-Benzes for the affluent, Volkswagens for their long-haired children. Season tickets for Redskins games, sideline standing room at the St. Albans–Landon football game. A flashy penthouse at the Watergate West, a mellow apartment at the Westchester. A subtly opulent gown fom Madame Paul's shop, a zany original from the Exit boutique. The opening of an art exhibit at the National Gallery, an opening at the Museum of African Art. The presidential box at the Kennedy Center Opera House, a stage-side table at the Cellar Door. Summer at your "cottage" in Newport, Rhode Island, an autumn weekend in a real cottage at Rehoboth Beach, Delaware. Justice William O. Douglas in the seat of honor at your dinner party, or Sonny Jurgensen. An invitation to dinner at the White House, an invitation to lunch in Kay Graham's private dining room at the Washington *Post*. Riding your Fuji 10-speed to the office, riding to hounds in Middleburg.

Washington society is a multiflavored, many-layered cake. The recipe is tricky. Add too many plutocrats and it will come out hard. Too many aristocrats will make the flavor bland. Too many strident strivers from the new meritocracy will turn it sour. But when the whole thing is properly balanced and blended, the results can be a pleasure for those who have such tastes.

10 GOVERNMENT WORKERS GALORE

One out of every three workers in the Washington metropolitan area draws his paycheck from the federal government. Of the other two, one makes his living from lawyering, lobbying, reporting, researching, or analyzing the activities of the government. Most of the remaining third of the labor force caters to the two-thirds who make their living directly from the federal establishment.

Take away federal employees, and Washington would be like Detroit without automobiles, Seattle without Boeing, or Houston without oil. In fact, Washington is the biggest "company town" in the world—outside of Peking and Moscow, where everybody works for the government. But unlike other company towns, there is no risk here that prosperity will be dimmed when a rich vein of ore runs out, a well goes dry, or the public stops buying the local product. The local product in this company town happens to be a vast array of government services, and the public demand seems to be insatiable.

This makes the civil servants of Washington a very secure group of people and keeps the local economy booming, through good times and bad. As a matter of fact, the hardships that spell trouble in the rest of the nation— unemployment, governmental rules, war, energy shortages—are often translated into growth of the federal bureaucracy in Washington, with the accompanying surge of spendable income. The federal civilian payroll pumps an estimated $435 million into the Washington economy each month.

There are about 348,000 civil servants at work around Washington in some 120 federal departments, agencies, bureaus, commissions, and government corporations. This includes an estimated 18,000 people at the massive suburban Virginia complex of the Central Intelligence Agency (CIA), whose employment figures (like its budget) are secret. Add in about 70,000 military personnel stationed at the Pentagon and bases in the area, and you get a grand total of more than 418,000 on the federal payroll. Another 100,000 or so area residents are living in whole or in part on civilian federal pensions.

The civil servants in the national capital area account for about 12 percent of Uncle Sam's total worldwide civilian roster of 2,832,000. (This percentage has been roughly constant for decades, at least since detailed records were begun in 1910.) Ranking behind Washington in the number of civilian federal employees are the metropolitan areas of New York City (123,000), Philadelphia (81,000), San Francisco (75,000), and Chicago (73,000). There are more federal workers in the Washington area than in any single state. California has 298,000; New York, 173,000; and Texas, 146,000.

Many a new President has come into office full of confidence that he is the one who can beat back the charging dragon of federal employment. Few have been successful. There was a substantial drop in the number of government workers between 1920 and 1930, and again at the end of the Second World

War (during which the number of nonmilitary personnel had hit an all-time high of about 3.8 million). There was also an 8 percent decline in total federal employment during the first three years of the Seventies. Aside from these dips, the trend has been steadily upward. But state and local governments have been expanding even faster. In 1950, about one-third of all government employees worked for Uncle Sam. Today that proportion is down to 19 percent and continues to drop.

THOUSANDS OF JOBS

There is no "typical" civil servant. The Civil Service Commission (CSC)—the hirer and overseer of the vast majority of Uncle Sam's employees—has counted more than 10,000 types of federal jobs grouped into 23 general occupational categories. There are men and women working for the government as game wardens, secretaries, psychiatrists, naval architects, lawyers, air traffic controllers, archaeologists, accountants, cancer researchers, pest control technicians, cryptographers, fish hatchery managers, telephone operators, meteorologists, astronauts, economists, historians, fingerprint identifiers, computer programers, janitors, deep-sea explorers, and interior decorators. Virtually every lawful occupation known to man can be pursued in the sprawling bureaucracy.

But the occupational profile of the people working for Uncle Sam in Washington is not quite as varied as elsewhere. As the headquarters of most of the agencies, Washington is full of civil servants who manage, administer, guide, and order. Much of this work is not highly visible to the outsider, and renders the bureaucrat vulnerable to charges of "paper shuffling." While federal employment outside the capital is about evenly divided between white-collar and blue-collar employees (including postal workers), the federal labor force in Washington is 84 percent white collar. This 84 percent has a median annual salary of about $16,000. The average male white-collar salary for federal employees in Washington is about $19,300, compared to $12,700 outside of Washington. Female white-collar federal workers average about $10,853 in the Washington area, while elsewhere they earn about $9,200.

The civil servants of Washington work in 523 buildings, 190 of them owned by the government and the remaining 333 leased, entirely or in part (which is a boon to the Washington construction and real estate businesses). The biggest concentration of workers is at the Pentagon, the largest office building in the world, where some 27,000 people work each day. The smallest federal office in the capital area is space for two Department of Agriculture employees in suburban Fairfax, Virginia.

About 42 percent of the area's U.S. employees don't work in the District of Columbia, but in the surrounding counties of Maryland (27 percent) and Virginia (15 percent). Some large agencies—like the Census Bureau in Suitland, Maryland—went to the suburbs years ago. The suburbanization of the bureaucracy was accelerated during the boom of the Sixties, when the social service agencies were expanding rapidly and large blocks of relatively cheap office space could be found more easily in the suburbs than in the District. Offices were leased just across the Potomac River in Rosslyn and Crystal City, Virginia, and about 6,000 employees of the Department of Health, Education and Welfare (HEW) were moved to the huge, privately owned Parklawn Building in Rockville, Maryland. The Bureau of Standards abandoned its old buildings at Connecticut Avenue and Tilden Street and moved to a sprawling campus near Gaithersburg, Maryland. During this exodus, the General Services Administration (GSA)—Uncle Sam's house-keeping and supply agent—came under fire from District organizations, who charged that its policies were hastening the decline of the inner city. Today, GSA is making a greater effort to find suitable space within the District before looking elsewhere.

Defense is number one in federal employment—civilian as well as military, in Washington and worldwide. In the Washington area, 85,000 people work for the Department of Defense, out of a world total exceeding 1 million civilian Defense workers. The second-largest federal employer in the Washington area is HEW, with 33,000 employees. Among the other large federal employers in Washington are the Postal Service (18,000), GSA (18,700), the CIA (possibly 18,000), the Treasury Department (15,500), the Justice Department (14,600), and the Department of Agriculture (11,129). Combining the professional staffs of the House and Senate with all the administrative, clerical, and support service staffs of the Capitol Hill complex, one sees that Congress is a massive bureaucracy in its own right. While the legislative branch is still dwarfed many times over by the executive agencies, it is one of the principal growth areas of the federal government. Twenty years ago there were only about 4,500 people working on the Hill, on a budget of $42 million. Today 16,000 congressional employees represent a budget of more than $330 million each year.

Worldwide, there is no federal agency that even approaches the Defense Department in total civilian employment. The Postal Service is second (703,000), followed by the Veterans Administration (196,000), HEW (130,000), Treasury (111,000), and Agriculture (80,000). Many federal agencies have staffs numbering just a few hundred, and some have far fewer than that. Probably the smallest of all is the Susquehanna River Basin Commission (a joint state-federal body), which has two full-time federal employees—a commissioner stationed in St. Thomas, Pennsylvania, and an assistant in Washington. A sampling of the smaller agencies includes the American Battle Monuments Commission (390), the Federal Maritime Commission (270), and the Commission on Civil Rights (200).

The highest-ranking people in federal service got where they are by a political route—either by election or by presidential appointment and confirmation by the Senate. The elected officials are relatively few: the President, Vice President, and 535 members of the House and Senate. Appointees include the Cabinet secretaries, under secretaries, and assistant secretaries; federal judges, heads of independent commissions, councils, agencies, and boards; and various miscellaneous officials like the Comptroller of the Currency, Architect of the Capitol, and Librarian of Congress. The total number of "patronage" positions in the federal government is probably fewer than 6,500, with barely 1,000 positions carrying policymaking authority. The situation today is a far cry from the "spoils system" that prevailed before the Civil Service Commission was established in 1883.

A couple of years ago, the CSC found that a miniature version of the spoils system had been operating illegally within the General Services Administration. A "special referral unit," created soon after the Nixon administration took over in 1969, gave preferential treatment to about 400 people who applied for GSA jobs covered by the merit system. All of the 400 were active in the Republican party, and most of the names were given to the referral unit by the White House, the Committee to Reelect the President, and GOP senators and congressmen. One CSC investigator noted that "in every administration there are people referred from various sources to departments and agencies; what was wrong in this case is that these people were systematically given preference in the hiring process." After its investigation, the CSC sought the dismissal of four high-ranking GSA officials and the suspension of four others, all of whom allegedly knew of the illegal unit. The GSA officials took their case to federal court to resist the CSC discipline, and the battle was still being fought in early 1975.

During this case, it became clear that political and personal favoritism in civil service hiring was not confined to the GSA during the Nixon years. Another investigation found unorthodox practices in the Department of Housing and Urban Development. Worst of all, it was discovered in early 1975 that even the three commissioners of the Civil Service Commission had occasionally pulled strings to help a well-connected applicant find a federal job. Learning of this, the penalized GSA officials charged that it was the "acme of hypocrisy" for the Civil Service Commission to fire or suspend anyone else for the same sort of quasi-legal things its own commissioners had done. Embarrassed by the whole situation, the CSC said it would draft new rules to explicitly prohibit its officials (and those of other federal agencies) from personally recommending applicants for civil service jobs.

About 90 percent of all federal employees—the rank and file of the bureaucracy—got their jobs by taking tests administered by the commission. (The largest group of federal employees who are outside of the Civil Service merit system are those who work on Capitol Hill, on the staffs of congressmen, senators, legislative committees, and administrative bodies like the office of the House doorkeeper. Most applicants for Hill jobs are not required to take exams of any sort.) For the low-level jobs, the tests are designed to determine mental aptitude and office skills. The Federal Service Entrance Exam, taken mostly by recent college graduates seeking jobs in the middle of the GS scale, resembles a College Board test. "Super-grade" prospects are not subjected to an exam but to an evaluation of their education and job experience. In fiscal 1974, the commission administered tests to about 1.8 million applicants for about 200,000 vacant jobs. A number of federal bodies—such as the Foreign Service, FBI, CIA, Postal Service, and VA Department of Medicine and Surgery—have specialized tests that are given instead of the CSC exam. Since 1944, military veterans have received a boost on their test scores. Ten points are added to the scores (if passing) of all job seekers with service-related disabilities, wives of disabled veterans who cannot work, and unmarried widows of deceased servicemen. Five points are added to the scores of all other veterans. There are special waivers of certain physical and educational requirements for veteran applicants, too.

Applicants are ranked by their test scores and put on an "eligible list." An agency's personnel department is obliged to interview the highest-ranking applicants with the necessary skills and select one of them. After preliminary selection, the applicant is subjected to a "suitability" check conducted by CSC investigators (before employment for upper-grade applicants, during provisional employment for lower-level workers). If the check turns up any derogatory information, the FBI is called in to conduct a "full field investigation." The investigation centers on the applicant's life style, political activity, and criminal record, if any. No longer are homosexuality, extramarital affairs, illegitimate children, and participation in campus protests considered to be automatic disqualifiers for all federal jobs (although someone applying for a particularly sensitive position might be ruled out for such things). In 1969, the CSC abandoned the requirement that each new employee take an oath of loyalty to the United States. Today, "free spirits" of all sorts can be found among the civil servants of Washington. The federal government is now probably more tolerant of superficial forms of nonconformity—such as long hair, beards, and mod attire—than private employers.

A JOB FOR LIFE

Top federal executives have complained for decades that it is well nigh impossible to fire their underlings. Basically, they're correct, short of major misconduct. After an employee passes his probationary period (usually one year), he has life tenure with Uncle Sam, barring some gross dereliction of duty. In a typical recent year, only about 22,000 workers—not even 1 percent of all federal employees—were fired. Whereas an employee dismissed from a private company usually has little recourse, civil servants have an elaborate appeals process. Some have two appeals within their agency and two more—sometimes three—to the commission itself. The average appeal takes about nine months, but there is a new proposal in the works to compress the appeals process into one appeal to the commission (which should take "only" three months). Of the 2,600 firings that were appealed in 1973, about 15 percent were won by the employees because of their bosses' "procedural errors" in dismissing them. As in every line of work, there are layoffs due to funding cutbacks and department reorganizations. The severance pay system is rather generous, though. Employees who have worked for the government for ten years or less are given a week's pay for each year. Those who have worked longer get the same amount for each year up to ten, plus two weeks' pay for each additional year, up to a maximum of fifty-two weeks.

One sure way for a civil servant to incur the wrath of his superiors—and maybe even get fired—is to blow the whistle publicly on bungling that he sees in his department. Take, for example, the celebrated case of A. Ernest Fitzgerald, the Pentagon cost-efficiency expert who told a congressional hearing in 1968 that Lockheed's C-5A jumbo transport plane would end up costing the taxpayers about $2 billion more than it was supposed to. Instead of being praised for uncovering this boondoggle, Fitzgerald was ostracized. A weaponry analyst of great skills, he was reassigned to a job in which he studied the cost overrun on a bowling alley in Thailand. His personal life was probed by the Pentagon's Office of Special Investigations. A year after his testimony on Capitol Hill, he was dismissed, on the pretense that a reorganization rendered his job unnecessary. He appealed to the CSC. Nearly three years later, it ordered the Air Force to reinstate him in his old job. The CSC investigation had found that Fitzgerald's job was the only one eliminated by the reorganization. It also found that the White House had had a hand in the firing. Alexander Butterfield, then a White House aide, had written H. R.

Haldeman a memo that stated, "Fitzgerald is a topnotch cost expert, but he must be given low marks in loyalty; and after all, loyalty is the name of the game." (Butterfield was the one who, during the Watergate probe, first revealed the existence of the tape recording system in the White House's Oval Office.)

Of course, the Ernest Fitzgeralds are a rare breed in every line of work, especially in government service. Most federal employees are team players who go to great lengths to protect themselves, their superiors, and their agencies from embarrassment and criticism. Confronted with a probing question from a reporter or curious citizen, many bureaucrats will clam up, declining to dispense information that anyone is entitled to receive. They prefer to go about their obscure daily tasks without the glare of publicity. Publicity involves risks. While it could lead to wider recognition of a job well done, it could also mean a disruption of the steady, certain advance up the GS ladder of promotion.

THE SALARY PYRAMID

At the top of the federal pay hierarchy is the Executive Structure of appointed officials, including Cabinet and sub-Cabinet officials, federal judges, and miscellaneous directors, chairmen, and commissioners of all sorts of executive bodies. Executive Structure salaries, which have not been raised since 1969, range from $36,000 (for heads of relatively minor agencies, such as the Indian Claims Board and the Panama Canal Company, and deputies of the Capitol Architect and the Librarian of Congress) up to $60,000 for Cabinet secretaries and Supreme Court justices. Between those limits are assistant Cabinet secretaries ($38,000), under secretaries and district judges ($40,000), members of Congress, circuit judges, and heads of major agencies, such as the AEC and the VA ($42,500). The only federal officials whose salaries exceed the five levels of the Executive Structure are the President ($200,000 plus $50,000 allowance for expenses incidental to his office, both taxable), the Vice President ($62,500 plus a $10,000 allowance, also taxable), the Speaker of the House (same salary and expenses as the Vice President), and the Chief Justice of the Supreme Court ($62,500).

Most of the white-collar men and women who staff the great bureaucracies are paid according to the General Schedule, with grades numbered from 1 to 18. (The upgrading of federal jobs has made GS-1 and -2 employees almost nonexistent.) This scale covers everyone from messengers, clerk typists, night watchmen, and telephone operators (ranging up to GS-7) to "super-grade" administrators and scientists at the level of GS-16, -17, and -18. Salaries on the GS scale currently range from $5,294 to $36,000, with the increments from grade to grade rather small at the bottom of the ladder and increasingly large toward the top. Between most grades there are ten pay "steps," enabling an employee to advance periodically to a slightly higher salary without being promoted to a higher GS level. The salaries for all GS grades are the same everywhere, so they are relatively more attractive in regions with a low cost of living (like the South) than in, say, an expensive region like Alaska.

Blue-collar federal workers (70 percent of whom work for the Department of Defense) have a wage scale that is geographically adjusted. Called the Federal Wage System (FWS), it attempts to match the prevailing wage rates for various trades in 138 parts of the country.

For white-collar workers not covered by the General Schedule, there are many other pay systems, such as one for federal judicial employees, the Foreign Service, the FBI, and medical professionals in the VA. They are all comparable to the GS system.

Fringe benefits are virtually the same for all federal employees, and they tend to be more generous than in private business—that is, equivalent to a higher percentage of a worker's base income. In addition to nine workdays off each year for national holidays, employees get thirteen workdays of vacation per year during the first three years of employment; twenty days off for their fourth through their fifteenth years, and twenty-six days off each year after that. Sick leave is the real bonanza: thirteen days per year, with no limit on accumulation of unused days. The government pays one-third of the premium on life insurance for every employee, with coverage equal to $2,000 more than the annual salary (rounded up to the next $1,000). Anyone making less than $8,000 is covered for $10,000. Low-cost health insurance is offered, too. All full-time employees work eight-hour days, forty-hour weeks, and must be given two consecutive days off each week (except in special cases, such as jobs with law enforcement agencies).

While more than half of all private businesses in the nation have no retirement plans, Uncle Sam provides federal pensions that are greater than social security. For most employees, 7 percent is deducted from their base salary each year and the government pays in a like amount. Upon retirement, workers receive an annual pension equal to a proportion (as high as 80 percent for a forty-one-year employee) of their salary during their three highest-paid years of employment. Federal judges get the best deal of all, a guarantee of the same salary for the rest of their lives, whether on the bench or in retirement. People who leave the government before they have worked the five years to qualify them for a pension may take with them the money they have paid into the fund (without interest). When Spiro Agnew resigned the Vice Presidency, he was three months short of qualifying for a $15,625 per year pension beginning at the age of sixty-two. His accrued pension payments totaled about $25,000.

THE FEDERAL SALARY BOOM

Federal pay soared in the Sixties, prodded by the Salary Reform Act of 1962, which established the goal of "comparability" between salaries in the public and the private sectors. During that decade—marked by about eleven hefty pay hikes—the federal payroll expanded three times as fast as the gross national product (which wasn't exactly standing still during the Sixties, either). These pay increases were voted by a Congress that was becoming increasingly sensitive to the power of the public employee unions, especially those of the numerically potent and well-organized postal workers and low-level white-collar bureaucrats. But in 1971, Congress extricated itself from the biennial hassle over federal salaries. It dumped responsibility for the whole thing into the President's lap—or more precisely, into the laps of two members of his team, the director of the Office of Management and Budget (OMB) and the chairman of CSC.

Under the new system, General Schedule salary levels are reviewed and adjusted each year to keep them on a par with nongovernment rates. The adjustment (invariably an increase) recommended by the OMB-CSC team takes effect automatically each October 1 unless the President proposes an alternative plan to Congress. Unless Congress disapproves the alternative plan within thirty days, it goes into effect. If it doesn't approve, the OMB-CSC increases are implemented. In 1972, 1973 and 1974, President Nixon sought, with varying success, to delay or cancel pay increases that he thought would aggravate inflation.

While General Schedule pay is reviewed (and usually increased) annually, bigwigs included in the Executive Structure have to wait at least four years for a salary hike. A presidential commission every four years makes a recommendation to the President, who passes it along to Congress. The proposal goes into effect automatically, unless either the House or the Senate vetoes it. Unfortunately for the federal judges and high-echelon bureaucrats who are wrapped up in one pay package with congressmen, Congress is sometimes reluctant to raise its own salaries (even by passively accepting someone else's proposal).

In early 1974 President Nixon suggested that all Executive Structure salaries be boosted 7.5 percent in each of three consecutive years (which would have raised congressional salaries to $52,800 by 1976). Considering the amount of inflation since Executive Structure salaries were last set in 1969, as well as the anticipated rate of inflation over the next few years, the proposal was hardly extravagant. But the Senate was afraid of public disapproval in an election year, especially the Year of Watergate, and vetoed the plan by a vote of 72–26. The senators wanted so badly to impress the voters with their frugality that they even killed a compromise plan that would have increased every salary in the Executive Structure except their own. As Senator Robert Dole (R-Kan.) pointed out, "the difficulty with pay raises in the Senate is that one-third of its senators are millionaires, one-third are statesmen, and the other third are cowards."

The question of whether civil servants are overpaid or underpaid relative to their counterparts in the "real world" is an endless, unresolvable debate. Most experts seem to feel that overpayment is common at the low and middle levels of the bureaucracy (especially considering the generous fringe benefits). But in the five higher levels and the "super-grades" of the GS scale, most employees could be earning substantially more in private business and the professions. After a few years of self-sacrifice in public service, many middle- and upper-level bureaucrats—especially lawyers at the regulatory agencies—cash in on their federal experience by jumping to lucrative jobs on the other side of the fence, with corporations, law firms, and trade associations.

Nearly every outstanding private citizen who is recruited for a high-level government job has to take a cut in salary (though his pay may be augmented by investments and other personal income). Sometimes, owing to strange misalignments between the power of a given job and the salary that comes with it, federal officials have to take a pay cut to be "promoted." When President Nixon moved George Shultz from Secretary of Labor to Director of OMB (which is a more powerful position), Shultz's salary dropped from $60,000 (Level I of the Executive Structure) to $42,500 (Level II). His wife reportedly quipped, "One more promotion like this, George, and we'll have to borrow money to live." Fortunately for the Shultzes, however, George was later moved to another Cabinet spot, this time at the Treasury, before retiring from government in 1974.

There's no better way to get a feel for the diversity of Washington's 348,000 federal employees than to meet a few of them and talk with them about the jobs they do, how they happened to get into federal employment, their leisure pastimes, their families. Here are a few of them:

Robert D. Larkin, forty-nine, a GS-13 electronics technician making about $24,000 (a grade above the great majority of federal technicians, most of whom get no higher than GS-12). Works at the Goddard Space Flight Center in suburban Greenbelt, Maryland. Personally constructed, at considerable saving to the government, a general-purpose digital computer that is used at the Center to simulate satellite-control operations. Born in Rochester, New York, father an optics specialist. After high school, worked as an office boy at a New York City advertising agency, then enlisted in the Air Force in World War II. Got out as a sergeant, worked in Los Angeles as a streetcar motorman and bus driver, and in a sheet metal plant and steel mill. Then took a job with North American Aviation as an analyzer of low-level flight test data. Entered federal service in 1950 as a GS-7 to do flight test work at the Patuxent Naval Air Station in Maryland. Learned all the electronics he knows on the job. Married, seven kids. Lives near the Chesapeake Bay, commutes 24 miles to work. Hobby: camping.

Mrs. Jeanne B. Simmons, twenty-six, black, a GS-7 secretary earning about $9,250. Works in the Office of Public Affairs at the Department of Health, Education and Welfare. A District native, her father a laborer and deliveryman. Graduated from high school and started federal service as a GS-2 clerk-typist. After taking some business school courses, qualified as a GS-4 secretary at the Food and Drug Administration. Then advanced to a GS-5 secretary in the HEW Office of the Secretary. Later promoted to GS-6 and GS-7. Her husband, twenty-nine, is studying for a master's degree in urban planning at Morgan State College, a predominantly black college near Baltimore. One son, four. Lives in Hillcrest Heights, just across the District line in Prince George's County, Maryland. Hobbies: sewing, bowling, wall painting, swimming, dancing.

Arthur Walker, thirty-eight, a GS-15 military budget analyst making about $29,000 (official title: Chief of the Budget and Operations Branch of the Budget Division of the Comptroller's Office of the Army Matériel Command). Born in Libertyville, Illinois, father a purchasing agent and executive for a small electronics firm. High school in Chicago, BA degree in business from Loras College, Dubuque, Iowa. Began federal service as a GS-5 Army management intern at the Red River Army Depot, Texarkana, Texas. Served as a budget analyst at Army installations in Kentucky, France, and Germany, rising to a GS-13. Spent a year at Syracuse University, 1969–70, getting a master's degree in business administration at the Army's expense. Transferred to the Office of the Comptroller of the Army, at the Pentagon, assumed present job in 1972. Married, four children. Lives in suburban Springfield, Virginia. Hobbies: reading, church activities, Cub Scouts.

Jacob W. Stevens, fifty-six, black, a letter carrier making about $12,500. Works out of a small office at the Dupont Circle Office Building in the District, where each morning the tenants pick up the mail that he began sorting at 5 A.M. Later in the day, he makes two deliveries through the halls of the building. Well liked by the building's tenants, who describe him as highly efficient, helpful, and cheerful. Born in Richmond, Virginia, father a career soldier who retired as a sergeant and then found work at the Washington Navy Yard. Three years of high school in the District. Four years of stocking railroad cars for the Pullman Company, then four years in the Army during World War II. Entered federal service as a clerk-messenger at the Library of Congress. Became a letter carrier in 1949. Married, one son (an apprentice draftsman for a construction firm). Lives in three-bedroom house in the Northwest part of Washington.

Robert L. Stock, fifty-two, a sheet-metal specialist with the General Services Administration, making around $6 an hour. (Because his wage is set regionally on a cost-of-living basis, his counterpart at a federal installation in Columbus, Georgia, gets $4.88; in Alaska, $8.89, and in San Francisco, $6.17.) Born, raised, and lived his whole life near Laurel, Maryland, in Prince George's County. Ninth-grade education. Worked as a heavy equipment operator, followed by six months in the Army during World War II. Started work with Uncle Sam in 1947 as a sheet-metal worker. Employed for a while at the now demolished Navy building on Constitution Avenue. Ten years at the National Security Agency in Odenton, Maryland, where he found the security precautions "nerve-wracking." Asked for a transfer, and spent the next ten years at the Pentagon. Lives in Levitt-built community called Belair. Pleased he can commute 24 miles to work without encountering a single traffic light. Married, one son (an electrician), one daughter (a school system supply specialist). Hobbies: fishing and hunting.

PUSH FOR EQUAL EMPLOYMENT

Minority-group citizens—blacks, Spanish-Americans, American Indians, Oriental-Americans—used to be virtually nonexistent in federal employment at all but the lowest levels. This situation has been vastly improved over the past fifteen years, though the percentage of minority employment still declines sharply with each step up the grade scale. Nationwide, the proportion of blacks in federal employment is about 16 percent—slightly more than the percentage of blacks in the American population—and Spanish-surnamed people account for another 3 percent. In GS grades 5 through 8, 16 percent are Negroes (up from about 10 percent in 1965); in GS grades 9–11, about 7 percent (up from 3 percent in 1965); in GS 12–18, about 4 percent (up from 1 percent). In the Washington area, the percentage of blacks is substantially higher in every grade level than in the rest of the nation: GS 1–4, 49 percent; GS 5–8, 25 percent; GS 9–11, 17 percent; GS 12–13, 8 percent; GS 14–15, 4 percent; GS 16–18, 2 percent. About 27 percent of all federal employees in the Washington area are black, roughly the same proportion of blacks in the entire metropolitan area. Every federal agency is required to have an equal employment program, with "goals" for hiring minority employees. (The CSC says the goals are not the same as quotas—which would technically violate the letter of the merit system—but the difference is more semantic than real.) A parallel thrust to the recruitment of minority applicants is the search for more women to staff middle- and upper-level positions.

Besides minority recruiting, the most important trend in federal employment is the growing power of public employee unions. Since President Kennedy signed an executive order in 1961 allowing limited union activity, federal union membership (not counting postal workers) has more than tripled. When the Postal Service was made into a public corporation in 1971, the postal unions traded their considerable leverage with Congress into collective bargaining muscle. The four unions that have exclusive national contracts with the Postal Service can negotiate all aspects of pay, fringes, and working conditions. Technically, they have no authority to strike, and wage disputes are settled by binding arbitration. The threat of an illegal strike is still present, however. In 1970, before the Postal Service was created, thousands of postal workers, angry over congressional delays in granting pay increases, walked off the job in the first large-scale postal strike in history.

By comparison with unions in the private sector (and the postal unions), the organizations of other federal workers are weak. They cannot bargain for salaries, major fringe benefits, or hours of work. At most, they can lobby the bureaucrats of OMB and CSC, attempting to influence their recommendation on the automatic salary adjustment each October. Or they can lobby the President to present a more favorable alternative plan, and try to influence Congress's approval of it. Federal labor leaders have dreams of talking Congress into giving certain "nonessential" federal workers the right to go on strike. The idea is gradually gaining ground on Capitol Hill, but acceptance is still a long way off. (Incidentally, the federal unions wield a lot of clout with congressmen who have big concentrations of civil servants in their districts, like those of the Maryland and Virginia suburbs of Washington.)

SOME DRAWBACKS

There are a lot of things that make federal service a pleasant career—job security, good pay, predictable raises (without having to muster courage to ask the boss for one), and good fringe benefits. But there are also some frustrations associated with federal service.

There's the Hatch Act, for example. Designed to keep partisanship out of the performance of routine public duties, the Act prohibits U.S. government workers from running for office (except for nonpartisan local offices) and participating actively in party politics. Federal employees may, however, contribute to partisan candidates.

Most federal careerists like their job security and have no interest in trading it for the greater power and uncertain tenure of an appointive position. But others live with the frustration of being passed over for the top jobs in favor of political appointees from the outside. A rare example of promotion from the ranks was the 1974 appointment of Irving M. Pollack to the Securities and Exchange Commission (SEC). Pollack, fifty-six, joined the SEC staff in 1946 (recruited by his older brother, who was personnel chief of the SEC). He rose through the ranks to become chief of the SEC's Bureau of Enforcement, where he had a reputation for toughness and integrity. Several times he was considered but passed over for vacancies on the five-member commission. Then Watergate hit the Nixon administration. The scandal led to the resignation of the SEC's chairman, G. Bradford Cook (who as general counsel had been involved in the Vesco affair and had been chairman for only ten weeks), and generally tarnished the SEC's reputation. The new chairman, Ray Garrett, Jr., resisted White House pressure to fill a commission vacancy with a pro-Wall Street choice, and President Nixon finally appointed Pollack (who is actually a Democrat).

A career bureaucrat has to endure the constant threat that programs he administers might be chopped to pieces—or reorganized—by a new administration or a current one that has changed its mind. Beyond the risk to the civil servant's job, there is the psychological blow of losing something in which he has invested so much of his energy and imagination. It's a feeling experienced by many on the staff of the Office of Economic Opportunity's Legal Services program (legal advice for the poor), when it fell out of favor with the Nixon administration and was severely cut. Many of the bureaucrats who ran volunteer organizations like the Peace Corps and VISTA were concerned that their esprit de corps (and funding) would be hurt by consolidation into the Nixon administration's umbrella agency, ACTION. Bureaucrats who oppose a particular cutback or reorganization can always find a friend on Capitol Hill, where every strong senator or congressman has a few pet programs he watches over.

Civil servants must accept the fact that cost-saving inventions and practices they devise will be rewarded far less generously than in the private sector. Officially, great cost-saving brainstorms can be rewarded with a prize of up to $25,000, and the Defense Department is supposed to pay an ingenious employee $1 for each $1,000 saved. In reality, however, incentive grants are small potatoes. In 1972, 91,000 federal employees were awarded special achievement prizes averaging $176, and another 56,600 got an average grant of $80 for cost-saving suggestions. There's a retired GS-15 engineer in Maryland who got $300 from the Navy for conceiving in 1957 a method—eventually refined by others and adopted—for test-firing Polaris missiles without losing them. Herman I. Shaller has claimed for years that Uncle Sam owes him $1.5 million for saving about $300 million and two years of research time. But the Navy, the U.S. Court of Claims, and the Supreme Court didn't agree with him, so he's now trying to interest Congress in overhauling the whole incentive-award system.

LIMITS ON FREE SPEECH

While many middle-level bureaucrats live comfortably with the don't-rock-the-boat ethic, others are annoyed by the shroud of secrecy that surrounds much of the work they perform—not because of national security, but because public exposure might embarrass their superiors. As William Rehnquist wrote in 1971 in the *Civil Service Journal* (before he was promoted from the Justice Department to the Supreme Court), "I think one may fairly generalize that a government employee is seriously restricted in his freedom of speech, with respect to any matter for which he has been assigned responsibility." A. Ernest Fitzgerald learned this during the C-5A scandal. So did Mrs. Jacqueline Verrett, a biochemist with the Food and Drug Administration who found a strong link between cyclamate artificial sweeteners and deformities in chicken embryos. After she gave a television interview on the subject (not prohibited by her bosses but strongly disapproved), she was twice publicly reprimanded by then HEW Secretary Robert Finch. Cyclamates were subsequently removed from general public use—not because of Mrs. Verrett's research, the FDA said, but because of the discovery of other unrelated deleterious effects.

The number of bureaucrats who contend daily with such sensitive issues as new airplanes and the safety of food additives is quite small. A much larger number of government folks have the opposite problem—dead-end jobs, underuse of their skills in overstaffed offices, giving them calluses and frustrations from too many years in the same harness. But these are problems shared by millions of workers these days, in corporate and industrial employment as well as government. On the whole, government workers are probably no more or less fulfilled, hard-working, and resourceful than their counterparts elsewhere. William Knudsen—a former president of General Motors and World War II head of the Office of Production Management—commented on the similarities of public and private employment when he said, "We have red tape in big business, too, but there we call it 'the system.' "

In any event, 418,000 government workers, civilian and military, hold jobs in the Washington metropolitan area. They are largely responsible for the tone of life in the nation's capital, and have a lot to do with calling the tune for the lives of 213 million Americans in all the fifty states. Whether this makes you happy or not, it is a fact of current life (and a growing trend, at that).

11 CONGRESS

The U.S. Congress—Washington's great slumbering giant—occasionally wakes up, looks around, and finds that the nation has changed quite a bit since it last took stock of itself. There ensues a flurry of reform, revitalization and general reassertion of Congress' power vis-à-vis the President. This has happened over the past three years, thanks to two jolting traumas: Vietnam and Watergate.

Vietnam was a painful demonstration of the impotence of Congress in the presidentially dominated field of foreign affairs and war-making. For nearly a decade the nation waged war without a congressional declaration of war. For nearly a decade Congress rubber-stamped White House requests for funding authority, all based on the Gulf of Tonkin resolution, which was hastily passed by both houses on the basis of incomplete information. And while all this was going on, Congress pursued a "guns-and-butter" economic plan, ignoring the mounting inflationary pressure that finally burst through the ceiling in the Seventies.

Congress eventually got tired of being pushed around by the President and the Pentagon. It also got tired of its own bad habit of appropriating money in the dark, with little sense of priorities or knowledge of where the revenue would come from to pay for its new social programs. So Congress made some changes. During the Ninety-third Congress it passed (and repassed over President Nixon's veto) a precedent-setting law that severely limits the President's ability to commit American troops to foreign action without prior congressional consent. And recognizing its own shortcomings, Congress created a budget apparatus, analogous to the White House Office of Management and Budget, to put some order into the obligating of federal funds. To better contend with the tangle of conflicting expert opinion heaped upon it during debates on complex scientific issues (civilian and military), Congress set up the Office of Technology Assessment. And for the first time ever, Congress adopted limits on private funding of federal elections and created partial public funding of presidential elections.

All of this overhauling was well underway when Watergate began seeping into the national consciousness. Congress was slow to get embroiled in the Watergate mess, but it eventually exercised very capably its privilege and duty of investigation (by the Ervin Committee) and indictment (by Representative Peter Rodino's House Judiciary Committee). The Ninety-third Congress made history with the nation's second impeachment proceedings against a President—the first impeachment attempt to be based upon carefully considered, legitimate criminal charges (rather than the transparently political complaints against Andrew Johnson in 1868). The Ninety-third Congress continued to make history by being the first one to try out the machinery of the Twenty-fifth Amendment to the Constitution, to fill the Vice Presidential vacancies created by Spiro Agnew's resignation and Gerald Ford's elevation to the Presidency.

Watergate was a prelude to the real fireworks of House reform that followed the Democratic sweep of 1974, which resulted in the largest roster of House Democrats (291) in a decade and the largest number of House freshmen (92) since 1949. The 75 new Democratic members—younger, more liberal, and less accustomed to taking orders from their seniors—quickly threw their weight behind veteran House liberals. Together they pushed reform after reform through the Democratic Caucus, chaired by Representative Phillip Burton (Cal.), a savvy, pugnacious and ambitious reform advocate (who probably has his eye on the Speaker's chair).

In a few weeks' time, the House Democratic Caucus effected a number of important changes. The power to make committee assignments was taken away from the House Ways and Means Committee and given to the twenty-four-member Steering and Policy Committee, composed of the House Democratic leadership and sixteen other key Democratic congressmen. House members were prohibited from chairing more than one committee at any one time. The Democratic allocation of seats on major committees was increased to two-thirds plus one, enabling more freshmen and other younger members to serve on them, and enhancing the chances of passage of liberal legislation. The machinery for electing committee chairmen was modified to make challenges against senior chairmen easier. The House Ways and Means Committee (with the farthest ranging jurisdiction of any committee in Congress), was expanded by 12 members and was forced to form subcommittees, a decentralization of authority long resisted by former chairman Wilbur Mills (D-Ark.) And on the first day of the new session in 1975, the House Democrats succeeded in abolishing the Internal Security Committee, which liberals and civil libertarians had been trying to get rid of for years.

The 1974 assault on the Ways and Means Committee had been plotted for a long time, and the plotting was made easier by the gradual decline of Mills's influence—which began waning even before his ludicrous presidential bid in 1972 and his increasingly obvious abuse of alcohol. It is typical of the House's cautiousness (some would say cowardice) that few members were willing to make a frontal challenge to Mills until his cavorting with stripper Fanne Foxe improved the odds of success. The big splash in the press over the Tidal Basin scandal gave the impression that Mills was being ousted from the Ways and Means chairmanship as punishment for personal impropriety (of which many congressmen are equally, if more discreetly, guilty). But Mills's fling with the "Argentine Firecracker" merely provided a convenient excuse. The real reason for Mills's demise was his colleagues' pent-up resentment over his autocratic and sometimes arbitrary use of power.

The same pent-up resentment among members, not all of whom were new or young, led to the deposing of three other previously powerful House committee chairmen. Wright Patman (D-Tex.), the most senior member of the whole House, was removed as chairman of the Banking and Currency Committee, to be replaced by Henry Reuss of Wisconsin. F. Edward Hebert of Louisiana lost his chairmanship of the Armed Services Committee to Melvin Price of Illinois. And W. R. Poage of Texas was unseated as chairman of the Agriculture Committee by Thomas S. Foley of Washington. Wayne Hays of Ohio managed to hold onto his chairmanship of the important

Administration Committee but only after severe challenge. And Jamie Whitten of Mississippi retained chairmanship of the appropriations subcommittee on agriculture only by giving up his jurisdiction over environmental and consumer protection. All in all, it was the most drastic intraparty house cleaning that anyone had seen on the Hill since the early 1930s. One conservative Democrat, Representative John Jarman of Oklahoma (a twenty-four-year House veteran), was so upset with the new state of affairs that he abandoned his party and joined the GOP, dropping the Democrats' House roster to 290.

Not to be outdone by the House, Senate liberals in early 1975 renewed their long campaign to modify the filibuster, which conservatives had used for decades against civil rights legislation and, more recently, to delay passage of bills for the Consumer Protection Agency and campaign finance reform. After a bitter fight, in which the pro-filibuster forces were led by skillful parliamentarian Senator James Allen (D-Ala.), the rule was changed to make it easier to cut off debate (cloture). In the first major change in the cloture rule since 1917, filibusters can now be cut off by vote of sixty senators, rather than two-thirds of those present and voting, as required before.

The Capitol Hill press corps, ever vigilant for signs of life in the ailing legislative branch, may have overestimated the changes that are likely to flow from these reforms. But one thing is already clear: Congress is indeed becoming a more feisty combatant in Washington. President Ford has already felt Congress' new independence in a stinging series of confrontations. And Secretary of State Kissinger, who has not been in the habit of consulting Congress on much of anything, had to journey up to the Hill late in 1974 to plead for postponement of a cutoff of U.S. military aid to Turkey, buying time to make yet another attempt at a lasting peace accord on Cyprus.

WHAT CONGRESSMEN DO

Congress may seem an enigma to many of its constituents, because it doesn't fit the textbook descriptions written about it. It is frequently untidy, and to those who are impatient for action on a specific issue, the legislative process seems ungainly and cumbersome. A few bills come out looking about the same as they went in, but most are trimmed or padded along the way. The resulting product is often unsatisfactory to all involved, proponent and opponent alike. Yet this, at its root, is the essence of the legislative purpose: to blend and balance the interests of the nation. No one has decreed that it has to be neat.

Anyone who harbors the romantic notion that Congress is a focal point for oratory and face-to-face debate is doomed to disappointment. Most people who visit Congress for the first time are struck by the relative emptiness of the legislative chambers. Frequently there are only a few of the 435 congressmen on the House floor. And over in the other wing of the Capitol, there may be only two senators on the floor—one talking, and the other paying not the slightest bit of attention. Small wonder that some visitors ask just what it is that these people do to earn their $42,500 annual salaries.

The truth is that representatives and senators do quite a lot to earn their keep. Their appearances in their respective chambers constitute only a small part of their working day, which ofttimes stretches to twelve or sixteen hours. The work day involves several hours attending committee hearings and "markup sessions," where bills are shaped for action on the floor. The lion's share of the work on legislation is accomplished in committee. The debate on the floor is the icing on the cake, and it rarely changes votes. The give-and-take, the compromising, whipsawing, logrolling and tradeoffs take place in the committee rooms. Most of this used to be done in secret executive sessions with the press and public excluded, but some recent rules changes have opened more of these meetings to the public.

There is still another aspect to the lives of representatives and senators. This is the role they play as the Washington contact point for people back home who have dealings with the federal government, be they state or local officials, businessmen, farmers, labor leaders, or "just plain citizens."

A PROFILE OF CONGRESS

Who are the 535 people whom American voters have chosen to represent their interests in the House and the Senate? Well, the vast majority of them are middle-aged, although there are a few House members in their twenties and more than a few members of both chambers in their sixties, seventies, and eighties. The 92 new House members elected in 1974 had an average age of only forty years, lowering the House average to below fifty—an alltime record. The Senate, by statute and tradition, has a higher average age.

All but nineteen members of the Congress are men. Fewer than five percent are part of a racial minority, including seventeen blacks, the Hawaiian delegation of mixed Oriental-Hawaiian ancestry, a Democratic congressman of Japanese descent (former San Jose, California, Mayor Norman Mineta), and a few members of Latin-American heritage. Unmarried people are a rarity in Congress (although quite a few members leave their spouses back in the home state and *act* as if they weren't married).

Virtually every major Western religion is represented in Congress, from Baptist and Mormon (including the whole Utah delegation) to Quaker and Syrian Orthodox (the religion of Congress' only member of Middle-Eastern descent, South Dakota Democrat Senator James Abourezk). The Ninety-fourth Congress has the largest number of Catholics (124) and Jews (24) in congressional history. The most overrepresented minority religion is the Episcopal church, which comprises a mere 1.5 percent of the national population but 12 percent of the House and Senate. Public displays of piousness make good politics, so only six members said (in a recent survey) they have no religious preference whatsoever.

As for education, members of Congress without at least a bachelor's degree are a negligible minority. There are a number of PhDs, and the House has several former Rhodes scholars, including Speaker Carl Albert. Financially, most members of the House and Senate are considerably better off than the citizens they represent—not just by virtue of their government salaries, but because of the success they achieved before going into politics. A few representatives and senators enjoy inherited wealth, but most made it themselves, primarily in law and business. While a few Hill politicians leapt right into federal office from the private sector, most started out in local or state politics and worked their way up.

Far and away the dominant pre-politics livelihood is law, which is a convenient occupation for a politician to fall back on if the electorate turns him out of office. The next largest occupational group represented in the House and Senate—and the most varied one—is business. Then comes educators—college professors, high school teachers, principals, administrators—whose ranks have swelled in recent years. (Twelve of the new House members come from academic jobs.) Another fast-growing "proving ground" for future representatives and senators is television journalism, a line of work uniquely suited to the politician's need for instant public recognition of name and face. A number of House members had appeared on TV as newsmen and commentators, and GOP Senator Jesse Helms was widely known in North Carolina for his conservative television editorials. There's even a meteorologist and former TV weatherman in the House, Democrat Dale Milford of Texas.

The Senate has no medical doctors, but the House has three: Thomas E. Morgan (D-Pa.), chairman of the Foreign Affairs Committee, Tim Lee Carter (R-Ky.), and freshman Larry McDonald (D-Ga.), a member of the John Birch Society and fervent foe of abortion. The ranks of the former professional athletes were thinned in 1974 with the defeat of pitcher Wilmer (Vinegar Bend) Mizell, a GOP congressman from North Carolina, and Olympic decathlon ace Bob Mathias, a Republican representative from California, but former star quarterback Jack Kemp has proved more durable as a Republican House member from New York State. Freshman Representative Edward Beard, a Rhode Island Democrat, is a former prizefighter.

Also sitting on the House side are seven clergymen (including two Catholic priests), a couple of pharmacists, a veterinarian, a former sheriff or two, several ex-officials of labor unions, two former State Department employees, and even a onetime U.S. Chief of Protocol (Missouri Democrat James Symington). Until early 1975, the House also had an alumnus of the CIA—Soviet specialist Robert Steele, Republican congressman from Connecticut, who ran unsuccessfully for governor.

The businessmen—Congress' wealthiest occupational bloc—represent an astounding array of enterprises. Most numerous are the bankers, and there are quite a few real estate operators and insurance agents, too. Many of the southern and western congressmen and senators have extensive agricultural and livestock holdings. There is a sizable contingent of newspaper publishers and owners of broadcast stations (good bases for launching political campaigns). Three House members used to be undertakers. Congress has former accountants, stockbrokers, FBI agents, lumber dealers, oil wholesalers, new and used car dealers, a housepainter, advertising and public relations men, social workers, and owners (or former owners) of an ice cream company, a brewery, a fleet of taxi cabs, department stores, and a circus. Until the start of the Ninety-fourth Congress, there was even a professional auctioneer, former Democratic Representative Kenneth Gray of Illinois, who also once piloted helicopters and owned an airport. Congress, while certainly not a mirror image of working America, is more than just a collection of lawyers—especially the House, whose occupational profile is considerably broader than the lawyer-laden Senate.

CONGRESSIONAL STAFFS

A representative or senator cannot be a topnotcher without topnotch staff aides, and they, in turn, can work effectively only with strong guidance from their boss. Elected officials are expected to formulate the general outlines of legislation they introduce and their own votes on the issues. But the under-pinning of the legislative process—the research that goes into casting a vote or drafting a bill, as well as the drafting itself—is done by professionals on the staffs of the members and the committees. Members of Congress, like the President and Cabinet officials, rarely write their own speeches, instead relying on aides who knows their bosses' policies and styles of expression. While representatives and senators sometimes handle constituent problems personally (especially those of bigwig constituents), the bulk of this service (called "case work" on the Hill) is handled by the office staff. A strong supporting staff leaves the elected official free to engage his colleagues in the high-level maneuvering and exchanges of ideas essential to the success of every legislative effort. (Both chambers have a good number of do-nothing legislators, content to coast along on the efforts of their staffs, offering mini-mal direction and imagination.) Most top staff aides have law degrees, and there are a lot of ex-journalists in key positions, too, especially as administra-tive assistants (the member's right-hand aides, called "AAs") and as press secretaries.

A congressman can have up to 18 employees and a total annual payroll of $204,720. Individual salaries range up to a maximum of nearly $35,500, but only one person on a congressman's staff can receive this maximum at any one time. Senators, on the other hand, are not limited to any given number of employees, and their office payroll allowances, which are based on their state population, run from $392,300 to nearly $752,000. Top pay for an individual on a senator's staff is $37,000, and only one aide at a time may receive this maximum. Years ago, senators and representatives recruited their staffs largely from their home states and congressional districts. Some still do bring a number of employees from home to Washington, but many now rely on a cadre of experienced Capitol Hill staffers who move from office to office, bring-ing with them a high degree of professionalism based on years of congressional service.

Both Democrats and Republicans run job placement services to help match senators and congressmen seeking professional staffers with Hill employees who are job-shopping because their present boss has announced retirement, has been defeated at the polls, or has died. Congress was embarrassed in 1974 when a reporter—Francie Barnard of the Fort Worth (Tex.) *Star Tele-gram*—unearthed the fact that the lawmakers had imposed equal employment opportunity rules on everyone else in the country while practicing illegal job discrimination in their own offices. A number of offices were discovered to be on record with the job-placement services as refusing to hire persons from one or more racial or religious minorities, requesting or excluding those born under specific astrological signs and, in at least one instance, turning down in advance any "unattractive females." The glare of publicity brought forth many protestations of innocence. While the discrimination probably has not been totally ended, it has been driven deeper underground.

Committee staffs, as might be expected, consist largely of people who are experts in the fields within the purview of the committee. Legal backgrounds are the most prevalent. Most of the committee personnel and budget are con-trolled by the panel's senior Democrats, but the minority (now Republican) members have a small budget for recruiting a few aides to assist them. Al-though it is not strictly legal, many representatives and senators use the committee personnel as extensions of their personal staffs, sometimes for assignments that are purely political and not related at all to the committee's jurisdiction. The salaries of committee staffers are comparable to those of a member's office staff. Job turnover among top committee aides is minimal, except when the chairmanship changes hands and the new boss brings in his own favorites.

The only two exceptions to the $37,000 ceiling on committee staff salaries are the $40,000 remunerations paid to Laurence N. Woodworth, chief of staff of the Joint Committee on Internal Revenue Taxation, and Alice M. Rivlin, director of the new Congressional Budget Office. No one begrudges them these higher salaries. Woodworth is one of the leading tax experts in Washington, Mrs. Rivlin is a top economist and budget specialist, and both could command much more than $40,000 in private employment.

HOUSEKEEPING

The people who hold the major House administrative jobs—"housekeeping" positions like Sergeant at Arms, Clerk of the House, and Doorkeeper—are elected by the majority party caucus and receive $40,000 salaries. The corresponding officials on the Senate side—the Secretary of the Senate, Sergeant at Arms, and Doorkeeper—receive $38,760. Working beneath them is a phalanx of lesser patronage employees, including doormen and elevator operators (some of whom are superfluous button-pushers on automatic elevators). The House doorkeeper has more than 300 people working under him, as pages, doormen, messengers, barbers, clerks in the document room, etc. For 27 years the job was held by William M. (Fish Bait) Miller, the Mississippian who chanted "Mistah Speakah . . . the President of the United States!" at the start of every State of the Union address. For years his reelection to the post was a foregone conclusion, but in 1974 he was turned out of office by younger, more liberal members who felt he was not serving their interests as well as he served those of the senior members. The new doorkeeper is James T. Molloy, a former disbursing clerk who managed House paychecks and expense accounts.

Each legislative body has an ordained Protestant clergyman on the payroll to serve as chaplain, having the principal responsibility of seeing to it that every session is opened with a prayer. For this, the current spiritual adviser to the House, the Reverend Edward G. Latch, D.D., receives $19,770 a year. His longtime Senate counterpart, the Reverend Dr. Edward L. R. Elson, however, receives only $16,000. (Until recently he was also fulltime minister of the fashionable National Presbyterian Church, which President Eisenhower used to attend.)

One of the most important administrative officials of Congress—the Architect of the Capitol—is appointed, ironically, by the President. This $38,000-a-year post carries responsibility for the physical condition of the buildings and grounds of the whole Capitol Hill complex, the maintenance of which keeps some 1,800 people busy every day. There is no statutory requirement that the Architect of the Capitol be an architect by education or practice, and from 1865 until 1971 the position was held by nonarchitects. But the current architect, George M. White, is a Fellow of the American Institute of Architects.

In the last Congress, both House and Senate entered the electronic age (albeit not without soul-searching and misgivings). The House took the most revolutionary step by installing electronic voting, which has cut the time of each quorum call and roll-call vote down to fifteen minutes. (Roll calls used to consume thirty-five to forty minutes, when clerks had to call out each name.) Representatives now carry plastic ID cards which are magnetically sensitized. There are stations scattered about the House floor into which the cards can be inserted, and the member then presses a button which records his vote as "yes," "nay," or "present." The computerized system guards against any attempts to vote the same card twice. It also provides lighted tally boards for viewing from the House floor and galleries, and produces a print-out of the final vote. The system is working well, although there are occasional complaints that votes have been wrongly recorded. And there have been suspicions of some proxy voting (members bringing over cards belonging to colleagues and voting for them—strictly against the rules).

For its part, the Senate installed a sophisticated sound system. For years spectators and press in the galleries strained to hear the give and take of floor debates. The new sound system provides a microphone at each senator's desk. The volume can be adjusted by an operator seated at a console in the northeast corner of the gallery overlooking the Senate floor.

In recent years the voters have shown a distinct preference for a Democratic rather than Republican majority in Congress, and the last election was an even more emphatic reaffirmation of this preference. Licking their wounds from the 1974 Democratic landslide, the Republicans could at least console themselves with the fact that the President's party (be it GOP or Democratic) usually loses a lot of House seats in off-year (nonpresidential) elections. The GOP loss of forty-three seats in 1974 was only five more than the average loss in such off-year elections (38).

Only twice in the past twenty-odd years has the electorate given the Republicans control of Congress—once in 1947–48 (the famous Eightieth Congress, against which President Truman ran so successfully for reelection), and again in 1953–54 (the first Congress after Eisenhower's landslide election in 1952). But Eisenhower lost control of Congress in the next election when the voters again switched to the Democrats. Going further back, the Democrats controlled both Houses of Congress from 1932, when Franklin D. Roosevelt swept the country in his first election, until 1947, two years after his death. Given that mandate over such a long span of time, you might think that the Democrats could have done as they pleased on legislation, since they had the votes to do it.

But Congress isn't quite as simple as just two major parties. Congress is actually run by three blocs: the conservatives, the liberals, and the moderates. The latter is the largest group and decides most of the big issues. It's an amorphous entity that includes both Republicans and Democrats. Its composition changes from bill to bill, depending on the make-up of the legislation. The occupants of the middle ground don't always follow their party leaders, and they shift so often from one position to another that, for practical purposes, they are not a group at all.

There are liberals and conservatives in *both* parties. There are also a few "independents," who technically belong to neither party, but are loosely aligned with one or the other. The best way for an independent to win, as

Conservative-Republican Senator James L. Buckley of New York demonstrated in 1970, is to let the major party candidates squabble between themselves and then beat both of them in a three-way race.

The late Senator Wayne Morse of Oregon moved from the Republican party to the Democratic party. He was a "Republican for Eisenhower" in 1952 but became disenchanted with Eisenhower's policies, so he switched to the Democrats after a confusing interim as an anti-Eisenhower "independent." Then he switched again and opposed Democratic policies, and he finally lost his seat in the Senate. Senator Strom Thurmond shifted from Democrat to Republican. Senator Harry Byrd of Virginia is an "Independent"—the only official, unhyphenated Independent currently in the Congress. Byrd was a Democrat until the Democrats in Virginia became too liberal for him, so he created his own "party."

CONGRESSIONAL DECISIONMAKING

On specific issues, members of Congress usually vote on legislation according to their constituents' wishes rather than on party allegiance. They are far better attuned to home folks' thinking than the home folks realize. Those who stay in Congress for years and years have a gifted ear for what people back home are thinking and talking about.

Many bills go through without a murmur of opposition. In fact, both houses have special days on which they pass legislation without debate. These are "unanimous consent" days. Committees have given such bills cursory consideration. If there seems to be nothing seriously wrong with the bills, they go on the unanimous consent calendar which is called up on the floor at regular intervals. Scores of measures pass this way. Each bill is called by number and name and, unless a member objects to it, the bill passes without a vote. Unanimous consent is vulnerable to abuse. Frequently in the hectic final days and hours of a session special interest bills that normally would not have a prayer of passage are sandwiched into a sheaf of "unanimous consent" bills and passed.

Another type of legislation that gets little notice is what is known as a "private bill." Most often such a measure repays a citizen for damage done by the government to his home or possessions, or permits an alien to stay here beyond his legal limit, or in some other way corrects an alleged wrong done to a resident. Slews of such bills pass without any more than perfunctory debate because practically no one in either House or Senate has the foggiest notion what they are about. Or cares. Naturally, in such a situation, there is room for monkeyshines, and there have been suspicions that in some cases congressmen have persuaded the government to pay off a poor soul for damages and then have split the payment with him.

Major, controversial bills are mauled and pawed over endlessly. It's a fair guess that any important piece of legislation takes from two to seven years to be enacted. Sometimes it takes longer, depending on the electorate's understanding of what is involved and the interest generated for or against a bill by special-interest groups that lobby Congress.

An issue such as national health insurance, for instance, has taken more than twenty years and *still* hasn't made the grade. But the Taft-Hartley Act was passed within the two years of a single Congress, even though it was assailed by the unions as a "slave-labor" law. A vast majority of voters supported it because they were fed up with nationwide strikes, particularly those led by miners' boss John L. Lewis. Similarly, the McCarran-Walter Immigration Act passed quickly because the electorate was fearful of an influx of "undesirables" from the Orient and southern Europe. (The quotas were later modified, but not until Senator McCarran of Nevada and Representative Walter of Pennsylvania had died.) President Truman vetoed both Taft-Hartley and McCarran-Walter, but the members of Congress read the strong message from the country and passed them over his vetoes.

THE LEGISLATIVE ROUTE

Many bills originate not in a congressional office, but in the executive branch as part of the President's legislation package. Bills are also born in the office of the legislative counsel of a trade association, corporation, labor union, or other special interest. The lobbyist then plants the bill with a friendly member of Congress who introduces it as "his" bill. Sometimes this is sinister, but often a committee staff will actually solicit drafts of "ideal" bills from several opposing lobbies and use them as source material for crafting a compromise bill.

Most legislation follows a tortuous path. A bill is introduced in one house (or both) and hearings are held by a committee that has jurisdiction over its subject matter. Public hearings are mostly window-dressing, used to generate publicity for (or against) bills of particular interest to the leadership of the committee. The most "successful" hearings are ones at which a flamboyant witness makes some sort of dramatic revelation, which the reporters present pick up and splash across the evening news shows and the next morning's newspapers (revelations, for example, of human suffering, corporate negligence, a federal boondoggle, or widespread abuse of some law).

Support or opposition by the President is often crucial to the fate of a controversial bill, but not always. Lobbyists swarm over the committees, some openly and some covertly. Some testify at the hearings, saying clearly why they favor or oppose the bill. Others go around to the back door and buttonhole the members hearing the bill. Because of personal friendships or campaign contributions, they are quite often more effective than the "front men" who have testified publicly.

Finally, if the committee approves the bill ("reports it favorably"), it may reach the floor for debate. In the House, the bill must go to the floor from the Rules Committee. This committee sets the conditions under which the House will consider it, the time each side may spend debating it, the types of amendments that may be offered, or even whether *any* amendments will be in order. The Rules Committee is a potent force, and has the discretionary power to give a green light to a bill or to let it languish in committee. Many a bill has been put in a drawer forever by inaction of the Rules Committee. In the Senate, the majority leadership schedules which bills will come up for debate, and in conjunction with the minority leadership, determines the amount of time that may be spent on the debate. Sometimes there is no limit set, and a small band of senators who strongly oppose a measure may tie up the proceedings so long that the leadership finally withdraws it. This is a "filibuster," for which the Senate is renowned.

Today's filibusters are tame in comparison to those of old, when red-eyed and bone-weary senators took turns reading from the Bible, literary works, newspapers, magazines, or encyclopedias, just to cling to the floor around the clock and wear down the opposition. Now the ground rules for filibusters have changed. Even when one is in progress, the Senate works a normal day. Filibustering senators no longer need hold the floor twenty-four hours a day. They need only withstand a number of cloture attempts—periodic ballots seeking sixty votes to end the "extended debate" (which is the polite phrase by which a filibuster is known today). If, after several attempts at cloture, the opposing forces seem deadlocked, efforts to pass the legislation are abandoned and the filibuster has succeeded.

There are between 10,000 and 15,000 bills introduced during the two years of a Congress. Many are duplicates, some are frivolous, and others are so blatantly partisan or directed toward some special interest that they are ignored from the moment they are born. Sometimes legislation is introduced simply to threaten or warn an industry about a practice that many people dislike, even though the sponsor has little hope of getting it passed. Other types of bills have an almost irresistible appeal once they get loose on the floor: increases in social security benefits, tax cuts, measures to "study" methods of reducing crime, and bills pushing new social welfare plans (although the soaring cost of these plans in an inflationary time has caused even the liberals to be less open-handed with federal funds than during the prosperous Sixties).

Some bills appeal only to the congressmen from a particular region of the country, but deals of mutual self-interest are often made that enable them to pass. For instance, a congressman from Rhode Island has scant interest in legislation that benefits soybean or cotton producers, but a colleague from an agricultural state will seek his vote on these bills in return for support on a bill he knows is of keen interest to the member from Rhode Island. This is an old institution known as "logrolling" or "back-scratching" ("you scratch my back and I'll scratch yours"). The members shake hands on it and the deal is made. Ultimately the day arrives when the deal is consummated and a "majority" of Congress passes a bill that benefits one or several parts of the country (and, ideally, does minimal harm to the others).

CONGRESS AND THE PRESIDENT

An amazing thing about Congress is that it is scared of the President. Because it is a large, often incoherent body with diverse interests, Congress can be led by the President (*whoever* he is)—a focal point of power in the nation. Members of Congress find it almost impossible to deal with him on equal terms. The Constitution considers Congress an independent branch of government, equal to the President and the judicial system. Indeed, Congress in a pique could conceivably trim or cut off the funds of the others, since it has the sole power to appropriate money and the other two branches are entirely dependent on its generosity.

But Congress seldom knows what it wants to do, and it takes a long time to make up its mind. A consensus is seldom apparent except when the country is furious about something or there is broad support for innovative legislation—conditions occurring only occasionally. And while Congress can cut off the executive's funds, the President likewise can refuse to spend money that Congress has appropriated. This so-called "impoundment" of funds has been done by numerous Presidents, most recently by Richard Nixon and Gerald

Ford, as an alleged anti-inflation measure. Meanwhile, the President is in a position to influence national thinking. He has television at his disposal during prime viewing hours and he can stir up mail to members of Congress on any subject merely by asking that the voters make their views known.

President Nixon's relationship with Congress was abominable, due in large part to the heavy-handed, arrogant way that his "palace guard" (Haldeman, Ehrlichman, et al.) dealt with congressmen and senators of both parties. The situation improved under Ford, formerly "one of the boys" from the House. Ford's White House staff is full of key advisers with extensive Hill experience, either as House members (Donald Rumsfeld and John Marsh) or staff (Bob Hartmann). But just because Congress likes Ford personally and enjoys his hospitality at White House parties, it has shown no signs of rolling over and playing dead. After a brief honeymoon, the Democrats (joined by many GOP members, too) ran up a string of veto overrides unprecedented in recent years.

During Nixon's five and a half years in office, Congress managed to overturn only five of his twenty-four vetoes. In the first four months of Ford's tenure, four of his first fifteen vetoes (made for ostensibly anti-inflationary reasons) were overridden. Veteran Washington observer James Reston of the *New York Times* was moved to comment, "Not since President Pierce in the 1850s has Congress rebuked the veto power so sharply." But the Ninety-fourth Congress is far from the "veto-proof" power that it was publicized to be after the 1974 elections. The Democrats' two-thirds bloc in the House, for example, is full of moderates and conservatives who will frequently buck party discipline to back the Republican President's veto.

THE LEADERSHIP

There are fewer powerful men in Congress today than there have been in many years. Only a handful can speak with authority and with real clout. Senator Barry Goldwater of Arizona, the Republican candidate for President in 1964, comes closest to this, for he epitomizes conservative thinking across the land. Yet he only seldom exercises his influence in the country or in the Senate. And Goldwater's power is nothing like the power that the late Senator Robert A. Taft of Ohio exercised over *both* Houses of Congress twenty years ago.

Lyndon B. Johnson was another man with tremendous impact, when he was Democratic majority leader of the Senate. He had a legislative genius for bringing moderates and liberals or moderates and conservatives together to pass legislation. He was a compromiser, which in Congress is a leader. His oft-repeated Biblical allusion "Come, let us reason together" usually meant he was going to take another member into camp by threats or persuasion. And he had an ally in the House—Speaker Sam Rayburn—whose prestige has been unmatched in modern times.

The current leaders of the House and Senate follow a workaday style which produces legislation only when presidential pressure is either very strong or very weak. Senate Majority Leader Mike Mansfield of Montana, while widely liked and admired, seldom puts pressure of his own on the membership, and exhibits none of the prima donna characteristics or high-flown ambitions of earlier Senate majority leaders. Senator Hugh Scott of Pennsylvania, as minority leader, likewise tends to lead by persuasion and moderation more than by strong direction. In many cases, the number two man, or "party whip," is the person who lines up the votes in specific and practical ways. The current majority whip, Senator Robert Byrd of West Virginia, is an effective operator in this role. The Republican (or minority) Senate whip, Robert Griffin of Michigan, has become more influential since the accession of Gerald Ford, whom Griffin helped to become Republican House leader.

On the House side, Majority Leader Thomas (Tip) O'Neill of Massachusetts, comes closer to the time-honored stereotype of the consummate politician than almost anybody in recent years. Friendly with members on both sides of the partisan aisle, he is an affable and effective backstage operator. But he is not a far-sighted, inspirational leader, and no one equates him with the strongest past holders of the job. Minority Leader John Rhodes of Arizona has assumed greater importance since his predecessor in the job, Gerald Ford, became Vice President and then President.

House Speaker Carl Albert is not one of the alltime heavyweights, but he is coming along. It takes time and perseverance and brains to sway a body as large as the House. He's getting there, but it's a long road, and his progress will depend heavily on how long he is Speaker. The job itself is not the power-house it used to be under Rayburn, Garner, and "Uncle Joe" Cannon, whose despotism led to a systematic reduction of the dictatorial perquisites that Speakers once enjoyed. Albert is a moderate, and thus a balance wheel in the House, and his ability is greatly underrated, partly perhaps because he is small and unprepossessing. He put his influence behind the 1974 reforms, largely because he knew his personal power would be enhanced by reducing the influence of the Ways and Means Committee.

Wilbur Mills was once the most influential man in the country on tax matters. He still has a knowledge of taxes unmatched in Congress, except perhaps by Senator Russell Long of Louisiana, who heads the Senate Finance Committee. But his personal power plummeted after the Tidal Basin affair, and he was ousted from the Ways and Means chairmanship in favor of Oregon Representative Al Ullman (whose economic views are not much different from Mills's).

Some of the more important congressmen are men whose weight within the House is greater than their public reputation: Barber Conable (R-N.Y.), chairman of the House Republican Policy Committee and a member of the Ways and Means Committee; John McFall (D-Cal.), majority whip; Bob Eckhardt (D-Tex.), chairman of the Democratic Study Group; John Anderson (R-Ill.), chairman of the House Republican Conference; the aforementioned Representative Phillip Burton, head of the Democratic Caucus; and George Mahon (D-Tex.), chairman of the powerful Appropriations Committee.

Contrary to popular conception, the caliber of most representatives is high, despite the empty public oratory and the obvious cases of petty bickering. In fact, the TV viewing public was favorably impressed with a group of formerly little-known members of the House Judiciary Committee when they appeared on the screen in 1974 during the televised impeachment inquiry. Most of them came across as honest and industrious lawmakers. That was one of the first times the public had gotten an inside look at a House committee in action, and it improved the House image considerably.

The best-known senators are those who have run for President, but these men often find their effectiveness back in the Senate is diminished by an abortive bid for presidential power. (The influence of former presidential aspirant Edmund Muskie, however, was enhanced in 1974 when the Maine senator was chosen to head the new Budget Committee.) The most powerful members of the Senate besides the party leadership are the Democrats who chair the important committees, like Russell Long (La.) of Finance, John McClellan (Ark.) of Appropriations, Herman Talmadge (Ga.) of Agriculture, John Stennis (Miss.) of Armed Services, William Proxmire (Wis.) of Banking, Housing and Urban Affairs, Henry Jackson (Wash.) of Interior, John Sparkman (Ala.) of Foreign Relations, Warren Magnuson (Wash.) of Commerce, Abraham Ribicoff (Conn.) of Government Operations, James Eastland (Miss.) of Judiciary, Jennings Randolph (W. Va.) of Public Works, and Harrison Williams, Jr. (N.J.) of Labor and Public Welfare.

The length of continuous service in the Senate and the House still determines, generally speaking, who becomes a committee chairman. (For only one committee is the chairman picked by the leadership—the Joint Committee on Atomic Energy.) In the Senate, the retirement or defeat of a chairman automatically elevates to the chairmanship the committee member with the most seniority. The House, however, officially abolished the seniority system a couple of years ago when House Democrats decided that chairmen should be elected by the Caucus at the start of each Congress. The major turnover in chairmanships at the start of the current session in January 1975 was the first use of this antiseniority mechanism.

House committee chairmen used to be virtual dictators over what their committees did or did not do on legislation. Often they could kill a bill single-handedly, even one which a majority wanted. But in 1973 the House adopted a rule stripping chairmen of this exclusive power and giving committee members the right to overrule their leader.

Changes come slowly in the rules of procedure by which the House and Senate operate. Most senior politicians are against significant changes because they see them as threats to their established power. And lobbies for entrenched interests see their own influence destroyed by breaking the status quo. In 1974, a study group chaired by Representative Richard Bolling (D-Mo.), a veteran House reform advocate, proposed a top-to-bottom reorganization of the committee structure. The Bolling plan would have, among other things, eliminated duplicative, fragmented jurisdictions by consolidating like functions in one committee. It also would have balanced committee workloads, which now vary widely from panel to panel. The Bolling plan, while it made a lot of sense, was greeted with anguished outcries from all corners, ranging from committee chairmen, who didn't want to lose any piece of their current jurisdictions, to lobbyists, who didn't want to have to cultivate a whole new committee staff if their pet issue were transferred to another panel.

SEPARATE HOUSES

Since their creation, the House and Senate have enjoyed a love-hate relationship. Nothing rankles the 435 members of the House more than to hear the House called "the lower body." And in debates on the House floor when it is unavoidable to make reference to the Senate, it is always called "the other body."

Across the Capitol, the Senate fosters the impression that because it is a smaller body, it is "elite" and more prestigious. Senators are not reluctant about referring to themselves as "the upper body." And there is at least one undeniable fact that lends credibility to the lofty status of the Senate. While there are many instances of sitting congressmen who have chosen to run for the Senate, no one can recall any sitting senator who has opted to campaign for the House.

The House and Senate operate as if there were no other legislative body. Their committees and subcommittees deal with the same bills with little regard for any action that may have been taken earlier by the other body. Witnesses from government departments and agencies, from trade associations, labor organizations, other lobbies, and from the public must in large measure repeat their testimony and answer many of the same questions in separate hearings before House and Senate committees. Reports on legislation by these committees, with rare exceptions, never allude to what the other body may have done in the way of amendments, etc.

In short, the only point of contact between senators and representatives— aside from chance meetings at the same social functions—is through service on a handful of joint committees, and in "conference committees" on legislation, where differences between House and Senate versions are reconciled.

Sessions of the House of Representatives normally open at noon. The House seldom has Friday sessions or puts important bills on the calendar for Mondays. This permits the operation of what has been dubbed the "Tuesday–Thursday Club," a tradition that allows members to spend long weekends back home in their districts. The Senate, on the other hand, quite often opens its sessions as early as 9:30 A.M. Because it has less strict rules for limiting debate, the Senate normally takes longer than the House to complete floor action on a bill. Saturday sessions of the Senate are not at all uncommon when there is a need to expedite certain legislation.

Since senators and congressmen cannot spend all their time in the Senate and House chambers, both bodies have bell and light signals to alert members to what is happening on the floor and whether their presence is required. These signals are seen or heard in individual offices and in public places, including the Capitol restaurants.

When the House is in session as the "Committee of the Whole," the presence of 100 members constitutes a quorum (as compared to the 218 members required to make up a regular quorum). The House normally sits as the Committee of the Whole when it considers amendments to legislation. At such times the Speaker of the House does not occupy the chair, but relinquishes it to another member. When all amendments have been considered, the committee "rises," and then the members, sitting as the House of Representatives once again and with the Speaker again presiding, vote on final passage. This is how much of the work gets done without burdening *all* members with the necessity for being present for *all* of the detail.

Mail to the members of Congress floods into the Capitol post offices every day. In fact, there is so much that the House zip code (20515) is separate from the Senate's (20510), to help the mail clerks speed the letters and parcels to each member. Each body has its own post office and separate postmaster. The House even has two postmasters, one appointed by the majority party and one by the minority party, proving that on Capitol Hill, at least, the Postal Service has not been removed from politics.

Queries on every conceivable subject come into the members' offices. Businessmen often write about legislation pending in one of the committees.

They also ask for guidance on matters they are involved in before one of the federal agencies. Frequently these are bucked to the member's administrative assistant, who usually has enough skill to deal with them discreetly, without putting his boss on a spot or appearing to apply "political" pressure on the agency. Most members of Congress are careful about this. Swashbuckling tactics can explode in a congressman's face, and they might even land him in Jack Anderson's column. Other letters sometimes praise the member for his stand on a public issue, deride him for it, or inform him of a situation at home that he might want to intercede in—perhaps the need for a new post office, additional flood control project, or highway.

Many constituents are proud of the "personal" reply they have received from their senator or representative. It may very well be a personal and individual reply, but then again it may not. When a great deal of mail is received on a single subject, a staff aide will usually draft a uniform response. From this, punched tapes are prepared and fed into a battery of automatic typewriters which rip off hundreds of individually typed letters in a short time. These letters are put in a "signature machine," which traces the signature from a die of the authentic signature and transfers it to a whole batch of letters at the same time.

THE SETTING

The congressional compound of Capitol Hill is like a miniature city—a collection of buildings spaced on beautifully landscaped grounds, connected by roadways and an underground rail system. Every day some 16,000 people come to work there. Besides having its own post office and zip code, each body of Congress has its own restaurant, bank, barber shop, newsstand, gymnasium, and stationery store. The 155-acre grounds of the Capitol and the surrounding land of the office buildings are patrolled by a thousand-member police force separate from all others in Washington. (Ever since a bomb exploded in a first floor men's room in the Senate wing a few years ago, the Hill policemen inspect all packages and attaché cases brought into the building.)

At the center of the congressional village is the great domed Capitol itself, perched on the edge of an 88-foot plateau once known as Jenkins Hill. In the first seven decades of its existence, the Capitol underwent frequent expansions, achieving its present shape just after the Civil War. The only major change since then—but one not noticeable to most observers—was a 33-foot extension of the East Front (where the presidential inauguration is held every four years) in 1961. There is a group in Congress today, including House and Senate leaders who desire more room for personal hideaway offices, who want to extend the West Front as well. So far, their plans have been beaten back by a consortium of historic preservationists, architectural purists, and congressional pennypinchers.

The Senate does business in the north wing and the House in the south wing, with their respective office buildings located nearby. The Senate used to call its two buildings the old Senate Office Building (or "Old S.O.B.") and the New Senate Office Building (or "New S.O.B."). A couple of years ago the buildings were named after two recently deceased senators (one from each party), Georgia Democrat Richard Russell (for the old building) and Illinois Republican Everett Dirksen (for the new one). The Senate thinks it needs more office space, so it is now planning a major annex for the Dirksen building. House members and many of its committees are housed in the Cannon, Longworth, and Rayburn buildings, all named after former Speakers. Seniority plays a large role in the assignment of office space, with senior members getting the quarters that are near the elevators closest to the Capitol.

The land between the buildings is honeycombed with underground passage-ways, so it is possible to spend a whole day on the Hill—walking from the Rayburn Building to the Capitol to the Dirksen Building, or anywhere else—without going out into the weather. For those in a hurry (or too lazy to walk), there are subway cars running between the Capitol and every other building except Cannon and Longworth. Anyone can ride the subways at no cost, but at times, when bells call the lawmakers to the House and Senate floors, the front sections of the cars are reserved for senators and representa-tives alone. The trip takes fifty-two seconds between Dirksen and the Capitol, about the same from Rayburn, and only forty-one seconds from the closer Russell Building.

The rest of the federal enclave on Capitol Hill is taken up by the white marble building of the Supreme Court (which until 1935 was housed in a small chamber in the Senate wing of the Capitol) and three buildings of the Library of Congress (whose Congressional Research Service is a boon to representatives and senators for everything from speechwriting to drafting legislation). The newest addition to the Hill is the Library of Congress' Madison Library, a building that the House leadership coveted for its own use and considered expropriating.

Congress' largess with federal subsidies applies especially to its own enter-prises on Capitol Hill. Goods and services purchased on the Hill—everything from a haircut to a meal in the House or Senate restaurant—cost less than "on the outside," and losses are subsidized with federal revenue. Food, by the way, is very good on the Hill. Whenever the restaurant is open, the Senate's savory bean soup is on the menu (which includes a recipe for those who want to try it at home). You can buy a beer on the House side of the Hill, but not in the Senate restaurants.

A NEW ERA FOR CONGRESS?

Many people around Washington, including members of Congress, have a hard time deciding just what role Congress should play and how much leader-ship it should exercise in making federal policy. In the early Sixties, it was fashionable among liberal political scientists to advocate congressional sub-servience to a strong chief executive. The President, after all, was considered the spokesman for All the People, while Congress was thought to be more easily swayed by nasty special interests. Then the intellectual establishment recoiled in horror at the excesses of President Johnson's crusade in Southeast Asia and President Nixon's imperious domination of domestic policy. It didn't take long for the liberal theorists to change their tune and call for a return to the days of more balanced power between Capitol Hill and 1600 Pennsyl-vania Avenue.

For the time being, the scales are moving more closely into balance. The impact of the 1974 House reforms in this balancing act is difficult to assess right now. One must keep in mind that the "reforms" of one period become the despised status quo of the next, requiring additional "reforms" to correct.

In 1910, House members revolted against the dictatorial ways of Speaker Cannon, and they vested tremendous powers in the hands of the committee chairmen. But six decades later, the power of the chairmen was deemed to have grown to dangerous proportions, so another series of "reforms" swept through the Democratic Caucus. One beneficiary of this reform wave is the Speaker, but the principal beneficiaries are the hundreds of House members who are not part of the leadership. The 1974 reforms have further diffused the already fragmented power of the House. It remains to be seen whether the reassertion of Congress' role will be helped or hindered by these changes. The effect will probably be much less miraculous than first expected. The reforms of December 1974 were chronicled in the press as a "hurricane in the House." But Congress has an inertia that resists reform, a fact that "Uncle Joe" Cannon expressed with the terse aphorism, "Rain don't always follow the thunder."

The Ninety-third Congress accomplished a lot of important things. But its legacy of unfinished business is a staggering challenge to the current crop of representatives and senators. The Ninety-third fought over—but didn't resolve—questions of tax revision, reform of the federal criminal code, national health insurance, guidelines for ecologically sound land use, a proposed Consumer Protection Agency, easier registration for federal elections, and a comprehensive energy policy. Some of this legislation passed one chamber but not the other, and some didn't get acted upon by either. All of these bills have awesome lobbies lined up for and against them.

Not until the high-spirited Ninety-fourth Congress has cut its teeth on these tough issues—and the problems of inflation and recession—will Washington be able to proclaim, or put to rest, the notion of a new era for the legislative branch.

12 THE PRACTICE OF POLITICS

Politics is what Washington exists for. Government, yes, but politics is the practical art of making policy through consensus, and the making and implementing of policy is what government is all about.

Since Washington is the political center of the nation, a politician arriving here has hit the big time, even though he may be starting on the bottom rung of a new and taller ladder. Whether he is a new congressman, senator or Cabinet member, he'd better know his stuff (or learn it fast), because suddenly he will be plunged into the explosive issues that seemed so easy to settle when he was back home. But the issues are rarely as simple as he once saw them, and Washington is strewn with the bodies of politicians who didn't make the grade.

It's a tough town.

Popular governors, like Henry Bellmon of Oklahoma, arrive in the capital on the crest of a Senate victory, but after the initial round of congratulatory parties, they find they are now small fish in a big pond. Famous athletes, after winning elections easily, are shunted onto obscure congressional committees and seldom heard from again. Great lawyers from back home, like former Senator Sam Ervin of North Carolina, come to Washington and spend years talking profundities to themselves (earning the respect of their Senate colleagues but hardly national fame) until someone else's wrongdoing fortuitously thrusts them onto the center stage of a televised congressional investigation. People bearing illustrious political names (like Senators Robert Taft, Jr., and Adlai Stevenson III, both thoughtful men with styles different from their famous fathers) discover they have no particular advantage over other newcomers. Even a renowned author like Clare Boothe Luce could get lost in the supercharged political atmosphere of Washington.

As a matter of fact, Washington is a graveyard of political ambition for *most* of the men and women who are sent here. Take George Romney, a self-made man who rose to the top of the auto industry and was elected governor of Michigan three times, in a series of campaigns based on old-fashioned Mormon honesty, frugality, and self-reliance. A few gaffes helped him lose the GOP nomination for President in 1968, but the victorious Richard Nixon appointed him Secretary of Housing and Urban Development, presumably because that department needed someone with missionary fervor to get it stirring. But the nation's policies in housing and urban affairs were more than even a Mormon missionary could straighten out, so Romney quit and left Washington.

But if Washington is the end of the line for most politicians, it is a giant springboard for the hardy few. Decades ago, a governorship was considered the best stepping-stone to the Presidency, but today it is the Senate or House in which a politician can drum up national recognition. Presidents Ford, Nixon, Johnson, Kennedy, and Truman all achieved their first fame through congressional service.

The main thing that distinguishes "politics" from "government" is the electoral process, which requires the politician to get a vote of confidence from a constituency before he can come to Washington to make policy. Every public official is "in government," but very few are "politicians." The only real politicians are the President, Vice President, and 535 members of Congress, since they are the only ones who must be concerned with the wishes of a constituency. But some nonelected officials, especially high-level presidential appointees, must practice the art of politics, too, because their wagons are hitched to the stars of politicians. If these bureaucrats care about their pet programs (and care about getting reappointed), they will help sell the voters on the value of the President's programs when the next election rolls around.

In essence, politics in Washington is built on the knack of doing what the homefolks want. Or even better, doing what they will want when they finally make up their minds. A first-rate politician knows his constituents so well that he can anticipate their wishes on most topics. The legislative performance of a member of Congress is supposed to reflect the views of the majority of his constituency, and usually does. Some liberals seem to forget this when they curse Senator James Eastland of Mississippi or Senator James Allen of Alabama for being such "damned conservatives." Some conservatives likewise forget it when they condemn Senators Kennedy and Brooke of Massachusetts for being "so damned liberal"—overlooking, perhaps, the fact that a majority of Massachusetts voters selected George McGovern for President in 1972. If an elected official decides to oppose his constituents' wishes on a hot issue, he'd better be a persuasive proponent of his position when he gets home.

Getting elected and reelected to a federal office requires a difficult blend of many factors, including shrewdness, stamina, personal charm, knowledge of the electorate's hopes and fears and economic interests, and rapport with local political leaders. Getting elected also requires money, in order to communicate the candidate's name, image, and (sometimes) policies to a constituency ranging from 500,000 (for a congressional district) to a few million (for a medium-sized state) to tens of millions (the national presidential electorate). Money by itself cannot buy the voters' approval, but it can buy their recognition of the candidate, and recognition is the first crucial step.

POWERFUL MONEY

The pervasive importance of money in national politics is nothing new, but the ante kept getting raised until, over the past couple of years, laws were passed to keep spending within reasonable bounds and make it more visible to the public.

More than fifty years ago—in April of 1924—the *Kiplinger Washington Letter* sent its readers the following note on campaign financing in the forthcoming presidential election: "Campaign contributions are being solicited. You will be asked soon by Republicans or Democrats. Numbers of business houses are referring to us letters and telegrams representing first steps in solicitation campaign. Republicans are using strong-arm tactics, setting quotas for each city and state, even quotas for individuals and business firms, forcing subscriptions by polite threats, mentioning the possibility of unfavorable future action on tariff and other matters."

By the time of the New Deal days of the late Thirties, fund-raising amounts had soared above their previous levels, even after the dampening effect of the depression years. The individual donations made in anticipation of diplomatic appointments, however, look quite modest compared with today's figures. The Democrats got $15,000 from Robert W. Bingham, who was later named ambassador to the Court of St. James in London, traditionally the most prestigious overseas post. By contrast, W. Clement Stone, the Chicago insurance magnate, contributed $2 million to the 1972 Nixon campaign fund, for which he received no appointment at all, let alone the ambassadorship to England that he reportedly wanted. In 1936 Joseph E. Davies (then married to Marjorie Merriweather Post) gave $17,500 and was named ambassador to the Soviet Union; in 1972 Washington businessman Kingdon Gould gave $100,000 and got an ambassadorship to the Netherlands. In 1936 a Washington newspaper correspondent named Leo Sack contributed $2,500 to the Democrats and received an appointment to Costa Rica; in 1972 Florenz Ourisman, a Washington real estate investor who desired an ambassadorship, chipped in $150,000 to the GOP coffers and didn't get any position at all.

Throughout American political history, big contributions—especially from business and labor groups—have rarely been made except in the expectation of (or as a reward for) favorable treatment in return. During the 1972 campaign the government announced a higher price support for milk shortly after the dairy industry pledged $500,000 to the Nixon reelection chest (and lesser amounts to key congressional Democrats, too). But this was nothing new. During the New Deal, the Roosevelt administration reduced tariffs on cigarette paper, saving the cigarette companies about $500,000 a year, and then cut the duty on Turkish tobacco (used for blending with American tobaccos), saving the companies another $2 million a year. Soon thereafter, executives of the R. J. Reynolds Tobacco Company "loaned" the Democrats $300,000, in addition to their regular contributions. More recently, there was the $100,000 gift from the Seafarers International Union to the Humphrey presidential campaign in 1968, made following the Justice Department's refusal to extradite to Canada a former official of the union who was charged with a Canadian crime.

During the Sixties, the rise of Madison Avenue campaigning methods—television, direct mail advertising, the entire "media blitz"—pushed the cost of politics through the roof. A few politicians made it to Washington without spending vast sums of money on advertising, like Lawton Chiles, who won a Senate seat by traversing the state of Florida on foot, shaking hands and chatting en route. (Success breeds imitation, however; today even this is a slick tactic of many campaigns, becoming almost a cliché.) But winning with a low-budget campaign is the exception, not the rule. The high cost of politics has given a special edge to independently wealthy candidates. While most candidates had to sell their souls for outside contributions, the wealthy ones merely sold some stock (or real estate, or any other liquid asset). They didn't always win, though. Witness the losing efforts of parking mogul Howard Metzenbaum in Ohio, food magnate Norton Simon in California, and New York's Representative Richard Ottinger, the congressman who spent nearly $4 million of his family's plywood fortune on a losing bid for a Senate seat.

In politics at all levels, especially national, the candidates and parties that need the money least—the incumbents—have the easiest time raising it, since contributors want to keep in the good graces of the winning team. After occupying the White House through two consecutive administrations, the GOP in 1928 elected Herbert Hoover and finished the campaign with a surplus in the party treasury. Roosevelt's campaign had excess cash after winning in 1936, 1940, and 1944. The prospects of Truman's winning in 1948 were so bad that Thomas Dewey had no trouble raising money, and Truman left the Democrats in a deep financial hole when he won. Adlai Stevenson ran deficit campaigns twice against Dwight Eisenhower. Incumbent Lyndon Johnson raised money with ease in 1964, but the Humphrey presidential bid in 1968 (plus debts of Robert F. Kennedy, which the Democrats assumed after his assassination) left the Democratic National Committee in debt to the tune of $9 million. But the $30 million campaign of George McGovern in 1972, while ending in one of the worst routs in history, did not swell the DNC debt at all. Another aberration in the pattern of deficit campaign spending was Senator Barry Goldwater's 1964 race; he didn't spend all the money raised in his behalf, and some of it was still available four years later for Richard Nixon's campaign. In most deficit campaigns, the party tries first to pay off all its "real" debts, like printing, television ads, phone bills, and staff salaries. Most of the remaining debt is usually in the form of "loans" made to the party by its biggest "fat cats." Many of these party loyalists can be convinced to forgive their debtors by converting the loans into donations. (But the IRS, understandably, doesn't allow this kind of defaulted loan to be written off like a conventional "bad debt.")

In the 1972 presidential election, the political spending spiral reached an all-time peak—probably a historic per capita peak never to be attained again. The Finance Committee to Reelect the President reported it raised a grand total of $60,200,000. The Democrats raised and spent less than half that amount on the McGovern campaign, but adding in all the money spent on House and Senate races by both parties, the nation was treated to its first $100 million election year. When the newspapers mentioned "big contributors" that year, they were referring to gifts in the high six-figure range. Five-figure amounts seemed old hat, and the Committee to Reelect the President raked in some 140 donations of $50,000 and above, and the Democrats convinced 45 people to part with similar amounts for the desperate campaign of Senator McGovern.

A NEW WAY

Of course, the election of 1972 will not be remembered primarily for the sheer amounts of money involved, but for the scandals that surrounded the solicitation of that money from questionable sources, and the spending of it on activities that ranged from unethical to illegal. It was the sins of Watergate, more than the soaring costs, that finally mobilized the citizenry to demand a change—a drastic overhauling of the traditional way of financing federal campaigns.

The reform movement had been slowly gathering steam for several years before Watergate. Congress took the first big step in 1971, when it approved a plan under which a federal fund for presidential candidates would be stocked with $1 allocations from every taxpayer who simply checked a box on his income tax form. To encourage small contributions, Congress allowed each taxpayer to take an itemized deduction for political gifts up to $100, with married couples allowed to deduct up to $200 (or to take a tax credit of up to $25 or $50, respectively). Other new legislation required the public disclosure of all donations of more than $100, set spending ceilings on the major forms of political advertising, and limited the contributions of a candidate and his family to his own campaign ($50,000 for the Presidency, $35,000 for the Senate, $25,000 for the House).

All of these reforms went into effect before Watergate, except the federal check-off fund, which—for obvious reasons of incumbency—the Republicans insisted be postponed until after the 1972 election. The disclosure measures made the financing of the 1972 election the most visible in history—after Common Cause won a court order requiring the reporting of millions of dollars that the Committee to Reelect raced to collect before the new rules became law.

But the 1971 reform left a gaping hole in the solution to soaring campaign costs: it put no ceiling on an individual's or political organization's contributions. Congress finally plugged that hole in 1974 with a bill that one of its chief sponsors, Representative Bill Frenzel (R-Minn.), hailed as "the greatest change in our political lifetime." Under the provisions of the new law, which will be used first in the 1976 election, an individual may donate to a congressional candidate no more than $1,000 per election (or a maximum of $3,000 for a candidate who competes in a primary, a runoff, and the general election). Organizations such as the "political action committees" of trade associations and labor unions may donate no more than $5,000 to a congressional candidate in each election. Individuals and organizations are limited to $1,000 and $5,000 donations, respectively, to each candidate for President. To put an end to six-figure giving by political fat cats, Congress set an overall limit of $25,000 on the donations that one individual may make to all federal candidates and all political action organizations in one calendar year. The limits on a candidate's contribution to his own campaign are the same as in the 1971 law. In addition to outside financing, each candidate for the Senate could receive up to $20,000 (House candidates, up to $10,000) from both the state and national campaign committees of his party. (Senatorial candidates in large states could receive even more than the $20,000, based upon a formula of $.02 for every state resident of voting age.)

The new law intends that there will be no more $60 million presidential campaigns. Each presidential candidate will be allowed to spend in a single primary an amount pegged to the voting population of the state—a sum ranging from about $200,000 for the New Hampshire primary to some $2 million in a state the size of New York. For the presidential general election, no candidate may spend more than $20 million (a large portion of which, in the case of a major party candidate, will probably come from the federal check-off fund). A minor party candidate can receive from the fund an amount proportional to his party's performance in past elections (providing it got more than 5 percent of the vote). Total spending limits have been placed, too, on House and Senate races. A House candidate may spend no more than $70,000 in a primary and an additional $70,000 in the general election. A

Senate candidate may spend an amount based on the voting population in his state, an amount ranging from $150,000 in a small state to about $1.7 million in California.

The proponents of campaign spending reform got a lot more out of Congress than they had expected, thanks to Watergate. About the only provision that wasn't included was federal funding of House and Senate elections, rejected by Congress because it would have made it easier for challengers back home to knock off incumbents. To enforce the new law, Congress created a six-member commission—two appointed by the President, two by the House, and two by the Senate—empowered to make audits, conduct investigations, and file civil suits against violators. To close one of the traditional forms of backdoor campaign funding—inflated honorariums for convention speeches and magazine articles—the new law specifies that no federal official may receive more than $1,000 per speech or article, and no more than $15,000 in a single year.

No one is sure, of course, just what effect the 1974 law will have on cleaning up the polluted electoral process. Loopholes have a way of appearing magically in even the tightest-appearing laws, once they are implemented. Some observers are concerned that business groups and unions might set up several dummy "organizations," each of which will be allowed to donate $5,000 to a federal candidate. This possibility looms as a danger unless the definition of a bona fide organization is made more explicit by Congress or a court ruling. But even if this loophole is not plugged, the new ceilings on overall spending will tend to prevent one candidate from overpowering another with funds from special-interest groups.

Passage of the 1974 spending law was by no means the last word in the intricate debate over the funding of federal elections. On January 2, 1975, the unlikely duo of liberal Democrat Eugene McCarthy and Conservative–Republican Senator James L. Buckley of New York filed suit against the new law. They charged that it is an unconstitutional abridgment of the right of free speech. Their challenge will probably go all the way to the Supreme Court, which in past cases has ruled that political advertising is tantamount to speech and therefore protected by the First Amendment. If the High Court accepts the case, a five-man majority could conceivably return the nation's political finance system to the pre-Watergate status quo.

COMMITTEES GALORE

The practical art of politics—electing and reelecting the candidates of one's choice—is an everyday occupation, year in and year out, of the Washington-based professional staffs of the Republican and Democratic parties. The role of the two national committees will not be altered much by the campaign finance reforms, because there has always been more to their responsibility than tapping rich people for giant donations. The national committees, at times, are propaganda factories. They collect, digest, and disseminate statistical information to local party officials on elections, party registrations, and the party's record of achievement in Washington. They act as jeering sections against each other. They each run annual fund-raising dinners, where, for a contribution of up to $1,000, party loyalists get a meal of steak, baked potato, peas and carrots, and ice cream, plus a lot of windy speeches and maybe some professional entertainment. Their biggest job is the organizing of the quadrennial nominating conventions. The fund-raising efforts of both national committees are continuous operations, dependent largely on small contributions solicited through direct mail advertising. The small gifts have a way of adding up to big money. In 1973, for example, the GOP national committee pulled in about $4 million in amounts of $100 and less, cultivating a computerized mailing list of some 800,000 names.

Practically everyone knows that in 1972 the Democratic headquarters was housed in the Watergate office building, and that some Republican zealots busted into it, starting the biggest political stink in modern times. Long before the break-in, Larry O'Brien, who was Democratic national chairman longer than anyone in recent years, used to swear he was going to move the committee out of the Watergate because the place was so expensive and the party needed to economize. But he never got around to doing it. It wasn't until after the scandal broke that the Democrats moved to less conspicuous, if no less plush, quarters in the Air Line Pilots Association building, at 1625 Massachusetts Avenue. The staff there numbers 85 to 100 people. The current national chairman is Robert S. Strauss, who as national treasurer did an amazing job of reducing the party's debt. He was elevated to the top spot when the moderate Democrats regained control of the party after Senator McGovern's defeat and the resignation of the senator's pick for the chairmanship, Jean Westwood.

The Democratic National Committee is much more "activist" than its GOP counterpart, frequently looking for ways to broaden grass-roots participation in its decisionmaking. These attempts at democracy have included regional conventions for drafting a new party charter and reform of anachronistic procedures at the national convention. (The innovations, it should be noted, are not generally popular with the old-guard Democratic regulars—like labor leaders and big-city machine pols—and have occasionally aggravated the party's longstanding problem of divisiveness.) Because of their shortage of cash in recent years, the Democrats have had to be more imaginative than the GOP in raising money. Their most successful trick has been to stage evening telethons (televised pleas for money), featuring the donated services of famous entertainers.

The Republican National Committee is located in its own small building at 310 First Street S.E., about three blocks from the Capitol and two blocks from the Cannon House Office Building. It's part of a little enclave of Republicanism known as the "Eisenhower Center," and is next to the Federal-style building that houses the Capitol Hill Club, a social club for Republican members of Congress. There are about 100 people working at the committee in nonelection years, but the ranks swell by as many as 200 additional paid and volunteer workers when the campaigns are under way. The GOP National Committee is currently headed by its first woman chairman, Mary Louise Smith of Iowa.

Each national committee focuses primarily on winning the White House, and when it succeeds, the new President becomes the symbolic leader of the party. This doesn't necessarily mean that all Presidents maintain good rapport with the national committee leadership of their parties. Lyndon Johnson had nothing but contempt for Democratic headquarters, preferring to go it alone. And President Nixon short-circuited his party's structure by setting up his own Committee to Reelect the President. Some people maintain Watergate would never have happened if his 1972 campaign had been handled by the GOP National Committee.

Each party has two congressional campaign committees (one for the House and one for the Senate) that are separate from the national committees, with independent fund-raising apparatuses. The amount of money that they can pour into a congressional race is now limited by law, but the allowable amounts could still be crucial in close contests. The committees try to allocate their funds to incumbents and challengers according to need, with the ultimate objective being winning as many new congressional seats as possible. Since a congressional campaign committee is often vying for the dollars of the same party stalwarts being courted by the national committees, their roles are sometimes more competitive than complementary.

When Lyndon Johnson was Senate majority leader, he took a personal interest in the dispersal of the congressional campaign funds. When he extended a helping hand to distressed Democratic senators facing reelection and "new boys" running for the first time, it wasn't purely altruism or party loyalty. It was practical politics. He wanted to make sure his party kept control of the Senate, and he also wanted the winning senators to know *how* they got their aid from Washington, and who sent it to them. They were supposed to remember this when he asked for their votes on a close issue in the Senate. The current majority leader, Mike Mansfield of Montana, has a different approach. He declines to get involved in the allocation of campaign funds, a job he leaves to the Senate members and staff of the Senatorial Campaign Committee.

Also headquartered around Washington are associations representing various subgroups and factions of the major parties. In the same building as the GOP National Committee, for example, is located the headquarters of the Young Republican National Federation, a "young" Republican being someone under forty years old. There is a corresponding group called Young Democrats, but it doesn't do much, perhaps because younger people tend to have a more important role in the regular Democratic party structure than they do in the Republican party. On the right fringe of the GOP is the very independent organization called Young Americans for Freedom, which has its own Washington office. On the other wing, also represented by a small Washington staff, is the Ripon Society, an association of moderate-to-liberal young Republicans founded in 1962 in Cambridge, Massachusetts, where it is still headquartered. Once labeled "little juvenile delinquents" by former Attorney General John Mitchell, this respected group opposed the Goldwater candidacy and was lukewarm on the Nixon-Agnew ticket. Ripon was generally supportive of the Nixon administration's policies, but not the President's opposition to busing, promotion of the ABM system, and nomination of G. Harrold Carswell to the Supreme Court.

On Capitol Hill, the Democratic and Republican parties are hardly homogeneous. Southern Democrats often have more in common ideologically with midwestern Republicans than with some of their own party colleagues, and the same is true of liberal Republicans and Democrats from the Northeast. So there are informal blocs of politicians on both sides of Capitol Hill, and in the much larger House, several semiformal organizations lend a certain cohesiveness to the blocs. The most important of these is the Democratic Study Group, with a membership of about 140 House liberals. Organized in 1959, the DSG has its own professional staff, which researches the issues and pre-pares fact sheets on current bills. A much smaller, more casual organization, is the Wednesday Group of liberal Republican House members. Occasionally the Wednesday Group of congressmen take a more or less unified stand on a particular issue, such as their call a few years ago for improved relations with Cuba. The newest intra-House organization is the steadily growing Black Caucus, an informal union of the Negro representatives. They often take common positions, hold joint press conferences, and help each other and black challengers in campaigns (and even visit the White House together, as they did at the start of Gerald Ford's term in office, when they tried to bury the hatchet after several years of ill will from—and toward—Richard Nixon).

Besides the strictly partisan political organizations, there are numerous Washington-based groups that are enmeshed in the political process as observers, educators, reformers, and promoters of the candidacy of particular kinds of politicians. The venerable League of Women Voters is a nonpartisan fountain of information about the electoral process, issues, and the candidates themselves. (Many incumbents consider the League's lengthy questionnaires about their positions to be a pain in the neck, but the information is a boon to voters.) John Gardner's Common Cause and Ralph Nader's Public Citizen, Inc., are active in procedural reform of Congress, and Nader's outfit also issues reports on particular members of Congress, supposedly unbiased, but usually more complimentary to liberals than conservatives. A nonprofit organization called the Citizens' Research Foundation, based in Princeton, New Jersey, and headed by Herbert E. Alexander, runs the National Infor-mation Center on Political Finance, located in Washington. The center keeps an up-to-the-minute tally on political donations by individuals and lobbies, and it circulates this information in easily digestible form to reporters and interested citizens all over the nation.

One of the most important, but publicly little-known, political pressure groups is the National Committee for an Effective Congress, founded in 1948. Based in New York City (and headed by Russell Hemenway, who commutes frequently to Washington), the NCEC raises money for liberals, especially those who are important to promoting a "liberal" foreign policy—disarma-ment, international cooperation, free trade, etc. In 1970 it raised more than $800,000 from its supporters across the country and distributed the money to liberal senators (and challengers) in very tight contests. In 1974, besides distributing money, NCEC deployed fifteen campaign consultants (under the supervision of David Brunell, a former aide to Representative Don Riegle of Michigan) to make sure its donations were being spent most effectively. As a lobby, it was a potent force behind the reform of campaign financing.

THE PROFESSIONALS

The increasing sophistication of political campaigning—especially the reli-ance on television—has given rise to an army of electoral technicians: profes-sional campaign managers, public opinion analysts (the fancy phrase for "pollsters"), filmmakers, direct mail advertising experts, and media con-sultants. For a fee, these specialists will do everything from selecting the candidate's wardrobe to writing his policy position papers. While some people consider the consultants' slick methods (like those described in Joe Mc-Ginniss's *The Selling of the President*) no more respectable than snake-oil huckstering, their stature in political circles is such that they even have their own professional group, the American Association of Political Consultants. Most consultants specialize in the candidates of one party or the other, or at least liberals or conservatives.

Since the consultants are a peripatetic lot, it doesn't matter much where they are based. But Washington offers better contacts than any other city, so many of the top people are headquartered here. Matt Reese started out as John Kennedy's campaign director in West Virginia in 1960, and later was a key man at the Democratic National Committee before going into consulting. Joseph Napolitan helped put Marvin Mandel and Milton Shapp into the governor's mansions of Maryland and Pennsylvania, but was on the losing side with 1968 presidential candidate Hubert H. Humphrey and Massachusetts gubernatorial candidate Kevin White. Washington-based filmmaker Charles Guggenheim, one of the best in the business, has had winners in Senators Edward M. Kennedy (D-Mass.) and Philip Hart (D-Mich.), but losing causes in George McGovern's presidential bid and the Senate races of Joe Duffey (Connecticut), Howard Metzenbaum (Ohio), and Albert Gore (the senator from Tennessee who lost to William Brock). Robert D. Squier, considered one of the best media consultants, couldn't do the trick for presidential aspirant Senator Edmund Muskie (D-Me.) or New York gubernatorial candidate Howard Samuels. For moderate-to-liberal Republican candidates, the leading Washington consultant is John Deardourff, of Bailey, Deardourff and Eyre, who has worked for the likes of Senators Charles Percy (R-Ill.) and Edward W. Brooke (R-Mass.), but couldn't save the inept candidacy of New Jersey senatorial hopeful Nelson Gross. Douglas Bailey (of the same firm) helped coordinate the campaign for state ratification of the feminist Equal Rights Amendment to the Constitution, under contract to the National Federation of Business and Professional Women's Clubs.

Other Washington campaign specialists include pollsters Peter D. Hart and John F. Kraft, consultant Mark Shields, and direct mail advertising advisers Guy Yolton and Richard A. Viguerie. Viguerie's computerized lists of conservative contributors have churned out millions of pieces of fund-raising mail for GOP candidates and a few Democrats, especially Alabama Governor George Wallace. Yolton's firm, which describes itself as "politically ecumenical," has helped raise money for both parties' national committees (at different times) and individual candidates ranging from conservative Republican to liberal Democrat. It also helped set up Common Cause's highly successful direct mail fund-raising apparatus. Though they are not consultants per se, demographic analysts Richard M. Scammon and Ben Wattenberg made a major impact on campaign substance and style with their 1970 book *The Real Majority,* as well as Scammon's *America Votes* series and Wattenberg's *The Real America.* Scammon, a former director of the Census Bureau, is head of the Elections Research Center, and Wattenberg is a recurrent political adviser (especially to Senator Henry "Scoop" Jackson, D-Wash.).

A number of the leading campaign technicians have their offices in other cities. One of the best pollsters is Robert M. Teeter of the Detroit-based Market Opinion Research Company. The New York area is home to poll-takers Oliver Quayle III, Louis Harris, Daniel Yankelovich, and the Roper Organization. (The Gallup firm, headquartered in Princeton, New Jersey, doesn't do privately commissioned polls for candidates, but takes the nation's pulse with polls for public consumption, and Opinion Research Corporation also measures attitudes on issues.) If a poll commissioned by a candidate shows him to be leading, you can bet it will be "leaked" to the public via a cooperative reporter. If it shows the candidate trailing, it will be hushed up and used in-house for exhorting the campaign staff to try even harder and perhaps for overhauling the campaign style.

New York City is also the headquarters of such prominent campaign consultants as conservative strategist F. Clifton White; Harry Treleaven, who works for moderate-to-conservative Republicans; David Garth, one of the top consultants to liberal Democratic Senate candidates; Roger Ailes, who concentrates on moderate Republicans (and like Treleaven, contributed to Richard Nixon's 1968 victory); direct mail specialist Walter Weintz, who is credited with pioneering the mass-mail solicitation concept during Senator Robert Taft's 1950 reelection bid; and Papert, Koenig, and Lois, Inc., an ad firm that handles liberals of both parties. Anne Wexler has an impressive reputation for Democratic political organizing in Connecticut. Other campaign craftsmen are scattered around the country, like Patrick Caddell and John Marttila in Boston; Tom Collins of the New York office of Rapp, Collins, Stone and Adler; Los Angeles-based partners Herbert M. Baus and William B. Ross, who engineered the successful California races of Richard Nixon in 1960 (primary and general election) and Senator Barry Goldwater's primary in 1964; and Alabama-based direct mail specialist Morris Dees, who raised $15 million for McGovern in 1972 and who signed on as a consultant in 1974 to Georgia Governor Jimmy Carter and Washington Senator Henry Jackson, both Democratic presidential hopefuls.

All the top consultants have mixed won-lost records. Their reputations are based on the spectacular wins (especially upsets), and people tend to forget the losses. The more sensible of them are humble about their trade. They acknowledge the difficulty—given the myriad factors that go into a success or failure—of pinning credit or blame on a particular television spot ad or clever slogan or any other campaign tactic. Despite the fact that political consultants became fat and happy on the soaring campaign costs of the Sixties (especially television budgets), many of them were personally concerned that the whole thing was getting out of hand. The American Association of Political Consultants generally supported the crusade for reform of the campaign spending laws. The new finance law, rather than trimming the consultant's sails, might actually increase the demand for his services. Candidates must now be even more careful that each campaign dollar is spent as effectively as possible. If television spots are shown less frequently, each showing must have greater impact.

Dirty tactics have been a part of American campaigning since the creation of the Republic. They still are, and can be even more devastating today when executed with all the skill Madison Avenue can muster. In recent years, television ads for Republican candidates have accused other candidates of everything from fostering crime in the streets to helping kill American GIs in Vietnam by encouraging trade with Communist countries (a charge used against Senator Vance Hartke, D-Ind., in a 1970 challenge by then Representative Richard Roudebush, now head of the Veterans Administration). The Democrats' media consultants have come up with their own share of demagogic appeals. In 1964 there was an infamous anti-Goldwater ad that featured the mushroom cloud of a nuclear explosion. And in 1968, Joseph Napolitan conceived a commercial that consisted only of the word "Agnew" on the television screen, with a sound track of hilarious laughter.

As a mild deterrent to dirty tactics, there exists in Washington an organization called the Fair Campaign Practices Committee, which acts as a clearinghouse for complaints about unfair tactics and asks all candidates to adhere to its Fair Campaign Code (a guide to decent campaigning that no one could possibly take issue with). The committee asks each side in a dispute for information about the charge, but does not make any ruling itself. If both parties agree to an outside decision, the complaint is turned over to the American Arbitration Association. The whole matter is dropped if either party refuses to arbitrate. Occasionally, the publicity generated by a complaint to the committee—or more importantly, a candidate's refusal of adjudication—has mattered in a close race.

A TOUGH BUSINESS

Politics is like no other profession in the world. In no other line of work must a successful practitioner subject himself, so continuously, to the scrutiny of the people he serves, needing their express approval before he can return to his job. In no other occupation is a star performer so constantly vulnerable to a challenge that could mean the loss of his job. Of course, politics offers particular safeguards for the incumbent, as evidenced by the return to Washington every two years of a vast majority of those congressmen who seek reelection.

But things can happen that are beyond the politician's control (or within his control, if he were not too smug to recognize the impending danger). Just ask those veteran Republican congressmen who were knocked off in the post-Watergate Democratic landslide of 1974. Just ask former Senator J. William Fulbright (D-Ark.), a powerful Washington figure who didn't keep his fences mended back home, and who didn't take the primary challenge of Governor Dale Bumpers seriously enough until it was too late. Or ask Representative Wilbur Mills (D-Ark.), once one of the most influential men in the capital. He could tell you that a smelly scandal in one's "private life," if it ever becomes public, can set in motion a chain of events that undoes the accomplishments of a distinguished career.

The political arena in the capital is not for people with thin skins. As we said, Washington is a tough place, and politics is the toughest game in town.

13 COURTS AND JUSTICE

At 10 A.M. on the first Monday in October, inside a white, neo-Greek temple at 1 First Street N.E., a packed courtroom audience rises to its feet as nine black-robed men take their seats behind a long, high bench. Shouting "Oyez! Oyez! Oyez!" the crier announces the start of another term of the U.S. Supreme Court, finishing his spiel with "God save the United States and this Honorable Court!" (The Court may have banned prayer in the schools, but it still calls for divine guidance in its own work.)

Over the following nine months, these nine justices will attempt to dispose of some 5,000 legal disputes, all of them involving federal statutes or matters relating to the Constitution. About 150 of the most complicated and novel cases will be subject to full oral arguments and decided with formal, written rulings. A handful of these precedent-setting decisions—the so-called landmark decisions—will set in motion a series of events that will change the very fabric of the nation.

The Supreme Court is America's single most powerful public institution. Its membership, of course, is determined by the President and Congress, who can and do influence the shape of future decisions through the nomination and confirmation of justices. But once assembled, the Court has power over the executive and legislative branches far surpassing their influence over the judiciary. The Court can order the President to do things he doesn't want to do, as was made perfectly (and painfully) clear to President Nixon in the Watergate tape case. The Court can void federal (as well as state and local) laws, and Congress' only recourse is modifying the law or, in very rare cases, passing a Constitutional amendment, which would require state ratification. Even Congress' own internal affairs are not exempt from Supreme Court review, demonstrated by the historic 1969 ruling that the House could not legally expel Representative Adam Clayton Powell, Jr. (D-N.Y.), or any other representative who meets the constitutional requirements of citizenship, age, and residency. But the Court can also boost the powers of its sister branches of government, as it did when it gave a very broad interpretation to the President's right to confer criminal pardons in just about any manner that he sees fit. (The ruling upheld President Ford's unique pardoning of Richard Nixon, which was granted even before any Watergate charges had been brought against the former President.)

The Supreme Court, ultimate arbiter though it is, is just the tip of the enormous iceberg of government bodies that deal daily with federal laws—making them, enforcing them, apprehending violators, and trying cases. The federal "crime and justice" establishment is rooted in all three branches, whose responsibilities are interlocking and—ideally—supportive of the others.

The Justice Department is the government's chief enforcer of federal laws—civil and criminal—in areas ranging from civil rights and organized crime to taxes and antitrust. The Justice Department is crucial to the implementation of Congress' laws and the federal judiciary's decisions. All the bold laws and bold rulings would not amount to anything if they were not backed up by a vigorous and tenacious enforcement effort at Justice. The department is a part of the President's executive team, so it's a "political" organization. The top people there are selected by the President to reflect his ideology. If the President tells the Attorney General to increase—or, conversely, soft-pedal—investigations and suits in a particular area, it will probably be done. Sometimes the White House "suggestions" are more explicit, as during the frequent communication between Nixon aides and the antitrust division in the ITT merger case. Lest anyone forget, the President is the Attorney General's boss. When Richard Nixon told Elliot Richardson, and then William Ruckelshaus, to fire Watergate Special Prosecutor Archibald Cox, their refusal to do so left them almost no alternative but resignation. The men who have held the post of Attorney General in recent years have tended to be successful lawyers who have been politically active in the President's party. President Ford made a departure from this tradition in his 1975 appointment of University of Chicago president and law professor Edward H. Levi. Widely respected as a legal scholar and authority on antitrust policy, Levi said at the time of his nomination that he couldn't even remember which party he had specified when he first registered as a voter years before.

The Justice Department has a different tone in each administration, activist in certain fields and reticent in others. The department under Attorney General Robert Kennedy obviously took different tacks from that of Attorney General John Mitchell. But below the top officials, there is a bureaucracy of middle-level lawyers—many of them holdovers from a previous administration—who have been known to resist new directives handed down from above. Sometimes they succeed in convincing their bosses to continue active enforcement in a given area; sometimes they're overruled. During the first Nixon administration, a group of young lawyers in the civil rights division chose to resign, with a noisy protest, rather than comply with what they felt to be a deemphasizing of federal initiative in civil rights enforcement.

When the U.S. government goes to the Supreme Court as party to a case, it is represented by the U.S. Solicitor General, the third-ranking official at Justice (behind the deputy attorney general). The Solicitor General (who in 1975 was Robert H. Bork) and his staff decide whether the government should appeal cases that it loses in lower courts, determine whether an issue is worth pursuing all the way to the Supreme Court, prepare briefs and give the oral argument before the High Court. It is usually the Solicitor General himself, attired in swallow-tail coat and striped trousers, who presents the government's case before the nine justices. (Former Solicitor General Erwin Griswold, who served under both Lyndon Johnson and Richard Nixon, has appeared before the Court on more occasions—114, including appearances during his long career as professor and dean of the Harvard Law School—than any other living person.)

Under the department's wing are such agencies as the Drug Enforcement Administration, Federal Prison System, Law Enforcement Assistance Administration (as its name implies, primarily a grantmaking body), Immigration and Naturalization Service, and Federal Bureau of Investigation. The FBI's hulking J. Edgar Hoover Building takes up a solid city block along

Pennsylvania Avenue. It towers over the building—across the street in the Federal Triangle—that is the headquarters of its "parent," the Justice Department. The relative size of the two buildings has more than symbolic meaning, because the FBI dwarfs every other division of the department in staff and funds consumed. It investigates all explicitly federal crimes—such as kidnapping and some forms of racketeering—and is called in on certain nonfederal crimes, such as murder, if there is a federal angle (such as depriving someone of his civil rights by shooting him). It has a very good batting average on apprehending fugitives, even if it has had a hard time locating Patty Hearst (still at large in early 1975).

Under its longtime director Hoover, the FBI operated virtually free of any supervision by Congress and Hoover's nominal superiors at the Justice Department. During the last years preceding his death, the FBI became heavily involved in the surveillance (and harassment, in some cases) of anyone Hoover deemed to be a threat to domestic tranquillity. When it was revealed that this definition encompassed numerous respected organizations and individuals (including public officials), Congress moved to curtail such programs. Whether they have actually been abandoned, under the directorship of Clarence Kelley, is not completely clear.

Congress gets into the "law and order" act through the House and Senate Judiciary Committees. They handle legislation for all particularly legalistic matters, from civil rights and impeachment (House Judiciary) to judicial confirmation (Senate) and interstate tangles (such as the legality of selling state lottery tickets across state lines). Congress sets the budget and staffing of the federal judiciary, adding judges when increases in population and case load require. Congress has power, too, over the size of the Supreme Court, since the number of justices isn't specified in the Constitution. Congress fixed it at nine in 1867, and there hasn't been a serious effort to change it since FDR's "court packing" bill was beaten back in the Thirties. Congress is also the arena in which attempts are made to circumvent unpopular decisions with new laws, such as bills banning the use of federal funds for busing, which the Court has ruled to be a permissible method of desegregation in certain situations. After the Court virtually outlawed capital punishment, President Nixon proposed—and the Senate Judiciary Committee approved—a bill to bring back its limited use. (Congress, however, has failed to act on the bill.)

Confirmation of Supreme Court nominees used to be almost automatic. Until the last decade, the only rejection in modern times was a 1930 thumbs-down vote on a nominee of President Hoover's. Then came a flood of hassles. President Johnson was forced, by a Senate filibuster, to withdraw the nomination of Associate Justice Abe Fortas to be Chief Justice (owing to questions about his outside financial affairs). President Nixon lost close Senate votes on nominees Clement F. Haynsworth, Jr., and G. Harrold Carswell (the former on financial conflict-of-interest grounds, the latter on civil rights and the "mediocrity" issue).

THE FEDERAL JUDICIARY

Below the Supreme Court is the pyramidal structure of the federal judicial system. There are 110 federal courts in all: 11 Circuit Courts of Appeals, 94 District Courts (including benches in Puerto Rico, Guam, the Virgin Islands, and Panama Canal Zone), and 5 special-jurisdiction courts (the Court of

Claims, Customs Court, Court of Customs and Patent Appeals, U.S. Tax Court, and U.S. Court of Military Appeals). Together they are presided over by nearly 600 federal judges, nominated by the President and confirmed by the Senate.

The concerns of these courts are anything involving a U.S. law or the Constitution, as well as certain civil disputes between citizens of different states. (Conflicts between two state governments go directly to the Supreme Court as "original cases.") Federal courts handle cases involving narcotics, interstate auto theft, bankruptcy, liquor taxes and "moonshining," forgery, counterfeiting, copyright and patent infringement, immigration, and all matters of interstate commerce. They also deal with labor laws, civil rights, airplane hijacking, social security, taxes, antitrust challenges, maritime matters, securities registration, and environmental quality. In short, their breadth of jurisdiction spans the entire range of federal activity. Persons convicted in local and state courts can have their cases reviewed by a U.S. District Court, if there is a reason to believe that the lower court's procedures (or the police) denied them their due-process rights under the Constitution.

It used to be that citizens set foot in a federal court only when Uncle Sam had a case against them. But today, increasing numbers of concerned citizens—banded together in public interest groups—are getting the goods on Uncle Sam and taking the government to court on their own. They are challenging federal statutes and allegedly lax enforcement in every area from environmental affairs to product safety. Congress has encouraged this brand of activism by writing into many new laws explicit provisions for citizen challenge of administrative standards.

This trend is making a lot more work for federal courts across the nation, especially at the U.S. District Court and Court of Appeals for the District of Columbia. The gray, massive, unadorned U.S. Courthouse at the foot of Capitol Hill is the scene of daily clashes between attorneys for every constituency in the nation—corporations, civil rights groups, ecology activists, trade associations, individual citizens, and the federal government itself. While serving, technically, only the 720,000 people of the District of Columbia, the District Court has fifteen judges (the fourth highest of the nation's ninety-four district courts) and the Court of Appeals has nine (the third highest among federal circuit courts). But these courts are really national courts, second in impact only to the Supreme Court. If someone sues a federal agency, the case will probably be tried in Washington, the home of that agency. The Court of Appeals for the District of Columbia handles all appeals from decisions by the regulatory and adjudicatory agencies, such as the Federal Trade Commission, Securities and Exchange Commission, and National Labor Relations Board. Congress has made the Court of Appeals for the District of Columbia the sole or principal arena for hearing disputes arising from several laws, including the Clean Air Amendments of 1970 and the Environmental Protection Agency's noise control standards. The law creating the Consumer Product Safety Commission allows someone to challenge its rulings either in the Washington district or in the judicial district where the challenger resides or does business.

With this volume of nationally important disputes, it's not surprising that the judges of Washington's District Court and Court of Appeals (the latter headed by the capable and liberal David Bazelon) are thrust into far greater fame than most federal judges ever attain. The name of Judge John Sirica, retired Chief Judge of the District Court, became a household word for his tough handling of the Watergate case, other parts of which were heard and decided by his colleagues Judge Gerhard Gesell and Judge Charles Richey. (Richey, appointed by Nixon as a supposed conservative, turned out to be a liberal, handing down significant decisions on such issues as the tax-exempt status of a Ralph Nader research group and confidentiality of reporters' sources.) In recent years, cases involving the Pentagon Papers, Amchitka nuclear test, Alaska pipeline, and bribery charges against former Senator Daniel Brewster have all been heard in Washington.

For these cases and every other with a substantial federal question, the end of the line is the Supreme Court. A tiny fraction of the nation's legal cases are ever filed with the Court, and of the cases that are filed, most are given merely a cursory review. The vast majority of them are dismissed for want of federal jurisdiction or because the Court feels that the lower court's ruling was sound. (Under the traditional but unwritten "rule of four," a case will be accepted for full review if four justices are in favor of hearing it.)

THE MEN OF THE COURT

The Constitution is a document of constantly changing meaning, with the direction of change determined by the nine members of the Supreme Court. By a bare majority of five, they say what the law is, and their ruling is usually the last word on the subject for a long time to come. A Supreme Court ruling is the product of nine very bright minds, nine different lives, and nine different conceptions of the role of government in society. Because of lifetime appointments and unusual longevity, only one hundred men have had the opportunity to put their imprint on the Constitution as members of the Court. All have been lawyers, although that is not a requirement of the job. Most have had prior judicial experience, although that isn't necessary either. (Chief Justice Earl Warren had been a prosecutor, state attorney general, and governor, but never a judge; today, four of nine justices had no previous experience on a bench.) While the Court is no longer called "Nine Old Men," the current crop is not exactly spring chickens. Their average age is sixty-five, ranging from Associate Justice William O. Douglas's seventy-seven years to Associate Justice William Rehnquist's fifty-one.

In years past, most justices were men who had been born into families of wealth and social standing. Today, that can be said of only two members, Potter Stewart and Lewis F. Powell, Jr. But the circumstances of a justice's birth are not a reliable guide to his judicial philosophy. Chief Justice Warren Burger, brought up in a poor home, is the leader of the conservative bloc, while lowly-born Associate Justices Douglas, William J. Brennan, Jr., and Thurgood Marshall are the nucleus of the liberal contingent.

Presidents almost invariably appoint to the Court members of their own political party, but not always: Brennan, a Democrat, was appointed by Eisenhower. Most members of the present Court were never active in politics, but Burger and Byron White were once active in the GOP and Democratic parties respectively (White rather briefly, during JFK's 1960 campaign). For decades it has been traditional for various constituencies to be "represented" on the Court. The "Jewish seat"—once held by Cardozo, Brandeis, Frankfurter, Goldberg, and Fortas—is now vacant. The "Catholic seat" is filled by

Brennan. Perhaps the arrival in 1967 of the first black justice, Marshall, marked the start of a "Negro seat," but it's too soon to tell. There is not now, and never has been, a "woman's seat" on the Court.

When the justices take their seats at the bench on the first Monday of each October, they can expect to be busy at the Court through June. The months of July, August, and September are the Court's vacation, which might seem to be a pretty soft deal for $60,000 a year ($62,500 for the Chief Justice). But most justices spend a good bit of their vacations going over briefs from last term's carryover cases and boning up on the issues to be faced in the coming term. The increase in case load has been enormous in recent years, up to some 5,000 from 2,313 in 1960. Burger feels that the situation is almost out of control. A few years ago he suggested that Congress create a sort of mini-Supreme Court to weed out obviously hopeless appeals and pass along the more promising ones. The liberals on the Court didn't like the idea at all, and Douglas, for one, thinks there is nothing unreasonable about the present work load.

For one thing, the justices get a lot of help in making up their minds and writing opinions. They have three clerks apiece, brilliant young men and women just out of the best law schools, where they undoubtedly ranked at the top of their classes. Most serve just one year—at about the same salary they would get in private practice, something in the midteens—and then go on to glory in private or public service. Two members of the current Court once clerked there: White, for Chief Justice Fred Vinson, and Rehnquist, for Associate Justice Robert Jackson. Other former clerks who achieved some degree of renown include former Secretary of State Dean Acheson, Ambassador to England and former Cabinet official Elliot Richardson, Washington attorney and onetime New Deal "Brain Truster" Thomas G. Corcoran, former State Department official Alger Hiss, Transportation Secretary William T. Coleman, Jr., Washington civil liberties attorney Joseph L. Rauh, Jr., law professor Charles Reich, who wrote *The Greening of America,* and the late publisher of the Washington *Post,* Philip L. Graham. Clerks research the cases, write memos on both sides of a case, discuss the issues with their bosses, and prepare preliminary drafts of opinions. Burger, besides having three one-year clerks, has created a new position of "permanent clerk," an idea that has yet to catch on with the other justices, who prefer a full transfusion of new blood each year.

During most of the nine months of the term, the justices alternate between two weeks of hearing oral arguments and two weeks of sitting in their chambers to think and write. Since the Supreme Court is primarily an appeals court, all the information the justices need should be in the briefs, which are more important than the lawyers' verbal eloquence. But when attorneys for each side step to the podium to give thirty minutes of argument each, the justices have a chance to refine their ideas through a vigorous give and take. (Lawyers appearing before the Court should *never* read their arguments verbatim, but instead refer to notes only occasionally.) The thirty-minute limit is strictly adhered to, and a red light on the podium tells an attorney that his time is just about up. The only lawyers who may represent a client before the Court are those who have been admitted to the Supreme Court Bar, a privilege open to anyone who pays a $25 fee, gets an introduction from two current members, and has belonged to his state's supreme court bar for three years.

On each Friday morning of the term, the nine justices meet for the most critical part of the whole process: the secret weekly conference, held around a table covered in green felt. It is there that the justices figure out how they line up on an issue, try to change each other's minds, and decide who will write the majority opinion—a task assigned by the Chief Justice if he is part of the majority. Even though the nine men start each conference by shaking hands with one another (a custom dating from the nineteenth century), the discussions are often ferocious. Positions change constantly, both during the conference and afterward, as drafts of various opinions begin to circulate among the justices. Sometimes a preliminary majority becomes a final minority, after several flip-flops and realignments in between. A justice's draft opinion might be revised as many as a dozen times, influenced by new ideas of his own, his clerks, and his colleagues. In a particularly murky ruling, such as the 1972 capital punishment decision, no justice trusts another to choose just the right words to reflect his own feelings, so the decision comes out in nine parts—the majority opinion and a concurring or dissenting opinion from the other eight. Needless to say, this splintering of consensus detracts considerably from the weight of the ruling.

The final opinions are prepared in the Court building by federal printers sworn to secrecy. The rulings are read to the world at 10 A.M., any day of the term except Fridays. Since a "leak" of a decision would be punishable by law, there is no such thing as a "scoop" by the Court press corps. A reporter makes his reputation there by explaining and analyzing the rulings clearly, as do such veteran Court observers as Anthony Lewis of the *New York Times,* Lyle Denniston of the Washington *Star,* S. J. Micciche of the Boston *Globe,* and Fred Graham of CBS. Most of the top Court reporters have law degrees themselves, like Graham, Micciche, and Warren Weaver, Jr., of the *New York Times.*

FROM WARREN TO BURGER

The late Chief Justice Earl Warren and his colleagues of the Fifties and Sixties left a remarkable array of decisions designed to redress social wrongs that they perceived in American life. There were landmark rulings in school desegregation, reapportionment (to correct rural domination of state legislatures), separation of church and state (the school prayer ruling), censorship (overturning pornography bans), and rights of accused criminals. The unpopularity of these decisions with certain groups accounted for the "Impeach Earl Warren" billboards one used to see along highways in the rural South and Midwest (not to mention southern California).

In the presidential race of 1968, Richard Nixon campaigned directly against the Supreme Court of Earl Warren, who was a fellow Californian and former GOP governor, but no political friend of Nixon. The strategy was politically sound, because the nation was divided over equal rights, worried more about crime than the social and economic causes of crime, fearful of youths who hated the Vietnam war, and puzzled by the "treason" of those who questioned the truthfulness of their government. Blaming the liberal Warren Court for much of the nation's problems, Nixon made it a political football to be kicked around as a campaign issue. He promised to "turn the Court around"—a campaign promise that would ordinarily not be deliverable, since no presidential candidate can guarantee the takeover of the Court as he can of the Cabinet. But as luck would have it, a series of retirements enabled the new President to name to the Court an uncommonly large number of new justices—four, including a new Chief Justice—during one presidential term. Once they reached full strength, in early 1972, these four conservatives— Burger, Blackmun, Rehnquist, and Powell—set about the long task of "turning the Court around."

The Court of the Fifties and Sixties was called the "Warren Court," not just because Earl Warren was its Chief Justice, but because he fashioned a majority by his own force of personality and legal vision. When Warren first took the reins, the Court was internally divided and its members were antagonistic toward one another—and toward him as a political appointee with no prior judicial experience. But Warren pulled the Court together, and within a year came the historic, unanimous decision in the *Brown* desegregation case. By this standard, it is difficult to call the present group of nine men the "Burger Court." Burger is often in dissent, an embarrassing position for the Chief Justice. When he is able to put together a majority, it is an ephemeral one, appearing and evaporating from case to case. More importantly, the Burger majorities are largely a gift from the former President, in the person of three other like-minded appointees. To constitute a majority, they have only to recruit one of the two "swing men" from the Warren Court—White or Stewart. Perhaps it would be better to call it the Nixon Court.

Underlying the Warren Court was the legal premise that individuals have to be protected from society, particularly the steamroller of majority rule and the cumulative weight of government. The Warren decisions tended to curtail the abusive power of government and its agents, be they overzealous policemen, racist school officials, or blue-nosed movie censors. But the underlying premise of the Burger Court is that society must be protected from its individuals, especially if they don't think and act as most people do.

Nixon liked to say that he believed in "strict construction" of the Constitution, but the concept of "strict construction" varies according to who applies it. Every member of the Court, past or present, is a "strict constructionist" in some selective ways, on his own terms. The phrase could be applied to those liberals on the Court who take an absolutist view of the Bill of Rights. What could be a "stricter" reading of the First Amendment than Douglas's refusal to consider any curtailment of free speech, short of (to paraphrase Chief Justice Holmes) "falsely shouting fire in a crowded theater"? Burger, on the other hand, considers himself a "strict constructionist" for believing that society sometimes requires some limits on freedom of the press and artistic expression.

A MIXED BAG OF DECISIONS

There are liberals who are occasionally heard praising the Burger Court for this or that "surprisingly liberal" decision. But most of those decisions found Burger on the dissenting side. There were some liberal rulings, of course, in which the Nixon appointees participated, like the decision that gave eighteen-year-olds the vote in federal elections. Or the unanimous ruling that Attorney General John Mitchell had improperly delegated his wiretap authority to subordinates. Or the permissive abortion decision, written by Blackmun, who tried to balance the mother's right to abort during the first six months with the government's interest in the child's birth at any time thereafter. Or the biggest blockbuster of all, the 8–0 ruling, written by Burger himself, that the President had to surrender his Watergate tapes.

But the liberal rulings from which Burger dissented are more numerous. The Court ruled that the *New York Times* and Washington *Post* should not be prevented from publishing the Pentagon Papers. The Court struck down as vague a Massachusetts statute against "treating the American flag contemptuously" (i.e., wearing it on the seat of the pants). The Court softened the standards for being a conscientious objector, adding moral and ethical standards to religious grounds. The Court ruled that prescribed lengths for maternity leaves were unconstitutionally arbitrary. It voided an Indiana loyalty oath that prevented Communists from running for office. It ruled that a student cannot be expelled from college for distributing an allegedly obscene newspaper (a matter that should go through local legal channels). All of these decisions were handed down during Burger's tenure as Chief Justice, but in virtually all of them, he and the other Nixon appointees were in dissent.

Cases in which the Warren legacy has been eroded are greater in both significance and number. On the obscenity question, a Burger majority in 1973 rejected the notion of one national standard of permissiveness and ruled that locales should be allowed to set their own "contemporary community standards." This led to a crackdown on pornography in many parts of the country, but it did not allow the Court to wash its hands of the whole matter, as it hoped it could. In 1974 it felt compelled to reverse an Albany, Georgia, jury that had banned the movie *Carnal Knowledge,* which was hardly sexually explicit.

In the antitrust field—in a ruling called the "modern Dred Scott decision"—the Court upheld the practice in professional sports of "buying" and "selling" players against their will and requiring that they play for their assigned team or not at all. Putting a chill on class action suits (the new form of legal activism), the Court imposed tough standards of class eligibility, including proof of "individualized injury" to each member of the suing class. The Court refused to outlaw the exclusive reliance on local property taxes to fund schools, a practice which opponents say causes educational inequities through uneven school budgeting. In the Pappas-Branzburg-Caldwell cases, the Court ruled that reporters do not have an absolute right to shield the identity of their sources during public investigations.

The heaviest attacks on the Warren precedents have come in the fields of civil rights and criminal procedures. Tipping the scales in favor of prosecutors, the Nixon appointees—joined by moderates White or Stewart—have approved criminal convictions by less than unanimous juries. They have ruled that an accused person does not have an absolute right to counsel during lineups. They have upheld the right of police without a search warrant to frisk an arrested suspect and use against him anything that is found, even if it isn't related to the crime for which he was arrested. They have ruled, too, that a suspect who has been given immunity—whether he wants it or not—can be compelled to give self-incriminating testimony if he is promised that it won't be used against him.

In civil rights, the Court has taken a states' rights stance on the matter of allowing racially discriminatory clubs to hold liquor licenses. It upheld both Maine's right to revoke such a license from the Elks and Pennsylvania's decision to let the Moose keep their license. In the critical area of school desegregation, Burger wrote the 1971 *Swann* decision allowing busing as a tool of merging de jure dual systems, but he didn't intend that the ruling apply to de facto segregation as well. So, when the Court later heard cases from Richmond and Detroit involving merger of city and suburban districts to remedy racial imbalances, it turned thumbs down on busing, with Burger writing the majority opinion in the Detroit case.

Two of the Court's most publicized rulings of recent years left thorny issues basically unresolved. The "nondecision" in the DeFunis case, on "reverse discrimination" in college admissions, virtually invited future cases. Whatever the final verdict, it will have a tremendous impact on "compensatory" programs in both education and employment. And the 5–4 ruling against the death penalty was based largely on the unevenness with which sentences have been imposed by judges and juries, not on capital punishment being a "cruel and unusual punishment" in every situation. The decision was made with the Nixon appointees in dissent. Stewart and White, who voted with the majority, indicated that they might uphold capital punishment if it were mandated by state law for specific crimes. Following the Court's death ruling, more than thirty states did enact such mandates, tossing the whole issue back in the lap of the Supreme Court. In late 1974 the justices agreed to hear the appeal of a man who was convicted of murder in North Carolina, one of the states that now requires a death sentence for first-degree murder, rape, and arson.

THE "NIXON COURT"

The "crime and justice" establishment in Washington, like everything else in the capital city, is essentially political, in the sense that the actions of the Justice Department and the congressional judiciary committees—and the Supreme Court—change in response to the popular will, as perceived by the President, Congress and nine justices. Judicial philosophies in Washington are like what they say about the weather in New England: "If you don't like it, wait around a while, and it will change." But change usually comes slowly to the Supreme Court, since few Presidents get a chance, as Nixon did, to replace nearly half the court in fewer than three years.

As for the current condition of law enforcement in America, some people see signs of repression, while others applaud the trend as a correction of undue permissiveness. The future shape of the Court, and hence its policies, will depend primarily on such factors as the health and age of its current members, and which political party controls the White House after 1976. But one thing is certain: the Supreme Court today is the most enduring legacy of President Nixon. Long after his Cabinet has left office, long after his legislative initiatives are forgotten, long after the turmoil of Watergate has subsided, the past and future decisions of the "Nixon Court"—a bundle of precedents—will still be exerting their influence on American life.

14 CORRUPTION OVER THE YEARS

Within the past fifty years, Washington has gone from Teapot Dome to Watergate. Yet the history of corruption in the nation's capital does not begin or end with these flagrant examples. Corruption has been a part of government for a long time. In every decade since the first colonists landed at Jamestown, Virginia, a few—relatively few—public servants have violated trust by putting personal financial gain ahead of "the public interest." Dishonest politicians have come in every size and shape—Republicans and Democrats, liberals and conservatives, independently wealthy leaders and officials just scraping by on their salaries.

Styles of wrongdoing change from era to era. They change as people's crucial needs change, and as government changes in its central powers and purposes. In the early colonial communities, corruption was found in the division of food and supplies. Later the focus was on bond issues and land grants. With the coming of the railroads, corruption was attached to the granting of franchises and rights of way. As the giant industrial monopolies grew, late in the last century, there were tempting incentives for government officials to wink at obvious restraints of trade. And in every war the United States has fought, there has been some profiteering in the supplying and pricing of military goods.

In this century, federal regulation of business has brought an increasing opportunity for corruption. Corruption has surfaced in every conceivable economic area—fuel sources (Teapot Dome), the stock market (fraud in Wall Street), housing (the FHA scandals), and routine federal contracts (the "five per center" scandals of the Truman administration). Ever-increasing taxes have provided venal bureaucrats and citizens with an almost perennial opportunity for wrongdoing. Putting the fix on an income tax case remains one of the most sought-after kinds of favoritism, but it is rarely successful. Indeed, the significant thing about corruption in Washington is that, given the innumerable chances for cheating, the actual number of known cases is relatively small.

WATERGATE

The Nixon administration didn't invent political corruption in America, but not in recent times has any other administration produced such a concentration of abuses as those which occurred in and around the Watergate affair. Never before did a President resign his office after virtually admitting that, over a year and a half of televised addresses to the nation, he had lied about his knowledge of illegal acts by his aides. Never before had so many top administration officials—including a Vice President, two Attorneys General, a Secretary of Commerce, a Secretary of the Treasury, and numerous White House assistants—been implicated in so far-reaching a pattern of corruption.

Even a nonfederal official in far-off California—former Lieutenant Governor Ed Reinecke—got caught in the web, and in 1974 was convicted of lying to the Senate Judiciary Committee. His transgressions involved the convoluted saga of ITT, its pledge of support for a GOP convention in San Diego, and its subsequent favorable settlement of an antitrust suit brought by the Justice Department. By early 1975, twenty-six former Nixon aides and officials of his reelection campaign had been convicted of or had pleaded guilty to Watergate-related crimes.

At first Watergate seemed to be a unique situation in the history of political corruption, to the extent that no one involved seemed to have been motivated by a desire for personal financial gain. The price exacted from individuals and corporations for special review of a tax problem, milk subsidy, or antitrust matter was not a payoff to a particular fixer, but a fat campaign contribution to the Committee to Reelect the President. (White House Counsel John Dean III did borrow a few thousand dollars of campaign funds from the bulging White House safe to pay for his honeymoon, but he subsequently paid it back.)

For a while, it looked as if members of the White House crowd were merely overzealous partisans. But then the nation saw Vice President Agnew resign and plead "no contest" in a tax case involving government contract kickbacks (received both before and after he became Vice President), a scandal technically unrelated to Watergate but coming in lock step with Watergate revelations. Subsequently, President Nixon found himself in hot water over his own income tax returns (which involved unallowable deductions, unreported capital gains, and backdating of documents). Then the President's friend Charles (Bebe) Rebozo was reported to have used campaign funds to pay for personal gifts to President Nixon and members of his staff. Finally, there came the shocking indictment of former Treasury Secretary John Connally for allegedly taking a bribe to lobby for a boost in the milk price support, but he was later acquitted on all charges.

But these episodes were just side shows of the Watergate scandal—the burglary of opposition offices, electronic surveillance of newspeople, forged campaign letters, rigged postcard polls, the making of lists for IRS harassment, and the systematic cover-up of these activities. The ominous thing about Watergate was not the individual venality but the institutionalized corruption—the corruption of the political process itself. To find a comparable power-for-power's sake scandal, you have to go back to the Republicans' "theft" of the presidency in 1877. In the election of 1876, the Democratic candidate, Governor Samuel J. Tilden of New York, had received 250,000 more votes than Republican Governor Rutherford B. Hayes of Ohio, and appeared to have won in terms of electoral votes. But the votes of Oregon and three southern states (still under Republican carpetbag rule) were in dispute. A deal was struck between congressional leaders of two parties. The southern Democrats promised that Hayes could have the disputed electoral votes, and the Republicans promised to withdraw federal troops from the South and not enforce the civil rights of Negro freedmen. Two days before inauguration day, a congressionally appointed electoral commission declared Hayes the winner by one electoral vote. The social impact of the deal echoed for nearly a hundred years thereafter in American race relations.

The number of officials indicted for standard types of political corruption has not varied much in recent years. The more conventional sorts of crimes—bribery, kickbacks, conflicts of interest—are almost a staple in political history. But today, the public tolerance of such behavior is wearing thinner, and this growing distaste may make routine venality more risky for future politicians. While the temptations to which congressmen and bureaucrats are subjected are no less enticing than they have been, the chances of being detected are rising. There are more news reporters covering every congressman and poking into obscure corners of the federal bureaucracy. There has also been a gradual decline in the kind of "loyalty" which said "my boss, right or wrong." The late Senator Thomas Dodd (D-Conn.) and former Representative J. Irving Whalley (R-Pa.) were both brought down in recent years by trusted assistants who finally got fed up with their bosses and decided to blow the whistle on them.

Though it may not seem obvious in this post-Watergate era, it is quite likely that Washington is actually "cleaner" than hundreds of statehouses, governors' mansions, county courthouses, and mayors' offices around the country. In state and local government—as scandals in Maryland, Texas, New Jersey, Florida, Illinois, New York, and elsewhere have shown—public officials have a more direct and personal control over the government business (awards of contracts, for example) than congressmen and high-ranking federal bureaucrats do. There is also some sort of inverse relationship between the size of a public official's salary and his vulnerability to a bribe. Uncle Sam's people, on average, are better-paid than other public servants.

IN EVERY BRANCH

No part of the federal government has been free of corruption or conflict of interest. Remember the 1969 Senate investigation into profiteering in the operation of servicemen's clubs in Vietnam? It involved, among other people, the Army's highest-ranking enlisted man, Sergeant Major William O. Wooldridge, former Provost Marshal Carl C. Turner, and Brigadier General Earl F. Cole (who was later demoted to colonel). Even the federal judiciary isn't immune from the temptations of unethical financial gain. Remember the downfall of Supreme Court Justice Abe Fortas? On his way (possibly) to the Chief Justice's seat, Fortas was stopped short by the revelation that he had accepted a $20,000 fee from a foundation created by financier Louis E. Wolfson, who was subsequently indicted for selling unregistered securities. Fortas returned the money a few months after the indictment and took no part in the Supreme Court's review of Wolfson's eventual conviction. All the same, Fortas's indiscretion led to his resignation from the Court.

The known cases of corruption in the upper levels of the federal bureaucracy are relatively few (with the exception of a couple of particularly rich periods—like the Grant administration, in which the whole Cabinet seemed to be lining its pockets). The only Cabinet member to serve time in jail for political corruption was Harding's Interior Secretary Albert Fall, convicted of taking at least $400,000 in bribes from oilmen involved in the Teapot Dome scandal. Harding's Attorney General, Harry M. Daugherty, was allegedly involved in all sorts of shady dealings—including the sale of liquor licenses and criminal pardons, as well as Teapot Dome. He resigned and was later acquitted. Navy Secretary Edwin Denby, who was implicated in Teapot Dome, was also cleared of wrongdoing.

The rarity of Cabinet-level indictments made it all the more startling when Watergate-related charges were brought against former Attorney General John Mitchell, former Secretary of Commerce Maurice Stans, former Attorney General Richard Kleindienst, and former Secretary of the Treasury Connally. Mitchell and Stans, who had masterminded President Nixon's 1972 reelection bid, were acquitted in 1974 of arranging an illegal campaign contribution from financier Robert Vesco at a time when Vesco was under investigation by federal authorities. After beating one rap, Mitchell was convicted with several White House aides in the cover-up trial, and Stans pleaded guilty to five misdemeanors related to his fund-raising activities. Kleindienst pleaded guilty to charges of "inaccurate testimony" concerning the ITT antitrust case and got off with a suspended sentence.

In recent decades, the biggest scandal unearthed in the federal bureaucracy (rather than among elected officials) concerned favoritism in the collection of income taxes and prosecution of tax cases. A congressional investigation led by 1951 to the firing or resignation of more than 150 employees of the Bureau of Internal Revenue, including Commissioner George J. Schoeneman. At the same time, President Truman fired T. Lamar Caudle, assistant attorney general in charge of taxes, who was subsequently sent to jail—along with Truman's appointments secretary Matthew J. Connelly—for conspiring to fix a St. Louis businessman's tax case.

A comparably broad bureaucratic scandal, but one involving no high-up Washington officials, was the tangle of corruption uncovered in the early Seventies in field offices of the Federal Housing Administration and its parent agency, the Department of Housing and Urban Development. More than 300 people—federal officials, contractors, real estate agents, mortgage bankers, and others—were indicted for bribery and fraud in more than twenty cities, including Richmond, New York, and Detroit. Most of the indictments charged the bureaucrats with helping private building contractors gouge poor families who were attempting to buy renovated inner-city homes with federal subsidies. Among those convicted of tax evasion and sent to jail was the director of the FHA's Philadelphia insuring office, Thomas J. Gallagher, Jr.

Vice Presidents of the United States have been involved in more than their share of unsavory business, most of it related to their activities before taking office. Aaron Burr set an early standard of treachery that would be difficult for any other Vice President to equal. While in office, he killed Alexander Hamilton in a duel in Weehawken, New Jersey, but was not prosecuted. (Soon thereafter, he presided at the impeachment trial of Supreme Court Justice Samuel Chase.) After leaving office, Burr launched an adventure in 1806 to seize the Louisiana territory and invade Mexico (presumably, to set up a new government with himself as president). When the conspiracy was found out, Burr was tried for treason. He was acquitted, but took refuge in Europe.

Vice President John C. Calhoun was investigated by the House in 1828 on charges that while Secretary of War he had profited from the award of a construction contract for a fort near Norfolk, Virginia. Although the House found wrongdoing on the part of a Calhoun aide, the Vice President was exonerated. Grant's Vice President, former Speaker of the House Schuyler Colfax, had been one of several congressmen to accept bargain-priced stock of the corrupt Crédit Mobilier company in the late 1860s. Grant made the issue of impeachment moot by dumping Colfax from his ticket for the second term. It is unlikely that the Vice President would have been impeached anyway, however, since most authorities agree that impeachment covers only offenses committed during tenure in an executive or judicial office, not before.

And, of course, there was the famous "Checkers" episode during the 1952 presidential campaign. Vice presidential candidate Nixon was attacked for allowing an $18,235 fund to be raised by a supporter who solicited donations from more than seventy California businessmen. The fund, Nixon said, was intended to help defray his senatorial office costs, and none of it had been used by him for personal expenses. (In 1968 the Senate revised its ethics code to make such office funds allowable.) In an emotional television broadcast, Nixon admitted accepting a personal gift from a Texan: "a little cocker spaniel dog . . . black and white, spotted, and our little girl Tricia, the six-year-old, named it Checkers." Nixon vowed, "I just want to say this, right now, that regardless of what they say about it, we are going to keep it." The broadcast brought an avalanche of support for Nixon. The next day, Dwight Eisenhower told him, "You're my boy," and his position on the ticket was assured.

PRESIDENTS, TOO

Presidents have always shown a remarkable knack for dissociating themselves from smelly scandals that hatch during their administrations, even those involving aides who were intimates and close advisers. President Grant urged prosecutors to "let no guilty man escape" punishment for the "Whisky Ring," a St. Louis conspiracy between federal revenue agents and distillers to evade liquor taxes. But it was soon shown that Grant's private secretary, General Orville E. Babcock, was deeply involved in the mess, and that some of the kickback money had found its way to Grant's campaign coffers. Grant's order that justice be done was compromised further by the revelation that he himself had accepted a gift of a carriage and trotting horses from John McDonald, the superintendent of internal revenue in St. Louis and a key figure in the ring. Babcock was acquitted of bribery charges, and Grant was not impeached.

President James Garfield, the twentieth president, ran an administration as clean as any, and the voters who elected him had apparently been willing to forgive past sins. It seems that Garfield had been one of numerous senators and representatives who had bought stock in the Crédit Mobilier at preferential VIP prices.

In the summer of 1923, President Harding set off across the country on a badly needed vacation. A few months earler he—and the nation—had begun to learn the extent of the skulduggery of the "Ohio Gang," the circle of old cronies that the former Ohio senator had brought to Washington to staff his administration. On his way back to the capital from Alaska that summer, the President took ill in San Francisco—first ptomaine poisoning, then pneumonia, and finally blockage of a blood vessel—and died in his hotel room. The biggest scandal of his administration—centering on the leasing of federal oil deposits in the Elk Hills, California, and Teapot Dome, Wyoming, reserves—did not break until after his death. Harding's epitaph might well have been his own remark: "I am not worried about my enemies; it is my friends that are keeping me awake nights."

President Harry Truman had some similar cause for worry. Investigations during his administration revealed that the awarding of Reconstruction Finance Corporation (RFC) loans was being influenced by E. Merl Young, a former $1,080-a-year federal messenger and husband of a White House stenographer. Young's wife received a mink coat from a company whose RFC loan had allegedly been expedited, and the gift gave the Republicans a handy symbol of Democratic corruption, contrasted a few years later with Pat Nixon's "respectable Republican cloth coat." The deep freezer became a symbol of corruption, too, when it was brought out that Mrs. Truman, presidential military aide General Harry Vaughan, Chief Justice Fred M. Vinson, and presidential appointments secretary Connelly had each accepted one as a gift from a client of alleged fixer James V. Hunt. (Hunt claimed he could arrange federal contracts for a 5 percent commission.) A Senate investigating committee had no quarrel with Mrs. Truman's acceptance of the gift, because of the long tradition of personal, corporate, and institutional gifts to First Families.

The whole issue of gifts to the presidential family surfaced again twenty-five years later when Maxine Cheshire of the Washington *Post* revealed that a few pieces of expensive jewelry given to Mrs. Nixon and her daughters by foreign potentates had not been properly recorded as "state gifts"—as required by a 1966 law—and were being used as personal possessions. Casual treatment of the "state gift" law was apparently bipartisan. When Senator Hubert Humphrey (D-Minn.) left the Vice Presidency in 1968, he took with him a 7.9-carat diamond that had been given to his wife by President Mobutu of Zaïre. Just before this was disclosed in 1974, Humphrey hastened to return the $160,000 gem to the State Department, which is the appointed repository of such gifts.

On no White House staff of recent years has any one man had as much influence as Sherman Adams, President Eisenhower's most trusted adviser. Ike was understandably shaken to learn that Adams had interceded with two federal regulatory agencies on behalf of a friend, Boston businessman Bernard Goldfine. In return, Goldfine had given Adams a $700 vicuna coat and a $2,400 Oriental rug and had paid more than $3,000 of hotel bills run up by Adams and his family (as well as hotel bills incurred by Senators Frederick G. Payne, R-Me., Styles Bridges, R-N.H., and Norris Cotton, R-N.H.). Eisenhower tried to keep Sherman Adams, claiming, "I need him." But before long, Adams was forced to resign. The senators were not disciplined in any way.

The most miraculous trick ever turned by a President in keeping clear of a close-to-home scandal was that of Lyndon B. Johnson after the Bobby Baker affair blew open. From the time he had come to Washington from Pickens, South Carolina, at the age of fourteen, Robert G. Baker had been like a son to Johnson. He advanced from Senate pageboy to become secretary to Senate Democrats at the age of twenty-seven. Baker was the right-hand man of the Senate's powerful majority leader, Senator Johnson of Texas. It turned out that Baker had long been using his position as an intermediary for campaign funds and legislative fixer to line his own pockets. With his only official source of income being a modest Senate salary, Baker had amassed a net worth of nearly $2 million, including the Carousel, a swinging motel and nightclub on the Maryland oceanfront where members of Congress were frequently entertained.

Senate hearings on the Baker affair failed to follow up any of the rich leads linking several senators to various Baker business deals. "This committee is not investigating senators," Chairman B. Everett Jordan (D-N.C.) stated huffily. The committee was not investigating Presidents, either, and it gave a perfunctory clean bill of health to Lyndon B. Johnson, who became President just about the time the scandal broke. It is widely believed in Washington that if Bobby Baker had told all he knew, or if the press had done a thorough job of sleuthing, President Johnson would have been ruined. Baker was convicted in 1967 of income tax evasion, theft, and conspiracy to defraud the government. He was sentenced to up to three years in prison, served approximately a year and a half, and is now a self-employed businessman and investor.

CAPITOL HILL CONNECTIONS

Congressional leaders can be just as adept as chief executives in dissociating themselves from wrongdoing that occurs in their Capitol Hill offices. The classic case of this in recent years involved influence peddling in the office of former Speaker of the House John McCormack (D-Mass.). All through the Sixties a New York lawyer named Nathan M. Voloshen used his close friendship with McCormack and Martin Sweig, the Speaker's administrative assistant, to arrange favors—some blatantly illegal and others merely shady—for clients that included some of the nation's largest corporations, Army privates seeking early discharges, and leaders of organized crime. Sweig and Voloshen were both convicted in 1970 of charges stemming from the influence-peddling investigations, but the reputation of the aged, soon-to-retire Speaker was somehow spared. So was the reputation of the late House Majority Leader Hale Boggs (D-La.), who had received about $45,000 worth of home improvements for $21,000, by courtesy of Baltimore contractor Victor H. Frenkil. A client of Voloshen, Frenkil was trying (futilely, it turned out) to get a $5 million cost-overrun reimbursement for construction of the garage under the Rayburn House Office Building.

Corruption in and around the White House is rarely more than a once-a-decade phenomenon, but almost every year some congressman or senator gets caught with his hand in the cookie jar. Most of them are let off with barely a slap on the wrist. Jail is usually considered an undue punishment to heap on a person who has already been disgraced, is probably washed up in politics, and maybe faces disbarment by the legal profession as well (which, for most congressmen, means a loss of their livelihood.)

Corruption in Congress takes many forms, some of them explicitly illegal and others merely unethical. You can read about it every day in Jack Anderson's column: congressmen who allow businessmen to pick up their tab on an expensive vacation; congressmen who arrange special meetings for big campaign contributors who happen to have contract or tax problems with Uncle Sam; congressmen who receive director's fees from banks and corporations over which their committees have legislative jurisdiction; congressmen who maintain ties with their back-home law firms (a practice considered unethical by the American Bar Association); congressmen who get salary kickbacks from their own aides; congressmen who are entertained by organized crime figures.

Nothing comes of 90 percent of the revelations of shady dealings described by Jack Anderson and other investigative reporters. They cause a minor ruckus for a few days and then sink into obscurity. Not because the charges are untrue, but because more people—legal authorities, congressional ethics panels, and the electorate—are reluctant to try to nail a member of Congress. The Senate is so reluctant to sit in judgment of its own that it has censured only seven members since its founding, and only two in the last forty-five years (Senator Joseph McCarthy, R-Wis., and Senator Thomas Dodd, D-Conn.). No member of the House has been censured since the unanimous vote in 1921 against Representative Thomas Blanton (D-Tex.), who had slipped an allegedly lewd speech into the *Congressional Record*. (He served another fifteen years or so after censure.) In 1967, however, the House ignored a committee recommendation that Representative Adam Clayton Powell, Jr. (D-N.Y), be censured for misuse of office funds, and instead took the more serious action of forbidding him to take his seat for the new session. It later relented (with prodding from the Supreme Court) when he was reelected in 1968, but took away his seniority and fined him $25,000. Powell was defeated in 1970 in a primary challenge by Representative Charles Rangel (D-N.Y.) and died in 1972.

The Senate's ethics committee, chaired by Senator John Stennis (D-Miss.), is soft on wayward senators. Take for example, the case of former Senator George Murphy (R-Cal.). It seems that Patrick J. Frawley, Jr., a wealthy businessman and supporter of right-wing causes, gave the actor-turned-politician unlimited use of a credit card, half the rent on a Washington apartment, and a $20,000-a-year salary—all illegal "gifts" from a private citizen to a federal official. All that Murphy did in return, according to the senator, was to view (on a screen installed in the senator's apartment) and "evaluate" movies made by a Frawley company. Stennis investigated the whole thing and said it was all right. Or take the case of the late Senator Edward Long (D-Mo.), who had been accepting about $2,000 per month from an attorney for Teamsters boss James Hoffa, then in jail. Long said the payments were "referral fees" for cases unrelated to Hoffa. Little supporting evidence was offered by Long. The Stennis committee conducted a closed investigation and exonerated Long. (Long was later defeated in a primary by Senator Thomas Eagleton, D-Mo.)

Congress is equally touchy about passing judgment on its federal partners in the Executive and Judiciary Branches. The difficulty of getting a majority of the House to agree to indict and two-thirds of the Senate to convict has made impeachment a seldom-used weapon against corruption. The likelihood of impeachment and conviction has sometimes led to a premature resignation, thereby short-circuiting the process itself (the end result of which, after all, is merely the removal of an official from office). Among former President Nixon's accusers, some were elated by his resignation, on purely practical grounds, but others seemed disappointed, on theoretical grounds, that the impeachment mechanism was halted in midstroke.

Judges have felt the weight of impeachment more than other officials. Since the first impeachment trial in 1798, nine of the twelve impeached officials have been judges, and all five men against whom impeachment was successful were judges. In the two most famous impeachment cases—against Associate Justice Samuel Chase in 1804 and President Andrew Johnson in 1868—the motives of the accusers were political and had nothing to do with impeachable acts of "treason, bribery or other high crimes and misdemeanors." Both men were acquitted, even though Johnson was saved by only one vote. In the Johnson trial, seven Republicans bucked the Radical Republican Senate leadership and voted for acquittal, risking their careers in the process, and all but one of those seven were defeated in their next reelection bid. Despite the threats of impeachment aimed by some congressmen at liberal jurists like the late former Chief Justice Earl Warren, former Justice Abe Fortas, and Justice William O. Douglas, the Senate has not sat as a court of impeachment since 1936.

VOTER REACTIONS

The American electorate has a mixed record in the business of voting out men who have been accused of impropriety. Senators Murphy and Long were defeated. Representative Powell was reelected once after his transgressions became public, but was defeated two years later. Representative Martin McKneally (R-N.Y.), a former national commander of the American Legion who somehow forgot to file any income tax returns from 1964 to 1967, was defeated for reelection in 1970, but just narrowly. Senator Dodd was denied his party's nomination after being censured and lost as an independnt candidate. Representative H. Carl Andersen (R-Minn.) was defeated in 1962 after it was revealed during the Billy Sol Estes scandal that he had sold the Texas phantom-fertilizer tycoon a share in a coal mine his family owned. Senator Daniel Brewster (D-Md.) lost a reelection bid to Representative Charles Mathias (R-Md.) in 1968, and soon thereafter the government went after him for accepting $24,500 from the Spiegel mail order company in 1967, while his postal committee was considering legislation favorable to the firm. Most Washington observers believe that if Brewster had been reelected he never would have been indicted, let alone convicted, as he was in 1972. The difficulty of trying and convicting public officials was illustrated when, in 1974, a U.S. court of appeals ordered that Brewster be given a new trial on the grounds that the lower judge's instructions to the jury had failed to make a sufficient distinction between a "bribe" and an "illegal gratuity," two crimes of differing severity.

In numerous other instances, the electorate has taken a forgive-and-forget stance. Representative James M. Curley, a popular former mayor and governor of Massachusetts, was convicted of mail fraud in 1946. His adoring constituents elected him mayor again, and he continued to hold that office while serving five months in jail. (Curley's sentence was commuted by President Truman.) In the Fifties, Representative Thomas J. Lane (D-Mass.) was convicted of income tax evasion and also won reelection. Then there was Representative Seymour Halpern (R-N.Y.), a member of the House Banking and Currency Committee, who in 1969 was in debt up to his nose to several banks (with most of the loans unsecured and at the prime rate) at a time his committee was considering bank holding company legislation. After his reelection the following year, he was "punished" with a transfer to another committee and a demotion in seniority. (He decided not to run for reelection in 1972.) In 1968 *Life* magazine charged that Representative Cornelius E. Gallagher (D-N.J.) had business ties with mobster Joseph "Joe Bayonne" Zicarelli. The magazine charged, too, that the body of a small-time hood who died at Gallagher's New Jersey home was stashed in the basement until it was removed by a Mafia henchman. At first Gallagher seemed to be finished in politics, but he fought back, sued *Life* (unsuccessfully), and won reelection in 1970. Two years later, however, amid new charges of misuse of party funds and tax evasion, Gallagher got only 15 percent of the vote in the primary. Soon therafter he pleaded guilty to the charges and went to jail for seventeen months.

Even as Watergate monopolized the nation's concern with political corruption, there were members of recent Congresses whose questionable activities led to criminal proceedings. Former Representative John Dowdy (D-Tex.) exhausted his appeals and was sentenced to jail in 1973 for accepting a bribe to squelch the investigation of a fraudulent home improvement company that had cheated hundreds of middle-income black families in Washington, D.C. Representative J. Irving Whalley (R-Pa.) was fined in 1973 for padding his staff payroll and forcing his aides to kick back the difference. Within one year, three New York congressmen were indicted for receiving illegal payments. Democratic Representative Frank J. Brasco was indicted in October 1973 for allegedly conspiring to receive a $27,500 bribe to help an underworld figure secure a federal mail hauling contract. He was convicted in a second trial after the first ended in a hung jury. In February of 1974, Republican Representative Angelo D. Roncallo was indicted for alleged participation—before his election to Congress—in a scheme to extort a contribution to the local Republican party from a building contractor who wanted a public construction contract. Roncallo was acquitted of all charges, but the electorate did not return him to Washington. Democratic Representative Bertram L. Podell was indicted in July 1973 for allegedly receiving a $41,350 bribe to influence the Civil Aeronautics Board to grant a Bahamas route to Florida Atlantic Airlines in 1969. He subsequently pleaded guilty to conspiracy and conflict of interest and was sentenced to six months in jail and a $5,000 fine.

The most startling recent case was that of former Senator Edward J. Gurney (R-Fla.), who was indicted by a federal grand jury in 1974 for bribery, conspiracy, and lying to the grand jury. He was charged with extorting—for personal and political use—some $223,000 from Florida developers who had dealings with the FHA and U.S. Department of Housing and Urban Development. The alleged crimes covered a period of more than three years, including part of the time that Gurney was a member of the Senate Watergate Committee. The Florida Republican, who withdrew from his reelection race at the urging of state GOP leaders, was the first senator in fifty years to be indicted on federal charges while holding office.

THE GRAY AREAS

One of the problems of contending with corruption in government is a lack of consensus on what constitutes corruption. Even a supposedly clear-cut charge like bribery is open to subtle interpretation. Besides the question of how the recipient used the money (for personal purposes or for campaign and office expenses), there is the matter of the giver's motive. In general, a bribe entails a gift made in the *expectation* of a *particular* favor, rather than in the abstract *hope* that the recipient would take a *generally* friendly stance toward the giver. This is the crux of the never-ending Washington debate over the desirability of funding the American electoral process with private contributions, especially massive doses of money from American corporations and from labor unions (through their tax-exempt "political action committees").

A more serious lack of consensus clouds the whole issue of conflict of interest on Capitol Hill. It is not at all uncommon for a senator or representative to have extensive investments in the industries that are under the legislative jurisdiction of a committee he serves on. Some congressmen on agriculture committees own farm lands (and have received large subsidies in past years). Congressmen on banking committees own bank stock. Senators who write oil depletion tax laws own oil stocks. Et cetera, et cetera. Some people are outraged by it, but most people around Washington seem to think that it's O.K., as long as a legislator doesn't use inside information to make a sharp investment and doesn't try to further a particular investment through a particular legislative action.

Acknowledging that "most of my income is from oil and gas," Senate Finance Committee Chairman Russell Long (D-La.) adds, "I don't regard it as a conflict of interest." His rationale: "My state produces more oil and gas per acre than any state in the union. If I didn't represent the oil and gas industry, I wouldn't represent the state of Louisiana." It sounds reasonable at first hearing, but do the senator's tax policies take into account fully the best interests of gas and oil *consumers,* who are many times more numerous than the owners and employees of all the energy companies combined?

Citizens would be a lot better equipped to decide for themselves what constitutes conflict of interest if there were stricter laws requiring disclosure of the personal finances of all elected and high-ranking appointed officials. Senator Clifford P. Case (R-N.J.), who discloses his own finances voluntarily, has long sponsored such legislation. The proposal has been broadly opposed as being an "invasion of privacy" and "unwieldy to administer."

DONATIONS AND APPOINTMENTS

Ordinarily, if someone demands and is given a particular favor in exchange for campaign donations, it is called "corruption." But if the favor demanded is appointment to an ambassadorship, few people seem to mind. The "selling" of ambassadorships to the highest bidder has been going on since the nation was founded. Both parties have done it, and neither seems inclined to stop. Both Watergate Special Prosecutor Leon Jaworski and the House Judiciary Committee, however, deemed the practice questionable enough to be included in the scope of their investigations of grounds for impeaching the President. And one of the charges to which "CREEP" attorney Herbert W. Kalmbach pleaded guilty was the explicit offering of a European ambassadorship to Maryland Republican J. Fife Symington in exchange for a $100,000 campaign contribution. (Symington never got the diplomatic post, but declined Kalmbach's offer to return the money.)

Large campaign donors usually are interested in appointments to the more prestigious European countries, so most of the smaller nations of the world are sent an American ambassador from our professional foreign service. President Nixon's 1972 campaign received at least $881,405 from people who held ambassadorships at the time of the donations, and another $418,367 from people who subsequently became ambassadors. Among the large donors whom Richard Nixon appointed to ambassadorships are Walter H. Annenberg (Great Britain), Shelby Davis (Switzerland), Fred J. Russell (Denmark), Ruth Farkas (Luxembourg), John Humes (Austria), Kingdon Gould, Jr. (Luxembourg and the Netherlands), Arthur K. Watson (France), Vincent de Roulet (Jamaica), Leonard Firestone (Belgium), and J. William Middendorf II (the Netherlands). In some of these posts, the cost of maintaining the embassy is so high that anyone without a sizable fortune is at a disadvantage.

Another gray area of ethics is the whole matter of public officials who move back and forth between private enterprise and public service. The upper levels of the federal bureaucracy—appointive positions, primarily—are full of men and women who used to have some degree of control over industries with which they deal as public officials. Some of them probably will be employed again by these industries when they leave office. Corporations are constantly raiding the bureaucracy for men and women whose expertise and friendships with key government personnel will be beneficial to their business. The practice is commonplace in almost all government departments and regulatory agencies. Critics of the practice are worried not so much about transfers of specific inside information as they are about a biased effect on government policymaking.

EFFECTS AND THE FUTURE

Is corruption any more prevalent—on a per capita basis—in government than in the other broad areas of American life? Probably not. Before pointing an accusing finger at politicians and bureaucrats, it is well to recall the cases of corruption uncovered in recent years in organized labor, in business, in entertainment and professional athletics. But corruption in government has far deeper consequences than wrongdoing in other fields of endeavor. Political corruption takes its toll not just in distorted policymaking and economic favors to special interests, but in the erosion of public faith in the governing process.

Long after big contributors to the 1972 Nixon campaign stopped trying to collect on their "investments," the legacy of Watergate continued to contribute to public apathy and cynicism. The scandal confirmed some of the people's worst suspicions about the honesty of all politicians and all political institutions. And the cynicism was heightened by post-Watergate revelations of other abuses of presidential power during the Kennedy and Johnson administrations. It was disclosed in 1975 that Attorney General Robert F. Kennedy, with the President's acquiescence, authorized IRS harassment and FBI bugging of steel executives in 1962, immediately after the industry raised prices against the President's wishes. And in 1975 the press revealed that President Johnson ordered the FBI to tap the phones of Robert F. Kennedy and the Rev. Martin Luther King, Jr. (during the 1964 Democratic convention) and to compile dossiers of unsavory information on foes and allies of the President.

Despite the shock of these disclosures, however, the public's worst suspicions are not generally warranted. The vast majority of public servants are honorable people. Breaking and entering and illegal surveillance are not the norm in American campaigning. Nor is IRS harassment or threat thereof. Neither is the solicitation of financial support from individuals who are under federal investigation. Nor is the circulation of scurrilous letters tagging political opponents with sexual improprieties—such as fake letters about Senators Humphrey and Jackson prepared and distributed by agents of the Committee to Reelect.

Various sorts of campaign shenanigans have been practiced by both parties in the past. Most have been milder and less widespread than the well-orchestrated barrage of GOP "dirty tricks" in the 1972 campaign. Others were blatantly illegal, like apparent fraud by Democratic workers at polling booths in Illinois and Texas on presidential election day in 1960. In any event, the recent spotlight on this sort of activity has probably put a damper on their use in the near future.

With each successive wave of corruption in politics, Washington has moved toward higher standards of behavior. This higher standard was undoubtably a factor—however important or slight—in the decision of Senator Edward M. Kennedy (D-Mass.) to sit out the contest for the 1976 Democratic presidential nomination. Kennedy's detractors and supporters alike agree that his explanation of the Chappaquiddick tragedy was too implausible to satisfy even the most gullible citizen in the post-Watergate era. While a rising trend of political morality may not have been apparent to the public, such a rise has in fact been taking place gradually over recent years. In the middle of the nineteenth century, Daniel Webster publicly acknowledged taking a payment from a major bank for his vote on a specific piece of legislation, and the practice was accepted by many voters and lawmakers as being "normal." Today, while it is sometimes practiced, it is not normal. It is a punishable offense.

Will Watergate result in further purification of the American political bloodstream? Well, it has already brought a revulsion against the use of power-crunch tactics as they were practiced by the Nixon "palace guard." And it has led to further laws limiting campaign spending and requiring public disclosure of contributions.

Whatever the short-run effects of the Watergate horror, the memory of it will serve as a constant reminder that honesty and decency are also good politics.

15 LAWYERS, LAWYERS, LAWYERS

There are some special things you should know about Washington lawyers. Many of them don't practice law.

Some of the law they *do* practice doesn't sound like Perry Mason. No courtrooms. No litigation. No standard pleadings.

Many of them earn their living with something called "administrative law." Which means they talk to hearing examiners (now called "administrative law judges"). And they write briefs for commissions instead of courts.

Some just talk on the telephone and advise their clients on what to do (certain clients simply want someone to "hold their hand").

Some give political advice (for a fee).

Some write legislation (which they plant with a cooperative congressman, who submits it to his subcommittee, whose chief counsel forwards it to the Legislative Drafting Service of the House or Senate, whose legal authors concoct a bill which, not surprisingly, comes out strongly resembling the legislation which the lawyer drew up in his downtown office in the first place).

There are about 17,000 lawyers in Washington. Roughly half of these are in the government. Of those 8,000-plus who are on the outside, about 7,000 are actively practicing law. (They occupy sixty-eight full columns of listings in the Yellow Pages of the Washington telephone directory.) More than half of these are involved in the routine law work involved in helping clients buy or sell a home, draw up a business contract, get divorced, or sue a delinquent debtor. Somewhere between 2,000 and 3,000 lawyers practice what has come to be known as "Washington law." Altogether, lawyers in Washington take in more than $200 million a year in legal fees.

Nowhere does the legal profession enjoy more employment than in Washington. Lawyers in the capital of the United States are a higher percentage of the population than in any other city in the world. It has been called a "lawyer's paradise," a "lawyer's garden of Eden," and even "a lawyer's Valhalla," since many lawyers, after spending their lives here, die here, and, undoubtedly, some do go on from here to heaven. Among American cities, Washington's legal population is the largest. Larger than New York's, for example, where corporate and financial law is dominant. Washington has more lawyers than other capital cities. More than London, Paris, Brussels, or Brasilia. And definitely more than Moscow or Peking (where contests and issues tend to be settled in other ways).

POLITICS AND LAW

The basic product of the capital city is politics, which is translated into policy, which ultimately becomes law or regulatory rules. Thus the distillation of politics is law, though admittedly the channels may seem devious and difficult to follow. More members of the House and Senate come from the law than from any other profession. Many corporate vice presidents in Washington are lawyers. So are trade association executives, and even an occasional newspaper man (like Clark Mollenhoff of the Des Moines *Register* and Warren Weaver, Jr., of the *New York Times*).

One thing that law training does is to establish an awareness of the competition between different interests and ideas. It probably creates a tolerance for varying points of view, a tolerance without which even the most adamant crusader or firebrand cannot long exist in Washington. Lawyers assume that anything can be (and probably will be) contested, denied, delayed, reviewed, litigated, contradicted, espoused, affirmed, or amended. In fact, in the democratic methods of American government, many subjects at issue on Capitol Hill ultimately find themselves amended out of existence, or at least amended beyond recognition. Whether legal textbooks recognize such a technique or not, it is a favorite approach of political-minded lawyers, and Washington lawyers are political-minded, if nothing else.

Washington lawyers practice constitutional law, labor law, tax law, corporate law, consumer law, environmental law, class-action law, international law, civil rights law, protest law, legislative law, administrative law, maritime law, and even "executive law" (which, since Watergate and other landmark cases, has come to be a separation-of-powers refuge for Presidents in distress).

WATERGATE—PLUS AND MINUS

The Watergate scandal brought prominence to Washington attorneys in a degree not seen since the Army-McCarthy hearings of 1954 and, before that, the legislative reform spree during the New Deal 1930s. During Watergate hearings, not only did lawyers chair and staff the Senate Select Committee; they also testified as witnesses with their own lawyers at their side who in turn spoke for other lawyers who were principals in the case. Seldom has the lawyer-client relationship been more thoroughly lawyer-to-lawyer. When John Ehrlichman (lawyer) appeared, he had by his side his counsel, John J. Wilson (lawyer), arguing the right of Richard M. Nixon (lawyer) to refrain from revealing the contents of tapes of conversations with the President's Counsel, John Dean (lawyer), about an alleged cover-up of activities involving G. Gordon Liddy (lawyer) and John Mitchell (top lawyer of all government lawyers).

Watergate showed how the legal profession lubricates the wheels of Washington (and occasionally gums them up). In terms of hourly billings, Watergate was a bonanza for the Washington legal establishment. But Watergate was hardly a boon to the public image of the profession. The public trial of so many lawyers for Watergate-related crimes hammered home the fact that persons trained in the law are not necessarily more obedient to it than the average citizen.

Since the practice of law in the capital does not provide much opportunity for courtroom experience, much of the Watergate case was prepared and tried by out-of-town lawyers, including Special Prosecutors Archibald Cox of Boston and Leon Jaworski of Houston; President Nixon's preresignation counsel, James D. St. Clair, from the Boston firm of Hale and Dorr; Albert Jenner, the Chicago attorney who served as counsel to the Republican members of the House Judiciary Committee during the impeachment inquiry; and

Richard Ben-Veniste, a former assistant U.S. attorney from New York City who was one of the government's principal prosecutors in the Watergate cover-up trial. But the most brilliant courtroom success—the acquittal of Maurice Stans in the Vesco case, tried in New York City—was pulled off by Washington attorney Walter Bonner, whose skill at manipulating a jury's minds and emotions is rare in Washington legal circles. (John Mitchell, Stans's codefendant, who was also acquitted, was defended in court by New York lawyers Peter Fleming and John Sprizzo, with supporting work by Washington attorney William Hundley.)

Sam Dash, the chief inquisitor of the Senate Watergate hearings, was recruited from the faculty of the local Georgetown University Law Center, and John Doar, majority counsel for the House Judiciary Committee impeachment proceedings, had a deep background in civil rights litigation at the Justice Department. Washington attorney Jacob Stein successfully represented another local lawyer, Kenneth Parkinson, the only defendant in the cover-up trial to win acquittal. One of the key Watergate prosecutors, Jill Volner, had previously worked in the organized crime section of the Justice Department and the racketeering division of the Labor Department. The chief government prosecutor, James F. Neal, came to Washington from a lucrative private practice in his native Tennessee, but he had previously spent a number of years at Justice, where he had been instrumental in convicting labor boss Jimmy Hoffa of jury tampering. Neal's sure grasp of the intricate Watergate details and his persuasive closing comments to the jury were a dazzling display of legal skill. John J. Wilson, the unsuccessful attorney for cover-up defendant Bob Haldeman, said after the trial that Neal was "the greatest lawyer I ever saw in a courtroom."

Where the Washington lawyers shone most brightly during Watergate was in backroom maneuvering and plea bargaining, which required the sort of shrewd compromise that they practice every day for their regular clients. Among the lawyers who excelled were Judah Best (one of the team that arranged the remarkable deal for former Vice President Spiro Agnew), Charles Rhyne (who represented former presidential secretary Rose Mary Woods both in and out of court), and Charles Shaffer (who handled John Dean's defense). Perhaps the cleverest job of negotiating was done by Herbert (Jack) Miller, the disarmingly affable lawyer (and onetime Justice Department prosecutor under Bobby Kennedy) who got former Attorney General Richard Kleindienst off light and helped arrange the pardon of former President Nixon.

While Watergate was a lucrative field day for most of the Washington lawyers connected with it, some suffered from their involvement, direct and indirect. The Washington office of Nixon's and Mitchell's old firm—New York-based Mudge, Rose, Guthrie and Alexander—no longer boasts of good connections with the White House. The firm of Morin, Dickstein and Shapiro, which former White House aide Charles Colson joined as a name partner before Watergate reached scandalous proportions, was jolted by Colson's eventual guilty plea (arranged by one of the firm's partners, David Shapiro, a respected former civil liberties lawyer with experience in defending accused Communists). Hardest hit of all was William Bittman, who, as counsel to Watergate burglar E. Howard Hunt, had received payment for his services—$210,000 in cash—from onetime Nixon personal lawyer Herbert Kalmbach.

After the story surfaced (in the Senate testimony of go-between Tony Ulasewicz), Bittman resigned Hunt's defense and, more significantly, resigned his partnership at the firm of Hogan and Hartson.

WHY WASHINGTON?

Legal scholars agree that the American governmental system does, in fact, foster the presence of lawyers in adversary proceedings and brings more of them to Washington than to the other major capitals of the world. British government, with its parliamentary form, settles more policy matters and conflicts between Whitehall and British citizens with less litigation and legal formality. To the degree that the rules of evidence and courtroom procedure are more flexible in Great Britain than in the United States, the saturation level of lawyers is comparably lower in London than in Washington. Even Paris, with its traditional Gallic love of disputation, manages to argue more and litigate less.

The American principle of separation of powers contributes to this high level of legal activity. The founding Americans, suspicious of royal authority, set up their now famous "checks and balances," with Courts checking Congress and presumably Congress checking the Executive. When conflicts arose, lawyers swarmed like stormy petrels, and Washington became their gathering place. When the British or French government, or the Canadian or German, encounter such conflicts as are engendered by the Watergate dispute over "executive privilege," the matter is resolved by a vote of "no confidence" in the Parliament or the Chamber of Deputies or the Bundestag, and the electorate makes the decision on whether to toss out the government. Not so in the United States and Washington. Here we turn it over to the legal types, where the issue is disputed ad infinitum, or until the next regularly scheduled election rolls around.

What a glorious setup for lawyers! (And the lawyers in Washington are among the first to admit it.)

THE MAJOR FIRMS

A few years ago, it was a simple job to pick the "top ten" law firms in Washington, and even today people try to pick their own list of the top ten. Yet, the city's law practice has expanded so enormously in recent years that any list of ten will leave out dozens of other firms that are preeminent in their own special fields and will, of necessity, omit a number of other individuals or small firms that have distinguished themselves in one way or another.

Still, on almost everybody's list, the rank of "Number One Firm" goes to Covington and Burling. The position is accorded to it by virtue of its age, size, reputation, and performance. Organized more than fifty years ago, it now houses more than 150 lawyers and has represented clients that range from the government of Iran to the Du Pont Company. Earnings range from a $16,000 to $18,000 starting salary for a young law graduate from a good law school to something over $200,000 a year for the most senior partners.

In recent years, Arnold and Porter (once Arnold, Fortas and Porter) has gained ground on prestigious Covington and Burling. Arnold and Porter now has about one hundred lawyers and a roster of clients somewhat less international than C&B, but also somewhat more "litigious." Founding member Thurman Arnold, now dead, liked nothing more than to be able to say, "Let's sue him." But Washington law does not give much opportunity for suit. More often, a case becomes a matter of representing a client before a government agency, and of knowing the ins and outs of negotiation rather than practicing courtroom tactics.

The second-biggest firm in Washington now is Arent, Fox, Kintner, Plotkin and Kahn, with approximately 125 lawyers, and it is still growing. The firm started with a strong bent toward antitrust and tax work, then strengthened its expertise in regulatory law with the addition of Earl Kintner after he resigned from the chairmanship of the Federal Trade Commission.

Hogan and Hartson is an old-line, traditionally Republican firm with strong business connections, both in Washington and throughout the country, with special Chicago affiliations. In size it is now third to C&B and Arent, Fox. Its roster was expanded in 1975 with the addition of former Senator J. William Fulbright and former Virginia Governor Linwood Holton.

Clifford, Warnke, Glass, McIlwain and Finney. This was once a one-man show, built around Clark Clifford, a former St. Louis lawyer who became counsel to President Truman and later Secretary of Defense under President Johnson. Paul Warnke was also in the Defense Department before throwing in his lot with Clifford. The firm has considerable political savvy, commands high fees, and has added some Arab oil countries to its list of clients.

Wilmer, Cutler and Pickering. Strong in corporate representation, the firm represents General Motors. The most conspicuous of the partners is Lloyd Cutler who has had run-ins with Ralph Nader over automobile safety legislation. The firm has approximately ninety-five lawyers.

Williams, Connolly and Califano. Another former one-man operation founded by Edward Bennett Williams, who made his reputation as a defense attorney (for clients ranging from ex-Teamsters boss Jimmy Hoffa to the Washington *Post*) and is now also president and part owner of the Washington Redskins football team. This is the firm that former Treasury Secretary John Connally turned to when he was indicted for bribery in the "milk fund" case, and Williams won acquittal for his client.

Jones, Day, Reavis and Pogue. A growing firm in taxes and in securities law (without which no big company can survive). Coming up fast in general practice. Now has between forty and fifty lawyers.

Steptoe and Johnson. An old-line Washington–West Virginia firm with many illustrious alumni, including both the founding members and a former Secretary of the Army, Stephen Ailes. Has grown in recent years to a staff of fifty lawyers.

Sutherland, Asbill and Brennan. Strong on taxes, with former Internal Revenue Director Randolph Thrower as an Atlanta partner.

Cox, Langford and Brown. Especially strong in international business (such as airlines) and represents a number of foreign embassies. Has recently taken in some new partners, including J. Edward Day, former Postmaster General in the Kennedy administration.

Corcoran, Foley, Youngman and Rowe. Strong Democratic orientation, but influential in any administration, owing to long experience of senior partners Tom Corcoran, Edward Foley, and James H. Rowe.

Ginsburg, Feldman and Bress. Also Democratic leanings, with former White House aide Mike Feldman as a persuasive representative.

Leva, Hawes, Symington, Martin and Oppenheimer. A group of old hands, growing older, but still potent. All the partners have had government service, in regulatory agencies, price control, etc.

Patton, Boggs, Blow, Verrill, Brand and May. A younger firm, in age of partners and its own tenure, but has doubled size in five years. Client interests range from sugar to Alaskan oil.

Verner, Liipfert, Bernhard and McPherson. A practice originally in transportation and trucking, now diversified and growing.

Sharon, Pierson, Semmes, Crolius and Finley. Built around a former Clark Clifford associate and an old Clifford client. Now works broadly for industrial clients.

Danzansky, Borkland, Margolis and Adler. Has local and national clients, strong in utilities issues.

Howrey, Simon, Baker and Murchison. A still-growing firm, specializing in antitrust, with strong roots in the Federal Trade Commission background of senior partner Edward F. Howrey.

SPECIALTY FIRMS

There are many other excellent firms that specialize in certain areas of Washington practice:

Radio and television (FCC): Cohn and Marks, one of whose partners, Leonard Marks, was head of the U.S. Information Agency; Fletcher, Heald, Rowell, Kenehan and Hildreth, a firm that has been growing under different names for nearly thirty years; and Pierson, Ball and Dowd, another of the leaders in the Washington specialty field.

Railroads and trucking and airlines (ICC, CAB): The Verner, Liipfert firm, mentioned earlier, is strong in this field. So also are: Jones, Day, Reavis and Pogue (especially in airlines); Mayer, Brown and Platt; Prather, Levenberg, Seeger and Doolittle; and Farmer and Ewing.

Energy and fuels (FPC, Department of the Interior, etc.): Too early to say which firms will emerge on top in this burgeoning field, but generally, the current will flow toward those with experience in petroleum, coal, and general corporate practice, like the aforementioned Patton, Boggs firm.

Taxes (IRS): Lee, Toomey and Kent is an oldtimer and a leader. Other major firms in the field include Ivins, Phillips and Barker, originally from Philadelphia but now firmly entrenched in Washington; Caplin and Drysdale, featuring former Internal Revenue Commissioner Mortimer Caplin; and Bogan and Freeland.

Maritime: A very specialized specialty, attracting a growing number of firms, such as President Nixon's own former firm, Mudge, Rose, Guthrie and Alexander, whose Washington partner, Arthur M. Becker, concentrates in this area. Also: Kominers, Fort, Schlefer and Boyer; Galland Kharasch, Calkins and Brown; Kirlin, Campbell and Keating; and Morgan, Lewis and Bockius, which is a top firm in labor law.

Patents: Several of the leaders are Schuyler, Birch, Swindler, McKie and Beckett; Cushman, Darby and Cushman; and Browne, Beveridge, DeGrandi and Kline.

PICKING A LAWYER

More important than the abstract ratings of law firms is the recurring question of how to pick one for your own purposes. Here are some general observations for your guidance. Use them with several grains of salt. Mix them with your personal knowledge and the advice of your local legal counsel. No one can pick a lawyer for you, and since you're the one who pays the bill (or gets stuck with an adverse judgment), you had better be the one to do the picking.

First: Consult your regular counsel to see whether he has an affiliated law firm in Washington.

Second: If the answer to the above is "yes," ask whether the Washington affiliate is experienced in the problem that confronts you at this time. If you face a major labor-management dispute, you'll need a lawyer with expertise at the National Labor Relations Board. If your problem relates to advertising claims, you had better have someone familiar with the Federal Trade Commission. But if your problem relates to broadcasting, you will want an attorney with communications background and a familiarity with the Federal Communications Commission. Being a good tax lawyer may not be enough to help a client through the labyrinths of the regulatory agencies.

Third: Ask what kind of fee arrangement the Washington firm operates on. Some work on a straight time basis, some on an arbitrary charge, some on the size or importance of the case to the client.

Fourth: Beware big talk about high connections. Some lawyers have them, to be sure, but in only a very rare case do the connections decide the case. More often, the solution will be on the basis of hard legal research, digging into past precedents, or simply pavement-pounding footwork.

Fifth: Beware the promise of a "sure thing." There are very few "sure things" in Washington. Most reputable lawyers will give you their objective judgment on a case, but not many knowledgeable or reputable practitioners will promise automatic satisfaction. Size up the lawyer on the basis of his candid estimate of your chances and his willingness to let you in on the procedures and efforts that will have to be undertaken.

Sixth: Tell your lawyer—and his Washington affiliate—*all* the facts as you know them. The problem may be simpler than you think, and if you detail it for him, he may be able to solve the question without going very far up the administrative ladder.

Seventh: Recognize that your problem with Washington may not be a legal problem so much as a matter of knowing where to go in the bureaucracy for the answer to your question. Thus, it may be shoeleather that is required, so before you commit yourself to expensive legal help, pin down the nature of the problem.

Eighth: Check with your trade association and other industry representatives to see whether other individuals or companies have had similar problems. Even if it is a tax case, you may find that there is a backlog of experience. Others may have found the answer before you started looking. (There's no need to reinvent the wheel.)

Ninth: Don't panic. Remember that the American governmental system is built on laws and nearly everybody has different interpretations of how to apply them. So if you seem to be in trouble, you're not the first, nor yet the last, and the overwhelming odds are that you'll come out all right.

None of these generalities tells you just which lawyer to pick, if any. But such prior consideratons set the stage for your choice. Frequently, you can handle your problem without a lawyer. Perhaps a few simple telephone calls will suffice. Don't be afraid to pick up the phone and call. More often than not, you'll get to someone in Washington who will help you.

How much should you pay a Washington lawyer? It will depend, of course, on his prominence, experience, and record of performance. Some younger Washington lawyers will bill their clients at the rate of $35 to $50 an hour. More experienced practitioners bill at rates ranging from $75 to $100 an hour. Within the law firm itself, for computing the fee, a senior partner's time may be valued at $150 or $200 an hour. But when the fee structure reaches these heights, the fee is probably not based on hourly rates so much as on a general appraisal of the importance of the case, its complexity, and the amount of money riding on it for the client himself.

Most senior lawyers agree that they have about 1,200 hours of "billable" time per year. (Some say this can be stretched to 1,400 hours, if you include some overlap and some weekend and evening work.) Thus, a top partner can be expected to generate for his firm a minimum of $120,000 a year (multiplying $100 times 1,200 hours). Junior members of the firm ("associates" who haven't yet "made partner") normally generate more client billings than they receive from the firm in salary, and this residue is divided among the partners. Of course, before the partners can start divvying up their profits, they must cover overhead costs like office rent (usually in a high-rent part of town), secretarial and paralegal staffs, extensive law libraries, etc. Not all Washington lawyers bill $100 an hour, but an elite few will bill much more, when they have a unique ability to deal with a particularly crucial case.

Washington law firms handle their internal affairs in ways ranging from the quiet, man-to-man discussion of Clifford, Warnke et al. to the more formal staff-type arrangement of Covington and Burling. Until recently, the Covington senior partners met weekly at the Metropolitan Club (just two blocks from their offices on 16th Street) to discuss cases in progress. Yet, with more than fifty-five partners in all, even this meeting had to be restricted to the senior-seniors, including such men as H. Thomas Austern, Charles Horsky, and Edward Burling.

The division of fees operates quite differently from firm to firm. In some larger firms, each partner is allotted a "share" or percentage of the whole, and the figure is set at the end of each year for the following year. The share is usually based on the partner's ability to bring in business rather than his legal scholarship or research capacity. Associates are paid a salary in the same way that a corporate counsel would be paid by his own corporation.

A few firms, however, allow individual lawyers to practice almost as separate law firms, sharing the library facilities and the expense of the younger researchers and associate lawyers. Covington and Burling, using a system like this, has occasionally been described as a "legal cooperative." Some of the partners pursue cases and clients very much on their own, keeping other partners casually informed along the way.

There are very few lawyers in Washington firms who are not male and white, although most of the top firms are now integrated (technically, at least) by gender and race. This trend is bound to accelerate as the new crops of law school graduates, in which women and racial minorities are increasingly prominent, work their way into government and private practice. (With the addition of a female partner, C&B had to move its weekly partners luncheon from the Metropolitan Club—which allows no women members and bans female guests until 6 P.M.—to the Sheraton-Carlton Hotel at 16th and K Streets.)

The legal practice of the nation's capital is not regularly reported as a news matter, yet it is written about from time to time. One of the most knowledgeable of such writers is Joseph C. Goulden, who authored a study of the subject in a book called *The Superlawyers,* published in 1971. Some years earlier, the subject was given an insider's treatment by Charles Horsky, a senior partner of Covington and Burling, in the 1952 book titled *The Washington Lawyer.*

HOW THEY WORK

Washington's law practice, on the whole, is less than glamorous. One morning recently, a Washington lawyer received a frantic phone call from one of his affiliate partners in Pittsburgh, asking how one of their clients could get an export license for a product on which he had a tentative order from a firm in Europe. The Pittsburgh lawyer, while experienced in corporate law, was mystified by the Washington bureaucracy and his confidence was shaken by the prospect of floundering in the federal morass in search of *the* one person who could give him the answer his client needed.

His Washington partner listened for a few minutes, noted the salient facts, and promised an answer. The Pittsburgh lawyer was sure the Washington lawyer had a pipeline to the top or, at the very least, a lifelong familiarity with the problem. But the Washington man had no such thing. What he did have was the standard Washington telephone directory, with every government listing. Not knowing who had the answer, he called the central number for the Department of Commerce and asked for someone in the Office of Export Administration. The first call got the wrong person, but he was directed to another number, which also proved to be off target. The third call got the officer who handled export licenses for the product in question. The lawyer asked if he could come down and talk to him. The expert, a middle-grade government employee and career civil servant, delighted at the prospect of a caller on this otherwise dull weekday morning, said, "Certainly. Come in the Fourteenth Street entrance, pass the main bank of elevators, and turn right."

Twenty minutes later, after an 85¢ taxi ride, the Washington lawyer was in the office of the export-license specialist, posing his client's problem. As it turned out, it wasn't much of a problem but the export license application required some information he didn't have. So he picked up the phone, called the client in Pittsburgh, and told him he was in the office of an international trade specialist at the Department of Commerce in Washington. He got the technical details he needed, and in less than half an hour the applicaton was filled out, filed, and on the way to being processed. Lawyer and government expert shook hands. Client was overjoyed. (And the Pittsburgh partner was astonished at the expertise of his Washington colleague.)

The Washington lawyer, in fact, billed the client only at his customary hourly rate of $100 plus two hours of subsequent follow-up and the cost of telegrams, telephone, taxi fare, and legal secretarial work. He might easily have billed him $2,000, which the client probably would have paid without question, marveling at the slick performance of his Washington lawyer in getting prompt attention to a vital piece of business.

Indeed, some attorneys do charge many thousands of dollars for a single telephone call. The famous onetime New Dealer Tom Corcoran is reputed to have billed a client $10,000 for one telephone call to a high-ranking official in the Department of Defense. Whether true or apocryphal, the story is plausible, and comparable billings could very well be worth the money to clients who need fast answers to important questions.

Such calls and such services usually do not require influence. But they do require that the high-ranking official take the call and give an answer. If the caller is unknown to him, he is likely *not* to take the call. The question, while easy to answer, would remain unanswered, and the client's business would be stalled until a routine inquiry worked its way tortuously through the maze of red tape and back out again. So prominence and friendship translate into "identifiability" and a better chance of getting through.

The movement of lawyers back and forth between government and private practice is so continuous that it raises eyebrows among a good many laymen. Yet it is part of the process of mutual education (and advantage) by which public work is accomplished. Some twenty years ago, however, during the Eisenhower administration, top administrators noted that the drain on their legal staffs was becoming a serious problem. As soon as a young staff member got his feet wet and began to get valuable to his agency, he was whisked away by some private firm and the government was left holding an empty bag and forced to train another neophyte. So a new policy was inaugurated, called the "four-year rule," and it was installed in a number of agencies, including the General Counsel's Office of the Treasury, some regulatory agencies, and the top echelons of the Department of Justice. Under it, an entering lawyer makes a gentleman's agreement to stay at least four years, so he can repay the government for the time it devoted to training him in his specialty. While the rule is not legally binding, the moral and ethical pressures on rising young aspirants are usually enough to keep it reasonably well enforced.

INTERNATIONAL PRACTICE

One of the most lucrative listings on the Washington legal hit parade now is international in character. Since World War II, with the enormous expansion in international trade, hundreds of Washington representatives have taken up the business of shepherding businessmen through the bureaucratic labyrinths. Sometimes the case involves high-level representation between governments, handled in an unofficial way to avoid the stickiness of public policy. Sometimes it involves advice to governments on how to approach other governments, or how to prepare presentations to the U.N. Usually it is a mixture of business and politics. One Washington lawyer recently handled a case involving an American aircraft company that wanted to build and operate an airfield in Bangkok, Thailand, with Japanese financing.

Another Washington lawyer was a go-between for a large foundry company in negotiations with the Soviet Union and the United States Department of Commerce for the construction of facilities to build trucks in the USSR. Another was involved in the efforts of Control Data Corporation to establish long-range computer manufacturing and sales relationships with the Soviet

Union. Many others have become active in Japanese trade and Japanese investment in the U.S., which has been a kind of mini-explosion in the U.S. economy in recent years.

The boom in imports (from Japan, Germany, Italy, and other parts of Western Europe) has created burgeoning commissions for Washington lawyers in representing both foreign clients and American concerns that operate overseas. Much of this business has gone to such established international firms as Covington and Burling; Cox, Langford and Brown; or Coudert Brothers (with Sol Linowitz, former OAS ambassador and ex-chairman of Xerox) and the newly reconstituted firm of Rogers and Wells (with former Secretary of State William P. Rogers as senior partner).

The growth of import business brings law practice to Washington from another source: the American companies that feel the need of protection from tariffs or special legislation such as the Burke-Hartke bill proposed a couple of years ago.

On the other side of the coin, the rapid rise in exports from the United States to Europe, Japan, and the Soviet Union has given many individual attorneys an opportunity to help hook up American business corporations with foreign embassies in Washington or commercial ministries at the other end of the line. One such attorney is Hobart Taylor, a successful black practitioner in the Washington upper levels, who speaks for such clients as Chrysler Corporation, Swindell-Dressler, and White Motors (the latter two in connection with intricate deals with the Soviet Union).

And Washington firms are sure to capitalize, too, on the growing number of high-level international disputes, including cases pitting the interests of one national government against another. Among the folklore of Washington law firms is the case of Pakistan and India, who found themselves some years ago locked in a dispute over control of the river waters flowing between them. Without any body of international law to guide them on water rights, they looked toward the United States, where water compacts had been developed between the states. For legal counsel, they engaged Covington and Burling, "the informal State Department," and senior partner John G. Laylin, who analyzed the situation in terms of a similar dispute between the states of California and Arizona over the flow of water in the Colorado River.

Strangely enough, Supreme Court practice is hardly a drop in the bucket of Washington law. Some 5,000 cases are sent to the high court each year, but the vast majority of them are summarily dismissed without a hearing. Barely 150 cases are subjected to full oral argument and decided with precedent-setting written opinions. Much of the oral argument is made not by Washington lawyers, but by the out-of-state attorneys who handled the cases in lower courts at the trial and appeal stages. Thus, for all the pomp and fanfare of the Supreme Court presence, it does not feature as a major source of legal revenue in Washington. Most top Washington lawyers, however, make a point of becoming admitted to the Supreme Court Bar (a pro forma process entitling them to argue before the Court). Such admission is a necessity for arguing before the Court or sharing fees for cases that reach the Court.

PUBLIC INTEREST LAW

Making a strong appearance on the scene now is the whole area of "public interest law," involving environmental cases before the EPA and Department of the Interior, all manner of pollution cases, stockholders' challenges before the SEC, consumerism, class-action suits, and other suits brought by public groups. Common Cause, under the leadership of John Gardner, has given prominence to some of the recent cases, and of course Ralph Nader is the patron saint (or devil) of similar challenges. There is even a private foundation, the Stern Family Fund, which has devoted a large share of its resources to this area by creating the Stern Community Law Firm. The most prominent public interest lawyers include Joseph L. Rauh, Jr., a veteran civil rights and civil liberties attorney; John Banzhaf, a consumer activist professor at George Washington University Law School who forced the acceptance of free anti-smoking commercials on television (leading in 1971 to the banning of all broadcast cigarette ads); and William Dobrivir, a Covington and Burling dropout who was instrumental in exposing the GOP "milk fund" and its relation to an increase in the milk price subsidy. (Dobrivir's halo was tarnished when, for a joke at a cocktail party, he played a portion of a White House tape that a court had entrusted to him in his professional capacity.)

As of now, however, public law is principally *pro bono publico* and is not yet a profitable branch of Washington law practice. Such practice, however, may become more profitable in the future if it follows the example of two recent cases. The firm of Joseph L. Rauh, Jr., and John Silard collected a fee of $97,500 (by court order) for handling a successful suit for the enforcement of school desegregation in seventeen states. And Gilbert Hahn, a former chairman of the District of Columbia City Council, won an even larger court-awarded fee for handling a suit to force the city to revise its tax assessments. For now, however, the practice of public interest law is dependent upon subsidies from foundations. One of Washington's most successful public interest firms, the Center for Law and Social Policy, has received Ford Foundation support since its creation in 1969, and in 1974 got a $1.1 million Ford grant for work in such areas as health, consumer affairs, women's rights, and the environment. Two other Washington firms, the Citizens Communications Center and the National Resources Defense Council, received 1974 Ford grants of $230,000 and $300,000, respectively.

MORE GROWTH AHEAD

Since Washington is still relatively young among the major capitals of the world (though perhaps it is now becoming slightly middle-aged), it is in various stages of growth and transition, and nowhere is this more noticeable than in the changing flow of legal practice.

Before World War I, law practice in Washington was unhurried, unspectacular, and also relatively unlucrative. It consisted mainly of patent law, a little mild antitrust prosecution, some legislative drafting, and sporadic cases involving railroad regulation, banking, and tariffs. Even most of these cases would be handled by New York law firms or by lawyers who regularly practiced for corporations and private clients in other cities. After World War I, during the cleanup of wartime situations, tax cases began to grow, but still most aspiring young lawyers looked to New York or Boston, Philadelphia, Los Angeles, and San Francisco to make their fortune in corporate law.

Then the depression and the Roosevelt New Deal burst like a rocket over the governmental scene, and lawyers flocked to Washington. There were Tommy Corcoran and Ben Cohen and Bob Jackson and Tom Clark and

Thurman Arnold and Paul Porter and Abe Fortas, and new justices of the Supreme Court, like Frank Murphy from Detroit and Felix Frankfurter from Harvard. Supreme Court cases involved the NRA, the AAA, and the SEC, and constitutional disputes were page-one headline news. It was the heyday of the legal profession in Washington—until today.

Now again, lawyers in the nation's capital are called upon to help individuals, corporations, labor unions, and organized citizens defend themselves or attack others, set new rules, or adapt to the ones already here. Economic controls in peacetime spawned thousands of commissions for lawyers, even as labor legislation did a generation earlier. And tens of thousands of new cases are being generated every year by the laws and rules regarding health, safety, pensions, taxes, pricing, import-export licensing, trade practices, packaging, labeling, franchising, copyrights, patents, labor contracts, broadcast licenses, advertising claims, the stock market, and myriad other areas and routines of modern life which are regulated by the federal government.

What next for lawyers in Washington?

Global law? Interplanetary law? Space agreements? Or will it be a more inward-looking practice involving the rights of individuals and their protection against intrusions of the government itself via wiretaps, secret investigations, and professional spying? Observers of the legal profession expect that public law, via class-action suits and group litigation, may be the next big frontier for Washington law. Where only a few now tread, the path may be widened into a broad highway over which hundreds of organizations and citizens groups will soon be traveling.

Whatever else this new phase of Washington law may bring—in terms of more court suits, new laws, and finely sharpened public sensitivities—the one most predictable outcome is simple: More growth in federal law, more opportunities for the Washington legal profession, and still more lawyers in what is already the most heavily lawyered city in the whole world.

16 LOBBIES AT WORK

Here is a simple guide to help you label the thousands of organizations in Washington that exist to influence federal policy:

1. If you agree with the aims of the group, it is a "crusader in the public interest," a "voice of the people," or a "force for good."

2. If you're indifferent to its cause, it is a "special interest group."

3. If you disagree with its position, it's a "lobby."

To many people around the nation, the word "lobby" is so distasteful that they reserve it exclusively for their enemies. But in Washington, lobby is not a dirty word. Savvy Washingtonians know that the vast majority of the lobbyists here bear no resemblance to the popular conception of a seedy fellow hanging around the corridors of Capitol Hill, peddling influence and offering bribes. But the stereotype is given a boost every few years by a new Capitol Hill scandal, like the discovery of the operation of Nathan Voloshen and congressional aide Martin Sweig (who during the Sixties conducted their illegal lobbying in the office and under the very nose of Speaker John McCormack.)

Lobbyists are the people who represent the interests of labor, agriculture, business, veterans, religious sects, welfare recipients, state and local sportsmen, automobile enthusiasts, foreign governments, animal lovers, ethnic and racial minorities, and taxpayers in general. Whatever your particular characteristics, whatever your cause, and whether you know it or not, there is a lobby in Washington representing your interests.

All lobbies have equal status before the law, but some are "more equal" than others. The clout wielded by a lobby depends on many things. The larger its membership the better, especially if the members can be reached by phone and urged to contact their congressman, and to tell him that they will remember how he voted on their pet issue when the next election rolls around. The National Rifle Association, headquarters of the "gun lobby," boasted a couple of years ago that it could trigger an instant avalanche of 500,000 letters from its members. Those who know the NRA's success against gun control legislation do not doubt the boast. Highly placed government contacts are indispensable to a lobbyist, too.

Above all, a successful lobby cannot exist without money: money for entertaining congressmen and high-ranking bureaucrats, money to contribute to the campaigns of cooperative politicians (and the opponents of uncooperative ones), money to pay for the research necessary to plead a good case before Congress and in the Executive Branch; money for an advertising campaign if an issue becomes hot enough to attract broad public attention. Some of the public interest lobbies—Ralph Nader, Common Cause, the environmental and consumer groups—do surprisingly well with lots of volunteer labor, press coverage, and small contributions. But they are the exceptions, and what they may lack in money, they make up in zeal.

While the word "lobbyist" is not an insult in Washington, most lobbyists would rather be called something else. In the words of Dale Miller, an old friend of the late President Lyndon Johnson and a representative of business interests in Texas and elsewhere, "It just isn't sophisticated to call yourself a lobbyist in Washington any more." Lobbyists who are lawyers in private practice would rather be identified by the name of their firm, not the name of a client. Lobbyists who are lawyers working full-time for a trade association or union often carry the title of "legislative counsel." Lobbyists who work for a particular corporation are often called "vice president for governmental relations" or "Washington representative." Many lobbyists say they are in "consulting" or "public relations." Public relations firms, incidentally, are nowhere near as effective lobbyists as law firms. An exception is the nationwide P.R. firm of Hill and Knowlton. Their lobbying team includes Liz Carpenter, ex-press secretary of Lady Bird Johnson, and Washington office chief Robert Gray, onetime secretary to President Eisenhower's Cabinet and an occasional social escort of former presidential secretary Rose Mary Woods. A Hill and Knowlton alumnus, Lawrence Merthan (once an aide to ex-Senator Eugene McCarthy), is now an executive of the Carpet and Rug Institute.

". . . BY ANY OTHER NAME . . ."

The NRA doesn't like to be called the "gun lobby"; the American Petroleum Institute isn't crazy about the term "oil lobby"; and the Pharmaceutical Manufacturers Association would rather be identified by its official name than as the "drug lobby." But these catch phrases are a convenient form of shorthand, especially to identify combinations of trade associations that work together toward common goals. If a reporter had to list all the components of the "highway lobby"—which includes the American Road Builders Association, American Trucking Associations, American Autombile Association, American Petroleum Institute, Motor Vehicle Manufacturers Association, Rubber Manufacturers Association, and many other groups—there would be no space left for the story. Some highway lobbyists (who for years were successful in opposing any diversion of funds from the interstate highway trust fund to mass transit) show a sense of humor by referring to themselves as the "road gang."

Because of the many hats that lobbyists wear, no one knows exactly how many there are in Washington. A reliable count would require an impossible consensus on definition. There's a law requiring Capitol Hill lobbyists to register with the Senate and House and report their expenditures, but the law defines lobbying so narrowly that it is virtually useless. Only those people whose "principal purpose" is the influencing of legislation need register, and most lobbyists prefer to define their principal occupational purpose in some other way. Clark Clifford—a powerful Washington lawyer, adviser to Democratic Presidents, and former Secretary of Defense—has never registered as a lobbyist. But for twenty-five years he has used subtle influence with high-level officials to plead—out of court—the cases of the nation's corporate giants.

Some of the most successful lobbyists work invisibly, pulling off major coups by knowing how and when to make their moves without ruffling feathers, muddying waters, or making waves. Other lobbyists, lacking access to key people with power, resort to the opposite techniques—public controversy and confrontation—to create a stir and get results.

In the last century and early decades of this one, congressional lobbying had the subtlety of a sledgehammer. It often entailed outright bribery. Railroad baron Collis Huntington once told some colleagues that legislation he needed from a newly convened Congress would cost only $200,000, because "this coming session will be composed of the hungriest set of men that ever got together." Bribery is not an extinct art on Capitol Hill, though today money is usually used not for cash gifts but rather to pay for goods and services (entertainment, travel, and small favors for public officials). Trade associations used to pay congressmen or senators as much as two or three thousand dollars to address their conventions, and some members earned twice as much from honorariums as they did from their congressional salaries. This came to an abrupt halt in 1974 when, in the wake of Watergate, Congress passed the Federal Election Campaign Act Amendments prohibiting any elected or appointed federal official from accepting an honorarium exceeding $1,000 or accepting aggregate honorariums exceeding $15,000 in a calendar year.

Some lobbyists used to offer congressmen use of their clients' private planes. Senator Vance Hartke (D-Ind.) was accused during the ITT scandal of using that company's plane as a private taxi service. Congressmen and senators could frequently be spotted at National Airport's Page Airways terminal for corporate and private aircraft, though in today's atmosphere, most senators and representatives are gun-shy about accepting such free transportation.

CULTIVATION OF BIGWIGS

High-ranking appointed officials, especially members of the regulatory commissions, get the royal treatment, too. Some of them, when confronted by reporters, deny that they ever discuss business at these social events, while others openly acknowledge that a strict separation of business and pleasure is impossible. In 1973 the governors of the New York Stock Exchange met in Washington and threw a fancy dinner party, attended by virtually everybody-who-is-anybody in federal securities regulation—leaders from the Hill, the Federal Reserve, the White House, and the Securities and Exchange Commission. Asked about the propriety of attending the dinner, SEC member Hugh F. Owens said, "It was a social gathering, pure and simple." But another commissioner, John R. Evans, acknowledged that he had "asked specific questions about what they'd do if we did certain things about their rate proposals." He said the dinner was a "great time to get their opinions; sometimes you can get answers privately you can't get at a public hearing."

Extracurricular socializing resulted in 1975 in the demotion of regulator Robert D. Timm, who for several years had been a member and then chairman of the Civil Aeronautics Board. (Although he was not reappointed as chairman by President Ford, Timm was allowed to remain on the board until the expiration of his term at the end of 1976.) In 1974 Washington *Star* reporter Stephen Aug had revealed that Timm took an all-expenses-paid golfing trip to Bermuda hosted by the chairman of United Aircraft (an airframe manufacturer), who also invited executives of Pan American, TWA, Western, and Braniff airlines. It was reported, too, that Timm had spent a weekend in

Portugal (at his own expense) with TWA's Washington vice president, Thomas K. Taylor. The Aviation Consumer Action Project, a Nader-sponsored watchdog group, got after Timm, and, even before his demotion, he was forced to withdraw from consideration of cases before the CAB which might affect United Aircraft.

Entertaining at big cocktail parties and conventions, however, is not nearly as effective a lobbying technique as the small, elegant dinner party, given either at the home of the lobbyist (if his client pays him enough to maintain a suitably gracious home) or at a private club. The seemingly random guest list of a lobbyist's dinner party was probably planned with more of an eye to commercial gain than social rapport. If a public official invited to such a party doesn't know at the time just why he was invited, the purpose will eventually be made clear to him—a few days, weeks, or months later. One of the favorite private clubs of lobbyists is the George Town Club, housed in a tiny, exquisitely paneled and furnished old townhouse on Wisconsin Avenue in historic Georgetown. It is owned, not coincidentally, by Tongsun Park, a nephew of the president of Korea, *bon vivant,* entrepreneur, and lobbyist with interests in shipping, rice, and oil. Some of the most social and best-connected lobbyists are members of the elite 1925 F Street Club, founded and run for decades by a grande dame, the late Mrs. Laura Merriam Curtis Gross, whose nephew, William Merriam, was a prominent lobbyist for the ITT Corporation. The most exclusive and little-known hangout for Capitol Hill lobbyists is a private club in a cramped, plain rowhouse at 116 Schott's Court, next to the parking lot of the Dirksen Senate Office Building. The 116 Club is a favorite luncheon spot for oil lobbyists and their congressional contacts.

COSTS AND CONTRIBUTIONS

In every election year, a lobbyist had better have a ready supply of cash for all the $100-a-head cocktail parties that are staged to raise money for congressional incumbents. Lobbyists grumble a lot about this custom, practiced equally by both parties, and call it "extortion" and a "shakedown." Others call it a "silver offering." But rather than risk angering an incumbent who sits on a committee with jurisdiction over his client, the lobbyist forks over the money and goes to the party. Despite increasing "Watergate sensitivity" about political contributions, lobbyists in 1974 were deluged as normal with invitations to parties for incumbent congressmen. Many lobbyists got letters of invitation that were ostensibly written on congressional stationery and apparently drafted by the well-known Republican senators whose signatures appeared at the bottom. The letters urged a contribution to a lesser-known House member. While the letters appeared to violate the law against soliciting political contributions from a government office, they were technically legal. As columnists Evans and Novak revealed, the letters were drafted on official-*looking* (but not official) Senate stationery by a conservative lobby called the Americans for Constitutional Action, which mailed them from its offices.

The $100 cocktail parties are just nickel-and-dime stuff in the high-stakes game of politics. The big campaign money comes from the so-called political action committees (known as PACs and pronounced "packs"). These are created by trade associations and labor unions to channel the supposedly voluntary contributions of their members into the campaigns of friendly congressmen or the opponents of unfriendly ones. In 1962, for example, the

American Medical Association induced physicians to contribute $3 million to AMPAC, which passed the money along to the opponents of incumbents who were pushing medicare legislation. But none of the incumbents who campaigned on an explicitly pro-medicare platform was defeated. Three years later, despite a rumored $12 million lobbying expenditure by the AMA over the course of the long battle, medicare was enacted. In every election year the AFL–CIO's Committee on Political Education (COPE) pours thousands of dollars—deducted virtually automatically from union membership dues—into the campaigns of each of its congressional friends, the vast majority of them Democrats.

While the lobbyist's use of money gets the most public attention, it is not the only weapon in his arsenal. There are many other more reputable—and often more effective—ways that a lobbyist can ingratiate himself with a public official. Since lobbyists are vast storehouses of information on esoteric matters, they are indispensable to congressmen and bureaucrats who need to draft guidelines, regulations, or laws affecting a certain area. The public official knows roughly the goal he wants to accomplish, and the lobbyist can given him the facts to implement it—facts that are selected, edited, and presented in a manner favorable to the lobbyist's client. Often lobbyists don't wait for a congressman to ask for their help. They conceive and draft a special-interest bill themselves, and then go up to the Hill to find someone to introduce it. Lobbyists play such a vital role in the legislative and executive processes that they have been called the "fourth branch of government" (or sometimes the "fifth branch," just below the Washington press corps). Lobbyists not only draft legislation but they also get witnesses for legislative hearings, and even make up lists of intelligent questions for committee members to ask each favorable and hostile witness. Many a representative's and senator's reputation for solid research and incisive questioning is based on a lobbyist's crib sheet. In 1974, while Congress grappled with the intricacies of the energy crisis, one federal oil analyst remarked privately, "Capitol Hill is so weak in staffing that any good lobbyist is a congressman's best source of information."

In many instances, effective lobbying consists not so much of persuading congressmen to espouse an alien point of view, but rather identifying members who are already friendly to the general proposition and providing them with enough material to serve as a rationale for voting the way they would have voted in the first place. This is known as "marshaling the forces" or "counting noses," and in sheer volume it probably surpasses every other technique for getting bills passed.

FORMER CONGRESSMEN

Many of the top lobbyists on Capitol Hill are retired or defeated representatives and senators, and a number of them lobby for the same interests that they once championed as congressmen. Andrew Biemiller, once merely a two-term liberal Democrat from Wisconsin, now wields considerable power as the director of the AFL–CIO's extensive lobbying effort. Frank Ikard, a former congressman from Texas, is president of the American Petroleum Institute. Former California Senator Thomas Kuchel has represented sugar and motion picture clients, and most recently lobbied (so far, unsuccessfully) for an antitrust exemption to permit a merger of the two professional basketball leagues. Florida's ex-Senator George Smathers has lobbied for shippers, the Association of American Railroads, and the American Horse Council. Ross Bass, a former senator from Tennessee, is an occasional lobbyist for the Recording Industry Association, and ex-Senator George Murphy of California has lobbied for Nationalist China. Former Kentucky governor and congressman Earle Clements is a tobacco lobbyist, and Graham Purcell, former Democratic congressman from Texas, represents sugar interests.

Former Oklahoma Senator Mike Monroney, who once chaired the Senate Commerce Aviation Subcommittee, now lobbies for airlines and natural gas firms. Carter Manasco, an ex-representative from Alabama, lobbies for the National Coal Association, and in 1969 helped defeat a four-cent-a-ton tax for mine safety and health research. Some defeated congressmen—if they are of the same party as the White House—are hired to lobby on the Hill for the administration's legislative program. Former Representative John Kyl of Iowa is doing this for the Interior Department, and ex-Representative Richard Roudebush, defeated in a 1970 bid for a Senate seat from Indiana, became a Veterans Administration lobbyist and in 1974 was chosen to head the entire VA.

The former congressman's big advantage as a lobbyist is camaraderie, being "one of the gang." He is entitled to eat in the members' dining room, use the members' lavatory, and can even walk onto the floor of the chamber any time except when a bill in which he has a direct professional interest is under consideration. Former Senator Albert Gore of Tennessee in 1973 told *Wall Street Journal* reporter Kerry North that, "as a member of the Senate, I felt resentment when a former colleague took advantage of our friendship and association to lobby for some special interest." Although the law firm he joined after his defeat in 1970 was registered as a lobbyist, Gore insists that he never lobbied personally, just gave his clients advice "about the ways of politics." Now, as a director of Occidental Petroleum and chairman of a coal subsidiary based in Cleveland, Gore still manages to spend some time in Washington.

Camaraderie works equally well in the labyrinthian world of the Washington military establishment. Most major defense contractors employ a handful of former generals, admirals, colonels, and captains to lobby their cause at the Pentagon and with members of the House and Senate Armed Services Committees. Many of them are effective lobbyists, others merely window dressing. The retired officers get a lot of help from other parts of the defense procurement lobby, including the labor unions of the electronics, weaponry, and aerospace industries, and the congressmen whose districts depend economically on the prosperity of these industries.

CORPORATE REPRESENTATIVES

The elite of the corporate lobbyists are the "Washington vice presidents." While virtually every American corporation is represented by a trade association with headquarters or a branch office in Washington, the largest companies also have their own eyes-and-ears here. Many of these corporate offices are staffed by several administrative aides, secretaries, and in-house counsels, leaving the top man—"vice president for governmental relations"—free to cultivate high-level contacts. This cultivation requires—among other attributes—stamina and an iron stomach to get the executive through the endless nights of cocktail receptions, dinners, and charity balls. And the vice president must be fresh enough the next day to be witty and well informed over cocktails and a long lunch with a key federal official. The executive's social life, of course, is funded by his corporate expense account—a boon to Washington's caterers and the expensive restaurants clustered along Connecticut Avenue and K Street.

Representatives of some 125 corporations on the *Fortune* top-500 list belong to an informal club called the "Washington Representatives Group." Handpicked by R. Hilton ("Dixie") Davis, a lobbyist for the U.S. Chamber of Commerce, the group meets every couple of weeks for briefings given by Davis at the chamber's headquarters on Lafayette Park, across from the White House. The briefings are a general intelligence report on things going on in the federal government that the corporate representatives should be aware of, if they aren't already.

The staff men in corporate lobbying hobnob with important officials and with other lobbyists, and the life is satisfying to many of them. But some ambitious business executives would rather not be assigned to the nation's capital. Washington is far removed from the intrigues of climbing the corporate ladder, and some executives would rather stay in the home office, to maneuver better for the top spot of president or chairman of the board. Other executives love the particular rewards of being a Washington representative, especially the freedom of running their own offices with minimal interference from headquarters.

More and more, Washington representation for the major corporations is getting to be a specialty of its own, not interchangeable with managerial jobs in the home office. And increasingly, the Washington vice president is an executive spokesman with genuine influence on corporation policy—concerning legislation, consumerism, and other public issues.

Who are the leading corporate practitioners in Washington? It would take a list of probably thirty or forty names to do justice to them all, in terms of knowledgeability and effectiveness. On almost everybody's list is Bryce Harlow, Washington representative of Procter and Gamble, and formerly on the Nixon White House team. So is William G. Whyte, vice president of U.S. Steel and a friend and informal adviser to President Ford. Others who rank high on the scale are L. Berkley Davis, vice president of General Electric; Rod Markley, vice president of Ford; Allan D. Cors, vice president and director of government affairs for Corning Glass; Kim Firestone, vice president of Firestone; Claude Hobbs, vice president of Westinghouse. Also James Pipkin, who held the unusually high rank of executive vice president of his company, Texaco, until his retirement in 1974; Theron J. Rice, of Continental Oil; J. Carter Perkins, vice president of Shell; Edd Hyde, vice president of Reynolds Metals; Carstens Slack, vice president of Phillips Petroleum; and K K Bigelow of Martin Marietta.

There is much more to these men's jobs than wining and dining government officials at fancy restaurants. Their duties more often find them in conference rooms, congressional hearing rooms, Capitol Hill offices, golfing at the Burning Tree Club, lunching at the Metropolitan Club, or the sacred precincts of their own Carlton Club (in the Sheraton-Carlton Hotel on 16th Street). And more often than not, they will be planning strategy rather than looking after the details.

A lobbyist must keep his client highly visible in private but absolutely invisible to the public eye (except to get brownie points for some corporate good deed). The worst thing that can happen to a Washington vice president is to involve his company in a scandal, complete with congressional hearings and splashy press coverage. Before the ITT affair of 1972, William Merriam was secure in his fiefdom. He was a dapper, well-connected, respected corporate lobbyist. Then came Jack Anderson's exposé of the Dita Beard memo, and a subdued Merriam was called before a Senate panel to discuss everything from antitrust matters and GOP contributions to ITT's alleged arrangements with the CIA to protect its investments in Chile. Soon after the furor died down, Merriam was transferred to ITT's branch office in Rome.

During the Watergate affair, Claude C. Wild, Jr., Gulf Oil's Washington vice president, admitted to a Senate hearing that he had arranged an illegal $100,000 corporate donation to the Committee to Reelect the President. (He had good company, however, in such corporate giants as 3M, Goodyear, Braniff, Ashland Petroleum, Phillips Petroleum, Carnation, and American Airlines, most of which were fined a mere $5,000.) Wild said he hadn't expected any particular favors for the money. "I would just like somebody to answer my telephone calls once in a while," he said. Soon thereafter, there was a shake-up in the Gulf Washington office, and Wild departed. In the ethics of Washington lobbying, the sin of Merriam and Wild was getting caught. The same techniques, practiced discreetly, would have made them heroes in the eyes of their superiors. (Wild's admitted $100,000 contribution turned out to be just the tip of a vast iceberg of illegal Gulf gifts spanning three presidential administrations. In early 1975 it was disclosed that the corporation had maintained a secret $10 million political fund from 1960 through 1974, and the Securities and Exchange Commission promptly charged the company with falsifying its accounts to hide the money.)

SPECIAL ISSUES

A fact of life in Washington is that the more complicated and obscure an issue is, the greater the lobbyist's opportunity to influence the outcome. A case in point is the setting of sugar quota formulas and price objectives, an arcane congressional ritual that has influenced the prices consumers have paid for vast quantities of sugar. The nation's cane and beet sugar industries do not produce enough sugar to meet the American demand, so some has to be imported. Until recently, when the U.S. price was higher than the world price, Congress restricted imports to keep the domestic price up. Foreign sugar producers clamored to get as large a share of the total import package as they could. Lobbyists would have their finger in the pot at every stage of the process. The representatives of the U.S. Cane Sugar Refiners Association and the U.S. Beet Sugar Association would tell the House and Senate Agriculture committees how much foreign sugar they believed should be let in, and their advice would be taken seriously. Foreign governments traditionally retain the best lobbyists they can afford. The fees are sometimes astronomical, but have usually been worth it to a sugar-producing nation. The process is so complicated that a sugar lobbyist once confided to columnists Jack Anderson and the late Drew Pearson, "There aren't five men in Congress that understand it." The lobbyist added, "I never talked to an individual member of Congress save one, Harold Cooley." The late congressman Cooley, longtime dictatorial chairman of the House Agriculture Committee, sometimes let sugar lobbyists sit in on sessions that were closed to the press and public. After his retirement, he became a sugar lobbyist himself.

For many lobbyists, tax revision is the favorite arena of covert operation. Take, for example, the genesis of a 1969 amendment that allowed corporations to deduct as business expense the cost of relocating their employees from one branch office to another. A few large corporations that constantly move executives around the country went to Jay W. Glasmann, a former tax lawyer at the Treasury Department who now practices privately. Glasmann enlisted the support of other large business lobbies, like the National Association of Manufacturers, and together they convinced Congress to change the law.

The classic example of a "special interest" tax change is a 1954 revision that was worded so explicitly that it covered only two people: movie mogul Louis B. Mayer and another executive of Loew's, Inc. The so-called Louis B. Mayer amendment saved him an estimated $2 million in taxes on the sale to Loew's of his lifetime MGM movie rights. As tax expert and former Treasury official Stanley Surrey has observed, few people know or are interested enough to oppose special-interest tax amendments that don't "hurt" anyone else except by diminishing the total pool of federal revenue. "When tax issues are technical," he has written, "the pressure groups act only as proponents and not as opponents." Surrey has asked rhetorically, "When the issue is a special provision for one group as against the taxpaying public as a whole, what pressure group is there to speak for the public?"

PUBLIC INTEREST LOBBIES

Until a few years ago, the answer to this question would have been "none." But today there are legions of so-called public interest lobbies at work in Washington. In a broad range of policy areas—especially the environment and consumer protection—these lobbies scrutinize proposed legislation and administrative actions, testify at hearings, confer with bureaucrats and congressional committee staffs, and monitor the implementation of new laws. These organizations are often funded by foundations and grass-roots donations, and volunteers supplement the full-time staffs. Unlike lobbyists for profitmaking interests, the public interest lobbies thrive on publicity.

The king of the public interest lobbyists is Ralph Nader, the intense, clean-living leader of a conglomerate of research groups that cover everything from aviation and cosmetics to auto safety and meat inspection. His organizations have separate staffs and identities—such as the Aviation Consumer Action Project or the Health Research Group—but they all derive their money from his central organization. A man of monastic tastes in living accommodations and social life, Nader funds his lobbying largely with public speaking fees and citizen contributions (gathered through a direct-mail solicitation apparatus called "Public Citizen Inc."). These days, when Nader sits down at the microphone to address a congressional hearing, he is invariably flanked by knowledgeable aides, one of whom probably wrote the testimony that he reads. While Nader continues to be a forceful dramatizer of issues, some of his supporters fear that his diversity of effort diminishes his impact by spreading his energy thin.

The most unusual public interest pressure group in Washington is Common Cause, which calls itself the "citizens' lobby." Using aggressive direct-mail solicitation (more than 18 million pieces mailed since its founding in 1970), Common Cause has more than 300,000 members who pay annual dues of $15. While other public interest lobbies focus on substantive issues, Common Cause concerns itself with procedural reform in such areas as campaign financing, the congressional seniority system, disclosure of the assets and income of major officeholders, complete registration of lobbyists and their spending, and citizen access to all congressional committee meetings. It has a network of state and local offices that are staffed, like the headquarters, largely with volunteers. Chairman John W. Gardner, founder and inspirational leader, is a former foundation executive and Secretary of Health, Education and Welfare in the Johnson administration. The group's biggest coup was winning a suit against the Committee to Reelect the President, requiring disclosure of donations made to CREEP before the current campaign spending law went into effect in the spring of 1972. It also played a major role in encouraging the unprecedented House reforms of late 1974 and early 1975.

There are many other lobbies in Washington that fall somewhere between, on the one hand, trade associations and labor unions and, on the other hand, the general public interest organizations. This catchall category includes lobbies that exist to further special interests, but interests that are not so much material as philosophical, social, and spiritual. The American Civil Liberties Union, for example, lobbies as the watchdog of individual rights and takes a stand on tens of national issues every year. (The ACLU was also in the vanguard of the campaign to impeach President Nixon, ostensibly in the constitutional interest of making impeachment a viable deterrent against misconduct rather than a rusty historical oddity.) The Americans for Democratic Action (liberal) and the Americans for Constitutional Action (conservative) lobby on legislation and periodically grade every member of Congress according to his adherence to their positions. The National Association for the Advancement of Colored People, the Urban League, and other civil rights organizations lobby for the legal and economic interests of black Americans. Then there are the local government lobbies, including the National League of Cities and the U.S. Conference of Mayors (which press for more federal funding for urban America) and the National Association of Counties.

HEALTH, RELIGION, AND ENVIRONMENT

Whatever disease you or your loved ones may be afflicted with, there is a lobby at work to spur federal research to conquer it. Mary Lasker, the spiritual leader of the "medical lobby," and her chief lobbyist, Mike Gorman, were influential in the growth of the National Institutes of Health during the Fifties and Sixties, later turning their efforts to the cancer crusade and, most recently, national health insurance.

Even churches get into the lobbying act. Their representatives are highly visible on such obviously religious matters as legislation allowing prayer in public schools. They work more subtly on other issues, like the Catholics' longtime support of military aid to the regime of Catholic dictator Franco of Spain, or pressure by Jewish groups to increase aid to Israel in its struggle with the Arabs and link Soviet trade concessions to emigration of Soviet Jews. Every religious group that operates its own schools—especially the Catholic church—joins in the push for federal aid to nonpublic schools. The Quakers were integral to the peace lobby during American involvement in Southeast

Asia. The Mormon church, which has a vast genealogical data bank so it can confer blessings on its members' deceased forebears, recently lobbied (quietly and successfully) for access to individual records of the 1900 census. And a few years ago, when legislation was drafted to require more humane slaughter of animals in meat packing houses, orthodox rabbis lobbied successfully for an amendment allowing special techniques of bloodletting required by religious ritual.

New national issues have a way of spawning new lobbies and rejuvenating old ones. Rising citizen concern about the environment in the Sixties gave lobbying muscle to such organizations as the Sierra Club (founded in 1892) and Friends of the Earth (a 1969 offshoot of the Sierra Club). It spawned groups like the Environmental Policy Center, the Environmental Action Foundation, and the League of Conservation Voters. The consumer issue gave birth to Ralph Nader, or vice versa. National interest in welfare reform and the guaranteed annual income has made many lobbies busy, including the National Welfare Rights Organization (which keeps pushing for a guaranteed income much higher than Congress and the President are likely to approve). The National Council of Senior Citizens, organized in 1961 to battle for medicare, is working now for greater social security benefits and for national health insurance, the controversial proposal that has drawn the support or opposition of such groups as the Committee for National Health Insurance, the American Medical Association, the American Hospital Association, and numerous others in the health field. The rebirth of the long-dormant women's rights movement led to the creation of a lobbying office of the National Organization for Women (NOW), followed by a consortium called, quite candidly, the Women's Lobby. As the revelations of Watergate unfolded, numerous liberal groups banded into an informal "impeachment lobby," with the AFL–CIO as a major participant.

THE "OTHER SIDE"

Since there are at least two sides to every issue, the creation of new lobbies always means more work for opposition lobbies. 1971—a year when the environmental groups were blocking offshore oil drilling, deep-water ports, supertankers, new refineries, and the Alaska pipeline—was also, not coincidentally, the year that the American Petroleum Institute moved its headquarters from New York City to Washington. Soon thereafter the industry's troubles—public relations, if not financial—were compounded by the energy crisis and an unprecedented degree of federal interest in their operations. The "oil lobby" had long been one of the most effective in Washington, managing to convince Congress for years that the health of the industry and national security depended on the depletion allowance and quotas on foreign oil. But prior to the move to Washington some oil executives were beginning to think that the small API lobbying staff was failing to meet the increasingly sophisticated challenges from environmentalists and congressmen. As one critic told the *New York Times* recently, "We needed people who would nose around, get to know the right congressional staff people and find out what API had to prepare for, how the industry should defend itself, how it should go on the attack with Congress." Since coming to the capital, the API, with an annual budget of $19 million, has increased its staff of registered lobbyists from five to eleven.

Sometimes a professional lobbyist creates his own lobby by spotting a trend or a piece of legislation that might have a heavy impact—positive or negative—on a particular industry. No matter that the legislation may not have a snowball's chance in hell of getting passed. The fact that the bill has been drafted, or is even being contemplated, constitutes a sufficient threat or promise to bring forth a new lobby. The lawyer or public relations man quickly solicits memberships in the new organization and tries to live comfortably on the fees as the organization's registered lobbyist. It is best for the lobbyist, of course, if the issue lingers for years. If it comes to a head too soon, he'll have to find another horse to ride.

Take for example, the Burke-Hartke bill that was kicking around Congress a couple of years ago—a bill to restrict imports and American investment overseas. Representative James Burke (D-Mass.), an old friend of the troubled New England shoe industry, privately conceded that he never intended the bill to pass in its original form, if at all. He kept the bill on the griddle as a countervailing force, to assure that enthusiasm for free trade did not obscure the plight of import-injured domestic industries and unions. But this was not widely known, and lobbies of multinational corporations and import-export firms sprang up overnight to do battle with Burke-Hartke.

Burke tells a story about attending a dinner meeting sponsored by one of these lobbies. The professional lobbyist who had organized it berated the congressman and went through a long song and dance about how the bill would ruin the economy. Burke waited until the lobbyist's spiel had run its course, and then said with a straight face, "Yes, Senator Hartke and I realize the shortcomings of our bill. We are seriously thinking about withdrawing it." The lobbyist, suddenly facing the loss of his guaranteed employment, stared in shock and said, "You wouldn't do that, would you?" He lapsed into an unhappy silence the rest of the evening, fearing that the goose that laid his golden egg was about to be killed.

NOTHING SUCCEEDS LIKE SUCCESS

Lobbying campaigns can be ethical or corrupt, blatant or subtle, broad-based or elitist, populist or patrician. But after disposing of value judgments, Washington appraises a lobby on the impartial grounds of performance—whether or not it accomplishes what it sets out to do. By this standard, one of the most successful lobbying campaigns in recent years is the continuing opposition of the National Rifle Association to gun control laws. By one means or another, the NRA has managed to convince large numbers of people that their constitutional rights and personal safety would be impaired by restrictions on the sale of handguns. When former Senator Joseph Tydings (D-Md.) was running for election in 1970, the NRA and local sportsmen's groups took aim on his gun control advocacy and flooded the state with derogatory bumper stickers. It was a big factor in Tydings's defeat.

Seldom, of course, does one issue defeat a candidate, and in this case several lobbies took credit. (Lobbyists have a habit of taking full credit for every success, while evading responsibility for anything that might have gone wrong.) Tydings had been active in the movement for population control, and the Catholic voters didn't take kindly to that. Since he had espoused tighter tax laws for horse farms, some people attributed his defeat to opposition from the horse breeders. Still others said the *coup de grace* was an accusation, leaked to *Life* magazine by ex-White House aide Charles Colson, that Tydings tried to pull strings for a corporation in which he owned a lot of stock. (The Justice Department cleared Tydings of any wrongdoing a week after his defeat by Republican Representative J. Glenn Beall.) But the most publicized single factor in Tydings's defeat was the NRA-guided campaign against gun control—the same campaign that today leaves handgun legislation languishing in committee, with no immediate prospect of action.

Among the legendary examples of ineffective lobbying is the AMA's crusade against medicare in the early Sixties, a crusade joined by many other groups, including the United States Chamber of Commerce. The AMA's choice of a theme for the attack was the threat of "socialized medicine"—a threat which, if demonstrable, would probably have helped the AMA cause considerably. But after more than thirty years of social security and other such federal programs, a plan for government-insured medical payments (restricted to the aged and poor) no longer frightened the average American voter. With passage of medicare and medicaid, the AMA suffered a serious black eye, and there followed an internal shake-up. The association now approaches the issue of national health insurance in a less strident way. Recognizing the broad appeal of the issue, the AMA has countered the federally controlled "womb-to-tomb" plans with its own "medicredit" version, allowing tax deductions for the cost of privately purchased health insurance. It all goes to show that failure can be a good teacher, and that old lobbies can learn new tricks. (But the AMA is not about to abandon the old trick of spreading around a lot of campaign money. Before the 1974 congressional elections, AMPAC and its state affiliates contributed more than $600,000 to pro-"medicredit" incumbent congressmen and senators and challengers. Some 205 members of the House—nearly half its roster—received AMPAC support.)

Every few years, especially after a major scandal, people start muttering, "Ya know, we ought to rid Washington of those damned lobbyists," as if lobbyists were troublesome houseguests who had overstayed their welcome. But the lobbyists of Washington are full-fledged tenants, and they have been paying their room and board faithfully since the government opened its doors here in 1800. Like an election, each lobbyist is a communicator of some small part of the public's collective will, a receiver and transmitter of messages that his friends back home send to Washington. Because of the varying numerical strength, fervor, and wealth of the senders, the messages arrive in different forms and are treated accordingly. Some are clear but faint, and they are usually ignored. Others are strong but fuzzy, and they are heard but soon forgotten. Some signals never arrive at all, jammed by more powerful ones on the same frequency.

People love to debate whether lobbying is or is not desirable but the simple fact is that lobbying is an integral part of the governmental process. In the future, lobbying might be more closely monitored and controlled, but there is not the slightest chance that it will disappear.

17 THE PENTAGON AT PEACE

The American military which calls Washington home is a peaceful organization these days. It fires no shots in anger or in defense. It operates on peacetime rules. It takes its orders from the President and gets its paychecks from Congress. It is not exactly a picture of joyful strength. Like the policeman in Gilbert and Sullivan's *Pirates of Penzance,* its lot "is not a happy one."

Following the expansion brought on by Vietnam fighting, the defense establishment now finds itself in an uncomfortable condition of restraint. It is saddled with chores of maintenance, in addition to its job of "keeping up with the Russians." Its volunteer army is composed of civilians who sign on as much for curiosity, vocational training, and the rates of pay as for dedication to a military career.

Today the military does a minimum of "ordering" and a maximum of persuading. While the chain of command remains intact, Defense does not have precedence over other parts of the government. To get its appropriations, it makes thousands of trips to Capitol Hill to mend political fences, meet with committee chairmen, and give pep talks to friendly congressmen. In preparation of its budget, it spends thousands of hours with the experts at the White House Office of Management and Budget, none of which conjures up a picture of bravado and derring-do. The Washington military life is desk work—paper-pushing and talk. Many an ambitious officer takes it as a dose of medicine, knowing that it's good for him and essential to his advancement, but happy when it's over.

THE PENTAGON

Today's volunteer defense establishment headquarters is at the Pentagon— that five-sided behemoth of a building that rises out of the Virginia flatlands across the Potomac River from the Capitol and White House. But the Pentagon today is a thinned-down place. From its World War II peak of 40,000 civilian and military personnel, its occupancy is now reduced to 27,000, of whom 13,000 are civilian Defense employees, 12,000 are military personnel, and 2,000 are employees who keep the place operating as an office center twenty-four hours a day.

Two-thirds of the Defense Department's top brass have their offices at the Pentagon. Here are the expansive offices and big desks of the Secretary of Defense, the Joint Chiefs of Staff, the Secretaries of the Army, Navy, and Air Force, the Defense Intelligence Agency, the service chiefs, and the budget officers who prepare the annual bill of $95 billion.

The Pentagon building itself is a marvel of self-sufficiency. It was built during World War II at a cost of $83 million, taking sixteen months in the construction, and was finished January 15, 1943. It was then—and still is—

the largest single office building in the world, large enough to hold two Chicago Merchandise Marts or three Empire State Buildings. Today, the twin towers of New York's World Trade Center contain more cubic space, but the Pentagon is still larger than either one of them alone. Its vital statistics read like a small city: 3,705,000 square feet of office space with 17½ miles of corridors, 19 escalators, and 150 stairways. And in another year, it will have its own underground stop on the Washington Metro subway. In the concourse of the huge building are banks, a bookstore, a florist, a beauty salon, and dozens of other shops and service centers for everything from optometry to railroad tickets. Because it is a military communications center, the Pentagon contains more than 87,000 telephones and radio facilities connecting it with 4,000 military installations in the U.S. and another 2,000 overseas.

For all of its superlative statistics, the Pentagon is not the only scene of defense activities in the national capital area. Scattered about the city and environs are 130 other military locations, including the Forrestal Building on Independence Avenue south of the great Mall, the Crystal City complex in Arlington, south of the Pentagon, and an underground "rock Pentagon" or "little Pentagon" in the Catoctin mountains of Maryland—known as Fort Ritchie—where the Pentagon operates its underground command center to be used in time of emergency. These are connected with the White House and other secret presidential command posts by supersecure communications systems.

All told, the Department of Defense employs 2,100,000 military people and approximately 1,000,000 civilians, with another 75,000 civilians and military people in related defense-type organizations. The 2.1 million military force is the smallest since before the Korean War—down 1.4 million from the Vietnam peak of 3.5 million in 1968 and down 556,000 from the pre-Vietnam year of 1964.

As a massive "paper factory," the Pentagon grinds out position papers on virtually every subject that is even peripherally related to defense, and this means almost everything under the sun. There are project papers, program papers, memoranda on contingency plans, objectives, alternatives, dissents, and appraisals of situations. Such papers bear classifications ranging from "eyes only" through "top secret," "secret," "confidential," and "no forn" (no foreign dissemination) to "cosmic" (for NATO members). The principal sound emanating from the doorways that line Pentagon corridors is the click of electric typewriters, augmented by the ticking of computers that crank out thousands of feet of printouts.

THE SECRETARY OF DEFENSE

Although the Pentagon is military headquarters, civilians dominate its policy. Far and away the most important civilian in the Pentagon is James Rodney Schlesinger, Secretary of Defense. At age forty-six, Schlesinger is young for that office, but he brought into it a wide experience in government and has proven to be a tough administrator.

Schlesinger was educated as an economist and holds a doctoral degree from Harvard in that field. He taught for eight years at the University of Virginia, then went to the Rand Corporation in the field of strategic studies. In 1969 he entered government service, becoming assistant director of the Bureau of the Budget and the Office of Management and Budget, when that office was created. He next was appointed chairman of the Atomic Energy Commission, and then served briefly as director of the Central Intelligence Agency. In his few months there, he shook the staid and bureaucratic intelligence headquarters to its roots and fired or retired some 1,200 employees.

Schlesinger came to the Pentagon in July 1973, better prepared for that post than any of his predecessors with the possible exception of General George Catlett Marshall. While at the University of Virginia he wrote a book, *The Political Economy of National Security,* on the role of systems analysis in politics and strategy.

In private life Schlesinger is quiet and disdainful of Washington protocol. He avoids large parties and even refuses White House invitations when possible. He prefers to spend his little free time with his wife and eight children or at his favorite pastime of bird watching.

The professional military staffs in the Pentagon accept new political appointees slowly. The generals and admirals prefer to watch and analyze newcomers while they judge their capabilities and weaknesses. Schlesinger has shown himself direct and forceful, sometimes to the point of rudeness, but generally willing to listen.

Like most Secretaries of Defense, Schlesinger has problems with the Congress. His military philosophy as reflected in the current defense budget and in his off-the-cuff comments in his appearances before some of the committees has led some members to brand him as a big spender. His principal budgetary problems are still before him and will remain chronic in the era of inflation-inspired budget squeezing on Capitol Hill and within the Executive Branch.

Shortly after Schlesinger arrived at the Pentagon and after the preparation of the budget was well under way, he created a minor furor by revising the national air defense policy. He reasoned that the manned bomber threat to the U.S. is now negligible, since the Russians have so many intercontinental missiles that they need not rely on bombers. His decision required the demobilization of all Nike Hercules antiaircraft missiles except the four batteries in Florida, and the reduction of the number of air intercept squadrons to a new low. The decision was his rather than that of the Joint Chiefs. He now gives indications of dissatisfaction with the apportionment of roles and missions among the services, which the chiefs have traditionally regarded as their own bailiwick.

THE MILITARY CHIEFS

However important the civilian Secretary is to overall policy and budgets, the uniformed military dominate the professional armed forces: Army, Navy, Marines, and Air Force. Even strong Defense Secretaries like Robert S. McNamara, who shook the Defense Department with whirlwind ferocity at times, have left little permanent effect upon nuclear strategy, budget planning, tactics, or weapons. It takes about two years to prepare a budget, guide it through Congress, and get the money committed.

The generals and admirals in the long run determine how the Army's 13 divisions, the Marines' 3 divisions, the Navy's 580 warships, and the Air Force's 1,000 ICBMs and 500 big bombers are organized and held in readiness—and in many instances how they are deployed and employed. The military are the experts, the technicians, the advisers, and the operators. The civilians make the policy decisions, but the military determine how the decisions are interpreted in the field and carried out.

The top brass—both civilian and military—tend to emerge from the same origins: the middle-class, conservative, traditional go-getters—establishment men who are aggressive, achievement-oriented, innovative but not iconoclastic, leaders but not adventurers. Many of the generals and admirals come from the South or Midwest. Many of the civilian leaders in the Pentagon are eastern establishment types from legal, industrial, or financial backgrounds, but they, too, are balanced by men from the Midwest, South, and West. Three of the past Secretaries of Defense were lawyers, three came from finance, three from industry, one was a general, one was a politician, and the incumbent, James R. Schlesinger, is an economist.

The Joint Chiefs (who are heads of the military services) and the Defense Secretary fashion defense policy, military strategy, military programs, armed forces and weapons, and budgets. But they don't have a free hand. Underlying their management of the military forces and the $95 billion budget are national policy and objectives set by the President with the advice of his National Security Council. In terms of money, Secretary McNamara always insisted that there was no fiscal ceiling imposed on the services during their budget preparations. Each service was instructed to include funding for all requirements in its draft budgets. The combined demands far exceeded the amount that could be expected to be available. The Defense staff would then scale them down, and McNamara would claim the difference as savings due to his efficient system.

BUDGETS AND THE NEW VOLUNTARISM

Despite the enormity of the numbers surrounding everything military in Washington, the relative cost of defense to the nation has been contracting in the past few years. Gone are the days of Vietnam, Korea, and World War II. In personnel, the military establishment has been on a decline since 1968, when the post-Vietnam tapering off began to take effect. In budget terms, the figures seem mountainous—$95 billion out of a total federal budget of $350 billion, representing about 27 percent of annual federal outgo. Yet it is only 7 percent of the total U.S. economy, compared with 9 percent during Vietnam, 15 percent during Korea, and 41 percent at the peak of World War II.

So the Pentagon is feeling poor. It also feels troubled:

Troubled by new problems of voluntarism in recruiting and command.

Troubled by the uncomfortable requirements of change—in methods of leadership, of patterns in dress and military codes, in the loosened ties of formality, loyalty, and dedication to career.

Troubled by charges that minorities have not been given complete opportunity.

Troubled by suggestions that its mission should be aimed as much at education and social service as toward the demands of making war.

The defense establishment is troubled also by the fact that it is top-heavy with military brass. As in every extended period of peace, the military services have built up a superfluity of high-ranking officers. As the numbers of enlisted and noncommissioned personnel have declined, the permanent corps of professional officers has become a larger percentage of the total, and the growing technological sophistication of nuclear warfare has encouraged retention of more military officers with "scrambled eggs" on their visors—men and women with the rank of lieutenant colonel, commander, and above.

Although the number of men and women in uniform has fallen drastically over the past few years, the military payroll has not. In preparation for an end to the draft, military pay was doubled between 1968 and 1972 and has continued to soar to attract new volunteers. The pay of raw recruits is now about four times that of a decade ago. Total military pay, for active and retired personnel combined, now comprises about one-third of the military budget.

HOW POLICY IS MADE

The National Security Council, guided by Henry A. Kissinger, has steered foreign and defense policy in the 1970s. It consists of the President, the Vice President, the Secretary of State, the Secretary of Defense, and two "statutory advisers," the director of Central Intelligence and the chairman of the Joint Chiefs of Staff. In fact, of course, these members are often represented in discussions by their deputies or assistants. The NSC staff prepares studies on various key issues—such as U.S. relations with China, the Soviet Union, or the Middle East—drawing on the State Department, Defense, Central Intelligence Agency, and other government agencies for information, estimates, and recommended courses of action, with assessments of risks and costs. After these NSC studies are hammered out, the President selects his options, makes decisions, and orders implementation.

The military services are represented on the NSC by the chairman of the Joint Chiefs or the deputy secretary. When the chairman has strong views on any NSC paper he frequently insists on expressing them personally to the President when the paper is briefed to him. When matters involving one or more of the armed forces are presented to the President, the chief of staff of that service is usually invited to be present. Sometimes friction develops. During the Cuban missile crisis in 1962 at such a meeting, President Kennedy directed Admiral George W. Anderson, then chief of naval operations, to pass on *detailed* instructions to the commander of the Atlantic Fleet then blockading Cuba. Admiral Anderson resisted, saying that the Navy gave only mission-type orders to fleet commanders. Subsequently, Admiral Anderson was not given the customary reappointment for a second tour of two years but was sent off as ambassador to Portugal.

The Joint Chiefs also collaborate on the massive preparation of the annual budget and the major defense programs, the strategic plans, and the contingency short-range and long-range plans by region and area around the globe.

The military planning process starts with assessment of the worldwide threats, based on national intelligence estimates of the potential adversaries. The chiefs emphasize enemy capabilities rather than intentions. How many ICBMs and submarine-launched missiles and bombers do the Russians have? How accurate and how effective are they as weapons? Where are they located and how are they deployed? How can the U.S. deter Moscow from using them? Against this background of potential threats, the chiefs count up U.S. national interests around the world, treaty commitments, and obligations or responsibilities. What does the U.S. have to defend and what are the priorities?

These defense problems—some 1,200 in a year—are handled by the Joint Chiefs with the help of about 1,330 military and 365 civilians. The chiefs agree on some 99 percent of these issues. Where they split—and these involve usually some deep differences over strategy or service rivalry—they submit their divergences to the Secretary of Defense for resolution. For example, the Navy's preference for aircraft carriers collides in tight budget situations with the Air Force's leaning toward bombers and land-based missiles and the Army's concern for conventional weapons.

Prior to Secretary McNamara, the chiefs were chronically split on a number of issues, mostly revolving around roles and missions. There was no practical way to resolve such splits, so papers on which the chiefs could not reach agreement were returned to the working groups. Some of them reappeared year after year without solution. McNamara insisted that split papers be sent to him with the views of all services. He then made decisions, taking the matter out of the hands of the chiefs. The chiefs quickly learned to work out their differences. That was probably McNamara's greatest single contribution toward the integration of the services.

Basic strategic thinking is organized in the annual JSOP—Joint Strategic Objectives Plan—which provides the strategic outlook over the next eight years, with emphasis on the plan for the last five years of the period. During the 1960s the plan tried to deal with what former Defense Secretary Melvin R. Laird called the 2½-wars concept—a major war in Europe, another major war in Asia, and a minor conflict elsewhere. Under the old concept the chiefs often forecast a defense budget of $100 billion or more. Laird scaled the planning down to 1½ wars—one major war in Europe and a smaller war elsewhere—but later stressed that planning should look toward "zero" wars or effective deterrence.

The change from a 2½-war basis to a 1½-war basis for planning does not in fact indicate a change in national policy but does give a basis for reducing active and reserve forces and ammunition and matériel stockpiles. The 1½-war planning basis is more realistic, since funds never were adequate to meet the 2½-war goals.

The chiefs work about 700 hours a year in what is called "the tank" (the gold-carpeted conference room on the Pentagon second floor near the river entrance). There they meet at least three times a week with their top planning officers, their "ops deps" or operations deputies, who are three-star officers, sitting in twelve maroon leather chairs around a boat-shaped walnut Formica table. At each place are a pad of paper, and yellow and red pencils, and on the table are small glass bowls of candy. Besides the JSOP, the chiefs deal with the JIEP (Joint Intelligence Estimate for Planning), the JLRSS (Joint Long-Range Strategic Study) that looks ten to twenty years ahead, and the JSCP (Joint Strategic Capabilities Plan), which covers the military forces and contingencies they might have to cope with in the next fiscal year.

JCS handles some 10,000 papers a year (besides about 750,000 messages) on subjects as diverse as extending the airfield on the island of Diego Garcia, in the Indian Ocean, to the policy of returning the Panama Canal to Panama.

A Joint Chiefs' paper can originate with any of the services or within the Joint Staff and is often written by a lieutenant colonel, colonel, or equivalent Navy commander or captain. It usually takes three weeks to a month for a paper to move through the staff routine—from a "flimsy" on white paper from the action officer on the Joint Staff to the "buff-colored" paper reviewed and revised by one-star generals or rear admirals, to "green" paper when the "planners" agree. The green papers go to the "ops deps" for approval—and they can "sign off" when there is no disagreement. If there is an objection by one or more of the services, the controversial paper is submitted to the Joint Chiefs. When the chiefs' O.K. has been given, the "green" paper is red-striped for referral to the defense secretary and the National Security Council.

Many of the papers, thus, originate with the ideas of younger officers in their thirties who are the "indians." The decisions are made on a higher level of three-star and four-star officers and later by civilians, but the paperwork is done by the more junior officers. So much of this paperwork is secret that the Pentagon's shredders chew up 10.5 tons of classified papers every day.

THE GATHERING OF INTELLIGENCE

One of the most controversial functions of the military, yet usually inconspicuous, is the collection of facts and judgments about the rest of the world. Such fact finding goes by the name of "intelligence," and parts of the job reside in the Central Intelligence Agency (CIA), the Defense Intelligence Agency (DIA), the National Security Agency (NSA), the intelligence branches of the armed services, and the State Department.

Strangely enough, despite the proliferation of intelligence functions throughout the government today, one of the original purposes of unifying the armed services after World War II was to centralize intelligence. In that conflict, different services had varying estimates of enemy capacities. In 1945 the Navy, through its ONI, believed that Japan was ready to collapse, but its chief of intelligence, Admiral Ellis Zacharias, found it difficult to transmit his estimate to the White House and later wrote that he had never been able to present his view forcibly to President Roosevelt. He believed that Roosevelt had relied principally on the other estimates, which forecast a prolonged war, and therefore ordered preparations for invasion of the Japanese mainland which, in fact, was rendered unnecessary by the Japanese surrender in August 1945.

However that may be, the unification of the armed services did not unify the intelligence branches. What it did was to add another layer, now known as the Central Intelligence Agency. The CIA, in sheer numbers, is one of Washington's largest institutions. Its headquarters, nestled in the trees on the Virginia side of the Potomac River, occupies the second-largest single building in the national capital area (after the Pentagon). Nowadays, its denizens are permitted to say that they work for the CIA, but until a few years ago, they had to say, cagily, "I work for the government." To those in the know, such a response, repeated again and again, was a dead giveaway. Still, there were "cover jobs," and many a Washington family has discovered, years later, that the friend they thought was in the State Department management service was actually a CIA operative.

While the CIA gathers information from the far corners of the earth by fair means and foul, much of its work, in fact, is routine. The agency employs hundreds of social scientists, historians, anthropologists, and other types of academicians who analyze daily developments around the world. Many of these analyses, while tightly guarded and classified "secret," are not much more secret than the contents of a daily newspaper.

The truly secret portion of CIA work embraces the highly controversial underground missions that occasionally surface, much to the embarrassment of the agency and the government. These acts of espionage and subversion—in such widely distant places as Chile, Vietnam, Italy, and the Middle East—have recently been downplayed. Many undercover missions of the clandestine services were hangovers from the traditions of the OSS (Office of Strategic Services) in World War II and such "cold war" counterrevolutionary actions as the Bay of Pigs invasion of Cuba in 1961. The clandestine services, honed to a fine polish during the term of CIA Director Allen Dulles (1953–61), were continued during subsequent terms of Directors Richard Helms and James Schlesinger. Now, however, they are being minimized under the directorship of William E. Colby, a lawyer by training, who has been in the CIA since the Korean War. There is irony in the fact that the "international dirty tricks" division is being soft-pedaled by Colby, because he once was deputy director of the CIA's clandestine "black operations." Still, the fact-gathering functions that once were carried out by the clandestine services can now be accomplished more accurately and faster by the sophisticated methods of satellite scanning and by information gathering through flights of the high-flying reconnaissance plane, the SR-71 (which last year flew from New York to London in one hour and fifty-six minutes).

Theoretically, all U.S. intelligence is brought together and unified by the United States Intelligence Board, which is responsible to the National Security Council, and ultimately, of course, to the President. In fact, the various military services, the CIA, and the State Department tend to rely on their own organizations for specialized information. The Defense Intelligence Agency, now headed by Army General Daniel O. Graham, employs 5,000 people, and reports mainly to the armed services. How many people are in the CIA (or closely involved) is not officially recorded, but a reliable estimate would put the number at something upwards of 18,000—in Washington and around the world. The CIA budget, not reported, is buried in hundreds of camouflaged budget items throughout the $350 billion federal budget. Estimates of the real cost of all U.S. intelligence have ranged from $2 billion to more than $6 billion, but since the end of the Vietnam war, the cost is probably in the middle of that range.

CIA morale reached an alltime low in early 1975. In the previous year it was shaken by the congressional outrage that greeted disclosure of the agency's role in the political affairs of Chile. Criticism was heightened by publication of the best-selling exposé *The CIA and the Cult of Intelligence,* written by former CIA employee Victor Marchetti and former State Department aide John Marks. Finally, in January of 1975, *New York Times* reporter Seymour Hersh broke the story that the CIA for years had spied on politically active American citizens and compiled dossiers on some 10,000 of them—in violation of its charter. Director Colby insisted that the illegal snooping was a thing of the past, but Congress and an ad hoc federal commission launched full-blown investigations anyway. Besieged though it is, the CIA continues to gather and interpret facts, and thanks to the electronic age, its estimates of enemy military strength are probably better now than ever before.

The Pentagon buys about $32 billion in goods and services a year. The $95 billion defense budget for fiscal 1976 includes $25 billion for military personnel, nearly $28 billion for operation and maintenance, $1.7 billion for construction, $1 billion for family housing, $3 billion for military aid to foreign countries, $17 billion for weapons and supplies, and $9.6 billion for research and development.

Of the defense total, the Army gets $21.4 billion, the Navy $26.2 billion, the Air Force $25.5 billion, and the rest goes to defense agencies. The money can be described also in terms of the kinds of force it supports: $7.6 billion is for strategic forces (the missiles and bombers), $36 billion for general purpose forces (conventional land, sea, and air forces), $7.3 billion for intelligence and communications, $1.6 billion for sea lift and airlift, $5.6 billion for the National Guard and Reserve Forces, and the rest for other activities.

The factories and munitions plants that supply the Pentagon employ more than 1.7 million workers. These industries turn out $6.8 billion in aircraft, $2.8 billion in missiles, $3.5 billion in ships, $3 billion in ordinance and combat vehicles, $1.4 billion in electronics, $2.3 billion in other hardware and software. Another $9 billion goes for research, and $3.5 billion is devoted to construction and building work.

In the U.S. defense industry, Lockheed Aircraft Corp. is the number one contractor with $1.6 billion in fiscal 1973, producing aircraft and the Navy's submarine missiles. Number two is General Electric Co. with $1.4 billion, making atomic power plants and aircraft engines and working on the Air Force B-1 bomber and Minuteman missile. Number three is Boeing Co. with $1.2 billion, making the Minuteman and SRA missiles, and bombers.

The vast buying power of the Pentagon resides in the military services, but the Defense Secretary has overriding control. The Secretary is advised by a Defense Systems Acquisition Review Council before making the critical decisions whether to proceed with research, engineering, development, testing, or production of new weapons and equipment. Each major weapon system is run by a project manager who is responsible for meeting quality, performance, and delivery and price goals. Examples of Pentagon big weapon systems: the Navy's proposed Trident missile submarine, $13.5 billion for ten submarines by the 1980s; and the Air Force's B-1 bomber program, $15 billion for 244 planes.

These weapons and equipment purchases arm the military forces of the U.S.—still considered the most powerful in the world despite quantitative advantages of the Soviet forces. The U.S. has 1,000 Minuteman ICBMs, 54 Titan II ICBMs, 41 Polaris submarines with 656 Polaris-Poseidon missiles (many carrying several warheads), 500 bombers, several hundred jet fighters, 16 Army Divisions, 3 Marine Divisions, 22 Air Force Wings, 13 Navy Attack Wings, 3 Marine Air Wings, 13 aircraft carriers, 68 atomic attack submarines, and 185 other warships.

The final say on military spending and on most important military programs rests with the Congress. The principal congressional review of military bills falls to the Armed Services committees and the military subcommittees of the Appropriations committees of the House and the Senate. Hearings on military bills are held by the Armed Services committees prior to coming before the Congress for vote. Hearings on appropriations are held by the military subcommittees of each house. The chairmen of the Armed Services committees are powerful figures in the process. The same is true of the defense subcommittees of the Appropriations committees. In both houses the chairmen of the Appropriations committees are the chairmen of the defense appropriations subcommittees.

Chairman of the House Armed Services Committee is Melvin Price of Illinois. He replaced longtime Chairman F. Edward Hébert of Louisiana, who has served consecutively in the House from the Seventy-seventh through the Ninety-third Congresses. Hébert, ousted from the chairmanship in the 1975 overhaul, is a strong proponent of a strong defense and ran his committee with a firm hand. In fact his "advice" to the Secretary of Defense carried almost the weight of law. Once he was offended by the eastern universities that dropped ROTC during the Vietnam war, so in the Ninety-second Congress he tried to write into the authorization bill a clause that would prevent any military spending at such universities. He failed, but he did put the recommendation in his report, and on that basis the armed services reduced their postgraduate input to those schools. They now support only medical students who have signed up for military service.

John C. Stennis of Mississippi chairs the Senate Armed Services Committee. He has been in the Senate since 1947 and is one of its most powerful members. Like his House counterpart, he is a staunch advocate of defense needs, but he is also sensitive to the high costs of the military establishment. During his long absence while recovering from gunshot wounds suffered in a street attack, the committee was chaired by Senator Stuart Symington of Missouri.

During the Ninety-third Congress, the House Armed Services Committee was expanded from thirty-nine members to forty-three, adding two liberal Democrats, Ronald V. Dellums of California, a black ex-Marine sergeant who generally votes against the chairman, and Patricia Schroeder of Colorado, a young lawyer and women's lib advocate, who resists military attempts to "educate" her. She declined an orientation visit to West Point and demanded a breakdown of the costs of the visit. The sharpest thorns in the side of the Pentagon are Representative Les Aspin of Wisconsin and Representative Otis Pike of New York, who frequently attack the military for wasteful spending (such as flight pay for desk-bound officers) and mammoth cost overruns on procurement contracts. (Aspin is an unusually knowledgeable gadfly, having received a PhD degree from M.I.T. and having served as a Pentagon aide to former Defense Secretary McNamara from 1966 to 1968.)

Chairman of the defense subcommittee of the House Appropriations Committee is George Mahon of Texas, whose committee also includes Robert L. F. Sikes of Florida, a supporter of strong defenses. Senator John L. McClellan of Arkansas is chairman of the Senate appropriations subcommittee. While supporting a strong defense, he has promised to cut the new military budget by $3.5 billion, and his cuts of the last budget indicate that he will probably get most of the cuts he wants.

CHAIN OF COMMAND

By law, these military forces and the 2.1 million men and women in uniform are commanded from the White House by the President as Commander in Chief. Some 573,000 of these troops are outside the continental U.S., organized under unified commands such as the U.S. Commands in Europe, the Pacific, Alaska, and the Southern Command (Panama Canal and Atlantic). Other commands are the Strategic Air Command, the U.S. Readiness Command, and the Continental Air Defense Command.

The chain of command runs from the President to the Secretary of Defense to the Joint Chiefs. The chairman of the Joint Chiefs in practice is the link from the Secretary of Defense to the unified commands around the world.

The command and control authority of the President is transmitted to the worldwide U.S. Military Commands through the National Military Command Center (NMCC) on the second floor of the Pentagon—a tightly guarded area of the Joint Chiefs. The center has the computers and the data banks jammed with military information necessary to carry out war plans, plus the communications links by land line, radio, and satellite. A few years ago a fire in the computer room of the Pentagon immobilized most of the computers and destroyed many of the files and programs. All critical files and programs are stored with duplicate computers at the alternate command post, and it was only necessary to switch computer operators there while repairs were made in the Pentagon.

The famous Moscow-Washington "hot line," initiated during the administration of President Kennedy after the Cuban missile crisis, also terminates in the NMCC, not in the White House, as commonly believed. Nevertheless, some of the cables go through the heart of downtown Washington and were nearly severed two years ago by excavators digging in the street for the new subway system. The "hot line," known to military men as "Molink," is not a red telephone or any other type of "do it yourself" device, but actually a bank of four teletype machines at each end of the line. Two are equipped with Russian Cyrillic alphabet keyboards and two are in English.

The NMCC is manned by five teams of nineteen people—officers, enlisted men, and secretaries. Each team is headed by a general or admiral. The remaining officers on the team are area specialists, Europe, Mideast, Russia, Southeast Asia, etc. Each team does six days of duty and then has three days off. The shifts are from 6:30 A.M. to 2:30 P.M., 2:30 P.M. to 10:30 P.M., and 10:30 P.M. to 6:30 A.M. After each six-day cycle the team progresses to the next shift so that no team is on the same shift more often than six days out of twenty-seven. The same system applies to the National Military Intelligence Center (NMIC), which is on the floor directly below the NMCC and is connected therewith by a stairway in the secured area. Access to these two areas is carefully controlled, and authorization is checked at each of two guarded gates. Authorized visitors must be escorted by one of the officers on duty in the area.

Both operational and intelligence communications worldwide feed into the two areas, where an initial analysis is made and displays are kept up to date to aid in the quick briefing of the Secretary of Defense and the Joint Chiefs of Staff. When the U.S. is not involved in actions the activity centers in the intelligence area. There the daily briefings are held for the high command, and there the situation reports are prepared for circulation to key staffs. During the Vietnam war the focus was in the NMCC, which is now relatively quiet. In fact, boredom there is something of a problem. This is alleviated by periodic communications tests and worldwide command post problems in which the staff work and communications of a simulated war are carried out to keep everyone sharp and to test for defects in the system.

The Pentagon's worldwide military command and control system can be alerted in less than three minutes. It can control U.S. forces in a limited war in Southeast Asia or the nuclear holocaust of missiles and bombers released against selective and precise targeting or in a spasm of massive retaliation (which is no longer contemplated in current strategic planning except as a deterrent against massive nuclear war).

During the Middle East war in October 1973, Secretary Schlesinger called a worldwide alert as a signal to Moscow that the U.S. was concerned about Soviet mobilization of its airborne troops. This was a relatively mild alert— "defense condition four"—which meant that troops and units were to be placed on advanced readiness status. Defense condition five is a peacetime posture, and the condition of readiness is accelerated to condition one, which is a wartime all-out preparation for combat with advance units moving forward to staging areas. A more serious alert was called in the autumn of 1962, at the time of the Cuban missile crisis. The Army and Air Force began assembling units in Georgia and Florida. Embarkation facilities were cleared, and an amphibious task force was made ready for the invasion of Cuba. Moscow got the message and dismantled the missiles.

In October of 1973, Moscow again got the message and no Soviet paratroopers flew to Cairo to help stop the Israeli march west of the Suez. The Molink hotline was not employed, but Secretary of State Kissinger flew to Moscow to reaffirm the policy of détente and the U.S.-Soviet accord to take all measures necessary to avert nuclear war.

Despite the costs of defense to the U.S. and the Soviet Union, the atmosphere of détente is nourished by both superpowers. Both nations and their allies are engaged in international talks to reduce troops and arms in central Europe, and to write some agreement that would assure peace and cooperation in Europe.

More significantly, both superpowers are continuing to grapple with the dilemma of the arms race, through Strategic Arms Limitation Talks (SALT). In the SALT I agreement of 1972, each side pledged that it would not deploy a massive antiballistic missile (ABM) defense system, which would have been staggeringly expensive and questionably effective. Over the following two years, the negotiators focused on limiting offensive nuclear weapons, particularly missiles equipped with multiple, independently targetable warheads (called MIRVs). In a surprise announcement in November 1974, Secretary of State Kissinger said the U.S. and Soviet Union had finally put a "cap on the arms race" with a "breakthrough" agreement to limit offensive weapons.

But when the terms of the SALT II accord were examined, some disarmament advocates were less than overjoyed. The agreement did put a ceiling on the total number of delivery vehicles, but the ceiling is substantially higher than the current number of missiles and bombers in each side's arsenal (allowing the Americans, for example, to expand their capability by about 10 percent to meet the new maximum). And since the Soviet missiles are larger than those of the U.S., and therefore able to carry more MIRVs per missile, some conservative critics fear that the Soviets will be able to far surpass American destructive capability without exceeding the SALT II missile ceiling.

So there is no end in sight to the mammoth expenditures on nuclear armaments, which now cost the U.S. some $18 billion a year. But both sides have left open the possibility of conferring again in a few years to discuss an actual reduction—or even elimination—of the nuclear stockpile. By then, the Communist Chinese will probably have deployed some sort of nuclear weapons of their own, adding yet another potential participant to the talks.

THE FUTURE OF DEFENSE

It is now more than two years since the discontinuance of the draft, and Washington is watching its military organization with a keen eye to see what its shape will be, what its mood will be, and what secondary roles it may develop. In social and racial mix, the armed services have been taking in more minorities not only in the enlisted ranks but in the officer corps as well. The branches have nineteen black officers of general or admiral rank (three Air Force, fourteen Army, and two Navy). There are four women generals and one woman admiral. Small as the numbers are, they are larger than they have been before.

In the summer of 1973, 35 percent of the new enlistees in the Army were black, and it began to look as though a majority of the new volunteer Army would be black, but after that the number of white enlistees increased and by mid-1974, black enlistment was running at 27 percent. The Marine Corps and the Navy, which encountered some sharp outbreaks of racial conflict in the ranks, turned special attention to the problem and have since made specific efforts to enlist qualified black men and women.

In the field of education and training, the military is rapidly becoming one of the country's most active institutions. A peacetime military finds itself going to school a large part of the time, preparing for things that the nation hopes will never happen. In the process, millions of young men and women become adept at handling electronics, communications, and paperwork, and if the volunteer military doesn't hold its enlistees, most of this training will find its way back into the stream of civilian work.

The Pentagon may not like its new role, cast in the peacetime mold, but the new look seems better to most American citizens. The prospect is that, in personnel numbers and percentage of the GNP, the military establishment will continue its downward trend.

18 THE MAKING OF FOREIGN POLICY

Foreign policy is tough enough for Moscow and Peking these days. And in times of growing food shortages, tight oil supplies, and shifts in world power, international decisions are increasingly complicated for New Delhi, Teheran, and Tokyo. Yet for all the uncertainties they face, their foreign policies fall into place more easily than those of the United States of America. Washington, capital of a populous democracy and a powerful industrial nation, with attachments to every part of the world, seems to have the hardest time of all in knowing just where its best interests lie.

The United States has shown a tendency to develop different foreign policies at different times—and even at the same time. In its domestic political disputes—over such issues as Vietnam, Cuba, the Middle East, and the Communist bloc—the U.S. often keeps its foreign neighbors on pins and needles wondering how the argument will turn out and how the result will affect them.

Yet such is the interplay of forces in a democracy, and despite its frequent turmoil, the United States manages to translate the conflicts into policy. The mechanisms for this are headquartered in Washington. Foreign policy gets applied in many places through the government, and some of the agencies would not be recognized as part of the foreign policy complex.

Foreign policy is affected by what happens elsewhere in the United States—in Sacramento, Atlanta, Chicago. What consumers ask for and buy at the store, for example, affects our foreign economic policy, tariffs, and balance of payments. Consumer transportation habits affect our national stance on energy and fuel, which, in turn, bears on our relations with the Middle East, Venezuela, and Mexico. Attitudes of ethnic blocs affect our relations with some of their former tormenters. In Washington, these attitudes and preferences are heard, measured, and somehow infused into foreign policy. In the process, more than four dozen agencies of government get into the act, but the most important of these are the Department of State, Congress, and the President.

The White House is, and always has been, the most powerful formulator of the general outlines of foreign policy. The President and his advisers have the resources of the whole executive branch at their disposal. In times of foreign crises, the President can move with a degree of speed, secrecy, and certainty that Congress cannot match. The White House foreign policy apparatus is the National Security Council (NSC), which was created—like the CIA and the Defense Department bureaucracy—during the Presidency of Harry Truman. The NSC, consisting of the heads of the major foreign affairs bodies, had formal functions under President Eisenhower, but was virtually ignored by Presidents Kennedy and Johnson. JFK and LBJ both relied more on an elite coterie of advisers, such as McGeorge Bundy and Walt Rostow. When Richard Nixon arrived in 1969, however, the NSC was rejuvenated into a potent mini-bureaucracy guided by security affairs adviser Henry Kissinger. Borrowing staff from several other agencies (including the State Department), Kissinger built a staff of more than a hundred people, headquartered in the White House and in the adjacent Executive Office Building.

The White House knows in advance about virtually every major foreign policy initiative, but it sometimes fails to keep other government departments fully informed and to solicit the advice of their experts. The disastrous Bay of Pigs invasion in 1961, for example, was a joint project of the Central Intelligence Agency (CIA) and the White House, with a minimal role for the Pentagon and little consultation with anyone at the State Department, except Secretary Dean Rusk (and Under Secretary Chester Bowles, who thought it was a terrible idea). The policy of intervention in Southeast Asia, conceived by Kennedy advisers and the CIA, was strongly opposed by the State Department's area specialists and a few chieftains like Under Secretary George Ball.

In 1969 the NSC began planning President Nixon's overtures toward Communist China, and for nearly two years kept it secret from almost everyone at the Department of State except Secretary William P. Rogers. Even Secretary of Defense Melvin Laird had no idea that the China plan was going to be hatched. While he was on a visit to Japan, Laird publicly mentioned the U.S.'s desire that Japan develop a nuclear capability of her own. This statement threw a small wrench into Kissinger's secret Peking negotiations, which, unbeknownst to Laird, were being carried on at that very moment. There are many, many other examples of White House policies—such as the pro-Pakistan "tilt" in the Indian-Pakistani war of 1971—that were made without, or against, the advice of the professional diplomats at the State Department.

THE ROLE OF CONGRESS

Congress, likewise, is often kept in the dark about White House foreign policy plans. In the Vietnam period, it gave President Johnson carte blanche war authority (through the Gulf of Tonkin resolution), with grave second thoughts later on. Later, Congress rubber-stamped the President's requests for more and more money, even while registering its growing disapproval by threatening to cut off funds. After seeing the results of its abdication on foreign affairs power to the White House, Congress is now beginning to take more initiative. One of the first such attempts was Majority Leader Mike Mansfield's move to form a congressional coalition for reducing American troop strength in Europe. In 1974 and 1975 Congress forced a showdown with President Ford to reduce military aid to South Korea, Cambodia, and Vietnam, and cut off aid to Turkey and Chile.

Most importantly, Congress put a limit on Export-Import Bank loans to the Soviet Union (no more than $300 million over a four-year period) and decreed—after prodding by Senator Henry Jackson—that preferential trade treatment would have to go hand-in-hand with increases in emigration rights for Soviet Jews. An angry Kremlin ended up rejecting the American trade agreement altogether. And the same 1974 trade bill took punitive measures against the Organization of Petroleum Exporting Countries (OPEC), in retaliation for Arab curtailment of supply in the winter of 1973–74. But by failing to make an exception for the South American OPEC nations that have remained friendly to the U.S., Congress caused a mini-crisis in inter-American diplomacy, especially with Venezuela, the U.S.'s chief foreign oil supplier.

President Ford and Secretary Kissinger, who had become increasingly annoyed by congressional muscle-flexing in foreign affairs, finally made their displeasure known in sharp public statements. Kissinger complained that congressional hyperactivity in the international realm could "so stultify flexibility that you have no negotiating room at all." And in his 1975 State of the Union address, Ford warned that "legislative restrictons, intended for the best motives and purposes, can have the opposite results, as we have seen most recently in our trade relations with the Soviet Union."

"Crisis management," while spectacular, is not the true function of foreign policy, of course. Committees of the House and Senate conduct daily work in international affairs. The Senate Foreign Relations Committee (for years the fiefdom of Senator J. William Fulbright, but now chaired by Senator John Sparkman of Alabama) has broad authority, including the review of treaties and the grilling of the President's ambassadorial nominees. The Senate Finance Committee and House Ways and Means Committee write foreign trade legislation, balancing such tricky concerns as the U.S. payments deficit, the health of threatened domestic industries, and the need for diplomatic rapport with exporting nations overseas. The agriculture committees help the Agriculture Department set trade policy for foodstuffs. Other committees have small pieces of the action.

In the American political tradition, foreign policy is supposed to be bipartisan or even apolitical, as in the old adage that "politics stops at the water's edge." It is questionable whether this was ever true, but it certainly has not been the case for a long time. Every time the President or Congress makes a move in the international arena, the impact of that action on public opinion—and, therefore, its political consequence—is analyzed carefully. President Truman's perceived need for the "Jewish vote" is thought to have influenced his policy on Palestine in the late Forties. President Kennedy confided to close associates that any plan to withdraw U.S. military advisers from Vietnam would have to be announced *after* his reelection in 1964, lest his GOP opponents tag him with being soft on communism. And Richard Nixon, seeking southern support in the 1968 campaign, reportedly promised South Carolina's conservative Senator Strom Thurmond that, as President, he would support development of an antiballistic missile system and try to help the American textile industry by trimming Japanese imports. So it goes. Politicians make hay with the voters, and with each other, on every foreign policy issue from oil import quotas to disarmament.

FOREIGN AFFAIRS BUREAUCRACIES

Among more than fifty federal agencies, commissions, departments, and administrations with foreign policy roles, some are clearly dominant and some are merely subordinate. The Defense Department is a giant in foreign affairs, since there is hardly any major international issue that doesn't have a "national security" angle. The Pentagon's representation in other countries is enormous. At American posts throughout the world, there are several thousand more Defense Department employees (military attachés and advisers) than employees of the State Department, who technically run the missions. The Pentagon also maintains military aid and training missions in dozens of nations, dispensing assistance valued at more than $3 billion each year.

In international economic affairs, the Treasury Department is dominant. The White House Council on International Economic Policy was influential under Nixon aides Peter Peterson and Peter Flanigan, but has declined somewhat in the Ford administration. The Commerce Department has a major role in negotiating international trade agreements. (Peterson, who was one of the more dynamic Secretaries of Commerce, negotiated the landmark trade pact with the Soviets in 1972. He was encouraged to resign soon thereafter, probably because of White House resentment at his growing influence.) The Office of Management and Budget is increasingly powerful in international affairs, since it is the gateway for the flow of foreign affairs funds to every branch of the federal government. The Civil Aeronautics Board shares with the State Department the responsibility for negotiating international controversies over air routes and landing rights.

The Bureau of Narcotics and Dangerous Drugs, a division of the Treasury Department, works with State to stem the tide of drugs from France, Turkey, Mexico, and any other country where they are grown and processed. The Export-Import Bank makes subsidized loans to foreign countries to help them buy American exports. The Justice Department's Immigration and Naturalization Service controls the entry (and sometimes exit) of aliens. The Atomic Energy Commission works with foreign countries in developing peaceful uses for atomic power. The Department of Agriculture has a role in AID's Food for Peace program. The Peace Corps (a division of ACTION) has 6,800 volunteers working overseas, primarily to train locals in such fields as agriculture, health, and education. The newest major participant on the foreign policy scene is the international division of the Federal Energy Administration, which is analyzing every angle of the American position vis-à-vis the cartel of oil-producing nations. The list of federal bodies with foreign policy interests goes on and on, from NASA to the tiny American Battle Monuments Commission (which inspects and helps administer overseas cemeteries where American soldiers are buried).

Then there's the intelligence establishment. Intelligence is usually regarded as a branch of foreign policy information, but over the past twenty-five years the branch has grown thicker than the trunk of the tree itself. When the CIA was created, for example, it was supposed to confine itself to the analyzing of international information gathered through every possible means, from sources public or clandestine. Its original mission was to report on things happening in other countries, not to take a participatory role in them. But "participate" it has, in country after country, year after year. In 1953 it played a principal role in deposing left-leaning Premier Mossadegh of Iran (restoring the exiled Shah to the throne). The following year it directed the overthrow of the leftist government of Guatemala's President Arbenz. It played the role of kingmaker successfully in the Congo and in several countries of Southeast Asia, but unsuccessfully when it tried to end Sukarno's reign in Indonesia. In 1972 and 1973 it put some $5 million into the Chilean movement to overthrow the Marxist government of President Allende (who was assassinated in September 1973 by Chilean rebels).

FOGGY BOTTOM

A tour of the federal foreign policy establishment eventually arrives at "Foggy Bottom," the Washington neighborhood (once slummy and swampy, now "renewed") that is home to the Department of State. The Founding Fathers gave the State Department the honor of being the first—and therefore senior—department of the executive branch. But in budget, staffing, and sheer power, the State Department is eclipsed in its own field by several other agencies (particularly Defense and the CIA). The department is full of capable diplomats, but diplomacy is not synonymous with the making of foreign policy. More often than not, the diplomatic skills of American foreign service officers are taxed to the full when they have to explain, sell, and implement policies that originated not in their home office, but at the White House, the Pentagon, in Congress, or somewhere else in the foreign affairs factory.

It is no secret in Washington that the State Department was humiliated when, during the first Nixon term, it took a distant back seat to Kissinger's National Security Council. The capable but low-key Secretary Rogers seemed to be a closer adviser to the President in domestic affairs than in foreign policy. After showing a brief but impressive diplomatic flair in the Middle East negotiations of late 1969, Rogers deferred more and more to Kissinger, the President's alter ego on all things foreign.

Being ignored by the Nixon White House was an indignity, but it was nothing new for the professionals at State. As a matter of fact, their stock had been declining steadily since peaking in the late Forties, when, led by Secretaries of State George Marshall and Dean Acheson, they had conceived the bold policies that reconstructed Europe and helped save several Western governments from communist takeovers. But these triumphs were followed by the "loss" of mainland China—which America was powerless to prevent, but was blamed on State. The rise of Joseph McCarthy, and his reckless charges against State Department personnel, forced the early retirement of many top experts and damaged the public's faith in its foreign service. Foreign policy during the Eisenhower years was controlled by Secretary of State John Foster Dulles, but he relied less on his department's expertise than on his own judgment and that of his brother, CIA chief Allen Dulles. Things were hardly better for State during the Kennedy and Johnson years of White House domination.

The department got a good shot in the arm when Henry Kissinger became Secretary in 1973, moving his office from 1600 Pennsylvania Avenue to the plain, modern buildings of State, at 22nd and C Streets. Kissinger brought a new style and a new glamor. More importantly, his physical presence in the State Department gave the professional diplomats an easier access to him and his ideas, before his mind was made up on a given issue. It should be noted, however, that Kissinger retained his leadership of the NSC and continued to use its staff as much as, if not more than, the State Department for research and judgment on everything from energy policy to international drug trafficking.

THE KISSINGER MYSTIQUE

For the first several years of his domination of American foreign policy, Henry Kissinger was treated like a demigod in Washington, and especially by the news corps. His every action was hailed as a brilliant move. But as things started falling apart for Nixon, Kissinger was given a closer look, too. Some critics contended that his concentration on improving relations with the super-powers—the Soviet Union and potentially powerful Communist China—has sacrificed rapport with traditional European allies. Critics argued that Kissinger badly neglected the problems of the Third World, the developing nations of Africa and Asia. They also complained that the Secretary's extensive experience did not include much international economics, which is increasingly crucial to understanding world affairs today. Finally, there have been a number of personal embarrassments to Kissinger, including the revelation that he probably authorized the tapping of his subordinates' telephones to find press leaks. Kissinger himself recognized some of the criticism in a talk to foreign service officers in Washington in November 1974, when he admonished them against thinking that foreign policy could ever be run by a single "superstar."

But even Kissinger's detractors cannot deny the individual brilliance and energy of his operations—especially in Peking and the Middle East. Back home in Washington, Kissinger has instilled in the State Department a feeling of importance and participation in the making of foreign policy. There is a new pride in Foggy Bottom, even if career officials there joke about his one-man missions and solo globe-trotting ("The State Department is in Cairo today, but he'll be back in Washington over the weekend"). Within the bare beige offices where most desk officers and lesser policymakers work, it is clear that the Secretary can be attending to only a few headline issues. Thousands of other daily decisions are being made by foreign service officers stationed in Washington and abroad. And it is Kissinger's announced goal to force these men to take on more of the load, to make decisions and take the rap for mistakes. He is trying to reduce the feeling of safety in numbers.

The Policy Planning Staff, for one thing, has been reemphasized and made an important part of the department. In the past, this group of thirty full-time policy professionals has been accused of hiding in an ivory tower, or of not being allowed out of the tower. Its ruminations about the shape of the future world have not been listened to. Kissinger has ordered the policy planners to augment their theoretical forecasts with practical advice, and he has instructed each division of the department to make this advice a big part of its decisionmaking process. Playing an important part in this is the Secretary's insistence that the policy planners also think in money terms all along the way. How much will a certain policy cost? And how much might it take away from some other vital effort? If the cash isn't available—forget it.

Kissinger insists that every person in the department try to *anticipate* problems rather than merely rush to put out fires when they flare. "I don't ever want to be surprised," he warns them. "If a bad situation is brewing—or if it *could* develop—I want you to be prepared for all the eventualities and ready with solutions." The reason for emphasis on this goes back to an old State Department problem: the desk officers who handle any foreign country or area naturally have to be men with experience in that part of the world.

That means they have served there as diplomats in the past. U.S. policies in that region are partially *their* policies. They have a vested interest in convincing themselves and everyone else that things are fine over there. They tend to put a rosy interpretation on reports from the area—or even to cover up disturbing reports.

Kissinger is a tireless, around-the-clock worker, and his aides are expected to be indefatigable, too. Many of them are now accustomed to getting a phone call from him at 11 P.M., asking them to have a report or a position paper on his desk at 8 the next morning. "I don't mind rushing down to the Department and working these hours," says one deputy under secretary. "But where do I get the stenographic help? The girls around here are strictly nine-to-five-thirty types."

One practical method of changing people's ways is Kissinger's insistence on eliminating the old-style staff meeting. It used to be the custom at every level in the department to hold meetings where one or two people specializing in a certain issue explained their views and everyone else nodded and expressed general agreement. Kissinger's attitude is: "We already know that. We can live without the self-congratulation. I want fewer people in each meeting, and I want them to act like an opposition party—trying for that little space of time to find flaws in what the expert is saying." He dislikes wishy-washy opinions. First he wants each person to advocate a line of action full force. The compromises—if any—will come later.

It is not yet clear whether Henry Kissinger will succeed in his announced goal of making such changes endure after his time. He wants to remake the department, so that the Kissinger ways become "institutionalized"—part of the system. All reformers dream of making their reforms permanent. Few succeed in a bureaucracy.

THE DIPLOMATIC ROUTINE

Disappointing as it may be to both its detractors and its admirers, the State Department is nowhere near as depraved or as heroic as many people may think. Inside the flat-faced buildings in their four-square-block unit are corridors and offices only a little less plain than the building's exterior. The Washington-based employees work longer hours than most of their fellow citizens, and only a few of them wear striped pants or attend elegant receptions. Far more of them brew endless cups of instant coffee on a table in the corner of their plain-walled offices.

The State Department's schedule of work is broad. Not only does it have to maintain relations with more than 130 nations (the number varies as colonial areas move up to nationhood while other small nations merge), it also covers many fields that are of special interest to some or all Americans. It has experts in petroleum, metals, and other major commodities, and it tries to prevent international decisions that would harm America's ability to get the materials it wants. It has fisheries experts. It contacts foreign governments about changing postal rates and rules. It has a large office that issues passports to Americans who want to travel, and there are consular services to guard the interests of those Americans when they are abroad. An American teenager who falls into the hands of foreign police for drug possession, or a U.S. citizen who runs out of money and can't get home when his prepaid charter flight is canceled—these and many other problems are the concern of the State Department.

There are two ways of getting into the foreign service: the up-from-the-bottom route (via the foreign service exam) or the "lateral entry" route, through which seasoned specialists from the private sector or other government agencies assume middle- and upper-level jobs at State. Lateral entry is becoming the preferred way of getting to the top in a hurry. In 1970 about 65 percent of all the State employees with ranks of FSO-1 and -2 (the top career staff) had entered "laterally" rather than through the exam.

But the process of written and oral examinations still brings in a new crop of some 180 foreign service officers each year. Only about 5 percent of all applicants pass. (The number of applicants declined through the 1960s and early 1970s, probably because of the sagging stature of the State Department.) The written exam, which can be taken in dozens of cities, is probably the most comprehensive test of general knowledge one could ever encounter. It includes questions on history, literature, economics, music, art, and many other subject areas. Those who pass it are further screened by a panel of interviewers who look for qualities of quick thinking, sound judgment, and clear expression.

The foreign service was once very elitist in its makeup, and is still a long way from being a cross section of the nation. Before 1925, about 65 percent of all American diplomats were graduates of just three colleges: Harvard, Yale, and Princeton. As recently as 1970, the alumni of these colleges and the other five in the Ivy League accounted for one-quarter of the new recruits. Midwesterners and southerners are underrepresented in the foreign service, as are women and blacks.

There is no ceiling on the age of a new FSO. All that is required is that the person be young enough to serve at least one full tour of foreign duty (usually two years) before retirement at age sixty. The average age of the new crop usually runs about twenty-seven years. There is no absolute requirement on formal education, either, yet virtually all FSOs are college graduates, and about 60 percent possess advanced degrees. An applicant need not be able to speak a foreign language to be accepted, but his chances of promotion are nil unless he eventually becomes fluent in at least one, through instruction paid for by the government. The American foreign service is not as strong linguistically as those of other countries (many of which require fluency in two tongues *before* acceptance), largely because the rest of the world has obliged the U.S. by learning English, the new dominant language of international affairs. The new recruits are usually classified FSO-7 or -8 and receive starting salaries ranging from mid-$9,000 to mid-$13,000, depending on prior skills and experience in other fields.

Officers can choose to specialize in any of four career areas: *Administrative* work, which covers the management of U.S. posts abroad, budget and fiscal planning, personnel, and all the other housekeeping from building a new embassy to operating the motor pool. *Consular* work, which means protecting and assisting Americans abroad. *Economic/commercial,* which means analyzing business and trade trends and negotiating commercial issues with foreign governments. *Political,* which covers the traditional diplomat's work of studying the policies of other nations, knowing what makes them tick, and carrying out U.S. policies to mesh with—or to block—those of other countries.

Most FSOs spend their careers alternating between a two- or three-year stint abroad and a comparable period as a desk officer back home in "Foggy Bottom." At any given moment, more than one-third of the 3,300 FSOs are on assignment in Washington (where they work side by side with more than 4,000 clerical workers and high-level specialists who are "on loan," many of them more or less permanently, from other federal agencies).

U.S. PRESENCE OVERSEAS

The 2,000 or so FSOs who are abroad at any given time staff some 280 American outposts—about 130 embassies (in the capitals), 130 consulates (in other principal cities), and 11 missions to international organizations. Besides FSOs, most of these outposts have employees of several other federal agencies attached to them—Defense, CIA, Commerce, Agriculture, Labor, etc.

The staffs of American diplomatic missions are invariably much larger— sometimes by a multiple of 10—than the counterpart staffs of the Western European allies. In a few major capitals, the U.S. has a total employment of 500 to 1,000, while other large nations make do in the same city with barely 100. America's far-reaching commercial and military interests obviously require more staffing than other nations deem necessary, but some U.S. diplomats feel that efficiency could be improved by trimming employment. There is a much-quoted story about the response of Ellis Briggs, American ambassador to Brazil in 1958, when he was told by Washington that his mission would soon be sent a man with a doctorate in physics to act as science attaché. Briggs wired back: "The American Embassy in Rio de Janeiro needs a science attaché the way a cigar-store Indian needs a brassiere." The attaché was sent anyway, and before long another arrived.

Most American ambassadors—about two-thirds in recent years—are chosen from the ranks of senior FSOs. But the other one-third, the political appointees, are assigned to most of the choice, glamorous assignments, such as Western European countries and exotic Caribbean islands. Most of the political appointees are wealthy businessmen who contributed to the campaign of the victorious President. Some, however, are elder statesmen from nondiplomatic fields of government (like former New York Senator Kenneth Keating, ambassador to Israel, and former Kentucky Senator John Sherman Cooper, a onetime ambassador to India whom President Ford appointed to open the first U.S. embassy in East Germany). Not all the wealthy ambassadors are diplomatic neophytes. Publisher Walter H. Annenberg may not have brought much international experience with him on his assignment to London, but his predecessor, the wealthy, well-born David K. E. Bruce, was a seasoned diplomat who was later chosen by President Nixon to head the first American mission to mainland China. Some political appointees prove to be better diplomats than anyone expected at first, including John Volpe, the self-made millionaire contractor (of Italian-American parentage) who was named by President Nixon to head the embassy in Rome.

One particularly difficult ambassadorial job that is *never* given to anyone but a real pro is the top spot in Moscow. Since the end of World War II, only the best-trained foreign affairs experts (all of them fluent in Russian and well versed in Soviet affairs) have been assigned to that post. The late Llewellyn (Tommy) Thompson served long tours of duty there. Others who distinguished themselves were George Kennan, the late Charles (Chip) Bohlen, Foy Kohler, and Jacob Beam. The flexible-minded Kennan devised the "containment" policy for coping with Russian aggression after the war, but then had the objectivity to see that it was time for his own brainchild to be phased out. Because the top men in Washington were less ready to change courses, Kennan resigned. Tommy Thompson had a long string of successes in foreseeing Soviet moves, including an advance warning to Washington that the Russians would move into Czechoslovakia to end the Dubcek flirtation with the West. In 1975 the Moscow post was occupied by Walter Stoessel, a top career FSO who had served twice before in Moscow.

One of the reasons for assigning wealthy men to the leading foreign capitals is Congress's stinginess in providing American embassies with entertainment money (called "representation allowances"). In recent years Congress has earmarked only about $1.2 million annually for official hospitality throughout the entire network of U.S. missions overseas. Most other major nations, with considerably smaller staffs, spend two or three times more government money on expense-account entertaining than the American embassies. So it's convenient (and in some cases, necessary) for the American ambassador to pick up part of the tab himself. When former Senator J. William Fulbright was nominated to be ambassador to Great Britain, many observers wondered how he would be able to afford the job. It soon became a moot point, however, when he asked that his nomination be withdrawn for other reasons.

REWARDS AND RISKS

Like any other group of people, the FSOs have their dullards, their shirkers, their petty bureaucrats who would rather lie low than take a risk that could ruffle feathers and jeopardize their advancement. Despite the aspersions cast on the foreign service by Senator Joe McCarthy in the 1950s, relatively few of them are homosexuals. But they've developed a sense of humor about the charge. When an American diplomat in East Europe was convicted of passing official secrets to a communist mistress a few years ago, people at State joked: "As soon as one of us has anything to with a *woman* he's thrown out and jailed."

The foreign service doesn't pay very well, even at the top. Most senior career diplomats could make a lot more money in private business, in, say, the management of multinational companies. It is their intense interest in diplomacy that ties them to the foreign service. One instance of such dedication was that of Alfred Jenkins, the senior U.S. diplomat who helped establish the new mission in Peking in 1973. Jenkins, who speaks fluent Chinese, was the key man in setting up the secret Kissinger visits to Communist China and then the spectacular Nixon tour. Jenkins brooded and toiled so hard that he began to look like a wraith in the weeks before everything finally jelled. Later he confessed to friends that for several nights before President Nixon's surprise announcement of a trip to Peking, he couldn't sleep a wink, going over and over the possibility that a step had been overlooked or that the whole project would produce a monumental thud.

The hazards of being an American diplomat overseas go far beyond jungle disease and cultural deprivation in some Godforsaken outpost. In an age of headline-grabbing terrorists, being an American diplomat in a tense country can be dangerous. Over the past ten years, a dozen U.S. diplomats have been killed on duty. The first American ambassador to be assassinated was John Gordon Mein, murdered by machine-gunning rebels in Guatemala in 1968. In 1973 Palestinian terrorists murdered in cold blood the U.S. ambassador to the Sudan, Cleo A. Noel, Jr., and the U.S. chargé d'affaires, G. Curtis Moore. In 1974 Rodger Davies, ambassador to Cyprus, was killed by a sniper (probably a Greek Cypriot) during the bloody Greek-Turkish fighting on the island. These men, and others who have died representing their country, are honored on a large stone plaque in the State Department. There is room on the plaque for more names, which, tragically and inevitably, will be added over the years.

FOREIGN AID

Besides scattering more diplomats around the world than any other nation, the U.S. dispenses a flood of dollars. In the twenty-five years following the end of World War II, America poured some $150 billion into other nations: about $52 billion in economic assistance channeled through the Agency for International Development (and its predecessor agencies), $42 billion of military equipment, $20 billion through the Food for Peace Program, $23 billion in contributions to international organizations, and some $13 billion in credit subsidies on loans made by the Export-Import Bank. In the late Sixties, the foreign aid program came under attack from all sides. Conservatives, many of whom never did like foreign assistance, argued that it was ineffectual and went beyond the U.S.'s appropriate sphere of responsibility. Many liberals argued that the money was often misspent, imperialistic, and—in the case of military aid—used to bolster dictatorships and foment wars between neighboring nations.

As a result of congressional trimming, U.S. economic assistance is down to about $3.5 billion a year, the lowest figure since the end of World War II, in terms of percentage of the GNP. About $1 billion of that is unilateral aid distributed by AID, a division of State with some 2,300 employees in Washington and another 2,100 scattered around the world. Most of the money is targeted on the neediest nations, such as Afghanistan, India, Bangladesh, Pakistan, Laos, and—especially—Vietnam. The aid is in both material assistance and technological training in everything from agriculture to setting up birth control programs (once controversial, but today taken for granted). Another major component of U.S. foreign aid—nearly $1 billion—is the U.S. contribution to multilateral international organizations, such as the World Bank, the development banks of the Americas, Asia, and Africa, and the United Nations (its Development Program and Relief and Works Agency). In recent years, U.S. funding of these groups has accounted for a smaller and smaller proportion of their total budgets, as Washington tries to convince other wealthy nations to pick up the slack. The remaining large chunk of American economic aid is about $1 billion of food supplied under the Food for Peace program. Adding military assistance brings the U.S. aid total to about $6.5 billion annually.

Though not officially a component of American foreign aid, the overseas sale of weaponry by American defense contractors has become an immense business and an unsettling factor in world order. In fiscal 1974 American firms sold a record $8.3 billion of armaments to other countries, more than twice the previous year's total. More than $4 billion of the 1974 amount was sold to the newly affluent Arab nations, and the flow of armaments actually increased in the following fiscal year. While these transactions (in new, modern armaments, not used surplus) were conducted by private corporations, they have been encouraged by Secretary of State Kissinger as an integral part of the U.S. diplomatic initiative of making friends and winning influence in the Arab world. Since these sales dwarfed U.S. aid to Israel, many politicians became concerned about the impact on peace in the Middle East. In February of 1975 Senator Edward M. Kennedy proposed a six-month moratorium on such sales until the Ford administration could explain its position and the whole issue could be debated, but Congress seemed reluctant to take up the matter.

THE NERVE CENTER

Though the biggest gatherers of foreign information are located outside of "Foggy Bottom" (at the Pentagon and CIA), the State Department has its own intelligence clearinghouse, the "Operations Center." Manned twenty-four hours a day by five professionals and a secretarial support staff, the "Op Center" looks like the headquarters room in the movie *Dr. Strangelove*. Information pours into the center by virtually every electronic communication method. There are tickers carrying the news from AP, UPI, Reuters, and FBIS (pronounced "FIBiss), which stands for Foreign Broadcast Information Service, a monitor of every major overseas news broadcast, like Radio Moscow and Radio Peking. There is direct telephone contact with the White House Communications Center and the National Military Command Center at the Pentagon. There is a battery of message receivers called SCAT machines, over which messages flow from U.S. sources overseas (including CIA agents). The messages are coded "Routine," "Priority," "Immediate," or "Flash." Adjacent to the main room of the center is the "telecom room," where a dozen or so people can sit and watch teletype messages from around the world thrown on large screens (used if telephone lines are suspected of being tapped).

The "Op Center" is concerned with matters both official and personal. It gets immediate notification, of course, of any change of government overseas, especially if it will jeopardize U.S. citizens or economic interests. (In the event that evacuation of Americans is required, the center has an "emergency and evacuation plan" on file for every nation on earth, including information on available airfields and the probable number of American tourists in the country at a given moment.) News of the death of every American citizen overseas is cabled to the center, and the center tries to contact a relative or close friend of the deceased to ask him to bring the news to the immediate family. If the Secretary of State or other high official is traveling abroad and needs something back home—anything from special documents to the white tie and tails that he forgot to pack—the center will get the things together and have them rushed out to the airport.

The center sometimes engages directly in sensitive diplomacy, as in the matter some years back when a small fleet of Cuban fishing vessels was damaged in a storm and foundered off the Gulf Coast of Texas. The Coast Guard wasn't too happy about helping them, but an Operations Center official talked it into treating the fishermen like guests of America, not prisoners. The

Czech embassy was used as an intermediary, since the U.S. has no relations with Cuba, and the fishermen were repatriated soon thereafter.

The center's biggest black eye was the case involving a Lithuanian sailor from a Russian ship who sought asylum on a U.S. Coast Guard vessel off the coast of Cape Cod, Massachusetts. The Coast Guard notified the Operations Center that it had a defector and that his Russian superiors wanted to board the American ship and retrieve him. The State official who took the call deliberated too long, and by the time he called the Coast Guard back to tell it to keep the defector, the Russians had already boarded the boat and forcibly repatriated the Lithuanian. The center reacted properly, but not fast enough, and reprimands followed. (In 1974, the Lithuanian was released by the Russians and came to the United States to live.)

In addition to serious matters, the center gets crank calls and nuisance calls. One night a telephone operator contacted the center (which takes all calls to the general State Department number during the night) and said she was trying to place a person-to-person call to Moshe Dayan from "a party in New York City." The center said it would take the whole thing over. The "party" in New York turned out to be just that—a loud, drunken gathering that decided to call Moshe. The center talked to the people at the party and took their message for Mr. Dayan, but diplomatically let the matter drop right there.

Each morning at 8:45, the senior watch officer leaving duty meets with the executive secretary of the Department of State (a little-known but often very important official). They go over all the significant items of the night before—not just intelligence, but everything of interest to the Secretary of State (including housekeeping matters in overseas offices). The executive secretary then briefs the Secretary of State when he gets to the office. The executive secretary is the first contact of the center in a matter of real emergency, and he, in turn, calls the Secretary of State. The executive secretary calls the Operations Center every night before he goes to bed, and he gets to the office early (about 7:30), so he is out of contact with the center only seven or eight hours.

WORLD OF THE FUTURE

International developments of the last decade have made the U.S. justifiably humble about its ability to shape the future of the world to its own liking. Vietnam has cured Americans, at least temporarily, of their tendency to leap to the aid of governments whose rapport with their own people is shaky at best. The reality of soaring prices at home has caused Americans to stop laughing at the double-digit inflation that was once thought to be the exclusive plague of developing nations (or "inept" European regimes). The precarious state of the U.S. balance of payments has led to a call for cutbacks in the number of American troops stationed abroad. American industry now finds it must compete, in the overseas sale of sophisticated products, against nations that were once just technological copycats. And the nation's feeling of invincibility was eroded by the display of Arab economic might when the OPEC nations clamped down on the stream of oil in the winter of 1973.

In the "global village" of tomorrow, the United States is not going to play sugar daddy to everyone. There just isn't enough candy to go around, and besides, many of the old recipients have changed their minds about the once unquestioned wholesomeness of the treat. One sign of the new U.S. attitude was the pronouncement, at the Rome world food conference in 1974, that the U.S. could not be the world's farm and granary, and that the developing nations had better put a lid on their population growth and step up their production of food.

But even if the U.S. takes a less interventionist role in other nations' business, it will still be, and cannot avoid being, the single most powerful force in world affairs. Since the American economy is inextricably linked to the world economy, the foreign policy factory in Washington will continue to be a major influence on life and death in every continent.

19 AMBASSADORS ON THE JOB

The evidence of the diplomatic presence is everywhere in Washington. Along Massachusetts Avenue and 16th Street, many of the most elegant buildings display painted shields and crests over their front doors, proclaiming the identity of the nation whose embassy is housed there. Automobiles with "DPL" license plates are a common sight on the streets—Mercedes-Benzes, Rolls Royces, Cadillacs, and hundreds of Volkswagens (for third secretaries and attachés). Foreign garb—saris, turbans, or tribal robes—doesn't turn heads on city sidewalks or in chic restaurants, although such attire is usually reserved for social occasions, conventional business suits being normal office wear. In the blocks of Pennsylvania Avenue near the International Monetary Fund, the World Bank, and the Inter-American Development Bank, a passer-by is as likely to hear sidewalk conversation in Spanish, French, or German as in English, though English is the common denominator of diplomacy today, in Washington and throughout the world.

There are countless reasons why Washington is the world's leading diplomatic center, and they all boil down to: Money and Power. As the wealthiest nation on earth, the U.S. contains 6 percent of the world's population and consumes 38 percent of the world's energy. It is the hungriest maw for the intake of the world's raw materials and manufactured goods. The U.S. is also a source of financial assistance to foreign nations—although Americans are becoming increasingly disenchanted with unilateral foreign aid. The Pentagon—administering the most powerful single military establishment in the world—is a major supplier of new and used armaments to foreign governments who fear that their neighbors (or some of their own citizens) may suddenly cause them trouble. Washington is the headquarters of the major world economic assistance organizations, staffed by economists, statisticians, political scientists, sociologists, and plain office workers from every part of the globe. Washington is where nations dicker with the World Bank for a development loan (in "soft currency") or with the International Monetary Fund for relief from a balance-of-payments crisis (in somewhat "harder" money).

As a result of all this, Washington has more foreign embassies than any other capital in the world, and these embassies are staffed by the world's largest concentration of topnotch diplomats. Even the poor countries—who are able to pay for only a handful of embassies—always have one in Washington. It is a "must" to have an embassy in the most important diplomatic center on the face of the earth.

Washington has enjoyed this diplomatic preeminence since World War II, when the U.S. emerged as the world's most powerful military force. This position was strengthened over the following twenty-five years by the massive outpouring of economic aid to virtually every nation on earth. But it took some years for Washington's prestige to catch up with its power. Far from being even the most glamorous city in America, Washington was once a cultural wasteland compared to such scintillating foreign capitals as London and Paris. Despite its obvious power, Washington was considered a "hardship post" by diplomats who were accustomed to a social climate of fine restaurants, theater, concerts, opera, and ballet. Today, thanks to the cultural boom that has engulfed the nation's capital, diplomats no longer look down their noses at Washington's performing arts.

But to many diplomats, the onetime hardship of cultural deprivation has been replaced by the hardship of crime—no worse in Washington than in most large American cities, but worse than in their own home capitals. Every year or so, a grisly tragedy—like the murder of a Belgian diplomat's son in Rock Creek Park in 1973, or the fatal shooting of a man inside the Italian Embassy a few years earlier—sends quiet waves of fear through the foreign community here. Crime is a major factor in the gradual shift of embassies away from the Meridian Hill neighborhood of 16th Street, Washington's "Little Embassy Row." The risk of crime is not entirely domestic, however. A couple of years ago, a secretary at the British Embassy lost a hand in the explosion of a "letter bomb," apparently mailed from overseas by the terrorist Irish Republican Army. The fatal shooting of an Israeli military attaché in front of his suburban Bethesda, Maryland, home in 1973 had not been solved nearly two years later. The apparently motiveless murder looked like the work of a terrorist, but there was no evidence to support this speculation.

Out of the total of 149 independent nations in the world, there are 125 embassies in Washington, employing some 5,500 people (2,000 diplomats and 3,500 supporting staff). Among the nonrepresented nations are several communist countries with whom we have never had formal relations, such as North Vietnam, North Korea, and the Castro regime in Cuba. (East Germany was removed from this list of the unrepresented in 1974, with the opening of her first Washington embassy on the eighth floor of a Massachusetts Avenue office building.) Relations with the Arab nations of Algeria, Iraq, and Syria were severed for several years, but recently Algeria and Syria resumed diplomatic relations with the U.S. Several of the unrepresented countries have agreements with other nations to serve as their "protecting power" in the U.S., much as the Swiss serve as America's intermediary in Cuba. Iraq's protector, for example, is India, and the Algerian government used to work through the embassy of Guinea during its period of nonrecognition.

The Communist Chinese have a mission here, but not with the status of an embassy. The Vatican City has a representative in Washington, too, housed in a stately residence on Massachusetts Avenue across from the U.S. Naval Observatory. But don't look for him on the State Department's diplomatic list—he's not officially an ambassador, minister, or even a chargé d'affaires, but is called the "apostolic delegate." The most precarious of all the diplomatic offices in Washington is that of Rhodesia, whose policies toward its black citizens led to a United Nations trade embargo. The U.S. abides by the embargo and doesn't recognize Rhodesia, but the nation has two representatives here who work out of something called the Rhodesian Information Office. Some black congressmen think they should be expelled from the U.S., but so far no action has been taken. Under an amendment guided through Congress by Senator Harry Byrd of Virginia, the U.S. accepts imports of chromium from

Rhodesia in defiance of the U.N. embargo. A consortium of anti-Rhodesian interests, including black congressmen and African diplomats, tried to get the Byrd amendment repealed in 1974, but couldn't muster enough votes. (Byrd feels that the government of Rhodesia is no more repressive than that of the Soviet Union, which is the only other source of American chrome imports.)

In addition to the individual embassies and the international economic organizations, Washington is the home of a slew of hemispheric groups, principally the Organization of American States, headquartered in the beautiful Pan American Union building at 17th Street and Constitution Avenue N.W. (which has a tropical garden, complete with parrots, in its center courtyard). In addition, there are Washington offices of numerous organizations based elsewhere, such as the International Labor Organization in Geneva, Switzerland, and the Inter-American Tropical Tuna Commission, headquartered in La Jolla, California.

THE PECKING ORDER

The prestige of an embassy in Washington is determined by several factors, such as the size and wealth of the nation, its historical ties with the U.S., the skill and social charm of its ambassador (and his wife), and the richness of its ambassadorial residence and offices. And not to be overlooked is the amount of trade that a foreign country does with the U.S., although this is not a guarantee of high prestige. Even though Canada is by far America's largest partner in trade and has a very capable staff here (headed by the well-regarded Ambassador Marcel Cadieux), its embassy lacks the magical aura of some lesser nations. Canada's geographic and cultural closeness to the U.S.— plus its general agreement with American foreign policy—causes her to be taken for granted. Another exception to the trade/prestige correlation is the Soviet Union, which, despite large percentage gains in trade and the potential for greater activity, is still a minor economic partner of the U.S. (about $1.2 billion annually, compared with some $32 billion of trade with Canada and $18 billion with Japan). But the Soviets hold a powerful place in the Washington diplomatic establishment, based on their military might and the influence (or control) they wield over so many other nations.

On the basis of mutual economic interests and cultural affinities, the nations of Europe stand higher in the diplomatic pecking order than any others—higher than the Latin American nations, the Asians, and the Middle Easterners. America's European roots are a binding force to England and France, however strained political relations may be for brief periods. The emergence of Japan as a worldwide economic power has been accompanied by a surge in its embassy's importance in Washington, politically and socially. Similarly, the Middle East oil crisis reminded the U.S.—painfully—of the need for friendly relations with the Arab nations, especially Iran.

Embassy staffs in Washington run the gamut from minuscule to sprawling. The smallest are those of Chad and Luxembourg, each of which has merely an ambassador and an office assistant. Luxembourg Ambassador Adrien Meisch is one of the busiest men in diplomatic Washington, simultaneously wearing the hats of cultural attaché, social host, economic attaché, and spokesman for his nation. More than most ambassadors, he uses embassy parties for real business, since they offer him a unique opportunity to talk with numerous other diplomats within a short period of time, all in one place.

(As if his duties here were not enough, Ambassador Meisch is also accredited to Canada and Mexico and must make periodic visits there.)

The largest embassy in Washington is that of the Soviet Union, which has a professional staff numbering about 110, not counting secretarial, clerical, and menial employees. The next largest are Great Britain (72 on the professional staff), Japan (60), Germany (60), France (53), and Canada (49). Some nations have embassy staffs that are disproportionately large, considering their populations and GNP. South Korea, for example, has a professional staff of about 40, Thailand, 35, and Greece about 30. (What these three nations have in common is an unusually strong reliance on American assistance, especially military.)

The titles of professional diplomats and the order of rank within the office vary little from embassy to embassy. The top person is the ambassador extraordinary and plenipotentiary. Next is the minister, followed by the counselor, the first, second, and third secretaries, and finally the attachés. A large staff might have several of every position below ambassador, and an unusually small staff might dispense with several steps in the succession. In the absence of the ambassador, either temporarily or permanently, the next-ranking diplomat has the phrase "chargé d'affaires ad interim" affixed to the end of his name.

SEASONED DIPLOMATS

Most major nations assign an experienced career diplomat to Washington, in contrast to the United States' penchant for sending wealthy campaign contributors to the important world capitals. Some of the top ambassadors were in the United States earlier in their foreign service careers, as a subordinate official of their embassy. This is true, for example, of Soviet Ambassador Anatoly Dobrynin, who was a minister in Washington during the Fifties, and Italian Ambassador Egidio Ortona, a minister here during the late Forties and Fifties. A number of ambassadors held their country's top posts in other nations before coming to Washington: former Belgian Ambassador Walter Loridan, who retired in 1974, had been ambassador to Mexico, the Soviet Union, and Germany; Irish Ambassador William Warnock headed embassies in Germany, Switzerland, Austria, India, and Canada; and French Ambassador Jacques Kosciusko-Morizet (a professor of French literature at Columbia University in 1946) was ambassador to the Congo. Many diplomats get their first exposure to the United States through an assignment at the United Nations in New York City. U.N. alumni include Dobrynin, Ortona, Kosciusko-Morizet, and Swiss Ambassador Felix Schnyder, who was chairman of the UNICEF executive committee. Several ambassadors were once in charge of their countries' foreign offices, analogous to our Department of State. This group includes Austrian Ambassador Arno Halusa and Jordanian Ambassador Abdullah Salah (who had also been ambassador to India and France). There is a diplomat in Washington who was once a head of government and one who was a chief of state. Jens Otto Krag, Head of Delegation of the European Communities, is a former prime minister of Denmark, and Galo Plaza, Secretary General of the Organization of American States, is a former president of Ecuador (and a onetime student at the Universities of California and Maryland, as well as Georgetown University).

But career diplomacy is not the only route to an ambassadorship in

Washington. Family connections help. The dean of the diplomatic corps, Nicaraguan Ambassador Guillermo Sevilla-Sacasa, is an in-law of the family that has ruled that country for many, many years. Iranian Ambassador Ardeshir Zahedi, a noted *bon vivant* around Washington (and formerly his nation's ambassador to Great Britain, 1962–67, and minister of foreign affairs, 1967–71) accelerated his already meteoric career by marrying the Shah's daughter (whom he later divorced, while remaining close to the Shah). Between parties with jetsetter celebrities (a photo of himself and singer Liza Minnelli hangs in a salon of the chancery), Zahedi is busy finding American investment opportunities for the Shah's vast oil wealth. One day he is negotiating for the purchase of a skyscraper in New York City; the next day he is trying to arrange a deal to make the Shah half-owner of a chain of filling stations across the United States.

Great Britain has often sent an ambassador with a nondiplomatic background. Former Ambassador John Freeman, for example, had been the outspoken editor of the *New Statesman* magazine (and a more than occasional critic of the United States). Former Ambassador George Rowland Stanley Baring, the Earl of Cromer, was a partner in the renowned investment banking firm of Baring Brothers, a government economic official, and chairman of IBM (United Kingdom). However, the current British ambassador, Sir Peter Ramsbotham, is a career diplomat who served during his career in the U.N., in Paris and Cyprus, and as ambassador to Iran.

The function of an ambassador varies greatly, depending primarily on the size of his staff. If he has a phalanx of aides—economic counselors, military attachés, agricultural ministers, and second secretaries for administation—his hands are free for selective contacts with high-level officials of the United States, the world economic organizations, and other nations. He can conduct his subtle diplomacy over lunch at the International Club or the Jockey Club restaurant or at late afternoon conferences at the State Department. The ambassadors of small nations have to do more of the nuts-and-bolts work themselves—negotiating loans at the World Bank and the U.S. Agency for International Development, attending hearings at the Tariff Commission, and drafting reports to the government back home about the state of the United States.

BUSY AMBASSADORS

Being an effective ambassador is hard work. As Adlai Stevenson, himself a skilled diplomat, once quipped, "An ambassador's job is composed of equal parts of alcohol, protocol and Geritol." There is hardly a night of the week on which he doesn't have a social obligation. And "obligation" is exactly how he sees most social events. His absence would be an insult to the host (be it another ambassador, a State Department official, or maybe a U.S. senator), and it could hurt his chances of securing a favor later. In addition, his absence would deprive him of the nuggets of information—ranging from real intelligence to sheer rumor—that every ambassador picks up over cocktails and canapés. So his attendance is a must, but it might be merely a token appearance. His chauffeur will keep the limousine warm at the curb, ready to whisk him away to the next of several receptions in one night.

Infinite are the varieties of embassy parties, ranging from the mob scene for several hundred guests to the intimate dinner for serious conversation.

Obligatory parties are given for the arrival of the nation's chief of state and for the arrival and departure of a new ambassador. Also obligatory is a large party on the national holiday, which might commemorate anything from independence (like France's "Quatorze Juillet") to the emperor's birthday (like Ethiopia's tribute to Haile Selassie each July 23, a tradition that was discontinued after he was deposed in 1974). At the British Embassy (still the top prestige invitation, despite periodic vogues enjoyed by exuberant Middle Eastern and Latin American embassies), the birthday of the queen is celebrated with a garden party every May 30, regardless of the current ruler's actual date of birth. The event is "veddy, veddy British"—gardens in bloom, striped tents on the lawn, and tables laden with mounds of fresh strawberries and Devonshire cream. There is not a month of the year without at least six official national days, and September is the leader (seventeen). With some 125 embassies in Washington, it is not surprising that some national days fall on the same date as others—like Switzerland and Dahomey on August 1, Austria and Iran on October 26.

Besides the standard social functions, embassies seize every conceivable occasion as a pretext for throwing a party and downing large quantities of liquor (free of U.S. taxes). The British, for example, hosted a party in 1974 for actress Jean Marsh when she toured the U.S. promoting the BBC television serial *Upstairs, Downstairs,* the sophisticated Edwardian soap opera that simultaneously titillated and educated American audiences.

Protocol is the social lubricant of diplomatic circles—although too much of it can gum up, rather than oil, the works. The order of precedence among ambassadors is determined not by the size, power, or even age of a nation, but simply by the order in which its ambassador arrived in Washington and presented his credentials. The most senior member of the diplomatic community is given the title of "Dean," and since 1958 it has been held by Ambassador Sevilla-Sacasa. The honorary position carries few privileges but several obligations, including attendance at more embassy parties than anyone else cares to attend. The dean also has the obligation of greeting the U.S. President at Andrews Air Force Base upon his return from every foreign trip. (The dean is invariably joined in this duty by the ambassador of each country the President visited on the trip.) Precedence determines where each ambassador sits at the dinner table. Some ambassadors personally couldn't care less where they sit, just so they're next to a beautiful and witty woman. One ambassador who cared tremendously, however, was former French Ambassador Hervé Alphand, who once threw a fit at a dinner where he felt he had not been seated according to precedence. When planning small dinner parties, the host embassy has to be very careful not to invite diplomats from countries that are not getting along at the time. A bad mistake in the invitation list could cast a pall over the whole evening, so this kind of caution—more a matter of common sense than protocol—is essential.

Having been ambassador to the United States since 1943, Sevilla-Sacasa has spent a larger portion of his life here than most American-born Washingtonians. His nine children were raised here, and they feel as much at home in the United States as in Nicaragua. In decades past, when foreign ambassadors settled in for lengthy stays in Washington, their children often became thoroughly Americanized. The classic example is Ahmet Ertegun, a son of former Turkish Ambassador Mehmet Ertegun, who came to Washington in 1934.

Ahmet attended Landon School in suburban Bethesda and became a devotee of American pop music. Today, as the head of New York-based Atlantic Records, he is one of the most powerful executives in the rock-'n'-roll recording industry, as All-American an enterprise as one could imagine.

These days, most nations change their ambassadors to Washington as often as they change their governments (much as the United States does when a different party wins the White House). Only twelve ambassadors on duty in 1975 arrived here before Richard Nixon became President in 1969. Of this group, the most important are the Soviet Union's Dobrynin, Switzerland's Schnyder, and Italy's Ortona. Besides being consummate diplomats, they have had the good fortune to be left in Washington long enough to learn their jobs fully, make important contacts, and gain personal prestige. But most ambassadors don't get to stay long enough to make any impact.

Some ambassadors make an impact quickly—but the wrong kind. Ortona's predecessor, former Italian Ambassador Sergio Fenoaltea, was very much disgusted by American policy in Southeast Asia, a disgust shared by many other ambassadors here. But unlike the others, who maintained a tactful silence, Fenoaltea made his personal feelings very clear. The U.S. made a few hints to Rome, and Fenoaltea was replaced. The most discreet silence on Vietnam was kept by former Swedish Ambassador Hubert de Besche. Despite his government's virulent opposition to the war in Vietnam, and its harboring of GI deserters, de Besche managed to remain one of Washington's most popular and respected ambassadors.

If, by chance or design, a diplomat does something not merely embarrassing but downright criminal, he is immune from prosecution. One of the precedent-setting immunity cases in international law concerned a Serbo-Croatian diplomat who cut a wide and disruptive swath in America in the Twenties. He got involved in everything from paternity suits to bigamy, but the courts ruled that he could not be prosecuted. If a diplomat does something sufficiently heinous, the State Department can label him "persona non grata" and escort him to the first plane bound for his home country. This rarely happens, however, since an offending diplomat is usually recalled by his country before the U.S. is forced to "PNG" him. The vast majority of diplomats never need immunity from anything worse than a parking ticket or speeding violation.

THE DIPLOMATIC UNDERLINGS

The lives of subordinate diplomats are far less glamorous than those of ambassadors (who, incidentally, have control over the staffing of the embassy). They must be part correspondent, reporting to their capital on the state of the American economy, pending trade legislation, tariff policy, military spending, and the general political climate here. (One diplomat recently quipped to an American journalist, "You know, we're in the same business.") They must be part lobbyist, too, informing the American government of their country's needs and particular problems and seeking assistance.

Cultural attachés arrange exchanges of students and visiting scholars, as well as exchanges of performing artists. Military attachés try to keep abreast of technological and strategic developments in the United States that would affect the security of the home country. They assist with arms purchases, although these transactions are more often handled by a special visiting mission. The Latin American embassies are traditionally top-heavy with military attachés, with first prize going to Argentina, whose fifteen army, navy, and air force aides outnumber the rest of the professional staff combined. (Landlocked Paraguay even has a naval attaché, as well as two attachés for the army and one for the air force.) Agricultural attachés try to get their home country's produce into the U.S. in large quantities without high tariffs.

Press attachés handle the embassy's public relations (often assisted by an American P.R. firm) and monitor every mention of their country in the American press. One young third secretary for a Latin American embassy searches the *Congressional Record* every day for comments about his nation made on the House and Senate floors. If he comes across a derogatory reference he looks up the speaker of it in the series of congressional profiles made by Ralph Nader's "Congress Watch," to determine why the congressman made the remarks and whether he has any clout on the Hill. Some foreigners in Washington have developed a healthy skepticism about what they read in the newspapers here, especially about the American government. One Hungarian diplomat, who had served in both Moscow and Washington, had little faith in the press of both countries, but for the opposite reasons. In Russia, he said, the press provides a constant barrage of governmental praise, while in the U.S. the press can find nothing to praise. He grew to like the United States very much, and thought the press should go easier on its elected officials. But most diplomats were riveted by the press's unearthing of the Watergate scandals—and astounded by the degree of press freedom that permitted such revelations to be published (a distinct contrast to the practice in many of their homelands).

The social life of the embassy staff is less formal and frenetic than the ambassador's, although staff members are often invited to parties given by other embassies with whom they have frequent dealings. Employees of the IMF and World Bank have their own country club, called Bretton Woods, situated on a hill above the Potomac River near Seneca, Maryland. The well-equipped club includes a golf course, tennis courts, swimming pool, bar and grill, and fields for cricket and soccer. Developed in the late Sixties, Bretton Woods has been a boon to the foreign economic diplomats, who are not usually stationed in the U.S. long enough to become members of private clubs in Maryland and Virginia (and a special boon to officials from Africa, who are not welcome at some of Washington's country clubs).

Many diplomats are inveterate tourists, and end up having seen more of the U.S. than most Americans have. In recent years a New York-based foundation, in conjunction with a recreational vehicle manufacturer, has sponsored three-week whirlwind tours of the American West for foreign diplomats, both from Washington and from New York City. On one such summer tour, thirty families drove in a caravan of camper vans through Yellowstone Park, the Redwood Forests, Indian reservations, and mountain ranges. They raved about what a good change of pace it was after the routine diplomatic grind.

Most embassy staffers live in homes and apartments throughout the Washington area, with the suburbs becoming more and more popular. A prominent exception is the staff of the Soviet Embassy. They tend to be very cliquish, and many of them live together in well-guarded apartment buildings.

The Communist Chinese emulated the Russians by buying an entire hotel, the former Windsor Park, on Connecticut Avenue next to Rock Creek Park. Some members of the mission live in a mansion in the Kalorama section—complete with a little-used tennis court—that the Chinese purchased from author-philanthropist Philip Stern.

Although a few poor nations like to put up a good front for their egos, the opulence of a nation's embassy (ambassador's residence) and chancery (staff offices) usually reflects its prominence in the world. The new, struggling nation of Bangladesh (formerly East Pakistan) has its chancery in the Brighton Hotel on California Street N.W., a modest old establishment favored by students visiting Washington on the cheap, and Ambassador M. Hossain Ali lives in a conventional suburban home in Bethesda, Maryland. At the other end of the elegance pole are the Massachusetts Avenue palaces of Canada, Iran, Indonesia, and Great Britain, the Kalorama Road mansion of the French ambassador, the Foxhall Road château of the Belgian ambassador, the embassies of Italy and Spain in the 16th Street corridor, and soon the new Japanese embassy on Nebraska Avenue. The Soviets' tall gray mansion on downtown 16th Street is about as austere as the no-nonsense diplomats who inhabit it.

Traditionally, foreign nations have established their embassies in mansions built by millionaires (or their heirs) who came to Washington at the turn of the century from New York, Pittsburgh, Chicago, and other industrial cities. Embassies have been a boon to architectural preservation in Washington, since foreign nations—and a few wealthy private clubs—are the only organizations that can afford to maintain architectural white elephants. The decaying, turn-of-the-century Lothrop mansion, which occupies a spectacular bluff at Connecticut Avenue and Columbia Road, was saved from an uncertain fate by the Russians who bought it in 1974 as an office for one of their diplomatic missions. The British Embassy, a Georgian brick palace that looks as if it were 200 years old, was actually built in 1931 by English architects, craftsmen, and laborers with materials largely imported from the Mother Country. In the past few years foreign governments have constructed as chanceries some of the most innovative modern buildings in Washington, such as the German office building on Reservoir Road (west of Georgetown), the Brazilian chancery on Massachusetts Avenue, and the Danish embassy on Whitehaven Street, just off "Embassy Row."

Since most large nations overflowed their original chanceries long ago, a lot of them rent office space in prosaic glass-and-steel office buildings in the booming business district along K Street and Connecticut Avenue N.W. The entire chancery of the South Pacific nation of Fiji is a suite in a building at 1629 K Street, and the African nation of Lesotho (formerly the British dependency of Basutoland) works out of a suite at 1601 Connecticut. Sweden moved its chancery to the penthouse suite of a building in the Watergate complex a few years ago, and other diplomatic tenants of the complex include Japan, Italy, and Yemen. (The doors into the Swedes' Watergate offices have exotic push-button locks, with combinations that can be changed as often as necessary for top security.)

LEARNING TO LOBBY

Until recently there was very little honest-to-goodness lobbying done by the embassies, just vague attempts to ingratiate themselves with federal bigwigs at fancy parties. The Communist nations ignored Congress especially, because their own governmental experiences with centralized governments taught them that legislatures had no power at all. What little lobbying was done on behalf of foreign nations was performed largely by American lobbyists.

Now foreign governments are getting into the lobbying swing. The Communist nations go up to the Hill to lobby for "most favored nation" status. (Even Soviet party chief Brezhnev wasn't above a little hard-sell trade lobbying here in 1973, as he demonstrated to a group of key senators and congressmen at a Blair House dinner in his honor.) The Japanese lobby on textiles and electronics, trying to fend off protectionist trade legislation that would limit their American markets. Ditto the meat-producing nations (such as Argentina, Australia, and New Zealand) and the leading dairy countries (like Canada and the Netherlands). Spain lobbies for more U.S. importation of shoes and olives. Every nation with a national airline lobbies for landing rights in more American cities (while resisting the granting of broader landing rights to American carriers). Israel, of course, keeps applying pressure to its friends on the Hill for enough modern weaponry to defend itself against its Arab neighbors.

Since most of America's trade partners have "most favored nation" status, it is more appropriate to describe the dozen or so nations that do not have it as "least favored nations." These countries—all Communist—have stiffer tariffs put on the goods they send to America, so the prices of their products are not as competitive. The Czechs complain, for example, that their beers, watches, and glassware—despite being of high quality—don't stand a chance in the American marketplace against similar products from, say, West Germany. So they try to convince Congress to grant them "MFN treatment." The Romanians, one of the most pro-U.S. of the Eastern European nations, have been lobbying hard for MFN, too. For a time their cause was helped by the warmth that Richard Nixon felt toward Romania, whose leaders showed him unusual courtesy when, as a private citizen and an apparently washed-up politician, he toured Europe after his defeat in California in 1962. When he rose phoenixlike and won the White House, he returned their kindness by paying a visit to Romania on a state visit to Europe in 1969 and hosting their chief of state in Washington the following year. For a while it looked as if the 1974 trade bill would pave the way to MFN for the Soviet Union and the Eastern European nations. But these countries were angered by the stiff conditions that Congress imposed regarding Jewish emigration (and in the case of Czechoslovakia, payment of damages to U.S. citizens for property confiscated during the Communist takeover after World War II). The Soviets and the Czechs both rejected the terms of the deal, but Romania seemed willing to increase Jewish emigration rights in exchange for MFN. (Yugoslavia and Poland both had been granted MFN privileges—years before and for different reasons—so their trade with the U.S. was not affected by the Jewish emigration stipulation in the 1974 trade bill.)

Several embassies—including those of Japan, Australia, France, West Germany, New Zealand, and Ireland, as well as the Washington office of the

European Economic Community—have aggressive agricultural staffs that keep in constant communication with the U.S. Department of Agriculture (USDA). They provide information about production in grains, dairy, and livestock in their home countries, and they try to ascertain what America's production will be. When U.S. cheese production was lower than usual in late 1973, President Nixon, on the recommendation of the Tariff Commission and the USDA, expanded import quotas to ten times the level of a year before. It was a boon to the foreign dairy producers—a boon that their agricultural attachés could see coming and make plans for.

In early 1974, when there was concern that U.S. wheat supplies might run out before the new crop was harvested, some attachés were in daily contact with USDA, to determine the possibility of an embargo on U.S. grain exports. Although no embargo was adopted, there were delays in U.S. grain shipments to several nations. But the constant flow of information between the U.S. government and foreign embassies in Washington enabled other nations— such as Canada and the European Common Market countries—to increase their export activity and take up the slack in American grain exports. These dairy and grain communications are the sort of routine work the embassies engage in daily. But the largest and most controversial agricultural deal in history—the Russian purchase of one-quarter of the entire American wheat crop in 1972—was negotiated not by Soviet embassy personnel and American bureaucrats, but by a special delegation from Moscow that worked out of hotel suites in New York and Washington and dealt directly with American grain dealers.

Although the embassies are becoming more adept at lobbying, they still rely heavily on Washington law firms to represent them before the U.S. government and the international economic organizations. Japan probably pours the most money into the Washington legal establishment, paying fees to such firms as Hogan and Hartson, Gadsby and Hannah, Daniels and Houlihan, and Stitt, Hemmendinger and Kennedy. Japan pays Hogan and Hartson a $36,000-a-year retainer, and is billed separately for the hourly services of the firm's lawyers and other expenses. The firm also represents, for a retainer of $24,000 a year, the Council of European and Japanese National Shipowners Associations, for whom it wrote a pamphlet entitled "Cargo Preference: Boon or Barrier"—an attack on U.S. laws that protect American shipowners from foreign competition.

The firm of Galland, Kharasch, Calkins and Brown is expert at representing foreign airlines in dealings with the Civil Aeronautics Board and the State Department, and in recent years has represented such carriers as Swissair, Lufthansa, Philippine Air Lines, Qantas, and Japan Air Lines. One of the busiest firms in foreign representation is Cox, Langford and Brown, which has worked for the embassies of India, Italy, Belgium, and Venezuela. Romania's campaign for MFN has been assisted by Walter Surrey of Surrey, Karasik and Morse. Arnold and Porter represents the government of Switzerland, as well as corporations in Germany and England. Covington and Burling has done work in the past for Iran and Hong Kong, and since 1967 has been assisting Guinea in securing loans from the U.S. and the World Bank, so the nation can exploit its rich bauxite deposits. Iran's legal affairs in this country are coordinated by Ralph Becker of the firm of Rogers and Wells. Preeminent among the international sugar lobbyists is the father-son team of Arthur L. Quinn and Arthur

Lee Quinn. Former Attorney General Richard Kleindienst, before his conviction in the Watergate scandal, made an agreement to represent the minister of industry and energy of Algeria, whose country did not at that time have diplomatic relations with the U.S. Minister M. Abdesselam, in an agreement made in November 1973, offered Kleindienst a retainer of $10,000 a month, plus expenses not to exceed $24,000 a year without specific authorization—a financial package that is very juicy even by the lush standards of Washington law firms. Clark Clifford assisted Algeria in reopening relations with the U.S., and has been retained for general services since then. The Soviet Union, strangely, employs the services of no Washington law firm, although it retains a patent firm and public relations counsel in New York City.

The only organization registered to lobby for Israel is the very effective American Israel Public Affairs Committee (AIPAC), whose 12,000 American supporters contribute about $400,000 a year to maintain an eleven-member staff in Washington. Its publication, *Near East Report,* is received by some 30,000 people, including the entire Congress (free of charge). Headed for more than twenty years by lawyer-journalist I. L. (Si) Kenen, AIPAC is now directed by Morris Amitay, a lawyer who was formerly an aide to Senator Abraham Ribicoff (D-Conn.).

No one knows exactly how many lobbyists are engaged in international affairs in Washington. More than 11,000 individuals and law firms—mostly Americans on retainer to foreign governments and corporations—are listed in a Justice Department registry, as required by the Foreign Agents Registration Act of 1938 (FARA). But FARA is as full of loopholes as the congressional rules on the registration of domestic lobbyists, so a great many people who represent foreign interests are not required (or don't bother) to register as official "foreign agents." The only tool of domestic lobbying that is not legally available to lobbyists for foreigners is the campaign contribution. It is frequently rumored, however, that foreign funds manage to find their way into American politics. There were indications in the Watergate tapes, for example, that Greek money may have been given to the 1972 Nixon reelection campaign, in appreciation for the administration's friendliness with the since-deposed military junta in Athens.

THE ECONOMIC ESTABLISHMENT

Allied to the diplomatic community but somewhat separate from it is the international economic community and its two basic organizations: the International Monetary Fund (IMF) and the World Bank Group, both of which grew out of the economic conference held in Bretton Woods, New Hampshire, in 1944. The IMF headquarters in Washington employs about 1,400 people of 90 nationalities, and the World Bank Group employs another 3,000 people of 100 nationalities, most of whom work at the Washington headquarters. An additional 1,060 people work for the Inter-American Development Bank, one of four regional banks similar in operation to the World Bank. The IMF's 126 member nations do not include any Communist nations except Romania and Yugoslavia, nor do they include Switzerland, an international banking power in its own right. The same nations are also missing from the roster of the World Bank Group, since it requires membership in the IMF.

The IMF provides liquidity for the world's trading system—short-term financial assistance to nations that are temporarily unable to meet foreign obligations, owing to trouble with their balance of trade and balance of payments. Member nations may not seek IMF funds to finance permanent development projects, or for military purchases. Some nations request "loans" (made in the form of currency exchanges) during seasonal declines in agricultural production, or when low world prices in their principal export commodities yield less revenue than they had expected. Funds are also sought when internal inflation and international currency speculation put their economy in trouble. The IMF can work fast to shore up a critical situation, acting on an emergency request within seventy-two hours. IMF assistance is an alternative to such steps, destructive to free trade, as restricting imports to improve the balance of trade. In addition to lending money, the IMF tries to improve the world economic climate by sending consultants to member countries to advise them on everything from reform of their internal tax systems to efficient statistical record keeping. The IMF, which has reserves of about $36 billion in gold, "special drawing rights," and foreign currencies, is headed by Managing Director H. Johannes Witteveen of the Netherlands, who succeeded ten-year Managing Director Pierre-Paul Schweitzer of France in 1973.

Distinctly different from the IMF, the World Bank and its affiliates exist to finance—to the tune of about $3.5 billion a year—development projects in member nations: roads, power plants, schools, tourism, birth control, railroads, telephone systems, agriculture, industry—virtually any project that would improve the general standard of living. Member nations borrow money from the World Bank at an interest rate (in 1974) of about 7.25 percent, considerably lower than prime commercial rates. Since 1960, countries with unusually low GNPs—less than $300 per person annually—have borrowed from the World Bank's International Development Association (IDA) with no interest charge at all. India and Pakistan have received more than half of all IDA funds, with the African nations receiving the next highest amounts. Some countries that are marginally above the $300 per capita GNP cutoff are nonetheless eligible for a "blend" of regular World Bank and no-interest IDA loans. World Bank economists based in Washington are constantly traveling to member nations to assess the value of an applicant's proposed project and the realistic prospects of loan repayment. The bank runs the Economic Development Institute, where annually about 200 government officials and businessmen from developing countries take courses in development methods.

Most of the funds that the World Bank lends out are raised through the sale of bonds in financial centers around the world. The bank has to pay more for this capital than its borrowers pay back in interest, but the gap is covered by contributions from the wealthier member nations. The "profit" generated by the nonprofit World Bank in every year of operation since 1947 is kept as an emergency reserve available for IDA loans. The United States, having contributed about 23 percent of the bank's "subscriptions," controls 23 percent of the bank's voting stock. (The U.S. has occasionally used its dominant voting power as an instrument of its own foreign policy, as it did when it thwarted bank aid to the Marxist government of Salvador Allende in Chile.) The president of the World Bank is Robert S. McNamara, former Ford Motor Company president and Secretary of Defense under Presidents Kennedy and Johnson.

Needless to say, ambassadors and embassy staffs must court the officials of the IMF and World Bank Group as assiduously as they do the U.S. government—probably more so, considering America's waning interest in dispensing foreign aid. The U.S. foreign aid program is administered by the Agency for International Development (AID), a part of the State Department. Other U.S. agencies with which embassies have varying degrees of contact are the Export-Import Bank (called "Ex-Im Bank") and the Overseas Private Investment Corporations (OPIC). OPIC lends money to American interests that wish to invest in new or expanded businesses abroad. OPIC also sells insurance against the sorts of risks—revolt, expropriation, currency crises—that tend to discourage American investment overseas.

Ex-Im is designed to promote American business by lending money to foreign governments and businesses, so that they in turn can buy American exports. The bank also offers American exporters subsidized insurance against the possibility of default by the foreign buyer. In 1974 Ex-Im came under attack from congressmen and senators who argued that the U.S. shouldn't be lending hundreds of millions of dollars to such wealthy nations as the Soviet Union and Iran (at a bargain interest rate of 6.5 percent) at a time when American corporations are suffering from tight credit, double-figure interest rates, soaring costs—and fierce trade competition from foreign nations. Ex-Im has since raised its interest rates to reflect the higher cost of money worldwide, and Congress has imposed certain limits on its lending freedom (such as the four-year ceiling of $300 million on loans to the Soviet Union).

CROSSROADS OF THE WORLD

The diplomatic importance of Washington is attested to by the intensity with which foreign diplomats covet and cultivate an assignment here, and how much they hate to leave the U.S. for assignments elsewhere. One Dutch economic counselor, transferred to a politically volatile (and not very significant) South American nation, wrote to an American friend, "I'm not worried about the guerrillas getting me, but I might die of boredom."

Few diplomats suffer from boredom in Washington, unless their nation has absolutely nothing it can secure from, or do for, the United States and her people. They may suffer from fatigue or frustration, but not boredom. For Washington is the city where the top foreign policy brains of the world meet, compare notes, struggle, and occasionally iron out differences. Washington is the world's diplomatic melting pot.

20 THE NEWS CORPS

They are everywhere in Washington, nearly as common as lawyers. They are heroes or villains, depending on whether or not you like what they're telling you. They are a nuisance to the ins and a boon to the outs. They have a thirst for the unusual and the unsavory. They seem to turn a cold shoulder to the daily stream of dull, constructive events that comprise the bulk of government activity in Washington. They are accused of being unduly liberal, but most are middle-of-the-roaders who studiously avoid showing their ideological stripes in their work.

They are the men and women of the Washington news corps.

They are hard to spot in the streets and hallways and hearing rooms of Washington, because they don't look much different from the newsmakers they cover. They don't have flushed faces, and they don't run around breathlessly in rumpled suits, with ties askew or collars loosened, or with a press pass sticking out of their hatbands. Some of them look as if they might be accountants or congressmen. Others resemble lawyers or actors or used car salesmen.

To see many of them at one time, you can cruise the corridors of the National Press Building (at 14th and F Streets N.W.), which has some 500 tenants, most of them newspeople, at work in tiny offices behind milky glass doors with old-fashioned gold-and-black lettering identifying the occupant. Or you could hang out in the sumptuous lobbies of new office buildings in the 1700 block of Pennsylvania Avenue near the White House, where the likes of Art Buchwald, Evans and Novak, and numerous newspaper and magazine people have their headquarters. If you want the feel of a newsroom, with banging typewriters and ringing phones, just slip into the back rooms of the Senate press gallery any weekday around 5 P.M. Or, for the price of an expense account lunch and an "in" with the maître d', Paul Delisle, you could spend an afternoon at Sans Souci, the chic French restaurant on 17th Street where dapper columnists and bureau chiefs swap (or pretend to swap) information with equally dapper White House aides and Cabinet members. A trip to the dining room or bar of the National Press Club would undoubtedly turn up some real journalists, but a good many of the men and women you'd see there would be associate members who are public relations representatives.

The people who gather, process, and interpret information about Washington exercise judgments many times a day about what is or is not important enough to pass on to the public as news. This power of selection sometimes makes the Washington press corps as instrumental as the newsmakers themselves in the presentation of public issues to the nation and the world.

The lenses of the press, through which the public observes Washington, are varied. Some give wide-angle views, such as a wire service's end-of-session review of congressional activity. Some give perspective, like a newspaper column or television commentary rich in historical allusions. Others are focused for close-up detail, like a trade journal account of a technical regulation that affects a particular industry.

To the general public, whose image of Washington is transmitted principally by television, the business of gathering news here must seem to be a nonstop sequence of dramatic events. The public gets a picture of Senate hearings at which reporters sit at long tables and jot notes on the witness's explosive testimony, and sidewalk confrontations between Cabinet members muttering "no comment" and broadcast journalists with jutting microphones. To the TV audience at home, it must seem that every Washington journalist works within view of the Capitol dome or the Supreme Court steps, because these majestic sights always loom behind the TV correspondent as he delivers his one-minute wrap-up.

SOURCES OF NEWS

But that's just the tip of the iceberg, and it is a small part of the news business in Washington. More often than not, the events staged for television are reactions to news stories that evolved through more routine and often tedious reporting. The real news out of Washington is derived from countless daily contacts between reporters and their sources—by telephone, over a casual lunch, during rambling conversation in a bureaucrat's office on a slow afternoon, in a chat with a congressman in the Speaker's lobby of the House, in a formal interview, or perhaps at a crowded party or reception.

The words "source" and "contact" suggest the passing of hush-hush information, and many major Washington stories start with this sort of reporting. A reporter may get a call from a junior congressman who has been snubbed by his committee chairman over a subcommittee assignment. In retaliation the congressman may pass to the reporter some bit of information damaging to the chairman's reputation, and that bit of intelligence might become the basis for a news story. Or a conscientious bureaucrat who learns that his pet program is going to be gutted by a funding cutback may pass the information on to a reporter in the hope that the reporter will publicize the story without revealing the source.

Usually, however, a reporter's sources are simply people with routine access to the information he needs for covering Washington. A source may be someone on the staff of the Senate Foreign Relations Committee who can give a cool evaluation of the prospects for passage of the new foreign aid bill. A source may be a woman at the Department of Housing and Urban Development who keeps abreast of the status of an urban renewal grant for a city in a particular paper's circulation area. A source may be a U.S. court of appeals clerk who can be relied upon to call as soon as his judge hands down a decision that interests a certain publication or radio-TV station.

The problem of becoming too chummy with news sources—especially if they are prominent people—is that the reporter's toughness and objectivity can be damaged by friendship. Pentagon reporter Richard Fryklund warned of this when he recalled a story he wrote which then Defense Secretary Robert McNamara said spoiled his whole lunch. "If I had been a close friend of McNamara," said Fryklund, "I would have worried about ruining his lunch."

There are risks, too, for reporters who meticulously report every little damaging thing they know about a public figure, even if it's all true. If such a reporter contacts the newsmaker's office regularly, he will start finding that his calls aren't returned, that he is no longer being notified of routine press conferences, and that the competing reporters on the same beat are being fed advance information that he isn't getting. This is called the "freeze," and it's used to make a particularly spunky reporter look bad in his editor's eyes by missing too many stories.

The freeze is practiced widely in Washington, from Capitol Hill to the White House to the Washington offices of major corporations. Stuart Loory, who used to cover the White House for the Los Angeles *Times,* was put into a deep freeze after he asked President Nixon a particularly pointed question at a press conference. The FBI under J. Edgar Hoover was notorious for giving a cold shoulder to reporters who wrote articles that the Bureau considered critical and rewarding cooperative reporters with leaked "scoops."

While reporters on a particular beat must walk a tightrope with the public figures they deal with daily, the at-large investigative reporter can work with hit-and-run freedom, with no need to maintain rapport with the officials he exposes. It's not surprising that the Watergate scandal was brought to light not by the high-paid veterans of the White House press corps, but by the *Post*'s aggressive team of local reporters, Bob Woodward, who used to cover District of Columbia affairs, and Carl Bernstein, who once covered suburban Virginia politics.

PROTECTION OF PRIVATE LIVES

Every reporter in Washington knows of senators, congressmen, bureaucrats, judges, generals, or White House aides who are lazy, dishonest, ignorant, alcoholic, lecherous, or emotionally unstable. Very often these personal habits are not merely harmless idiosyncrasies, but debilitating problems that severely hamper the public figure's performance. Even though the public should know about these problems, the reporters best qualified to report them—those on a beat—are the least able to do so without getting the freeze.

There is an unwritten understanding on the part of many Washington reporters to protect the so-called private lives of public men. Juicy information on the personal lives of Washington figures may find an outlet with Jack Anderson or the Washington *Post*'s Maxine Cheshire, but on the whole it is ignored. Even Anderson will withhold derogatory information about a newsmaker if the person agrees to tell all he knows about a larger fish in the pond. "We'll give immunity to a very good source as long as the information he offers us is better than what we've got on him," Anderson admits.

Sometimes reporters sit on valuable stories because they feel that premature release would jeopardize national security. Several journalists (including Seymour Hersh, who pulled no punches in unearthing the Mylai massacres and CIA's domestic spying) knew in advance, but did not write, that American planes would soon be flying from American bases in Thailand to bomb Hanoi—a major step in the escalation of the Vietnam war. *New York Times* columnist James Reston knew about American U-2 flights over the

Soviet Union for a year before pilot Francis Gary Powers was shot down in 1960. And the *Times* intentionally underplayed a story about CIA participation in the upcoming Bay of Pigs invasion of Cuba in 1961.

Most recently, some of the nation's major news organizations acquiesced to the wishes of the CIA by withholding a story about the agency's secret attempt (partially successful, it later turned out) to recover nuclear warheads and code books from a Soviet submarine that sank in 1968 in deep waters near Hawaii. The press's voluntary embargo on the story began crumbling when the Los Angeles *Times* printed an abridged account of the salvage project in February 1975 and Jack Anderson gave it even wider circulation the following month. The rest of the press quickly followed suit, including the *New York Times,* whose reporter Sy Hersh had been working quietly on the story since late 1973 (and trying in the meantime to convince his editors that disclosure of the multimillion-dollar project would not damage national security).

As large as the Washington press corps is, its coverage barely scratches the surface of the federal government. There are many reporters—probably too many—covering the same stories. Newspeople are a gregarious lot. They enjoy the camaraderie of covering the big stories together, and their editors and bureau chiefs, who often make coverage assignments, want to be sure their paper has the same stories that will be played up big in other papers. At the same time, somewhere else in town, a ruling at the Federal Trade Commission or passage of a little-known bill in the House may go unnoticed and unreported, except perhaps for a few paragraphs on the wire service tickers of the Associated Press (AP) or United Press International (UPI). Much of the problem of duplicated coverage stems from the desire of out-of-town newspapers to have their own correspondent at the White House press conference, or on the trip to Peking, or sitting through hours of Watergate testimony, just so the reader will see his paper's own byline on the story. The public would be better informed if Washington bureau chiefs deployed their forces in other ways.

FRICTION BETWEEN PRESS AND PRESIDENT

Presidents and the press have never been overly fond of each other, and they're not supposed to be. They see things from different angles. The news corps must pry and question and be a devil's advocate to illuminate the President's positions. The President, however, wants publicity for programs he feels are in the public interest. The President wants his words to be taken at face value, but a good reporter must balance those words with the opposing opinions and skepticism of other officials who will be playing a role in shaping policy. There is a natural antagonism, and some of it is inevitable.

Nearly all Presidents have felt they were being treated unfairly by the press at one time or another. President Kennedy, who generally got along well with the press, was angered by David Halberstam's prophetically pessimistic dispatches from Vietnam in the early 1960s, and leaned on the *New York Times* to recall him. Kennedy aides, with or without the President's approval, used FBI agents to try to track down embarrassing leaks to the press. And of course, the Johnson years saw the coining of the phrase "credibility gap" to describe the chasm between official explanations and reality in the administration's Vietnam policy.

President Nixon generally received a good press during his first administration. Nixon's early domestic programs—such as the guaranteed annual income, executive reorganization, and revenue sharing—and his foreign initiatives like the trips to China and Russia were reported favorably.

But top Nixon aides proved to have a particularly thin skin for criticism. It became increasingly difficult for reporters to arrange interviews with key aides, let alone drop in casually for a chat. Nixon himself became secluded, and even before Watergate, the number of news conferences dropped to an all-time low. The tense but respectful press relations of previous administrations were replaced by a new coolness. Many Presidents have complained about the press, but the Nixon administration set out to do something about it.

It was in November 1969 when then Vice President Agnew made the first of several speeches that accused the news media of an elitist, liberal bias. Dean Burch, then chairman of the Federal Communications Commission, personally called network executives and asked for transcripts of commentaries on one of the President's Vietnam speeches. The Subversive Activities Control Board called TV stations and asked for a log of pro- and anti-administration editorials and news items. A group of GOP businessmen, including presidential intimate Charles (Bebe) Rebozo, challenged the license renewal of a Florida TV station owned by the Washington *Post,* a frequent Nixon critic. And then there was the Pentagon Papers case, in which the Justice Department made the first formal attempt—albeit unsuccessful—at prior censorship of news in peacetime. It was later revealed that bugs were placed on the phones of two *New York Times* reporters, Neil Sheehan and Tad Szulc, who were involved in the publication of those papers.

Things simmered down for about a year, primarily because Agnew assumed a lower profile. But the battle was renewed during the campaign of 1972. The White House was apparently not assuaged by the fact that the press was taking George McGovern to task for dumping vice presidential nominee Thomas Eagleton, equivocating on key economic issues, and conducting a disorganized campaign.

WATERGATE

Then came Watergate. In the summer of 1972, the Washington *Post* revealed ties between the Watergate break-in and the Committee to Reelect the President. The White House responded by castigating the paper for "shoddy journalism." (Press Secretary Ron Ziegler later ate his words, and on April 30, 1973, Nixon gave credit for the exposing of Watergate to a determined judicial system and a "vigorous free press.") As 1972 drew to a close, White House communications aide Clay Whitehead urged local television stations to demand of their networks more "balance" in their public affairs programing, and suggested that a lack of "balance" could be held against the local stations when their licenses come up for renewal. Public broadcasting, which has long suffered from underfunding, was attacked by the White House as a carrier of liberal bias in its public affairs programs. Administration supporters on Capitol Hill acted to curtail all public TV programing that might contain political discussion.

Apart from these major initiatives, there were earlier skirmishes, such as the FBI investigation of CBS correspondent Daniel Schorr for an alleged high-level federal job that was later admitted to be bogus, or the phone-tapping of several White House aides who were suspected of leaking inside information to *Time* magazine. Congress had got into the act in 1971 when the House Interstate and Foreign Commerce Committee tried unsuccessfully to subpoena the unedited film of a CBS documentary, "The Selling of the Pentagon."

The press was socked by the Supreme Court's decision (in the Caldwell-Branzburg-Pappas cases) declaring that newspeople do not have an automatic First Amendment right to withhold from a grand jury the identity of their sources of confidential information. The five-man majority in this case was composed of all four Nixon appointees and Justice Byron White. The decision was followed by the introduction in Congress of numerous newsman's privilege bills, giving reporters the right to withhold source information from grand juries, but not from a trial itself.

The personal friction between President Nixon and the press reached an apex in 1973 when the President said, after the firing of Special Prosecutor Archibald Cox, that he had "never heard or seen such outrageous, vicious, distorted reporting in twenty-seven years of public life." He later told a press conference, "Don't get the impression that you arouse my anger; you see, one can only be angry with those he respects." Gasps and muttering were heard from the reporters present.

The question is asked whether the challenges to the press during the Nixon years actually diminished its freedom and ability to inform the public effectively. There is no sign that this happened on a broad scale, although there were some danger signals. There was something ominous, for example, in CBS's decision in June 1973 to abandon its custom of providing commentary immediately following the President's major policy speeches. (The "instant analysis," however, was later reinstated, and continues today.)

Relations between the White House and the press improved significantly after the Nixon resignation and the ascent of Gerald Ford. The improvement was not due to a change of politics (if anything, Ford is more traditionally conservative than Nixon) but to a change of personality and style. Whereas Richard Nixon throughout his career had been secretive and distrustful of the press, Ford as President has continued to be as open and matter-of-fact with the press as he was while serving in the House as minority leader. And Ford knows, too, that the White House press operation must be run by professional newspeople, not the likes of Nixon press spokesman Ron Ziegler, a former advertising executive who had never worked in news reporting of any kind. Ford started off on the right foot with the appointment as press secretary of J. F. terHorst, who had previously been the respected Washington bureau chief of the Detroit *News*. But terHorst soon began to feel that he was not being kept fully informed of inside policy at the White House, and resigned immediately following President Ford's pardon of Richard Nixon. He was replaced by NBC White House correspondent Ron Nessen, the first broadcast journalist to become a presidential press secretary. President Ford has been hit hard by the Washington press corps, especially as the recession of 1974–75 deepened, but the situation hasn't deteriorated into the personal acrimony that marked the Nixon period.

What do Washington newsmen think about the charges leveled against them that they put a liberal slant into their reports? Walter Cronkite, one of the most objective of the network stars, has written that "we acknowledge that all men, not excluding journalists, harbor bias and prejudice, but it is the mark of the professional newsman that he recognize these in himself and guard against their intrusion into his reporting." Peter Lisagor, the Chicago *Daily News*'s savvy Washington bureau chief, agrees. "I know some of the most prejudiced people in this town who are straight, honest, objective reporters . . . I know people who hate given government officials and write very straight accounts about them."

Within the American news establishment there is another balance wheel that helps keep the news flow from going too far in one direction. This is the tension between the reporters (who may be vaguely "antiestablishment") and the publishers and networks bosses (who are likely to be more conservative). The vast majority of the nation's papers have moderate-to-conservative editorial policies. In 1960, 78 percent of the dailies that endorsed a presidential candidate endorsed Nixon, and these papers had 80 percent of the nation's total circulation. In 1968, 80 percent endorsed him, and in 1972 the rate was 90 percent.

Management's views occasionally find their way into the news pages or onto the airwaves. Many Washington reporters have experienced the frustration of having a story killed or played down because it would embarrass a politician who is close to the newspaper's or broadcast station's owner, or because it would alienate an important advertiser. Although the Nixon administration complained of a liberal bias in reporting, surveys of media bias, conducted by journalism schools, have more often found a slant toward the conservative point of view.

THOUSANDS OF JOURNALISTS

The Washington news corps is unique in two ways. First, it is the largest group of newspeople in any one city in the world. Second, its vast output is prepared largely for consumption outside of the capital city itself. Washington residents never see the stories written by most of the city's press corps, and newsmakers see a story about themselves, or one derived from them as sources, only if they happen to subscribe to a clipping service or to the out-of-town paper in which the story appeared.

Washington, of course, has a local press corps composed of the "metropolitan staffs" of the Washington *Post* and Washington *Star* (which absorbed the Washington *Daily News* in 1972), the independent and network-affiliated local radio and TV stations, the Washington *Afro-American* and several well-regarded suburban papers (including the Montgomery County, Maryland, *Sentinel* and the Alexandria, Virginia, *Gazette*). The local press corps is full of topnotch news people, because job-hunting reporters come to Washington from all over the nation, looking for a broad audience of influential readers for their copy. A local paper gives them a foot in the door for national recognition.

There are close to 5,000 people in Washington engaged daily in the news business. About an equal number of men and women on the federal payroll are engaged in what is called "press information" work in the Executive Branch, Congress, and the White House. The press information officer is referred to by irreverent reporters as a "flak" (short for "flak catcher"), which describes the manner in which he often absorbs, deflects, or refutes journalistic attacks on his agency or his superiors. The press information officer is, more often than not, the anonymous "department spokesman" to whom guarded explanations are attributed in many news stories.

For all the frustration that public information personnel can cause reporters, they are now a permanent part of the news and information system. Since most press information officers—like the public relations men who serve Washington representatives for large corporations—are refugees from the relatively low pay of journalism jobs, they can appreciate the reporter's need to get the facts quickly.

Who are the 5,000 or so newspeople in Washington? Most are men, although the number of women is rising. They are overwhelmingly white, since it is only recently that minority groups have come into the press corps in any numbers. They are from all parts of the country, and they are not a "northeastern liberal elite." Most were educated at big state universities. Some have had little or no college. NBC's David Brinkley grew up in North Carolina and became a newspaper reporter at the age of eighteen without the benefit of a college education. Harry Reasoner, a native of Iowa, also started without a college background. Walter Cronkite and Frank Reynolds (who, like Reasoner, had long stints as Washington correspondents before being promoted to network anchormen in New York) attended college but did not graduate. While the *New York Times* staff is unusually laden with northeasterners, former Washington bureau chief James (Scotty) Reston grew up in Dayton, Ohio, and columnist Tom Wicker came from North Carolina. While the Washington *Post*'s young Watergate ace Bob Woodward is a Yale graduate, his partner Carl Bernstein is a dropout from the University of Maryland.

If there is a northeastern establishment flavor to be found in Washington journalism, it is supplied primarily by the columnists. Notice the places of birth and education of the following: Joseph Alsop, the recently retired veteran columnist (Connecticut, Harvard); Rowland Evans, Jr. (Pennsylvania, Yale); Tom Braden (Iowa, Dartmouth); and Joseph Kraft (New Jersey, Columbia). For balance of background, however, we have Marquis Childs (Iowa, University of Wisconsin); Carl Rowan (Tennessee, Oberlin); Robert Novak (Illinois, University of Illinois); Hugh Sidey (Iowa, Iowa State); and James J. Kilpatrick (Oklahoma, University of Missouri).

WHAT THEY'RE PAID

Most of the senior Washington newspeople are paid between $25,000 and $40,000 per year, a salary range which puts them in the top 5 percent of salary earners in the U.S. The salaries in newspaper work are considerably lower than those in broadcasting, and many young correspondents for small newspapers, magazines, and news services work for considerably less than $15,000. The best-known broadcast stars are paid salaries well into six figures, with Walter Cronkite and David Brinkley receiving about $250,000 per year. Columnists normally split their gross income 50-50 with the organizations that syndicate the columns, but a pundit carried by a few hundred large papers can clear well above $100,000.

The journalists of the printed word are numerically dominant in Washington and have always harbored a certain resentment of the television types, partly because broadcast news sometimes seems more like entertainment than journalism. But the truth is that more people derive their view of the national government from television and radio than any other medium. This has come about within the past fifteen years. In 1959, about 57 percent of the people queried in a major national poll said newspapers were their primary source of news. By 1971, however, TV had supplanted newspapers as the main information source for 60 percent of the people. Newspapers were the favored news source of only 48 percent.

If anyone doubts which news medium is considered the most powerful by the newsmakers in Washington, he should see the deference they accord the electronic journalists compared to the lowly pencil pushers. A press conference, demonstration, or corridor interview is a bust if no TV cameras or tape recorders appear. Press briefings and congressional hearings have been known to grind to a halt while a TV crew changes the film in its cameras. Politicians and bureaucrats can weather all sorts of damaging revelations on the news pages or critical judgments on the editorial pages, but are wary of sardonic commentary by CBS's Dan Rather and Eric Sevareid or ABC's Howard K. Smith. In the words of Nixon speechwriter Pat Buchanan, "It's all over if you get chopped up on the networks. You never recover. The newspapers can beat the hell out of you and you've got no problems."

Yet, for all its impact on the views of the American people, television is not a prime originator of great news stories out of Washington. It is usually a dramatizer of news dug up by enterprising newspaper reporters. Take, for example, the CBS report in 1971 called "The Selling of the Pentagon" about the military's public relations campaigns. The subject of Pentagon propagandizing of the American people had already been treated extensively in a book by former Senator J. William Fulbright (D-Ark.) and in a front-page feature in the *Wall Street Journal* a few months before. But the CBS report created a furor that none of these written accounts had generated. The most devastating piece of investigative reporting of the past decade—on the Watergate conspiracy—was done primarily by newspaper reporters. Still, the full seriousness of it did not hit the American people until the broadcast media gave the story top billing.

Walter Cronkite, who anchored the first half-hour network news program in 1963, acknowledges the limitations of his medium. "We are a prime news medium in the order of a headline service," he said in a 1973 interview. "We offer the viewer speed—showing, in a limited amount of time, the persons and places that make the news. But in most other senses we're a supplemental service."

Most Washington-based network newsmen had brief stints with newspapers early in their careers before achieving prominence in radio and TV. Some of them have a deep knowledge of their specialty derived from formal education and firsthand experience. One such formidable figure is CBS's diplomatic correspondent Marvin Kalb, who has done graduate work in Soviet studies and the Russian language, once served as press attaché for the American Embassy in Moscow, and has authored several books on international affairs.

Radio, far from being eclipsed by the visual impact of television, is still a source of Washington news and commentary for millions of people. There are about as many radios in America as there are people, and over 100 million of these are car radios on which people get at least a few minutes of news each hour and, on the growing number of all-news stations, a much heavier diet. These stations are served by a number of special news-gathering organizations, including the Mutual network and Westinghouse Broadcasting, whose veteran Washington pundit is Rod MacLeish. A very few of the nation's AM and FM radio stations—about 100 out of 7,667—have a reporter of their own in the capital to interview local congressmen and keep track of things that affect the home area. On the vast majority of stations, news from Washington is presented in the "rip and read" style, in which an announcer reads the lead sentences of a few dispatches he has torn off the station's wire service ticker. Items on complex national and international events are often so brief that they defy comprehension.

Public television has yet to become a major force on the Washington news scene, but its influence is rising. Its most notable success of recent years was the rebroadcast each evening of the Senate Watergate hearings, giving its affiliate stations the highest ratings they had ever achieved.

Ironically, the most popular public affairs television program in Washington (and in numerous other cities where it is syndicated) is a discussion show composed largely of print journalists sitting around in an unfettered bull session—"Agronsky and Company," hosted by veteran broadcast correspondent Martin Agronsky. His four regular participants—Carl Rowan, James J. Kilpatrick, Hugh Sidey, and Peter Lisagor—were already respected writers before they took to the airwaves. Now their weekly televised squabbles (unrehearsed and generally good-natured) have made them mini-celebrities, with faces and personalities familiar to millions.

THE WIRE SERVICES

In the print medium there are two organizations doing the lion's share of Washington reporting that fills the front pages of the nation's daily newspapers. They are the Associated Press (AP) and United Press International (UPI), the wire services to one or both of which virtually every daily in America subscribes. With news staffs of over one hundred each in Washington, AP and UPI do the most comprehensive job of covering all official Washington activities. Only some 470 newspapers—about 27 percent of the nation's dailies—have any sort of Washington correspondent, so the vast majority of papers must use wire copy exclusively for national news. Actually, even the 27 percent with correspondents rely heavily on the wires for coverage of the big stories, and use their own bureau for supplementary articles on Washington events with some special interest to the local region.

Knowing that the wires cover so many events so competently can be a bad crutch for the lazy Washington correspondent to lean on instead of doing his own reporting. Longtime UPI Washington manager Julius Frandsen likes to tell the story of a "reporter for one of the larger newspaper bureaus who was assigned to cover a hot, complicated Senate hearing—so hot it was being televised live. He sat through the session reading newspapers and magazines, taking few notes. He was confident that he could write his story from memory—memory and the UPI ticker copy that he would find back at his office. But he had forgotten about the live TV coverage. His bureau chief had been watching him on the screen—and hid all of the ticker copy."

Writing for the wires is hard, unrewarding work. The salaries tend to be lower than those paid to bureau members of large, out-of-town papers. Since many papers have a policy of not putting bylines on wire stories, many good wire reporters are denied broad public recognition. For every assignment that could be considered glamorous, the wire reporter spends a lot of time "watch-

ing rat holes"—keeping abreast of routine situations that might never materialize into a story, on the outside chance that something newsworthy just
might happen. Since most Washington reporters work for either a morning or
an afternoon paper, they have just one deadline a day. But the wire reporters
must write their stories quickly throughout the day, because at any given
moment, somewhere in a different time zone of the United States and the rest
of the world, an editor is waiting for a hot story to run on his front page
before his paper is "put to bed."

WASHINGTON CORRESPONDENTS

Working side by side with the wire reporters and doing in-depth stories on
their own are the correspondents for the nation's most prestigious papers and
chains, such as the *New York Times*, St. Louis *Post-Dispatch*, Los Angeles
Times, Knight newspapers, *Wall Street Journal*, Long Island *Newday*, Des
Moines *Register*, Chicago *Tribune*, and Detroit *News*, to name just a few.
While all of these papers have reporters in their Washington bureaus who act
as hometowners, doing localized versions of Washington news, they also have
correspondents who cover the major national stories out of the White House,
Supreme Court, Pentagon, Congress, and the bureaucracy. This latter group
of reporters enjoy a prestige among their colleagues and sources—if not
among the public—rivaling that of the columnists.

The two major dailies of Washington—the *Post* and the *Star*—have so-
called national staffs that function much the same way as the bureaus of
out-of-town papers do, leaving the local coverage to the metropolitan staffs.
Through aggressive recruitment of top reporters from other bureaus, and
through the discovery of star material in their own news room, *Post* owner
Kay Graham and executive editor Ben Bradlee have built a national staff
second to none in Washington, including that of the *New York Times*. While
the *Post* does not have the large out-of-town circulation of the *New York
Times*, it is thoroughly read every day by more Washington policymakers, as
well as the reporters of all the major papers and wire services, who use it
freely as a source of ideas for stories of their own. The *Post* was set back in
its rivalry with the *Times* by getting a hold on the Pentagon Papers several
days too late, but its tour de force on Watergate humbled the *Times* and made
it the hero of American journalism. The Washington *Star*, which once ruled
the local Washington market in circulation, is no match for the *Post* these
days, either editorially or financially. But it is still considered a fine paper, compared to the bulk of the nation's press.

Even less heralded than the wire-service reporters are the mass of news
people who write for smaller papers among the 470 dailies with some sort of
Washington bureau, or who may work for the bureau of a large paper or
chain but concentrate on Washington. Many of these so-called hometowners
or specials work solo. They concentrate on things of local interest. How did
Senator Jones vote on the recent wage-price control? How will the proposed
military base cutbacks affect our local army supply depot? What's holding up
Smithville's urban renewal grant? How will the Supreme Court's ruling on
abortion change procedures in our local hospital? Is Betty Ford going to cut
the ribbon at our state fair next month? These and countless similar assignments—usually submitted to the reporter in a long-distance call from the local
editor—make the hometown correspondents some of the busiest newspeople

in Washington. Some of the reporters work solely for one paper, while others try to boost their earnings by juggling several clients, often requiring that they be in several places at the same moment.

Since the hometowners' stories never appear in Washington papers, the caliber of their reporting and writing is largely unknown to their colleagues in the press corps. The best of them, however, can find solace in being well known to the hometown readers and knowing that their stories can have a profound impact on the political careers of congressmen in their circulation areas.

The hometowner's dream is to unearth a Washington story with national significance far beyond his local beat. After the scoop appears in some small daily in the hinterlands, national news outlets like AP, UPI, the networks, and the *New York Times* and Washington *Post* may pick it up, maybe (or maybe not) with credit given to the originating reporter and newspaper. In 1960, for example, correspondent Don Larrabee uncovered a sensational story that three Navy sailors, who had sunk to the bottom of Pearl Harbor on the battleship *West Virginia* on December 7, 1941, had survived for nineteen days, trapped in an airtight storage room, before finally succumbing. Larrabee's eerie scoop appeared first in the small New Bedford, Massachusetts, *Standard-Times,* and later on front pages around the world. More recently, news of President Nixon's extraordinary tax returns—a major factor in the crumbling of his public support—surfaced first not in Washington but in Rhode Island, on the front page of the Providence *Journal.*

There is another important, though small, subgroup of reporters in Washington whose work determines how the rest of the world reacts to Washington. These are the journalists who write and broadcast for audiences in other countries. There are about 110 foreign newspapers and news services and about 20 broadcast organizations accredited to cover Congress. In the number of news organizations at work here, the Germans are at the top (with some 18 newspapers and services represented). England is in second place, followed by Japan, Australia, and Canada. The foreign press corps is primarily concerned with fine points of American economic and trade policy that are often life-and-death matters for the economies of their countries. Domestic matters (like Watergate) are covered when they become juicy enough to interest people across the seas.

REPORTERS FOR BUSINESS

Business and labor readers around the country are served by a lesser-known group of reporters whose specialty is practical economics and policy. Such organizations and publications as McGraw-Hill, Dow Jones, the *National Journal, Wall Street Journal, U.S. News and World Report, Nation's Business,* the *Journal of Commerce,* and the BNA services are in this group, along with smaller trade journals whose Washington bureaus focus on government policy affecting virtually every kind of economic activity in the world. Among the 125 members of the periodical press galleries of Congress, for example, are publications with such names as *American Dairy Review, Computerworld, Modern Tire Dealer, Leather and Shoes Magazine, Public Utilities Fortnightly, Rubber World, U.S. Medicine,* and *Western Stamp Collector.* Of the special newsletters that are read by business, labor, and professional people, the *Kiplinger Washington Letter,* founded in 1923, is the largest and best-known.

While the trade press reporters are unknown to the general public, many are high-salaried specialists whose stories are read intensely, both inside and outside Washington. The output of the trade press is not entertainment, but it forms a basis for decisions by businessmen, labor leaders, and consumer advocates.

THE MAGAZINES AND COLUMNS

General-interest news weeklies—like *Time, Newsweek,* and Dow Jones's *National Observer*—play a role similar to television news programs, giving perspective to stories that have been carried piecemeal by daily publications. The usefulness and influence of the news weeklies' Washington reporting seems to be greatest in areas where the local papers do an inadequate job of covering national affairs.

Some of the most provocative Washington reporting in recent years has been done by some of the freelance and staff writers of the political, intellectual, and literary periodicals, including the *New Republic* (with the perceptive writing of John Osborne and Richard "TRB" Strout), *Harper's,* the *Atlantic* (occasionally featuring the Washington fiction of Ward Just), *Commentary,* the *Nation* (with columns of Robert Sherrill), the *Washingtonian, The New Yorker* (with columns by Richard Rovere), the *New York Times Magazine,* the *National Review,* and the *Washington Monthly* (a relatively young muckraking publication whose startling scoops include Christopher Pyle's 1970 piece on Pentagon surveillance of American citizens and politicians).

Every reporter in Washington probably lusts for the fame, prestige, broad circulation, high pay, and freedom of expression enjoyed by those prima donnas of the press corps, the columnists. But the pitfalls of column writing are many. There is, for example, the dual and often contradictory requirement of being both wise and lively several times a week, on cue. A columnist cannot survive on pontification alone. He must dig up significant tidbits of inside information to analyze and expound upon. While a columnist needs sources in high places to keep him supplied, he must be careful that the contacts aren't using him to disseminate unreliable information for their own benefit.

There are columnists in Washington to suit every imaginable political taste, short of anarchy. Conservatives used to have to make do with William F. Buckley, Jr. (who actually holds court in New York), but now there are the well-conceived columns of James J. Kilpatrick in the *Star* and William Safire in the *New York Times.* (An ex-speechwriter for Nixon and Agnew, Safire is one of the best wordsmiths in town.) The most quotable and persuasive new columnist in Washington is conservative, undogmatic George F. Will (syndicated by the Washington *Post*), who once taught political science at Princeton and wrote for Buckley's *National Review.* Fervent liberals are delighted by the likes of Tom Wicker in the *New York Times,* the *Star*'s Mary McGrory, and two less predictable liberals—Joseph Kraft and David Broder—in the *Post.* Irreverent left-of-liberals make a point of reading the superbly written, often bitter columns of Nicholas von Hoffman (who appears not on the *Post*'s editorial pages, but on the front of the paper's arts-and-living section called

"Style"). Evans and Novak, authors of the widely read "Inside Report" column, take a conservative slant but at one time or another have ruffled the feathers of every newsmaker in town, liberal, conservative, and in between.

And then there are the humor columnists, whose raw material is the folly of Washington officialdom. The most popular of these columns is the verbal slapstick of Art Buchwald, but many Washingtonians prefer the dry understatement of the *Times*'s Russell Baker. The fictitious situations in Buchwald's columns, preposterous as he tries to make them, ring so true that he has been accused at times of using privileged information. "I once wrote that President Johnson had announced a new plane which could go very fast and was top-secret and everything," Buchwald is fond of recalling. "The reason he announced that, I said, was because he didn't want to announce the real plane that we were developing, that flew so slow nothing could shoot it down. It only went 130 miles an hour. And no jet could hit it. A week later, I got a letter from Fairchild Aircraft which said, 'How did you know we were working on such a plane?' "

In a class by itself in breadth of readership is the daily muckraking column of Jack Anderson and his partner Les Whitten. Anderson has maintained the hard-hitting tone of his predecessor, Drew Pearson, while avoiding Pearson's tendency to go easy on personal favorites and hold grudges against enemies. Anderson and his staff serve as a national grievance center for the collection of bits and pieces of information exposing the foibles of politicians, bureaucrats, and the top brass of the Pentagon. The column's most important exposés of recent years include the secret donation of $400,000 by the ITT Corporation to the Republican party ("the Dita Beard affair") and the revelation—through leaked transcripts of high-level meetings—of a pro-Pakistan bias in the White House during the 1971 Indo-Pakistan war. Anderson sometimes takes small liberties with the facts for the sake of flamboyance, but his accuracy batting average is surprisingly good. His chief blunder of recent years—and a very bad one, indeed—was the 1972 publicizing of "secret" drunk driving charges against vice presidential candidate Senator Thomas Eagleton (D-Mo.) that later proved to be fake.

HOW TO READ WASHINGTON NEWS

Now that you have met some of the Washington news gatherers, and looked over their shoulders while they worked, here is some advice for *you*. Advice on how to read the Washington news you get in your papers and magazines, and how to listen to the news on radio and television.

Don't mistake a "trial balloon" for a fully developed, agreed-upon course of action. Very often an official (either anonymously or on the record) makes a policy proposal for the sole purpose of finding out what the public response would be. In the fall of 1973, for example, White House aide Melvin Laird said that tax increases were among the alternatives under discussion for inflation control. He probably knew full well that Congress and the public would scream bloody murder, and the response to his statement confirmed this. (Another person distressed by Laird's "trial balloon" was Treasury Secretary George Shultz, the administration's top economic coordinator; from Tokyo, where he was attending an international trade meeting, Shultz fired back a warning to Laird to "keep your cotton-picking hands off economic policy.")

Keep in mind that there's always a time lag between error and correction.

Any person can make a charge against a prominent official. If it is bold enough, it will get a big play in the papers and on the airwaves. It may be days, weeks, or months before the accused gets his story told, and his response probably won't get the same treatment accorded to the original charge. Most newspeople in Washington are skeptical of unsavory information brought to them by unproven sources, and they demand thorough verification. They have to be especially careful that the information is not being planted with them by someone who stands to gain from discrediting a particular public official. Occasionally, however, even a careful reporter—operating under the pressures of deadline and his boss's desire for a hot story—will unwittingly pass on to the public erroneous information.

Beware of "official denials" and "cover stories." The first of these ploys is a blanket denial of charges in a fast-breaking news story, made in the hope that the whole thing will blow over soon. If there's a good chance that the controversy really will blow over, the denial is better than a "no comment" response, which is considered tantamount to confirmation. But official denials have a way of coming back to haunt their creators. When the U-2 was shot down over Russia in May 1960 during the Eisenhower administration, the first reaction from the U.S. was a flat denial from NASA authorities that there had been any intentional intrusion into Soviet airspace. Subsequently, the spy mission was acknowledged by the U.S., but as a consequence, the summit talks in Paris broke down. A "cover," often used in conjunction with a blanket denial, is a fabricated story designed to cover the facts and divert the press's and public's attention. In the first few weeks of the Watergate affair, the White House's "official denial" was accompanied by the "cover" story that the burglary had been planned by Cuban refugees who feared that a Democratic White House would be soft on Castro. Advice to the reader: suspend final judgment until you have learned more.

Watch out for the "Monday morning plant"—big administration announcements that appear in the Monday news (or on Tuesday with a Monday dateline). They are often less important than they seem to be at first glance. Since weekends and Mondays are slow news days, some news-savvy government officials will select them for planting the announcement of a new project, knowing it will not be crowded out by "real" news. President Johnson was fond of this technique, and if his name or his administration was not on page one every Monday morning, his press secretary would get a good chewing out.

Finally, not all of the pitfalls in the path of your news comprehension are the fault of deceptive public officials. A chief culprit is "negative distortion"—the journalist's penchant for playing up the bad news. It is a problem that afflicts all newspeople, not just the Washington press corps. It is a problem that afflicts liberals and conservatives equally. Take, for example, reporting of the riots and burning in Washington that followed the assassination of the Reverend Martin Luther King, Jr. Most Americans apparently thought the entire capital city was a battleground engulfed in flames and lawlessness. But the disorder (serious though it was) was confined to a relatively small area of the city and caused negligible disruption of the daily routines of hundreds of thousands of federal and private employees. Or take the Watergate crisis, which was widely thought to have "crippled" or "paralyzed" the federal government. Well, the whole sorry mess did sap national energy that could have been devoted to pressing problems, and did result, for the first time in

American history, in the resignation of a President, but Uncle Sam was hardly crippled. The federal bureaucracy showed the keep-on-plugging inertia that is both its greatest strength and its worst weakness.

"Bad news" distortion stems from competition for the reader's and listener's limited attention, from the need of all news media to attract followers, to be first with everything, to dramatize each story as though it were the beginning of the millennium or the end of the world. While the news profession gropes for a way to cope with the problem, you can ponder the alternative—a state-controlled press, spewing out nothing but praise for the government and its leadership. The alternative is so unappealing that we can afford to gag on some of our own imperfections, a small price to pay for freedom of information.

21 WOMEN IN WASHINGTON

More and more women are making names for themselves in Washington these days—on their own merits and by their own initiative. It's a trend that became noticeable in the early Sixties and gathered steam as employment barriers started to crack and fall. In past decades, there had been a handful of hardy women in government, the arts, law, journalism, lobbying, and other fields in Washington, but their impact was slight. Today, their voices have multiplied and are heard more clearly. Yet, despite substantial female gains in middle-level federal employment, women do not occupy many genuine policy-making positions.

Women have always played an active role in the life of Washington, going all the way back to the capital's first great hostess, the beautiful and witty Dolley Madison. But until recently, the important women derived their impact largely from inherited wealth and/or the power of their husbands. If Jacqueline Bouvier had not married young, ambitious Senator John F. Kennedy, she probably would have become just another attractive society woman, but not a stylesetter imitated by chic women around the world.

Many of Washington's important women of decades past were very capable in their own right, but they used wealth and good connections as springboards to prominence. Some were noted hostesses, including mining heiress Evalyn Walsh McLean and Mrs. John Henderson, a senator's wife who was a prime mover of real estate and mansion-building in Washington. Eleanor (Cissy) Patterson was an inheritor who became as powerful in newspaper publishing as she was in society. Eleanor Roosevelt, going far beyond the call of a First Lady's duties, was a driving force in civil rights. And Mrs. Marjorie Merriweather Post—heiress, hostess, patron of the arts—was a sharp businesswoman who took an active interest in the development of the General Foods corporate empire.

Women have outnumbered men in Washington for years, as they do, on average, throughout the entire population. But the preponderance in Washington has been accentuated by the magnet of government jobs. Single women traditionally have flocked to Washington to work in the government, which discriminated against them slightly less than employers in the private sector. Also, Washington was (and still is) considered a good place for a career girl to find a husband among the bright young comers on Capitol Hill and in the Executive Branch. Until recently most of the jobs for women were clerical, secretarial, or on the lower administrative levels. Now there is a gradual movement up the ladder, but what "woman presence" there is at commission level, Cabinet level, and White House level is more of a sprinkling than a solid representation.

The first woman elected to Congress was Jeannette Rankin, a suffragette from Montana, who served in the House from 1917 to 1919 and again from

1941 to 1943. The first woman member of the Senate took her seat under touching—and rather ludicrous—circumstances. She was Rebecca L. Felton, an eighty-seven-year-old former schoolteacher, writer, and widow of a Georgia representative. In 1922 the governor of Georgia, as a "graceful gesture," appointed her to fill a vacant Senate seat. After serving two days, Senator Felton was replaced by a duly elected senator. The next woman senator was Hattie Caraway of Arkansas, who succeeded her husband after his death in 1931. In 1972 Louisiana Governor Edwin Edwards appointed his wife to fill the Senate seat left vacant by the death of Senator Allen Ellender (D-La). She served for three months, until the election of Senator J. Bennett Johnson (D-La.). Some women who have participated in public affairs as wives—like former Senator Margaret Chase Smith (R-Me.) and, most recently, Representative Corinne Boggs (D-La.), widow of House Majority Leader Hale Boggs—were later elected by their home constituencies. But the past few years have seen the election of such vigorous self-starters as Representatives Bella Abzug, Shirley Chisholm, and Barbara Jordan. While women candidates appear to be acceptable to most electorates, the House of Representatives in 1975 has only 19 females among the 435 members. Since the defeat of Senator Smith of Maine, the Senate has had no women.

In the Executive Branch, there is an increasing proportion of women, though here again the tide is rising slowly. The federal government has been pressing private organizations to take "affirmative action" to recruit women and minorities for top jobs, but it has not been putting as much pressure on itself. The federal government is the largest employer of women in the Washington area. Women work in every department, agency, bureau, and commission, and men outnumber them in all but the lowest categories of work. The Civil Service Commission publishes a fascinating catalog of federal jobs and the number of women holding them (for example: fifty-three law clerks, three archaeologists, one railroad safety inspector, and no foreign agricultural specialists).

It is more meaningful, however, to look at salary levels, since they provide an index to the importance of these jobs. As is the case with racial minorities, the percentage of women on each level of the federal white-collar job ladder decreases with each step up in responsibility and salary. In federal employment worldwide, women occupy roughly 70 percent of the jobs from GS-1 to GS-6, jobs that are largely clerical and secretarial. In the middle-level administrative and technical jobs (GS-13, -14, -15), there has been a sharp increase since 1967—more than 40 percent—in the absolute number of women workers. But men still occupy about 96 percent of all federal jobs rated GS-13 and above. Only about 2 percent of the "super-grade" bureaucrats (GS-16, -17, -18) are women.

President Nixon in 1973 hired a consultant, Jill Ruckelshaus, whose job was to try to recruit women for high government posts. When asked once about the status of women in the federal government, she skirted the question by saying, "If you were crossing a river and had asked an alligator to take you across, it isn't very good politics to comment on how scaly his back is." (Ms. Ruckelshaus continued to hold her job for several months after her husband, former Deputy Attorney General William Ruckelshaus, was fired when he refused to follow President Nixon's order to dismiss onetime Watergate Special Prosecutor Archibald Cox. She left the White House in early 1974, however, citing a desire to "spend more time at home" with her five children, aged six to thirteen.)

After a two-decade absence of women in the Cabinet, President Ford in 1975 selected Carla Anderson Hills to be Secretary of Housing and Urban Development. A corporate lawyer from Los Angeles, Mrs. Hills had previously been an assistant attorney general in charge of the Justice Department's Civil Division (and the first woman to hold that high a position at Justice since the administration of Woodrow Wilson, who appointed two female assistant attorneys general). The only previous women Cabinet members were Oveta Culp Hobby, the Houston *Post* publisher who served as HEW Secretary under President Eisenhower, and Frances Perkins, Labor Secretary during the New Deal. There are a few women hovering just beneath Cabinet level as commission members and assistant secretaries of this or that department. President Nixon's years in the White House were marked by the appointment of an unprecedentedly large number of women to middle- and upper-level positions.

There is, for example, Dixy Lee Ray, a former chairman of the Atomic Energy Commission who is now assistant secretary of state for oceans and international environmental and scientific affairs. Dr. Ray, a marine biologist from the West Coast, was named to the AEC job by President Nixon, at the recommendation of her predecessor, James Schlesinger (now Secretary of Defense). At first her atypical life style (she and her two dogs share a mobile home in rural Virginia) belied her talent, but she subsequently has proven her skill both as an administrator and as a political infighter. Until 1973, Marina von N. Whitman was one of the three members of President Nixon's Council of Economic Advisers and the first woman to be on that panel. She has since returned to the University of Pittsburgh. But before she left, Ms. Whitman and CEA Chairman Herbert Stein told Congress's Joint Economic Committee that women nationwide earn 10 to 20 percent less than men in comparable jobs for no better reason than pure discrimination.

Carol Laise, a career foreign service officer and former assistant secretary of state for public affairs, was appointed in 1975 to be the first female director general of the U.S. Foreign Service. As such, she oversees personnel policy for the 7,000-member American diplomatic corps. Miss Laise previously served as ambassador to Nepal while her husband, Ellsworth Bunker, was ambassador to South Vietnam. Barbara M. Watson served as administrator of the Bureau of Security and Consular Affairs, with the rank of Assistant Secretary, from 1968 until early in the Ford administration. Of the five female American ambassadors serving overseas in 1975, three—Eileen R. Donovan in Barbados, Jean M. Wilkowski in Zambia, and Nancy V. Rawls in Togo—are career diplomats. Ruth L. Farkas, ambassador to Luxembourg, is a member of the family that controls Alexander's department stores in New York City and contributed $300,000 to former President Nixon's 1972 campaign. The American ambassador to Ghana, Shirley Temple Black, has been active in Republican politics and served on the U.S. delegation to the United Nations.

Anne Armstrong, former co-chairman of the Republican National Committee and counselor to the President under President Nixon, stayed on in the same position at President Ford's request, but resigned in late 1974. She recruited women for policy posts and took on special duties related to the National Bicentennial. Gwen Anderson, long active in the Republican organization of Washington State, works at the White House on political liaison, and Mrs. Patricia Lindh is a special assistant to the President for women's affairs. Virginia Knauer is special assistant to the President for consumer affairs, as well as director of the Office of Consumer Affairs in the Department of Health, Education and Welfare. Jayne B. Spain is vice chairman of the Civil Service Commission. Virginia Y. Trotter, formerly vice chancellor of the University of Nebraska, is assistant secretary of HEW for education, the federal government's top education position. Vice President Rockefeller's chief of staff (with a salary of $42,500, as much as members of Congress are paid) is Ann C. Whitman, who was once President Eisenhower's personal secretary.

Other prominent women figures in government include Helen Delich Bentley, the hard-bitten marine affairs reporter for the Baltimore *Sun* who became chairman of the Federal Maritime Commission; Charlotte T. Reid, a onetime radio singer who served in Congress from Illinois for ten years before losing an election and becoming a member of the Federal Communications Commission; Virginia Mae Brown, appointed by President Johnson to the Interstate Commerce Commission; Catherine Bedell, chairman of the U.S. Tariff Commission; and Beatrice Willard, member of the Council on Environmental Quality. Betty Southard Murphy, a top Washington labor lawyer, was appointed by President Ford in 1975 to be the first woman member of the National Labor Relations Board. Previously she had served in the Labor Department as administrator of the Wages and Hours Division.

Barbara Franklin, formerly consumer affairs director for the Singer Company and a onetime talent scout for the White House, is vice chairman of the Consumer Product Safety Commission; another member of the Commission is Constance Newman, former head of VISTA, the volunteeer antipoverty agency. The assistant secretary of commerce for science and technology is Betsy Ancker-Johnson, formerly a research scientist and executive with Boeing Aircraft. Mary Gardiner Jones, a longtime member of the Federal Trade Commission, resigned in 1973 and was succeeded by Elizabeth Hanford, who had previously been deputy director of the Office of Consumer Affairs. Bennetta Washington, wife of D.C. Mayor Walter E. Washington, has a PhD in education, is active in civic affairs, and has served as a Labor Department executive during the Johnson and Nixon administrations.

FIGUREHEADS AND POWER WIELDERS

The importance of women varies from department to department. At Treasury, the top women tend to be figurehead administrators—like Mary Brooks, a Republican politician who is director of the mint, Romana Acosta Banuelos, a Spanish-American businesswoman who was treasurer during most of Nixon's administration, and current Treasurer Francine I. Neff, a GOP national committeewoman from New Mexico before she accepted the $36,000-a-year post. Frances G. Knight exercises considerable power as director of the Passport Office.

At the Pentagon, there are five women with the rank of general or admiral, most of whom are in charge of distinctly female military operations. (Three other women who achieved such ranks are now retired from active duty.) The highest woman military officer is Major General Jeanne Holm, director of the

Air Force's personnel council. Brigadier General Mildred C. Bailey is director of the Women's Army Corps (WAC). The top officers of the various nurses' corps are Brigadier General Lillian Dunlap (Army), Brigadier General Claire M. Garrecht (Air Force), and Rear Admiral Alene B. Duerk (Navy). The Women Marines, Women's Air Force, and Coast Guard Spars are directed by lower-ranking female officers.

All too often, the highest woman in an agency or department is in charge of either equal employment opportunity (in which case, she is usually black), consumer affairs, or, as at the Labor Department, the Women's Bureau. Ruth Bates Harris was once the highest-ranking woman in the National Aeronautics and Space Administration. A black woman, Ms. Harris was deputy assistant administrator for Equal Opportunity. She and two aides accused NASA of not moving fast enough in hiring women and members of minority races and prepared a 40-page report to support their claim. After discussions with NASA Administrator James Fletcher about the report, Ms. Harris was fired in October 1973. While NASA officials denied that the report had anything to do with her dismissal, Ms. Harris successfully sought relief from the Civil Service Commission, with assistance from the NAACP Legal Defense Fund.

The past few years have seen the elevation of women to top positions in the two major political parties. Jean Westwood of Utah served as chairman of the Democratic National Committee during the period of Senator George McGovern's candidacy, and the current head of the Republican National Committee is Mary Louise Smith, former co-chairman of the Women's Political Caucus of Iowa.

Breaking the sex discrimination barrier also has its humorous aspects. Jewel Lafontant, a black Chicago lawyer, became the first woman deputy solicitor general in December 1972. Male Solicitors General are required to wear a tail coat and striped trousers when they present themselves before the Supreme Court, but no one knew what Mrs. Lafontant should wear. She was told to design her own costume, which she did, appearing at the Court attired in a modified cutaway jacket and striped sheath skirt.

FEMALE LEGISLATORS

The women in the House of Representatives call themselves the Women's Caucus, but they do not necessarily vote as a bloc, except on women's issues, and not always then. Their interests are as disparate as their backgrounds. Of the nineteen women serving in the House, fourteen are Democrats and five are Republicans. One-third of them are in their first terms, and most of the others still haven't accumulated enough seniority to be legislatively potent. Representative Leonor K. Sullivan of Missouri is the only woman chairing a committee. She was elected to the House more than two decades ago, after the death of her husband, a congressman from Missouri, for whom she had been administrative assistant. She is now the third-ranking majority member of the House Banking and Currency Committee, as well as chairman of the Merchant Marine and Fisheries Committee. She was a principal champion of the truth-in-lending and truth-in-packaging consumer laws.

Much of the power wielded by women on the Hill was dissipated by the retirement in 1974 of the House's three senior women—Representatives

Edith Green of Oregon, Martha Griffiths of Michigan and Julia Butler Hansen of Washington.

A former teacher, Representative Green had been chairman of the Special Education Subcommittee of the House Education and Labor Committee. She didn't get along with other Democrats on the committee, however, and transferred to an education subcommittee of the House Appropriations Committee. She exercised considerable control over all education bills. Representative Shirley Chisholm, rounding up support for legislation to extend the minimum wage requirements to one million domestic workers, mostly women, said of her, "I knew that Edith had the most influence. I begged her. I said: 'Edith, this is a cause for a woman. You're very well respected in this House. When you get on the floor, the men will listen.' And they did."

Representative Griffiths, an attorney who served in Congress for twenty years, was the fourth-ranking majority member of the powerful Ways and Means Committee, and a well-versed, vocal member of the Joint Economic Committee. Long interested in equality for women in areas like social security benefits, Representative Griffiths became prominent as the chief proponent of the Equal Rights Amendment. She was also chief House sponsor of a broad, federally operated national health insurance plan.

Representative Hansen was chairman of the appropriations subcommittee which handles funding for the Interior Department. A politician from Washington State, her interests include synthetic fuels, resource management, and the Trans-Alaska pipeline, but she was particularly concerned about the Indians who fall under Interior Department jurisdiction. When Bureau of Indian Affairs officials came to her to plead for money, she donned jewelry given her by the various tribes she visited over the years and asked sharp questions about conditions on the reservations.

The most important nonelected woman on the Hill is Alice Rivlin, the first director of the Congressional Budget Office, Congress' answer to the White House Office of Management and Budget. Mrs. Rivlin, who has a doctorate in economics from Radcliffe, served in the Johnson administration as an assistant secretary of HEW and spent more than ten years at the Brookings Institution, where she became widely known as an expert in analysis of the federal budget and reform of policies in health and welfare.

There are very few women in key staff positions on Hill committees, but an increasing number of representatives (especially the female ones) and senators are appointing women to responsible jobs as administrative and legislative aides on their personal staffs. Frances Henderson, who is well versed in the labyrinthine politics of New Jersey, is the administrative power in Senator Clifford P. Case's office. Vernice Holifield controls access to her husband, Representative Chet Holifield of California, chairman of the House Government Operations Committee. (Officially, she is his receptionist.) Arlene Horowitz was a member of Representative John Brademas's staff when she became concerned about discrimination against women in education. Since Brademas was a member of the Select Subcommittee on Education, Ms. Horowitz drafted antidiscrimination legislation which is under consideration in both houses. (She now works for the National Council of Jewish Women.) Lola Aiken, wife of the recently retired senior senator from Vermont, was also his administrative assistant.

Women are active in the governments of the District and its suburbs.

Probably the most important woman in the District government today is Barbara A. Sizemore, superintendent of schools. New to her job in 1973, Mrs. Sizemore inherited a difficult situation fraught with controversy and dissension. Her selection split the school board. An outspoken woman, Mrs. Sizemore came to Washington after twenty-six years in the Chicago school system, where she most recently headed a three-school decentralization project on Chicago's South Side. Her chief interests are community control of the schools and the problems of minority students. "Education is always political, never neutral," commented Mrs. Sizemore shortly after she got her Washington job. "It is used to achieve the ends of government."

There is no jurisdiction in the Washington area that does not have women on the elected governing board, from the D.C. City Council to the Montgomery County (Maryland) Council. In Fairfax County, Virginia, the chairman of the board of supervisors is Jean Packard. Women are prominent on the area school boards, as well as in the state legislatures of Maryland and Virginia, as delegates from the Washington suburbs. Several years ago, the D.C. police force began recruiting women—not just to write parking tickets and direct traffic, but to be full-fledged, gun-toting law enforcers. Today the more than one hundred D.C. policewomen are highly visible in the city, and many a patrol car carries a two-person team mixed by both sex and race. In 1974 a black policewoman was fatally shot by a robbery suspect in downtown Washington, marking the first on-duty death of a policewoman in American history.

In the Washington area labor force as a whole, there are 10 percent more women than men: 1,039,413 women over the age of sixteen (either working or looking for work) versus 934,419 men. Of the women, about 10 percent work for the government (100,735 in 1971), mostly as clerks, typists, office assistants, etc. Others are now moving into the middle and upper ranks of private business and the professions as administrative assistants, executives, lobbyists, lawyers, broadcasters, news correspondents, securities analysts, and personnel administrators. While there are still inequalities of pay and responsibility, much of it stems from ingrained patterns and unconscious reflexes more than overt policy.

Of the million working women in the Washington area at the time of the last census, 106,887 were professional women, that is, lawyers, professors, journalists, architects, doctors, etc.; 12,628 were nurses, and another 5,491 were health workers of other kinds; more than 30,000 were elementary and secondary schoolteachers; 23,916 had managerial or administrative jobs; more than 30,000 were salespeople; 62,941 were service workers, such as waitresses; and 20,662 were household workers. Most women holding jobs in the last two categories live in the District, where Negroes outnumber whites on the female work force by more than two to one. Black women are generally less educated than white women (the median years of education for black women in the District is 11.4, compared with 13.2 for white women). In secondary education, only 3 of the 86 Washington-area public high school principals are women, and only 12 of the 131 junior high principals.

WOMEN IN JOURNALISM

More and more women are breaking away from the traditional staples of women's reporting—consumer affairs, food, fashion, society, and spicy interviews with the great and near-great—and are getting into general reporting of government and politics. The old distinctions are becoming blurred. Women can now join the formerly male National Press Club, and men can join the Washington Press Club, formerly the Women's National Press Club. (In 1974 the latter club elected its first male president, Ron Sarro of the Washington *Star*). Among the important journalists in Washington are Mary McGrory, a syndicated columnist for the Washington *Star;* Elizabeth Drew, a television interviewer, freelance writer, and former correspondent for the *Atlantic;* Meg Greenfield, editorial writer for the Washington *Post* and *Newsweek* columnist; Eileen Shanahan, who covers economic and tax matters for the *New York Times;* and Marilyn Berger, a foreign affairs reporter for the *Post*. Vera Glaser, Malvina Stephenson, and Wauhillau LaHay cover political figures in their syndicated columns and radio broadcasts. UPI's Helen Thomas (Martha Mitchell's favorite telephone contact) and Frances Lewine of the AP cover the White House, as does Bonnie Angelo of *Time*. (In 1975 Helen Thomas achieved the distinction of being the first woman elected to membership in the Gridiron Club, a venerable collection of bureau chiefs and columnists, and— more significantly—the first woman elected president of the White House Correspondents Association.) Jane Denison churned out much of the UPI copy on the Watergate hearings and tape transcripts over the many months of the scandal. Some of the most spunky questions asked at the President's press conferences come from the mouth of the irrepressible Sarah McClendon, a veteran reporter who covers Washington for a few obscure newspapers and radio stations in Texas. (In 1974 Mrs. McClendon was elected vice president of the National Press Club.)

However, many of the prominent women journalists in Washington still work basically in an extension of the old "Women's Page" feature. Sally Quinn, whose penetrating interviews appear in the *Post*'s style section, did a brief stint on the CBS *Morning News,* in competition with NBC's Barbara Walters of the *Today Show*. To the satisfaction of both CBS and herself, however, she returned to the *Post* in 1974 (after a comical turnabout in which she joined and resigned from the Washington bureau of the *New York Times* in the space of a few weeks). Kandy Stroud covered Washington parties and personalities for *Women's Wear Daily* until she left *WWD* in early 1975. (An interview she did in 1972 with presidential candidate Edmund Muskie's wife, while perfectly harmless in itself, served as the basis for a cruel attack on Jane Muskie—by William Loeb in the Manchester, New Hampshire, *Union Leader* —that reduced the candidate to tears in public.) Betty Beale of the *Star* is Washington's senior chronicler of the social scene, and former police reporter Maxine Cheshire of the *Post* is skilled at uncovering the embarrassing peccadilloes of Washington newsmakers.

The most important woman in newspaper publishing, locally and nationally, is Katharine Graham, publisher of the *Post*. Taking over upon the death of her publisher husband, Mrs. Graham has been active in all aspects of the paper's operations (including, at the height of Watergate, defense of her paper's aggressive reporting of the scandal). Late in 1972, Elsie Carper, whose journalistic career had included covering District affairs in Congress for the *Post,* became that newspaper's first woman assistant managing editor. At the *Star* the national desk editor is Barbara Stubbs Cohen, and Mary Lou Werner Forbes is co-editor of the metropolitan desk. The staff of

Changing Times, the Kiplinger consumer magazine, includes Managing Editor Marjorie E. White and Associate Editors Margery A. Crane and Ellen Roberts.

Marian Burros, a *Post* food writer and WRC-TV commentator, has proven that the subject of food, nutrition, and grocery shopping can be elevated from the traditional rut of promotional puffery to a level of serious journalism. Washington has one of the very few woman sports columnists in the nation, the *Star*'s Joan Ryan (whose husband, Frank Ryan, had an outstanding career as quarterback of the Cleveland Browns). Mrs. Ryan writes intelligently about athletics in general, with no particular emphasis on women's sports.

The city's most prominent woman fiction writer is octogenarian Katherine Anne Porter, the author of *Ship of Fools* and *Pale Horse, Pale Rider.* Judith Viorst, wife of *Star* political columnist Milton Viorst, writes witty light verse and humorous essays.

Women have had a hard time breaking into television journalism in Washington, but now they are all over the airwaves. For a long time, the only visible woman television reporter broadcasting nationally out of Washington was Nancy Dickerson, who now works a light schedule for Newsweek Broadcasting. Today all of the major network bureaus have women giving reports from the field, including CBS's Marya McLaughlin, Lesley Stahl, and Connie Chung, and NBC's Catherine Mackin (who in 1972 was the first woman to broadcast political convention coverage from the floor, and later proved to be one of the hardest-hitting correspondents on the presidential campaign trail). Ann Compton of ABC became in 1974 the first woman television journalist to be assigned to the White House full time. The important positions of news director and producer in Washington are still held almost exclusively by men, but Sylvia Westerman of CBS had a major role in coordinating the network's coverage of the Senate Watergate hearings. On Washington's local stations, women have proliferated as both field reporters and anchorpersons (with the impetus of discrimination suits against some stations). Local female television personalities include Rene Carpenter, ex-wife of astronaut Scott Carpenter.

LAWYERS AND LOBBYISTS

Numerically, women do not do very well in the Washington law establishment. The District has 1,095 women lawyers compared with 13,881 men. Few of the major firms have a woman for a partner. Arnold and Porter does—a cigar-smoking tax expert named Carolyn E. Agger, who also happens to be the wife of another prominent Washington lawyer, former Supreme Court Justice Abe Fortas. Patricia Roberts Harris, once dean of Howard University's law school, ambassador to Luxembourg, and a member of the U.S. delegation to the U.N., is a partner in that very Democratic firm of Fried, Frank, Harris, Shriver and Kampelman. Ms. Harris was chairman of the committee responsible for seating delegates to the 1972 Democratic convention, an assemblage remarkable for the number of women, blacks, and young people who participated.

Gladys Kessler, of Berlin, Roisman and Kessler, is one of the small number of influential women practicing public interest law. Nancy Truscott is in the firm of Howard, Poe and Bastian. Other well-known women lawyers in private practice are Dovey Roundtree and former local judge Marjorie

Lawson. Jill Wine Volner, a young Columbia Law School graduate, acquired a reputation as a knowledgeable, tough-minded lawyer while serving on the staff of the Watergate special prosecutor. Women judges on the U.S. District Court for the District of Columbia are Judge June L. Green and Senior Judge Burnita Shelton Matthews.

In the lobbying profession, Dita Beard of ITT may have given women lobbyists a bad name, but most are considerably less flamboyant and more effective. Jim Grant, now Representative Richard Bolling's wife, was known for her cigars and tough language, but was also a successful lobbyist. Some other women lobbyists: Evelyn Dubrow, legislative representative of the International Ladies' Garment Workers Union; Dorothy Ellsworth of the Brotherhood of Railway, Airline and Steamship Clerks; Carol Burris of the Women's Lobby; Leslie Jerould of the League of Women Voters; Joan Claybrook of Ralph Nader's Congress Watch; Ann M. Roosevelt of Friends of the Earth; Louise C. Dunlap of the Environmental Policy Center; and Ruth M. Saxe of Common Cause. LaDonna Harris, wife of former Senator Fred R. Harris, actively lobbies for Indian legislation (she is a full-blooded Comanche). Ada Deer, a Menominee Indian, has been in Washington for a couple of years working for legislation for her tribe. A delegation of Alaskan native women spent 1970 and 1971 in Washington lobbying for the land claims settlement legislation that brought their people nearly $1 billion. Mary C. Gereau, a veteran legislative representative for the National Education Association, now represents the National Treasury Employees Union.

The fight in 1973 to extend the minimum wage to domestics was coordinated from a suite belonging to Representative Shirley Chisholm (D-N.Y.). Thirty-nine organizations, including the ILGWU and the Women's Lobby, worked together. The National Organization for Women (NOW), the National Women's Political Caucus, Common Cause, and the League of Women Voters were among the organizations which lobbied Congress for passage of the Equal Rights Amendment to the Constitution, now facing difficult ratification challenges in the state legislatures. (The only organized female opposition to it has come from Phyllis Schlafly, a veteran advocate of conservative causes.)

The following individuals and organizations are also active in women's rights in Washington: Dr. Bernice Sandler, a psychologist now heading up the Association of American College Women's "project on the status and education of women"; Daisy Fields, a founder in 1968 and now executive director of Federally Employed Women (FEW); the Women's Equity Action League (WEAL), in which Dr. Sandler, Arvonne Fraser (wife of Representative Donald Fraser), and others have been active; political scientist Irene Pinker at the Federation of Organizations for Professional Women; Barbara Kilberg, once a member of John Ehrlichman's Domestic Council staff and now vice president for academic affairs at Mount Vernon College, who tried to keep the lines of communication open between the Nixon administration and women's groups; and Dr. Fann Harding of the Heart and Lung Institute, organizer of the Association of Women in Science.

One of the newest women's rights organizations is the International Institute of Sex Identities, a prime mover of which is lawyer Cathy Douglas, wife of Supreme Court Justice William O. Douglas. The institute collects and analyzes data on the nature of femininity and masculinity. On a completely different level, Washington Opportunities for Women (WOW) has for several years run a job information center that helps women with résumés and keeps files on available jobs in the public and private sectors.

BUSINESSWOMEN

In the business community, some fields are wide open to women. One is real estate. Millicent Chatel handles Capitol Hill and Georgetown property. Other large Capitol Hill real estate firms are run by Barbara Held and Rhea Radin. And one of the biggest in northern Virginia belongs to Routh Robbins. Flaxie Pinkett, a black civic leader, heads the real estate and insurance firm built by her father, John Pinkett. Among the area's investment houses, Ferris and Co. has been a leader in promoting capable women; Julia M. Walsh (a former governor of the American Stock Exchange) is the firm's vice chairman of the board, and its senior vice presidents include Gail H. Winslow and Sally A. Behn. Phyllis Peterson is a partner in Sade and Co., and Grace Taylor, an investment counselor with Loomis Sayles and Co., has been vice president of the Washington Society of Investment Analysts. Jean Sisco, until recently a vice president of Woodward & Lothrop, one of the area's largest department stores, is now a government affairs consultant to the American Retail Federation. (She is also the wife of Joseph J. Sisco, a high-ranking State Department official.) Woodward & Lothrop's vice president in charge of consumer affairs and public relations is Julia M. Lee. Liz Carpenter, who was Lady Bird Johnson's press secretary, is a key member of the Hill and Knowlton public relations firm in Washington, and a well-known speaker of witty political jibes. Esther Peterson, consumer affairs adviser to President Johnson, is now vice president for consumer affairs for Washington-based Giant Food, Inc. Jane E. Marilley, president of Courtesy Associates, has built her firm into one of Washington's largest in the field of telephone answering, convention management, travel planning, and public relations. Greenwood's Transfer and Storage Company, Washington's oldest major black business (with 1973 annual sales of $1.5 million), is managed by Helen Greenwood Allen, daughter of the founder.

PHYSICIANS AND ACADEMICIANS

Women comprise about one-seventh of the total number of physicians in the Washington area (about twice the national percentage of women doctors), but are only one in forty among the clergy. There are more than twenty times as many male architects as female and almost eighty-five times as many male civil engineers. Conversely, there are three times as many women librarians as men, and forty times as many are nurses. (One of Washington's few successful women architects is Chloethiel Woodard Smith, who has designed everything from townhouse clusters in the new town of Reston, Virginia, to apartment buildings in the Southwest redevelopment area and office buildings along Connecticut Avenue.)

In academic Washington, there are a few women who have made notable contributions to their particular disciplines. One of these is Dr. Thelma Lavine, chairman of the philosophy department at George Washington University. Jean Camper Cahn is dean of the Antioch Law School in Washington. Dr. Janet G. Travell, a specialist in pharmacology and cardiovascular disease, served as White House physician to Presidents Kennedy and Johnson and remained in Washington to teach at the medical schools of George Washington and Georgetown universities. Dr. Mary Louise Robbins is professor of microbiology at the George Washington School of Medicine and Health Sciences. Dr. Frances Welsing is an assistant professor of psychiatry and pediatrics at the Howard University School of Medicine, and has done controversial studies on the roots of white racism and its effect on black children. The chairman of the Howard University history department is Lorraine Williams, whose specialties are the Civil War and Reconstruction periods.

One of the more colorful women in the Washington health establishment is Dr. Estelle Ramey, an endocrinologist at Georgetown University Medical School. She took on Senator Hubert Humphrey's friend and personal physician, Dr. Edgar Berman, when he argued that women are biologically unsuited to serve as President of the United States. Dr. Ramey has also objected vociferously (and successfully in one case) to the *Playboy*-center-spread type of illustrations used in some medical textbooks. Dr. Ariel C. Hollinshead is director of the Laboratory for Virus and Cancer Research at the George Washington University Medical Center. Dr. Roselyn Epps, a pediatrician, is head of the Division of Maternal and Child Health Care in the D.C. Department of Human Resources. Preterm, the city's leading nonprofit abortion, vasectomy, and sex-counseling clinic, was founded and is run, appropriately, by women. Its founding mother was Nan Tucker McEvoy, and its current director is Judy Jones. Helen P. Wright is a past president of the National Association for Mental Health (and wife of influential Federal Circuit Court Judge J. Skelly Wright).

In the social research organizations in Washington, there are few women among the top professionals. But Karen Davis, a health economist who took her PhD degree at Rice University, is a fellow at the Brookings Institution. Nancy Teeters, a former Brookings economist who specializes in the federal budget process, is now in the economic studies office of the Library of Congress, and was a participant in President Ford's 1974 "summit meeting" on inflation.

WOMEN IN THE ARTS

The performing and visual arts are fertile fields in Washington, and women play an important role in both. Zelda Fichandler is founder and producing director of the Arena Stage, one of the nation's best-known repertory theaters. Ms. Fichandler took her troupe to the Soviet Union for an official performance tour in 1974. The National Ballet, a fine company which went out of business in 1974, was founded and headed (and funded through most of its ten years of life) by Mrs. Richard J. Riddell. Hazel Wentworth was a cofounder and director of the now defunct Washington Theater Club, which suffered large financial losses before folding in 1974. Naomi Eftis is producing director of the experimental Back Alley Theater. Frankie Hewitt is executive producer of Ford's Theatre (where John Wilkes Booth shot President Lincoln), which was renovated and reactivated under the aegis of the Interior Department. A recent addition to the local theater scene is the Washington Area Feminist Theater, which is holding a bicentennial contest for women playwrights, the prize to go to the author of the best one-act play about women who have performed some service in the cause of liberty or helped to improve the lives of their fellow women.

Washington's women artists were long overshadowed by the fame of such local artists as Morris Louis, Kenneth Noland, Gene Davis, Rockne Krebs, and Sam Gilliam. Until a few years ago, only two women artists—Anne Truitt (a seminal figure in the "minimal" style of hard-edge painting and sculpture) and Alma Thomas (an abstract expressionist)—had large followings. The recent blooming of Washington's women artists was heightened by the Conference for Women in the Visual Arts, held at the local Corcoran Gallery in 1971. The conference led to the formation of two groups, the D.C. Registry of Women Artists and the Washington Women Art Professionals. Ironically, the first major group shows spotlighting Washington's women artists were held, in 1973, in New York City. Rising stars (several of whom exhibited at the two Manhattan shows) include painters Cynthia Bickley, Enid Sanford, and Sheila Isham; sculptors Jennie Lea Knight (who works in polished wood), Joan Danziger (who has done fantasy figures in rag mâché), Rosemary Wright (modulated cardboard sculptures); video artist Patricia Moella; and mixed media painter-sculptor Mary Beth Edelson, who is the informal leader of the feminist movement in Washington art.

Important art administrators in Washington include Jane Livingston, chief curator at the Corcoran Gallery of Art, and Adelyn D. Breeskin, recently retired as curator of contemporary art at the National Collection of Fine Arts and now a consultant to its department of painting and sculpture. Women run several of the important commercial galleries in Washington: Barbara Fendrick, of Fendrick Gallery; Nesta Dorrance, the Jefferson Place Gallery, which went out of business in late 1974; Bernice Weinstein, Jacob's Ladder; Henrietta Ersham, Henri Gallery; and Jane Haslem, of the gallery bearing her name. Alice Denney has been Washington's pioneering organizer of exhibits featuring extremely avant-garde art. Artist Marian Van Landingham was the moving force behind (and is now the director of) the Torpedo Factory Art Center, a onetime Navy factory on the Potomac riverfront in Alexandria, Virginia, that has been renovated into a complex of low-rent artists' studios, workshops, and exhibition galleries.

There is a sizable representation of women in the National Symphony Orchestra. Ballet dancers Christine Knoblauch, Susan Frazer, Carmen Mathe, and Michelle Lees met with critical acclaim with the National Ballet, but scattered to other companies when it collapsed.

Women are important to the arts in other ways. Probably the most significant person on the national arts funding scene is Nancy Hanks, chairman of the National Endowment for the Arts, the chief dispenser of federal subsidies to the arts. Mrs. Jouett Shouse, long active in government and politics, established Wolf Trap Farm, a summer concert pavilion near Reston, Virginia. Mrs. Polk Guest is instrumental in fund raising for the John F. Kennedy Center for the Performing Arts. Peggy Cooper is a leading black arts impresario and co-founder of Workshops for Careers in the Arts (as well as an associate producer at WTOP-TV). The late Marjorie Merriweather Post gave generously to the Washington National Symphony during her lifetime and left a priceless collection of imperial Russian art to the U.S. government at her death in 1973.

Mrs. Post was a notable figure in Washington for several decades. Heir to the $20 million Postum Cereal Company fortune at her father's death, Mrs. Post left an estate more than six times that size when she died. A shrewd businesswoman who had four husbands (and in the end took back her maiden name), Mrs. Post learned everything there was to know about cereals at an early age, and then expanded her company to include other products. She is credited with having first recognized the potential of frozen foods, buying out the struggling Birds Eye Company and incorporating it into her domain. At the first state dinner she gave as wife of American Ambassador to Moscow Joseph Davies, her guests were afraid to eat the food for fear the new freezing process would poison them. "Come along to the kitchen," said Mrs. Post, and she showed them how it was done.

A FEW MORE WASHINGTON WOMEN

There are a few women from Washington who are nationally and internationally prominent in athletics, including teenage Olympic swimmer Melissa Belote and gymnast Roxanne Pierce.

Some well-known women are hard to categorize. A few have become famous because their husbands were, like former First Lady Pat Nixon, or because their bosses were, like presidential personal secretary Rose Mary Woods, who worked for Richard Nixon longer than anyone else, since 1951. Others are prominent because they entertain, like Gwen Cafritz and Polly Logan, or because they are entertaining, like Barbara Howar, the swinging party-giver, talk-show hostess, wit, and author. In Washington, such women can be important.

Take Alice Roosevelt Longworth, the daughter of President Theodore Roosevelt. "Princess Alice" was a headstrong, hoydenish young woman with a penchant for bons mots who married the Speaker of the House, Nicholas Longworth, in a White House wedding more than sixty-five years ago. Though a cousin of Eleanor Roosevelt, she viewed the First Lady with some distaste. She campaigned successfully against American entry into the League of Nations, and less successfully against the candidacy of President Franklin D. Roosevelt. But Alice Longworth, now in her nineties, endures. Long after the league and the New Deal have become history, Washington still chuckles over her latest witticism.

Traditionally, the woman most frequently thought of as the symbol of Women in Washington is the First Lady, but there is no typical First Lady. Eleanor Roosevelt was active in political and social movements; Mamie Eisenhower was not. Jackie Kennedy personally supervised cultural programs (not to mention the total redecorating of the White House) and set a national style in fashion and entertaining; Bess Truman kept hands off such matters. Lady Bird Johnson, while keeping an astute eye on her million-dollar businesses in Texas, promoted park development and urban beautification; Pat Nixon, on the other hand, eschewed the activist role and was content to stand in her husband's shadow. Never really at ease in public life, she nonetheless attended every social function and gave every little speech that was asked of her, never once getting caught in even a slight faux pas.

Betty Ford's style is a distinct contrast to Pat Nixon's. The present First Lady is relaxed in the public eye and matter-of-fact in her dealings with the press. Whereas Pat Nixon never volunteered a personal opinion on any public issue, Mrs. Ford, soon after arriving in the White House, called a press conference at which she voiced opinions—firmly but not stridently—on a wide range of subjects, including abortion, on which she at first took a liberal stance but later equivocated. (She also said she assumed her children had tried marijuana, and that she wasn't too concerned with a little youthful experimentation.) Her self-confidence might be rooted in the things she achieved early in her life, before she was a politician's wife. She studied modern dance with Martha Graham, first at Bennington College and then in New York City. Having begun modeling part time at a Grand Rapids, Michigan, department store at the age of fourteen, she later was a professional Powers model in New York and a fashion coordinator in Grand Rapids. She had done a lot of living on her own by the time she, at age thirty, married Gerald Ford, after divorcing her first husband of five years. (Mrs. Ford, incidentally, is not the first presidential wife to have been divorced, a distinction that belonged to Mrs. Warren Harding.)

WHAT LIES AHEAD?

In a numerical sense, the status of women in Washington and in the federal government has improved markedly over the past decade. But women still do not play significant roles in most of the federal policymaking processes. In 1970 Daisy Fields told a House Special Subcommittee on Education: "It cannot be said that there are not more qualified women who could fill positions at these levels; rather, the root of the problem lies in our social customs, traditions, life patterns, and the perceptions of the male and female role—the stereotypes we perpetuate." Over the next few years, however, the stereotypes are sure to be altered, and the promotion of more women administrators into policymaking levels appears likely.

Like men in Washington, women in Washington come in various political, economic, racial, social, and cultural shades. They form no solid bloc, not even on legislation. As the American colonists of 1776 really wanted only the "rights of Englishmen," the current crop of women activists are seeking merely the "rights of citizens." In Washington, the tide is now running in their direction.

22 CONSUMER CAPITAL

Since every voter is a consumer, it might seem that consumers would have the biggest lobby in Washington and speak with the loudest voice. Yet until fairly recently, consumer interests were represented vaguely throughout the federal system—in boards and regulatory agencies—without much focus in politics and law. The 1960s changed all this. Like an idea whose time had come, consumerism burst upon the Washington scene and created a steady stream of reports, recommendations, bills, and laws.

The reasons for the change were partly economic, partly political, and partly a product of personality. Economically, the two decades of prosperity that followed World War II had built a large body of affluent and well-informed consumers. People who had once cared only about the source and amount of their incomes were becoming concerned about spending their incomes wisely. On the political front, consumers found a growing number of senators and congressmen attempting to balance the scales between buyers and sellers in the marketplace. Then came the catalytic ingredient of personality: Ralph Nader. His presence in Washington galvanized young people into action, provided a kind of messianic leadership, and kept the pressure on business and government day after day.

These factors combined to make consumerism one of the most potent issues in Washington. Consumerism spawned dozens of new citizens organizations and lobbies. It has been both a boon and a headache to trade associations and Washington corporate offices, which have had to expand their staffs and budgets to meet consumer challenges directed at industry after industry. And consumerism has enriched Washington law firms, which have the regulatory law experience needed to represent associations and corporations in consumer proceedings before federal agencies and commissions. On Capitol Hill, the burgeoning issue has led to the creation or bolstering of consumer subcommittees. Of principal importance are the House Banking and Currency Committee's Subcommittee on Consumer Affairs and the Senate Commerce Committee's Subcommittee on Consumer Affairs, chaired by Senator Frank E. Moss (D-Utah), under the benevolent wing of the full committee's chairman, longtime consumer champion Senator Warren G. Magnuson (D-Wash.). The House consumer panel was chaired for several years by consumer crusader Representative Leonor K. Sullivan (D-Mo.), but she was deposed in the 1975 House shake-up in favor of Representative Frank Annunzio (D-Ill.), who hadn't even been a member of the subcommittee previously. The members who voted against Representative Sullivan didn't criticize her administration of the subcommittee, but said they wanted to spread the chairmanships around, and she was already chairman of another full committee.

The consumer crusade of the past fifteen years has changed the very way that government relates to the people. Citizens were encouraged by consumer activists to expect complete information and prompt satisfaction in the marketplace, and they began to demand the same of their servants in Washington. So trouble-shooting offices were set up in virtually every federal department, agency, and commission. Outgrowths of the old Office of Public Information, most of the new ones are called "offices of consumer affairs." Some agencies have an "ombudsman." The U.S. Postal Service, a government corporation, has both an ombudsman and "customer relations" personnel.

Whatever the name, the function is the same: to answer questions, explain government rules, untangle and cut red tape, hear complaints, and pass them along to someone who can find out what's wrong. Instead of getting the old runaround or brushoff, the angry citizen gets a sympathetic ear. (Whether he gets results is another matter, but it's an improvement nonetheless.) At the Civil Aeronautics Board the consumer affairs office takes complaints from citizens who have been bumped from overbooked flights, whose children were stranded in Europe by fraudulent charter tour operators, and who think they were overcharged on a long flight with sections on different airlines. At the Interstate Commerce Commission, the public information office takes complaints about the cost and reliability of household moving companies. And so it goes at an increasing number of agencies around town. Citizens who don't know the bureaucratic maze well enough to figure out which agency has jurisdiction can direct their questions and complaints to Uncle Sam's central consumer information agency, the Office of Consumer Affairs.

Filling the roles of instigator, irritant, and monitor are the citizen pressure groups of the consumer lobby. They run the gamut from old guard (the National Consumers League, founded in 1899) to establishment (Consumers Union) to iconoclast (the multibranched organization led by Ralph Nader). Virtually all of the groups—with the conspicuous exception of Nader's—take a role in the Consumer Federation of America, an alliance of consumer bodies from labor unions, rural organizations, professional societies, religious groups, and miscellaneous citizen organizations. Over the past couple of years, the CFA has become torn by intramural battles, mainly over the dominant role within it of the labor unions and Consumers Union. Its effectiveness as a force on Capitol Hill has been hampered by limited budgeting and staffing.

Some consumer groups started as the personal crusade of one fervent reformer and later grew into full-fledged organizations, with continuous funding and full-time staffs. Ralph Nader, who wrote his auto safety exposé *Unsafe at Any Speed* in a rented room near Dupont Circle, today heads an organization of twenty-one pressure groups with a total budget of about $3 million a year. While Nader's personal impact has been lessened by the breadth of his scatter-gun attacks, it has been more than offset by the vigilance of his hundreds of staffers, who serve as a countervailing force to trade association lobbyists. The success of Ralph Nader with auto safety reform induced other crusaders to attempt similar campaigns against consumer evils. Nader aide Jim Turner wrote *The Chemical Feast,* an exposé of alleged laxness in the Food and Drug Administration, which led to the founding of a citizen lobby called Consumer Action for Improved Food and Drugs. Capitol Hill testimony by a solo crusader named Robert Choate spotlighted the nutritional deficiencies of breakfast cereals that are consumed in large part by children. Choate later broadened his field of interest to include general nutrition, advertising aimed at children, and the quality of children's television programing.

Besides the activist groups, Washington is home base of several privately published consumer publications. Most of them—like *Of Consuming Interest* (a weekly newsletter published by Federal-State Reports, Arlington, Virginia) and *Consumer Newsweek* (published by Arthur Rowse)—are progress reports on legislative developments in the consumer movement. Washington is the home, too, of Kiplinger's *Changing Times,* a pioneering consumer magazine begun in 1947 to help families spend their money more effectively.

THE EARLY YEARS

The consumer action of the Sixties and Seventies—such as the Kefauver-Harris drug amendments of 1962, the cigarette health warning and broadcast ad ban, truth-in-packaging, truth-in-lending, auto safety reforms, and bans on certain chemical additives and insecticides—would never have been possible without legislative foundations laid tens of years earlier. The tide of consumer activism has ebbed and flowed several times in this century. Traditionally, it has risen when citizens, already upset about general economic conditions, are politicized by a particular horror story of corporate disregard for consumer safety.

The first organization resembling a consumer movement was the National Consumers League, founded in 1899. It was more concerned with working conditions—wages, sanitation, and child labor—than with the quality of goods produced by American manufacturing. But in the same period, Populist and Progressive reformers were beginning to point out that the efficient blessings of technology and mass production were resulting, all too often, in shoddy merchandise, unwholesome food, and monopoly prices. The muckraking journalists, publishing their exposés in such magazines as *McClure's* and *Collier's Weekly,* took aim on every form of corruption in business and politics, focusing especially on the food industry.

As early as the 1880s, the U.S. Department of Agriculture conducted tests on chemical food additives used to give an illusion of freshness. (Formaldehyde was used to "embalm" meat and dairy products in transit to the market, and canned peas often derived their lovely shade of green not from Mother Nature but from copper sulfate.) The first pure food legislation was introduced in the Nineties, but for nearly a decade it foundered, passed one year by the House and not the Senate, the next year by the Senate but not the House. The appearance in 1906 of Upton Sinclair's *The Jungle* finally got results. Its tales of rats being ground into sausage meat and slaughterhouse workers falling into vats of boiling lard (never to be retrieved) turned the nation's stomach. The sale of meat products fell by one-half in the United States, and foreign markets were jeopardized, too. The meat industry relented in its opposition to the bill, and the Pure Food and Drug Act and Meat Inspection Act passed in 1906.

The decade of the Twenties was a period of general consumer satisfaction with an economy that was pouring out products that most of the nation could afford. But the boom was buoyed by a high-pressure sales climate, dependent on clever advertising and lots of it. A minor backlash was triggered by the publication in 1927 of a best-selling book entitled *Your Money's Worth: The Waste of the Consumer's Dollar.* The book gave impetus to product-testing laboratories, the best known being Consumers' Research, Inc., founded in 1929 by coauthor F. J. Schlink. (Consumers' Research exists today as publisher of *Consumers' Research Bulletin*.) Six years later, a split within the organization gave birth to the Consumers Union, today the nation's foremost nonprofit testing group and publisher of the monthly *Consumer Reports,* as well as a strong legislative advocate and underwriter of research into consumer problems.

More than all the exposés on advertising techniques, however, it was the depression that turned the American citizen into a thrifty, discriminating, and conserving consumer (at least for a while). When a new suit of clothes had to last five years, you could bet that it was chosen with an eye for durability more than style. The New Deal administration, finding that the Pure Food and Drug Act had been gradually rendered ineffective by court rulings and technological changes in food processing, began a campaign to tighten it up. The proposed legislation was radical for the era, and included requirements of ingredient labeling, uniform quality grades on food labels, and proof of advertising claims. The Food and Drug Administration tried to incense the nation with an exhibit of the dangers of doctored foods, faulty cosmetics, and quack medicines. This 1937 "chamber of horrors" included photos of a lovely young woman who had been blinded by a brand of mascara called Lash Lure. But like thirty years before, passage of the bill depended on a public shock— this time provided by the death of more than a hundred people from a deadly elixir of sulfanilamide put on the market in 1937 before adequate testing. The following year, a new FDA bill passed—gutted, however, by deletion of important sections on grade labeling (a concession to the food industry).

Consumer activism was blunted by World War II, which required that consumers and industry pull the same oar of conservation, price controls, and rationing. And when the war was over, citizens were too elated with the increasing availability of consumer goods to be very concerned about rising prices and slipping quality. The Fifties was a period of calm in consumerism, caused by general prosperity and broad public respect for the goals and methods of the business establishment.

But a storm was gathering. The average education level of the American people was rising, and well-educated buyers were becoming more skeptical and demanding. Prosperity brought an ever increasing choice of consumer goods, differentiated more by advertising claims than by design and quality. The spread of charge accounts and easy credit (with interest charges skillfully hidden) lured many families into unneeded purchases, and consumer debt soared. By the end of the Fifties' boom times had spawned consumer bewilderment and questioning of American values in many areas (including corporate responsibility, race relations, and environmental protection).

THE CONSUMER SIXTIES

In 1962 President Kennedy enunciated a "Consumer Bill of Rights," calling for the right to safety, the right to be informed, the right to choose, and the right to be heard. The Kennedy consumer legislation package included an overhaul of the Food and Drug amendments of 1928, which were found to be inadequate in the testing of drugs prior to marketing. Drug industry opposition hamstrung this reform, championed on the Hill by Senator Estes Kefauver (D-Tenn.). Then came the thalidomide scandal and the tragic sight of grotesque infant deformities. A few months later, in October of 1962, the legislation cleared Congress and was signed into law.

The early Sixties saw the birth of government groups that would mold a new consumer consciousness. President Kennedy appointed a consumer advisory board in 1962, and two years later, President Johnson appointed a special assistant for consumer affairs. His choice was Esther Peterson, who had been a legislative specialist at the Amalgamated Clothing Workers Union and an assistant secretary of labor. She became an outspoken consumer advocate. In 1967 she was replaced by Betty Furness, a onetime television star ("You can be sure if it's Westinghouse") who had been making a name for herself as a spokesman for consumer interests. (Today Mrs. Peterson is both consumer affairs director for the Washington-based Giant Food chain and head of the National Consumers League, bridging the business-consumer gap.)

The growing consumer consciousness was beginning to be felt on Capitol Hill even before the New Frontier and Great Society. In 1960 Congress passed a law requiring clearer labeling of household products that contained lethal and other hazardous ingredients. In the same year Senator Paul Douglas (D-Ill.), one of the staunchest consumer supporters on the Hill, introduced a consumer credit protection act. (The timing was premature, but eight years later his concept reached fruition as the truth-in-lending law.) In 1961 Senator Philip Hart (D-Mich.) introduced a truth-in-packaging bill that was a few years ahead of its time. In 1964 Congress got to work on President Johnson's package of recommended laws, including reforms in meat and drug inspection, interest charge disclosure, and pesticide control. But consumerism was still an amorphous feeling more than a movement. It lacked the cohesive pressure groups—the citizen outrage—necessary to joust successfully with highly organized, experienced trade associations and corporate lobbyists.

Hearings on highway safety were held on the Hill in 1965, but the auto and tire industries were successful in pinning virtually all the blame for the soaring death and collision statistics on bad driving habits. Then Washington was hit by a one-man tornado named Ralph Nader. He arrived in Washington in 1964, an obscure young lawyer with a passion for improving the design of automobiles, which he felt to be rolling hazards to the nation's health and safety. The auto industry and the public were shaken from their complacency by publication in 1965 of Nader's *Unsafe at Any Speed,* an attack on auto design that focused on the General Motors Chevrolet "Corvair." General Motors responded to the attack by investigating Nader's life, hoping to turn up something derogatory, but the disclosure of their tactics backfired on them and only strengthened Nader's position. Congress responded by passing two bills, the National Traffic and Motor Vehicle Safety Act of 1966 (which gave the government authority to set safety standards for auto design and construction) and the Highway Safety Act of 1966 (aimed at improving the design of highways).

Reading the handwriting on the wall, the auto industry stepped up its own safety campaign by installing seat belts (on all 1964 models), flexible windshields (1966), and collapsible steering columns (1967). All the while, however, the automakers moaned that federal standards would be a severe blow to the industry. "If we have to close down some production lines because they don't meet the standards," Henry Ford II warned in 1966, "we're in for real trouble in this country." But Detroit, like all the other industries that struggled against consumerism, is learning to live with the standards, while lobbying to make them palatable to themselves. In 1974 the auto industry was given an unexpected anti-safety dividend, when Congress, under heavy pressure from exasperated motorists, voted to rescind the requirement that all cars have interlocking ignition and seat belt systems. Many drivers apparently found such devices to be a paternalistic infringement upon their right of self-injury.

The mid-Sixties were by far the most productive years, legislatively, in the history of the consumer movement. Sixteen consumer protection measures were passed from 1966 to 1968, and the Ninetieth Congress came to be known as "the consumer's Congress." The Truth-in-Packaging and Labeling Law was passed, giving consumers some idea of what and how much was inside packages on the store shelf. The Child Protection Act of 1966 (strengthened in 1969) banned the sale of unusually hazardous toys. The Flammable Fabrics Act of 1967 strengthened federal authority to set up standards and broadened the list of items covered. The Wholesale Meat Act of 1967 and the Wholesale Poultry Products Act of 1968 required that states set up purity inspection systems (for goods processed and sold intrastate) comparable to federal standards for interstate packers. The Truth-in-Lending Act was passed in 1968, eight years after prototype legislation was introduced by Senator Douglas. The Interstate Land Sales Full Disclosure Act of 1968 required developers to provide prospective buyers with the information they need to evaluate the property for sale. The Natural Gas Pipeline Safety Act of 1968 authorized the setting of safety procedures for pipeline transporting of flammable, toxic, and corrosive gases. The Radiation Control for Health and Safety Act of 1968 required standards for testing the radiation emissions of everything from X-ray equipment to color television sets.

While all of this was going on, the consumer movement was building organizations to gather information, mobilize public opinion, and lobby for legislation. Several existing groups—like the venerable National Consumers League—joined with labor unions to form the Consumer Federation of America in 1967. But "Lone Ranger" Ralph Nader continued to work apart from the consumer establishment (yet closely with Congress), aided by a growing staff of bright young lawyers. His parent organization, the Center for the Study of Responsive Law, harbored many small research projects bearing such names as the Center for Auto Safety, the Health Research Group, and the Congress Project (Nader's only foray into the realm of politics, consisting of a report on how effectively Congress—and individual members—performs its job). Groups of college students tagged as "Nader's Raiders" spent summers in Washington investigating the functioning of several executive agencies, most notably the Federal Trade Commission.

All of this activity was financed through Nader's personal speaking and writing fees, plus contributions solicited through a direct mail advertising apparatus (Public Citizen, Inc.) and grants from social activist private foundations. The Nader organization is credited with being the principal influence behind passage of the consumer protection bills in the areas of auto safety, meat and poultry inspection, gas pipeline safety, and radiation emissions. Nader and his lieutenants became masters of the new art of lobbying by agitation: creating as large a ruckus as possible through sensational exposés and press coverage. The press, always interested in a flamboyant story, was more than willing to cooperate. During the heady consumer boom of the late Sixties, hardly a week passed when a headline didn't scream "Nader Attacks Baby Food Additives," "Nader Urges Trust Action Against GM," or "Nader Charges Senator Betrayed Mine Workers."

THE NIXON YEARS

When Richard Nixon arrived in 1969, he appointed Virginia Knauer his special assistant for consumer affairs (following a very brief stint by the Good Housekeeping Institute's Willie Mae Rogers, who resigned under fire). Mrs. Knauer, long active in Republican women's circles, had been a Philadelphia councilman-at-large and director of the Pennsylvania Department of Consumer Protection. Two years later, the President's Committee on Consumer Interest was replaced by a White House Office of Consumer Affairs.

In 1973 the Office was transferred to HEW, with Mrs. Knauer still at the helm. Today it is primarily a clearinghouse for consumer complaints, but other functions include consumer education, monitoring the progress of consumer bills, prodding industry to provide better consumer protection, and acting as administration spokesman on consumer affairs. It is not a powerful consumer advocate or policy formulator, and the transfer from the White House to HEW was considered by many observers to be a demotion. In the drafting of a Nixon administration position on the proposed Consumer Protection Agency, Budget Director Roy Ash's opposition to the bill was more influential than Mrs. Knauer's support of it. Legislatively, the Nixon years did not maintain the breakneck pace of the Sixties, but several important consumer protection measures were signed into law in the early Seventies. The Fair Credit Reporting Act of 1970 gave citizens the right to inspect financial reports on themselves at credit bureaus, challenge inaccuracies, and learn to whom the reports had been distributed. The Postal Reorganization Act of 1970 banned the mailing of unordered merchandise. The 1970 amendments to the Federal Deposit Insurance Act prohibited the issuance of unrequested credit cards and limited the consumer's liability for fraudulent use of a lost or stolen card to $50. The Securities Investor Protection Act of 1970 offered protection to investors against the failure of brokerage houses. The Poison Prevention Packaging Act of 1970 authorized standards for child-proof medicine containers. The Lead-based Paint Poisoning Prevention Act of 1970 was aimed at stopping the lead poisoning of children who ate chips of old paint, especially in urban slum apartments. The Little Cigars Act of 1973 extended the 1965 ban on cigarette broadcast ads to cover cigars the size of cigarettes. The 1972 Motor Vehicle Information and Cost Savings Act authorized, among other things, minimum durability standards for front and rear auto bumpers. Perhaps the most significant consumer reform in this period, however, was the 1972 law that created the Consumer Product Safety Commission.

With the early Seventies came a rejuvenation of the Federal Trade Commission, which had long been a toothless watchdog of consumer interests. Its staff rarely initiated major investigations, but merely followed up on citizen complaints. Crippled by its own red tape and lacking statutory enforcement powers, the FTC took sixteen years to get the "Liver" out of Carter's Little Liver Pills, and nearly as long to force the makers of Geritol to stop promising to cure "tired blood." The commission's defects were glaringly revealed in two studies released in 1969—one by a Nader team (that included President Nixon's future son-in-law, Edward Finch Cox) and the other by an American Bar Association committee. These two very different groups arrived at a surprisingly similar verdict: overhaul the FTC or abolish it. The FTC's rebirth began under the brief tenure of Caspar Weinberger (who soon moved to the Office of Management and Budget and then became Secretary of HEW), and was accelerated by the appointment of Miles W. Kirkpatrick, the Philadelphia lawyer who had headed the ABA investigation.

The FTC began to act more vigorously in consumer matters. Consumer specialists were dispatched to regional offices to help develop new cases at the grass roots. Consumer groups were allowed for the first time to intervene on the public's behalf in FTC cases against corporations. The commission's Bureau of Competition launched new antitrust litigation against giants in the oil, cereal, and copying machine industries. The Bureau of Consumer Protection formulated requirements for factual substantiation of advertising claims, and began ordering companies to run corrective ads to atone for past deceptions. Congress gave the commission a new enforcement weapon, in the form of authority to secure federal court orders against deceptive trade practices that threaten public health and safety. (Previously, the commission's only weapon was the cease-and-desist order, which often went ignored through many rounds of legal appeals.) The commission gave a green light to the practice of "comparative advertising," in which a product's competitors are named in its ads.

Realizing the inefficiency of analyzing and passing judgment on each company's advertising and sales practices in a piecemeal fashion, the FTC began setting industry-wide trade regulations to spell out in advance what is and is not an allowable marketing tactic. (The commission's statutory power to impose these regulations was challenged in the courts, but was finally upheld.) The FTC drafted rules covering mail order sales (specifying allowable period of time for delivery of the ordered goods), door-to-door sales (setting a period during which the buyer can change his mind after the sale), and book clubs (regulation of the "negative option" plan, under which books are delivered unless the buyer says he doesn't want them). This faster pace is continuing under Lewis A. Engman, who became chairman in 1973, following a time at the White House as assistant director of the Domestic Council. Since 1970 the commission has gone after everything from misleading aspirin ads to trade practices at a Navajo trading post. It has launched major investigations of pyramid franchise schemes, misleading warranties, and unauthorized disclosure of consumers' credit reports. There is no corner of the marketplace that the FTC now feels to be outside its area of jurisdiction.

While the FTC has undeniably emerged from its pre-1970 lethargy, its effectiveness is still questioned by some consumer activists. They point out that the commission—in the interests of time and money—is frequently willing to let offenders off the hook with a "consent decree," a legal device under which an accused company promises it won't commit any of the sins enumerated in the FTC's complaint, but never admits that it committed the sins in the first place. Some FTC programs have a way of fading into the woodwork after they are announced with great ballyhoo. The advertising substantiation program, for example, has fallen far short of expectations, since most of the data submitted as proof turn out to be so voluminous, complex, and vague that the commission staff has no way to deal with the material. As is the case in other bureaucracies, FTC procedures of complaint, response, accusation, hearing, and final decision are slow-moving and involved. FTC defenders argue that the actual win-loss record of the commission is not as important as the general climate of surveillance. They claim that FTC forays against deceptive advertising have led to stronger self-policing of the advertising industry, which is ultimately more effective than random FTC complaints.

While the FTC tries to protect the consumer's pocketbook, the Consumer Product Safety Commission is working to protect his health and safety. The newest of the major consumer agencies, the CPSC is responsible for safe design and construction of an estimated 10,000 manufactured products, ranging from children's toys to mobile homes. According to Commission Chairman Richard Simpson (a former Commerce Department official and an engineer by training), "Our mission isn't to eliminate all risk, but all unreasonable risk." Acknowledging that people can always find a way to hurt themselves through misuse of a safely designed product, the commission is trying to make a dent in the statistics of 20 million annual injuries and 30,000 deaths attributed to consumer products. It is giving special attention to products that can be hazardous to children, such as toys, cribs, swimming pools, playground equipment, sliding glass doors, power lawnmowers, and gasoline-powered minibikes. The commission also sets flammability standards for everything from toys and clothing to carpets and building materials. The first citizen complaint filed with the commission was the professional football players' case against artificial turf, which they claimed caused orthopedic injuries and skin burns.

The CPSC does some of its own research and also relies on outside testing services. (One of its members is Lawrence Kushner, former deputy director of the National Bureau of Standards, one of the government's principal testing agencies.) It has also used accident reports from hospital emergency rooms and police stations to determine the frequency and seriousness of injuries resulting from various products. Actions that the commission can take range from a mild warning printed on a product to an outright sales ban (as has been leveled against some types of toy stoves and games with darts and arrows). It can recall products suspected of being hazardous and can order redesigning. It can also authorize consumer refunds and punitive actions— fines and jail terms—against manufacturers who flout commission rulings.

THE BUSINESS RESPONSE

The rise of consumerism in the mid-Sixties took American business by surprise. Mistaking consumer complaints for an indiscriminate attack on the institution of free enterprise, many trade associations in Washington responded with broad-brush counterattacks. Consumer advocates—even respected senators and representatives—were condemned as enemies of business, and every new piece of legislation was flatly opposed. But business began to change its tune when it saw the ease with which Congress was passing politically popular bills which the trade associations, by virtue of their outright opposition, had had little role in shaping.

In 1967 the U.S. Chamber of Commerce established an in-house consumer affairs committee, and in the next five years virtually every trade association in Washington followed suit. The purpose of these committees is twofold: publicizing each industry's voluntary actions to improve quality and service, and lobbying Congress and the consumer agencies to make federal regulation easier for business to live with. Many Washington offices of national corporations set up consumer affairs divisions, as did some of the leading public relations firms. (Carl Byoir and Associates sends its clients periodic reports on the status of consumer legislation and regulations.) Symptomatic of the changing business attitude toward consumerism was the 1973 move to Washington of the Council of Better Business Bureaus, which had long had a do-little image. Today it has become a positive force in consumer affairs, aided by education programs for businesses and a computerized consumer complaint system.

Corporations have seen that consumer activists are busy in state and local governments across the nation, pressing for consumer regulations that have not yet received a very hospitable reception on Capitol Hill. The dismaying prospect of hundreds of varied and overlapping state laws, each with different requirements, makes business amenable to federal legislation that would supersede state action. The quest for national legislation has led the American Insurance Association and State Farm Mutual Automobile Insurance Co. (the nation's largest automobile insurer) to press for federal no-fault insurance standards, to preempt the field from the more than twenty states that now have no-fault programs. (The national legislation is being opposed by a segment of the legal profession that has thrived on personal injury suits from auto accidents.)

After an impressive string of legislative victories in the late Sixties, Washington's consumer advocates and lobbies began pushing for a crowning achievement: creation of an independent Consumer Protection Agency (or Agency for Consumer Advocacy, as it is named in a Senate version of the legislation). Led on the Hill by Representative Benjamin S. Rosenthal (D-N.Y.) and Senator Abraham Ribicoff (D-Conn.), the CPA supporters are not satisfied with an Office of Consumer Affairs buried deep within the enormity of HEW. They want an agency that will be an unabashed, hard-hitting consumer advocate. The agency would intervene on the consumer's behalf in proceedings before the regulatory agencies—the FTC, FDA, Federal Communications Commission, Federal Power Commission, and most other agencies whose decisions will affect the citizen's position in the marketplace. In addition, the CPA would seek judicial review, in federal court, of these agencies' rulings. It would also have the power to obtain written responses to questions put to businesses pertaining to any matter affecting consumer health and safety. (One federal agency that would be off-limits to meddling by the CPA staff would be the National Labor Relations Board, which organized labor—which likes the status quo just fine—got exempted from both the House and Senate versions of the CPA bill.)

Corporate lobbyists have been active on both sides of the debate over creation of an independent Consumer Protection Agency. Most of them have opposed the legislation, arguing that consumers are protected adequately by consumer-oriented members of the regulatory commissions and don't need a spokesman to represent them before these bodies. This tack has been taken by such business groups and corporations as the U.S. Chamber of Commerce, the Grocery Manufacturers of America, the National Association of Manufacturers, Sears, Ford Motors, and General Mills. But many corporations support the legislation, including Quaker Oats, Montgomery Ward, Zenith, and Kimberly-Clark. Ralph Nader has thrown his personal influence and staff resources into the battle for the CPA.

After being kicked around Congress for more than five years, the CPA bill came close to passage in 1974. The House cleared it, but Senate conservatives mounted a filibuster, and supporters of the legislation narrowly missed invoking cloture to bring the issue to a vote. The bill was withdrawn, but its backers made another try under a new Congress in 1975 (with the prospect of Senate passage vastly improved by liberalization of the cloture rule). Debate over the CPA bill dramatized the Nixon and Ford administrations' internal dissension and ambivalence about consumer affairs in general. The White House position waffled from outright opposition to lukewarm support, but was never very clear. Gerald Ford opposed the legislation when he was in the House, and he continued to oppose it as President.

HERE TO STAY

In the last session of Congress, more than 200 consumer bills were introduced in the House and Senate. They covered an incredible array of issues: warranties, nutritional labeling, dating of perishable foods, school bus construction standards, vitamins, class action suits, children's television advertising, bottled water, and many, many more. Some of these bills were merely congressional plays to the grandstand of public opinion, and had little chance of passage. And some of them were attempts by Congress to strengthen authority already vested in one or more regulatory agencies.

The sheer volume of proposed consumer bills, however, attests to the fact that consumerism has taken its place in Washington alongside the interests of industry, agriculture, labor, transportation, housing, and health as one of the ongoing concerns of government. In time, consumer protection—like other governmental functions—may become bureaucratized, routinized, and ponderous. But for now, in its growing phase, it is a vigorous young giant astride the Washington scene.

23 THE BLACK PRESENCE

Washington is the center of black America.

Not solely on a basis of population, for there are half a dozen American cities with more Negro residents.

Not just for its role in equal rights, for more grass-roots work and suffering took place in such cities as Birmingham, Selma, Atlanta, and Memphis.

Nor has Washington been the birthplace of Afro-American music, art, and culture, which found more fertile soil in New Orleans and Chicago (for jazz), New York City (for dance and literature), or Detroit and Memphis (for rhythm-and-blues).

Washington is the center of black America today because it is where the power of the ballot box comes to rest. It is the political pressure point for 24 million Negro American citizens. At the end of 1974 there were more black members of Congress than ever before (eighteen in all—sixteen representatives, one delegate, and one senator).

Washington is the home of a larger number of influential, intellectual, and affluent black Americans than any other city. It has the highest proportion of black residents of any large city in the United States. The city itself (the District of Columbia) is 72 percent black. The Washington metropolitan area is 23 percent black. Predominantly black colleges in the District, led by venerable Howard University, enroll some 22,000 Negro students every year. And Washington is now the home of several black-oriented cultural organizations, like the D.C. Black Repertory Theatre and the Museum of African Art. All of this stands alongside a deep-rooted black social structure dating back 200 years to colonial America, and more recently infused with new-style activists, professionals, and political leaders from most of the nation's fifty states.

All of these factors account for the special significance of Washington to Negro Americans—a significance as much symbolic as concrete. It was in Washington that Lincoln signed the Emancipation Proclamation. Martin Luther King, Jr., conceived his "dream" in the South, but he came to Washington to enunciate it for all the world to hear, from the steps of the Lincoln Memorial. And it was in Washington that civil rights victories won in the South were cemented into federal law during the Sixties.

But Washington has always had trouble living up to its symbolic role as an oasis of Liberty and Justice for All. Until a series of court edicts in the Fifties opened all the District's public accommodations to blacks, the city was as segregated as any in the deep South. Negroes were not allowed in the city's finest hotels, restaurants, and theaters. Real estate covenants—tacit or explicit—prevented blacks from buying homes in the Washington suburbs as well as in the more prosperous areas of the District west of Rock Creek Park. Until the Forties, many federal office buildings were equipped with separate drinking fountains and restrooms for the limited number of black civil servants in the bureaucracy. Segregation was even enforced at the dedication of the Lincoln Memorial in 1922, at which black dignitaries, including those who spoke at the ceremony, were seated in a separate area across a road from the white audience. Negro Washington was, in the words of local historian Constance Green, a "secret city"—a mass of people whose experiences, attitudes, and customs were unknown to most white Washingtonians.

This situation was aggravated by the fact that, for a century (from the 1870s until 1974), Washingtonians—white and black—had little say in the administration of the District of Columbia. All the shots were called by four congressional committees, chaired until recently by southern congressmen and senators, who had no political incentive to serve their Washington "constituents" who couldn't vote. Today District residents enjoy some semblance of self-government, but the power of the purse is still held by Congress. Social activists—black and white—continue to call the District "the last colony."

VARIETY IN BLACK WASHINGTON

"Black Washington" is just as diversified as "white Washington." The 760,000 blacks of the Washington metropolitan area represent an infinite variety of attitudes, incomes, occupations, and aspirations. The black community includes intellectuals on college faculties. It includes young men and women working in drug control and tenant rights in the Shaw, Anacostia, and Adams-Morgan neighborhoods. It includes the mass of apolitical civil servants, secure in their bureaucratic jobs. It encompasses the "street scene" along the decaying corridors of 14th and 7th Streets—a world of numbers games, soul music, drug addiction, welfare checks, fortunetellers, and pimps with long white Cadillacs.

"Black Washington" is also the cliques of well-to-do lawyers and doctors, many of whose fathers and grandfathers were professionals before them. It covers the church establishment, ranging from the old-guard African Methodist Episcopal to Black Muslim. It contains the black business community of bankers, real estate developers, insurance agents, undertakers, and liquor dealers, whose values are much the same as those of white businessmen. Washington is the headquarters, too, of national civil rights lobbyists and administrators, who work for the Negro cause and equal opportunity for all minorities. It is home base for local politicians and rival factions vying for dominance in the District's new "home rule" government. "Black Washington" is rich and poor, but mostly it is middle class. It is composed of hundreds of thousands of Americans who go to work every day, raise their families, watch the Redskins and the Bullets on TV, and strive for a reasonably comfortable life.

About three-quarters of the Washington area's Negro citizens live in the District of Columbia, and the rest live mostly in the areas of Maryland's Prince George's and Montgomery Counties that lie close to the District line. While the proportion of blacks in the District has risen sharply over the past two decades—from about 35 percent in 1950 to 72 percent today—their proportion of the whole metropolitan area has held constant at about 23 percent since before 1920. The black proportion of the area's suburban population was a falling percentage from 1900 through the Sixties. Recently it has turned around, rising from about 6 percent at its low to 8 percent in 1974.

Some 15 percent of the District's black workers make their living in professional, managerial, and technical occupations—the highest percentage among blacks in the nation. This accounts for the relative well-being of about half of the city's black population. About 17 percent of D.C.'s Negro families earn more than $15,000 a year, and 3 percent have incomes over $25,000 (twice the national black average in that income bracket). More than 300 black families had incomes exceeding $50,000 in the early Seventies.

But nearly half of the District's black residents have incomes below $8,000, and it's difficult to live comfortably on that income in the inflation-ridden economy of the nation's capital. A profile of this group is essentially a description of the problems that plague every large American city—rising welfare costs, illegitimacy, slum housing, street crime. In 1972 half the black births in the District were out of wedlock (compared with 11 percent of the white births), and in 1970 nearly one-quarter of all the children in the city were in families that received some sort of public welfare payment. The low-income blacks account largely for the District's shocking infant mortality rate, one of the highest in the nation, and an incidence of venereal disease that is several times the national average. The problem of the undereducated poor in Washington is primarily the difficulty of finding enough unskilled jobs in a city where most of the work is white-collar.

A large portion of the black labor force works for the federal government, which offers a degree of job security unknown to blacks in cities whose economies are mostly industrial. While Washington Negroes traditionally held only low-level jobs in the federal bureaucracy, the civil rights push of the Sixties opened up an increasing number of middle- and upper-level administrative positions.

TOP BLACK OFFICIALS

During the New Frontier and Great Society days, there was a sudden appearance of black appointees in high federal offices. Robert Weaver became the first black Cabinet member and first Secretary of Housing and Urban Development. Andrew Hatcher was appointed associate press secretary to President Kennedy. Carl Rowan, now a columnist and television commentator, was made director of the United States Information Agency (and later ambassador to Finland). Andrew Brimmer was appointed to the Federal Reserve Board, and Thurgood Marshall became the first black justice of the Supreme Court.

The Nixon administration did not appoint Negroes to the highest government offices with the same vigor shown by Presidents Kennedy and Johnson (perhaps because President Nixon had difficulty finding qualified blacks who shared his more conservative positions on domestic policy). But he appointed an abundance of blacks to jobs carrying such titles as "deputy assistant secretary" and "deputy director" of this or that federal agency. Many of them are in charge of the "equal opportunity" divisions of their offices or are involved with minority affairs of another sort. The best-known of Nixon's black appointees, former CORE leader James Farmer, put in a brief stint as assistant secretary of Health, Education and Welfare, before resigning in disgruntlement. Economist Brimmer served at the Fed until the middle of 1974, when he accepted a professorship at the Harvard Business School.

President Ford selected a prominent black lawyer, William T. Coleman,

Jr., to be his Secretary of Transportation. Coleman, whose appointment was widely hailed as an ideal choice, is a Philadelphian with deep experience in civil rights and urban affairs, as well as corporate law. Among top black officials are HEW Assistant Secretary for Human Development Stanley B. Thomas, Jr.; HUD Assistant Secretary for Housing Management H. R. Crawford; Assistant Secretary of Transportation Benjamin O. Davis, Jr. (a former Army general); Jefferson Banks Young, on the U.S. Tariff Commission; Constance Newman, of the Consumer Product Safety Commission; John H. Powell, Jr., until early 1975 chairman of the Civil Rights Commission, of which Colston A. Lewis is a member; Benjamin L. Hooks, on the Federal Communications Commission; Air Force Lieutenant General Daniel (Chappie) James, Jr., deputy assistant secretary of defense for public affairs (and probably the best-known black military figure today); James R. Cowan, assistant secretary of defense for health and environment; and National Labor Relations Board member Howard Jenkins, Jr., a leading labor lawyer. There are six Negroes serving as American ambassadors: W. Beverly Carter, Jr. (Tanzania); C. Clyde Ferguson (U.S. representative to the United Nations Economic and Social Council, former dean of the Howard law school, former ambassador to Uganda); David B. Bolen (Botswana and Lesotho), who replaced another black ambassador, Charles Nelson; John E. Reinhardt (Nigeria); Terence Todman (Guinea); and O. Rudolph Aggrey (Senegal and Gambia).

The White House aide who acts as President Ford's (and previously President Nixon's) liaison with black national leadership, consultant on black affairs, and talent scout is Special Assistant Stanley S. Scott, who is assisted by John Calhoun. Scott, a former UPI reporter, once got honorable mention in the Pulitzer competition for his coverage of the assassination of black separatist Malcolm X in 1965. He is a member of a prominent Atlanta, Georgia, family that owns several black weekly newspapers, including the Atlanta *World,* a conservative paper that has traditionally supported GOP candidates.

BLACKS IN CONGRESS

Capitol Hill is the home of the Black Caucus—an informal discussion and strategy group of seventeen black representatives from every part of the country, from Georgia to Michigan, New York to California. On the Senate side of the Hill, Edward W. Brooke, Republican of Massachusetts, could hold his own black caucus in a telephone booth, being the only Negro member of the Senate. (Brooke was raised in a comfortably well-off Washington family, graduating from the District's Dunbar High School and Howard University.) The Capitol also houses an office for a nonvoting representative from the District, Delegate Walter E. Fauntroy. The black congressmen most important to the people of the District are Representative Charles C. Diggs (D-Mich.), chairman of the House District Committee; committee members Delegate Fauntroy, Representative Ronald Dellums (D-Cal.), and Representative Charles Rangel (D-N.Y.); and House District Appropriations Subcommittee member Representative Louis Stokes (D-O.). It is these men—and their white committee colleagues, especially District Appropriations chairman William Natcher (D-Ky.)—who draft the laws and budget under which the District operates.

Fifteen years ago, it was difficult to find a Negro employed on a Capitol Hill staff in anything but a secretarial job, and even black secretaries were few. Today there are some thirty black men and women—many of them lawyers— in professional jobs on the staffs of senators and Senate committees. Their salaries range from about $10,000 to $30,000, and their titles include "legislative assistant," "caseworker," "urban specialist," and "document clerk." Some senators complain that they can't entice qualified blacks to work on the Hill for salaries substantially below what they could earn in corporations and law firms. The black professional corps on the House side of the Hill is considerably larger, with most of the aides working for black members.

LOCAL AND NATIONAL LEADERS

Since there was no elective politics in the District until the late Sixties, there were no genuine D.C. politicians. The role of politician was filled by black civic activists, ministers, appointed officials of the D.C. government, and Negroes prominent in other fields. With the coming of "home rule," however, many of these people have emerged as political leaders.

The most visible elected official of the D.C. government is Mayor Walter E. Washington, who served as appointed "mayor" from 1967 to 1974, when he became the District's first elected mayor in more than a century. Other blacks well known in local politics include Delegate Fauntroy, a minister and political rival of Mayor Washington, whose power base is the economically depressed Shaw area of the city; City Council Chairman Sterling Tucker, a past executive director of the Washington Urban League; City Councilman Julius Hobson, a perennial gadfly, advocate of statehood for the District, and the first elected school board member in 1968; and Clifford Alexander, Jr., a Harvard University and Yale Law School graduate, former counsel to President Johnson, former chairman of the Equal Employment Opportunity Commission, a partner in the prestigious firm of Arnold and Porter, and a strong challenger to Walter Washington in the Democratic primary for mayor.

Then there's City Councilman Marion Barry, Jr., an alumnus of the Student Nonviolent Coordinating Committee (SNCC), founder of Pride, Inc. (a grass-roots organization now run by his wife, Mary, that manages inner-city businesses with manpower from the ghetto) and former president of the D.C. school board; D.C. Human Resources Director Joseph Yeldell; labor leader Bill Lucy, secretary-treasurer of the union of state, county, and municipal employees (and chairman of Walter Washington's campaign for mayor); City Councilwoman Willie Hardy, a key figure in far Northeast Washington; lawyer Charles T. Duncan, a close friend and adviser to Mayor Washington; statehood advocate and school board member Charles Cassell, an architect by profession; the Reverend Douglas Moore, City Councilman, teacher, itinerant urban preacher, onetime radical activist, and founder of the Black United Fund; Julian Dugas, a lawyer, former school board member, a confidant of Walter Washington, and power-behind-the-throne at city hall (with the title of City Administrator); and City Councilman John Wilson, a veteran of SNCC who managed Walter Fauntroy's first campaign and worked for Georgia legislator Julian Bond.

The national civil rights organizations are active behind the scenes in Washington, pressing Congress for stiffer laws to guarantee political and economic equality, and pressing the Executive Branch for vigorous enforcement. M. Carl Holman, a former English professor and federal official, is president of the National Urban Coalition. Ronald Brown is director of the Washington office of the National Urban League. James O. Gibson, a race relations consultant at the Potomac Institute and onetime executive secretary of the Atlanta, Georgia, NAACP, is chairman of the D.C. Bicentennial Commission, which plans to make its 1976 activities meaningful to black Americans. The National Welfare Rights Organization, which has been in the forefront of the fight for a guaranteed annual income, is based in Washington and headed by executive director Ms. Johnnie Tillmon. The National Council of Negro Women is led by Dorothy Height, a social worker who has held numerous advisory positions in the federal government, ranging from the State and Defense departments to presidential commissions on employment of the handicapped and the status of women. One of the most respected men on the national civil rights scene, Clarence Mitchell, Jr., has for years directed the Washington bureau of the NAACP. He was so ubiquitous in the halls of Congress during the civil rights legislative battles of the Sixties that he was dubbed the "101st Senator." Mitchell's family is something of a dynasty in Maryland black politics. His brother, Representative Parren Mitchell, is a Democratic congressman from Baltimore. His wife, Juanita Jackson Mitchell, is a former head of the state NAACP. One of his sons, Clarence M. Mitchell, is a Maryland state senator.

PRESENT AT THE CREATION

There has been a black presence in Washington dating from, literally, the creation of the District. One member of the six-man team that conceived the city plan for the new capital in 1791 was Benjamin Banneker, a sixty-year-old black mathematician, inventor, and astronomer. When the mercurial leader of the D.C. planning committee, Pierre L'Enfant, quit and ran off with the maps, Banneker's remarkable memory enabled him and Andrew Ellicott to reconstruct the plan. (Born a free man in Maryland, Banneker was the grandson of an English woman who came to America as an indentured servant and later, after buying her own freedom and acquiring two slaves, married one of the slaves.)

Although Washington was the heart of the Federal Union, it always had a southern flavor. Slaves were owned in the District even after the Civil War began, until a congressional act of emancipation in 1862. In the ante-bellum decades, free black residents were repressed by severe curfews and occupational prohibitions, but many managed nonetheless to make comfortable livings as craftsmen, barbers, restaurateurs, and hoteliers. The end of the Civil War saw the founding of Howard University and Freedmen's Hospital, the enfranchising of black citizens (short-lived, like the voting rights of all D.C. citizens), and the arrival of a succession of black senators and congressmen, totaling twenty-two by the end of the century. Washington developed an elite of black intellectuals, professionals, government leaders, and businessmen second to none in America. Negroes made fortunes in business, and some of them were members of the then exclusive Board of Trade. Most, if not all, of the District's public accommodations were open to all citizens, regardless of race. A few impressive-sounding, but powerless, federal positions—such as register of the treasury, marshal of the District, and D.C. recorder of deeds—were the exclusive preserves of black appointees, including such notables as abolitionist and diplomat Frederick Douglass and former Mississippi Senator

Blanche K. Bruce. At Washington's Georgetown University in 1874, a black Jesuit priest named Patrick Healy (the son of a Georgia slave and a white planter) was made president by a board of trustees that was probably unaware of his racial origins.

But as federal enforcement of civil rights laws diminished and finally ceased in the 1880s and 1890s, Washington lapsed into the patterns of Jim Crow segregation that spread across the South. Not only were blacks barred from privately owned hotels, restaurants, and theaters, but they were even forced to use separate-and-unequal facilities in public parks, schools, and federal office buildings. Except for a few encouraging but abortive improvements in D.C. race relations during the New Deal and the Truman administrations, blacks led lives entirely apart from D.C.'s white majority until integration of all public accommodations in the middle Fifties.

This very integration has been a prime factor in the drain of Washington's white majority to the surrounding suburbs, leaving D.C.'s Negroes with almost as little contact with whites as they had experienced under segregation. To say that blacks lived lives apart from whites does not mean, however, that they all led lives of deprivation. Many did, of course, especially the wretchedly poor alley dwellers who crowded into the Southwest, Foggy Bottom, and Capitol Hill neighborhoods during the northward migration of rural southern blacks that began after World War I and continued unabated into the Fifties.

HOWARD UNIVERSITY

But all through the decades of segregation, Washington's black middle and upper-middle classes continued to nurture their long tradition of superior education and cultural achievement. Howard University, a national bastion of black learning, attracted to its faculty some of the most outstanding black intellectuals in America. Literary critic Alain Locke—Harvard graduate, Rhodes scholar, and leading figure in the "Harlem Renaissance" of the Twenties—was for many years chairman of the philosophy department at Howard. Carter Woodson, sometimes called "the father of black studies," was the mainstay of the history department. The sociology department was anchored by the late E. Franklin Frazier, whose studies of the "black bourgeoisie" were critical of the black middle class's neglect of their less fortunate brothers.

The dean of the Howard law school from 1939 to 1946 was William H. Hastie, the first Negro appointed to a federal judgeship (in the Virgin Islands) and later a federal court of appeals judge in Philadelphia (he retired in 1971). Dr. Charles Drew, a native of Washington and father of the blood bank, taught at the Howard medical school. Ralph Bunche was chairman of Howard's political science department before beginning his long career in international affairs. Former Howard President James Nabrit, Jr., a noted civil rights attorney, served as a member of the U.S. delegation to the United Nations during the Sixties. John Hope Franklin, an outstanding historian at the University of Chicago, taught at Howard earlier in his career. Other illustrious Howard scholars, some of whom still teach occasionally from semiretirement, include poet and literary critic Sterling A. Brown; historian Rayford W. Logan; Todd Duncan, the great opera singer (and creator of the role of Gershwin's "Porgy"), who has taught music at Howard since 1931;

Mercer Cook, who interrupted his romance languages teaching during the Sixties to be American ambassador to Niger, Senegal, and Gambia; and Flemmie P. Kittrell, a renowned home economist who served as a United Nations nutrition consultant to several developing nations, including India, Liberia, and the Congo.

Equally remarkable is the roster of Howard alumni who went on to fame in many fields. Sociologist Frazier studied at Howard, as did D.C. Mayor Walter E. Washington and black activist Stokely Carmichael. So did Senator Brooke of Massachusetts, actor-playwright Ossie Davis, playwright-poet Imamu Baraka (a.k.a. LeRoi Jones, author of *The Dutchman* and *The Slave*), and Claude Brown, the ex-juvenile delinquent from Harlem whose acclaimed novel *Manchild in the Promised Land* was published in 1965, the same year he graduated from Howard at the age of twenty-eight. Among the best-known graduates of the Howard law school are Supreme Court Justice Thurgood Marshall, U.S. District Court Judge William B. Bryant, and U.S. Court of Appeals Judge Spottswood Robinson III, onetime dean of the school. Some of Howard's outstanding alumni are obscure, even if their achievements aren't. Take, for example, James Bland (1854–1911). The son of an examiner in the U.S. Patent Office, Bland studied music at Howard and later became a successful minstrel comedian and songwriter of such ditties as "In the Evening by the Moonlight," "Oh, Dem Golden Slippers," and "Carry Me Back to Old Virginny," which was adopted by Virginia as its state anthem in 1940.

Howard gave the city an intellectual tone that attracted creative black men to the nation's capital. Paul Laurence Dunbar, the first nationally famous poet who focused on black themes and dialect, worked at the Library of Congress and lived in the LeDroit Park neighborhood of the District (above Florida Avenue, just south of Howard) in the late 1890s, a few years before his death at age thirty-four. Freedmen's Hospital, affiliated with Howard, served as a similar training ground and magnet for the nation's finest black physicians and medical researchers. One of these was Dr. Daniel Hale Williams, who is credited with performing in 1893 the first successful heart surgery, at the Provident Hospital he had founded in Chicago. Dr. Williams taught at Freedmen's from 1894 to 1898.

The brightest star in the Freedmen's galaxy was Dr. Charles Drew, chief surgeon there during the Forties, as well as professor of surgery at the Howard medical school. Born and raised in Washington, Drew attended the elite Dunbar High School, the city's only college preparatory school for Negroes, a school whose alumni list reads like a "Who's Who" of black America: Senator Edward Brooke, Delegate Fauntroy, former HUD Secretary Robert Weaver, critic Sterling Brown, Judge William Hastie, former Ambassador Mercer Cook (the son of Washington composer and band leader Will Marion Cook), and many others. Like his classmates Hastie and Cook, Drew went on to Amherst College, where he was an All-American halfback and captain of the track team. After taking his medical degree at McGill University in Canada and a short teaching stint at Howard, Drew joined Dr. John Scudder of Columbia University in blood research. In 1940 they discovered that plasma could be separated from the blood and stored for later use. Soon thereafter, Drew went to England to set up the first blood bank, an innovation credited with saving the lives of thousands of Allied soldiers during World War II. Until his death in an automobile accident in 1950,

Drew taught surgery at Howard to many young doctors who later achieved prominence, including Dr. LaSalle D. Leffall, chief of surgery at Howard, and Dr. Jack White, director of Howard's Cancer Center. Drew's widow, Lenore, still lives in the District, where she teaches at the Washington Technical Institute. Of their four children, one daughter is a housewife, another is a neurobiologist at the National Institutes of Health, another is a lawyer with the NAACP's Legal Defense Fund, and his son teaches school in the District.

A DIFFERENT STYLE

But far from the ivory towers of Howard University there has always been another part of black Washington that derives its vitality from the viscera rather than the cerebrum. It is the black Washington of the common man. Bars and shops along 7th Street and 14th Street. Playground basketball and sandlot football. Stage shows at the old Howard Theatre on T Street. This was, and is, the black Washington of blues bands, the daily numbers payoff, poolrooms, and storefront churches. This was the Washington of Bishop C. M. (Sweet Daddy) Grace and Elder Lightfoot Solomon Michaux—the "Happy Am I" preacher whose Georgia Avenue Church of God sermons on radio station WJSV ("Willingly Jesus Suffered for Victory") and Griffith Stadium baptisms were the ultimate in grass-roots religion during the depression. Going back to the 1890s, this was the Washington where Bill (Bojangles) Robinson worked as a stableboy and danced on the sidewalks for pennies, years before he made movies with Shirley Temple and was billed as "The King of Tap Dancers."

Most of Washington's Negro intellectuals scorned, at least ignored, this subculture of their hometown. One who didn't was Jean Toomer, who was born and raised in the District and educated at the University of Wisconsin and City College of New York. (One of Toomer's grandfathers was P. B. S. Pinchback, a black governor of Louisiana during Reconstruction.) He wrote of the honky-tonk scene on 7th Street in his poetry and in his novel Cane, which sold only 500 copies upon publication in 1923 but is revered today as a literary masterpiece. Toomer, a light-complexioned man whose intellectual tastes were far-ranging (including the philosophy of Russian mystic Gurdjieff), lived most of his life either in Europe or among the Quakers of Bucks County, Pennsylvania, and he wrote very little after Cane.

Another young Washingtonian who liked this side of the city was Edward Kennedy (Duke) Ellington, a son of middle-class Washington parents. After turning down a scholarship to study art at Pratt Institute, Ellington became a sign painter and jazz pianist. He went to New York City in 1923, ended up a few years later at the famed Cotton Club, and the rest is history. Black Washington has always been good to jazz musicians, offering them encouragement on their way to the top and solace when their stars are fading fast. If you knew your way around the stage theaters and small nightclubs of Washington in the Thirties, you might have come across little-known singers Ella Fitzgerald and Pearl Bailey, or one named Billy Eckstine, who won an amateur contest at the Howard Theatre in 1934, before becoming a famed vocalist and band leader. Or you might have come across a down-and-out Ferdinand (Jelly Roll) Morton, who during the late Thirties ran an obscure D.C. nightclub and recorded jazz piano and reminiscences for the music archives of the Library of Congress.

These people, like popular singers Marvin Gaye and Roberta Flack (a onetime D.C. teacher who rose to prominence singing at the Mr. Henry's nightclub on Capitol Hill) are some of the "favorite sons" and "favorite daughters" of black Washington. So is jazz pianist Billy Taylor, the son of a D.C. dentist. There are many others in many different fields. The man who was the Army's highest-ranking black officer until his retirement in 1974 is Major General Frederic E. Davison, a native Washingtonian who was once commanding general of the 8th Infantry in Europe. (Davison was slated to become Mayor Washington's principal administrative aide, but withdrew from consideration after it was revealed that he hadn't filed D.C. tax returns for several years in the mid-Sixties.) In athletics, there are light heavyweight world champion Bob Foster; pro golfer Lee Elder (the first black to qualify for the elite Masters tournament), who used to teach at D.C.'s Langston public course; young Cornelius ("Flamboyant") Greene, the black quarterback who went from Dunbar High to Ohio State, whose team he led to a Rose Bowl victory in his sophomore year. Washington's reputation as one of the nation's richest veins of basketball talent is amply upheld by such pro greats as Elgin Baylor, Dave Bing, and Austin Carr, and collegiate star Adrian Dantley of Notre Dame.

WHO'S WHO TODAY

The composition of the local black leadership today is not essentially different from its traditional shape. It consists of the most prominent educators, doctors, lawyers, businessmen, journalists, ministers, politicians, and a smattering of arts supporters, civil rights activists, and scions of old families respected as much for their ancestry as for achievement.

The black educational establishment of Washington consists primarily of the professors and administrators of Howard, whose president is James Cheek; Washington Technical Institute, where Cleveland L. Dennard is president; and Federal City College and D.C. Teachers College, both of which are headed by Wendell Russell. All four are public colleges funded largely by the federal government. Another Washington-based college with a substantial Negro enrollment is the Antioch School of Law, whose dean is a black woman, Jean Camper Cahn.

There is increasing concern in the black community about the declining quality of Howard University. Its enrollment is dropping, as is the academic preparation level of its entering classes (both situations being due, like the drain of top black professors, to the competition of newly integrated white colleges). Instructors complain of chronic absenteeism and apathy among their students, and Howard's law graduates have a high rate of failure of the D.C. bar exam. The college's administration believes a large part of the problem is the tight-fisted budget Congress gives the school. Other observers feel that Howard must make a choice between being an open-admission remedial school or a top-flight university that imposes tough academic standards.

The quality of the D.C. public school system, whose enrollment is about 97 percent black, has fallen so drastically in recent years that many well-to-do black families prefer to send their children to such private schools as Sidwell Friends, Georgetown Day School, Maret and St. Albans, or to boarding schools in New England. There is hope, however, that the public schools can make a comeback under the forceful leadership of the black superintendent, Barbara Sizemore. But hope was dimmed by a 1974 power struggle between Mrs. Sizemore and the school board over the superintendent's proposal that the budget be trimmed through sizable layoffs of teachers and administrators.

THE BENCH AND BAR

About one-third of the District's local judges—on the D.C. Superior Court and Court of Appeals—are blacks. Negro members of the District's federal courts are the above-mentioned Appeals Judge Spottswood Robinson III and District Court Judge William Bryant, who is joined on the lower bench by black judges Barrington D. Parker, Aubrey Robinson, and Joseph Waddy. Supreme Court Justice Thurgood Marshall first came to the public's attention through his work two decades ago on the historic *Brown* school desegregation suit in 1954. Before his appointment to the High Court in 1967, Marshall had been a federal appeals court judge and U.S. Solicitor General.

The best-known black lawyers in Washington today include several former public officials whose government experience and contacts have been valuable to their clients. There is, for example, Hobart Taylor, Jr., a former aide to President Lyndon Johnson and a past director of the Export-Import Bank, whose clients include overseas interests; Samuel C. Jackson, a former assistant secretary of HUD; the aforementioned Clifford Alexander, Jr., of the firm Arnold and Porter; Vincent Cohen, the first black partner at the prominent firm of Hogan and Hartson and manager of Alexander's mayoral campaign; and Patricia Harris, a former Justice Department lawyer, ambassador to Luxembourg, alternate delegate to the U.N., Howard law school dean, and today a partner in the prominent firm of Fried, Frank, Harris, Shriver and Kampelman.

Marjorie Lawson, a former civil rights adviser to Senator John F. Kennedy and a D.C. juvenile court judge, practices with her husband Belford V. Lawson, Jr., in the firm of Lawson and Lawson. Herbert O. Reid was formerly dean of the Howard law school. Tyrone Brown is general counsel to the Post-Newsweek broadcasting stations in Washington. Charles T. Duncan, son of Todd Duncan and a former District corporation counsel, is now dean of the Howard law school. A young black couple with an unmistakably bright future in law are Wesley S. Williams, Jr., and his wife Karen, who is the daughter of Judge William H. Hastie. The son of a Washington lawyer, Williams is an associate at the high-powered D.C. firm of Covington and Burling. Mrs. Williams clerked at the Supreme Court for Associate Justice Marshall in 1974–75.

MEDICINE

As has been the case for more than a century, most of Washington's leading black physicians today are associated with Howard and its teaching hospital. (In 1975 Howard opened a totally new hospital on Georgia Avenue and dropped the name Freedmen's, calling it the Howard University Hospital.)

The leading Negro doctors include Dr. Marion Mann, dean of the Howard medical school, and longtime medical professors Drs. Paul Cornely and W. Montague Cobb. The corps of black surgeons includes Dr. Burke Syphax, former chief of surgery at Freedmen's and chairman of Howard's department of surgery; Dr. William Funderburk; the aforementioned Drs. Leffall and

White; and Dr. Samuel Bullock. (Dr. Bullock was a lifelong friend of Dr. Charles Drew, and survived the 1950 auto crash that was fatal to Drew, who was driving a group of D.C. physicians to a meeting in Atlanta.) Drs. George Jones and C. Warfield Clark are well known in urology, and Dr. Roland Scott and his student Dr. Angella Ferguson are pediatricians who have been instrumental in sickle-cell anemia research at Howard. Other well-known pediatricians are Dr. Blanche Bourne and Dr. Nolan Owens.

Among the leading black internists are Dr. Lewis Atkinson and Dr. Edward Mazique. Dr. Henry Wicker, who teaches eye surgery at George Washington University medical school, and Dr. Pearl Watson are considered top ophthalmologists. One of the pioneering black psychiatrists is longtime Howard professor Dr. E. Y. Williams, now retired. Other noted psychiatrists include Dr. Charles Prudhomme, Dr. Frances Welsing, Dr. Eva Townes, and Dr. Alyce Gullattee. Other black physicians prominent in their fields are ear-nose-and-throat specialist Dr. C. David Hinton, urologist Dr. Frank Jones, obstetrician Dr. Alvin F. Robinson, and Dr. Hartford Burwell, an elderly doctor who once owned one of the three private hospitals that treated Negroes in the days when hospitals in the District were segregated.

In some old black families, careers in medicine are a proud tradition passed from generation to generation, and some families have several siblings who all became doctors. Dr. C. Herbert Marshall, Jr., an elderly physician who lives and practices on P Street in Georgetown, is the son of a successful physician and scion of a family that has had extensive Georgetown property holdings for decades. The Clark family—brothers Charles H. and John F. J. and sister Harriette (Chambliss)—are all physicians and practice together. The most awesome couple in black medical circles are orthopedic surgeon Dr. Charles Epps and pediatrician Dr. Roselyn Epps, who married after finishing their undergraduate and medical studies at Howard. He is chief of orthopedic surgery at Howard, and she is director of the D.C. division of Maternal and Child Health. The son of a schoolteacher and a housewife, Charles worked his way through college as a cab driver, railroad porter, laborer, and waiter. Roselyn was born into a distinguished family of southern educators. Her father was president of Savannah (Georgia) State College, her mother was an elementary school principal and college instructor, and her maternal grandfather was the first Negro graduate of Brown University and later president of Alabama State College.

Relative to the other professions, there are very few black architects in Washington. The most prominent black firm is Bryant and Bryant (headed by Charles I. and Robert E. Bryant), whose 1973 receipts totaled about $1 million.

RELIGIOUS LEADERS

The church establishment has always been very important to the black community, dating from the days when it provided surrogate political leadership before the rise of black electoral strength. This leadership was evident as early as the Reconstruction era, when the first Negro U.S. senator—Hiram Revels (R-Miss.)—and an early congressman—Richard H. Cain (R-S.C.)—were ministers. The power base of the late Representative Adam Clayton Powell, Jr. (D-N.Y.), was the enormous Harlem congregation of the Abyssinian Baptist Church. Despite the generally waning influence of organized religion in the lives of Negroes as well as whites, the church leadership continues to play an active role in local Washington politics. Channing Phillips—the first Negro ever placed in nomination for presidential candidacy (a "favorite son" gesture of the D.C. delegation to the Democratic convention in 1968)—is a minister, and so is D.C. Congressional Delegate Walter E. Fauntroy, who still preaches every Sunday at the New Bethel Baptist Church. When Walter Washington announced his candidacy in the District's 1974 mayoral contest, it was no coincidence that the dais and audience at the press conference were packed with black ministers, whose support Washington knew to be valuable to his campaign.

Among the black clergymen who are prominent in local civic affairs are the Reverend Jerry A. Moore, Jr., a member of the D.C. City Council and pastor of the Nineteenth Street Baptist Church (and a Republican, a rarity in local black politics); the Reverend David H. Eaton, minister of All Souls Unitarian Church and host of a local TV talk show; the Reverend Theodore S. Ledbetter, of the Plymouth Congregational Church; and Bishop Smallwood E. Williams, of the fundamentalist Bible Way Church. Until his death in 1974, the Reverend E. Franklin Jackson, of the John Wesley AME Zion Church, was one of the mainstays of the local civil rights establishment.

Although much less numerous than the Baptists and Methodists, the 75,000 black Catholics of the Washington diocese (D.C. and suburban Maryland) comprise about 20 percent of the diocese's total membership and are pressing for a more distinct identity and leadership structure. They have a crucial stake in keeping open the inner-city parochial schools, which offer an appealing alternative to the D.C. public schools. Bishop Eugene A. Marino, auxiliary bishop of the Roman Catholic Archdiocese of Washington, was the youngest bishop in the nation and one of only three black bishops when he was elected at the age of forty in 1974. One of the highest-ranking black Episcopalians in the nation is Bishop John T. Walker, suffragan bishop (second in command) of the Washington diocese. Despite the fact that his congregation is almost entirely white, Bishop Walker takes a deep interest in black civic affairs. He spoke before congressional committees in favor of home rule legislation and supported the antidrug programs of Hassan Jeru-Ahmed's controversial Blackman's Development Center.

The Black Muslim community in Washington is tiny compared to the Christian denominations, but it has a cohesiveness unmatched by other faiths. Its leader is the Reverend Lonnie Shabazz, onetime chairman of the Atlanta University mathematics department and now minister of Muhammad's Mosque No. 4. Washington also has a splinter group of Hanafi (Orthodox) Moslems. Their existence was unknown to most Washingtonians, black or white, until a January day in 1973 when several assailants entered their religious center and killed seven members of the sect (five of them small children) in the worst mass murder in Washington history. Four Black Muslims from Philadelphia were convicted in the murder, the alleged motive being revenge for Hanafi criticism of Black Muslim leader Elijah Muhammad. (The scene of the crime was a large house, in a pleasant neighborhood on upper 16th Street, which the sect rented from basketball star Kareem Abdul-Jabbar, a Hanafi member.)

THE BUSINESS ESTABLISHMENT

Despite the high percentage of Negro population in the District, black business is still small potatoes. Fewer than a tenth of all District businesses are owned by Negroes, and they account for only about 4 percent of the city's total business revenue. The most substantial black-controlled business is the forty-year-old Industrial Bank of Washington, which ranks fifth in assets among black banks nationally (about $39 million) and first in profits (about $668,000 in 1972). Now headed by B. Doyle Mitchell, son of founder Jesse H. Mitchell, Industrial had until recently a very conservative lending policy toward minority individuals and businesses. By comparison, Independence Federal Savings and Loan, founded in 1968, is the leader among D.C. savings institutions in the percentage of assets loaned to inner-city homeowners for mortgages—around 85 percent. Headed by William Fitzgerald, Independence has deposits of about $23 million. The smallest black commercial bank is United National Bank, headed by Samuel L. Foggie, a former Industrial Bank manager. One of Washington's newer black-controlled financial institutions is Community Federal Savings and Loan, which opened in 1974. Its president is Orlando W. Darden, a real estate executive who was the city's first black mortgage banker. The new Hemisphere National Bank also has substantial black representation in management and ownership.

The largest of D.C.'s nonbanking Negro businesses is Capitol City Liquor Company, a wholesale dealership with annual sales of about $12 million. It is headed by Chester C. Carter, a former U.S. deputy chief of protocol and ex-executive with the Seagram distilling company. William T. (Tommy) Syphax, who twenty-five years ago started the Arlington, Virginia, construction and real estate management companies that bear his name, now grosses about $8 million from the two firms. The only black-owned auto dealership in the Washington area is Wilson-McIntosh Buick-Opel Inc., with annual sales of about $6 million in 1973. Ed Feggans closed his Oldsmobile franchise— D.C.'s first black-owned auto dealership—in 1974, citing the inner-city location, energy crisis, and employee theft as contributing factors to the failure. Other major black-owned firms are Manhattan Laundry and Dry Cleaning; Capitol Cab taxi cooperative; Big V supermarkets; Clean-Rite Maintenance Company; Greenwood's Transfer and Storage; and John R. Pinkett, Inc., a thirty-seven-employee real estate and insurance company headed by D. C. Board of Higher Education chairwoman Flaxie Pinkett, whose father founded the company in 1932. One of the most successful black funeral homes is McGuire's, owned by R. Grayson McGuire, whose father founded it in 1912. (The McGuires are a Catholic family whose Washington roots go back four generations, including a member of the first graduating class from Howard and the owner of one of D.C.'s first black pharmacies.)

There are several black consulting firms in Washington, much of whose revenues come from government contracts in urban affairs studies: A. L. Nellum and Associates; the BLK Group, directed by cofounder Marie Barksdale; One America Inc., headed by Elaine B. Jenkins (whose husband, Howard Jenkins, Jr., is a member of the National Labor Relations Board); Sam Harris Associates (headed by Samuel E. Harris, who ran for D.C. mayor as an independent); and the National Institute for Community Development, headed by Larry Brailsford. One of the city's most successful public relations firms is

Ofield Dukes and Associates. A former political aide on the Hill, Dukes has done minority relations counseling for the likes of AT&T and the National Bankers Association, and regular P.R. for such clients as the Washington Bullets basketball team and Anheuser-Busch.

A list of leading Negro businessmen would include Emmett J. Rice, senior vice president of the National Bank of Washington; Bill Washington, head of Dimensions Unlimited, one of the biggest producers of rock-'n'-roll and soul music concerts in the Washington area; Cornelius C. Pitts, who owns Pitts Motor Hotel, the largest black-owned inn in Washington; Berkeley Burrell, president of the National Business League and proprietor of a dry-cleaning company and a black greeting-card firm; real estate executive William S. Harps; Theodore R. Hagans, Jr., who has six firms engaged in real estate development and sales management; and Ed Murphy, proprietor of Ed Murphy's Supper Club and principal in the development of a black-owned hotel to be built near Howard University.

BLACKS IN THE MEDIA

There are probably more black journalists at work in Washington, on mass circulation newspapers and in broadcast stations, than in any city in America. The "dean" of this contingent is Simeon Booker, bureau chief of the Johnson Publishing Company (*Ebony* and *Jet,* among other magazines) and a Group W Radio commentator. The second black Nieman Fellow at Harvard, Booker joined the staff of the Washington *Post* in 1952 as its first black reporter and moved to Johnson two years later. The best-known black journalists in Washington include syndicated columnists Carl Rowan (who appears in the *Star*) and William Raspberry (in the *Post*). Both local papers have an unusually large number of black reporters, and the *Post*'s Dorothy Gilliam and Robert Maynard have editorial responsibilities. Top-ranking blacks at the *Star* are Warren Howard, a former assistant city editor who now selects stories to put on the *New York Times* service wire, and Bernie Boston, the paper's chief photographer. Blacks are highly visible as anchormen and reporters at all of the local television stations. The evening news program is co-anchored at WTOP by Max Robinson; at WRC by Jim Vance and "roving anchorman" Fred Thomas; and at WMAL by Paul Berry. Also prominent on the local airwaves are TV newswomen Angela Owens, J. C. Hayward, Maureen Bunyan, and Carol Randolph.

The Washington bureaus of all the major networks have black correspondents, including ABC's Bill Matney (a former NBC White House reporter and twelve-year veteran of TV news), CBS's Bernard Shaw and Harold Walker (who first appeared on Washington station WTOP-TV in 1963), and NBC's Gordon Graham. Some of Washington's black journalists and federal press information aides are members of the Capital Press Club, founded in 1944, in an era when blacks were excluded from the National Press Club as well as the press facilities in the Senate and House.

The white news media's awakening of interest in black affairs during the Sixties has lessened the community's dependence on the black press as its principal source of daily news. But blacks can still get fuller accounts of black-oriented happenings from the Washington *Afro-American* and neighborhood tabloids like the *Capital Spotlight, Observer,* and *Informer* (which is published by Calvin Rolark, a black activist who heads the D.C. Black United

Fund, a fund-raising drive for inner-city social services). Among the most widely read magazines in black Washington are *Ebony* and *Jet,* for which reporter Fannie Granton covers D.C. social affairs and travels with the First Lady on campaign and diplomatic trips. Washington's four black-operated radio stations—WOL, WOOK, WHUR-FM (owned by Howard), and WUST—supply a steady diet of rhythm-and-blues, gospel, and jazz, along with black news and commentary.

BLACK CULTURE

The black arts have burgeoned in Washington over the past ten years. Among the relatively new and vibrant black cultural organizations are the D.C. Repertory Dance Company (led by Mike Malone and Louis Johnson) and the D.C. Black Repertory Theatre, directed by Robert Hooks, a native of the District's Foggy Bottom neighborhood who became a successful television, movie, and stage actor. The Capitol Ballet, headed by Claire Haywood and Doris Jones, is a predominantly black company with a classical repertoire. The ballet's prima ballerina, Sandra Fortune, won acclaim in 1974 at the international dance competition held annually in Varna, Bulgaria. In 1966 Howard drama professor Paul Allen founded the New Theater of Washington as a community-oriented organization that would be an outlet for his graduating drama students.

Among Washington's best-regarded visual artists are black painters Sam Gilliam and Alma Thomas, sculptor-painter Ed Love, and printmaker Lou Stovall. Ms. Thomas, an octogenarian who taught art at Shaw Junior High in the inner city, began painting in earnest after her retirement. Today her abstract paintings are in many private collections and such museums as the Whitney in New York City and the Corcoran in Washington. One of the moving forces in encouraging young blacks to develop their artistic abilities is Peggy Cooper, co-founder of Workshops for Careers in the Arts. (Miss Cooper, who is not yet thirty years old, is a native of Alabama, where one of her brothers is the mayor of a small town and another is a member of the state legislature.) She was instrumental in convincing D.C. officials to convert Western High School into a special school for instruction in the visual and performing arts. The school's artistic director is Mike Malone, who, besides co-directing the D.C. Repertory Dance Company, has choreographed such shows as *The Great White Hope* and *Owen's Song.* One of the nation's richest repositories of Afro-American culture is the Museum of African Art, located on Capitol Hill in the townhouse occupied by Frederick Douglass in the 1870s. The history of Anacostia, a neglected area of the District across a river from the heart of town, is relived in exhibitions at the Anacostia Neighborhood Museum, a Smithsonian Institution project directed by John Kinard and housed in a converted movie theater.

In Washington musical circles, the most prominent black is James De-Preist, principal guest conductor of the Washington National Symphony. A winner of the Mitroupoulos International Competition for conductors and a former assistant conductor of the New York Philharmonic, DePreist took a master's degree from the University of Pennsylvania's Wharton School of Finance before he decided on a career in music. Todd Duncan, retired from teaching at Howard, is an elder statesman of vocal coaching.

In terms of local recognition (bordering on adulation), the most prominent

Negroes in Washington are professional athletes, particularly football stand-outs like the Redskins' Larry Brown, Ken Houston, Verlon Biggs, Roy Jefferson, Charley Taylor, Manny Sistrunk, Brig Owens, Mike Bass, George Starke, Herb Mul-Key, and Harold McLinton. Ironically, until the recruit-ment of veteran receiver Bobby Mitchell in 1961, the Redskins were the only team in the National Football League without a black player, because owner George Preston Marshall was under the impression that the white Washington sports fan was not ready to accept black players. (Today Mitchell is the Redskins' director of professional scouting.) Other well-known black athletes in Washington include Elvin Hayes, Phil Chenier, and Wes Unseld of the Washington Bullets basketball team. One of the very few blacks in professional hockey is twenty-year-old Mike Marson, a native of Toronto who plays wing for the hapless NHL Capitals. Except at the predominantly black colleges, the coaching and managing staffs in Washington are mostly white. Notable excep-tions are the Bullets coach, former Celtics great K. C. Jones, and Georgetown University basketball coach John Thompson, a former collegiate star at Providence College and member of the Celtics.

THE SOCIAL SCENE

As in white Washington, the leisure pastimes and social life of Washing-ton's blacks depend primarily on one's degree of wealth, professional stature and depth of family roots. The poor have to make do with drinks in the neighborhood bar, church socials, television, the conviviality of sidewalk socializing on sweltering summer nights, and an occasional movie at the Republic or the Booker T theaters on U Street. Black teenagers can take in a soul show at the D.C. Armory, the Coliseum, or the Capital Centre in suburban Largo, Maryland. In the summer, the outdoor Carter Barron Amphitheatre in Rock Creek Park comes alive with the sounds of jazz and rhythm-and-blues.

For the black establishment of Washington, the social options are far broader. Well-to-do black professional and business leaders have a social structure as stratified and status-drenched as white society anywhere. The geographic center of this structure is the upper 16th Street corridor, where Negro "cave dwellers" live in such neighborhoods as the "Gold Coast" (between 16th Street and Rock Creek Park), Shepherd Park (north of Walter Reed Hospital, between 16th and Georgia Avenue), and North Portal Estates (sometimes called the "Platinum Coast"), an area next to the District line, across from Silver Spring, Maryland.

In large homes along such streets as Blagden Avenue, Kalmia Road, Argyle Terrace, and Colorado Avenue, affluent Negroes entertain one another with a sumptuousness rivaling the parties of white socialites in Spring Valley and Georgetown. As housing discrimination declines in D.C. neighborhoods west of Rock Creek Park, well-to-do blacks are moving in small numbers to Cleveland Park and Forest Hills. Many of the younger professionals, who have grown up with integration and don't need the security of the old en-claves, are settling in racially mixed apartment and townhouse complexes in Southwest D.C. and in the new towns of Reston, Virginia, and Columbia, Maryland. (The black families of Columbia have a median income of about $22,000—$3,000 higher than the town's white median income.) One socially prominent black couple, Alvin and Jacqueline Robinson, moved from the city to a McLean, Virginia, residence on land that Dr. Robinson's family has owned for years. Their contemporary house on affluent Crest Lane was the scene a few years ago of their daughter's wedding, a fancy lawn affair with buffet dinner served under a huge tent.

In decades past, being "in" necessitated membership in one or more of the well-known Negro social clubs, such as "What Good Are We," the "Girl Friends," the "Sappy Sues," and the "Regular Buddies." The many local graduates of Howard continued to socialize in later years with friends from their undergraduate fraternities—like Alpha Phi Alpha and Kappa Alpha Psi—and sororities—like Alpha Kappa Alpha, Delta Sigma Theta, and Zeta Phi Beta. "Must" social events included the Kappa Alpha Psi annual boat ride in the summer and the Kappa Dawn Dance, which began each year at 12:01 A.M. after Easter Sunday. Because most local hotels refused to rent their ballrooms to Negro social groups, big dances were held at such dance halls as the Lincoln Colonnade (beneath the Lincoln Theater on U Street), Murray's Casino (on U Street between 9th and Vermont Avenue), and a building at 1320 G Street N.W. After integration in the Fifties, the largest hotels in town were the sites of the annual black debutante balls, put on by the "Girl Friends" and the "Bachelor-Benedicts," a men's club.

But most of the black debuts were discontinued in the late Sixties as the daughters of the black elite came to regard such copying of white society as Uncle Tomism. Large weddings declined in popularity, too, except those with African themes. For the wedding a few years ago of Ernest Wilson, Jr., and his bride, who had been Peace Corps volunteers in Africa, a tribal chief was imported from New York to perform the ceremony at Howard University. The men and women guests—all barefoot—were seated on separate sides of the room, but mingled later for feasting and dancing.

In years past, many affluent Washington Negroes spent summer weekends at their cottages at such Chesapeake Bay resorts as Highland Beach, Arundel-on-the-Bay, Columbia Beach, and Eagle Harbor, or on Martha's Vineyard at the Oak Bluffs colony. (The oldest of these, Highland Beach, founded in the 1880s by a son of Frederick Douglass, was so exclusive during the Twenties that dark-skinned Negroes were barred by the light-skinned social establishment.)

These resorts still have their followings, but the increasing legal and financial freedom of blacks has opened up more and more social alternatives, decreasing the elite's dependence on their traditional clubs and vacation spots. Today, prosperous blacks can and do travel to ski resorts, the Caribbean, and Africa, and in their own hometown enjoy a wide range of cultural offerings and night life. They patronize all the restaurants that are favorites of well-heeled white Washingtonians, as well as black-owned spots like Billy Simpson's, Ed Murphy's, Chez Maurice, Face's, and Chez Brown, a chic restaurant near the National Theatre that features French cuisine and live opera singing (and is enjoyed by a large white clientele). Boat ownership is increasingly popular, and prominent black businessmen like developer Ted Hagans, ex-auto dealer Ed Feggans, and electrical contractor William Chandler keep their yachts at the Seafarers Club, a black social organization near Annapolis. Tennis is booming among Washington blacks as well as whites, as much for social status as for exercise. Despite the general decline in importance of the Negro social clubs, some of them—like "What Good Are We," the "Girl

Friends," and the "Guardsmen" and the "Huntsmen"—continue to thrive. A few of the women's clubs—such as the "Continentals," "Moles," and "Links" —throw parties not just for the fun of it but to raise money for black causes like the Urban League and the NAACP.

SOCIAL ELITE

Who are the members of the black social elite? They include many of the men and women mentioned above, because there is naturally a high coincidence between achievement and social prominence in black Washington. Some socially active black couples seem to have everything going for them—brains, professional success, good looks, good deeds, and the right connections. Take, for example, surgeon William Funderburk and his beautiful, chic wife Marilyn, who is friendly with Mrs. Edward M. Kennedy (and, like Joan, an alumna of fashionable Manhattanville College). Special deference is accorded to black people whose families were leaders of Washington in the last century—scions of the Cooks, Terrells, Langstons, Wormleys, Douglasses, Bruces, and others. Several of the numerous Syphax cousins (including longtime Dunbar High School teacher Mrs. Mary Hundley) are descendants of William Syphax, who in 1870 founded the first D.C. high school for Negroes. Born in 1825 of slave parents on the Arlington, Virginia, plantation of George Washington Parke Custis (grandson of Martha Washington), William Syphax was freed as an infant and educated in private schools in the District, eventually becoming one of the city's most respected education administrators. One of the oldest of Washington's Negro aristocrats is ninety-two-year-old Portia Washington Pittman, a daughter of Tuskegee Institute founder Booker T. Washington. A longtime choral music teacher at Tuskegee, Mrs. Pittman (former wife of the black Washington architect William Sidney Pittman) has lived in Washington intermittently over the years and has been a White House guest of four Presidents.

Some members of the black social elite earned their positions much as some white hostesses do, through hard work on charity balls and other fund-raising benefits. One such hostess is Annelee Willoughby, whose husband, Dr. Winston Churchill Willoughby, is a successful Trinidad-born dentist. Active in embassy social circles, Mrs. Willoughby chaired the SOS Desert Ball, which raised $70,000 for drought-stricken African nations. Hostess Marguerite Mazique, a psychologist and wife of physician Edward Mazique, is a former model who used to organize fashion shows to raise money for the NAACP. A Washington native, Mrs. Mazique was a student at Hampton Institute when she met and married a handsome Navy sailor named Harry Belafonte. She supported her struggling actor-husband and their two daughters through a few years of difficult marriage, but the match dissolved before Belafonte achieved stardom. (Today Belafonte and Mrs. Mazique—and their spouses— are all best of friends, and the children of the two couples consider themselves to be part of one big family.)

Socially, there is more contact today between the races in Washington than in years past. This is especially true among white and Negro professionals who meet in their work—or on the boards of civic organizations and at their children's private schools. Many of them form friendships that are transferred from office to the home. The trend is most conspicuous among the younger, more educated Washingtonians. Nevertheless, total integration of "white society" and "black society"—with their separate social clubs, individual traditions, and "cave-dwelling" families—is something yet to come.

A LOOK TO THE FUTURE

As citizens of the national capital, the black residents of Washington—and their parents and grandparents—have seen many great events in the history of the nation's largest minority race: the 1922 march of 1,500 Negro leaders through the streets of Washington, a silent protest against the rising toll of lynchings in the South; the 1939 concert of black contralto Marian Anderson at the Lincoln Memorial, before an audience of 75,000, after the Daughters of the American Revolution had refused her the use of Constitution Hall; the 1963 March on Washington, 300,000 strong, both Negroes and whites.

Washington has also been the scene of traumatic crises, like the post-World War I race riot, sparked by a crime wave that whites blamed on the District's black minority. On a Saturday night in July 1919, more than a hundred off-duty white soldiers invaded the slums of Southwest Washington, attacking its Negro residents, many of whom fought back. By the time order was restored five days later, several people had been killed and many injured in rioting through the downtown area. Nearly fifty years later, in 1968, the rioting and burning that followed the assassination of the Reverend Martin Luther King, Jr., left hundreds of stores and shops in the business district destroyed, and today—seven years later—the area still contains the unrestored carcasses of that outburst of grief and anger.

Today, the people who are most concerned about Washington's urban ills are the black residents of the District, especially those of the marginal middle class. They are concerned about street crime, committed mostly by young, unemployed black males against other blacks. They are troubled that their children are exposed to drugs and violence in the "normal" course of growing up in certain parts of the city. They are dismayed by the low quality of education in a city that was once famous for its public schools, black as well as white.

To the District's well-to-do white minority, most of whom live west of Rock Creek Park, the debate over the administering and financing of the D.C. government is a remote, academic issue. They can pay, out of their own pockets, for the social services that less-well-off citizens depend on the local government to provide.

But to the Negro middle class, home rule is a "gut issue." Unlike D.C.'s wealthier whites and increasing numbers of well-to-do blacks, they can't afford to move away from the problems of the District. Many of them have a financial equity in their small, tidy homes, yet not enough to buy them a more tranquil environment in a more expensive neighborhood of the District or the suburbs.

The future of Washington as a black center depends as much on the rest of the nation as it does on itself. The willingness of Congress to let District citizens govern themselves (real home rule, not the strings-attached variety practiced now) will hinge on how each congressman thinks his constituents would like him to vote, and how liberal he thinks they are in matters of race relations. While the new elected government of the District is a big step toward self-determination, Washington is still under the thumb of congressmen and senators in whose elections District residents have no voice.

In the bicentennial year of 1976, Washington will be on display to the world. Many Americans—from the prairies, the coasts, the mountains, the bayous, and the boundaries with Canada and Mexico—will realize that their capital city is a peaceful black-white city. Whether this comes as a shock or an inspiration will reveal whether their eyes are cast toward the past or forward toward the nation that American can—and probably will—be.

24 EQUAL OPPORTUNITY

Over the last three decades, Washington has set in motion a human relations revolution that has come to be known as "equal opportunity." In the most basic sense, "equal opportunity" means the right of every citizen to realize the full human potential, unimpeded by individual and institutional biases.

The federal government, often moving only with reluctance and in the wake of heavy pressures, but at other times acting with unexpected initiative, has created a body of equal opportunity laws, executive orders, court decisions, agency regulations, and administrative guidelines. The full implications of these are yet to be realized. But at the least, it seems certain that they will reshape the economic, social, and political contours of the nation. There is hardly any area of life in America that is untouched by Washington's commitment to equal rights for all. Federal regulations cover employment, education, housing, voting, and access to public accommodations like restaurants, hotels, and transportation facilities.

Much of what has occurred under the name of equal opportunity has been for many years traditionally categorized under the heading of "civil rights." But the civil rights movement is generally perceived as the struggle of the nation's black populace to move up from slavery, out of second-class citizenship and into the American mainstream. Today equal opportunity laws protect many ethnic and racial minorities besides Negroes: American Indians, Spanish-Americans, Orientals, and others. The laws cover people whose religion might impede their acceptance in the job, housing, or educational institution for which they are otherwise suited. Washington watches out, too, for the interests of children with mental handicaps by insisting that local school systems provide some sort of special education programs for them. The rights of the physically handicapped, as well, are being asserted in Washington, with requirements that federally funded buildings be built with special facilities for people in wheelchairs.

Equal opportunity no longer pertains only to a conglomeration of minorities. As a result of a comparatively recent emphasis on guaranteeing equal opportunity for women and the middle-aged, the fact is that what Washington has wrought directly influences the lives of an American *majority*. Take, for example, the field of employment policy. Equal employment opportunity laws and regulations now cover about 60 percent of the nation's labor force. Besides racial minorities, they cover women, who constitute 38 percent of the work force, and those in the age bracket of forty to sixty-five years, who comprise 40 percent of it. (Both of these groups, of course, overlap with each other and with segments of the racial minorities.) Federal contractors, for whom the equal opportunity statutes are particularly stringent, consist of 250,000 separate business firms that provide the government annually with

$50 billion in goods and services and employ fully one-third of the total work force.

There are those who may question both the need and the desirability of such a national obligation. There are racists who detest it, male chauvinists who laugh at it, and others who merely seek to avoid it. But equal opportunity is the law of the land, and those who ignore it or disobey it do so at their own risk. For if the federal government cannot legislate how we *feel about* one another, it has found that it can legislate what we *do to* one another. And with persistent prodding from equal opportunity's potential beneficiaries (or at least from the activists who represent them), Washington is beginning to make the law stick.

"Equality" and "opportunity" are ideals that are, for Americans, at least as old as the Republic. They are what brought many of our ancestors to these shores in the first place. But the United States of America emerged as a limited democracy of white male property owners. They could vote, but women, debtors, and Indians could not. Enslaved blacks were completely out of it: the Supreme Court designated them to be three-fifths human.

It took the massive upheavals of the Civil War, the Industrial Revolution, and the great migrations of Americans to the West and to the cities to set the stage for the creation of a constitutional base on which popular democracy and the potential for equal opportunity could be built.

That base consisted of four constitutional amendments. The Thirteenth Amendment, ratified in 1865, abolished slavery. The Fourteenth Amendment, approved in 1868, extended to all Americans the guarantees of due process and equal protection of the laws. The Fifteenth Amendment, ratified in 1870, provided that the right to vote could not be denied "on account of race, color or previous condition of servitude." And the Nineteenth Amendment, ratified in 1920, finally gave women the right to vote.

But it was not until the nation's entry into World War II that the federal government began to write the rules of equal opportunity into specific statutes affecting the conduct of specific institutions. From the end of Reconstruction until 1941—the constitutional amendments notwithstanding—Washington's role in the equal opportunity struggle was one of neutrality. To be neutral, however, was to condone the continuation of a policy of repression against many Americans. Since World War II, some obviously great and momentous governmental decisions have been made in the name of equal opportunity. Other federal actions in this area seemed almost trivial at first, but have turned out to be of unexpectedly great significance. Taken together, they add up to a massive jolt to the mixture of myth and reality that we call the American Way of Life.

These decisions and actions did not occur in a vacuum. They were the products—direct or indirect—of many factors: marches on Washington, both real and threatened; the assassinations of a President and major figures in the black civil rights movement; sit-ins, demonstrations, and confrontations in the South; urban riots in the North; astute lobbying and politicking—and a blunder or two—in Congress; a President from the South with an unprecedented personal commitment to equal opportunity, and—certainly not least—a Supreme Court, led by the late Earl Warren, that carved out a niche for itself in the history of American jurisprudence.

In chronological order, here are landmark actions that have emerged from Washington over the last four decades:

Executive Order 8802: Issued by President Roosevelt in 1941, the order banned job discrimination in the federal government and in private companies that produced goods for the war effort. This was motivated, in large part, by Roosevelt's desire to prevent a mass protest march on Washington, a demonstration that Negro civil rights leaders threatened to stage if it was not issued. While the order carried minimal enforcement provisions, it was a harbinger of the changes to come.

Brown v. *Board of Education of Topeka:* This historic Supreme Court decision in 1954 outlawed racially segregated dual school systems, ending the doctrine of "separate but equal" facilities established by the Court in 1896. It did not, however, address the problem of de facto segregation.

Civil Rights Act of 1957: This law reinforced the right of blacks to vote in federal elections and established two agencies that have been in the vanguard of the equal opportunity battle ever since, the Commission on Civil Rights and the Civil Rights Division of the Justice Department.

Equal Pay Act of 1963: A "sleeper" law whose impact was not felt until nearly a decade later, it prohibited wage and salary differentials based on sex. It is now a prime weapon in the women's fight for equal job opportunity in both the private and the public sectors.

Civil Rights Act of 1964: Conceived by President Kennedy and pushed through Congress by President Johnson, this sweeping legislation outlawed job discrimination on the basis of race, color, sex, and national origin. It also explicitly barred discrimination in any "program or activity" funded by the federal government.

Executive Orders 11246 and 111375: Issued by President Johnson in 1965 and 1967, these measures gave notice to private employers with federal contracts that passive nondiscrimination was no longer adequate compliance with the law. The orders set a new requirement of "affirmative action" to correct the results of past discrimination in hiring and promotion.

Age Discrimination in Employment Act of 1967: Another "sleeper" law that exploded in the Seventies, it prohibited employment discrimination against persons in the age bracket of forty to sixty-five.

Civil Rights Act of 1968: This law patched the last major hole in the fabric of the equal opportunity crusade—housing. It bans racial discriminaion in the sale and rental of virtually all of the nation's housing, public and private.

Equal Employment Opportunity Act of 1972: This law gave real enforcement powers to the Equal Employment Opportunity Commission (EEOC), which had been established as a conciliation agency with only the power of persuasion.

Equal Rights Amendment to the Constitution: Passed by Congress in 1972, this proposed constitutional amendment would extend existing sex discrimination bans to virtually every corner of American life. While its chances of state ratification by 1979 are still in doubt, its passage reflects the resurgence of the women's rights movement as a force in the equal opportunity effort.

Education Amendments of 1972: This measure prohibited sex discrimination in all federally assisted education programs, covering the students and faculty of the vast majority of the nation's institutions of learning, from preschool to college and vocational schools.

INTERESTED PARTIES

There is a lobby in Washington for every imaginable special interest, and the equal opportunity field is no exception. The most venerable are the black civil rights organizations, such as the NAACP, Urban League, and the Leadership Conference on Civil Rights, whose lobbyists are joined by the representatives of other minorities, including Chicanos and American Indians. The old people's lobby has a voice in the American Association of Retired Persons, and the women's rights movement is directed by such groups as the National Organization for Women (NOW) and the Women's Lobby. The freedom of an individual to not join a labor union is promoted, with limited success, by the National Right to Work Committee, a group with substantial financial backing from wealthy conservatives. The rights of handicapped people, too, are championed before Congress by several groups. And the American Civil Liberties Union finds itself in the middle of many battles in the human rights arena.

It is almost axiomatic in Washington that every lobby spawns an opposing lobby. (When the feminists push for liberalized abortion laws, for example, they run up against the equally determined women of the National Right to Life Committee.) Lobbying against civil rights is a very touchy undertaking, since all Americans these days are expected to at least pay lip service to the broad concepts of equal opportunity. But when a proposed law or guideline threatens the status quo in employment practices, education, housing, or anything else, lobbies leap forward, urging Congress to take a "gradual" approach, to let people settle their problems without interference from Washington. Just as you can't legislate morality, the lobbies argue, you can't force people to treat their fellow men fairly. This is the tack taken by business groups and unions trying to water down the fair employment legislation, and by the National Association of Home Builders back in the early Sixties, when it opposed open housing laws (which it has since come to live with, perhaps because the impact has been less than it once feared). And this is the drift of the antibusing argument, after the rhetoric about community schools is stripped away.

In one sense, every federal agency in Washington is involved in the equal opportunity effort, because each one has an obligation to promote fair hiring and promotion within its own labor force. The overseer of this commitment is the Civil Service Commission, which has the power to approve or disapprove each federal agency's affirmative action program. While Washington pressures the rest of the nation into compliance, it is not exactly a paragon of virtue itself. In practically every agency, the representation of minority employees and women decreases sharply with every step up the ladder of salary and policymaking power. An effort is being made, though, to beef up the under-represented groups. In 1973 the U.S. Commission on Civil Rights noted that over the past few years there has been a "modest improvement in the employment practices of federal departments and agencies."

The antidiscrimination business engulfs Washington because of the dispersion of monitoring and enforcement responsibilities over at least five Cabinet departments and three independent commissions. In just one area—fair hiring—some nineteen agencies have been delegated some degree of power to ensure that private firms, colleges, and other institutions with federal ties comply with job opportunity laws.

EEOC

The most important of these federal bodies, especially in the field of open hiring, is the Equal Employment Opportunity Commission. This presidentially appointed five-member panel (of which no more than three can belong to the same party) was hamstrung for eight years by its lack of enforcement powers. Commission members who tried to put some teeth into its operations were rebuffed by antagonistic congressmen. In 1969, for example, Senator Everett M. Dirksen (R-Ill.) had a heated run-in with then EEOC Chairman Clifford Alexander, Jr. The powerful senator threatened the young Negro lawyer with the loss of his job if the commission didn't quit, as Dirksen put it, "punitive harassment" of businessmen. Soon thereafter, Alexander resigned in disgust, charging that "vigorous efforts to enforce the laws on employment discrimination are not among the goals of this [Nixon] administration."

Finally, in 1972, the civil rights bloc on Capitol Hill gave EEOC the tools necessary to do its job—in particular, the power to initiate suits against alleged violators. Additionally, the new amendments extended the commission's jurisdiction to an estimated 18 million additional workers—in state and local government, education, and business firms with as few as fifteen employees (rather than the previous minimum of twenty-five).

Most actions by the EEOC originate from complaints of employees (or job applicants). In 1974 the commission had a backlog of some 90,000 complaints, many of them against the same large national companies and labor unions. (One as yet unnamed firm has been the target of an estimated 2,000 complaints.) The commission attempts to investigate the charge and, if a probability of illegal discrimination is found, resolve the dispute through voluntary conciliation. If the alleged violator does not cooperate with the EEOC negotiators, the final recourse is the filing of a commission suit against the employer in a U.S. district court. If the court rules in favor of the complainant, it can order the company to cease and desist, as well as pay back wages.

Between 1972 and mid-1974, the EEOC had initiated more than 240 suits. The commission's National Programs Division, staffed by forty-five lawyers divided into task forces dealing with particular sectors of the economy, tries to consolidate complaints and give top priority to suing companies that seem to have deep-seated patterns of job discrimination.

One measure of the boom in the federal equal employment bureaucracy is the exponential growth of the EEOC budget and staff. In its first year of operation, fiscal 1966, it had a budget of $2.5 million and a staff of 190. Today it spends about $53 million a year and employs some 2,400 people. The acquisition of enforcement powers in 1972 has swelled the staff of attorneys from about 40 to 280 today. The commission has thirty-two district offices and five litigation centers spread around the nation. While the EEOC structure has grown rapidly since its inception, most observers feel that it is understaffed and underbudgeted to do its job effectively.

JUSTICE AND HEW

While EEOC has supremacy in the hiring-discrimination realm, the enormous burden of implementing school desegregation falls primarily on the shoulders of the Civil Rights Division of the Justice Department and the Office for Civil Rights of the Department of Health, Education and Welfare (HEW). HEW's particular club over the head of segregated education is the threat of a cutoff of federal aid. The Justice Department is the litigating force—Uncle Sam's agent for working out mutually agreeable desegregation plans with state and local governments, or hauling them into court if they refuse to cooperate.

The Justice Department is also the protector of the voting rights of millions of southern blacks and other minority groups. The voter registration campaigns that it has watched over have been instrumental in boosting the number of black officeholders throughout the nation.

Justice's Civil Rights Division and HEW's Office for Civil Rights both have extensive powers in the area of equal employment opportunity. While much of Justice's past responsibilities in this field are now shouldered by the EEOC, it still has primary jurisdiction over complaints against state and local governments, having filed more than twenty cases against Uncle Sam's sister governments between 1972 and 1974. HEW is the primary recipient of job discrimination complaints against educational institutions.

The Department of Housing and Urban Development, too, has a major role in the equal opportunity structure. It receives, investigates, and adjudicates complaints of discrimination in the sale and rental of housing.

LABOR

Two of the most important, but publicly little known, equal opportunity agencies are housed within the Department of Labor: the Office of Federal Contract Compliance (OFCC) and the Wage and Hour Division. The latter is concerned with equal employment opportunity for women and the elimination of job discrimination based on age. The division's jurisdiction under the Equal Pay Act includes private employers, labor unions, schools, hospitals, and other public institutions. In earlier years, the act extended only to persons covered by the minimum wage law, but in 1972 it was amended to include executive, administrative, and professional personnel and college and university professors. The division may bring civil suits on behalf of employees, who may also institute enforcement suits of their own, individually or as a group.

The Age Discrimination in Employment Act gives the division jurisdiction over private employers with twenty or more employees, labor unions, employment agencies, and, under a 1974 amendment, federal, state, and local governments. The division has more than 1,000 compliance officers located in some 400 cities and towns across the country.

The bailiwick of Labor's OFCC is promoting equality of hiring by the 250,000 firms that provide goods and services to the federal government. In 1968 the office adopted a regulation that has provided many headaches for companies and labor unions that were dragging their feet on job opportunities for blacks and women. It told every employer under its jurisdiction to submit written "affirmative action programs," including specific goals and timetables for hiring target groups, as a means of eliminating past discrimination.

OFCC delegates its monitoring of federal contractors and the responsibility for supervising the affirmative action programs to nineteen federal agencies, each of which is assigned certain categories of industry. Each category is given a Standard Industrial Classification (SIC) code number. For example, petroleum refining and related industries are coded SIC 29 and are assigned to the Department of Interior for compliance monitoring.

OFCC itself deals with the construction industry (employers and labor unions). It seeks to arrange voluntary local agreements, called "hometown plans," for increasing minority hiring. When employers fail, in OFCC's opinion, to make a "good faith" effort to reach a plan's goals, OFCC can impose mandatory goals. Failure to make an effort to achieve mandatory goals can—but rarely does—result in the suspension, cancelation, or termination of a federal contract or in debarment from obtaining future federal contracts. (In late 1974, the government proclaimed virtually all of the existing "hometown plans" to be fiascos and moved on to the next stage of compulsory goals.)

A 1973 evaluation of OFCC by the Commission on Civil Rights found that the agency "has not yet provided federal agencies with adequate mechanisms for resolving compliance problems." In 1974, Representative Martha Griffiths (R-Mich.) made public a report prepared by the General Accounting Office (GAO) which found that of 120 employers' affirmative action programs reviewed by GAO, nearly half did not meet OFCC's criteria, although they had been accepted by the federal agencies delegated by OFCC to monitor them. Representative Griffiths called OFCC's enforcement effort "puny," noting that only one contract has been terminated for noncompliance in OFCC's history. She suggested, as the Commission on Civil Rights has in the past, that OFCC's functions be passed to EEOC. Congress thus far has balked at the idea.

COORDINATORS AND CRITICS

It is probably evident, from the roster of aforementioned agencies, that the federal civil rights apparatus is highly fragmented and full of overlapping responsibilities. In 1972 Congress made a stab at the problem by creating the Equal Employment Opportunity Coordinating Council, with a mandate to put some consistency into the policies of all the agencies involved. The council consists of the Attorney General (representing the Justice Department's Civil Rights Division); the Secretary of Labor (in the same capacity for the OFCC and the Wage and Hour Division); and the chairmen of the EEOC, the Civil Service Commission, and the Commission on Civil Rights. The council's main activity has been an effort to work out new guidelines for regulating the employment practices of public and private employers and labor unions—particularly those practices concerned with the selection of new employees and testing of job applicants. Indicative of the complexity of the issues involved is the fact that, by the fall of 1974, after two years of work, the council had produced two drafts, both of which have been found inadequate by business, state, and local governments and psychologists concerned about employment interviewing and testing procedures.

In a 1973 evaluation, the Commission on Civil Rights said: "There is no government-wide plan for civil rights enforcement. There is not even effective coordination among agencies with similar responsibilities in, for example, the employment area. The Equal Employment Opportunity Coordinating Council, created by Congress for this precise purpose, had not addressed any substantive issues in the first six months of its existence."

No review of Washington's equal opportunity establishment would be complete without a reference to the Commission on Civil Rights, which is probably the severest critic, in or out of government, of that very establishment. The six-member, presidentially appointed, bipartisan commission has no power to make policy, enforce laws, or adjudicate individual complaints. It is primarily an information clearinghouse, an investigator, and an evaluator of the performance of its sister agencies. The highly respected commission, headed in 1974 by former HEW Secretary Arthur S. Flemming, is an energetic producer of reports, more than 200 in all. These influential critiques have, in the words of Washington lawyer Berl Bernhard, "prodded Congress, nagged the Executive, and aided the Courts. Above all, [the commission] has lacerated, sensitized and perhaps even recreated the national conscience."

IMPACT ON BUSINESS

Despite the organizational defects of the federal civil rights program, it is not just a machine churning out meaningless regulations and spinning its wheels. The mountains of laws, guidelines, and court decision are changing the way America conducts its affairs. Especially, they are changing the way that businesses do business. For employers, the question is no longer what they *can't* do, but what they *must* do. Washington's demand is for "affirmative action": the elimination of discriminatory employment systems coupled with a positive effort to hire minorities and women. That demand has cost major U.S. firms a total of more than $100 million in back-pay and wage-adjustment settlements over the past couple of years.

The implications of the government's new approach became clearly visible in January 1973, when the EEOC, in a joint effort with units of the Departments of Labor and Justice, worked out a landmark settlement with the American Telephone & Telegraph Company—the nation's largest private employer. AT&T agreed to pay a total of $43 million in back pay and wage adjustments, in response to charges that the company discriminated against women and minorities in its employment practices. (AT&T would not concede formally that it was guilty of the charges, and the settlement was reached through a consent decree.)

By the fall of 1974, EEOC, working through the federal courts in cooperation with the Labor and Justice departments, had won similar settlements from such major national firms as Corning Glass, Uniroyal, the Bank of America, and—for a second time—AT&T. Another settlement was worked out with nine major companies comprising the bulk of the steel industry, along with the industry's labor union, the United Steelworkers of America. And EEOC let it be known that it was filing charges of discrimination against each of the automobile industry's "Big Three" (Ford, General Motors, and Chrysler) and their union, the United Auto Workers; Sears, Roebuck; the National Electrical Contractors Association; and the three major electrical workers' unions. EEOC doesn't ignore the violations of small fish in the business pond, either. It has prepared charges againt Stan's Sandwich Shop in Atlanta, Georgia.

With the stakes already high and getting higher every year, mastering the complexities of affirmative action has become a must for business executives, labor leaders, state and local government officials, educators—and citizens who want to know their rights. For many corporate executives around the country, a two-volume, 158-page EEOC publication, *Affirmative Action and Equal Employment: A Guidebook for Employers,* has become a familiar desk manual. The book is a guide to overhauling an entire personnel system, since the EEOC feels that "the most pervasive discrimination today results from normal, often unintentional and seemingly neutral practices throughout the employment process."

The language of the EEOC guide is replete with such bureaucratic jargon as "criterion related validation," "disparate effect," and "differential prediction," but the message is clear: shape up *before* Uncle Sam comes calling. The EEOC emphasizes that it is not interested in good intentions: "the most important measure of an affirmative action program is RESULTS—measurable, yearly improvement in hiring, training and promotion of minorities, and females in all parts of your organization." The EEOC warns that recent court cases have put the burden of proof on the employer to show that an under-representation of minorities and women (in relation to their proportion of the population and/or labor force) is not the result of discrimination.

The affirmative action boom has given rise, in Washington and other large cities, to a new breed of specialist: equal employment opportunity consultants (many of whom, not surprisingly, are women). One such consultant—Todd Jagerson of New York City—wastes no time in laying it on the line with prospective clients, warning them, "It's not a question of *if* you have problems, but *where*. It's not *if* you're going to be confronted, but *when*. And it's not *if* it's going to cost you money, but *how much.*"

There are many gray areas between the poles of permissible employment practices, but here is a list of "dont's" adapted from a questionnaire published by EEOC:

An employer:

• cannot refuse to hire women who have small children at home;

• cannot generally obtain and use an applicant's arrest record as the basis for nonemployment;

• cannot prohibit employees from conversing in their native language on the job;

• cannot, if most employees are white and male, rely solely on word of mouth to recruit new employees;

• cannot refuse to hire women to work at night because of a desire to protect them;

• may not require all pregnant employees to take leave of absence at a specified time before delivery date;

• may not establish benefits—pension, retirement, insurance, and health plans—for male employees that differ from those for female employees;

• may not hire only males for a job even if state law forbids the employment of women for that capacity;

• must attempt to adjust work schedules to permit an employee time off for a religious observance.

The courts have ruled, in some cases, against:
• minimum educational requirements for employment, such as a high school diploma;
• firing of an employee after his wages have been garnisheed;
• physical prerequisites that may have a "disparate impact" on certain groups (for example, a minimum height requirement that may work against women or Mexican-Americans);
• labeling jobs as "men's" or "women's"—unless sex is a "bona fide qualification" for a job (for example, a wet nurse);
• denying employment to married women if married men are hired.

WOMEN AND OLD FOLKS

Even more than black employees, women have been the principal beneficiaries of the equal employment push. The second settlement with "Ma Bell," for example, involved $7 million in back pay to 7,000 female employees, plus $23 million in first-year wage adjustments (of which 60 percent was paid to women and minority employees, with the rest going to white male employees who had promotion complaints). About one-third of the discrimination complaints filed with the EEOC each year are from women.

The Equal Pay Act, requiring equal pay for equal work by men and women, has been on the statute books since 1963, but it wasn't taken very seriously by employers until the women's movement gathered steam in the late Sixties and federal agencies began enforcing the law. A provision banning sex discrimination in hiring was inserted into the Civil Rights Act of 1964, ironically, by opponents of the bill who thought the concept would seem so ridiculous to Washington's lawmakers that the entire bill would be defeated. But the times have changed, and today there is nothing ridiculous about it. The Labor Department's Wage and Hour Division, which administers the Equal Pay Act, reports that in just three years, from 1969 to 1972, the number of discrimination complaints from women tripled, as did court-ordered payments of back wages. Today there are so few jobs that are considered inherently male or female that the distinction, legally, has all but disappeared.

Older workers—those in the forty- to sixty-five age bracket—have found a protector in Washington, too. In 1972 the Wage and Hour Division (administrator of the Age Discrimination in Employment Act) won a case against Pan American World Airways that required an award of $250,000 in damages to 29 employees. Two years later, the Standard Oil Company of California was ordered to pay $2 million in back pay to 160 older workers. Since 1969, some 200 similar cases have been filed, and the Labor Department had another 400 in the preliminary stages in 1974. In one recent year, nearly 9,000 older Americans were hired, rehired, or promoted after federal action against their employers or would-be employers.

In an attempt to head off discrimination against older workers, the Labor Department has published a pamphlet which says that studies have demonstrated that:

• older workers' attendance is likely to be better than that of younger persons;

• older workers are less prone to change jobs;

• even though some older workers may have longer spells of illness, they are apt to be ill or disabled less frequently than younger persons;

• in manufacturing jobs, the output of persons up to age sixty-five compares favorably with that of younger workers;

• in office jobs, there were minimal differences in output by age group, among 6,000 workers checked in one study;

• learning ability does not decline significantly with age; ability to learn at ages fifty and sixty is about equal to that at age sixteen.

One of the thorniest angles to the equal opportunity movement is the endless debate over "quotas." The first big flap concerned the "Philadelphia Plan," conceived by the Nixon administration in 1969, which required building contractors and unions in that city to hire specific percentages of Negro workers on federally funded projects. And the controversy continued with the EEOC's affirmative action programs and the Labor Department's "hometown plans." The Washington equal rights agencies insist that there is a difference between quotas, on the one hand, and "numerical goals" and "timetables" on the other. An interagency statement issued in 1973 maintains that "under a system of goals, an employer is never required to hire a person who does not have qualifications needed to perform the job successfully." Many observers, however, feel that the differences between quotas and goals are a semantic quibble. Some of the Jewish organizations fear that goals designed to boost the employment of an underrepresented minority—like blacks—could work against a high-achievement minority like Jews, who are represented in some fields (such as education and law) in numbers far exceeding their percentage of the population.

Related to the quota dispute is the question of "reverse discrimination." The EEOC has been getting a growing number of complaints from white males who charge that federal guidelines are causing employers to discriminate against them. The most celebrated case to date is that of Marco DeFunis, Jr., a white, male, Phi Beta Kappa graduate of the University of Washington who was denied admission to the university's law school under a system that treated minority applicants separate from white applicants. The Supreme Court in 1974 ruled that the case was moot, since DeFunis was later admitted to the law school under a court order. Eventually, the Court will have to come to grips with the issue squarely, and the ruling will probably have a greater impact on equal opportunity than any in recent years.

In 1975 the Supreme Court made a landmark ruling in a social security case that had elements of discrimination against both women and men. Throughout almost the entire history of the social security system, survivors' benefits had been paid to widows of deceased workers with children, but not to widowers in the same situation. The High Court ruled that this procedure discriminated not only against the deprived widower and his motherless children, but also against every working mother, since her earnings (which have always been subject to the same social security taxes as men's) provided much less future protection to their surviving family members than did the earnings of working fathers. In a unanimous ruling, the Court decreed—expensively for the social security system—that widows' and widowers' benefits must be equalized.

EDUCATION

Open access to good educational facilities has long been the keystone of the Negro civil rights effort, because fair hiring and open housing are largely irrelevant if an individual hasn't got the qualifications to get a decent job and earn a decent living.

In recent years the civil rights battleground has shifted from de jure segregation (dual school systems) to de facto segregation (racial isolation caused by patterns of housing, income, and residential preference). The busing issue has become a tug of war between the courts and Congress. The Supreme Court (in its 1971 *Swann* decision) has ruled that intracity busing is one permissible means of achieving racial balance, but it has also disapproved of busing plans that cross city-county boundaries, as in Richmond, Virginia, and Detroit, Michigan. Congress, meanwhile, has been very sensitive to broad public opposition to all forms of busing. Over the past three years it has passed laws blocking the use of federal funds to implement busing plans (unless local officials request it) and banning the busing of children to any school farther than the second-closest one.

Both Presidents Nixon and Ford have been opposed to a broad federal attack on de facto segregation. President Nixon strongly supported congressional measures to ban the use of federal funds for busing. At the height of the Boston desegregation riots of 1974, President Ford gave unwitting encouragement to opponents of busing by reiterating his opposition to it.

The White House's opposition to a hard line against racial imbalances has made it very difficult for the federal agencies that are responsible for enforcing court orders and the major laws passed in the Sixties. The Nixon administration decided in 1969 that it would back off from the vigorous use of federal aid cutoffs (and threats of cutoffs) to force compliance with desegregation guidelines, preferring to work out voluntary plans with school districts and use lawsuits sparingly as a last resort. The HEW Office for Civil Rights has initiated funding cutoff proceedings against more than 600 districts in the ten years since the 1964 Civil Rights Act. But in 1973 the Civil Rights Commission detected a trend toward "lower compliance standards for elementary and secondary schools, and what appears to be the elimination of the threat of fund termination, which has rendered [HEW's] enforcement program ineffective." The commission did not blame HEW, but said the slipping of desegregation enforcement is due to "policy decisions, made at the highest levels of the administration, with which [HEW] officials are obliged to comply."

Since 1968, the Justice Department Civil Rights Division has filed some fifteen suits against nonsouthern school systems—the main trouble spots in de facto segregation—including those of Indianapolis, Pasadena, California, and Omaha. At the college level, Justice sued the state of Louisiana after negotiations between the state and HEW's Office for Civil Rights broke down (HEW's talks with eight other states resulted in acceptance of voluntary plans to desegregate their higher education systems.)

Racial balance is not the only educational concern of the federal equal rights establishment. Following a 1974 Supreme Court decision on equal opportunity for non-English-speaking children, HEW began a study of the New York City public schools to determine the need in certain neighborhoods for classroom teaching in the Spanish and Chinese languages. Similar studies are planned for the schools of Chicago, Houston, Los Angeles, and Philadelphia.

Another dimension of the equal education issue, with a potentially far greater impact on the nation's schools than racial desegregation, is the issue of women's rights. HEW has issued guidelines that affect every aspect of higher education: student recruitment, admissions policies, student organizations, extracurricular activities, financial aid, faculty and staff employment, school services, and athletics. The most significant one is a requirement that all single-sex colleges receiving federal assistance integrate their student bodies with the opposite sex by 1979. In the area of competitive sports, colleges would be required to offer either separate teams for males and females or one team open to both sexes; the goal of "equal athletic opportunity" is hazily defined, and doesn't specify that expenditures for men's and women's sports be precisely equal.

FULFILLING THE PROMISE

The mandate of Washington's civil rights agencies is the most challenging one ever conceived in the capital. Their mission is to translate the lofty promises of the Declaration of Independence and the Constitution into hard reality. The challenge is awesome, because it requires the balancing of one person's rights against the rights of others. The choices available to one group can rarely be broadened without narrowing the choices available to others. To put it more concretely: an employer's right to refuse employment to anyone he doesn't like for any reason has been curtailed, increasing the freedom of minorities and women to secure jobs of their choice. Every equal opportunity issue involves tradeoffs between the rights of different people.

The equal rights movement is relatively young and has yet to accomplish any miracles. Job barriers and income differentials still prevent minorities and women from realizing their full potential. The nation's schools are still a long way from being integrated. Open housing laws have made hardly a dent in the racial isolation of the cities and the suburbs. The progress that is being made is largely the result of the concerted effort of the civil rights lobbies and the federal watchdogs. Ideally, the equal opportunity establishment in Washington could be self-liquidating, if the nation ever reaches the point where fair treatment of all citizens becomes an ingrained national norm, needing no monitoring by Uncle Sam. But that day is a long way off, so we had all better resign ourselves to a continuing stream of rules and regulations from Washington governing our ways of dealing with one another.

25 MANAGING THE ECONOMY

Every weekday in Washington, half a dozen members of President Ford's Economic Policy Board meet at the White House or in the Executive Office Building next door to take the pulse of the nation's economy and decide what to advise the President to do next. In times like these, the job is one of the most sensitive in the federal government. The decisions made at the White House, and modified by the Congress, affect the livelihood of 213 million Americans, and they strongly determine the political fortunes of the President himself, his Cabinet, the Congress and thousands of other functionaries at state and local levels.

For while the results may not always seem to justify the effort, it is still true that Washington spends as much time trying to manage the economy as it does on any other of its manifold responsibilities. From one administration to another, it does what it thinks will satisfy the needs of the moment, as these needs are perceived by the economists, friends, elected officials, and appointed administrators who surround the President and in whom he places his confidence.

But for those who live at the other end of the economic chain—whether they are businessmen, union members, self-employed farmers, or do-it-yourself housewives—the results in recent years have been a see-saw series of inflations and recessions, leaving consumers wondering whether Washington really knows what it's doing.

In the first few months of the Ford administration, the White House and the nation were treated to a condensed version of almost everything that had happened to the economy since the end of World War II—compressed into one short period from late 1974 to early 1975. Within this span, the U.S. economy was whipsawed by energy problems, an anemic stock market, shortages of raw materials, accumulations of inventories, tight money, a housing and auto slump, rising unemployment, falling production—in short, boom and recession tumbling all over each other.

As Ford moved into the White House, he found the U.S. economy pivoting between inflation and deflation. And when he looked around to take inventory of what he had at his disposal to deal with the situation, he found U.S. economic policy in a holding pattern. Following Watergate, the Nixon administration was being dismantled. The chairman of the President's Council of Economic Advisers, Dr. Herbert Stein, was getting ready to leave. George Shultz, President Nixon's former number one counselor on economic affairs, had already left as Secretary of the Treasury. Only Arthur Burns, chairman of the Federal Reserve Board, remained out of the original "triad" of potent Nixon advisers on economic affairs. A fourth economic operative, Roy Ash, was still on deck as director of the Office of Management and Budget (OMB), but his position was in question, and he subsequently left in 1975, to be succeeded by James T. Lynn, former Secretary of Housing and Urban Development. President Nixon's "moderator" of economic advice, Kenneth Rush, was waiting to be appointed something else (and subsequently became ambassador to France).

For the new President, economics was paramount, exceeded in importance only by the crucial matter of war or peace in the Middle East (which also had its economic side, in view of the 1973 oil embargo). Confronted with the dilemma of rampant price inflation and signs of recession, Ford faced a particularly difficult quandary. He believed in a free economy, a minimum of government interference, and cuts in federal spending. He did not believe in wage and price controls. His predecessor had tried controls, then taken them off, leaving him with the worst consequences of both policies.

Into this vacuum, Gerald Ford drew a new cast of characters. After a brief shakedown period, in September 1974 President Ford set up an Economic Policy Board, with Secretary of the Treasury William Simon as chairman. Ford's old Michigan friend, accountant L. William Seidman, was named executive director and deputy chairman—clearly the "master of ceremonies" of the ongoing show. Ford signaled that Seidman was to be the policy coordinator by simultaneously naming him deputy chairman of four other top administration economic policy committees. In the earliest days of his administration, Ford made it plain that the key men were Simon and Seidman and Alan Greenspan, chairman of the Council of Economic Advisers. These were men who were particularly attuned to the proposition of governmental budget restraint, and when inflation was the "number one enemy" their voices were heard most frequently. The Executive Committee would hold its daily meetings in Seidman's office, and the sessions would usually include OMB Director Roy Ash, Federal Reserve Board Chairman Arthur Burns, and Dr. Albert Rees, director of the Council on Wage and Price Stability. From time to time, other Cabinet officers or their deputies would sit in. This was the first "think group" in whom President Ford put his trust for economic advice.

Like Nixon's advisers, these men were "noninterventionists," who believed in a stable money supply, restraint in federal spending, and encouragement to new investment. Democratic critics derisively said "the old-time religion" would not work in time to save the economy from tearing itself apart. Even as "the new boys" began their task of setting the economy right, they had two strikes against them. Their reliance on budget restraint militated toward further dampening of business activity, which already was cooling too fast for comfort. Yet anything they might do to offset the slowdown could have the opposite effect on prices and simply add more fuel to the inflationary fires. It obviously was a tough time for the true believers in a hands-off economic policy. Democratic critics like John Kenneth Galbraith, Walter Heller, and Arthur Okun took the Ford economists to task for what they considered an overly simplistic approach.

In this climate, President Ford presented the Ninety-fourth Congress with his State of the Union message, and the follow-ups on energy and the economy. While he talked about tax cuts, emergency public jobs, consumer moderation on fuel consumption, and governmental budget restraint, the newly reinforced Democratic majority in the House and Senate was preparing darts to throw at the Republican trial balloons, and presented its own program of tax cuts and other stimulants to economic activity.

THE ROAD AHEAD

The debate over economic policy once again pointed up the fact that management of the economy is always an Achilles heel for Washington because it consists of so many "iffy" variables: money supply, interest rates, taxes, tariffs, quotas, subsidies, price supports, loans, incentives, labor rates, and—underlying everything else—the budget of the federal government.

Most of the variables have their ups and downs, but the budget and spending go mainly up. Yet now, even as federal spending takes off on another rise, management of the federal budget is undergoing a change—and one which may have more long-range significance than anything that has happened in Washington in recent years. For the first time, Congress has some machinery for looking at the budget as a whole—and looking at it all at one time instead of piecemeal.

In past years, spending bills in Congress appeared on the legislative calendar hit or miss, in order of their introduction. Nowhere did Congress have a method for collecting them at one time, adding up the totals and weighing the relative importances. Programs with "political sex appeal" could carry the day without reference to the final cost tab. Nowhere did Congress have a formal technique for studying future costs of programs it initiated. Nowhere did it have a reliable method for figuring out the heights of taxation to which a given program might escalate. Nowhere did Congress have a practical way of answering the question: Can we afford it?

The millennium is not yet here, but Congress did—in 1974—vote a budget control plan under which proposed expenditures can be studied and future costs estimated. So at the congressional end of Pennsylvania Avenue things are stirring that may eventually give the federal government a better chance of bringing federal spending into focus.

At the White House end of Pennsylvania Avenue, a change has taken place that dovetails with what Congress has done. One of President Ford's first actions, as an "old congressional hand," was to initiate a procedure to bring the White House and the leaders of Congress into consultation on the budget at earlier stages of the planning. While it could not prevent confrontations on policy, it did let each side know what the other was thinking.

Before the recession pushed inflation worries temporarily aside, a surprising consensus had begun to emerge among economists—liberal, conservative, and in between—on the question of federal spending. The economic thinkers of various persuasions started saying that inflation could be brought under control only if government stopped spending so much. Indeed 1974 may be remembered among economists as the year when John Kenneth Galbraith, the guru of liberal circles, found himself in agreement with Milton Friedman, the conservative guru, as well as with Herbert Stein, Paul McCracken, and Arthur Burns, leading Republican middle-grounders. What they agreed on was the need for setting priorities in spending and limiting the size of the federal budget. Not a surprising conclusion, but surprising in the roster of characters who found themselves in agreement, including Democratic Senator Edmund Muskie, who said in September 1974: "The single most important test that the American people are posing for their leaders is economic stability, and that has got to depend on budgetary restraint." While their protestations evaporated in the antirecession atmosphere of 1975, their brief popularity signaled a growing realization that government did, indeed, need to watch its spending habits more carefully.

A HOUSE DIVIDED

What makes economic management doubly difficult in Washington is the way in which power for dealing with elements of the economy is scattered. Congress votes to spend. The President spends or "impounds." If he spends, he is an accomplice to congressional spending. If he impounds, he is criticized for overruling the will of the people. On the other hand, the President initiates the formal budget. If he wants to present a balanced budget, he leaves out some obvious things that Congress, politically, feels obliged to reinstate. When Congress reinstates the left-out bread-and-butter items, the President can accuse Congress of having caused the budgetary red ink. But if the President sends up a realistic budget, including the red ink, it is he who takes the abuse for putting the government in the red. And so it goes, between President and Congress.

In the matter of money supply and regulation of banking, neither Congress nor the President is the responsible party. Here it is the Federal Reserve Board, an independent agency whose members are appointed by the President and confirmed by the Senate. While the chairman is usually sympathetic to the general economic views of the President, he may not act in complete agreement with the President's current political priorities. And so it goes, "downtown."

Whatever these divided houses do about the economy—whether to spend, tax, subsidize, or economize; whether to expand or contract the money supply; to drive interest rates up or encourage "cheap money"—whatever they do affects the take-home pay and purchasing power of every American citizen. Federal direction of the economy touches the working life and home budgets of 213 million people in the U.S., however they may or may not like it. The influence is so pervasive that it is entangled in every piece of legislation that passes Congress, even if it doesn't bear the label "economic." Regulation of working hours by the Department of Labor affects the conditions of 92 million people in the labor force. Guidelines for hiring practices are set by the Department of Health, Education and Welfare (in antidiscrimination regulations). Both departments affect the cost of doing business, and this has an effect on prices. Minimum-wage legislation, also an influence on costs, touches about 60 million people directly, and everyone else indirectly. The Federal Home Loan Bank Board (an independent agency like the Federal Reserve) sets interest rates payable by savings and loan associations. Other agencies influence the rates on mortgages and consumer loans. The reins may be loose or tight, but the underlying power to guide the economy is there— however scattered.

Federal involvement in management of the economy has grown most spectacularly in the past forty years. With the advent of the Roosevelt New Deal, Washington came on center stage. The volume of government lending rose to head off bankruptcies (though the Reconstruction Finance Corporation, which did the lending, had been instituted by President Hoover). Agricultural prices were propped up. A floor was put under wage scales. And most importantly, the federal government intentionally undertook a program of spending to stimulate the whole economy.

Until the middle 1930s federal spending had been regarded as a simple case of paying the bills to provide basic national services. From that day forward, however, federal spending by Washington also had the purpose of pumping up economic activity, creating jobs, and underpinning the strength of corporations and unions. Government was actively operating in the economic arena, not just setting the rules or being an umpire, not just guarding the money supply, but actively manipulating economic activity.

It was a sharp break with American tradition, though it was applauded by a majority of American voters, who were less afraid of government economic management than they were of unemployment and economic catastrophe.

It was an Englishman who had provided the rationale for the new spending doctrine: John Maynard Keynes, a University of Cambridge economist who had contended, in his *General Theory of Employment, Interest and Money*, that individuals saved too much, invested too little, so there was a gap that had to be made up by government spending. No theory could have been better formulated to appeal to the political mood of the times. And so, by 1971, President Richard Nixon, a Republican and presumed conservative, could say, "I am now a Keynesian."

Keynes gave political economy its marching orders, and Washington took them to heart. For forty years—through the depression of the Thirties, World War II, postwar reconstruction and industrialization of the underdeveloped nations, right up to the worldwide inflation of the Seventies—government spending was a heavy determining factor in economic ups and downs. And Washington was in the business up to its neck, producing "full employment budgets" and measuring the allowable spending limits by how much it would take to reach the theoretical "full employment balance."

FINE TUNING

As a consequence of the growing sophistication of government economic involvement, Washington became more and more adept at twisting the dials to produce specific results in specific parts of the economy. Capital spending was lagging? Then pass a tax credit for new investment. Home building was sluggish? Then let interest rates come down. Auto sales were looking weak? Then relax regulation W and extend installment loans. Steel is scarce? Then let in more from overseas. We have too many nails and reinforcing bars? Then shut them out. "Fine tuning" of the economy became the watchword.

But when the big crunch of worldwide inflation approached, "fine tuning" began to lose some of its glamor. Raw materials supplies did not respond to such tuning. Arab governments did not answer to the "persuasion" of the U.S. State Department, Congress, or President. The droughts in Russia and the floods in Bangladesh were no respecters of American economic planners. So the economists began to talk more about "underlying conditions" and the "economic essentials," such as just how far and how fast could we go in reaching the promised land with our limited supply of raw materials, machines, and labor. It was a sobering set of thoughts.

Complicating the job of the economic managers in Washington are the frequent changes of direction by the top men themselves. It is a fascinating fact that political leaders often change their economic policies more easily than they shift some other ones. When Franklin Roosevelt was running for the Presidency in 1932, he castigated Herbert Hoover for being economically profligate, for letting government costs rise too high, for putting too heavy a burden of government on the backs of the people. He pledged to reduce federal expenses and reduce taxes. His record, of course, turned out somewhat differently.

Again, in 1968, Richard Nixon ran on a free-enterprise platform of non-involvement by government in the affairs of the economy. Government, once again, was to pull back, to return to its proper role as a mediator, a monitor, and an umpire in business, leaving the main driving force to private initiative. Again and again he reiterated his determination not to inject government into economic decisions on prices and wage controls.

In June 1970, President Nixon told the nation in a telecast: "Now here is what I will not do: I will not take this nation down the road of wage and price controls, however expedient they may seem." Early in 1971 he said, "I do not plan to ask for wage controls or price controls." On August 4, 1971, he said he opposed controls. Eleven days later he froze the economy. Richard Nixon, a Republican and an economic conservative, became the first U.S. President to impose wage and price controls in peacetime. Surely, the gods had decreed that "fine tuning" was not working, and the Washington managers of the economy were stumped.

BACK TO THE FUNDAMENTALS

So Washington's role in managing the economy started swinging back toward restraint. After forty years of stimulating wages, prices, industrial production, investment, home building, auto sales, employment, and growth in the money supply, Washington centered its sights on inflation control. Quite a change—especially in view of the fact that every administration since 1946, Republican and Democratic, has subscribed to the Employment Act of 1946, sometimes characterized as the "Full Employment Act." The Employment Act said employment came first; other elements are subordinate. But as prices soared, Washington decided that Anti-Inflation would come first and other things would be subordinate. In effect, the economic management of the U.S. lived for forty years in fear of a depression through deflation. It lived on policies set to avoid slowdowns, to avoid a crash "like '29." Then, as the creature of those policies, the economy became confronted by another monster—a fire-breathing dragon named Inflation. Pity the poor economic managers who must do battle with this dragon, even as they try to avoid slipping into a rut of recession.

The epicenter of the new effort is the Office of Management and Budget, familiarly known as OMB. As a part of the Office of the President, it answers to him, and is a part of the Executive Branch. Thus it shares the duty of initiating requests for spending, and is suspect as an accomplice in the sin of overspending—except that no one in any administration is likely to see it that way, because OMB is the watchdog that guards the gate into the final budget which goes up to Capitol Hill with the President's imprimatur. Thus, the OMB fellows with the sharp pencils are devils to the budget officers from the individual executive departments, the budget persons from HEW and HUD, from Agriculture and Labor, from Transportation and Defense.

OMB has an especially hard row to hoe, since its professional staff numbers only 425, compared with many times that many budget men in the other executive offices. Outnumbered, the President's budget men have to be especially sharp, and they make up in "clout" what they lack in numbers. For some years, the Budget Bureau, as it was then called, would gather up the requests from all the departments, give them a little cosmetic cleaning, and pass them along to the President for transmittal to Congress. Gradually these "shopping lists" by the federal departments started to come under closer scrutiny. The director of the budget would make reductions, culling out "nonessentials" here and there, exercising judgment on what would pass muster. In these judgments, he would have prior instructions from the President: "hold the line," "loosen up," "stimulate." Following such instructions, the Budget Bureau—as an extension of the President's role of "Economic Manager"—became more than just a financial housekeeper.

The Budget Bureau was created during the presidential administration of Warren Harding. To be the first director of the budget, Harding picked a stern-faced Chicago banker named Charles G. Dawes, later Vice President under Calvin Coolidge. Dawes had been a general in World War I and occasionally punctuated his remarks with the mild expletive (not deleted) of "Hell 'n' Maria." He also played the violin, but as the symbol of his new appointment as budget director he adopted the image of the broom to dramatize his intentions of making "a clean sweep." Dawes believed, in the best tradition of the early 1920s, that the best government was the least government, and he operated the Budget Bureau on that principle. In the years following World War I, the budgetary function was not treated as a matter of any serious impact on the civilian economy. The Republican administrations of the "roaring Twenties" did not consider economic management as one of the Constitutional requirements of the Presidency. The budget director and his bureau, therefore, were in the simple business of accounting for what went out and what came in—and insisting that the two be in balance.

The attitude of the Twenties did not last through the ensuing depression, of course, but the first director of the budget did. Charles Dawes, a retired banker in Chicago, lived well beyond World War II, and in 1949, seeing pictures of President Truman swearing in his budget director, Frank Pace, Dawes said to a friend, "That man must be a fool." Not knowing which man the General referred to, his friend said, "Who do you mean, General?"

"I mean that man being sworn in as budget director," said Dawes.

"Oh," said his friend, "that's a very able man—why do you say he's a fool?"

"Well," said the first director of the budget, "he's smiling while being sworn in as budget director, and no man who takes the job of budget director should smile."

The Dawes philosophy lasted until 1933, when, in the depths of the depression, the U.S. launched into a new era of economic management. It was then that government set about to stimulate the economy. Inflation—now, in the 1970s, a dirty word—was then almost a hope. President Roosevelt began listening to an agricultural economist from Cornell University named George F. Warren, who preached that farm depression had planted the seeds of the industrial depression and that low farm prices, followed by low commodity prices in general, had triggered the plunge of the industrial world into the abyss of depression. The cure, said Warren, would be to make money cheap, let everybody have enough purchasing power to put grease on the wheels of commerce. It was too early for the terms "demand pull" and "cost push," but the meaning of his message was to stimulate prices through stimulation of demand. It seemed quite logical to FDR, who bought the principle, lock, stock, and barrel—except that, in practice, the principle seemed to lack something. The economy stayed sluggish. The economic managers of the first and second New Deals found that trying to pump up prices through making money available was as hard as trying to push a piece of wet spaghetti through a nail hole. The simple availability of money didn't make people want to put it to economic use. In this stage of our national life, profit had become a dirty word. The incentive to borrow and employ money was lacking, and it was not until after World War II that money managers, businessmen, investors, government officials, labor officials, and consumers managed to put together the formula to carry out economic expansion that had been envisioned in the 1930s.

THE FULL EMPLOYMENT GOAL

One by one after World War II, governments around the world began to adopt full employment as their economic goal. Whenever economies showed signs of sagging, they were bolstered by spending or borrowing or lowering of taxes. The Truman administration succeeded the Roosevelt administration in Washington. A Labor government was in office in Australia. In Great Britain, a Labor government under Clement Attlee succeeded Conservative Winston Churchill. People's governments and Socialist regimes came into power on the European continent. Economists stressed consumption. In Washington, a coterie of progressive business leaders formed the Committee for Economic Development (CED) to assist the government in the transition from war to peacetime production, and one of its major emphases was on consumer purchasing power. Easy credit was an ingredient of the new prosperity. And much to their surprise, businessmen found themselves enjoying prosperity. In the postwar years, while damning Harry Truman, business experienced the highest level of profits they had known since the middle 1920s—and (proportionately) higher than anything since then. In 1948, under the Keynesian doctrines of government spending, business profits were 8 percent of the gross national product. By contrast, in 1974 they were less than 6 percent.

With the new emphasis on the postwar consumer economy, price inflation became a constant companion. Sumner Slichter, a Harvard labor economist, shocked the economic fraternity and most "right thinking" businessmen and government officials by suggesting that a little bit of inflation might be inevitable, in time of prosperity. Some inflation, he said, may be the price we have to pay for a burgeoning economy. Expansion, he intimated, may not be possible without it.

In 1946, at the suggestion of President Truman and his advisers, Congress passed the "Employment Act," which for the next twenty-eight years served all American administrations and Congresses as the gospel. It was in these years that the economic managers in Washington—and many economists elsewhere—began to believe that a little bit of inflation wouldn't hurt. Economists wrote books specifying the amount that was "tolerable." At that time, 1½ percent per year was "tolerable." A few years later, Dr. Paul

Samuelson, the M.I.T. economist and former economic adviser to President Kennedy, issued a revision of his college textbook and raised the "tolerable" figure to 2–2½ percent. In later editions, he hinted that higher rates might be tolerable, but even he did not foresee the 12 percent that erupted in 1974.

INFLATION RAMPANT

The administration of President Gerald Ford came into office proclaiming inflation to be its number one domestic enemy. In delivering his opening address to the Congress in August 1974, Ford declared, "We have a lot of work to do." And he was speaking of economic management. For despite the generally pro-business leanings of the Nixon administration, it had failed in dealing with high costs, high prices, high interest rates, and the shrinking purchasing power of the dollar at home and abroad.

Noting the situation, Ford said international policies would be continued, but domestic inflation, he implied, would require some fresh thinking. So inflation became the first item of business of the new administration. Other matters—including the selection of a Vice President, the war on Cyprus, and the fleshing out of the executive staff—were dealt with, but the ominous threat of an economic blow-up dominated the thought processes of the new President and his staff.

Cliques and blocs began to develop around the presidential office, but they were not neatly arranged by ideology. Director of the Office of Management and Budget (OMB) Roy Ash, a former businessman, held to a fairly optimistic view that monetary restraint and budgetary moderation would be enough to tame the inflationary beast. Arthur Burns, chairman of the Federal Reserve Board and a former academic economist, viewed the situation as more serious.

Burns told President Ford that he had perhaps sixty days in which to devise some stern and effective measures to bring runaway prices under control, or at least start to slow the tide of rise and prevent financial collapse. In addition to tight money, he said, the administration would have to employ methods to increase the supply of goods and services. It would have to take bold steps to improve productivity, either by tax incentives to spur capital investment or by rationing of credit to the "neediest" businesses. Other suggestions included the reinstatement of a Cost of Living Council with real powers of subpoena, and activation of a program of public jobs for the unemployed. Burns thought these steps, not part of the traditional Republican bag of tricks, would be needed to do the job.

In all of this, Burns had tacit support on Capitol Hill from the influential chairman of the House Ways and Means Committee, Wilbur D. Mills, the Arkansas Democrat. Mills had once been a much-sought-out congressional oracle and authority on economic affairs, but President Lyndon Johnson neglected to cultivate him, and then President Richard Nixon gave him the cold shoulder. Mills's influence was further diminished by revision of procedures within his own powerful House committee. Eventually he lost his chairmanship entirely, but at that time there was no better ally on Capitol Hill in matters of economic policy.

Step by step, President Ford did ask for most of the things Burns advised. In his speech to Congress on the Monday night after his swearing in, President Ford asked Congress for an anti-inflation task force to monitor the cost of living. Within two weeks, this passed Congress and President Ford appointed the Council on Wage and Price Stability.

Spending restraint through budgetary control was elusive. After much "who-struck-John" between Capitol Hill and the White House, a budget of $305 billion passed the Congress (though events later made it a virtually fictional figure).

An "Economic Summit Meeting" was held at the White House, with business and labor present—along with bankers and economists—and the President exacted promises of good behavior on wages and prices. "Jawboning," ineffectual as it was, helped to set the tone of what the administration hoped to do. As the scenario unfolded, prices were maddeningly unruly. The calendar ticked off the third and fourth quarters of 1974, but the consumer price index rose further and finally finished the year with a rise of 12.4 percent. The fire was still hot.

Ford did a lot of listening. He listened to his friend William G. Whyte, Washington vice president of the U.S. Steel Corporation. He listened to Paul McCracken, who had been a member of the Council of Economic Advisers during the administration of President Eisenhower and chairman of the council under Nixon. He listened to George Meany, president of the AFL–CIO, and Frank Fitzsimmons, president of the potent Teamsters Union. He solicited advice from Bill Seidman of Grand Rapids, Michigan, a successful accountant, now his economic policy coordinator. He called for ideas from his Cabinet: Secretary of Commerce Frederick Dent, Secretary of the Treasury William Simon, Secretary of Labor Peter Brennan.

In addition to the advice that he solicited, the new President was favored with an abundance of free advice from his Democratic opposition, Senator Proxmire, the Wisconsin Democrat, then chairman of the Joint Economic Committee of Congress, now chairman of the Senate Banking Committee, told the new President to cut the federal budget to the bone (as though Ford—in his earlier role as congressman—hadn't been saying the same thing for more than twenty years).

President Ford, never a giant in the field of economic management, now found himself besieged with economic advice. Gone were the newspapermen's neat descriptions of the Nixon three-man advisory councils on economic affairs, which had been labeled as the "troika" (Secretary of the Treasury George Shultz, OMB Chairman Roy Ash, and chairman of the Council of Economic Advisers Herbert Stein). Gone, too, were the cute references to the "augmented triad" or "quadriad" which included Federal Reserve Board chairman Arthur Burns. The orderly chain of command was supplanted by task forces, ad hoc committees, Cabinet meetings, and "economic summit meetings," all part of the start-up confusion in a new administration. Not far removed on the sidelines were other Ford associates and friends such as former Senator Charles Goodell of New York who helped to put together an informal group of economic advisers from the business and banking world as an "Economic Kitchen Cabinet."

FORD'S TURNAROUND

President Nixon had his economic "Phase I," followed by phases two and three in the direction of loosening controls over the economy. President Ford also had his "phase one," consisting of the campaign to "whip inflation now" (WIN). But even as he was passing out WIN buttons, recession began to take the upper hand over inflation. When unemployment rose above 7 percent in December 1974, the cool heads at the White House saw the handwriting on the wall and decided on a change of policy. President Ford signaled the change in his State of the Union message calling for tax cuts, tax rebates, and public service jobs. For him, this was "phase two." But phase three emerged as Congress reshaped the President's recommendations on taxes, energy, and jobs, and under this mixture of White House initiatives and congressional revisions the country began to work its way slowly toward a higher level of economic activity.

The new emphasis on stimulating the economy was hard for some White House economic thinkers whose preoccupation had been on fighting the demon of inflation. But they made the shift. Secretary of the Treasury William Simon, who had threatened to resign if the deficit ever went above $30 billion, said he had changed his mind and testified before a congressional committee in favor of the President's proposals for tax cuts and tax rebates. The economic pragmatists in the White House, while preferring a balanced budget, acknowledged the recession as serious and threw their weight behind policies to stimulate business rather than cool it down. With auto sales slumping and housing starts below one million a year, business was already cool enough.

Economic writers and editorialists declared that President Ford had effected a 180-degree turnaround in economic policy. A few argued that it was "only a 179-degree turn," but clearly the new administration, after five months in office, had been forced to ease up on the brakes and start pressing down on the accelerator.

STATISTICAL MACHINERY

Behind every administration's show-window policies are thousands of hours of drudgery, statistics gathering, policy mulling, and analysis of historical records. Economic policy is no exception to this, and the economic policy machinery of the federal government is a widespread mechanism with roots in every executive department. HUD (Housing and Urban Development) is expected to speak up on the need for mortgage money (and to keep track of its ups and downs). Agriculture, obviously, speaks for farm income and collects figures on production and marketing. Commerce contains the statistical machinery of the Bureau of Economic Analysis and the Bureau of the Census, which gathers monthly and yearly statistics on business. Treasury keeps track of the revenues from taxes. The State Department speaks on the effect of tariff policy, trade agreements, prices, wages, and interest rates on our relationships abroad. Defense spends more money than any other department, so has a tremendous impact on the whole economy. Interior controls the federal government's land resources and many of its mineral reserves, including coal, oil, copper, gold, silver, and natural gas. The Labor Department, through its highly respected Bureau of Labor Statistics, provides records on employment and unemployment, hours of work, average hourly pay, and other work statistics. It also collects the monthly figures for the Consumer Price Index (CPI), familiarly known as the Cost of Living Index. The Department of Health, Education and Welfare, including the Social Security Administration, pours out statistics on welfare payments, monthly social security volume, and the ups and downs of health expenses, while the Department of Transportation (the baby among federal Cabinet offices) deals with figures on rail and truck activity, barge traffic, airline passenger volume, and other indices of economic performance. Taken together, the executive departments are a huge machine for collecting, analyzing, and dispensing figures on how we are doing in our efforts to make a national living.

Government statistics are closely guarded secrets until the very moment of their release. The most dramatic example in handling of government statistics is the secrecy surrounding the release of the monthly Crop Production Reports by the U.S. Department of Agriculture. These reports are issued year round, but the crucial estimates on wheat, corn, soybeans, and cotton come in July, August, September, and October, and they lead immediately to frenzied trading in the affected commodities all over the world. Shortly before the 3 P.M. release time on the scheduled dates, more than a hundred bureaucrats, trade association people, commodity analysts, and just plain speculators gather outside the USDA crop report lockup room in the basement of the department's huge South Building. Another fifteen to twenty reporters are given the report at the same time in a press room across from the lockup. Within minutes of when the big minute hand on the press room clocks goes straight up, the news on crop yields and probable production is being sent to the world. A half hour later, USDA officials meet the press to give their version of what the report means.

Surveys of crop conditions begin ten to fifteen days before the report comes out. They involve questionnaires which are sent to thousands of farmers, spot checks by USDA's Statistical Research Service, and computerized projections from USDA state offices. These are summarized and sent to Washington by USDA state statisticians in the form of punched cards, magnetic tapes, and written reports. All this information is put in double-sealed envelopes addressed to a special mailbox which has two locks. There are only two keys to these locks, one carried by the secretary of the Crop Reporting Service and the other by an assistant to the USDA Secretary. On the appointed day, the two key holders meet as early as 3:30 A.M., unlock the mailbox, and bring the information to the six-member Crop Reporting Board for evaluation. The makeup of the board varies from month to month, depending on which crops are most important in the report. For August, USDA state directors from key corn states such as Illinois or Iowa usually take part, along with three more or less permanent board members from Washington, D.C. In reviewing the information from the states, the board often has sharp differences. It's not unusual for arguments to last several hours before a consensus is reached.

The final word on what goes into the report (and what stays out) is left to Crop Reporting Board chairman Bruce M. Graham, a career USDA employee who is also deputy administrator of the Statistical Reporting Service. Before the board even opens up the state returns, all telephone service is cut off in that section of the USDA complex. Doors are locked and guarded, and windows are closed and sealed, with shades drawn. The Crop Reporting Board and the facts they have are locked up for ten to twelve hours—until 3 P.M.

The only serious security "leak" in the reports was back in 1907 when a USDA employee who handled the cotton estimates arranged a system so that he could signal to two outside accomplices whether a crop was up or down by opening and closing Venetian blinds in the lockup room. This hanky-panky continued for several months until one of the outsiders suspected that the other two men involved were making more money on the deal than he was and reported them to the USDA Secretary.

Even beyond prerelease secrecy, some economic activities of the government are kept secret until long after the fact. The number one example of this kind of ex post facto release is the record of the Federal Reserve Open Market Committee, which consists of all the Federal Reserve Board members and representatives of five Federal Reserve Banks who meet in Washington to decide how many government securities the Federal Reserve System should buy or sell (or whether to just sit tight). Since the decision influences the amount of money that banks will have to lend out, the action affects the liquidity of the banking system and the rates of interest that banks will charge. Obviously, advance information (or even concurrent information) would sharply affect the price of stocks, bonds, and commodities, so the Federal Reserve keeps the record of these decisions locked up for ninety days afterward. It is only in retrospect that economists, businessmen, and bankers can know for sure whether "the Fed" intended to expand the money supply, contract it, or hold it level.

MEASURING BUSINESS

Statistics on such things as manufacturers' inventories, employment, capital spending, and advance orders for durable goods (considered a good indication of things to come) are summed up regularly and given to the President as part of a running briefing on the economy. Some of the bundling of statistics is done by the Council of Economic Advisers, some by the secretary of commerce, some by members of the White House inner staff. The Commerce Department sends the President a monthly sampling of opinion that it gets from members of the Business Council, a group of approximately ninety top executives in major companies (manufacturing, retailing, railroads, banks, etc.). In staff parlance, these are called "instant readings." "Flash GNP forecasts" also go to the President every three months. These are advance estimates of the gross national product for the quarter just ended and are regarded as an important business indicator. They reflect the total output of goods and services and payments of all kinds that go to make up the economic activity of the United States. The "GNP"—now also a household expression among followers of the economy—serves as the ultimate thermometer of economic activity, having supplanted the National Income figures which are now only a part of the GNP.

The prominence of statistics as a basis for economic management—and the current abundance of such statistics—is a product of the past fifty years in Washington. Prior to the Twenties, economic statistics were slow and relatively scarce. But with the appointment of Herbert Hoover as secretary of commerce in 1921, government statistics gathering began to grow. Hoover, an engineer, believed in trying to act on known conditions. While his reputation for prediction suffered as President during the depression, his performance as secretary of commerce laid the groundwork for much of the federal government's present system of statistical information. What Hoover started embryonically between 1921 and 1928 was greatly expanded during the Roosevelt New Deal years, so that by the postwar years Washington had become accustomed to statistics as the raw materials of economic analysis and policy-making. Today, any businessman or housewife can "talk economics" by throwing around such terms as "GNP," "CPI," capital spending, and consumer intentions.

THE ONGOING JOB

While the quality of economic management may be subject to question— and the current inflation-recession is the prime example—Washington continues to try to guide the economy. There are those who think things would be better if Washington would just put the gears in neutral and let the big economic machine go its own way, but the interconnections between government and business have gone beyond the point of no return. While the private sector of the economy strains to adjust, Washington is being held responsible for the large economic policy decisions—on money, taxes, spending, interest rates, and production incentives. New York may make the financial deals, but the crucial policies on which the deals are predicated are made in Washington. Pittsburgh and Chicago make the steel, but many of their production and expansion decisions turn on what comes out of Washington. Detroit manufactures automobiles, but the kind and number they sell will hinge on decisions in Washington. So it is with the manufacturers of aircraft in Seattle, the growers of wheat in Kansas, and the producers of oil in Texas and Alaska.

Whether Washington will eventually earn good marks or a failing grade on the big economic test remains to be seen. In its bag of tricks, it carries an impressive array of devices. It has taxes and spending to use as dampeners or stimulants. It can call on rapid depreciation and depletion allowances, or it can abolish them. It can impose "windfall profits" taxes or offer investment tax credits (or both). It has the tools of government underwriting and loan guarantees. It can push interest rates up or down, put quotas on exports and imports, spend more or less. It can pay more in social security, retirement and unemployment benefits, or hold the line.

In deciding which of these options to use, or in what combination, the government will get plenty of advice from the sidelines: from organized labor, from "think tanks" like the Brookings Institution, Resources for the Future, and the Committee for Economic Development; from business groups such as the National Association of Manufacturers and the Chamber of Commerce. It will hear from consumers, from businessmen, from academic economists, from housewives and bankers. Each will give government its own message. And in the periodic political accountings called elections, every administration will stand or fall on the condition of the economy at the time. More than anything else except war, economics decides the grades that voters give when the final marks are put down on the political report card.

In today's climate, the effect of economic conditions is politically more potent than it has been at any time since the depression years of the 1930s. For the direction in which the economy is trending is more important to politics than the actual level of business at the time. If the economy is high but trending downward, the uneasiness is greater than when it is low and moving up. The wise heads around the White House know this, and that is why, as the presidential election of 1976 looms ahead, the American electorate can rest assured that economic policy out of Washington will put more of its chips on expansion than on fighting inflation. Given the choice between inflation (with lots of jobs) and recession (with people out of work) Washington's choice is obvious. Washington knows which side its bread is buttered on.

26 DOING BUSINESS WITH THE GOVERNMENT

If you have business you would like to transact with the government—whether for profit, persuasion, or just plain information—the first rule is: go ahead.

In far too many cases, citizens regard the government in Washington as unapproachable. In some instances, people with problems or questions are afraid of being confused by the complexity of bureaucracy. Sometimes they think they'll be pushed aside, ignored, or rebuffed by officials too busy to be concerned. Most such ideas are misconceptions.

The federal government is not an easy institution to extract things from, but with perseverance, guidance, and a little bit of luck, there's almost nothing that can't be found somewhere in Washington. Most government agencies, in fact, are eager to get their story across to the public. Far from trying to hide their light under a bushel, most departments and bureaus and commissions have special information offices set up for the express purpose of serving the public. The trick is to find the right one at the right time.

HOW TO GET INFORMATION

The Government Printing Office is the government's big fountain of information, in the form of written matter. While its list of publications runs to tens of thousands a year, you can get catalogs of special subject matter, broken down by topics and availabilities.

It is possible to get from Washington the printed records of all the public acts of Congress, the executive departments, the courts and independent agencies, as well as an encyclopedic collection of background information on every subject under the sun. The trouble is, you won't have time in your life to read it all, so you will have to be selective. As a general introduction to the government, including guidance on how to get government information, you can buy the *United States Government Manual,* updated every year. It is available at $4 a copy from the Superintendent of Documents, Government Printing Office, Washington, D.C. 20402. Or if you have a government bookstore in your city, you can buy it there. Look in your telephone directory under "United States Government," then check for Government Printing Office, Government Bookstore, or Federal Information Center.

The most comprehensive listing of government documents is the *Monthly Catalog of U.S. Government Publications.* $27 a year (includes index). Single copy $1.85. Available from the superintendent of documents in Washington, 20402, or any government bookstore. As publications are issued, the government compiles a list of those published during the preceding month. The most popular of these, or the ones with the greatest current appeal, are listed, biweekly, under the title *Selected U.S. Government Publications.* This is also available through the superintendent of documents, as above.

The third general source on what's available is a series of mimeographed "subject sheets" which will be sent to you if you write or call asking what the government has available on a given subject, such as gardening, cancer treatment, mathematics, geography, space science, or whatever. These will be sent free of charge, giving title and price of publications in your interest field.

If you make your inquiry to the Government Printing Office in Washington (or the superintendent of documents), use zip code 20402, and allow about four weeks for delivery, since the GPO now receives about 60,000 letters per day.

The government also has regional distribution centers outside Washington—at Philadelphia, Pennsylvania, and at Pueblo, Colorado. These offices are especially equipped to supply the 120 documents listed on the biweekly selected list. When ordering from either of these centers, try to give all the pertinent information, including catalog number or stock number.

As a general guide, most of the local government information offices are in or near the Federal Building, the federal courthouse (if any), or the central post office building in your city.

If you are interested in continuing information on business conditions, with general economic indications, month by month, you can subscribe to three regular publications:

Economic Indicators. Monthly. This is a compilation of information on business volume, retail sales, bank loans, employment, prices, wages, order volume, and similar material. It is available at all government bookstores. If none of these exists in your area you can write the Superintendent of Documents, GPO, Washington, D.C. 20402. Price 85¢ a single copy. $10.10 a year.

Construction Review, $1.25 a single copy. $14.50 a year.

Monthly Labor Review. $1.90 a copy. $22.35 a year.

On veterans' affairs, there is a basic booklet covering services offered by the Veterans Administration titled *Federal Benefits for Veterans and Dependents.* Revised yearly. Available from Superintendent of Documents in Washington, local government bookstores (see above), or any Veterans Administration office. Current price is 60¢, but this is subject to change with rising costs.

GOVERNMENT CONTRACTS

If you have never had any business dealings with the government, either as a buyer of surplus goods or as a seller of products and services, it may be well to get yourself oriented first. Government business is not exactly gravy. Government purchasing agents are tough, and sometimes the red tape is enough to drive you to distraction. On big contracts, you may be subject to renegotiation or cost auditing. Nevertheless, many individuals and companies find that their products and services are adapted to government use and the government is a natural customer. Other firms may use government business as a filler or to help them cover overhead while they sell the rest of their output in specialized private markets. Whatever the motive or incentive, it is well to know what you're getting into.

The primer in the field is a free government publication called *Doing Business with the Federal Government.* You can get it simply by calling, writing, or visiting one of the Business Service Centers maintained by the

General Services Administration. There are such centers in Boston, New York, Philadelphia, Washington, Atlanta, Chicago, Kansas City, Fort Worth, Denver, Los Angeles, San Francisco, and Seattle. For the address, look in the telephone book under United States Government, General Services Administration.

The comparable publication specializing in defense business is titled *An Introduction to the Defense Supply Agency,* and it contains all the statistics on what they buy, how much they buy, and how you should go about getting in on it. For a free copy, write: Headquarters, Defense Supply Agency, Cameron Station, Alexandria, Virginia 22314.

As for government surplus property, there is still a lot of it available to buy, and you can get a line on what it is and where it is by contacting the General Services Administration through the Business Service Centers listed above. Ask them for *Disposal, Surplus Real Property* or *Buying Government Surplus Personal Property.* There is no charge for either.

Military surplus is sold to the public by the Defense Property Disposal Service, Battle Creek, Michigan 49016, but before you approach them it would be a good idea to get and read the publication called *How to Buy Surplus Personal Property from the Defense Department.* Send 40¢ a copy to the Public Documents Distribution Center (PDDC), Pueblo, Colorado 81009. Ask for item no. 16M.

TAXES, REGULATION, AND OTHER PROGRAMS

Nothing is so chilling to the average taxpayer—individual or business—as the word that the Internal Revenue Service is challenging his tax return. Yet such challenges are commonplace, and will probably become more frequent as the IRS develops sophisticated new methods of examining returns, frequently by computer. The first rule to remember is: Don't panic. It happens to many people, and your return may have been audited simply on a random basis.

If the problem appears simple or the amount small, cooperate and produce the records that the agent wants to see. Try to make them as complete as possible. If the amount is sizable or the problem complex, call on a tax lawyer immediately. Most of this kind of tax auditing is done in your own city, so Washington won't be involved (unless the case drags on into an appeals phase or goes to Tax Court). If you do get a lawyer, don't send the IRS any documents without his express instruction and advice. It can be damaging to send more than enough, or some of the wrong things.

In the realm of government regulation, some new things have been added in the past several years. Most notable of these are the Occupational Safety and Health Administration (OSHA) and the Product Safety Commission, which are steadily on the prowl to see that business maintains proper standards of safety (and health) in working places and produces and sells goods that are up to safety standards for the public.

OSHA inspectors have authority by law to visit any workplace and issue citations if they feel that violations are present. They receive their authority under a 1970 law, and their agency is a part of the Department of Labor. To protect yourself in advance against inadvertent violations, get a copy of the checklist by writing OSHA, Department of Labor, Washington, D.C. 20210. In large cities, you can get a copy by calling or visiting an OSHA regional office, listed in the telephone directory under United States Government, sub-listing Department of Labor, OSHA. No charge for the list.

On product safety, the Consumer Product Safety Commission (CPSC) has authority over thousands of items, including such things as lawnmowers, heaters, book matches, playground equipment, etc. If you have questions as a user, maker, or seller, you can write to the Office of the Secretary, Consumer Product Safety Commission, Washington, D.C. 20207.

Antipollution controls are now being promulgated in a steady stream—relating to air, water, noise, ocean dumping, etc. To know what's what, write Maurice Eastin, Environmental Protection Agency, Washington, D.C. 20460.

One general source of help on new rules and regulations of all kinds is the *Federal Register*. It is too much to read regularly or search through aimlessly, but if you are looking for something specific or have reason to want to check the actual details of a regulation, it can be very useful. The subscription price has been $45 a year, but an increase is on its way. It is available through the Superintendent of Documents, GPO, Washington, D.C. 20402.

CONSUMERS AND SMALL BUSINESS

The government is now producing more written matter for consumers than ever before. Until recently, most such publications came from the Department of Agriculture or from subdivisions of other major departments. Now they have been coordinated by Virginia Knauer, the government's consumer affairs specialist, and made available through the General Services Administration. A catalog or index of such materials, 12 pages long, plus order blank, can be obtained by writing the Superintendent of Documents, GPO, Washington, D.C. 20402, or by visiting any of the GPO bookstores throughout the United States. Copies may also be obtained through the Public Documents Distribution Center, Pueblo, Colorado 81009. No charge for the catalog. About half the publications themselves are free. Publications topics range from passengers' rights, fair housing, home safety, buying hints, and construction guides to such subjects as health, auto safety, energy conservation, personal finances, and child care.

In the realm of small business, there are many services from the government, including assistance loans, lease guarantees, venture capital help, and technical help. Information on these services is available at Small Business Administration field offices around the country, listed under "U.S. Government" in the telephone directory. If there is no field office in your community, you can get more information by writing to the Small Business Administration, 1441 L Street N.W., Washington, D.C. 20406.

Among privately published books for businessmen interested in Washington, one of the most comprehensive and useful is *The Businessman's Guide to Washington* by William Ruder and Raymond Nathan, Collier Books, 1975, $4.50. Written by two former businessmen and public officials, it deals in practical terms with the sources and pipelines of information that businessmen are most likely to need.

SPECIAL BUSINESS HELP

Sometimes problems arise in business that you can't dispose of within your own company or industry. Import competition may be one of these, and in today's scramble for worldwide markets, such competitive pressures are on the rise. If the competition is fair and square, there may be nothing that anyone can, or will, do about it. But if you suspect that it is out of line with U.S. policy, you should make your views known. The person to contact is K. R. Mason, Secretary, U.S. Tariff Commission, 8th and E Streets N.W., Washington, D.C. 20436.

If you believe that foreign governments are unfairly or unlawfully blocking your exports into their markets by tricky regulations or gimmicks, you may be able to get help. Write Allen H. Garland, Trade Negotiations Office, 1800 G Street N.W., Washington, D.C. 20506. Be sure to give him the details of the problem.

Another good Washington contact on export trade problems is John P. Kearney, in the Department of Commerce. His address: Office of the Ombudsman for Business, Department of Commerce, Washington, D.C. 20230. Telephone: 202-967-3176. He may not be able to handle the problem all the way, but he can steer you through the government maze, suggest the proper agency to get in touch with, and identify specific officials in charge of special areas.

On the opportunity side, there are a number of government programs and offices that are set up to help expand business, especially overseas. To find out about new business prospects in foreign markets—Europe, Japan, Soviet Union, Eastern Europe, China—you can visit a Department of Commerce field office in your nearest large city. Or you can write Washington. Address your inquiry, specifying your field of interest, to: E. J. Krause, Director, Office of International Marketing (BIC 210), Commerce Department, Washington, D.C. 20230. He'll tell you what opportunities are opening up.

As a general proposition, when you need guidance on a Washington problem, or where to find something in the big federal system, try first to contact an association or group with which you are affiliated. A trade association, professional association, cause organization, or special alliance—if it has an office in Washington—is usually willing to help you find what you need, especially if you are a subscriber or sympathizer. This applies whether you are a businessman, union member, retired teacher, farmer, retailer, or plain consumer. Somewhere in Washington, there is an organization that represents your concern and knows where the information you want is likely to be.

FRIENDS ON THE HILL

It's a good idea to get to know your own congressman or one of your senators. Go up and shake his hand sometime when he is home in the district. As a politician, he will appreciate (1) your friendliness and (2) your recognition of him. Just because you did not vote for your congressman, and may not especially like his political views, don't ignore him or treat him with disdain. He doesn't know *how* you voted (unless you are conspicuous about it), and his inherent sense of politics will cause him to assume that you are a friend.

If you agree with him, let him know. You might consider giving him a contribution the next time he runs for office. (You can give him up to $100 without anyone's finding out. If you give more, your name will be on the list that he is required to file, and this list may be scrutinized by reporters working in Washington for your local newspaper.)

Corporate executives should make a special effort to know the congressmen from their area. Union leaders do, even if they don't support them. It gives them a lot of clout when bills come along in Congress that will affect their membership. There are lots of measures that affect businesses, so being able to phone a congressman directly in Washington and talk on a one-to-one basis (perhaps even first name) is a valuable thing for a company executive. He can explain how the bill will help or hurt his firm, reminding the congressman of the size of the payroll there—a reference that is quite legitimate, since it indicates that not only the company will be affected but also its workers.

Most congressmen honestly do not know how all the legislation that comes along in a session will touch their constituents. They appreciate being told the consequences, so that they can bear them in mind when it comes time to vote. Deal with your senator or representative as you would anyone in a responsible position—your banker, the postmaster, your clergyman, or doctor. He works for you, tries to protect you in Washington, and if he knows you, even distantly, he may do a far better job in your behalf.

Your representatives and senators are interested in keeping the goodwill of home folks, so don't be shy about asking them for help. They and their aides have access to every office, department, and bureau in Washington, and a little prodding from them can expedite your dealings with the bureaucracy. They can also give you valuable pointers on where to find the information you need. Congressional offices are attuned to offering constituent service on almost any subject, but don't expect miracles. If you're an average citizen, your congressman won't get you an interview with the Vice President or the head of the IRS. He can, however, get you into the White House on a VIP tour, if you give him enough advance notice of your trip to Washington. If he knows you personally, he might even take you to lunch in one of the Capitol dining rooms reserved for members of Congress.

When you write, address your note to your congressman by name. Use his office number if you know it. If you don't, you can address your letter to Representative So-and-So, U.S. Capitol, Washington, D.C. 20515. (The code for senators is 20510.) Give him the pertinent facts, and tell him clearly what your problem is. Or if you want to talk to him, dial 202-224-3121 and ask for him by name. You may be surprised what the two of you can accomplish.

27 WHERE YOUR TAXES GO

If you were given the job of counting the money, in $100 bills, that the federal government will spend this year, it would take you over fifty years. Even so, you could do it by then only if you counted nonstop at the rate of two bills a second, without a break and without sleeping. That's clearly impossible, but it will give you some idea of how much $315 billion is, which is about what the government probably will cost from July 1, 1974, to June 30, 1975.

Obviously, the government has grown over the years. The current federal budget is almost 600 times as big as it was at the turn of the century, and the end is not in sight. The trend is up. During the past seventy-five years, the government has cut back its spending in only twenty-one years. A third of those years were bunched after the two world wars, when wartime spending was reduced to peacetime levels. In the last twenty years, federal spending has gone down in only one year (1965), and even then it was an infinitesimal reduction.

But a strange thing about the federal budget is that it has taken a fairly constant part of the nation's output of goods and services in recent years despite the steady increase in dollars. When measured against the gross national product, the federal segment has been accounting for about 20 percent over the last two decades. In some years the percentage has been slightly higher or lower than that, but it hasn't varied very much. One can safely assume that as the country's output grows further, the government will grow in proportion.

Not very long ago the biggest chunk of federal spending went for defense. This is no longer true. Now the largest portion is for social welfare—for health, education, old-age benefits, unemployment pay, and similar programs. Defense has slipped into second place. It now takes less than 30 percent of the budget as compared with over 40 percent in 1965. This doesn't mean that it has gone down in terms of actual dollars. In the same period, actual spending for military and defense-related activities has risen from $50 billion to more than $90 billion.

Those figures omit a lot of outlays that some experts consider a part of the same package. For example, most of the public debt has been incurred to pay for wars. A year's interest on the debt now costs over $30 billion, approximately 10 percent of the budget. Then there are the costs of veterans' benefits, which are a direct outgrowth of past military activities. And there are the costs of foreign economic aid, which is closely tied to defense. Adding this type of indirect defense expenditure to the direct outlays once again makes the defense portion the biggest part of the federal budget. Nevertheless, there is no question about the rapid rise of the nondefense portion. There has been a virtual explosion of federal benefits of one kind or another.

Payments for health services rose from under $2 billion in 1965 to $26 billion in the 1975 fiscal year. This includes medicare and medicaid as well as research grants, medical education scholarships, public health services, and medical care on Indian reservations. Social security benefits, unemployment pay, the federal portion of public assistance payments, school lunches for children, grants to the states for social services, and similar expenditures add more than $100 billion, four times the amount in 1965. Federal programs in education have been rising just as rapidly. They more than quadrupled between the fiscal years 1965 and 1975, mainly because of new and bigger outlays for elementary schools, high schools and colleges, and vocational training for adults.

Surprisingly, some government expenditures are now going down after a period of steady increases. The peak is past in space research and technology. Aid for farmers is being cut back as the era of farm surpluses has given way to shortages. And sharp cuts in the Food for Peace program are holding down the overall total of foreign expenditures. These are the exceptions, however, and they are only a small stumbling block in the inexorable rise of total federal spending.

A NEW STYLE OF THINKING

What is more significant about the trend is the changed underlying attitude of politicians. Big budget increases once were proposed apologetically by whatever administration was in power. They were to meet an "emergency" or to meet special conditions. Administration officials blamed the Congress, and congressmen blamed the administration for boosting expenditures and running deficits. In recent years this view became muted as a result of two developments: (1) the acceptance of inflation as a fact of life and (2) the acceptance of Keynesian economics by conservatives as well as liberals.

It wasn't very long ago that most politicians rejected the inevitability of inflation. The target was no inflation at all, or at most 1 percent to 1½ percent a year. Relative stability of prices was a goal to be desired and was considered achievable. Instead, the aim now is much more modest—merely to bring down the increases to something nearer 5 percent, both in government spending and in prices. The acceptance of inflation has led, in turn, to an acceptance of rising federal budgets. Higher general prices mean more spending by the government for the things it buys and the programs it sponsors.

The economic theory of the government as a balance wheel in the economy has been the other important factor in the changed attitude. There are few economists in or out of government who have not come around to thinking that the government should stimulate business in times of recession and dampen it in times of boom, and even the politicians no longer argue the point. But politicians being what they are, they have found it easier to use the budget to stimulate in recessions than to dampen in booms. No one wants to take the blame for cutting off prosperity, so the result is that the stimulants are seldom removed once they are implanted. Federal spending rises faster in some years than others, but it rises nonetheless. And as new federal programs are voted into law, they tend to become untouchable with the passage of time. They give rise to so-called uncontrollable spending, which at the present is estimated to be about 75 percent of the budget.

Regardless of feelings on the subject, it is hard to find anyone with a say in the matter who expects the federal budget ever to be reduced. The only question they have is how much faster it will go up in the future and how much deeper it will intrude on everyone's life.

BUDGETS AND INFLATION

One new element in the U.S. budgetary situation is the recent return to an attitude of respect for restraint in government spending as one way to reduce some of the pressures of inflation. Where once this was a bone of contention between liberals and conservatives, the recent pace of price increases has created a slender bond between economists of different persuasions. At the 1974 White House economic presummit conferences, both liberal John Kenneth Galbraith and conservative Milton Friedman recommended that government hold the line on expenses until the inflation fires were dampened. Whether this is achieved or not, it is significant that two such widely differing advisers would come forth at the same time with similar counsel. The vogue for governmental restraint, however, does not signify an abandonment of the basic theory of government as the economic balance wheel. It suggests only that some economists and government officials in this country are beginning to face up to the necessity of "balancing down" for a while, instead of "balancing up," as they have been doing for the past generation.

Still, in other countries of the world, spending restraint is not catching hold. While the doctrine is espoused by conservatives, and some national leaders have given lip service to the idea, the full-employment philosophy has more political appeal. Reinforced by labor unions and labor parties, European governments are stimulating their economies rather than restraining them. In the rest of the world even more than here the tide is still running toward larger government budgets.

Getting the federal budget "under control" is the modern-day version of the quest for the Holy Grail. Most politicians agree that the cause is a noble one, and some even expend considerable energy in the search, but it continues to elude even the most dedicated of them.

THE "UNCUTTABLE" EXPENSES

Much of the budget, in fact, is "out of control" in the sense that certain outlays are required by law or contractual agreement. To reduce federal spending would therefore require the repeal of laws or the abrogation of contracts made by the government, and many of the programs involved are politically inviolate.

The $30 billion a year of interest on the federal debt is an example of a contractual arrangement. To cut the amount would require the government to refuse to pay all or part of the interest on bonds and other securities it has sold to the public under its promise of a stipulated return. As interest rates rise, the cost of refinancing the same debt also rises. Failure of the government to pay the higher rates demanded by the public would require it to pay off the principal as it came due. This would require it to raise taxes. Failure to pay the interest on the debt already outstanding would make it virtually impossible to sell new securities and, in effect, would be the equivalent of declaring federal bankruptcy. So the cost of carrying the federal debt continues to go up.

The government is similarly locked into other spending programs such as social security, veterans' pensions, medicare, and unemployment compensation. The lock is not as tight on these because the payments under them are set by law and laws can be changed or repealed. But here too there is a contractual obligation to present beneficiaries. And to reduce the benefits for future beneficiaries is an action that no politician interested in getting re-elected relishes.

Even with no new programs, federal outlays will continue to rise for years in the future, because future outlays are decreed by existing laws. And now inflation is adding to the cost of everything: armaments, food, clothing, and supplies for the military, which cost more even without any upgrading of quality. Government pay goes up just as does pay for workers in private employment. The cost of maintaining and repairing federal buildings rises along with nonfederal. The price of paper, fuel, typewriters, laboratory equipment, desks, electricity, and everything else that government uses keeps up with the price of similar items used in the private economy.

Federal spending in the fiscal year ending in July 1976 will be more than $350 billion, or about 10 percent more than spending for the fiscal year 1975, but the larger number of dollars will buy about the same number of programs, materials, and services. Thus, notwithstanding the national rhetoric about "economizing on government," the overall sums that flow through the federal coffers continue to expand.

Yet, as was said earlier, the federal budget accounts for a fairly constant 20 percent of the gross national product, year in and year out. Of the industrialized countries, only Japan runs a smaller percentage. Others are as high as 45 percent. Whether you consider government "big," "too big," or "about right," look now at federal income and spending for the 1975 fiscal year and see where the money comes from and what it pays for.

WHERE THE MONEY COMES FROM

The largest chunk of federal revenue comes from income taxes paid by individuals—44 percent. Another 29 percent comes from social security taxes and other insurance or pension payments (shared approximately half and half by individuals and employers). The third-largest income source is corporate income taxes, amounting to 16 percent. Excise taxes (federal sales taxes) account for 6 percent, and estate and gift taxes 2 percent. The other 4 percent comes from customs duties and miscellaneous sources. In time of deficits, of course, the government augments its revenue flow by borrowing.

Of the major category of revenue—individual income taxes—the largest proportion, 23 percent, comes from people with incomes between $10,000 and $15,000. The second-largest chunk comes from incomes of $15,000 to $20,000 (17 percent). The highest-bracket incomes, over $100,000, account for 8.5 percent. Even though the tax brackets are higher, the amounts netted are lower because there are fewer taxpayers with incomes of this size.

WHERE THE MONEY GOES

The largest outlay of "federal money" goes for what the budget officers call "income security," meaning social security payments, pensions and support benefits, and various federal contributions to supplement unemployment payments. These account for 33 percent of federal spending. Veterans' benefits and services take another 4 percent. The national defense budget, handled largely by the Defense Department, accounts for slightly more than 28 percent of the budget. Interest on the national debt takes about 10 percent, and health services account for a little more than 8 percent. Education, job training, and other manpower costs take a little under 4 percent. Commerce and transportation take about 4 percent; community development and housing take 2 percent; revenue sharing with the states (for local use), 2 percent; and the "general costs of government," 2 percent. Other expenses are split among international affairs and finance, slightly more than 1 percent, space research, 1 percent, natural resources and environment, 1 percent, and agriculture and rural development, 1 percent. (These figures add up to 101 percent, because some of the numbers have been rounded off, but the proportions are essentially correct.)

While some percentages may seem like small potatoes, the amounts of actual money are somewhat more impressive. Agriculture's 1 percent, for example, amounts to $3 billion, at current levels of spending. Natural resources and the environment come out to $3.1 billion. Space research and technology take $3.3 billion. Even the small percentages build up a lot of dollars.

WHO COLLECTS THE MONEY

Federal money is budgeted by the White House Office of Management and Budget, appropriated by Congress, and spent by thousands of departments, bureaus, offices, and agencies, but it is collected by the Treasury. Specifically, it is collected by the Internal Revenue Service, a part of the Treasury with its own boss. During the Watergate affair, the commissioner of Internal Revenue was under pressure from the White House to "bear down hard" on some suspected administration adversaries, but the final evidence was inconclusive. Considering the 117 million tax returns that are processed every year, it is remarkable that there are not more instances, or at least charges, of unequal treatment, favoritism, or discrimination in the collection of federal taxes.

The Internal Revenue Service consists of 75,000 people. Headquarters are in Washington, but there are seven regions, with offices located in New York, Philadelphia, Atlanta, Cincinnati, Chicago, Dallas, and San Francisco. There are also district offices in 58 cities around the country. The regions are, in fact, nearly autonomous, and taxpayers in different jurisdictions sometimes find that rulings on similar tax situations do not precisely match. These disparities spring from interpretation of the regulations, and probably would exist even if all returns were processed and audited in one location. A taxpayer who is aggrieved, or who challenges an Internal Revenue agent's ruling, can take it to the agent's supervisor. If he is not satisfied, he can go to the administrative appeals section of the service, and then he can appeal further to the federal courts.

More and more, tax returns are being selected for audit by computer. Corporate returns are even being partially audited by computer, at least in the case of larger companies. Audits are conducted in several categories. The tax returns of large companies are always audited, because a small difference in interpretation or in arithmetic can net large amounts of tax money when the error can be made to favor the government. Treasury lobbyists have often said, in testimony before committees of Congress, that every additional dollar appropriated for agents and auditing time yields more than a dollar of additional revenue. Among smaller companies, audits are conducted on a random basis or when an "eyeball" examination reveals some figures or percentages that don't seem to ring true.

Individual returns are audited on several grounds. Some kinds of taxpayers are watched especially closely, including doctors, dentists, and various groups of self-employed. The Treasury has discovered that where large amounts of cash are received, they may not be fully accounted for. Some taxpayers are audited on a random spot-check basis, like sticking a hat pin into the pile, just to turn up any occasional examples of carelessness or miscalculation. The Internal Revenue Service claims that it is just as anxious to straighten out errors in the taxpayer's favor as it is to extract more money, but it is hard to convince the average taxpayer that this is true.

A LOOK AHEAD

On the basis of current percentages (and there's reason to believe that the proportions will remain pretty much the same), the biggest chunk of "federal money" will continue to go for income security and it will amount to more than $118 billion in the 1976 fiscal year. Of this, more than $81 billion will be for retirement and disability payments, mainly through the social security system. Nearly $16 billion will go for "public assistance," or what is popularly called "welfare." About $7.5 billion will go for the federal portion of unemployment compensation. Another $8 billion will go for veterans' pensions and disability payments (budgeted separately from other pension and security programs).

In the field of health, the federal government will spend $28 billion to help provide medical services through "medicare" and other programs. Veterans' hospitalization and medical care will take more than $4 billion in addition.

In the second biggest category of expenses, national defense, the Defense Department will have a budget of about $92 billion, of which $26.5 billion will be for personnel costs alone. Another $27 billion will go for operations and maintenance, and nearly $18 billion for procurement of the various weapons of war, fuels, parts, machines, and materials. In addition, nearly $10 billion will go for research and development. Atomic energy costs will be slightly more than $3 billion. All defense items, including international military aid, will total $95 billion.

These three general functions—income security, health, and national defense—will account for almost $245 billion out of the $350 billion or more that the federal government will probably spend in the 1976 fiscal year. When you add $30 billion for interest on the national debt, over which there is no discretionary power, $275 billion of spending is pretty well set, leaving roughly $75 billion for all the remaining functions of the federal government. These remaining functions include: the conduct of foreign affairs, international finance, space research, agriculture, natural resources, environmental control, commerce, transportation, housing, community development, education, labor, revenue sharing, the courts, Congress, and general operations of the government. (For a detailed listing of all federal revenues and expenses, you can write the Government Printing Office, Washington, D.C. 20402, and ask for "The U.S. Budget in Brief—1976.")

In any such huge aggregation of income and spending, some waste is inevitable. Chances are that the tendency to play fast and loose with the public's money is greater when the budget is expanding fastest—during wars and during years when the government is intentionally stimulating the economy. In times like the present, some popular programs get squeezed or sharply curtailed. Still, there are tricks to the budget trade, and many experienced bureaucrats know them all. If the previous year's budget is not fully spent by the end of the fiscal year (June 30), then contracts are let in a great rush, supplies are bought, and even (it is said) fuel is burned in the midst of a heat wave. One of the heinous sins of officialdom, in the eyes of some bureaucrats, is to have money left over from last year's budget, because when the fiscal year has ended the money can no longer be spent, and this "surplus" may be "used against you" when you go back to plead for a comparable amount next year.

But such flagrant practices of waste are isolated, not the general rule. Where genuine waste occurs, it is probably caused more by inertia than by conscious wastefulness. Programs are continued beyond their reasonable life simply because they are in existence, and this means there are people whose livelihoods depend on their continuation. It is said that the most permanent thing under the sun is a government program which has outlived its usefulness. If government programs had a family escutcheon, the shield could be emblazoned with the motto: "Many are started and few are ended."

Where your tax money goes, from now on, will be more carefully watched than at any time in the past thirty years—more than at any time since before the Great Depression of the Thirties, World War II, and the expansionary period of the 1950s and 1960s. Even though spending has risen to counteract recession, the Executive Branch is watching the dollars more closely for anti-inflation reasons, and now Congress has passed a budget reform act under which it is obliged to handle its budgetary affairs in a more orderly way. At regular intervals throughout the year, it must add up the amounts it has appropriated and see whether they are likely to run the government into the red. If they do not, well and good. If they do, Congress must take special—and conspicuous—action to let the override run.

Whether the new inflation consciousness and budgetary control system will make for economizing remains to be seen, but henceforth you will have an easier time finding out where your money is going.

28 WHAT YOUR GOVERNMENT KNOWS ABOUT YOU

Washington gobbles up huge mounds of facts and figures, digests them, and disgorges them for almost every purpose under the sun. From each individual, business, farm, and organization in America it collects bits and pieces of information, some of it vital, some of it useful, some of it trivial, some of it malicious.

The federal government is a hungry "factocrat." It says it needs all of these data to serve the people—to tax them, to pay them a variety of public benefits, to protect them from the criminals and subversives in their midst, to record the ups and downs of their economic activity, to chart their future from the experiences of their past. Like a computerized pack rat, Uncle Sam can't bear to throw away any of his precious information. Long after most people have forgotten it is there, it still occupies an infinitesimal spot on a magnetic tape in some federal data bank.

The federal government knows when and where you were born, and it knows your father's name and your mother's maiden name. It knows what you do for a living and how much money you earn. If you were ever in the armed forces, it has a set of your fingerprints. It knows if you've ever been arrested for a major crime, or have received a federally funded scholarship. It knows if you've ever had your driver's license revoked. It knows if you own a firearm or a boat, fly a private airplane, operate a ham radio, or have a passport.

It knows if you've made any transaction with a foreign bank amounting to more than $5,000, and the nature of that transaction. It can find out very easily, if it cares to, whether you pay your bills promptly and how many debts you have (from credit records), and whether you drink or smoke (from health and life insurance records). It can get your bank to show photostats of every check you've written recently. If you have an FHA mortgage on your home, it might have a file assessing the stability of your marriage. If you've ever applied for a federal job, Uncle Sam still has a file on you with extensive information about how you live. It has a similar file on you if you've ever worked for a company that does business with the federal government. One of the nation's leading data-bank authorities, Arthur R. Miller, has estimated that the average American citizen is included in ten to twenty federal files.

A 1965 House survey of federal information gathering arrived at the conclusion, after months of searching, that some twenty federal agencies maintained more than 600 substantial data banks of economic, social, criminal, and individual facts. A Senate survey the following year attempted a more ambitious (some would say futile) survey to determine the actual number of federal files on individual Americans contained in federal data banks, and arrived at the grand total of 3.1 billion.

The decisions that determine what information should be collected and how that data will ultimately be used are made in tens of federal offices in the Washington area, such as the Census Bureau headquarters in the suburb of Suitland, Maryland; the FBI's massive J. Edgar Hoover Building on Pennsylvania Avenue, midway between the Capitol and White House; the Civil Service Commission offices at 19th and E Streets N.W.; the Federal Triangle offices of the Internal Revenue Service; the Department of Defense's sprawling Pentagon, across the Potomac River from the District; the Social Security Administration's offices on Independence Avenue S.W., at the foot of Capitol Hill, and the templelike National Archives on Constitution Avenue N.W.

DECENTRALIZED STORAGE

The billions of items of information collected by the government have all passed through the nation's capital at one time or another, but relatively few of these data find a final resting place in Washington. The FBI's enormous arrest and fingerprint data banks are in Washington, and so are the Department of Transportation's files of driver's license revocations and the Census Bureau's mass of statistics on everything under the sun.

But Uncle Sam's data-storage system is very decentralized, for a variety of reasons. Locating data banks elsewhere in the country makes the files safer in the event of an enemy attack on the capital and also tends to spread the economic benefits of this thriving federal activity over many communities. Hence we have the IRS National Computer Center in Martinsburg, West Virginia; the immense Social Security Administration data bank in Baltimore, Maryland, and the Civil Service Commission and Defense Department personnel records in two buildings, 12 miles apart, in the St. Louis, Missouri, area. (One of these buildings and a large number of the military personnel records it houses were damaged in 1973 in a fire of suspicious origin.) Individual census schedules are transferred onto microfilm at an installation in Jeffersonville, Indiana (a suburb of Louisville, Kentucky), and the only post-1900 census records keyed to individual identity are stored in Pittsburg, Kansas.

Much of the information that Washington gathers is compiled into aggregate statistics that are impersonal and anonymous. The government is very generous with this kind of information. It dispenses it in small pieces to anyone who asks, and it dispenses a great deal of it to business either free or for a fee. Uncle Sam's open-handed policy on aggregate information doesn't extend to individual information. Sure, the government will allow you to examine some of the files it has compiled about you, but most of them are routine information you gave to it yourself—like census, social security, and tax returns. But the government has a lot of information about you that you didn't supply, at least not knowingly or directly. It got this information from many sources, like your employer, your state and local government, your friends, credit bureaus, schools you've attended, insurance companies, banks, and organizations you belong to.

Until recently it was next to impossible to find out if such information about you even existed in federal files, let alone get a look at it yourself. While Uncle Sam was stingy about showing this information to you, he has been surprisingly free about passing "confidential" data around to anyone in his own family of bureaucrats, as well as state and local officials and even businesses that can claim some sort of "need to know."

Uncle Sam has been collecting data on the American people since the first census in 1790, but the sheer volume of information gathering and processing that goes on today was not possible until the development of the electronic computer. From its first computer purchase in 1951 (the Census Bureau's Univac I), the federal government went on to become the largest buyer and user of data-processing equipment in the world. There are about 7,000 computers installed in federal agencies around the nation. Relatively few of them are used to process and store information about the American people and their activities. Most are engaged in routine housekeeping matters like payroll computation, materials inventory control, and processing millions of checks for the recipients of federal benefits. The Washington area alone employs some 52,000 people to program, operate, and administer computer systems.

THE CENSUS

The first and largest of Uncle Sam's legion of fact finders is the Census Bureau. Everyone knows that the Census records the statistical characteristics of the American people in the first year of each decade, but few people realize how many other surveys the Census undertakes for itself and other federal agencies. The biggest of these is the Current Population Survey, in which some 55,000 households are queried each month on such subjects as income, education, change of residence, and family size. Four times a year, in the Quarterly Household Survey, Census canvassers knock on the doors of 15,000 households to determine whether they have purchased any automobiles, television sets, washing machines, and other appliances recently, or whether they intend to.

But the Census doesn't survey only households and individuals. It surveys every imaginable economic enterprise—construction, manufacturing, mining, communications, agriculture, retailing, transportation, and foreign trade—and it even surveys state and local governments (which combined now employ nearly three times as many people as the federal government). These periodic economic surveys (including the Weekly Retail Trade Report, the Monthly Selected Services Receipts Report, and the Current Wholesale Survey) ask the managers of every major business in America for information on how many employees they have, how much they are paid in total, the amount of materials consumed, the value of their manufactured products or sales, the size of inventories, etc. In the category of manufacturing alone, there are 425 different industries for which the Census compiles detailed information, covering some 11,000 different products. For the American labor force, the Department of Labor's Bureau of Labor Statistics does comparably exhaustive surveys of earnings, hours of work, unemployment, and other relevant factors.

The major periodic Census surveys include the monthly Survey of Construction, in which about 3,000 home builders and 800 building permit offices are queried on the number and type of housing units started and sold; the monthly Current Medicare Survey, in which 6,000 households are asked questions about their use of medicare, the costs, and their assessment of its efficiency; the annual Health Interview Survey and Health Examination Survey, in which more than 50,000 households are questioned about illness and injury during the previous year; the annual National Crime Survey, which gathers information on the type and frequency of major crimes, through interviews with victims; and the Cotton Survey, a monthly tally of cotton production at more than 3,700 gins. (To prevent leaks of this information to cotton speculators, statistics are compiled into the monthly report only four hours before public release, by a team of Census employees who are sequestered in a locked room.)

Businesses use Census surveys to predict the demand for their products, so they can adjust production or purchasing accordingly. A company thinking about opening a new branch plant will analyze census figures to determine if the region has a labor force that's adequate in size and training. Retail establishments use census surveys to discover whether the income level of the populace will support the type of merchandise they intend to sell in their new store, and to evaluate the annual sales of existing stores of a similar type.

A year's subscription to the *Census Catalog* (four quarterlies and twelve monthly supplements) can be obtained for $10.90 from the Superintendent of Documents, GPO, Washington, D.C. 20402. It describes and gives the price of every publicly available statistical report and computer tabulation compiled by the Census, as well as related reports of other federal agencies. The catalog tells how to order everything from a 40¢ demographic profile of young married couples to a $1,440 taped tabulation of "U.S. imports of sorbic acid and potassium sorbate" for 1972, keyed to the country of origin.

Ever since the first census was taken in 1790, Americans have been squeamish about laying bare the vital statistics of their lives. The uneasiness increased as the questionnaire got longer and the questions more personal. The questionnaires reached their apex of length and nosiness in the late nineteenth century and have actually been trimmed since then. (The 1890 census schedule, for example, required that American Indians specify the percentage of white blood in their parentage, and whether they "live in polygamy.") In this century, the most significant addition to the census schedule was a question on total household income, added in 1940.

CENSUS SAFEGUARDS

The Census Bureau is probably the only federal agency that absolutely refuses to share its information about individual American citizens and businesses with its sister agencies—not with the FBI, the CIA, the Civil Service Commission, or anyone. In 1942 the War Department asked the Census for the names and addresses of all Japanese-American citizens living on the West Coast, so they could be detained for security purposes. The Census refused to reveal them. The confidentiality of the Census's information was briefly threatened by a 1961 Supreme Court ruling that the Federal Trade Commission could subpoena a corporation's carbon copy of a financial report it sent to the Census. But the following year Congress specified explicitly that "your census reports cannot be used for purposes of taxation, regulation or investigation." Census officials say that, despite the bureau's reputation for confidentiality, they still get a few queries every year from federal investigators—most of them rookies, the Census assumes—who hope to get a look at someone's schedule.

The people who run Census economic surveys try to make sure that aggregate information they dispense will not accidentally reveal the identity of a business or facts about it by process of elimination, thereby giving an unfair advantage to competitors. For example, they would not give out statistics on the profits of all heavy construction companies in a given county if there were only one such company in the county, or even if there were two or three such companies. In the latter case, the managers of one or two of the companies would be able to determine the other's profits by subtracting its own profits from the Census's "anonymous" figure.

While the Census shields your responses from the eyes of others, it allows you to retrieve any information about yourself that has ever been submitted to it. All you have to do is fill out an application for a certain piece of information and send it, along with $5, to the bureau's "age search" division in Pittsburg, Kansas. Each year several hundred thousand people ask the Census for information about themselves, mostly for verification—for social security, pensions, passports, etc.—of when they were born and where. The Census will also send you information about your parents or grandparents, so long as they are deceased.

Census records are not confidential forever. Any curious and patient person can go through the decennial census schedules from 1790 through 1880, which are complete with the names of people who were questioned. The 1890 returns were almost completely destroyed by fire, and all the records since 1900 are still covered by the blanket of confidentiality. The 1900 schedules were opened in late 1973 to bona fide historians, genealogists, and certain family members detailed in a particular schedule. This move was approved by the Justice Department after a campaign by genealogical societies and the Mormon church (which maintains computer files on its members' lineage). It was opposed by the Census Bureau, which argued that the nearly 7 million living Americans who are profiled in those records might resent such an invasion of privacy. The bureau still feels that the period of confidentiality should exceed by a wide margin the nation's average life expectancy.

Despite the bureau's safeguards of privacy, a few Americans every ten years refuse to answer the mandatory questions, risking a fine of $100 and sixty days in jail. The agency doesn't like to prosecute those who balk, and will send official after official to the resister's home to try to convince him to cooperate. Most of them eventually give in. During the 1970 census five people were prosecuted, including a member of the Delaware legislature. The Census has always won its cases except when convictions in several Honolulu cases stemming from the 1970 census were set aside on the grounds that the Census had unfairly singled out these particular defendants while failing to prosecute others. The Census is now making informal plans to prosecute resisters more often to avoid the appearance of discriminatory justice.

TAXES AND SOCIAL SECURITY

Only slightly less vast than the Census files are the data banks of the Social Security Administration and the Internal Revenue Service. If you possess a social security card, which nearly every postadolescent American does, there is a file on you containing information about the date and place of your birth, sex, race, father's name and mother's maiden name, lifetime earnings, and benefits (if any) paid to you. There is supposed to be no disclosure of this information to anyone outside of the SSA except for "national security" purposes (a gaping loophole that we will examine later).

The IRS's Martinsburg, West Virginia, computer center has a master file of more than 80 million taxpayer accounts, coded by social security number so they can be compared with information the IRS receives about money—wages, interest, and dividends—paid to you by your employer, bank, and corporations in which you might own stock. Warehouses maintained by the National Archives contain corporate tax returns going as far back as 1902.

Moving from the general to the particular, we come to the U.S. Department of Transportation's National Driver Register (NDR). The register is not, as the name suggests, a master file of all licensed drivers in the nation. It is a data bank containing names and vital information about every person whose license has been suspended or revoked by any state in the nation. Each state that withdraws a resident's license notifies the register headquarters in Washington, and every state can check its applications for new licenses against the list. There are more than 3.5 million files on magnetic tape in the register, and in recent years the number of requests for file searches have run close to 70,000 per day. In addition to vital information about drivers (date and place of birth, color of eyes, etc.), the file specifies why his license was revoked, such as for reckless driving, conviction for a felony, hit-and-run, and driving under the influence of alcohol.

POLICE AND THE FBI

Until about five years ago, criminal record keeping was for the most part manual and decentralized among the nation's 40,000 law enforcement agencies. The only national criminal index was the FBI's National Crime Information Center (NCIC), a computerized data bank with information on stolen items and wanted persons. The NCIC contained about 3 million files, of which only about one-tenth were records on active criminals. In addition, the FBI maintained about 190 million identification and fingerprint files keyed to more than 80 million citizens (with about half of the fingerprints coming from the Selective Service records of military inductees). The bureau also had about 20 million criminal offender records in manual files outside the NCIC systems.

The FBI is now in the midst of assembling a computerized superfile that will link computer terminals in police departments of every state to a central clearinghouse to receive and dispense information. There are vast differences in official estimates of the number of Americans on whom there will be information in the master file. The FBI says there will be about 5 million by the end of 1975, while the Law Enforcement Assistance Administration estimates the number might run to 20 million—nearly one-tenth of the total population. The FBI says it will include complete files only on interstate offenders who commit "serious" crimes, but the states that are now feeding information into the computer don't yet have standardized definitions of "serious" crimes.

Some data bank expert estimates indicate that 35 percent of the FBI's arrest data fails to indicate the final disposition of charges—whether the accused was convicted or acquitted, or whether the charges were dropped because of insufficient evidence. Critics of the system argue that records of arrests that do not lead to convictions should be purged from the data banks, lest an unjustly arrested citizen be penalized later in his life for having a "criminal record." (There is legislation pending that would, among other things, enable a citizen to see his own criminal records and correct errors in them. These proposals would also prohibit the dissemination to other public agencies of records that are not marked as to the disposition or current status of cases, and would require the retiring of records that are several years old, provided the subject has not committed another crime.)

FEDERAL JOB FILES

As closely as Uncle Sam keeps tabs on the average American citizen, this effort is paltry compared to the scrutiny he gives the members of his own vast family—the 2.8 million men and women who make up the federal bureaucracy. Not just Cabinet members, executive directors, budget analysts, and division heads but also clerks, secretaries, janitors, and truck drivers. Among the 95 million records that the Civil Service Commission (CSC) maintains, mostly at the National Personnel Records Center in St. Louis, are about 80 million personnel folders for former employees and retirees. There is also an investigative file on every person who has sought employment with the federal government since 1939, but who did not actually take a job. The commission says it is more efficient to keep these files, numbering in the millions, than to go through the whole investigation process again if some previous applicant seeks a federal position years later.

When a person applies for a federal job and is tentatively considered acceptable, CSC investigators, sometimes aided by FBI agents, conduct a thorough character evaluation. This includes confidential interviews with his past and present employers, neighbors, old friends, and anyone who can shed light on the applicant's trustworthiness and suitability for the job. The commission has contractual agreements with many commercial credit bureaus around the nation, under which its investigators are furnished with information about the applicant's personal finances. Interviews with the applicant's associates can cover a broad range of personal matters, including hygiene, drinking habits, and sexual conduct.

If in the course of investigating an applicant the commission comes across derogatory information severe enough to disqualify him for employment, he is called in for an informal interview, accompanied by a lawyer if he wishes, and confronted with the information (but not the source of it). An arrest record is not in itself grounds for rejection at the hiring end, the CSC says. It also says it has hired numerous recent college graduates whose investigative reports indicated participation in antiwar demonstrations. The CSC's investigative authority extends to already employed civil servants as well.

The tragedy of the late foreign service officer Charles Thomas offers a dramatic, if atypical, example of the dangers of no-access personnel systems. A few years ago Thomas was fired from the State Department at the age of forty-eight, long before his retirement age, because of negative information in his file, the specifics of which he was not allowed to learn. Despondent at being fired and not finding new employment, he committed suicide. It was later discovered that the derogatory information in his file wasn't about him at all, but rather another foreign service officer with a similar name. Partly as a result of this, the State Department has revamped its personnel procedures, which are independent of the Civil Service Commission.

The Department of Defense, in addition to maintaining files on its 1.1 million civilian employees, has service records on the more than 6 million active and reserve military personnel stationed in the U.S. and abroad. And the Veterans Administration maintains medical, pension, and education records on about 29 million veterans and about 6 million dependents of veterans.

If the data banks described above—most of them routine files necessary to keep the nation's housekeeping functioning smoothly—were the extent of Uncle Sam's record keeping on the American people, this federal activity would not have become the emotion-charged issue that it is in Washington today. Federal record keeping became controversial when it was revealed, beginning in the mid-1960s, that millions of dossiers and bits of information were being stored on citizens considered for a variety of reasons to be potentially dangerous to the "national security."

Many of the individuals on the federal lists of "subversives" seem to have been included solely because of activities that are thoroughly legal and well within the protection of the First Amendment right of free expression, such as participation in protest demonstrations and writing letters to the editor critical of government policy. In 1974 the FBI admitted in court that it compiled a "subversives" file on a sixteen-year-old New Jersey schoolgirl. As part of a social studies project at her high school, she had written to the Socialist Labor Party and requested some printed material. After copying her name and address from the envelope (the FBI screened all of the party's incoming mail and investigated the senders), an agent investigated her family's employment, credit rating, and police record, and went to her high school to check on her attitudes and interests.

A 1966 Senate study of known files compiled for national security purposes arrived at the astounding estimate of 188 million. This estimate did not include, of course, whatever files are maintained at the suburban Langley, Virginia, headquarters of the Central Intelligence Agency. In the words of right-of-privacy expert Vern Countryman, "It is probably quite literally true that God only knows what is contained in the files of the CIA." The alarmists' worst suspicions were confirmed in December 1974, when the *New York Times* disclosed that the CIA had been maintaining files on some 10,000 American citizens, in defiance of its charter, which limits it to international information gathering and domestic intelligence pertaining to bona fide foreign agents. CIA director William Colby said that the practice had been discontinued before it came to light, but a full investigation ensued.

It was later learned that for twenty years (from 1953 to 1973) the CIA, with the full cooperation of the U.S. Postal Service, had opened and read every piece of mail—personal, business or otherwise—between the U.S. and communist countries. This operation, conducted in New York City and San Francisco, was strictly illegal, under the federal law prohibiting the opening of first class mail by any government agency without a specific court order of search and seizure. (It was not immediately known whether the names of Americans involved in correspondence with people in communist countries were incorporated into a CIA file and, if so, whether the file still exists.) In a comparably illegal program, the CIA opened the domestic mail of many pacifist activists, including Representative Bella Abzug (D-N.Y.), whose CIA file was maintained from the early Fifties until the early Seventies.

The Civil Service Commission has a file of some 2 million people who are suspected of subversive activity. The Secret Service, whose mandate is the protection of the President and other high government officials, has a highly sophisticated computer file covering more than 47,000 people. Among the guidelines for inclusion of an individual in this top-secret file are intent to "embarrass the persons protected by the U.S. Secret Service," a past history of making "irrational statements" or "abusive statements" about high-ranking officials, and a tendency to "insist upon personally contacting high government officials for the purpose of redress of imaginary grievances." Former Senator Sam Ervin (D-N.C.), a leading right-of-privacy advocate, once quipped that he himself is eminently qualified to be in the Secret Service's subversives file. "I have written the President and other high officials complaining of grievances that some may have considered 'imaginary,'" he said, "and on occasion I may also have 'embarrassed' high government officials."

When the President is scheduled to make an appearance in a given place, the computer can tell the Secret Service if any of the questionable individuals in its files live or work nearby. "You take a waiter in a hotel dining room where the boss is going to speak," a Secret Service spokesman explained a couple of years ago. "Let's say the computer turns up his name and we investigate and decide it would be better for him to be assigned to some other duties. No one has a constitutional right to wait on the President, you know." When the President goes to cultural events in Washington, the Secret Service demands in advance the birth dates and social security numbers of people who will be occupying nearby seats in the concert hall or theater, so they can be checked out through the central file.

In 1970 the *Washington Monthly* revealed that for four years the U.S. Army had deployed more than 1,000 plainclothes soldiers—some of them posing as student activists in beards and sloppy clothes—to keep tabs on political demonstrations all across the nation. The Defense Department admitted that the Army had compiled, at Fort Holabird in Baltimore, Maryland, computer files containing the names of 25 million citizens, including civil rights activists and public figures who were known to associate with political dissidents, such as Senator Adlai Stevenson III (D-Ill.) and Representative Abner Mikva (D-Ill.). The Army's activity had clearly violated the prohibition against military involvement in political affairs, and it promised to discontinue the Fort Holabird central index and transfer portions of the files to the Department of Justice. It was never established conclusively, however, whether the central files were erased, put in storage, or merely transferred to decentralized files at other Army computer centers.

Preeminent among the national security information gatherers, of course, is the FBI, which for decades has been assembling—with almost no congressional guidance or supervision—files on all sorts of persons it deems to be undesirable for some reason or another. In addition to keeping track of some 11,000 members of the American Communist party, 100,000 "communist sympathizers," and countless chieftains of organized crime, the FBI has extensive files on activists of all sorts. In 1969 the bureau revealed that it had tapped the phone of Martin Luther King, Jr., for four years before his assassination in 1968. The file on King was just one of an estimated 5,500 in a special category on prominent black Americans, including several entertainers. According to a Washington *Post* report in 1972, one such file on a popular black singer noted that she was "suing her husband for a divorce as a result of Mrs. —— catching her husband in bed with ——."

The files on black Americans didn't exactly outrage Congress, but in 1975 the Hill was rocked by news (delivered through reporter Ron Kessler of the Washington *Post*) that the FBI had been collecting highly personal information on numerous representatives and senators. Most of the derogatory intelligence, former FBI officials disclosed, had been gathered toward the end of the long tenure of Director Hoover, who occasionally made special targets of congressmen who dared to criticize him or the FBI. One such target, reportedly, was former Representative William Anderson (D-Tenn.), a retired Navy commander who championed the antiwar Berrigan brothers against Hoover's charges that they had plotted to kidnap Henry Kissinger. (The two priests were eventually acquitted of the charges.) There was no evidence that the FBI's derogatory information files had ever been used to blackmail a congressman into silence, but the very existence of the files raised that ominous possibility.

MORE DATA BANKS

The congressional investigations of federal information gathering conducted over the past eight years unearthed an amazing array of data banks that few people outside of the compiling agencies themselves had any idea existed. The following are a few of them (some of which have reportedly been recently discontinued):

• the Federal Housing Administration's files (totaling more than one million) on FHA mortgage holders, which include information on their marital stability, presumably because divorce is a leading cause of defaulted payments;

• the Customs Bureau's file of suspected smugglers;

• the Department of Health, Education and Welfare's lists of politically outspoken scientists who should not be awarded federal research and consultant contracts, and a similar file maintained by the National Science Foundation;

• the Department of Housing and Urban Development's "adverse information file," a catch-all for data critical of people and organizations with whom HUD has done or might do business.

SHARED INFORMATION

The Census Bureau's refusal to disclose information about individuals to any other federal agency is unique in Washington. Other agencies say they have similar confidentiality regulations, but upon close examination these rules are invariably found to contain an escape clause of some sort, usually referring to "national security" or a "legitimate need to know."

The U.S. Postal Service has been very willing to oblige its sister agencies of government—not just federal, but also state and local—by recording the origins of all mail received by certain individuals, organizations, and businesses in the U.S. This kind of surveillance, called a "mail cover" (which does not entail the opening of mail), is legal only when done at the request of a law enforcement agency that has a particular need to obtain criminal evidence, apprehend a fugitive, or protect national security. But the mail covers set up in 1974 on some 4,400 American citizens and businesses included many that were requested by government bodies not usually thought of as law enforcement agencies, such as the Interior Department, Labor Department, and state and local agencies dealing with real estate and welfare.

The FBI can somehow manage to get a look at virtually any bit of information that Uncle Sam possesses, and the flow of information between it and other agencies is more or less reciprocal. In addition to giving federal personnel files to the FBI, the Civil Service Commission will divulge their contents to "authorized officials of federal agencies having a legitimate employment or security need for information." The commission claims it will not make its files available to state or local governments or private individuals or companies under any circumstances.

The Internal Revenue Service is more generous with its sister governments around the nation than the CSC is. Computer tapes of tax returns are routinely made available to the tax officials of virtually every state, so they can be checked for discrepancies against state and local returns. The IRS also makes returns available to congressional committees (including in the past the now defunct House Internal Security Committee) and to any other federal officials by executive order. There is reason to believe, however, that returns are occasionally examined by individuals who have not been explicitly authorized to see them. For example, when prize-winning investigative reporter Clark Mollenhoff (who has now returned to his old job at the Des Moines *Register*) was briefly a White House assistant to President Nixon, he examined individuals' tax returns without authority granted by a formal executive order. When questioned about this, Mollenhoff alleged that similar examinations were made when John F. Kennedy was President.

The White House may have indulged in unauthorized examination of personal tax returns, but it did not consider turnabout to be fair play. When President Nixon's tax returns surfaced in the Providence, Rhode Island, *Journal-Bulletin* in late 1973, precipitating the furor over his questionable deductions, the IRS launched a major search for the employee who leaked the information. An investigator traced photocopies of the Nixon returns to a particular copy machine at the IRS computer center in Martinsburg, West Virginia. The employee quit his job under threat of dismissal, and the investigator was given an award for "noteworthy contributions to the effectiveness and efficiency of the Department of the Treasury."

The Nixon White House, the public has now learned, was not immune from the very sort of illegal leaks and unauthorized phone-tapping that it has used against its opponents. It was revealed, for example, that Joint Chiefs chairman Admiral Thomas H. Moorer received top secret documents from Yeoman Charles E. Radford, a former member of Henry Kissinger's National Security Council staff at the White House. And Kissinger, concerned about leaks to the press, is alleged to have ordered wiretaps on the phones of some of his assistants.

The subversive activities files of the House Internal Security Committee (known until 1969 as the House Un-American Activities Committee) had one of the most extensively consulted files in the federal government, covering an estimated 750,000 Americans. About twenty-five federal agencies could see their files under authority of the Federal Loyalty-Security Program. In 1970, reporting on the frequency of their use of the committee's data banks, the Department of Housing and Urban Development said it consulted the files about once a month; the Department of Health, Education and Welfare, several times a week; the Department of Defense, about 120 times each week; and the CSC, more than 280,000 times each year. In 1975 the House Democrats voted to abolish the committee, and its old files were transferred to the Judiciary Committee.

The FBI, which shares information so freely with its fellow federal agencies, has occasionally been accused of leaking information from its investigative files to favored members of the press—always to further a particular goal of the bureau. The Justice Department admitted in 1971 that an FBI agent had "confirmed" for a *Look* reporter information alleging ties between San Francisco Mayor Joseph Alioto and organized crime. Alioto charged that the FBI had not merely "confirmed" the information, but had initiated the story by planting information with *Look*. The FBI agent involved was reprimanded and forced to retire. Former Representative Cornelius E. Gallagher (D-N.J.) charged that the FBI had intentionally leaked information to *Life* magazine that alleged ties between him and organized crime.

One of the perverse ironies of the right-of-privacy crusade in Congress is that it was led, during the Sixties, by Gallagher and the late Senator Edward Long (D-Mo.), both of whom, it was later learned, had very personal reasons for guarding their own privacy. Gallagher was convicted in 1973 of income tax evasion arising from misuse of political funds. Long was discovered to have been receiving periodic secret payments, for an undisclosed purpose, from the lawyer of convicted Teamsters boss James Hoffa.

In 1973 the first cracks appeared in the wall of secrecy surrounding FBI files on many famous criminal cases that were closed long ago. Elliot Richardson, then attorney general, issued an order that FBI investigatory files more than fifteen years old and no longer needed for prosecution be made available to historians, after minimal deletions to protect the privacy of innocent people mentioned in them. Smith College professor Allen Weinstein was to have been given large portions of the 53,000-page file on accused Communist agent and convicted perjurer Alger Hiss. Weinstein and a television producer also sought access to the 25,000-page file on Julius and Ethel Rosenberg, who were executed in 1953 as atom bomb spies. But Richardson's order was not carried out. After delivering only about 250 heavily censored pages from the Hiss file, the FBI produced nothing further from it or the Rosenberg file. When Weinstein protested to Richardson's successor, former Attorney General William Saxbe, Saxbe said the whole matter was in the hands of FBI Director Clarence Kelley, who refused to honor Weinstein's requests. The professor, represented by the American Civil Liberties Union, responded with a suit, still pending in early 1975.

At some federal agencies, lists of people who have particular characteristics are sold to commercial solicitation companies for use in mail order sales campaigns. Among the lists of names and addresses that have been sold in recent years are the Federal Communications Commission's list of 265,000 amateur radio operators; the Federal Aviation Administration's list of 680,000 licensed pilots; the IRS's list of 143,000 gun dealers and collectors; the Coast Guard's list of registered boat owners; the General Services Administration's list of subcontractors who have worked for the federal government; the Veterans Administration's list of recently discharged veterans; and the Immigration and Naturalization Service's list of recently naturalized citizens.

Looking to the future, it is still the dream of many computer technologists, not to mention the efficiency experts in Uncle Sam's bureaucracy, to implement some sort of national data bank. When the Bureau of the Budget began talking hopefully about this in 1966, it envisioned not a master file of individual dossiers, but merely a repository of impersonal statistics. Intent aside, the whole proposition raised visions of Orwell's *1984,* and the outcry killed the idea for years to come. Some experts warn, however, that certain of the existing data banks that store both state and federal information—such as the FBI's master crime files and the Transportation Department's driver license revocation files—have already taken on the characteristics of a national data bank. In 1973 an HEW advisory committee stated that, despite the current technological improbability of developing a single national data bank, public concern is "well founded."

The HEW committee noted that a federal superfile of any type would require that each citizen be identifiable by a unique number within a common code, a number known in data jargon as a standard universal identifier (SUI). The committee strongly urged that no SUI system be established now or in the near future, and also recommended a halt to the spreading practice of using the social security number for this purpose. This practice, it said, "deepens the anxieties of a public already suffused with concern about surveillance."

Civil liberties aside, the social security number would not even be a reliable SUI. The Social Security Administration estimates that more than 4.2 million people have been assigned two or more numbers, and many people have been issued or use the same number as someone else. One infamous duplicate number, 078-05-1120, appeared on a sample social security card that came in a popular make of wallet sold nationwide beginning in 1938. Thousands of buyers of the wallet apparently thought it was their own number. In 1943, it appeared on the wage earner forms of 5,755 people, and in one year during the Sixties was still being listed on thirty-nine different IRS tax returns.

The startling revelations of the past few years—everything from Watergate to illegal spying by the Pentagon, CIA, and FBI—heightened the already mounting interest in the right-of-privacy legislation on Capitol Hill. The advocates of protective legislation span the ideological spectrum. (The principal House champions, for example, are liberal Representative Edward Koch, D-N.Y., and moderate-conservative Representative Barry Goldwater, Jr., R-Cal.) A flurry of bills was introduced on both sides of the Hill. One bill proposed banning the sale and rental of federal lists to direct mail advertisers. Another would allow a citizen to refuse to divulge his social security number to anyone except a federal agency specifically authorized to use the number. This, say its sponsors, would relieve citizens of the burden of giving their numbers for such diverse purposes as registering to vote, renting an apartment, giving blood, enrolling in college, getting a fishing license, and opening a charge account.

One right-of-privacy measure—the so-called Buckley Amendment—

slipped through largely unnoticed and soon caused a furor in higher education. As conceived by Senator James L. Buckley (Cons.-R-N.Y.), the amendment allowed students to peruse all files maintained on them by their colleges, including medical and psychological records and copies of parents' federal tax returns (in scholarship files). Parents complained that the amendment, intended to protect the students' rights, was an infringement on their own privacy. Similar complaints were heard from professors (about confidential letters of recommendation to graduate schools) and physicians (about certain medical files that should not be shown to students still under treatment). Senator Buckley was embarrassed by the unforeseen ramifications of his amendment and led the campaign to modify it to meet valid criticisms.

At the end of 1974, Congress passed and President Ford signed the first broad legislation aimed at curbing abuses in federal information gathering. It allows the citizen to examine individual files maintained on him and, if need be, challenge inaccurate information contained in them. To assist the citizen in finding data on himself, a list of all agencies that maintain individualized dossiers will be published periodically in the Federal Register. The new law also puts restrictions on the passing of personal information from agency to agency and to organizations and individuals outside the federal sphere.

The new law has a gaping hole in it, however. The right of perusal and challenge does not extend to any files of the FBI and CIA. And administration of the citizen access program will be left to each federal agency, with no watchdog body to see that it is being carried out in good faith. Attempts to include nonactive criminal and "national security" files in the bill were opposed by the Ford administration. While the President has singled out the right-of-privacy issue as one of his top priorities, his actions have not lived up to his promises. Ford vetoed, for example, amendments to the Freedom of Information Act that would make government information more accessible to academic researchers. (Congress overrode the veto.) And administration officials have quietly opposed measures that would limit the dissemination of arrest records and restrict the right of banks to disclose information about their customers' private accounts.

Except for a few subversive activities files that shouldn't exist at all, the most unsettling thing about federal data banks is that we know so little about them. In the modern mood of euphoria about the technological possibilities offered by the Computer Age, we sometimes fail to see that feasibility is not synonymous with desirability, that the most efficient way to do something may not be the socially and legally wisest way to do it.

Federal information systems, undeniably, are a useful tool for performing tasks on which the nation is dependent. They are not about to go away, nor does any responsible observer hope they will. As a matter of fact, some of the people who scream loudest about the burgeoning of federal data banks seem oblivious to the fact that their favorite social service programs, existing and proposed, require vast networks of information gathering to function without honest error and fraud. There is nothing wrong with Uncle Sam's insatiable demand for information that couldn't be cured with public knowledge of the existence and purpose of each data bank, guarantees of citizen access and correction rights, and stringent safeguards against unauthorized disclosure. In the quest for "total information," there must still be room for the individual's right to privacy.

29 LABOR HEADQUARTERS

Labor is now a member of the Washington Establishment, with the full panoply of rights, privileges, and perquisites thereunto appertaining. It won this position with the turbulence of organizing conflicts in the Twenties and Thirties, culminating with passage of the Wagner Act in 1935. It cemented it during the war years of the Forties and the prosperity of the Fifties and Sixties. Today, the craft and industrial unions—once arch rivals for the leadership of American labor—are united more or less harmoniously in the AFL–CIO, joined by the newer unions of service employees and government workers. Union membership totals more than 20 million plus another 2 million in related organizations—the highest level in history.

Labor used to have to fight for its position. Now it has it. The National Labor Relations Board (NLRB) is no longer a battleground for angry exchanges between employer and employee. Disputes are settled in the same low-key way that disputes are settled in other regulatory agencies, like the Interstate Commerce Commission and the Federal Trade Commission.

In politics, the labor influence has grown enormously. In 1944, FDR coined the famous phrase, "Clear it with Sidney," meaning Sidney Hillman, chairman of the CIO's Political Action Committee, which some authorities regarded as the labor wing of the Democratic party. Such concentration of power in a single labor leader is rare today (George Meany of the AFL–CIO comes closest), but unions still have plenty of clout. Labor is the best-organized, best-funded lobbying machine on Capitol Hill, and its support is essential to the Democrats in every election year. No economic controls policy was proposed by the Nixon administration until the President was sure that AFL–CIO chief George Meany would go along with it. The wage-price freeze of 1971 and the Phase II controls did not materialize until the "Two Georges"—Meany and George Shultz—had come to an understanding after a few rounds of golf at Burning Tree Club. And Gerald Ford did not let a week go by before he polished up his relations with George Meany at the beginning of the Ford Presidency.

Physically, organized labor is a highly conspicuous presence in Washington. The gleaming temples of union headquarters loom large at the foot of Capitol Hill and in the blocks surrounding the White House, expensively sheathed in marble and limestone and trimmed in bronze. These are impressive reminders to federal officials of the power that labor can mobilize when it wants to. Washington is home to 40 of the AFL–CIO's 110 member unions, and all of the rest have some sort of office here, ranging from one or two people to large staffs for such giants as the Steelworkers. Washington is home, likewise, to two of the major non–AFL–CIO unions, the Teamsters (largest in the nation at about 2 million members) and the United Mine Workers (whose new, reform-minded regime says it wants to move the headquarters to West

Virginia). The unions not based in Washington are those whose members are concentrated in a particular area—like the Auto Workers (Detroit), Rubber Workers (Akron), and Steelworkers (Pittsburgh).

AFL–CIO headquarters, recently expanded to twice its original size, occupies most of a city block on 16th Street, due north of the White House across Lafayette Park. Its limestone mass dwarfs the only adjacent neighbor, historic St. John's Church, "The Church of Presidents." The building's enormous lobby (austere as an airline terminal) sports two vast mosaic murals depicting the brawny, bare-chested rise of organized labor. Upstairs the feel is suitably bureaucratic—thousands of square feet of movable-partitioned offices. George Meany, from his top-floor suite, has a picture-postcard view of the White House. In the next block of 16th Street, next to the Sheraton-Carlton Hotel (John L. Lewis's old haunt) stands the Laborers' building. Within a radius of a few blocks are the headquarters buildings of the Machinists, Air Line Pilots, Communications workers, and Retail Clerks. The union presence near Capitol Hill—including the Railway Labor Building and that of the Carpenters and Joiners (not to mention the Labor Department itself, in its newly completed headquarters building)—is dominated by the Teamsters' white marble structure. (Its top floor boasts a tree-decorated terrace outside the elegant presidential office where Jimmy Hoffa once held court.)

Scattered all over downtown Washington are the headquarters of such diverse unions as the Asbestos Workers, Firemen and Oilers, Insurance Workers, Electrical Workers, Newspaper Guild, Pattern Makers, and National Football League Players Association. The leaders who inhabit the union palaces of Washington have salaries not too unlike those of other top executives. (Meany's salary is $90,000 a year.) Union officers also receive expense accounts. Like prominent lawyers, association executives, and corporate lobbyists, they can be seen lunching with government contacts at such popular 16th Street spots as the Hay-Adams Hotel dining room and Trader Vic's in the Statler Hilton. Their residences in suburbs like Bethesda and Silver Spring, Maryland, or Arlington and Alexandria, Virginia, are anything but proletarian. (Some sport circular driveways and columned porticos.)

MEANY

It doesn't embarrass the eighty-one-year-old Meany that people think he and most of organized labor are now part of the establishment. He worked hard to get the AFL–CIO where it is, and this involved the loss of some friends on the Left and the acquisition of some dubious new friends on the Right. Never overly fond of the ultramilitancy that characterized the old CIO, Meany has understood that as the American worker moved up on the economic scale he also grew more conservative. Fatter and fatter wage settlements have given the worker more and more to conserve, to protect against threatening reforms of the New Left.

George Meany became president of the AFL in 1952 upon the death of William Green, and then president of the AFL–CIO at the time of merger in 1955. Under Meany's leadership, the AFL–CIO has lent its weight to most of the "liberal" reforms that surfaced in Congress, especially civil rights legislation during the Sixties. The AFL–CIO lobbied hard for the Civil Rights Act of 1964, even though many of its lesser officials and even more of its rank and file were dubious or flatly opposed. While many unions, especially in the building trades, have dragged their feet on admitting blacks to membership, Meany feels they have moved as far and as fast as any group in the free society can be compelled to.

Meany has been accused of being blasé about the steady decline in organized labor's share of the American labor force—which has dropped from about 36 percent in 1945 to a current 27 percent of the nonagricultural labor force. Meany brushes off the criticism by saying that a few hundred thousand more members would not greatly strengthen labor's power in Washington. He also says that the workers now outside of the labor movement are the hardest to organize—low-paid service employees and clerk-typists or high-salaried professionals and managers. Meanwhile, large numbers of workers once considered "unorganizable"—such as schoolteachers and state, local, and federal employees—are joining unions in droves, becoming significant powers within the AFL–CIO.

George Meany is not the head of a union, and never has been. Despite his early days as a plumber, Meany has been a labor executive most of his working life. As chief of a superbureaucracy, he is labor's appointed ambassador to the federal government. Meany tells the truth when he says the member unions of the AFL–CIO are "autonomous." They run their own internal affairs and fight their own battles at the bargaining table. They also fight among themselves, especially on the question of which affiliate has jurisdiction over unorganized workers. The AFL–CIO is a loose confederation of sometimes warring elements. The industrial unions have little or nothing in common with the public workers or other white-collar groups. The building trades are sometimes in conflict with both. And a passel of small, impotent unions—many of them holdover craft alignments from simpler days—have little in common with *any* of the others.

Autonomous though the member unions are in their internal affairs, Meany is the unchallenged spokesman for the AFL–CIO's positions on national issues. Officially, these positions are set by the thirty-five-man Executive Council, but it is more or less a rubber stamp. There is rarely dissent, and there are rarely surprising positions taken, because Meany, like every skilled politician, seldom gets uncomfortably ahead of his constituents. The positions he asks the Council to take are generally in line with what the members— individually and collectively—believe in. On foreign policy, Meany has had his most difficult (and most adroitly accomplished) job of reconciling internal differences. He himself represents the right wing of labor, opposing détente with Russia and China, amnesty for draft dodgers, free trade, and arms reductions. He backed Nixon on Vietnam, but opposed him on accommodation with the Communist world. For many AFL–CIO unions, these are painfully out-of-date positions, yet Meany's strength is such that few have openly fought him. The rise of foreign competition, via imports and U.S. investment abroad, has helped to mute some of the opposition.

The council, composed largely of union presidents, meets quarterly—once in Washington, two other times in random American cities (Chicago being a favorite), and invariably in Bal Harbour, Florida, each February. The council eschews cities that aren't served by good passenger rail service, because Meany hates to fly. En route to the quarterly meetings, he plays a little gin rummy or poker and sips a drink or two. The meeting in Bal Harbour (usually described as a "posh" or "plush" community just north of Miami Beach) is held at the Americana Hotel. There, across the street from the local branches of Neiman-Marcus and Abercrombie & Fitch, in a meeting room a few steps from the hotel's cabana-and-swimming-pool playground, the council puts in two to three hours of work each morning for a week or so. There follows a noon press conference, at which Meany spars good-naturedly with the press. Then he goes off to the golf course. National political figures attend, much as barons and earls used to come to court when the monarch was in residence. Those Meany especially favors are given long audiences; lesser lights are dismissed in a half hour or so. (Some never make it inside.) Senator Henry (Scoop) Jackson's rising eminence as a presidential hopeful was demonstrated, for example, when he was included among a handful of Democratic senators given the "inside" treatment at the council's Chicago meeting in 1970.

Meany's control over the Executive Council was severely tested in 1972, when he talked it into a no-endorsement, "neutral" stance in the Nixon-McGovern race. (Before the Democratic convention, Meany had shown rare indecision over whom to endorse for the nomination, coming out too late for Hubert Humphrey.) Never before had organized labor failed to endorse the Democratic nominee for President, if it endorsed anyone, not even when labor leaders were lukewarm about Adlai Stevenson. Neutrality gradually became neutrality-for-Nixon as the campaign progressed. Meany was accused of jeopardizing the AFL–CIO's clout with the Democrats, simply because he couldn't stomach George McGovern and the New Leftism that the senator seemed to embody. (But many labor leaders, not just Meany, were burned that McGovern's people seemed to go out of their way to snub labor at the Democratic convention.) Meany's policy of neutrality was more than a matter of personal pique. Meany felt sure that McGovern could not win, that Nixon obviously would, and that this was no time for kamikaze loyalty. Besides, by concentrating labor's money and efforts to reelect its friends in Congress, the AFL–CIO could strengthen its hand on Capitol Hill.

A small band of dissident unions backed McGovern in defiance of Meany, but he casually dismissed their revolt as something they were free to indulge in. Vindicated by the McGovern defeat, Meany was courted by the White House and carefully consulted on every development in the economic controls program. Occasionally stung by charges that he was getting too chummy with the arch-enemy, Meany saw to it that labor got paid—in wage settlements—for its cooperation with the administration. He stayed with Phase II until most major unions got what they wanted from the Pay Board. Then he resigned, along with all other union leaders except Frank Fitzsimmons of the Teamsters, blasting the "inequities" of the economic control program. That was the first step in the long journey of dissociating organized labor from the Nixon administration and its economic policies. Even before Watergate made it easy to do, Meany was leading the AFL–CIO back to its traditional posture of measured hostility toward the Republicans, culminating in the 1973 call for President Nixon's impeachment. In the meantime, labor had fences to mend with the Democratic party apparatus. Relations were somewhat improved by the gradual purging of McGovern supporters and the installation of moderate Robert S. Strauss as national chairman.

But the fence-mending collapsed when it became apparent that Strauss was more interested in holding together the party's precarious new coalition than in welcoming back the AFL–CIO. The culmination came at the Democrats' "mini-convention" in December 1974 at Kansas City, where much the same forces that had pushed through the original McGovern reforms took charge once again. There they fought off AFL–CIO efforts to defeat the rules guaranteeing equal representation to women, blacks, and other minorities—a move Meany saw as intended to cancel out the heavy influence his own forces once had in the party.

Privately, AFL–CIO officials conceded there was little they could do, once the vote was in. Even though some Meany loyalists threatened to withdraw from their official Democratic National Committee positions, some unions decided to go along with the reforms. There was no disguising the fact that the Democratic party remains the home base for most of the union membership. Unless and until the Republicans offer something better, they have nowhere else to go. This fact of life was underscored by the continuing split in the ranks of the AFL–CIO itself. Several of its members that had backed McGovern in 1972—such as the State, County and Municipal Workers, the Communications Workers, and the Machinists, plus the nonaffiliated Auto Workers—supported the Kansas City compromise after trying to get Meany to soften his opposition.

Gerald Ford, a lifelong conservative, has never been a friend of organized labor. During his years in the House, Ford's rating of support for labor's interests hovered around 10 on a scale of 100. But Meany respects President Ford as an honest, pragmatic opponent, and Ford has gone out of his way not to alienate labor in overt ways. The arm's-length respect between the two men is a notable change from the contempt that Meany felt for Nixon toward the end.

In early 1975, however, the AFL–CIO stepped up its attack on the Ford administration's economic policies, calling them a "formula for more unemployment, extended recession, and prolonged inflation." Ending the recession became the number one priority of organized labor. It put all its weight and muscle behind programs to stimulate the economy with massive tax cuts and with direct federal spending to create new jobs. Recession, besides being an individual hardship for jobless workers, is a blow to the organizational strength of the unions. When workers are laid off, union membership falls, dues income drops, recruitment comes to a standstill, and service to members decreases. Numerous unions, like their corporate adversaries, had to lay off professional staff in 1974 and 1975 to keep within their budgets.

THE AFL AT WORK

As with every other bureaucracy, the real work of the AFL–CIO is done by the behind-the-scenes professional staff, composed mostly of men (and a few women) who once held similar positions on the staffs of member unions. Ex-newspapermen manage the publications and publicity operations; university-trained economists run the research operations; longtime union organizers keep in touch with the state and regional labor councils. Its lobbying efforts are skillfully coordinated by a former congressman, Andrew Biemiller.

Labor's attention focuses more on Capitol Hill than on the White House, Labor Department, and other executive agencies that labor must do business with. Labor's influence over Congress waxes and wanes in proportion to the Democrats' margin of control in the House and Senate. Not all Democrats are friendly to labor, however, especially the southern Democrats who still dominate many committee chairmanships by virtue of seniority. Some northeastern Republicans, like Senator Clifford P. Case of New Jersey and Senator Jacob K. Javits of New York, champion the cause of labor and are duly rewarded when the campaign funds are divvied up each election year.

On legislation that would affect the collective bargaining power of either employer or unions, management and labor have been in a stalemate for over two decades. The last law that trimmed the sails of labor was the Labor-Management Relations Act of 1947, familiarly known as the Taft-Hartley act, which the unions helped bring down on themselves through strike excesses of the Forties. But labor has long since demonstrated that it can live and prosper with Taft-Hartley, despite continued denunciations. The law's injunctive power against strikes, applicable in secondary boycotts and "national emergencies," has not been used much. And labor has made clear to Congress that it will fight tooth and nail any extension of that power or its blood relative, compulsory arbitration. The Landrum-Griffin Act of 1959 (Labor-Management Reporting and Disclosure Act) grew out of the Teamster scandals exposed by the Senate's McClellan Committee (chief counsel of which was young Bobby Kennedy) and brought a split in labor's ranks. The Teamsters and a few other unions fought it vehemently. They called its provisions (which included full disclosure of union financial holdings and democratic procedures inside unions) an attempt to "union-bust." But George Meany and Walter Reuther supported it, on the grounds that racketeers had no place in organized labor. The law did nothing to weaken legitimate union power, and it did help throw Jimmy Hoffa in jail.

The AFL–CIO put its all into a 1966 effort to repeal the "right to work" section of Taft-Hartley, which impedes union organizing, especially in the South. It failed. On the other side of the coin, the big business lobbies have not been able to convince Congress to adopt a single statute to curtail the power of unions since Landrum-Griffin. The fact is that labor and management are comfortable with the present arrangement. In boom times, labor can easily exact the wage increases from business, and business can turn around and recover its higher costs in higher prices. Aside from holding hearings on such matters as emergency strike legislation, bills to broaden the union rights of public workers (which have not yet passed) and bills to enable unions to organize nonprofit hospitals and to bargain for employer-paid legal services (which did pass), the labor subcommittees of the House and Senate are pretty quiet. Their legislative output is low, through no fault of their own.

So the labor lobby spends less time on labor law than it does on national issues that affect all Americans, not just union members. Organized labor is the strongest force behind increases in the minimum wage, because these increases automatically push up all other wages. Unions lobby for a big national defense budget, because defense cuts mean cuts in union jobs. Ditto for the federal highway program, which benefits everyone from the Auto Workers to the Painters (who do roadside billboards) to the construction trades. The unions are pro-consumer and pro-environment, except when reforms would jeopardize union jobs. (Ralph Nader's attacks on the auto industry, for example, were not popular with the Auto Workers, who were worried about the effect his blasts would have on auto sales.) AFL–CIO unions are behind the push for protectionist trade legislation and curbs on foreign investment. As a matter of fact, the Burke-Hartke bill that was a hot issue a couple of years ago was conceived at AFL–CIO headquarters. The non–AFL–CIO Auto Workers, more socially minded than most other unions, were a holdout against this protectionist trend for a long time. But when Detroit's sales plummeted during the energy crisis of 1974, even the free-trade UAW came calling on Congress to hold auto imports to the average level of the previous three years.

The unions are sophisticated lobbyists. Most of the lobbying is low-profile, but the AFL–CIO can mobilize phalanxes of labor spokesmen to come to Washington and tug at the lapels of their congressmen. And it instructs local leaders at home to write, phone, or otherwise inform the congressional delegations of the impact their votes will have on the economy of their districts. (It took business lobbies years to catch on to this simple method of making congressmen more "accountable," but now Capitol Hill is besieged by groups of out-of-town businessmen too.) The federation saves its biggest guns for special occasions. George Meany makes a provocative witness—wry, witty, harsh, grating, or ingratiating, as the occasion requires. Democratic committee chairmen like to have him come up to the Hill, since he can usually guarantee at least a few headlines for an otherwise dull hearing. Other union presidents are on constant call for hearing appearances, and for flattering or threatening visits to the offices of congressmen with large union blocs in their districts. President Leonard Woodcock of the UAW, trying to wear the social activist mantle of the late Walter Reuther, is a frequent hearing advocate of liberal legislation, like national health insurance.

POWERFUL COPE

Behind labor's lobbying campaigns stands a mountain of money. The AFL–CIO's mountain is called COPE, for Committee on Political Education. Each of its affiliate unions, as well as the independents, has a similar campaign fund, as do trade associations (which call them "political action committees," or PACs). The coffers are filled with the "voluntary" contributions of union members, who have no say over how the money is allocated among congressional incumbents and challengers. Those decisions are made by the leadership. At the AFL–CIO, this control rests largely in the hands of COPE director Alexander Barkan, considered to be one of the most powerful men in Washington, although little known to the public. A tough-talking political realist (who majored in philosophy at the University of Chicago in the Thirties, before embarking on a lifelong career in the labor movement), Barkan runs his office autocratically, enjoying the complete confidence of George Meany. The vast majority of the politicians whom Barkan selects to benefit from COPE's largess are Democrats. COPE, like other lobbies, compiles ratings of House and Senate members. COPE rates them on such issues as minimum wage increases; food stamps for strikers; voter registration by postcard (which would benefit the Democrats); national defense ("nuclear parity" with Russia); overturning the President's veto on vocational rehabilitation legislation; and leaving the present procedures of union political donations untouched by campaign spending reforms.

COPE's support can range from a few hundred dollars to tens of thousands of dollars, depending on how badly organized labor wants its favorite congressmen reelected and how close their contests are. In 1972 nineteen Democratic members and two Republican members of the House Judiciary Committee (which has jurisdiction over impeachment) received more than $190,000 from COPE. The Democratic gifts, which averaged about $10,000, ranged from a token $250 given to Representative Elizabeth Holtzman (the New Yorker who upset longtime Judiciary chairman Emanuel Celler) to a $30,923.03 contribution to the campaign of current committee chairman Peter Rodino, Jr., of New Jersey. COPE's contributions to 1974 congressional campaigns totaled about $2 million—the largest amount it had ever poured into House and Senate races. All but four recipients of this largess were Democrats. (In future elections, of course, COPE—like all other fund-raising organizations and individual contributors—will have to keep its gifts within the limits specified in the recent campaign spending law.)

The AFL-CIO demands a lot more from its friends in Congress than it can really expect them to deliver. Labor asks for repeal of all tax incentives on foreign investment; breakup of the oil industry into production and marketing branches; Federal Reserve Board allocations of bank credit for low-cost housing; massive public service employment programs; extended unemployment insurance for jobless casualties of the energy crisis and business recession. Labor doesn't expect to get all these measures, but it knows that the resulting compromises will be a lot more palatable if it aims high to start with.

Despite the AFL–CIO's reputed leadership of the so-called impeachment lobby, it soft-pedaled the issue with Congress. True, Meany asked for and easily got a ringing call for President Nixon's impeachment from the 1973 AFL–CIO national convention. True, too, a series of impeachment papers were featured in federation publications and distributed all over Capitol Hill. But for months thereafter, Meany deliberately held back from launching an all-out lobbying campaign. He didn't make impeachment a matter by which labor would judge the loyalty of its congressional troops. He knew it would be unwise to pressure labor's friends, who were waiting for constituent opinion to crystallize before putting themselves on record for or against impeachment.

The degree of labor's contact with the upper echelons of the Department of Labor depends on who occupies the Cabinet position of Secretary of Labor. Traditionally, about the only qualification required of a Labor Secretary is some experience with labor relations, regardless of which side of the bargaining table he has worked on. Arthur Goldberg, President Kennedy's first Labor Secretary and later a Supreme Court justice, was a staunch labor advocate (and former counsel to the AFL–CIO). Willard Wirtz, a labor lawyer and professor who had the longest tenure of any recent Secretary, presided over the department during most of the Sixties, when new job-training programs were adopted as part of the War on Poverty. President Nixon's first Secretary of Labor, George Shultz, is a labor economist with extensive mediation experience, and he enjoyed the respect of both labor and business. When Shultz left the department to begin his job-jumping odyssey through the high levels of federal service, he was replaced by James Hodgson, who had been in charge of labor relations at Lockheed Aircraft.

Ironically, labor's rapport with each of these past Secretaries was warmer than it was with Secretary Peter Brennan, who happened to be the first one chosen from the ranks of union leadership in more than twenty years. During 1972, ex-painter Brennan, then president of the New York Building and

Construction Trades Council (AFL–CIO), rallied hard-hat support for the President (and even came to Washington to present Nixon with an honorary flag-decaled hard hat). After the election, the White House decided that the appointment of Brennan as Labor Secretary would flatter organized labor (and serve the subsidiary purpose of weaning conservative Wallace-leaning rank-and-file members of labor unions away from the Democratic party). But the magnanimous gesture backfired. Meany regarded Brennan as an insignificant, reactionary labor leader not worthy of being Secretary of Labor. Meany thought the White House had insulted the intelligence of labor by thinking it wouldn't see through the ploy. Brennan was ignored—by the White House as well as Meany—ever after. The AFL–CIO chief continued to rely on Shultz as his main line of communication with the White House until Shultz's resignation as Treasury Secretary in 1974.

The power and prestige of the position of Labor Secretary was restored in early 1975, when Brennan was replaced by John T. Dunlop. A longtime professor of economics at Harvard, Dunlop had been an on-and-off fixture on the Washington scene for three decades. He served on numerous federal panels dealing with labor relations and economic planning (most recently, the Cost of Living Council, of which he was executive director in 1973–74). A master at negotiating jurisdictional disputes between unions, Dunlop enjoys excellent rapport with Meany and the other chieftains of labor.

LOBBYING THE BUREAUCRACY

So organized labor pays more attention to the Labor Department's internal bureaus than it does to Department leadership. Labor monitors the department's activities in such fields as occupational health and safety; manpower training (under programs going back to New Frontier days); and enforcement of minimum wage statutes. Labor keeps an eye on the mounds of data compiled by the Bureau of Labor Statistics—especially the Consumer Price Index, which gives unions ammunition for their charges of administration inaction against inflation, and to activate the inflation-escalator clauses in the contracts or to secure them in upcoming negotiations.

The National Labor Relations Board used to be an arena where the game of Lions vs. Christians was played out with some frequency. Today things are quieter. It gets into the news when it makes a ruling against some staunchly antiunion company—like the J. P. Stevens textile firm in the South or the Farah clothing concern in Texas—for intimidating or firing employees who attempt to organize their fellow workers, a right guaranteed by federal law. But most of the labor law precedents are well established and many of the "unfair labor practices" are minor, giving the NLRB the air of a family relations court.

The NLRB has an enormous case load, and decisions are sometimes handed down several years after the cases began. Critics of the board charge that its slowness and lightness of penalties enable antiunion firms to continue "unfair labor practices" with impunity, since the cost of legal battles, fines, and back pay for workers fired illegally usually amounts to less than the company would have to shell out in higher wages under a union contract. The Taft-Hartley law gives employers the right to file charges against unions for unfair practices, too, but the bulk of the cases are union-initiated. The board is composed of five members, with a three-member majority of the President's party. Thus the NLRB occasionally swings from "pro-labor" to "pro-management," but in the past couple of decades the ideological slant of the board has changed little from administration to administration.

Lately unions have begun paying more attention to the Equal Employment Opportunity Commission, a once-toothless agency created by the Civil Rights Act of 1964. In 1973 it was given a set of dentures by Congress in the form of power to seek court enforcement of its own orders. Both labor and management are feeling the bite. Heads swiveled when AT&T settled "out of court" for $43 million, after class-action charges were brought by EEOC on behalf of Ma Bell's female work force. Unions helped lobby the Civil Rights Act through Congress but now have come to understand that it can hit them too. Traditionally male strongholds are under attack by militant women, to say nothing of the longstanding Negro struggle for equal foothold in the unions. In November 1974, the federal government acknowledged that the twenty-eight voluntary plans for minority recruitment had failed to make any dent in the problem of discrimination and began moving toward mandatory plans. In a related development, a federal court in 1974 revoked the NLRB certification of two unions on grounds of illegal hiring discrimination. The NLRB repealed this unprecedented action and the matter was pending before the Supreme Court in early 1975.

Several other government departments get close attention from labor. The seagoing and longshore unions have ties to the various maritime agencies and to the congressional committees that oversee them. Maritime unions were closer to the Nixon White House than most others, after Nixon in 1972 announced a new shipbuilding program to beef up the U.S.-flag fleet. And the unions demonstrated their clout on the Hill in 1974 by helping to ram through a bill requiring that 30 percent of all oil imported into the U.S. be carried on American ships, which operate with higher wages than foreign vessels, thereby adding to the cost of the nation's oil supply. President Ford unexpectedly denounced the bill as a boondoggle and vetoed it.

The airborne and ground-crew unions of the airlines watch the CAB and FAA, occasionally intervening in rate and route filings. The ICC and National Mediation Board (the latter with jurisdiction over airline and railroad labor matters) are important to all transportation unions. The building trades, once the most powerful arm of the AFL, keep an eye on the Department of Housing and Urban Development, but are more concerned with the government as heavy-construction contractor, a role played by the Department of Defense (all sorts of military construction), Department of Transportation (highways and mass transit), and the Department of Health, Education and Welfare (hospitals and funding for school construction), to name a few. And, of course, the national AFL–CIO staff keeps close tabs on the policymaking of every federal agency that affects the daily lives and prosperity of working people—which is just about every agency in Washington.

NEW BLOOD

As labor became part of the establishment, there was a change in the kind of men who controlled organized labor. Today there are few of the rough-hewn, spellbinding giants left, men like John L. Lewis, Jim Carey, Sidney Hillman, Phil Murray, and David Dubinsky. Several generations ago, the struggle between labor and management was more than rhetorical, and defiance was the badge of heroism. The leaders were not merely theoreticians but also tough organizers who had once stood, as workers, shoulder to shoulder with the men they later led. Their names were often in the newspapers, and their faces, personalities, and goals were known to millions of average citizens.

Today, since the death of the UAW's Walter Reuther and the forced retirement (perhaps not permanent) of the Teamsters' Jimmy Hoffa, George Meany remains the only labor boss who could be considered a household name in America. And yet Meany's power—tremendous though it is—is significantly different from that of the old labor giants, since it grew out of years of service to the federation, not to a particular constituency of workers.

The rest of today's labor leaders are a mixed bag, largely unknown to the public. Some are elderly union presidents who came up the long, hard way, like the Steelworkers' I. W. Abel, who went into the mills after high school and organized for Lewis's embryonic CIO during the depression. Some of the younger leaders "paid their dues," too, like the United Mine Workers' reform president Arnold Miller, a West Virginia coal miner, who has black lung to prove it. Unlike their predecessors, many of the new leaders attended college and have an intellectual bent—men like Leonard Woodcock of the UAW, Albert Shanker of the American Federation of Teachers, and Jerry Wurf of the American Federation of State, County and Municipal Employees (who graduated from New York University and lectured at Cornell). AFL–CIO secretary-treasurer Lane Kirkland worked in the merchant marine for a few years, then went through the Georgetown University School of Foreign Service and joined the federation staff as a researcher when he was twenty-six.

A caveat about the labor leaders of today: they may be less colorful than the old giants, their grammar might be better, and they might prefer persuasion to defiance, but most of them are tough as nails.

The future of organized labor is a future without George Meany. Until he passes from the scene, which he now dominates as no one has since Lewis, the "labor movement" is not going to move in any startling new directions. One of the reasons for this is that none of the would-be innovators is foolish enough to take on Meany in head-to-head combat.

So what happens when Meany is gone? Well, the Executive Council, like the College of Cardinals, can guarantee continuity and stability in the event of the pontiff's untimely departure. It will most likely convene and name one of its members as acting president, until the next national convention (held every odd year). It might choose someone like I. W. Abel—respected, solid, incorruptible, elderly but vigorous, and close to Meany's views on most major issues. (Abel, who is close to retirement himself, said in 1975 he would decline a nomination to succeed Meany, but some observers feel he might be prevailed upon to take the position during a brief interregnum.) If Meany decides to retire (no sign of this at present), he might ask the council to name his protégé, Lane Kirkland, as interim president. Then the maneuvering for the permanent top spot would begin in earnest. Each strong bloc of unions within the federation will probably champion the candidacy of one of its own men, someone who will protect its interests. If internal jealousies result in a stand-off, they might turn to Kirkland as a compromise. Having spent virtually his whole career with the federation, Kirkland lacks a powerful constituency, but he also lacks powerful enemies. Smart, articulate, but tough, he is equally at ease with the old-timers and the new breed. He might be the compromise that could spare the federation the embarrassment of a knock-down-drag-out battle for leadership (something that Meany's grip has forestalled for years).

As a loose federation held together by a few common goals, the AFL–CIO is strongest when confronted by hostile forces. For a while, the bad blood between labor and the Nixon administration was enough to ensure a united front. But there are strong tensions building within the federation that may create fissures in the post-Meany era. Oddly, the strongest bond is between the two basic groups that split apart in the Thirties and remerged in 1955: the old AFL craft unions and the old CIO unions, in which members were grouped less by their specific occupation than by the industry in which they worked.

Potentially disruptive pressures for consolidation, reform, and more zeal-ous organizing come from the "public employee" bloc, dominated by Jerry Wurf's State, County and Municipal Employees and the American Federation of Teachers, led by Albert Shanker, who rose to prominence as head of the AFT's powerful New York City local. Both Wurf and Shanker are dynamic, ambitious men with bigger-than-ordinary egos. As the two youngest members of the Executive Council, both aspire to being the most influential labor leader in America. They both say that white-collar and government workers are the labor movement of the future, and they think the federation should put more emphasis on organizing these employees.

Wurf, as head of the AFL–CIO's most rapidly growing union, pushed within the Executive Council for the Public Employee Department that was finally set up in the fall of 1974, to stand in the federation beside such traditional departments as the Industrial Union Department, the Maritime Trades Department, and the Construction Trades and Service Department. As a first step, Wurf has tried to build a loose alliance of other government employee unions. So far, the efforts have made little headway and have been a thorn in Meany's side. Shanker hopes to merge the AFT with the larger (1.4 million members) National Education Association, which is not in the AFL–CIO and is not officially a union, but which is an increasingly militant spokesman for teachers' rights. A merged AFT–NEA would be the biggest union in the nation, even bigger than the current membership champion, the Teamsters. Shanker, a militant organizer who has twice been jailed in New York City for defying court antistrike orders, has been patient within the federation and has ingratiated himself with Meany by being a good team player. He was rewarded with a seat on the Executive Council even before becoming national president of the AFT.

CHALLENGES AHEAD

The leadership at the federation, whoever takes over, will have its hands full of problems. It must decide what to do about stagnating or even shrinking membership in mass-production industry and many craft lines. It must develop new ways to organize traditionally nonunion employees in the grow-ing service sector of the economy. Everyone knows that hand labor is on the decline and the demand for skilled labor and managerial talent is rising. But more than that, the relative demand for labor is declining as the American economy becomes more capital-intensive. The automation panic of the Fifties and early Sixties has faded into memory, chiefly because the dire predictions of mass technological unemployment did not pan out. But were they only premature? In organized labor, at least, the shrinkage in the traditional industrial unions is already apparent and is accelerating.

Some unions have tried to fight the trend through the most obvious forms of featherbedding. Others are following the early example of John L. Lewis, who foresaw the inevitable mechanization of the coal mines and chose to make the most of it. There would be fewer miners, Lewis decided, but they would be the highest paid miners in the world. The steelmakers paid a high price to the Steelworkers for the freedom to replace men with new machines, though mechanization still has a way to go in that industry. None of the old unions is immune from concern over shrinking membership, and not all of the shrinkage is due to technological competition. In the building trades, for example, the Labor Department estimates that only 45 percent of the carpenters in the nation belong to a union. The AFL–CIO continues to chalk up annual growth in total union membership, but this statistic hides a crucial fact: soaring growth in the public employee unions is offsetting an across-the-board membership loss in the private sector. Passage of a federal statute to govern labor relations at the state, county, and municipal levels—legislation that public-employee unions are fervently lobbying at present—could greatly speed this transition. Backers of the proposal think its passage is inevitable; just when, no one can say.

From a total of 135 AFL–CIO affiliated unions at the time of the merger in 1955, the federation is down to 110 unions, with the loss due to consolidations. But of the remaining unions, possibly a third of them could be called redundant—small, shrinking, tied to a dwindling trade or industry, clinging to what is left of their sovereignty. Many of them overlap each other's jurisdiction and compete for the right to organize the same workers. The AFL–CIO used to take a hands-off stance toward jurisdictional squabbles among its members but now submits the more troublesome ones to its own special mediation panel. But it lacks any official mechanism for effecting mergers and settling differences. So this sort of bickering—which involves material livelihoods as well as egos—continues to sap energy that could go into more effective and rational organizing. One effect of the 1974–75 recession has been an acceleration of the merger trend. Meany assigned one of his personal assistants to the job of matchmaker.

As organized labor grows more and more affluent, more "establishment," it has had to tone down much of the old rhetoric of mass struggle. A good many nonunion "middle Americans," who earn less than most plumbers or assembly-line bolt tighteners, don't feel much sympathy for the unions. They're bothered by strikes, even when the strikes are remote in place and impact. They think labor, with all its legal rights, is at least on a par with employers at the bargaining table—maybe more than par.

While the issue of "labor monopoly" has long since been rejected as a legal concept and sidetracked as a vote getter, who can say it might not be reawakened if the public becomes convinced that unions have acquired too much power? The issue is occasionally revived when Congress must deal with a "national emergency" strike that Taft-Hartley has failed to prevent—as in the case of railroads, covered by a separate labor statute. Then there is hot debate over compulsory arbitration in one guise or another as a "permanent" solution to strike impasses. So far, labor has been able to persuade Congress not to go that route, but its luck may not hold forever.

And there's the matter of the independent unions. The mighty Teamsters were ousted in 1957 for corrupt practices, after the Dave Beck scandals. They are headed today by Frank Fitzsimmons, who was picked by Jimmy Hoffa to mind the store while Hoffa did time in jail. Fitzsimmons, to Hoffa's surprise, quietly maneuvered himself into real power by easing out Hoffa's henchmen and ingratiating himself with the White House. When President Nixon granted Hoffa clemency in late 1971 after less than five years in jail, one of the conditions was that he not hold union office before March 1980. Hoffa sued the government in 1974, charging that this condition was designed to prevent him from unseating Fitzsimmons and was arranged in exchange for a Teamsters endorsement of Nixon in the 1972 presidential race as well as large, secret financial donations. If Hoffa can circumvent the ban on holding union office, he intends to run for the presidency of the Detroit local and someday challenge Fitzsimmons. However the saga of Jimmy Hoffa ends, it is doubtful that the AFL–CIO would want the Teamsters back in the fold. They continue to be tainted by the smell of racketeering. And their aggressive, sometimes thuggish intrusions against other unions (such as their campaign against Cesar Chavez's United Farm Workers) make them less than popular with the rest of organized labor.

The United Mine Workers haven't been part of the AFL since 1947, when Lewis, who couldn't stand either then President William Green or the increasingly powerful Meany, stomped out after Meany faced him down at a convention and made him look soft on communism. There followed the era of Tony Boyle's corrupt leadership, with pension fund scandals and the grisly murder—arranged by the union officials in Washington—of Boyle's chief challenger, Jock Yablonski. Today, under the reform leadership of Arnold Miller, the Miners are still far from united. It may take several years for the UMW to regain strength and stature as a union, although the soaring demand for coal—due to the energy crisis—will help. In the meantime, the federation would rather not be bothered with the Miners' internal problems, which persist despite the gains made in their 1974 contract settlement.

Finally, there are the United Auto Workers, the 1.4 million-member one-time social conscience of organized labor. It split off in 1968, amid charges by Reuther that the federation had forfeited labor's traditional role as a force for liberal reform in America. Like John L. two decades earlier, Reuther found it impossible to accommodate his ambitions to George Meany's pragmatic leadership. Woodcock espouses most of Reuther's concepts about social change, but is hardly messianic. There is a good chance that he will bring the Auto Workers back to the federation before long (not that such rapprochement is necessary to the prosperity of either organization).

REALIGNMENT

The coming realignment of power within the federation may take time to develop, but it will be fundamental. Strong forces from below—the service-oriented and government unions—will slowly but surely push their way upward through the weakened strata until a new peak appears. If the older unions choose to fight off what seems inevitable, the process could be volcanic, seriously impairing labor's influence in Washington. The main reason that unions wield such great political influence is that they are able to speak with one voice on the major issue and concentrate resources where they can have the most impact. No one within the AFL–CIO or the independent unions wants this to end, not even the most ambitious climber.

Despite growing wealthy and conservative, the federation tries to keep alive the spirit of an embattled movement, the feeling of being the perennial outsider. Ceremonial utterances are still sprinkled with the florid jargon of class struggle, as if "antilabor" forces are always lying in wait to spring a trap. However anachronistic the theme may have become, it still serves to unify the disparate elements of the federation. "Strength-in-unity" served the unions well in the early days when they really were oppressed, when most of the problems were external. It still serves in an era when labor has prosperously "arrived," when many of the severest challenges it faces come from within the family of labor itself.

Whether the Washington labor leadership concentrates in the future on the bread-and-butter issues or again champions political and social issues will be determined by the new crop of officials who are emerging. After a relatively quiet labor decade, Washington will soon be jumping with this new generation of labor leaders—college-educated and issue-oriented. In this, labor will be in step with other parts of the Washington establishment, of which it is now such an integral part.

30 ASSOCIATIONS FOR ALL

In the Washington, D.C., Yellow Pages, sandwiched between "Asphalt Tile" and "Astrologers," is a category entitled "Associations." It consists of thirty columns of single-spaced, fine-print listings that take up eight pages of the phone book. Virtually all of the listed organizations include in their titles such words as "Society," "Foundation," "Council," "Institute," "Committee," "Commission," "Union," "Federation," "League," "College," "Alliance," "Convention," "Academy," and, of course, "Association." More often than not, the titles also include the words "American," "National," "U.S.," or "International."

These more than 1,600 organizations have nothing specific in common with each other. But they all share the same general goal, method of operation, and reason for being in Washington: promotion of the common interests of the organizations' members. Because the federal government is taking an increasingly active role in everything that anybody does in this country, Washington is the headquarters of more national associations than any other city in America. Trade associations annually pump some $900 million into the area economy in salaries and expenditures of all sorts.

As the watchdog of its members' interests, an association assumes many different roles. It is a lobbyist, keeping in touch with (and entertaining) congressmen, congressional committee staffs, White House aides, and bureaucrats. It is an information gatherer for its members, sending out reports, newsletters, and memoranda, and taking long-distance phone calls from members who need specific information in a hurry. It is a peacemaker that brings together the heads of its member organizations, so they can iron out differences and decide on a common course of action. It is a genial host whose welcome mat is always out. It holds conventions and serves as an informal meeting place for its members when they come to Washington for business or pleasure.

If you ask an association executive what irritates him most about the press coverage his organization gets, he'll probably complain that the press ignores every function of his association except lobbying. And when the press writes about an association's lobbying, the executive complains further, it won't mention the day-to-day routine informational services rendered by associations to the people who make laws and regulations. Instead, it will concentrate on the occasional all-out campaign to kill an unfavorable bill or promote some special-interest legislation.

HOW THEY CAME ABOUT

Associations are nothing new, not in Washington or in the rest of the nation. As a matter of fact, European social critic Alexis de Tocqueville observed 140 years ago that Americans have a penchant for seeking out other people who have similar interests and forming organizations in which they can talk shop, share experiences, have fun, and think up better ways to pursue their common goals. Besides the ubiquitous trade associations, de Tocqueville wrote, Americans have "associations of a thousand other kinds: religious, moral, serious, futile, general or restricted, enormous or diminutive."

The signs of association activity are everywhere in Washington. On any given weekday, the streets of the 16th Street and upper Connecticut Avenue hotel districts are crowded with people who have rectangular plastic name badges pinned to their suit lapels and dresses. The badges proclaim that they are attending any one of the hundreds of conventions that take place in Washington each year, virtually all of them sponsored by trade, professional, religious, and civic associations. (Many of these conventioneers keep their badges on even when they leave the work sessions to venture out on the town in the evening, making them easy to spot in the lobby of the National Theatre, dining at Blackie's House of Beef, or ogling the strippers at the Silver Slipper on 13th Street.)

Besides the visual presence of associations, their names, initials, and jargon are omnipresent in the working vocabulary of the capital. As if a newcomer to Washington didn't have a difficult enough time keeping up with the acronyms of federal agencies—like OSHA (Occupational Safety and Health Administration), LEAA (Law Enforcement Assistance Administration), and Sally Mae (Student Loan Marketing Association)—he has to contend with association initials, too. The ATA could be either the Air Transport Association or the American Trucking Association, but the latter group is commonly known as "the Truckers." The ABA could be the American Bar Association or the American Bankers Association, but the latter group is usually just called "the Bankers." Then there are the "Chamber" (U.S. Chamber of Commerce), "the Brewers" (United States Brewers Association), and "the Canners" (National Canners Association).

Associations account for a large share of the local economy, ranking behind the federal government and tourist-related businesses as the third-largest employer in the metropolitan area. And virtually all of that employment is white-collar. Actually, the association establishment is almost an arm of the tourist industry in Washington, considering the amount of convention business it brings into town.

It is not coincidental that the proliferation in Washington of plush, expensive restaurants during the 1960s paralleled the boom in association budgets. A good many of the bills at these restaurants, especially at lunch, are covered by the expense accounts of association executives, corporate representatives, and lawyers. When association executives want to get away from the routine of lunch with their contacts at the Hay-Adams Hotel, Harvey's, the Rotunda, the Sheraton-Carlton, Jean-Pierre, or Duke Zeibert's, they can huddle with their own kind for drinks and a meal at the Association Executives Club, located in the Statler Hilton Hotel on 16th Street.

There is an association in Washington for every conceivable form of human activity, be it economic, spiritual, cultural, or recreational. Most branches of the food industry have associations to spread the gospel of the tastiness and high nutrition cost ratio of the foods they grow, process, or market: the Poultry and Egg Institute, the Peanut Butter Manufacturers and Nut Salters Association, the National Ice Cream Mix Association, the National Association of Margarine Manufacturers, the National Soft Drink Association, the National Turkey Federation, and the Salt Institute, to name just a few.

There are associations that promote leisure-time activities, like the Sport Fishing Institute, National Bowling Council, National Swimming Pool Institute, National Rifle Association, and National Jogging Association. There are associations to unite professional people in similar lines of work, like the Society of Women Geographers, the National Catholic Music Educators Association, and the Federal Statistics Users' Conference. There are associations that unite people who have nothing more in common than their ages or marital status, like the American Association of Retired Persons and Parents Without Partners, Inc. And there are associations that defy pigeonholing, like the National Investigations Committee on Aerial Phenomena. There is even an "association of associations," the formal name of which is the American Society of Association Executives.

VOICES OF BUSINESS

By far the most prolific type of association in Washington is the trade association, an organization of businesses that manufacture similar products or provide similar services. Usually the association name leaves little doubt about the kind of business the association members are engaged in: the American Hot Dip Galvanizers Association, the Cast Iron Soil Pipe Institute, the Tire Retreading Institute, or the National Association of Metal Name Plate Manufacturers.

Many of the associations here are low-budget outfits consisting of one or two people, plus a secretary, working out of a modest office in one of the older downtown buildings. In some cases the association's Washington "office" consists merely of a lawyer who represents it on a retainer while handling many other clients at the same time.

At the other end of the pole are the old, well-established associations that represent the largest industries in American business, and even American business itself, as is the case with the U.S. Chamber of Commerce and the National Association of Manufacturers. Each of the twenty-two largest associations in America—many of which are headquartered in Washington and most of which represent manufacturing industries—has an annual budget exceeding $5 million and a staff numbering between 100 and 400 people. Each probably occupies several floors of an elegant new office building downtown (in a fashionable block of Connecticut Avenue, K Street, or 16th Street) or in one of the fast-growing commercial sections of a suburb like Rosslyn, Virginia, Chevy Chase, Maryland, or in the "new town" of Reston, Virginia.

Many of the best-known associations—such as the American Institute of Architects, the National Rifle Association, the National Association of Broadcasters, and the Air Line Pilots Association—own their own office buildings and occupy all or part of them. The National Association of Home Builders, the voice of the enormous housing industry, recently completed its ultramodern National Housing Center (headquarters plus displays open to the public) near Massachusetts Avenue and 15th Street. Trade associations exist on the dues paid by member corporations. The most common practice is to assess each corporation a share of the association costs proportional to its share of the industry's total sales.

Most associations were conceived in the region where a particular industry was born and thrived. The National Cotton Council of America, for example, was founded and is still based in Memphis, Tennessee; the Motor Vehicle Manufacturers Association is headquartered in Detroit, Michigan; and the American Textile Manufacturers Institute is based in Charlotte, North Carolina. New York City, as the national center of commercial finance, is the headquarters of a number of major industrial associations. In the days before air travel, Chicago was a convenient headquarters for associations, because of its equidistance between the East and West coasts and its prominence in the national railway network. Chicago is still the home base of most of the food associations, such as the Millers' National Federation and the American Dry Milk Institute. It's also the health association center of the nation, with such organizations as the American Medical Association, the American Hospital Association, and the American Dental Association.

THE TIDE CONTINUES

But every year sees the defection to Washington of more and more of the major national associations, and even before this mass migration began, the larger trade associations headquartered in other cities maintained sizable staffs here.

Before the Great Depression, most corporate executives viewed associations as superfluous organizations that held enjoyable conventions and published magazines with ego-boosting stories about the industry and the personalities that dominated it. The staffs were small and the dues were low, because the member corporations didn't want much from the associations in the way of representation, leadership, or "legislative engineering" (lobbying). Each corporation spoke for itself, hired its own lobbyist, and felt it was conducting its business as well as 6 competitors in the same industry. Then the crash and the election of FDR changed things. The National Recovery Administration, with its industry codes, put a premium on cooperation among competing companies. Like World Wars I and II, the depression forced corporations to work together more than they ever had before, and trade associations were given a boost.

After the Second World War, however, trade associations settled back into their traditional pattern of expansion when times were flush and contraction when the going got rough. When profits were down, instead of looking to their association for guidance, some corporations dispensed with membership altogether, much as they would eliminate a wasteful frill. Association staffs were cut, and dues were lowered or held stable.

Then, in the middle of the turbulent Sixties, several popular movements—all of which could be generally termed "antibusiness"—converged and gave trade associations a tremendous shot of adrenaline. Explaining this situation ironically, one association official insists that "the patron saint of trade associations is Ralph Nader." Movements like consumerism, product safety, job safety, and environmental concern—which this association leader conveniently lumped together under the symbolic umbrella of "Ralph Nader"—gave business a mild case of paranoia. Corporate executives thought twice about standing up and stating their company's position loud and clear, risking being tagged as an apologist for pollution, deceptive labeling, or dangerous toys. The idea of hiding anonymously behind the shield of an industry trade association seemed much more appealing. More and more companies decided to keep their heads down and send their association staffs out of the trenches to catch the flak.

Trade associations prospered as never before, and the migration from New York and Chicago increased. Additional personnel were hired to analyze— and if need be, oppose—the many new bills introduced to correct alleged flaws in business practices. The mini-recession of 1968–70 was the first time in the history of trade associations that their staffs, budgets, and salaries, rather than being cut in hard times, actually soared. The advent of wage-and-price controls in 1971 further strengthened the hand of the trade associations. The Cost of Living Council relied heavily on association staffs to help devise wage-price guidelines (and formulas for computing the guidelines) that took into consideration the accounting and marketing peculiarities of each industry.

A good case study in the growth of the association establishment in Washington during the past decade is offered by the experience of the Grocery Manufacturers of America (GMA), which represents an industry that accounts for about 10 percent of the nation's total economic activity, with members ranging from Nabisco to Colgate-Palmolive to Seven-Up to Scott Paper. Headquartered in New York, the GMA did not even have a Washington office until 1966, when it opened a two-man office here. GMA President George W. Koch commuted between New York and Washington. But with the onslaught of consumerism—unit pricing, nutritional labeling, dating of perishable products—the GMA decided in 1970 to move to the capital, for easier lobbying of congressional committees and agencies like the Food and Drug Administration, the Federal Trade Commission, and the Department of Agriculture. Today its small but highly effective staff numbers about thirty people. Symbolizing the continuing tilt-toward-Washington was the move in 1973 of the National Association of Manufacturers, which brought its whole operation from New York to the capital, "where the action is."

ASSOCIATION EXECUTIVES

Before the boom of the Sixties, any association could hire an ace executive for about $50,000. Not so today. The top men of the leading trade associations in Washington now earn salaries hovering around $100,000, with a high of about $125,000. The average executive director's salary for the twenty-two associations with the largest budgets is about $72,000. (The salaries for executives of public service associations are generally lower.) Some association directors are actually paid more than the executives of the corporations they represent.

In years past, association posts were favorite jobs of defeated or retired congressmen and high-ranking federal officials who lost their appointments with a change of party in the White House. They got job security and the association got prestige, plus the benefit of their government contacts. Among the association heads with this background are Frank Ikard, a former six-term congressman from Texas who became vice president and then president of the American Petroleum Institute; Carl Bagge, a former Federal Power Commission commissioner who runs the National Coal Association; Paul Ignatius of the Air Transport Association, a former secretary of the navy and executive of the Washington Post Company; Stephen Ailes of the Association of American Railroads, formerly a secretary of the army and partner in the prominent Washington law firm of Steptoe and Johnson; Jack Valenti, a former advertising executive and aide to President Lyndon B. Johnson who now heads the Motion Picture Association of America; Walter E. Rogers, a former Texas congressman who is president of the Independent Natural Gas Association of America; and Richard Lyng, a former assistant secretary of agriculture who is now the head of the American Meat Institute. Most recently, the Motor Vehicles Manufacturers Association (which has a large Washington office) hired as its new chief William D. Eberle, a corporate executive who served for three years under Nixon and Ford as director of the White House Council on International Economic Policy.

Associations that don't hire a former government bigwig often seek a corporate executive with years of experience in the industry represented by the association. But there seems to be a trend away from hiring people from either of these backgrounds. Some associations have found that the value of previous federal contacts is overrated and that any diligent person can learn the particular problems of an industry without spending his life in it. Among the educational backgrounds that predominate on association staffs are law, business administration, and journalism. Job jumping among Washington association men sometimes resembles a game of musical chairs. Since all the associations here run on a mix of lobbying, information gathering, and entertaining, the skills developed at one association are readily transferable to another.

GOOD NEWS FOR LAWYERS

Associations are a boon to the Washington legal establishment. Not only do they employ hundreds of lawyers full time, as in-house counsels and lobbyists, but they also are lucrative clients of the city's large corporate law firms. Even though the nation's largest corporations retain Washington firms individually, there are occasional industry-wide challenges from Uncle Sam that require a unified response coordinated by the trade association and the law firm it hires.

The Motor Vehicle Manufacturers Association, for example, retained Lloyd Cutler of Wilmer, Cutler and Pickering to fight a federal antitrust suit that charged it and the Big Four automakers with conspiring to hamper development of antipollution devices. (The suit was settled through a "consent decree" without a trial.) The Pharmaceutical Manufacturers Association hired the same firm, plus the services of Thomas (Tommy the Cork) Corcoran, to battle in the halls of Congress against stringent federal regulation of the marketing and advertising of drugs. The National Canners Association for years has staved off legislation for uniform quality labeling of canned goods, in large part through the efforts of H. Thomas Austern, a senior partner of the prestigious law factory of Covington and Burling.

The costs of such representation run very high. The U.S. Brewers Association, the voice of the beer industry, faced no particular legal crises in 1973, but managed to pay some $200,000 in legal fees, a large part of that going to Covington and Burling. Among the law fees paid in 1973 by the International

Snowmobile Manufacturers Association, a young organization representing a relatively small industry, was $70,000 to Patton, Boggs and Blow (one of whose partners is the son of the late House Majority Leader Hale Boggs, D-La.).

Associations that represent competing industries sometimes bury their differences long enough to form alliances of convenience on particular issues. The Wool Bureau, for example, spends a lot of time and money every year trying to sell American industry and consumers the idea that its product is superior to all others, and the National Cotton Council of America makes similar claims for cotton. And there are giant chemical companies trying to convince America that synthetic fibers are better than natural materials. But along came a volatile new consumer issue that's laden with emotion: fabric flammability, especially of children's clothes. Suddenly the various fiber associations—joined by the American Textile Manufacturers Institute and the American Apparel Manufacturers Association—found themselves in a common predicament. A tenuous, temporary bond was formed to try to shape the inevitable federal regulations in a manner favorable to American industry without appearing to be callous about the safety of small children.

There are similar overlaps of association concern on the environmental issue of disposable versus returnable cans and bottles, in which the competing glass container and aluminum container manufacturers—plus the National Soft Drink Association—have common interests. Or the American sugar industry, in which the U.S. Cane Sugar Refiners and the U.S. Beet Sugar Association—joined by the associations of commercial sugar users, like the candymakers and the soft drink manufacturers—have a big say in determining how much foreign sugar is imported into the U.S. each year and at what price. The retailing associations and the restaurant associations join forces to keep the lid on the minimum wage for teenage employees. Virtually all manufacturing associations have a common stake in the fast-approaching conversion to the metric system. In all their collaboration, however, trade associations have to steer clear of activities that smack of antitrust violation.

CORPORATE SPOKESMEN

Trade associations exist to promote a total industry, to further the goals that their member corporations have in common. To further the goals of a particular corporation—often in competition with the other companies within its own trade association—there exists a creature unique to the nation's capital, variously called "vice president for governmental relations" or "vice president for Washington affairs," or simply "Washington representative."

Known for their lavish expense accounts for entertaining and their suave but tough personalities, these corporate executives are sent to Washington to make sure that the home company gets its fair share (or hopefully more) of government contracts; is not impeded by antitrust suits as it swallows up small competitors; is not harassed by long and costly federal tax claims; and is not maligned in the public's eye by embarrassing congressional inquiries or complaints from the Federal Trade Commission.

While corporate vice presidents and association executives cooperate on many industry-wide issues, there can be built-in jealousies and tensions between them stemming from overlapping purposes. Both groups get paid from the same source, the corporate treasury. Both groups want to prove their indispensability. Often after a successful legislative campaign, each group will take credit for victory and pooh-pooh the effectiveness of the other.

Every major trade association in Washington has a "political action committee" (PAC), and the trustees of the PAC—usually the staff of the association—decide which politicians it will support, on the basis of their voting records on issues of concern to the industry. Not surprisingly, each industry's PAC pours money into the campaigns of cooperative politicians who sit on the committees that regulate that industry. The American Bankers Association's "Bankpac," for example, has given thousands of dollars to the campaigns of each amenable member of the Senate Committee on Banking, Housing, and Urban Affairs. (The practice is much the same with organized labor.)

The major problem with PACs is that the supposedly voluntary contributions their members pay in are hardly voluntary. Both unions and corporations put pressure on their members and employees to chip in a specified amount of money. Often corporations secretly use company funds to reimburse their executives' personal campaign contributions, in violation of federal law. Investigation of the Watergate scandals revealed that numerous corporations didn't even bother in 1972 with PACs or under-the-table reimbursements, but made direct contributions from company funds. In lieu of, or in addition to, a conventional campaign contribution, many associations engage political figures to address their conventions, for which the officials can be paid a personal honorarium not exceeding $1,000. By keeping all of their political activities under the PAC umbrella, associations maintain their status as tax-exempt organizations.

RESULTS COUNT

It is impossible to assess the effectiveness of every trade association staff, but it is reasonable to assume that staffs would not be expanding and budgets would not be soaring if the member corporations didn't think they are getting their money's worth for their dues. Not that the effectiveness is proportional to budget, however. Some of the biggest associations are hampered by their high profile and diffused concern for many general issues. Some of the most effective representation is done by relatively low-budget associations whose concern is the well-being of one specialized, unglamorous industry.

Finally, if you ask a Washington association executive to assess his own effectiveness at influencing legislation, don't expect a straight answer. His response will vary according to who is asking the question. To the average citizen or inquisitive reporter, he'll say, "Oh, our association didn't really do much at all on that issue; our role in the passage [or defeat] of that regulatory bill was really minimal, despite what you read in the papers." But when he talks to the officers of his association—the corporate figures who pay his salary—the association's role is suddenly inflated to something like St. George slaying a dragon that threatened to devour the whole industry. The truth, as always, lies somewhere between the false modesty and the big boast.

31 THE EDUCATION VINEYARDS

American education ain't what it used to be—not necessarily better or worse, but definitely different. Every level of education is being wrenched by changes: declining enrollments, desegregation, attacks on property tax financing, questioning of the value of a college education, parochial school closings, new theories of "open education," teacher strikes, and the demand for equality between the sexes. In each of these challenges, Washington is in the middle of the fray, either as the principal instigator or as a bystander who got caught up in the struggle against his will.

The extent of the federal government's involvement with education today cannot be measured in dollars alone, for federal aid to education has rarely amounted to more than 10 percent of the nation's total annual spending on education, and is usually about 7 or 8 percent. But those dollars are Washington's foot in the doors of the schoolrooms, especially those of relatively poor states, where federal aid accounts for anywhere from a quarter to a third of the education budget. Despite the Nixon administration's attempts to phase out detailed categorical grants in favor of consolidated grants and revenue sharing, the federal aid pouring into virtually every school district in the nation has many strings attached. The failure of a college to comply with Uncle Sam's specific or general requirements can mean a loss of federal support on which the institution has grown dependent.

Federal aid to education is put into areas that Congress and the administration (coached by the education lobbyists who inhabit Washington) feel to be in greatest need of bolstering. Federal funds go to school districts that have a high percentage of poor people and are unable to raise enough money through property taxes to support their schools adequately. Federal funds pay for 80 percent of the Head Start preschool program, which reaches some 380,000 children each year, trying to prepare them for kindergarten. In many school systems, federal aid pays for the milk that students drink with their morning snack and for the hot meal they eat for lunch. Federal aid is targeted at handicapped children and youths who desire vocational training instead of college-preparatory studies. And there is a special category of federal aid to school districts which have a large enrollment of children of federal employees (mostly military personnel) who live on federal installations and therefore contribute nothing to the local tax base. Colleges, too, are the beneficiaries of federal generosity, but in recent years more aid has been channeled to college students—through scholarships and loans—than to the institutions directly.

Education is one of those activities that has always been jealously guarded by local and state authorities, so each new and deeper federal intrusion into education is viewed with not a little uneasiness. Since education was not mentioned in the Constitution as an enumerated power of the federal government, there has traditionally been a consensus in America that the federal role should be minimal. No national school system. No uniform national curriculum (although standardization of college entrance requirements has resulted in essentially that). No federal requirement of a minimum number of years spent in school. No monitoring of individual scholastic achievement (although the federal government, through the National Assessment of Education Progress, helps fund the testing of students who are then ranked on a broad regional basis).

In the middle 1950s, the federal government began to abandon its hands-off stance toward education. It then became popular to regard education as the key—or the obstacle—to the reaching of a broad range of national goals. (Ten years before, an entire generation of young men, back from World War II, got a chance to go to college under the GI Bill, but the government hadn't yet plunged into institutional aid.) If all Americans are to have an equal chance to realize their human potential, the Supreme Court ruled in 1954, the separate-and-unequal system of segregated schools must be abolished. If the United States is to keep abreast of the Soviet Union's achievements in space, a whole nation agreed after the surprise of Sputnik in 1957, then the nation's science curriculum must be beefed up—with the aid of federal dollars.

This spirit of Uncle-Sam-to-the-Rescue grew even stronger under the social planners of the New Frontier and Great Society. Justice Department attorneys filed suit throughout the South to dismantle the dual school systems that still flourished a decade after the *Brown* v. *Board of Education* decision. Washington took on the massive task of trying to even out per pupil expenditures on education by granting funds to districts with high densities of poor children. Head Start was born. And the planners discovered that a hungry child has a hard time being an adequate student, so they expanded the school milk and lunch programs and started a new one for school breakfasts. Higher education was not ignored, either. The soaring cost of going to college spawned programs of grants, loans, and work-study assistance, not to mention construction grants, graduate student fellowships, and research grants in particular fields deemed to be in the national interest (especially the sciences).

Any of these programs, of course, could conceivably have been implemented by state and local governments, using higher property taxes, state income taxes, and sales taxes. But instead they were born in Washington and financed with federal income tax revenue. Gradually, every level of education in every state became beholden to Washington to a degree that varied with its dependence on federal aid. To secure obedience to Justice Department desegregation plans in the South, Congress had only to prohibit the granting of federal education funds to school districts that still practiced de jure separation of blacks and whites. The same tactic is being used today to secure equal opportunity for women in higher education, in every area from balanced enrollment to equal expenditures on men's and women's athletic programs.

For more than twenty years, education policy has been inextricably meshed with constitutional issues of equal protection of the laws and equal opportunity. Because of this, the U.S. Supreme Court—which has no bureaucracy, no enforcement powers, and hands out rulings rather than federal grants—has probably stimulated more basic change in education than any other government institution. Take race relations in the schools. It struck the first blow against de jure segregation in 1954, and in the early Seventies it refused to hand down an outright ban on the busing of school children to achieve racial balance, although it rejected busing between the city and suburbs in the Detroit and Richmond cases. In 1971 the Court backed the IRS in its refusal to grant tax exemptions to private schools that discriminate by race—an attack on the all-white academies that sprang up all over the South in the late Sixties and early Seventies.

Or take the perennial controversy over government aid to parochial schools. For years their financial plight has been worsening, especially as they employ more and more lay teachers who, unlike nuns and priests, are not willing to work for an ascetic salary. To slow down the trend of parochial school closings—which further burden the public schools—several states began looking for ways to support the Catholic schools without running afoul of the constitutional requirement that affairs of church and state be kept separate. But the Supreme Court has taken a hard line on such state support. Generally, it has allowed only aid for noneducational services (such as transportation to school, driver-education courses, and health services) and educational functions that don't risk "excessive entanglement of church and state" (the supplying of textbooks for academic courses and federal construction grants to Catholic colleges). In 1971 the Court emphatically turned thumbs down on the Pennsylvania and Rhode Island systems of subsidizing teachers' salaries in parochial schools. President Nixon was displeased by the decision, and pledged thereafter to find some constitutional way to help Catholic schools with general operating expenses (in the name of "educational diversity"). He left office before he could find a solution to the dilemma.

There are many other ways in which the Supreme Court has affected the education establishment, some trivial and others crucial. There was the pro-women's rights ruling that a school district may not force a pregnant teacher to take a leave of absence until very late in her pregnancy. The Court ruled unanimously in 1974 that school districts must make a special effort to help students who do not speak English well enough to absorb normal classroom instruction—a ruling that had far-reaching impact on school districts from San Francisco's Chinatown to the Spanish-speaking neighborhoods of New York City and Miami.

There are times, however, when the Court prefers to sidestep a hot issue in education. In the 1974 *DeFunis* decision, a majority of the Court refused to grapple with the thorny problem of quotas and reverse racial discrimination in college admissions procedures, on grounds that the case was rendered moot by later events. The Court has been equally cautious about one of the most controversial matters in education today: intrastate equalization of per pupil expenditures on elementary and secondary education. The conservative bloc of the Court prefers to take a states'-rights tack, letting each state decide as it pleases whether to equalize spending among all districts or let the wealthy school districts thrive while schools in poor neighborhoods are strapped for revenue, owing to inequalities in taxable property. In 1973 the Court ruled 5–4 that Texas could continue relying on the local property tax to fund schools, despite the obvious inequalities. But soon thereafter, the Court let stand a New Jersey state supreme court ruling that required scrapping of the property tax in favor of statewide funding and equalized spending.

While the job of arbitrating thorny education issues falls to the nine men of the Supreme Court, the everyday task of running the federal education machine is in the hands of a bureaucracy called the Education Division of the Department of Health, Education and Welfare (HEW). The division contains two main parts, the U.S. Office of Education and the National Institute of Education, a relatively new and precariously funded research-and-development body that commissions and funds experiments in new educational techniques. It is presided over by the Assistant Secretary (of HEW) for Education, Virginia Trotter, a career educator and former vice chancellor of the University of Nebraska.

The Office of Education, with a staff numbering nearly 3,000 people, is the administrative arm of the federal education effort. Its mandate is to implement and monitor the effectiveness of most of the old and new federal aid programs dreamed up by Congress (and by the Office of Education itself). The HEW Education Division spends about $6 billion each year—roughly 40 percent of the more than $15 billion that Uncle Sam spends on everything directly or indirectly related to education. A big chunk of the other $9 billion or so is spent by other divisions of HEW, including the Office of Child Development (which funds Head Start with about $420 million a year), the Social Security Administration (which pays educational benefits to college students who have lost one or both parents), and the National Institutes of Health (which, among other activities, funds postgraduate research and the training of medical personnel). More than 35 percent of the federal government's educational expenditures are made by three agencies other than HEW—the Department of Defense (which trains military personnel in everything from exotic foreign languages to basic electronics), the Department of Agriculture (which runs the school nutrition programs), and the Veterans Administration (which administers educational grants under the GI Bill).

The federal government funds and oversees several entire colleges, including the military academies, Howard University, and Gallaudet College (America's only college for the deaf, located in the nation's capital). Uncle Sam even operates a unique institution called the U.S. Department of Agriculture Graduate School. This school, which has little to do with agriculture anymore, has 21,000 part-time students (mostly federal bureaucrats, but open to anyone), offers 600 courses (everything from languages and architectural history to speed reading and physics), grants no degrees, has no campus (holding its day and evening classes in office buildings all over Washington), gets no government appropriation, and charges tuitions as low as $16 per credit hour. Students have ranged from Supreme Court Justice Byron White (who took a "reading improvement" course in 1961, before being appointed to the bench), to clerk-typists trying to get ahead in their careers.

The Office of Education, usually called OE, has long had the reputation of being a headstrong, immovable bureaucracy that functions more or less independently from the rest of HEW, perhaps because it had existed since 1867 under several different names and for decades in the Interior Department, of all places. The first Secretary of HEW, Mrs. Oveta Culp Hobby, was so dismayed by the office that one of her assistants suggested that she "fire everybody down there and start all over again." OE is headed by the commissioner of education, a position held in 1975 by Terrel H. (Ted) Bell, a former superintendent of suburban schools from Salt Lake City, Utah. Most commissioners have been rather obscure men, not the best-known educators. And they have not normally been part of the President's inside circle, to say the least. President John F. Kennedy, upon learning of the resignation of his first commissioner, is reported to have said, "Why, I've never met the man, and now he's leaving town." Quipped aide Arthur Schlesinger, Jr.: "That may be why he's quitting."

But a few top education officials have been better known, both before and during their tenures in Washington. JFK's second commissioner, for example, was Francis Keppel, a longtime dean of the education faculty at Harvard. After a stint as President Johnson's assistant HEW secretary for education, he became head of General Learning Corporation, a profitmaking company in the education research-and-development field. Another of the better-known commissioners (and later assistant HEW secretary for education) was Sidney P. Marland, Jr., a longtime school superintendent who served under President Nixon until taking the top position at the College Entrance Examination Board in New York City. President Nixon's first commissioner was James E. Allen, Jr., who had previously been commissioner of education for New York State. He split with the administration over several major issues and left Washington after one year, to take a teaching post at Princeton University.

THE JOHNSON ERA

During the Johnson administration, OE was a hotbed of experimentation with new kinds of federal aid to education and new techniques of teaching. It was during this period that Congress and OE teamed up to conceive the array of categorical grants that are still in force today. Research into theories and techniques of education—which OE had been dabbling in since 1954—became a major federal pastime. The country was blanketed with a network of "educational R&D centers," located at universities, and "regional education laboratories," designed to disseminate the new methods among local school systems. Dozens of new ideas in education were given a try: the "new math," the "open classroom," team teaching, teaching machines, television, "performance contracting," and vouchers, to name a few.

In performance contracting, a school system contracts with a private corporation to take over the teaching of a particular problem area, such as reading or mathematics. The contractor "guarantees" that the children will perform at a certain level of competence by the expiration of the contract. If the level is not achieved, presumably, the contract is not renewed. If the level is exceeded, the contractor sometimes gets a bonus. Under the voucher system, parents are given a certificate good for "tuition"—up to the local average per pupil expenditure—at a number of different schools in the district. The participating schools are restructured (some remaining "traditional," some turned into "experimental schools," others specializing in particular subject areas) so the parents and students have a choice of educational styles that they can buy with their vouchers. (The only full-fledged experiment with a voucher system was made in the schools of Alum Rock, California.)

In the ten years since the federal government jumped into education research, there has been much controversy over the effectiveness of virtually every experiment. Where performance contracting was tried, it almost always cost more than conventional teaching, and it has yet to produce significantly higher test scores. In a few cities, there were suspicions that the contractor tried to boost scores by drilling pupils in the same material that would appear on their tests soon thereafter. Even the much-heralded "new math" ran into criticism, namely that some students suffered a loss in simple computation proficiency while acquiring a better grasp of mathematical theory. Defenders of the educational experiments point out that new programs are constantly plagued with resistance from teachers (individually—and collectively through their unions), and they tend to feel especially threatened by such programs as performance contracting and vouchers.

Teachers were not crazy, either, about the National Assessment of Educational Progress, a sampling of student achievement conducted by the Education Commission of the States (an offshoot of the Council of State Governments), with substantial funding from OE. Each year since 1969 about 100,000 pupils in four age groups have been tested in two of several academic subjects (reading, math, science, music, etc.). The exam for each subject is repeated once every five years. Many teachers feared that detailed breakdowns of test scores—by state, school district, or even individual schools—would result in parents holding teachers accountable for poor achievement. Their fears were largely allayed by the decision to report assessment scores only on a regional basis. Hence it is possible to compare, say, the math skills of nine-year-old boys in the Far West with those in New England, but not nine-year-olds from Chevy Chase, Maryland, with those from Winnetka, Illinois. Although the assessment has not been going on long enough to determine a trend in scholastic achievement over time, many people have been shocked by the low level of basic skills demonstrated by large numbers of the sample group, particularly in a test of English composition that required writing a brief essay.

NIXON'S EDUCATION POLICIES

The Nixon administration arrived in 1969 with a determination to "reduce, redirect, or eliminate education programs that are outdated, have failed to achieve their objective or are not reaching high-priority targets." To an education lobby that was reasonably content with the status quo in federal aid, these were fighting words. Not that Nixon proposed cutting total federal support of education. On the contrary, the total dollar amount soared in the following few years (with the administration's moderate increases pushed higher and higher by Congress). But the Nixon team had different ideas about allocating those dollars, and this meant trouble. By the middle of 1971, officers of the National Education Association, the powerful unionlike organization of schoolteachers, were calling the Nixon administration the most "antieducation" in many years.

The Nixon administration wanted to give local school systems more choice in how they could spend their federal aid money, but it ran into trouble with Congress by attempting to consolidate many "categorical" programs into education revenue sharing. (It is estimated that almost one-third of the money passed out to the states in "general revenue" over the past few years has been spent on education.) The categorical programs had many powerful advocates on the Hill. The administration also ran into a stone wall when it attempted to trim, and eventually eliminate, most kinds of "Impact Aid," the federal payments to school districts which contain federal installations. While impact aid is an expensive program, the money flows into schools in more than half of the nation's congressional districts, and it is a very popular program on the Hill.

Instead of showing disenchantment with the R&D programs that proliferated in the Great Society years, the Nixon administration suggested that Uncle Sam was not spending enough on education research. In a message to Congress after one year in the White House, the President said, "We must stop pretending that we understand the mystery of the learning process, or that we are significantly applying science and technology to the techniques of teaching, when we spend less than .5 percent of our education budget on research, compared with 5 percent of our health budget and 10 percent of defense." Nixon proposed a National Institute of Education, to be a co-equal of the Office of Education in the new HEW Education Division. Congress bought the plan, somewhat reluctantly, and NIE was begun in 1972. NIE supports research into virtually every learning problem, with special emphasis on reading skills, increasing the productivity of teachers, improving the relevance of education to career goals, and reaching such disadvantaged groups as handicapped and bilingual students.

Congress has been skeptical of NIE all along, preferring to skip the fancy research and put more money directly into the schools. Charging that NIE doesn't enjoy much support among teachers, Senator Warren Magnuson of the Senate Labor–HEW Appropriations Subcommittee engineered a 50 percent cut in NIE's 1974 appropriation. T. Keith Glennan, NIE director until his resignation in November 1974, said Congress's attitude was "shortsighted," and argued that "an investment in the future of education, in improvement in the coming decade, as opposed to improvements in the next six or eight months, is something worth doing."

In the field of higher education, the Nixon administration proposed greater assistance to the individual college student and less aid to the colleges themselves. Federal aid for the construction of college facilities shrank drastically during the early Seventies, as did federal research grants and teaching fellowships. The chief exception to this broad deemphasis of institutional support has been the colleges that are predominantly black in enrollment. These have received greater federal aid to help cope with the impact of competition with newly integrated white universities.

In the area of scholarship aid to individual college students, the Nixon administration has pushed for implementation of what it calls the "basic opportunity grant" (BOG), designed to guarantee that no qualified student is denied a college education for lack of money. Under the law creating the BOG, each college-bound student is eligible for an annual $1,400 grant, minus an amount that he and his family are deemed able to pay, based on their income. In reality BOGs have ranged from about $50 to $800. The grants may not exceed one-half of the cost of the student's annual education costs. The rest of the amount can be raised through a variety of other federal loan and work-study programs (or through scholarships granted by the college itself). In the first two years of the BOG program, it was plagued by hassles over funding and a broad lack of awareness of its existence on the part of high school guidance counselors, colleges, and students themselves.

Despite President Nixon's lukewarm attitude toward federally enforced integration, his Justice Department made major headway against separation of the races at all levels of education. Integration is now much further advanced in the Deep South than in the North and West, where segregation is traceable to de facto patterns of income and housing rather than deliberate design. In 1972 more than 46 percent of the southern black schoolchildren were in white-majority schools, while the comparable figure for the northern and western states was 28 percent. Desegregation was extended to those states which maintained dual systems of white and black state colleges in 1973 when a federal judge ordered integration of higher education in ten states— eight in the South, plus Pennsylvania and Oklahoma. Only the state of Louisiana balked at submitting a desegregation plan to HEW, and soon thereafter it was sued by the Justice Department.

The Nixon administration got its reputation for being "antieducation" not so much from its reorganization action as from the President's pugnacious vetoing and impounding of education appropriations bills. Some of these executive actions were taken for policy reasons—as was the President's veto of a bill that would have put Uncle Sam into the day-care center business in a big way. But most of the impoundments of school aid were explained on grounds of "anti-inflation." Whatever the reason, these acts raised the ire of the education lobbyists and their legislative allies on Capitol Hill, all of whom had come to regard federal education aid as a sacred cow that no President would dare veto or hold back.

THE SUPPORTING LOBBIES

One of the better ways to understand the place of Washington in the educational galaxy is to look at the lobbies—the multifarious councils, unions, groups, and associations that express the views of everyone from educational administrators to parents, teachers, researchers, and the industries that have burgeoned in an era of high educational priority.

The education lobby is probably the largest lobby in Washington. It is easily the most diverse and fervent. This should not be surprising, considering the enormity of the American education establishment. There are more than 14,000 public school districts in the United States. Total public, private, and parochial school enrollment totals about 50 million elementary and secondary school students. Add in nearly 9 million college students and more than 3 million teachers and administrators at all levels of education, and you've got 30 percent of the American people engaged in education. So headquartered in Washington there is an organization attempting to further the interests of every small and large part of that mass of people. About the only major education organization not based in Washington is the National School Boards Association, now centered in Evanston, Illinois, but it is contemplating a move to the nation's capital in 1976, budget permitting.

Different education associations have different policy positions, and many of these conflict with one another at times. But the groups manage to cooperate in loose coalitions when success on the Hill requires a united front. The broadest and most effective coalition in recent years has been the Committee for Full Funding of Education Programs, originally named the Emergency Committee for Full Funding of Education Authorizations. It was set up in early 1969, when it first became apparent that the new President was going to upset the lucrative apple cart of federal aid to education. The committee's goal was to persuade Congress to appropriate as much money (i.e., "fully fund" the programs) as Congress had authorized in the outpouring of education bills during the heady days of the Johnson administration.

Charles W. Lee, an affable, rotund man who had been Senator Wayne Morse's education expert for many years, was hired to run the committee on a financial shoestring. (Many organizations in the continually shifting coalition were reluctant to jeopardize their nonprofit tax exemption by putting too much money into lobbying.) Lee was holed up in an office near the Capitol, forever chain-smoking cigarettes and talking on the phone. He exhorted his troops at the ungodly hour (for Washington) of 7:30 A.M., at strategy breakfasts held once every week, come filibuster or floor amendment. He rallied grass-roots support in every congressional district in the nation, since there isn't one district without a public school, if not a library or community college. It soon became obvious that the "emergency" that had prompted the creation of the committee was going to be a long-term situation, so the word was dropped from the title.

In 1974, when the Full Funding Committee toasted Charles Lee at a fifth anniversary cocktail-buffet in the Rayburn House Office Building (at $25 a head, plus cash bar), its membership had swelled to some eighty education associations. The party for Lee, incidentally, had been postponed for several weeks while Congress, the White House, and the committee worked out an agreement which finally allowed the President to cut as much as 5 percent from some of the federal aid programs if, in return, he would agree to release the money he had previously withheld, and to attempt no further massive impoundments.

The Full Funding Committee has more than a few "odd couples" in its membership, such as the National Education Association (NEA), representing more than a million teachers, and the American Federation of Teachers (AFT), an AFL–CIO affiliate with only a fifth as many members. The AFT, whose emerging power is New York local president Albert Shanker, has been growing fast at the expense of the NEA, mainly in the big cities. The NEA has cut its ties with "management"—the organizations of school superintendents and administrators who formerly dominated its affairs—but it still balks at joining the AFL–CIO. Here and there, there have been a few mergers of AFT and NEA locals, but the national organizations still disagree on who is to merge with whom, who is to lead the new organization, and whether a cessation of their members' work is properly called a "strike" (AFT) or a "withdrawal of services" (NEA). In most respects, the two teachers' groups are arch-rivals, but as Full Funding Committee members in Washington, they often act as one when federal outlays for education are on the congressional calendar.

There are divergent interests, too, among the various organizations of the higher education establishment in Washington. The interests of two-year community colleges, for example, are not identical to those of four-year colleges. The broadest gulf is between the public and the private colleges. To simplify a complex situation: The public institutions would like federal money to flow directly to them, so they can keep their tuition down. But the private and religiously supported colleges, unable to get tax support, must raise their tuition to keep up with inflation. They prefer federal aid in the form of grants, loans, and payment for part-time work, so students can meet their higher tuition. Of course, every type of college has been smarting for the past few years from the sharp decline in institutional aid for construction, research, and teaching fellowships, so the organizations of public and private colleges find themselves working together on the Full Funding Committee.

The geographic hub of the nation's education lobby is Washington's Dupont Circle, the befountained park at the intersection of Massachusetts, Connecticut, and New Hampshire Avenues. As a matter of fact, one of the largest office buildings on the Circle—"One Dupont Circle"—is labeled the National Center for Higher Education. (Informally, One Dupont Circle is sometimes called "The Mother Ship," or "the higher education secretariat.") This white marble edifice is the home of the American Council on Education (ACE), the venerable (founded during World War I) association of college associations. ACE occupies the top floor of the building, the rest of which contains the offices of more than forty organizations dealing with higher education. All of the large, potent groups are there: the American Association of State Colleges and Universities, the Association of American Universities, the American Association of Community Junior Colleges, and the National Association of State Universities and Land-Grant Colleges, to name just a few. Also headquartered there are groups representing such diverse constituencies as college registrars, public relations officers, law schools, admissions officers, physical plant administrators, medical schools, music and art schools, engineering colleges, and accreditation officials.

The whole higher education lobbying establishment can't fit in one building, so other groups are scattered around Washington. In the immediate Dupont Circle neighborhood are such organizations as the Association of American Colleges, the National Student Lobby, and the National Student Association. There are representatives, too, of the noncollegiate sector of higher education (which is increasingly called "postsecondary education" in academic jargon): the Association of Independent Colleges and Schools (proprietary business schools), National Association of Trade and Technical Schools, and National Home Study Council, to name a few. Also headquartered in Washington are the two teachers' groups, the NEA and the AFT. Colleges and universities are also represented individually in Washington.

Starting in 1965, with the opening of a University of California office in Washington, more and more individual institutions are flocking to the capital to set up liaison offices. The purpose of these offices, which now represent more than fifty colleges, is to locate federal money and channel it back home. Some colleges, instead of staffing their own Washington offices, retain consulting firms that are specialists in this kind of "grantsmanship," and some form groups that represent several institutions together.

The main reason the Nixon administration had such a difficult time trying to consolidate categorical grants into general, no-strings-attached aid to elementary and secondary schools is that every specific grant has a constituency lobbying for it in Washington. Each lobby wants to make sure federal aid is spent on its specialty, not for some other purpose at the whim of a local district. Take, for example, the National Audio-Visual Association (NAVA), the trade group of the manufacturers, distributors, and salesmen of educational films, slides, tapes, records, etc. Working on its own and as a member of the Full Funding Committee, NAVA has blocked administration attempts to phase out or merge a particular section of the National Defense Education Act that provides tens of millions of dollars each year for the purchase of its members' teaching materials. And administration efforts to eliminate Title II of the Elementary and Secondary Education Act—a section that has yielded hundreds of millions of dollars for library development—have been thwarted by book publishers and the American Library Association (ALA), whose Washington director, Eileen D. Cooke, is a vice president of the Full Funding Committee. Her predecessor at the ALA, a legendary lobbyist named Germaine Krettek, spent fifteen years on Capitol Hill boosting federal aid for libraries from a mere $2.5 million a year to a couple of hundred million dollars at its peak in the late Sixties. (In 1963, Miss Krettek used her influence with the Senate leadership to keep the Senate in session for a few additional minutes on the afternoon of President Kennedy's assassination, until a library aid bill was reached on the consent calendar; as soon as it was passed, the Senate adjourned to mourn the late President.) But like several specialties, federal library funding has dropped off rather sharply over the past five years.

Though still headquartered in the Midwest, the National School Boards Association (NSBA) has a skilled Washington lobbyist in August C. Steinhilder, a quick-thinking lawyer who was once in the Office of Education. There was a time when the NSBA's members—the more than 14,000 boards of concerned laymen who call the shots in the nation's public schools—were very skeptical (sometimes hostile) toward the whole concept of federal aid to education. They didn't mind accepting Uncle Sam's money, but they resented the federal supervision that accompanied the windfall. Over the years, however, the school boards have come to accept the inevitable (out of a dire need for the revenue as much as any philosophical change of heart), and today the NSBA is an enthusiastic member of the Full Funding Committee. Since school boards are the employers of teachers and other school personnel who are now showing a tendency to organize and occasionally strike, the NSBA keeps a close eye on proposed labor legislation that would broaden public employees' right to strike.

The pressure points for all of this lobbying energy are the congressional committees that draft education legislation—the House Education and Labor Committee, the Senate Labor and Public Welfare Committee—and their corresponding appropriations subcommittees. The Senate normally shows more largess toward education aid, so the crucial battles are on the House side of the Hill. When a close vote is approaching on an "omnibus" bill (containing a little something for everybody), the education coalition produces quite a spectacle. The corridors of the House Office buildings and hallways around the House chamber are clogged with an array of school board chairmen, college administrators, unionized teachers, school superintendents, textbook publishers, overhead-projector dealers—anyone whose last-minute contact with a congressman could serve to remind the legislator of education's clout back home.

CHANGING PATTERNS FOR THE FUTURE

Some of the biggest challenges facing education today have little to do with politics, but are basic matters of demographics and changing public attitudes. For one thing, the nation's birth rate has been dropping for several years, and continues to drop. This means there will be a smaller school-age population, affecting different levels of education at different times. In New York State, higher education officials are predicting that the number of high school graduates will peak late in the Seventies and might decline by as much as 36 percent until 1990. While in some parts of the country the percentage of high school graduates going on to college continues to rise, the national percentage in 1973 was 49, down sharply from 55 percent in 1968. (It is uncertain, of course, how many youths are merely deferring college until after a period of work or travel.) All of this indicates, in any event, a contraction or, at least, a leveling out of educational demand.

While shrinking enrollments may ease the need for expansion of schools' physical plants, education at all levels will continue to experience inflationary pressures in everything from textbooks to teachers' salaries. Economy-minded school boards that work for the taxpayers will undoubtedly try to stabilize or trim the number of teachers—an effort that will bring them into conflict with the expansionist teachers' organizations. Helen D. Wise, NEA president, has urged the group's 9,000 local and state units to "work to prevent school boards from using declining enrollments as an excuse to keep class sizes large and reduce the number of teachers." On the teachers' side will be new federal mandates to improve education for the poor, handicapped, and culturally disadvantaged, since improvement often entails lower pupil-teacher ratios and individualized instruction. And increasing unionization of teachers cannot help but result in higher salary costs, which already account for about three-fourths of all elementary and secondary school expenditures.

In higher education, shrinking enrollments are already taking their toll in several ways. Competition for students is getting stiff, and this competition often entails "buying" students with offers of financial aid that they don't really need. Young college professors are having a lot harder time getting tenure, and many older untenured professors are being weeded out to make room for "new blood." Colleges of all sorts are having trouble finding money to offset the federal research money that flooded their campuses during the Sixties.

So the money crunch will continue to plague education at all levels for a long time to come—perhaps indefinitely. Where will it come from? The local property tax is already washed up as the sole source of this money. The states are now spending on average about 40 percent of their total revenues on education, mostly on higher education, and they will undoubtedly be called on to cough up even more money from income and sales taxes. Then there's Uncle Sam, traditionally the junior partner of America's education enterprise. Federal aid is bound to increase, but it's debatable whether the level of increase will merely keep pace with inflation, or serve to increase the federal share of the nation's total education spending.

In a 1974 speech to the American Association of School Administrators, then Acting HEW Assistant Secretary of Education Charles B. Saunders, Jr., warned that "no large-scale federal involvement is just around the corner, awaiting the election of right-thinking politicians." A massive program to equalize per pupil expenditures on a national basis would have to await a verdict on the "willingness and capacity of the states to meet their responsibilities for equalization of educational opportunities," he said. Until then, he added, the government is likely to remain the subordinate partner, providing leadership in research and targeting money into special problem areas (the poor, handicapped, bilingual education, etc.), but not paying for basic public education.

Whatever the specific role of the federal government in the educational process, education itself will become more pervasive than it is today in the lives of American citizens. While total enrollments will fluctuate from time to time—depending on birth rates, wars, and patterns of population—the per capita demand for education will continue to rise in a society which depends upon technology for its livelihood. Even the young Thoreaus and Walt Whitmans, the organic gardeners, the lovers of wilderness, and the latter-day Edna St. Vincent Millays will thirst for the kind of education that satisfies their own needs.

Whether the mechanisms are those of revenue sharing, "basic opportunity grants," categorical or bloc grants, the combined force of the education movement will see to it that Washington will be even more important than it is now in the shaping of the educational future.

32 SCIENCE AND THINK TANKS

Washington is the research capital of the world, because the federal government is the largest user of advice in the world. The research that it commissions and consumes is scientific and social, military and civilian, basic and applied. It encompasses every imaginable human concern, from the cost of housing to the temperature of the surface of Mars. Whether they know it or not, millions of citizens' lives are affected by this research in many ways, trivial and crucial.

Washington is the center of this studious activity, not just because of the immense volume of research conducted in and around the capital, but also because Uncle Sam is the primary source of funds for research carried on everywhere else in America—at colleges, corporations, hospitals, "think tanks," and consulting firms across the country.

In terms of employment and dollars, research is one of the top industries in the local Washington economy. It is not a highly visible industry, however, because its products—piles of papers and stacks of reports—don't have much bulk and are not found in the average American home. On the Washington scene, the signs of the research establishment are subtle. Some of the oldest social and scientific research groups (like Brookings, Carnegie, and Resources for the Future, all of which are located along or just off a stretch of Massachusetts Avenue called "Egghead Row") can be identified by the dignified bronze plaques beside the doorways: "Center for the Study of This-or-That," or "The Such-and-Such Institution."

The computer-oriented research firms, based in parklike settings in suburbs such as Rockville, Maryland, and Tyson's Corner, Virginia, sport titles with fancily concocted, pseudoscientific words, starting with the syllables "cyber-," "dyna-," "syner-," or "tele-," and ending with the suffixes "-etics," "-istic," "-metrics," or "-tron." The urban affairs consulting firms can be found in the suites of new office buildings along downtown K Street, and the lettering on the doors invariably reads "John Doe and Associates" or "Jones Associates, Inc." At the supersecret military think tanks, located in suburban Virginia near the Pentagon, employees wear plastic ID badges around their necks and curiosity seekers are turned away by armed guards at the reception desk.

It is estimated that a total of $36 billion was spent in fiscal 1975 on American research and development in all fields and by all organizations, public and private. Of that total, some $20 billion—55 percent—came out of the federal tax coffers in Washington. No nation in the world (with the possible exception of Russia, whose budget is secret) spends as much on research and development (R&D) as the U.S., either in absolute terms or as a percentage of GNP or the national budget.

The ways in which that $20 billion of federal research support was spent say some interesting things about the nation's priorities, at least as they are perceived by Washington's legislators and budget setters. Slightly less than half of the amount was spent on military research, primarily the development of new weapons like the Trident missile submarine, the B-1 strategic bomber, and new fighter planes for the Air Force and Navy. Aerospace research, overseen by NASA, accounted for about $3.3 billion. It was focused on the upcoming American-Russian space docking venture, on weather satellites, and on continuing development of the "space shuttle," a vehicle for repairing satellites in orbit and recovering them for overhaul and reuse. Together, defense and space R&D account for about two-thirds of the federal research dollar.

The other one-third is spread over all the government's civil R&D programs, in every field from energy and health to law enforcement and transportation. The civilian percentage of the research budget looks small, but it is a rising proportion. In fiscal 1966, for example, it comprised less than one-quarter of Washington's research spending. All R&D spending continues to rise in Washington, but the giant military and space segment is not growing as rapidly as the others.

The more than $6 billion spent on domestic research programs in fiscal 1975 was about evenly divided among three areas: health, energy, and miscellaneous social welfare programs (such areas as agriculture, housing, and transportation). The biggest gainer in this group has been energy research funding, which leaped 80 percent—an increase of $900 million—from 1974 to 1975. About half of all the energy money went to the Atomic Energy Commission for nuclear R&D. The Interior Department and Environmental Protection Agency got big boosts to find ways to expand the nation's use of coal without substantially hurting air quality. In the health field, most of the money goes into research to conquer the major killer diseases, particularly cancer. Funds are also given to the Food and Drug Administration to develop better ways to evaluate the safety of food additives and prescription drugs. The $2 billion or so channeled into the so-called social sector includes funds for tests of various versions of national health insurance, income maintenance, and housing allowances. New technology in crime prevention is funded, too, through research funds dispensed by the Law Enforcement Assistance Administration.

INTRAMURAL RESEARCH

Before the Second World War, virtually all federal research programs were carried on by federal agencies, staffed by civil servants, at laboratories and offices owned and operated by Uncle Sam. But the situation has changed today. A very small portion of the $20 billion federal research budget is spent on projects conducted by federal agencies themselves. This is not to say there aren't a lot of federal agencies engaged directly in R&D. A 1969 survey counted about 650 separate federal research stations, most of them pretty small (300 with budgets under $1 million a year). The largest government-owned and operated research sites are the major space centers, at Cape Canaveral, Houston, and Huntsville, Alabama.

Uncle Sam got involved in research in a variety of ways, some pragmatic and some accidental. Such agencies as the National Geodetic Survey and the Geological Survey have their roots in an agency founded in 1807 to facilitate maritime commerce, and today they are into such things as the study of gravitation, magnetism, and earthquakes. The Naval Observatory in Washington was likewise founded to assist navigation, but in later decades became involved in more sophisticated branches of astronomy. Today it is one of the world's principal timekeepers, using atomic clocks accurate to a millionth of a second. One of the first events that plunged the U.S. into scientific research was accidental—the fortuitous gift to the U.S. of the entire estate of an Englishman, James Smithson, who had never set foot in America. The first head of the Smithsonian Institution was Joseph Henry, a scientist who made discoveries in electromagnetism as important as Faraday's. He lobbied for a pure research role for the new agency, but was overruled. Today, the Smithsonian undertakes studies running the gamut from anthropology to astrophysics.

Some federally operated research programs are fairly obscure, like experiments at the hatcheries of the National Marine Fisheries Service. Others have a daily relevance, like weather-forecasting research conducted by the National Weather Service, based in suburban Suitland, Maryland. The "Beltsville turkey," a high-yield fowl enjoyed by millions of Americans on Thanksgiving Day, is just one of the successful by-products of work done at the Department of Agriculture's sprawling research farms in Beltsville, Maryland, outside of Washington. In the social sciences, essential economic and sociological studies are conducted by employees of the Department of Labor (in the Bureau of Labor Statistics), Department of Commerce, and Department of Health, Education and Welfare (in such divisions as the Social Security Administration and Office of Education). Research into product durability done at the U.S. Bureau of Standards in Gaithersburg, Maryland, has had direct applications in manufacturing. The National Institutes of Health, while farming out many projects to private researchers, do a substantial amount of work—employing several Nobel-winning scientists—at labs on their own campus in Bethesda, Maryland.

HIRED BRAINS

Despite the variety of federally run research programs, the vast majority of the R&D funded by Washington is conducted by independent organizations employing private citizens. All over America—especially in enclaves of southern California, around Boston, and in the Washington area—there are think tanks and consulting firms whose budgets have grown fat with contracts for extramural federal research. Some of them are nonprofit, while others are profitmaking corporations. Some of them—like the jack-of-all-trades Arthur D. Little firm—derive a large portion of their revenue from other sources, such as contracts with businesses. Others are almost totally dependent on research grants from Washington. The incestuous relationship between Washington and many think tanks raises all sorts of troubling questions about the validity of the conclusions reached by their studies. To what extent, for example, might a research team tailor its findings to suit the commissioning agency's preconceived plans, in the hopes of pleasing the agency and assuring the award of future contracts? Private researchers always deny, of course, that they've ever engaged in this sort of thing, but people who know the business say it happens all too frequently.

In terms of the dollar volume of work done, the smallest participant in the American research business—ranking behind the private organizations and federal agencies—is the academic community. Research grants specifically earmarked for projects at universities totaled about $2.2 billion in fiscal 1975, with most of it coming from HEW and the National Science Foundation, the principal conduit of federal money for basic "pure" scientific research. While the university allotment amounts to only a little more than 10 percent of the federal R&D budget, it is vitally important to hundreds of colleges around the nation. The 1975 amount was an increase of only 7 percent over the previous year—not even enough to keep pace with inflation—and many colleges have had to stabilize or cut back their basic research programs. Military research contracts were once a major source of money for many colleges, but some institutions reduced (or shut down) their defense-related projects because of student and faculty protests against them in the late Sixties.

The closest relationship between Washington and the research industry is in the realm of national defense. Much of the Pentagon's money is contracted to several so-called Federal Contract Research Centers (FCRCs). While their employees are private citizens, these nonprofit organizations are essentially arms of the federal government, since they were started by the government and get virtually all of their funds from Washington. The best-known of these, the Rand Corporation in Santa Monica, California, works almost entirely under Air Force contracts. The Institute for Defense Analyses (IDA), located near the Pentagon, does top-secret policy studies for the office of the Secretary of Defense (and in recent years, has broadened its activities into such nonmilitary areas as transportation and urban affairs). The Mitre Corporation, based in Cambridge, Massachusetts, with a large office in the Washington suburb of McLean, Virginia, is an FCRC of the Air Force.

The military uses its FCRCs—and independent think tanks like the Hudson Institute (New York), Battelle Memorial Institute (Ohio), and Stanford Research Institute (California)—as its hired brains. They ponder the toughest questions and plan the most complex new programs. Rand, for example, was heavily involved in all stages of both the Vietnam war and the space program. It laid the groundwork for the nation's earliest system of intercontinental ballistic missiles. And several of its staff—including Daniel Ellsberg—were hired away by the Defense Department to research and draft the once secret Pentagon Papers.

The entire scope and substance of the military research is known to few people outside the Pentagon and perhaps the White House. There is no regular congressional monitoring of it, and occasionally congressional committees have been refused access to secret reports within their specific areas of jurisdiction. Former Senator J. William Fulbright was incensed when his Committee on Foreign Relations was denied a look at an IDA report on the Gulf of Tonkin incident, the event that prompted Congress to give President Johnson a free hand in Vietnam. And as author Paul Dickson points out in his eye-opening book *Think Tanks,* the Pentagon spent some $4.5 billion on antiballistic missile research between 1956 and 1968, before Congress really debated the desirability of deploying such a system. Congress, of course, needed sound judgments on which to debate the merits, but the information it got was curiously one-sided. When the issue finally came to the floor of the House and Senate, the ABM backers were bolstered by mountains of pro-ABM reports from such groups as Rand, IDA, and the Hudson Institute, while the opponents were caught flat-footed, having to scrounge up their own experts. With the growth of the military think tanks, Dickson warns, "anonymous analysts and scientists with no direct responsibility to the electorate for their decisions . . . have been given some of the powers of government itself."

CIVILIAN RESEARCH

There are government-initiated research groups in the civilian sector, too, such as the network of FCRCs created a few years ago by the Office of Education to cooperate with local school authorities in experiments with new teaching techniques. One of the most important urban affairs think tanks, the Washington-based Urban Institute, was launched in 1968 with leadership from the Johnson White House and Cabinet and substantial funding from such agencies as HUD, HEW, and the Office of Economic Opportunity. But it also got a lot of money from foundations (especially Ford) and has an independence from the government not found in the FCRCs and other government-initiated centers. It has published meaty reports on such topics as welfare reform, land use, garbage collection, birth control, and police-community relations.

An organization whose research reports have, from time to time, exerted a major impact on public policy is the National Academy of Sciences, headed by Philip Handler. Housed in a stately marble temple on Constitution Avenue, the NAS is best known for the highly prestigious memberships that it bestows on a mere handful of the nation's most outstanding scientists. Officially, the NAS is a private organization, but it was chartered by Congress in 1863 with a functional as well as an honorary purpose: to act, on request, as the federal government's official adviser on matters of science and technology. The advising is done by ad hoc teams of NAS members, working under the aegis of the Academy's National Research Council (NRC). With about 80 percent of its budget coming from the government, the NRC has done work on such civilian issues as power plant siting and clean air standards, as well as military matters (defoliation and weapons systems) and social problems (freedom of choice in housing programs).

In the past, the federal agencies that requested research reports from the NRC could do anything they wanted with them. They could publicize a report that came to the "right" conclusion and bury one that didn't. The Food and Drug Administration commissioned a 1968 NRC review of prescription drugs and used it as the basis for removing from the market more than a hundred ineffective compounds. But when an NRC panel gave the supersonic transport plane (SST) a clean bill of health on one narrow point—the danger of sonic booms—its findings were distorted by SST backers into a general approval of the whole project. In 1970 another NRC team helped correct the misunderstanding (and scuttle the SST) with a warning that the plane might lower the radiation shield of the atmosphere and increase the risk of skin cancer. (A three-year study released by the Department of Transportation in 1975 contradicted this warning, saying that even a large fleet of SSTs would not harm the atmosphere.) Today the Academy has countered this problem of selective use of its reports by insisting upon the right to publish, on its own initiative, any report that it prepares for a federal client. In 1974, at the urging of some of its members, the Academy launched a study of the effects of Freon, the aerosol propellant and refrigerant which is thought to be a risk to the earth's ozone radiation shield.

The government has been farming out civilian projects to outsiders longer than anyone can remember. (Some experts trace the practice back to 1832, when the Treasury asked the Franklin Institute in Philadelphia to find out why a certain kind of boiler on American steamships had a tendency to blow up.) No one knows the total number of reports commissioned over the years, but a repository of the most requested ones—the National Technical Information Service in Springfield, Virginia—has more than 800,000 separate studies for sale. Some were significant to their era, others downright ridiculous. In 1974 there was a brief flap over a federal study, costing the taxpayers many thousands of dollars, that determined how children injure themselves on tricycles. The findings: injuries occur when children fall off, either by losing their balance or colliding with something.

The Russians' launching of Sputnik in 1957 triggered a ten-year boom in aerospace and military research, and the ghetto riots of the Sixties spawned a whole corps of "instant experts" in urban affairs. Urban consulting firms proliferated in Washington, feasting off research contracts dispensed by such federal bodies as the Office of Economic Opportunity (OEO), HUD, and (later) the Law Enforcement Assistance Administration. Many of the firms provided solid research and valuable, imaginative judgments, but some were merely masters of (in the words of James Kalish, a former urban consultant) "double-talking, flimflamming and feathering their own nests." The Government Accounting Office, Congress's auditor of the bureaucracy, has found far too many instances of studies that were vague, pointless, and overpriced. Despite the severe cutbacks at OEO, the urban affairs field is still prospering in Washington. Some of the older practitioners have been joined by organizations that were once primarily scientific and military, like Rand and Stanford Research Institute.

WITHOUT FEDERAL SUPPORT

The federal dollar is dominant in research funding, but there are a number of Washington-based organizations conducting and sponsoring research of all kinds with little or no reliance on Uncle Sam. They depend instead on such sources as their endowments, foundation grants, membership dues, and the sale of publications. Take, for example, the National Geographic Society, the great popularizer of science. With the tax-free dues (magazine subscriptions) of its 9 million members, it has funded such projects (usually flamboyant, with built-in mass appeal) as the underwater explorations of Jacques-Yves Cousteau and the African digging of the Leakey family, whose findings of early human skulls have rewritten the anthropology texts.

The Carnegie Institution, founded in 1902 with Andrew Carnegie's gift of $10 million, does research in the physical and biological sciences, conducted by seventy-five faculty members and some eighty-five postdoctoral students. Headed by Philip H. Abelson, Carnegie has several out-of-town facilities (including the Hale Observatories, operated with Cal Tech), as well as two research centers in Washington, the Geophysical Laboratory and the Department of Terrestrial Magnetism, both located on spacious sites along upper

Rock Creek Park. Carnegie's work over the years has contributed to the development of an array of things from hybrid corn to radar.

Of the many groups representing scientists and engineers in Washington, the largest is the American Association for the Advancement of Science (whose modern headquarters on Scott Circle, incidentally, has vertical window blinds that automatically move with the sun throughout the day). Besides its ongoing programs of membership meetings, seminars, awards, and "science-in-the-schools" programs, the AAAS occasionally commissions its members to do special research reports. One such report, a 1970 study of the effects of U.S. defoliation on the people and ecology of Vietnam, was a major influence on the decision to phase out military herbicide use.

There is a wide range of independent organizations in the social sciences and political research fields, too. The National Planning Association, founded during the depression, brings together the forecasting expertise of business leaders, economists, and government officials. Since 1960 it has prepared and sold highly regarded forecasts entitled the "National Economic Projections Series" and the "Regional Economic Projections Series." The American Enterprise Institute for Public Policy Research, founded in 1943 and funded largely by corporate donations, publishes reports on issues stretching from tax reform and defense policy to criminal justice and the performance of the news media. Among its best-known programs are "Rational Debates"—spirited discussions before live audiences, pitting well-known spokesmen for opposing views against each other (for example, Senator James L. Buckley versus former Pentagon official Paul C. Warnke, on the subject "Strategic Sufficiency: Fact or Fiction?").

Located in a small building near Dupont Circle is Washington's premier civil rights think tank, the Potomac Institute, created in 1961. Funded primarily with foundation grants from the Mellon family, the Institute has programs for and advises every level of government on such subjects as voter registration, equal employment opportunity, and school desegregation. In the areas of energy and the environment, the leading research group is Resources for the Future, which lives primarily off Ford Foundation funds but also does contract work for governments in the U.S. and other countries. Created in 1952, it has studied (and funded outside studies on) everything from water resources in Latin America to urban growth in the U.S.

Among the broad, public-policy research groups in Washington that accept no federal contracts, there are a few that are pigeonholed by their informal identification with one or the other end of the political spectrum. The American Enterprise Institute is considered to be conservative. Georgetown University's Center for Strategic and International Studies, which exists largely on corporate contributions (including, reportedly, a lot of oil money), has normally taken a politically conservative stance in its foreign policy recommendations. On the far left is the Institute for Policy Studies, a think tank that ponders and suggests (with foundation funding) radical alternatives to the status quo in virtually every area of public policy. It is, not surprisingly, the most casual and free-form of all the think tanks in Washington. The entry hall of its headquarters, an old townhouse near Dupont Circle, has radical handbills and notices of "counterculture" events posted on the wall. During the Watergate crisis, one could purchase anti-Nixon bumper stickers there ("Nixon: Put the Tiger in the Tank").

In a class by itself—in terms of the quality of its staff and the impact of its research—is the Brookings Institution, the nation's oldest public affairs research center. Founded (under a different name) in 1916 by a wealthy St. Louis rope manufacturer, Brookings has a large endowment (bolstered in recent years by the Ford Foundation) but derives about a tenth of its budget from federal contracts. Its studies, conducted by full-time fellows, have been responsible over the years for such innovations as uniform federal budgetary practices (during the Twenties), implementation ideas for the Marshall Plan (late Forties), and a presidential transition plan used by John F. Kennedy for a smooth succession in 1961. The concept of federal revenue sharing was developed in 1964 by a presidential task force headed by Brookings' resident tax expert, Joseph Pechman. An annual Brookings publication called *Setting National Priorities*—an analysis of the federal budget, complete with suggested alternatives—is always one of the most widely read books in Washington's highest policy circles from Capitol Hill to the White House. Brookings also conducts educational seminar series for businessmen and federal bureaucrats.

Although Brookings insists that its work is strictly nonpartisan, the organization has had a Democratic flavor in recent years. Its president, Kermit Gordon, was director of the Bureau of the Budget under Presidents Kennedy and Johnson. Other fellows who went from the Johnson administration to Brookings include another former budget director, Charles L. Schultze, and Arthur Okun, former chairman of the Council of Economic Advisers (CEA). (Herb Stein, on the other hand, left a senior position at Brookings to become a member and later chairman of President Nixon's CEA.) The deep antipathy that the Nixon crowd felt for Brookings is best illustrated by the disclosure during the Senate Watergate hearings of a bizarre White House plan—never carried out, and perhaps never taken seriously—to burglarize and set a fire at the Institution's headquarters, a large office building along "Egghead Row." Apparently the proposed break-in and diversionary fire were part of an attempt to locate secret defense papers thought to be in the possession of two Brookings fellows, Morton Halperin and Leslie Gelb.

LITTLE CENTRAL PLANNING

How much central control does the federal government exert in overseeing and setting priorities in its massive research establishment? Surprisingly little. In 1973 Congress took its first step to contend with the problem by opening a new Office of Technology Assessment, directed by former Representative Emilio Daddario, who had worked long on the legislation for it. Keeping its full-time staff small, the Office will put together ad hoc study teams of the best outside experts it can find, to advise Congress on thorny science issues. Its congressional board is a rarity on the Hill: equal numbers of senators and representatives, Democrats and Republicans.

At the White House, the first official science adviser was appointed by President Eisenhower soon after Sputnik. Ike also revived the President's Science Advisory Committee (PSAC), a panel of the nation's top scientific minds created under President Truman. President Kennedy added the White House Office of Science and Technology (OST), which worked with budget officials and other federal science chiefs to coordinate, avoid duplication, and set priorities in the federal research realm. President Nixon found the OST and the PSAC rather nettlesome. The OST staff, for example, besides agitating to get the U.S. out of chemical and biological warfare, was dead set against the SST that Nixon wanted so badly. (OST Director Lee Dubridge eventually backed the President on the SST, but so lukewarmly that no one was convinced, and OST opposition is credited with being a major factor in the plane's defeat.) The fiercely independent members of the PSAC had a penchant for raising ruckuses that messed up the President's plans in several areas.

So, in 1973, Nixon simply abolished the OST, PSAC, and the position of Presidential Science Adviser. He said the coordinating role of OST would be served equally well by the National Science Foundation and that NSF Director H. Guyford Stever would be, in effect, the White House science adviser. The howl from the science community in Washington was loud and sustained, but as of late 1974, the White House was still without a science structure of its own. President Ford, however, seemed more respectful of scientific opinion than Nixon had been and was seriously considering reinstating some sort of office, perhaps one proposed by the National Academy of Sciences in 1974.

But even with a renewed effort at the White House and a new review body on the Hill, the federal research effort—especially in military affairs—remains highly decentralized, virtually impossible for anyone to know thoroughly, monitor, or rechannel in new directions. Spending priorities are determined mostly by the persuasion of lobbies and their allies in Congress, where the dollar amounts are set—in esoteric, largely private deliberations—by numerous committees with fragmented jurisdictions.

WHAT LIES AHEAD?

The American scientific community has become a very gloomy and alarmist bunch over the past few years. They had been exhilarated, of course, by the hefty annual hikes in basic research funding during the late Fifties and early Sixties (amounting to 25 percent a year for university research). But then the rates of increase leveled off and dropped as the Vietnam war and soaring social welfare budgets vied for funds. The Nixon administration boasted that its fiscal 1975 research budget contained the largest one-year dollar increase in a decade, but scientists pointed out that the increase—10 percent over the previous year—was virtually canceled out by double-digit inflation.

While the American R&D budget remained fairly static over the last ten years, Japan and the nations of Western Europe were beefing up their commitment to science (still, however, falling far short of the U.S. in absolute amounts and proportion of the GNP). America continues to lead in every index of R&D achievement, such as Nobel prizes and the "patent balance" (patents issued abroad for American inventions, compared to patents issued here for foreign ones), but the gap between the U.S. and the other developed nations is narrowing. A narrowing gap is fine, of course, as long as it's due to foreign gains rather than American deterioration.

With leaner federal budgets (that is, smaller increases) coming in all policy areas, the research establishment will undoubtedly feel the ax like everyone else. The ax should fall primarily on duplicative and trivial programs. But care must be taken not to apply parochial standards of "relevance" in research. Basic scientific research, by definition, involves fishing expeditions that often yield nothing of immediate applied value, but sometimes discoveries that are of world-changing importance years later.

Finally, the nation must not put all its faith in the omniscience of R&D. Technology is blind. It has no inherent judgment and sense of values. In the field of housing, for example, new techniques of construction won't make a bit of difference unless the government comes to grips with the decay and abandonment of existing housing, caused by such nontechnological factors as suburban growth, tax policy, and a lack of cash in inner-city pockets. In the words of former Brookings fellow Harold Orlans, "Detroit produces only cars; the traffic jams are produced by taxpayers who will not allocate sufficient funds for efficient public transportation, and by governments too timid to tax, regulate, and police traffic so as to prevent them."

R&D is just one tool in Washington's bag. It can be a crucially important underpinning of policymaking, as the size and power of the Washington research complex demonstrates. But in the final analysis—in Washington as anywhere else—decisions are often made on grounds that are more emotional, political, and economic than scientific.

33 REGULATING BUSINESS

Buy an airline ticket, a railroad or bus ticket. Tune a radio or television set. Take out a loan. Put some money in a savings account. Pick up some aspirin at the drug counter. Any one of these actions, or any one of a thousand more, is influenced by a federal regulatory agency in Washington.

In fact, there are very few things you do that are not affected by one or more of the regulatory agencies that inhabit the Washington scene. Washington, through its "alphabet agencies," sets or approves the price of natural gas, the interest permitted to be paid on certain accounts, and shipping rates. It monitors the purity of foods and pills, the safety of textiles and toys, the working conditions in manufacturing plants, the quality of water in navigable streams, and the antipollution devices on your car. Washington mediates power struggles between big unions and big corporations. Washington can sue or close down a company for putting too many pollutants into the air or for putting the wrong substances into the water. Washington's regulatory power affects virtually everything that moves in the stream of commerce, coast to coast.

The regulatory fervor in the U.S. began in the reform mood of the 1880s and resulted first in the Interstate Commerce Act, which created the Interstate Commerce Commission. Then came the big trust-busting fever which brought into being the Sherman Antitrust Act of 1890, and in 1914 the Clayton Act, to be enforced by the new Federal Trade Commission. The Roosevelt New Deal, in the 1930s, produced another surge of regulatory legislation, creating the Securities and Exchange Commission (SEC), the National Labor Relations Board (NLRB), the Civil Aeronautics Board (CAB), the Federal Communications Commission (FCC), and others.

Now, after these successive waves of legislation, Washington can order a company to hire more women and minority workers, can review advertising claims and credit contracts, can prohibit two firms from joining forces, and—on occasion—can put the whole economy under regulation, including wages and prices in every sector. Full wage-price control was imposed during World War II, the Korean War, and from 1971 to 1974, and it could happen again.

Regulatory agencies are the instruments of this economic clout. While Congress created them as "independent regulatory agencies," they are hardly independent of the other branches of government. The President shapes regulatory policy by filling the top-level jobs with appointees who suit his ideological bent. Congress puts up the money, occasionally tries to meddle in their operations, and often comes to the aid—through special legislation—of a regulated industry that is displeased with an agency's verdict.

Federal courts have the power of final review over regulatory rulings. The agencies don't fit neatly into the separation-of-powers pigeonholes. They are hybrids of legislative, judicial, and executive functions. Most of them are empowered to make rulings with the force of law, monitor compliance with these rulings, and then sit in judgment of companies that do not obey.

Despite this permeating power, federal regulatory bodies operate with an obscurity that is true of few other governmental institutions in Washington. Most people have little idea of what, why, and how the agencies do what they do. Even some longtime Washingtonians have never been in the offices of a regulatory agency. Few people could even name the location of most of the agencies—except for a couple of conspicuous ones, like the Federal Trade Commission at the apex of the Federal Triangle downtown. Mostly, the regulatory agencies exist in the public consciousness as a jumble of initials: FCC, CAB, ICC, FDIC, FPC, EPA, FTC, FMC, and many more.

Though their work may be ignored by the general press and broadcast media, their every action is chronicled in great detail by the trade journals of the affected industries. Most of the regulatory bodies' staffs and budgets are too small to permit careful study of multibillion-dollar industries. And the constant turnover of middle-level staff members (many of them being lawyers and economists who leave to take jobs in the firms they once regulated) makes it difficult for long-range policies to be conceived and followed through. At the highest echelons are commissioners who all too often are appointed more for their faithful service to the President's party than their analytical skills.

Probably the most far-ranging of all the regulatory agencies is the Federal Trade Commission, whose bailiwick is not any one particular industry but the entire business community. Its mission is divided between consumer protection and antitrust enforcement (a function shared with the antitrust division of the Department of Justice). Until the Commission was overhauled during the first Nixon term, its antitrust section was virtually moribund, and the consumer protection bureau was mainly concerned with matters of no great danger to consumers. (The FTC once nearly issued a complaint against the manufacturer of an obscure brand of denim overalls called Red Fox, charging that the label could mislead the consumer into thinking there was fox fur in the pants; the charge was abandoned before it was formally issued, but not soon enough to save the FTC from public ridicule.) The commission still spins its wheels a lot on small matters, but its Bureau of Competition has had the audacity to seek a breakup of the giant breakfast cereal industry (in 1972) and the most gigantic of all industries—the production, refining, and marketing of oil (in 1973). Both cases, now in litigation, are certain to keep armies of government attorneys, industry lawyers, lobbyists, and economists busy for several years.

HOW THEY WORK

Most of the regulatory agencies share certain structural and operational traits. They have professional staffs that actually develop the agency's cases. They have administrative law judges (formerly called hearing examiners), who conduct trials—complete with testimony, presentation of evidence, and examination of witnesses—and then make a ruling. This ruling is then either sustained or overruled by the highest authority of the agency, usually a panel of commissioners but sometimes a single administrator. In the rate-setting bodies, like the ICC and the CAB, the regulated companies file applications asking permission to charge a certain fare or begin service in a new geographic area. Interested parties—ranging from trade associations and regulated companies to citizen groups and federal agencies—are invited to file comments on the proposal, pro and con. Then the administrative law judge holds his hearings, makes his preliminary ruling, and sends it on to the commission.

Some regulatory bodies—the prime example of which is the FTC—act as both accuser and jury. When FTC staff investigators spot an infraction of a law under their jurisdiction, they present their case to the full commission. The commission then decides whether to issue a formal complaint. If the complaint is made, the FTC staff serves as prosecutor and the commission itself serves as the jury.

The intricate legal operations of the regulatory agencies are codified in a 1946 law called the Administrative Procedure Act, which was designed to make sure each side in a contest airs his case in an orderly, judicial setting. The act transformed the previously rather informal agencies into miniature federal courts. If the 1946 law made the agencies more fair, it also made them painfully slow (and made their rulings vulnerable to court reversal if every step is not followed painstakingly). It also gave a new impetus to those lawyers who specialize in regulatory law. The Administrative Procedure Act is sometimes called a welfare program for Washington lawyers.

The men and women who sit on regulatory commissions are hardly household names to the American public, and most of them are barely known to knowledgeable Washingtonians. Although it is considered bad form for the President to appoint someone who has actually worked in the industry which he will regulate, a prospective appointee is always cleared with the industry first—quietly. Some nominees are confirmed by the Senate despite an absolute lack of qualifications in an appropriate field. Former *Wall Street Journal* reporter Louis M. Kohlmeier, Jr., in his book *The Regulators,* tells of a nominee to the Federal Communications Commission who candidly told a Senate hearing, "I don't know anything about communications; I came to Washington expecting to be appointed to the Federal Power Commission."

If many commission members arrive at their jobs with scant prior knowledge, they learn a lot before they leave. And this knowledge—or at least the inside contacts and prestige—is worth a great deal to the regulated industry. Many former commissioners go right from federal service to a corporate or trade association position, at several times the $40,000 or so they got from Uncle Sam. Most agencies have rules against a former official's appearing before them to plead a new employer's case (at least for a few years), but nothing prevents him from taking a job with a regulated company or giving advice in the background.

In 1961, when Newton Minow was being reviewed by a Senate panel as a nominee for a position on the FCC, he was asked what his qualifications were. "Two things," Minow responded. "First, I'm not looking for a job in the communications business; and second, I don't want to be reappointed." After that display of eccentricity and independence, Minow went on to declare commercial television a "vast wasteland" and alienate most of the industry. He left the FCC before completing one term.

There is as much social hobnobbing between lobbyists and regulatory officials as there is between lobbyists and congressmen—perhaps more.

Commissioners are often invited to give speeches before trade association conventions, are entertained at banquets, and sometimes are taken on trips to inspect some new facility of a company in their regulated industry. Most commissioners are flattered by all of this attention. They are largely ignored by the general public, so they enjoy being pampered by people who know how important they really are—important, at least, to the economic interest of a particular industry. Commissioners who rock the boat are not appreciated, as Nicholas Johnson found out as gadfly chairman of the Federal Maritime Commission and later as a member of the FCC. Figuring there must be some reasonable alternatives to paying a subsidy to support America's woefully inefficient merchant marine, Johnson suggested a number of innovations which quickly made him very unpopular with every segment of the shipping industry. He was no more popular at the FCC, where he attacked commercial TV programing and later championed more competition between conventional TV and cable systems. After leaving the FCC, Johnson ran unsuccessfully in a 1974 Iowa congressional primary and then returned to the Washington broadcasting arena—not in the industry's employ, but as head of the National Citizens' Committee for Broadcasting, a nettlesome challenger to the status quo.

OUTSIDE INTERFERENCE

Despite the so-called independent status of the agencies, they are frequently contacted by members of the Congress and the White House staff, who like to "inquire about the status" of pending cases. Sometimes the congressmen or presidential aides in fact want nothing more than general information about a case. But sometimes the purpose is influence more than information. Commissioners are especially sensitive to the wishes, however subtly expressed, of the chairmen of the House and Senate committees that control the agency's appropriations. Sometimes the meddling is not so subtle. Sherman Adams, President Eisenhower's closest adviser, got into hot water when he interceded on behalf of textile executive Bernard Goldfine in proceedings before both the FTC and the SEC. Financier Robert Vesco tried for months to arrange an interview between his lawyer and Chairman William J. Casey of the SEC, which was investigating Vesco. He succeeded only after giving a secret $200,000 to the Committee to Reelect the President and securing an entrée through then Attorney General John Mitchell. (Mitchell and CREEP treasurer Maurice Stans, who allegedly attempted to get the SEC to water down the charges against Vesco, were acquitted of trying to influence the SEC investigation.)

When an industry can't get the ruling it wants from a regulatory agency, it can always go to its friends on Capitol Hill, many of whom are more than willing to short-circuit the regulatory process by pushing through a special-interest bill. Congress leaped to the aid of the soft-drink bottlers when the FTC made antitrust rumblings against exclusive regional franchises. It went to bat for the tobacco industry when the FTC first proposed that cigarette packs carry health warnings. (Congress passed a health warning law, but not as strong as what the FTC had in mind.) The broadcasting industry got Congress to tell the FCC to keep its hands off regulation of the proportion of commercials shown per hour of TV programing. The commercial banking industry persuaded Congress to prevent the spread of the so-called NOW accounts, a kind of interest-paying checking account that was pioneered by savings and loans in Massachusetts and New Hampshire, with the acquiescence of the Federal Home Loan Bank Board. And recently the New York Stock Exchange persuaded Congress to give the SEC power to limit trading of exchange-listed stocks on the over-the-counter market, whose rising volume the NYSE saw as a threat. Congress was even willing to come through with a specific antitrust exemption to allow merger of what were then the nation's only two professional football leagues, the NFL and AFL. (A few years later, the Hill had second thoughts, and refused to approve a merger of the two pro basketball leagues.)

The common thread in most of these cases was Congress's willingness to help a well-entrenched segment of an industry fend off the competition of a newer branch. The regulatory agencies are normally more than willing to do the same thing, but Congress lends a hand when they don't go far enough.

TOO MUCH REGULATION?

Many people in Washington who have given thought to the matter have concluded that the American economy is overregulated, and probably to the detriment of the consumer. Ironically, the calls for deregulation don't come from the giant corporations in the regulated industries. True, they complain about the rules and requirements imposed on them, but many large firms in closely regulated industries—such as transportation, communications, and banking—have come to depend on the federal regulators to preserve their shares of the market against competition from newer, more aggressive companies or industries. In recent years, the deregulation proposals have come not from big business but from consumer activists (such as Ralph Nader) and conservative free-market economists. They have been joined by firms that have not fared well in contests before the regulatory commissions. Disparate as these voices are, they agree on one idea: the regulators' motherly stance in rate setting and limits on entry discourages competition and adds a hidden charge to the price of America's goods and services. The argument has not yet swayed Congress but may make progress in the years ahead.

The most ringing indictment of regulatory agencies by a top federal official in recent years was made in 1974 by, ironically, Chairman Lewis A. Engman of the Federal Trade Commission. (Engman saw no irony in his attack, since he considers the FTC to be a "deregulator," fighting the kinds of monopolistic practices that are fostered by its sister agencies.) "Most regulated industries," Engman said in a widely publicized speech, "have become federal protectorates, living in a cozy world of cost-plus, safely protected from the ugly specters of competition, efficiency and innovation." Federal regulation is a major contributor to the inflation crisis, he said, and the consumer is "paying plenty in the form of government-sanctioned price fixing." Engman said, "Our airlines, our truckers, our railroads, our electronic media and countless others are on the dole; we get irate about welfare fraud, but our complex system of hidden regulatory subsidies makes welfare fraud look like petty larceny."

Probably the most criticized of the regulatory agencies is the oldest one, the Interstate Commerce Commission, created in 1887. It sets rates and allocates routes for surface shipping, including railroads, trucks, canal barges, and oil pipelines. If a trucker wants to get into interstate business, he can't just buy a few rigs, solicit customers, and negotiate some mutually agreeable rates. He must apply to the ICC, specifying exactly what he intends to carry and the routes he will drive, and then make a case that certificating him would be a convenience to the public. The commission sometimes certificates a trucker to work a route in only one direction, not both ways, and this results in trucks returning from a destination empty, because returning with a full cargo would "compete unfairly" with another company.

In attempting to preserve the market share of all the modes of surface transportation, the ICC has prevented each mode from doing what it is equipped to do best. Over certain distances, with certain kinds of cargo of certain weights, railroads have a natural advantage over trucks, and vice versa. Likewise, barges have the edge over trucks and railroads in certain situations. But ICC rate structures negate these comparative advantages. In 1961, the Southern Railway asked that it be allowed to use a new, large lightweight grain car called "Big John," which would enable it to carry more grain for less money; other railroads and the barge companies screamed "bloody murder," and the ICC stalled for four years before allowing the cost-cutting innovation to be adopted. The ICC's faulty monitoring of railroad boxcar supplies has aggravated the chronic shortage of boxcars. And the ICC is credited with allowing the railroads to abandon passenger service that could be economically competitive with other passenger modes if properly managed.

SAVINGS THROUGH DEREGULATION?

It is argued that partial or total deregulation of surface transportation would result in mammoth savings. Economist Thomas Gale Moore estimated a few years ago that deregulation of trucking rates and free entry by new firms could cause rates to drop as much as 20 percent. And the President's Council of Economic Advisers has estimated that $2 billon per year could be saved by the partial deregulation of the surface freight industries.

Other agencies exhibit an equally protective attitude toward various segments of their industries. The Federal Communications Commission has taken a benevolent attitude toward the broadcast companies, to which it has allocated positions on the radio and television frequency bands. Unlike every other regulatory agency, the FCC exerts no control over broadcast rates and profits, so securing a VHF television license is like discovering a rich vein of gold. The profits of network affiliates often run 20 percent of annual revenue, compared to about 8 percent in most industries. Some regulatory critics have suggested that the FCC grant broadcasting licenses through competitive bids, which would at least generate a lot of revenue for the federal treasury.

When community antenna television (also called cable television) reared its competitive head in the late Fifties, the FCC's inclination was to leave it alone to compete with conventional television as it was able to. But after the broadcast industry complained to Congress, the FCC took CATV under its wing. The FCC makes no bones about feeling a primary allegiance to conventional broadcasting, and says it will permit cable TV to be only a supplemental service. But do the broadcasters need all the protection that the FCC was so eager to lavish on conventional television? In 1974 there were indications that CATV was having great difficulty breaking into the lucrative urban markets, owing primarily to the high cost of wiring a city with cables. After the frantic bidding for urban cable franchises, many cable systems are having a hard time signing up customers.

Then there's the commercial aviation industry, whose watchdog is the Civil Aeronautics Board, created in 1938. The enacting legislation was virtually drafted by the Air Transport Association (then a new organization) or, more precisely, by its legal counsel, Covington and Burling. The ATA's purpose was clearly anticompetitive. The first ATA president, Edgar S. Gorrell, asked Congress for a commission that would offer "protection against fly-by-night companies . . . with a lot of secondhand planes [that try to] cut prices right out from under legitimate operators." And protection is just what the ATA got from the new board. The nation's air routes were divided among the eighteen ATA carriers that existed in 1938, and CAB rules stipulated that no new scheduled-service airline may be created unless the board finds it to be a matter of "public interest, convenience or necessity." Few would-be airlines have met this artificial standard over the decades, and in recent years, the number of new certifications has been far exceeded by the number of mergers among existing airlines. All of the new certifications have been for regional carriers. The CAB has not approved the formation of one new trunk (nationwide) airline since the commission was founded.

Although the CAB permits more than one carrier to fly the same routes, it has been reluctant to allow one carrier to substantially undercut the others on the route to capture a larger share of the passenger traffic. The air traveler has choices of schedules and frills like fancy meals and in-flight movies, but the basic New York-to-Los Angeles flight costs roughly the same, no matter what airline he flies on. In the late Sixties, the CAB authorized more airlines to fly the same routes, and the percentages of seat occupancy dropped to grossly unprofitable levels. As empty seats multiplied further in the recession days of 1975, the CAB took an uncharacteristically bold step. It allowed American Airlines to cut its transcontinental fares by as much as 25 percent to generate more air travel, and gave a green light to National Airlines' sharply reduced fares for no-frills transportation between New York and Florida.

Proponents of free competition in air travel point to the California situation, where a handful of CAB-exempt carriers travel the high-traffic corridor between Los Angeles and San Francisco. Many of the intra-California fares are half what the CAB sets for interstate trips of the same distance. The California Public Utilities Commission, which exerts minimal control over fares, does not limit entry or exit of airlines. The mortality rate has been high for California airlines, but the efficient carriers, such as Pacific Southwest and Air California, have prospered by charging fares that the CAB would consider too low.

Since the scheduled carriers are more or less harmoniously united in the Air Transport Association (competing with each other in everything except price), the real struggle in commercial aviation is between the scheduled carriers and the nonscheduled charter airlines, called "supplementals." From 1955 to 1964, the charter carriers were permitted by the CAB to run a limited number of individually ticketed flights each month, but since 1964 they have been limited to charter flights under stringent rules of registration far in advance, membership in "affinity groups," and advance deposits. The degree to which these rules have been flouted by the public indicates that Americans—like their European cousins—crave budget air transportation and are willing to forgo some convenience in the interest of lower fares. The CAB fears that loosening of charter regulations would jeopardize the scheduled carriers, but in early 1975 the board took steps to liberalize charter rules, figuring, perhaps, that if it didn't do this, Congress would take the initiative by passing a pro-charter bill sponsored by Senators Howard Cannon (D-Nev.) and Edward Kennedy (D-Mass.).

Regulation of the banking system is conducted by several agencies in Washington, including the Comptroller of the Currency, the Federal Reserve Board, the Federal Deposit Insurance Corporation, and the Federal Home Loan Bank Board, whose various powers range from ruling on the establishment of new banks to setting maximum interest rates allowed to be paid on savings accounts. These regulators make rulings designed to preserve the operational distinctions between banks and savings institutions, which are constantly vying for the consumer's deposits. In the securities industry, the Securities and Exchange Commission requires registration of corporate stock offerings, supervises the operation of stock brokerage houses, and oversees the setting of sales commission rates by stock exchanges (which traditionally fixed rates uniformly, but now allow negotiable rates).

CONSUMER PROTECTION

Not all agencies are empowered to control entry of new firms and specify the rates they may charge. Some of them are concerned instead with protecting the consumer from hazardous products and practices. This group includes such varied agencies as the Food and Drug Administration, the Department of Agriculture's meat, eggs, and poultry inspection program, the Consumer Product Safety Commission, and the Federal Deposit Insurance Corporation (which insures bank depositors against loss of their money in the event of a bank failure). The consumer safeguard agencies do not have enough staff to evaluate the thousands of new products put on the market each year, not to mention periodic monitoring of quality control in food and drugs. Critics of the FDA have long charged that it is slow in issuing warnings about possibly hazardous substances and reluctant to ban a product altogether, except if confronted with overwhelming evidence of danger. (The classic example of FDA procrastination was the issuance of its 1970 list of unsafe toys three shopping days before Christmas.)

Regulatory reform advocates always exempt the consumer protection-type agencies from their grand plans for deregulation of the economy. Ralph Nader, for example, calls for abolition of the ICC and its rate-setting sister agencies, but simultaneously urges that larger budgets and stiffer enforcement powers be given to the consumer watchdog bodies. Nader feels that free competition will take care of the pricing of goods and services, but federal surveillance is necessary to assure decent quality.

PROS AND CONS

What are the arguments in favor of federal regulation? Well, there are certain kinds of services, requiring unusually high initial investment and system-wide uniformity, that are natural monopolies—such as local telephone service and electrical generation. Nearly everyone agrees that the rates of these industries need to be regulated by someone, be it a state or federal agency. And few people quarrel with the concept of allocating the positions on the radio and television spectrums (although there is room for debate on the proper method of assigning). In the industries where there is reasonably easy opportunity for new firms to enter the market, the argument for regulation usually centers on economic stability and evenly spread service. If the CAB, for example, allowed open competition among all commercial airlines, some of them would undoubtedly go out of business, causing financial hardship for their owners and employees (although the expansion of more efficient carriers would, presumably, take up the employment slack and prevent a net loss of jobs). Since airline regulation entails a lot of "cross-subsidization," under which high fares on densely traveled routes make up for losses on sparsely traveled routes, deregulation would probably mean the loss of air service to some isolated parts of America.

Or take the matter of fixing the interest rates that banks and savings institutions may pay their depositors. This form of regulation is allegedly designed to protect small institutions in general, and savings and loans in particular. If the rates were competitive, the commercial banks could pay more interest than savings and loans, because they can command generally higher rates on their loans than the savings banks can get on mortgage loans, to which they are limited. To prevent a flow of funds into commercial bank accounts, savings and loans would have to jack up the interest they charge on mortgages, which would adversely affect the housing industry.

Opponents of federal regulation argue that the consumer's interest in lower prices would be better served by vigorous enforcement of the antitrust laws. Antitrust policy and federal regulation often run at cross purposes. Antitrust action is designed to promote competition, while the regulatory agencies often see their purpose as softening of the effects of "pure competition." In the words of Clay Whitehead, formerly the White House's chief adviser on telecommunications, "the regulator's definition of competition is little more than what I would call market division."

Antitrust officials of the Justice Department are constantly taking potshots at the government's longtime infatuation with business regulation. Former Deputy Assistant Attorney General Donald I. Baker told an audience in 1973 that "almost every time a regulated monopolist is faced with competition, it tends to argue that the noncompetitive arrangement subsidizes some other wonderful public benefit." But even if these benefits are worthwhile, the antitrust proponents say, it would be more honest to subsidize them openly and directly, instead of through covert subsidies in the form of higher prices for all users of a particular service.

ANTITRUST AT JUSTICE

Practicing what it preaches, the Justice Department Antitrust Division during the Nixon administration injected itself into regulatory policy and proceedings with unprecedented enthusiasm, led by Assistant Attorney General Thomas E. Kauper. It threatened action against the New York Stock Exchange's fixed commissions and backed off only after the SEC began its own moves toward requiring negotiable commissions. It consistently supported the policy of former FCC Chairman Dean Burch to allow microwave companies to compete with the American Telephone and Telegraph monopoly in supplying long-distance, private-line telephone service. It has examined applications of power companies seeking AEC approval for joint development and ownership of nuclear power plants. It has been a party to cases at the

Federal Maritime Commission and the ICC in which carriers have sought permission to merge or pool facilities. It has filed suit against the television networks, seeking to bar them from producing their own entertainment programs.

The Antitrust Division has also declared war on joint ownership of television, radio, and newspaper properties within one community, and has sought (generally unsuccessfully) to block FCC license renewals on these grounds. Since these initiatives coincided with worsening relations between the Nixon White House and the mass media, there was reason to suspect an attempt to intimidate the networks into going easy on President Nixon. While this may have been the case with the network suit, it is reasonably clear that the cross-ownership suit was motivated primarily by a desire to counteract economic concentration in the industry which provides the public with access to the news.

In addition to its saber rattling against regulated industries, the Justice Department has directed some sharp thrusts against conglomerates in unregulated industries. LTV was prevented from taking over Jones & Laughlin Steel, and ITT had to make a few divestitures in order to keep the Hartford Fire Insurance Company. The Justice Department's assault on computer giant IBM was begun in 1969 and will probably drag on for a long time. Justice has also taken a hard look at price fixing of fees in the professions, such as civil engineers, architects, real estate agents, and certified public accountants. After years of reluctance to attack anticompetitive practices in their own profession —the law—Justice Department attorneys initiated several suits against state bar associations for illegal fixing of fees. Justice's busy pace was almost matched by the FTC's ongoing attempt to break up the cereal industry and the largest oligopoly of all, the oil industry.

In November of 1974 the department announced the boldest antitrust challenge in history—an attempt to break up the American Telephone and Telegraph Company, world's largest privately owned business. The suit seeks the company's divestiture of Western Electric, its manufacturing subsidiary. It also aims to force AT&T out of either the long distance telephone business or local service (which it controls through total or partial ownership of twenty-three systems around the country). "Ma Bell" denied that its monopoly constitutes an illegal restraint of trade and vowed to fight the suit to the end.

ATTEMPTS AT REFORM

Much to the surprise of some of its business adherents, the Nixon administration showed more interest in changing the regulatory agencies—through both procedural reform and limited deregulation—than any administration in recent years. The most publicized effort was the report of the so-called Ash Commission on executive organization, chaired by former Litton Industries president Roy Ash, later director of the Office of Management and Budget. The report recommended, among other things, that agencies with similar responsibilities be consolidated for coordinated policymaking. (The ICC, CAB, and FMC, for example, would be merged into a new Transportation Regulatory Agency.) The regulatory process would be streamlined by shortening the hearing process, replacing multimember commissions with single administrators, and creating a new Administrative Court, staffed by specially qualified judges, to review some of the agencies' rulings. After a flurry of discussion when the report was released in 1971, the Ash proposals sank into the same oblivion that swallows most regulatory reform proposals.

A more modest attempt at procedural reform was made by Congress when it drafted the legislation that created the Consumer Product Safety Commission in 1972. It wrote into the law explicit rules to correct some of the problems that plague other agencies. The CPSC, for example, was given much stronger enforcement powers, including criminal fines and jail terms (which will be little-used, certainly, but might have a deterrent value). The commission is required to answer all citizen petitions within 120 days, whereas other agencies can let them molder indefinitely. To prevent CPSC employees from casting hungry eyes toward a job in the private sector, Congress prohibited middle- and upper-level staff from going to work, within one year of leaving the commission, for any company whose affairs are under the jurisdiction of the commission, whether or not it has any matter actually pending before the commission.

The members of the first commission have taken their mandate very seriously. They run the most open agency in town, with a maximum of public meetings. They feel the citizen role should be participatory, not just reactive. Instead of merely filing comments on the agency's proposals (as at other regulatory bodies), citizen and business groups are actually invited to help write industry-wide safety codes. Finally, Chairman Richard Simpson publicly complained when he felt the Nixon staff at the White House was trying to exert political influence over the filling of key staff positions (a practice not uncommon in other agencies).

The Nixon administration—and the agencies whose members it appointed —made a number of attempts to encourage competition in regulated industries. Several of the deregulation proposals, however, fell into the category of wishful thinking. The Whitehead report on cable television, for example, urged that the embryonic industry be given a free rein to compete with conventional broadcasting, but the recommendations have yet to be implemented by the FCC. Deregulation proposals sent to Capitol Hill have a way of getting lost in the shuffle. Nothing has come of the 1972 bill to allow more flexible rate setting in surface transportation. And nothing has come of a bill, sponsored by the Treasury Department, that would eliminate many of the current distinctions between commercial banks and savings and loans—such as higher interest rates on accounts at savings and loans and checking accounts exclusively at commercial banks. Predictably, neither the banking industry nor the savings and loan industry has embraced the bill in its entirety, since both are reluctant to give up any of their exclusive advantages. The status quo seems safer.

President Ford has shown an unusually strong interest in both antitrust action and deregulation. The basis of his concern is the hidden cost that monopolistic practices add to the price of many goods and services—a cost that is bad enough in a stable economy and intolerable in a period of soaring inflation. Ford has endorsed vigorous antitrust enforcement in several major economic addresses and, like several previous Presidents, has said that the whole question of rate regulation could use a close examination by a disinterested federal study commission.

IT WON'T DISAPPEAR

The deregulation spirit is blossoming all over Washington these days. Ford administration officials at Justice and Transportation talk enthusiastically about deregulating both surface and air transportation. Congress is hurrying to get into the act, too, prodded by such longtime antitrust specialists as Senator Philip Hart (D-Mich.). The mood is reflected in a congressional drive to repeal federal authority for "fair trade" laws—those state statutes that allow manufacturers to set the retail prices of their products. But amid the flurry of deregulation publicity, one should keep in mind that there have been numerous past periods of interest in making American business more competitive and free of federal interference. Washington is littered with the recommendations of study commissions, task forces, and blue-ribbon panels that grappled with the issue in years past.

Governmental regulation is a staple on the government scene, both the "popular" kinds (like consumer safety and environmental protection) and the more basic and less well known kind (market control). The supporters of market-control regulation are well organized, while its foes have not been able to get the average citizen worked up about the extra money that he pays in hidden subsidies. Most people apparently believe that the agencies are a more reliable guardian of their economic interests than unregulated competition and a vigorous antitrust program. The concept of "Washington to the Rescue" has been seductive for a long time, ever since the ICC was created to curb the monopoly power of railroads. The same concept was especially seductive in hard times of the Thirties, which saw the greatest burst of new regulatory agencies.

However far from their original missions the regulatory agencies may have strayed, they are protected from abolition by government's traditional inability to stop anything it has started, or to diminish its own domain. So in realistic terms, the odds are that Washington will continue to muddle along in its present mode of regulatory action. Business, labor, and consumers will continue to pick away at various issues and complain about various techniques, making small changes here and there, but leaving the mammoth regulatory structure as ponderous and implacable as ever.

34 GOVERNMENT AND ENERGY

When Gerald Ford started grappling with the economic problems of the Presidency, it was not entirely clear to him whether inflation or recession would turn out to be the nation's "number one enemy." While he was engaged in making up his mind—and changing it in the process—another basic problem kept turning up on both sides of the issue: Energy.

On the inflation side, the high cost of imported oil (which quadrupled from 1973 to 1974) was clearly one of the culprits which helped push prices up to double-digit levels. Yet on the deflation-recession side, high oil prices were also to blame for taking more purchasing power from consumers and businesses just to pay for the same volume of heat, light, power, and raw materials. As petroleum demanded more from their budgets it left less for other things, so while contributing to inflation, it also accelerated recession by dampening the demand for goods and services all along the line.

It was this irony that finally gave energy policy a top billing on the nation's agenda. After years of promises from various U.S. Presidents, in 1975 energy claimed the position that it had deserved all along.

Richard Nixon had promised an energy policy during his first term, but the unwinding of Vietnam kept the issue in the study stage. During his abortive second term, Watergate interfered, yet finally an energy report did emerge in November 1974 (after Nixon had resigned). It suggested better governmental mechanisms for reaching decisions, but the decisions themselves were yet to come. Even now, many of them are yet to come—despite the moves by the President and the Congress to impose import duties on foreign crude oil, special gasoline taxes, and levies on windfall profits of energy producers.

GOVERNMENT'S DILEMMA

To understand why Washington has pussyfooted on fuel policy, you need to know a number of things about energy and the democratic process.

First, you need to realize that—except in time of war or clear-cut economic crisis—democratic government is poorly equipped to lay down any deep-cutting thou-shalt-nots to a consuming public that is accustomed to making up its own mind. Energy policy is not something separate from other policies. It is, in fact, a composite of all the policies of the nation, and it deals with the whole life style of a people. Energy policy embraces policy on transportation, construction, exports and imports, interest rates, taxes, city planning, zoning, housing—everything involved in people's daily habits. In the final analysis, energy policy affects the freedom of individuals to decide where to live, where to work, how to pattern their lives.

These are things that a totalitarian government is better equipped to handle. Governments that operate from the top down can—and do—have unified energy policies. The Soviet Union is economical on energy because people use it only when—and as—the government decrees. But democracies like the U.S. must struggle along with a patchwork of directives, persuasions, incentives, and penalty taxes.

The second thing to know about energy is that it is closely related to world affairs—so closely that the two can hardly be separated (as the events of the past two years have amply demonstrated). For this reason, many of the elements are not within the control of any one government.

The third thing is that energy and population—like food and population—are inextricably bound together. Food is essential to human life. Energy is essential to the life of modern technological society. Energy is the food of our industrial system. Without huge amounts of coal, oil, gas, uranium, and hydrogen—or some substitutes for them—our modern civilization would crumble.

The fourth thing is that energy and environment are tied together as closely as energy and population. The kind and quality of fuel we use affect the quality of the air and water around us and, ultimately, the quality of the entire atmosphere of our earth. So energy policy and ecology policy are part of the same problem.

These are things that Washington has to deal with in trying to come up with a consistent, workable policy for the U.S. on fuel. And while Washington is admirably suited for some things, it is not well suited for setting hard and fast priorities. Gradually, the message is sinking in: we can't always have our cake and eat it, too. We can't have the big cars and the multiplying roads at the same time that we have all the air conditioning we want. We can't have the maximum competition among overseas airlines and still have enough fuel for domestic consumption. We can't import all the oil we want and still be able to pay for all the other imports we might like to have. Some choices will have to be made, and Washington would rather not lay out such tough choices in advance of an election (and there is always an election just around the corner).

Nevertheless, Washington is trying. Washington, for all its cumbersome mechanisms, is trying to make some sense out of the conflicting demands on our dwindling oil resources. Washington, through a rearranged administrative setup, is trying to stimulate research and exploration. Washington is trying to encourage conservation—by individuals, by industries, and in the design of our automotive equipment. Washington will continue to try—with greater or less success, depending on the understanding of the voting public.

THE BUREAUCRATIC MECHANISM

The federal administrative setup for energy policy is new, having been established by the Energy Reorganization Act signed October 11, 1974. Under the act, the Energy Resources Council with Secretary of Commerce Rogers Morton as chairman is at the top of the heap. Secretary of the Treasury William Simon, the former energy policy coordinator, is an important member of the council. Executive of the council is Frank Zarb, head of the Federal Energy Administration and formerly an associate director of the Office of Management and Budget for energy. The FEA is charged with trying to carry out the policy. But before the policy can be executed, it has to be set—endorsed by the President and authorized by Congress.

In the meantime, the Energy Research and Development Administration goes ahead with its search for long-term alternatives. Under the directorship of Robert Seamans, former secretary of the air force, ERDA combines a number of agencies that formerly were scattered throughout other departments of government. Input will come from the Department of the Interior and the Department of Commerce, which deal with import controls and international payments problems.

The roots of government interest in energy policy go back to the beginning of the republic. The ordinance of 1787 for the Northwest Territory reflected the traditional sovereign rights of government over waterways, and waterways were then the principal source of power. Over the years, other legislation dealt with public lands and mineral resources, and in the Mining Act of 1866 Congress declared that public lands should be free and open for exploration for minerals and for mining. This, of course, affected the production of coal and, subsequently, oil, gas, and uranium. Some back pressure on this "free and open" policy was exerted by President Theodore Roosevelt, and in 1906 Roosevelt directed the Secretary of the Interior to withdraw more than 60 million acres of known coal land from any exploitation. In 1946, the Atomic Energy Act reserved the uranium ores on public lands, though subsequent amendments established procedures for leasing them to private industry for production of ore, which is then sold back to the AEC.

Running through this continuing tug of war between interests and values is the pattern of the current conflict among power needs, ecology, natural conservation, food production, and other competing priorities of modern life. Each of these interests is represented by agencies within the federal government, often in conflict among themselves. In any final solution there will be tradeoffs among agencies, policies, and priorities.

Despite the obvious need for energy policy coordination, a 1973 report commissioned by the Senate Interior Committee said: "A survey made by the Congressional Research Service of the major federal reorganization proposals of the past forty years reveals no specific consideration of fuel and energy matters until the relatively modest energy recommendations of the Ash Council." So when President Ford signed the Energy Reorganization Act as one of the first major moves of his administration, the action set a new course for the government on energy.

PROBLEMS AND PITFALLS

The recent history of the energy issue in Washington shows some of the deficiencies of the governmental process. After the Arab oil embargo in 1973, the Nixon administration commissioned a study of alternative paths to energy self-sufficiency and the relative costs of different approaches. After nearly a year of work, the Federal Energy Administration—then headed by John Sawhill—produced the report called "Project Independence." Released in November 1974, after Nixon's resignation, the report put heavy emphasis on conservation as the first step toward substantial savings of fuel. By the time the report was released, however, Sawhill himself had announced his resignation and the Ford administration's first nominee as a replacement, Andrew E. Gibson, subsequently had to withdraw, when he disclosed he was on an oil tanker company's severance payroll. Early in 1975, President Ford presented his energy message to Congress stressing new oil exploration, user taxes, import duties on foreign oil, and windfall profits taxes on fuel producers.

Farther down the road he saw relief in the form of nuclear power, and in the meantime, he called for research to make coal a viable tradeoff fuel in ways that would not seriously damage the environment. Power from oil-shale and coal gasification receded somewhat into the background as technical difficulties began to look more formidable.

But for all the straining to find a coordinated U.S. policy on fuel, it may turn out that worldwide exploration and developments already under way in the North Sea, Alaska, and elsewhere will provide the relief that governments so earnestly seek. As in other matters, it may be that market forces and supply-demand considerations will answer some of the questions before any changes in government policy begin to take effect. At an outlook conference in June 1974, economist Arlon Tussing of the Senate Interior Committee called attention to the possibility that within five years the world may face an absolute glut of oil. If this should come about, as the result of the enormous production soon to flow out of the North Sea, Alaska, and Mexico, oil prices could come down sharply. As he pointed out, most of the new oil production will be outside the Persian Gulf countries and the other OPEC nations who pushed up crude oil prices more than 300 percent in less than a year.

SOME UNDERLYING FACTS

While the decimal places and percentages change from year to year, it is possible to look at some recent figures and get a general idea of where the U.S. stands in fuel needs, supplies, and prospects.

The U.S. was self-sufficient in energy until about 1950, but since then has drawn more and more heavily on external sources. Coal production today is still at 1940 levels, yet there are estimates of a 300- to 400-year supply of coal under U.S. soil, if ways could be found to mine it economically and burn it without detriment to the environment.

Crude oil production has been declining within the United States since 1970, and natural gas consumption has been exceeding new discoveries since 1968. As of 1974, 39 percent of our oil came from overseas. Only about 17 percent of our oil, however, has been coming from the Arab countries. Other foreign sources are Venezuela, Mexico, and soon the North Sea. All of the foreign sources, however, either belong to the OPEC combine or follow OPEC in its pricing policy, so there is little solace in the fact that they are geographically separated.

In terms of oil reserves, the North Slope of Alaska gives a prospect of easing the U.S. bind, and after production starts there, North Sea production promises the U.S. and other industrial nations some relief. One single American oil company has reported potential production of half a million barrels a day from wells that will be drilled off the coast of Scotland. This kind of production, multiplied by competing companies and nations, could break the Middle East dominance sooner than most people realize. In the meantime, however, the Middle East countries have 60 percent of world oil reserves and currently produce 70 percent of world oil exports.

The U.S., with its importation of 39 percent of its oil needs, is still far better off than the European nations of France and Germany, who rely almost wholly on imported oil. Japan brings more than 90 percent of her requirements from the Middle East alone. Another factor which mitigates the oil squeeze for the U.S. is that petroleum accounts for only about half of the nation's total fuel needs. Coal accounts for about 17 percent, gas about 30 percent, with less than 5 percent accounted for by uranium (nuclear) and water power. The future for uranium, however, is *up*. Dr. Glenn Seaborg, former chairman of the Atomic Energy Commission, puts it very forcefully: "Civilization as we know it will grind to a halt unless we can develop nuclear power."

Several major studies of the energy situation within the past year have come out with surprisingly similar conclusions. Originating with the Ford Foundation, the Federal Energy Administration and the Committee for Economic Development, they all conclude that the U.S. will have to slow down its growth of energy usage. They also agree that it can be done, though they set different figures for the amount of conservation that will be required.

As a bench mark, they start with the fact that the U.S. has been increasing its use of energy by 4.3 percent per year. The C.E.D., a business-oriented organization, recommends that this growth be limited to 2.9 percent. The Ford Foundation study suggests a more drastic curtailment, to a 1.9 percent annual growth rate by 1985. The Federal Energy Administration, while not specifying a figure, also emphasizes conservation.

All studies point out that more efficient use of energy could be achieved by research, technology, more modern design of equipment, better production techniques, and by the practice of conservation by ultimate users—individuals, business, government and large institutions.

Compared with today's import level of 39 percent of our total oil supply, the Ford study recommends a cutback to a 15 percent reliance on foreign sources. The C.E.D. recommends a top figure of 10 percent. Such reductions could be brought about by limiting the growth in energy use and by stimulating domestic production through tax incentives and decontrol of prices. These approaches, however, will not be quick-acting, and Washington, as the focal point of energy policy, will be involved in basic energy questions for as long ahead as anyone can see.

Dr. Dixy Lee Ray, when she was chairman of the Atomic Energy Commission in 1974, said to a Washington group that "it will take twenty to thirty years for research and development to come up with usable power from renewable sources instead of fossil fuels, but it can and will be done." By the year 2000, she estimated, the U.S. could derive 60 percent of its energy needs—1.2 billion kilowatts—from 1,000 nuclear power plants. And the plants, she said, would be safe. "An earthquake that could flatten Chicago wouldn't disturb Commonwealth Edison's new nuclear plants there," she said. Beyond the year 2000, Dr. Ray forecast we will start taking our power from solar, fusion, and geothermal sources.

So the energy story is not a doomsday tale. There is coal in the ground, oil and gas under the surface, hydrogen in the water. There is sunlight in the air. And there is man's ingenuity. For in the longer run, there is reason to believe that a mixture of research and restraint can bring mankind's need for energy into balance with consumption, even though the cost will be materially higher than it is now. The problem for government is the short run.

Washington, through its newly vitalized Federal Energy Administration, its Energy Research and Development Administration, and its White House

Energy Resources Council, has proposed conservation as the first step, stimulated production as the second, and research as the ace in the hole. Eventually, research will rise to the number one position. In the meantime, persuasion will be the principal weapon of Washington, coupled with the price mechanism which assumes that people will conserve oil if it becomes more expensive. But "jawboning" has seldom been enough in itself to bring about major changes in consuming habits, and the price mechanism may be too slow a process to produce timely results.

So Washington is studying other—harsher—methods for divvying up the limited supply of fuel. These other means include mandatory allocations for business and rationing for individual consumers.

Rationing and allocations would have their greatest value in putting a ceiling on the amount of oil imported into the U.S. Each barrel of imported crude petroleum requires an outflow of $10 or more for the raw material itself. President Ford's proposal to cut the importation of oil by one million barrels per day from the Arab Middle East and Venezuela would reduce U.S. payments to these countries by more than $70 million a week, or nearly $4 billion a year. With careful conservation, and without crimping U.S. industry, this outflow could be stemmed.

This is the reasoning behind President Ford's goal of reducing U.S. reliance on foreign oil. And this is the thinking which lies behind the contingency planning for rationing and allocations. If the public does not curtail its consumption via persuasion and higher prices, more stringent moves are sure to come. For slow as it has been in taking shape, a consensus is finally arriving. In essence, the proposition is that—one way or another—government must lead the nation toward a more efficient use of energy, and that—as far as possible—the U.S. fuel supply must not be subject to a sudden cut-off by powers outside our own control. While the goal is not likely to be reached soon—if ever—the crystallization of opinion has given Washington its marching orders.

35 FOOD, FARMERS, AND THE GROCERY BILL

Food is in the forefront in Washington today as it has not been for more than a generation. Agriculture, besides being a star performer in the American economic production drama, is also a major force in world politics. In response to the rise in world hunger, voiced at the World Food Conference in Rome, U.S. agricultural policy now calls for all-out production.

Within four years, U.S. farm policy has gone through the most dramatic turnaround since farmers "killed little pigs" and plowed under their crops in the Great Depression years of the 1930s. Now, few farmers are urged to restrict their output in return for subsidy payment. Unlike the agricultural policies of the past forty years, which were engineered to control food output and prevent burdensome surpluses, there are no mandatory "set-asides" or "diversions" to enable farmers to qualify for assistance.

A generation of high consumer purchasing power around the world—accompanied by exploding population—has created world demand that did not exist forty years ago. Per-capita food production in both the developed and less-developed nations has been gaining during the past two decades, but millions still go hungry every day. And to add further urgency to the problem, the world has recently suffered crop failures through drought, frost, and floods, which have shoved food into the headlines of newspapers from Washington to New Delhi.

The U.S. needs high food production for both domestic and foreign consumers: at home, to hold grocery bills in line; overseas, to earn export dollars and help pay for the oil that we import. In the government fiscal year 1974, U.S. farm exports totaled $21.3 billion and produced a net favorable balance of agricultural payments sufficient to pay the $10 billion that the U.S. needed to cover its oil imports.

Farming is no longer the old-fashioned problem child of the economy. Indeed, the farm problem today is not a matter of chronic overproduction (which at one time cost taxpayers a million dollars a day to store). The problem of the Seventies is a mixture of rising production costs and ways to finance the ever more sophisticated and ever more corporatized methods of American agriculture. This is the problem to which Washington now addresses itself.

Experts believe that the production revolution in U.S. agriculture is finally being overcome by an even more powerful revolution in consumer demand. This will mean fewer tax dollars going to federal farm programs (but more paid out at the store and marketplace). Since the New Deal farm programs of the Thirties, the U.S. Treasury has shelled out $84 billion to support farm incomes.

THE ROAD TO THE PRESENT

U.S. agriculture's oversupply problems can be traced to the farm technology advances of the Twenties and Thirties when gasoline tractors replaced horses, finally freeing 90 million acres which had been supplying fodder for draft animals. Hybrid seeds and commercial fertilizers paid off in better yields. Finally, fewer farmhands were needed. Surplus production and manpower problems, tied to the Great Depression, led to "temporary" farm programs, starting with the Federal Farm Board in the Hoover administration in 1929 and the Agricultural Adjustment Administration, the Triple A, in 1933. Since then, there has been a succession of programs, none of which actually halted overproduction or solved farm income problems.

The technological revolution in agriculture has not slowed. Major breakthroughs are still emerging. Production per acre is 60 percent greater than it was twenty-five years ago. Many of these advances come from United States Department of Agriculture research at various stations throughout the U.S. and at the 10,000-acre Agricultural Research Service facility in Beltsville, Maryland, just northeast of Washington. Although there is some excess capacity in U.S. agriculture, the slack is being taken up, and in the future there will be little concern about extra acres not needed for crops or ranges.

The 1970 farm act—passed in the first Nixon administration—was the landmark legislation that allowed farmers to choose their own planting patterns in place of mandatory allotments. Farmers reacted by changing their cropping practices on an estimated 70 million acres of cropland—switching to crops which they could most efficiently and profitably raise. Then the 1973 farm act went a few more steps toward market orientation, retaining the set-aside concept for idling cropland when necessary, keeping commodity loans at low levels, and adopting target prices as protection against disastrously low markets. These changes prepared agriculture to enter the era of today, in which policymakers believe there will be solid cash markets for the full productive capacity of U.S. grain farmers.

The fact is that the old high-support, rigid production control programs usually failed to prevent surpluses. Farmers would take the required number of acres out of production and produce like mad on the rest, to take advantage of high prices. Benefits of government payments were translated into higher farmland prices, making it difficult for younger people to enter farming. Farmers had to buy their way into the programs. Thus, Washington's efforts to boost farm incomes became a cost of production, and restrictions on planting interfered with efficient operations of farms.

At the direction of Secretary of Agriculture Earl L. Butz, the Agriculture Department went to a full-production policy in 1971, turning loose government acreage allotments and marketing quotas. Assistant Secretary of Agriculture Clarence D. Palmby—now a vice president of the world's largest grain exporter, Continental Grain Company, New York—was the mastermind of the new policy. The next year, 1972, set-aside restrictions were freed up, in a move to get more production. Even with all the program-scrubbing in recent years, there are a few remaining planting restrictions under the peanut, rice, and long-staple cotton programs. Everything else that the government can do to lure full farm production has been done.

Palmby, a longtime expert in grain export marketing and sales development, was the program designer who worked with the White House and Congress to break off the shackles of the old crop controls and high-support policies. He was succeeded at USDA by Carroll Brunthaver, who worked out the fine points of the 1973 farm act and basic USDA policy on international grain reserves before returning to Cook Industries (Memphis, Tennessee), one of the giants in the world grain market.

THE DEPARTMENT OF AGRICULTURE

While USDA is regarded as the "farmers' department," most of its budget outlays now go for food programs: food stamps, child nutrition, commodity donations, supplemental family feeding, and nutrition education. This is a fact that irks Earl Butz and other agriculturally oriented officials on the topside at the agency. Of USDA's 1975 budget of $9.2 billion, a whopping 64 percent ($5.9 billion) is for food-aid programs. Expenditures for the feeding plans have skyrocketed since 1969, when only 14 percent of the USDA outlays went into food aid. By 1970, this jumped to 19 percent ($1.6 billion) and then up to 34 percent in 1971. In 1974, when the food programs finally accounted for half the USDA budget outlays, Butz asked that they be shifted over to the Department of Health, Education and Welfare. He is bothered by criticism of the department's huge spending from people who mistakenly blame it on farm subsidies, crop surpluses, and boondoggles. Butz wants the food programs set up as a separate budget, treated as welfare, and transferred out of his department. If they are not changed, food programs will account for four-fifths of USDA spending by 1980.

The department's payments for the major crop programs—wheat, feed grains, and cotton—have been dwindling even more steadily than food-aid costs have been climbing. In 1972–73 (the time of the massive Russian grain sales), farmers complying with government farm program rules withheld more than 60 million acres from production to avoid what were expected to be major surpluses following the big corn crop of 1971. Federal farm program payments in 1972–73 cost a startling $3.5 billion.

Then came red-hot demand for U.S. food and feed, a demand fueled by crop problems in Asia and Russia, by devaluation of the dollar, and by growing population and affluence in many parts of the world. U.S. farmers were encouraged by strong prices to produce full tilt and to ignore government land diversion or set-aside schemes. As a result, crop payments in 1973–74 tumbled to $2.4 billion and in 1974–75 are expected to slump to about $600 million, most of which will be crop disaster payments (because of rain, drought, and frost damage).

In the years ahead, farmers will continue to receive less of their income from government programs and more from the marketplace. From time to time, farmers will grow more of certain crops than can be sold at a profit, and USDA's Commodity Credit Corporation will be forced to extend loans to farmers until the crops are sold at a better price, or differential payments will be made between the average market price and a predetermined government target price.

In the spring of 1975, with grain and cotton prices sliding and the costs of farm machinery, fertilizer, pesticides, and other supplies at record-high levels, rural congressmen pushed hard for more farm income protection. Within the framework of the 1973 farm act, they wanted higher loans and government-guaranteed prices. The USDA—combined in an unusual alliance with urban congressmen and some consumer groups—fought the changes. They charged that the amendments would force up grocery bills and be costly to the government. Butz threatened to recommend a presidential veto if Congress approved the higher support levels. But the new chairman of the House Agriculture Committee, Representative Tom Foley of Washington, did a good job of convincing his colleagues that the amendments were not a major departure from the free-market orientation of the 1973 law.

SECRETARIES OF AGRICULTURE

Wide gaps between supplies and demand, plummeting prices, high costs, transportation problems, and antagonism between agricultural producers and other businessmen are troubles which every Secretary of Agriculture has faced since Abraham Lincoln chartered the Department of Agriculture in 1862.

Various USDA Secretaries have approached similar problems from many different angles and with scores of grand plans and a few gimmicks. When Henry Cantwell Wallace, editor of a successful midwestern magazine, *Wallaces Farmer,* became Agriculture Secretary under Harding and Coolidge, he was described as being "redheaded on his head and in his soul." Wallace was convinced that farmers lacked good business know-how, and he significantly expanded government agricultural reporting and forecasting, partly to discourage overproduction. He also started the USDA annual Outlook Conferences, which were criticized for being dominated by interests hostile to farmers. Wallace felt that the farm problems of the 1920s would be quite temporary and proposed a series of relief measures, including exemption of farmer cooperatives from some antitrust regulations.

Ten years later, Wallace's son, Henry A., was stewing over the same problems during his tenure as USDA Secretary (1933–40). But "Henry Jr.," who had made his mark as a hybrid seed expert and farm editor, was more of a politician than his father, more caught up in New Deal "solutions" and inclined to controls on output and farm income supplements. He was an idealist, aloof from the day-to-day activities and convinced that the job of USDA's information department was to teach farmers how to improve their own public relations. Wallace urged the adoption of the Agricultural Adjustment Administration to regulate farm production through government planning. He dramatized surpluses through reports of cotton being plowed under and baby pigs being slaughtered. His rigid production control ideas set the direction of agricultural policy for almost forty years. The "Triple A" plans, as they were known, were actually developed by agricultural economists from Cornell University. Wallace went on to become FDR's Vice President and Secretary of Commerce and was succeeded by Claude R. Wickard, a dour Hoosier, who had worked up through the ranks as a USDA farm administrator. He was eventually demoted to administrator of the Rural Electrification Administration.

Truman replaced Wickard with one of his poker-playing chums, congressman Clinton Anderson of New Mexico, who turned out to be a very capable administrator. But Anderson quickly ran into trouble with the National Farmers Union and with his own farm committeemen when he supported Republicans Cliff Hope and George Aiken in their campaign for more flexible price supports. And when his Forest Service ran into controversy over the way it was handling mining claims, Anderson packed the mining responsibilities and problems off to the Interior Department. In 1948, Anderson won a Senate seat and was succeeded by Charles F. Brannan as Secretary. Brannan, who was an assistant secretary under Anderson, had close ties to the Farmers Union. He was the originator of the "Brannan Plan" of differential payments to farmers based on average market prices and government guarantees. The scheme was rejected in the late 1940s but substantially accepted in the 1970s.

One of the most colorful of the Secretaries of Agriculture was the gutsy, pompous, stubborn Ezra Taft Benson, who served during all eight years of the Eisenhower administration in spite of almost weekly reports that he was about to be fired. Benson, a leader in the Mormon church, was intense—a man of strong convictions. He was opposed to farm subsidies, and he was in tune with Farm Bureau philosophy. Through the farm act of 1954 and the farm act of 1958, he nudged agriculture away from acreage allotments, marketing quotas, and high price supports to lower price supports and land retirement. Benson's much-maligned Soil Bank Plan was a Farm Bureau-conceived plan to retire whole farms in exchange for government payments as a means of reducing the tremendous surpluses which nagged the Eisenhower administration. The controversial Soil Bank idea was scrapped due to opposition from midwestern politicians who feared it would weaken small towns and the family farm concept. Fifteen years after Benson left office, his basic philosophy is being carried out by one of his former assistant secretaries, Earl L. Butz.

Orville L. Freeman, President Kennedy's ag Secretary, had few ties to agriculture but had been a three-term governor of Minnesota and was a favorite of the National Farmers Union. The White House gave Freeman a relatively free hand in farm matters. He responded by steering agriculture back to protective loan programs and production controls. By 1965, however, the Johnson administration and Congress were beginning to nudge over to more market-oriented policies. The general farm act of that year substituted direct payments for high and rigid price supports. However, acreage allotments and bases were still key elements of the farm programs, and the level of price supports for the different crops often decided what farmers would plant. Freeman was constantly trying to balance consumption with production, and it was because of the great need to get rid of surpluses that he pushed the Food for Freedom foreign food-aid programs (P.L. 480). He did not lack sensitivity to human needs, however, and spent endless hours to revive the food-stamp program and expand domestic food-aid programs in the final years of the Johnson administration. Freeman fought a losing battle for tough farm bargaining legislation, but his administration did accomplish major improvements in wholesome meat and poultry laws.

The swing back to more conservative farm policies was evident when Richard Nixon was elected and University of Nebraska Chancellor Clifford M. Hardin was named Secretary of Agriculture. Hardin relied heavily on his top aides for program advice and ran into political turmoil in the fall of 1971 when corn prices collapsed. He left USDA to become vice chairman of the board at Ralston Purina Company, St. Louis, moving up to a six-figure salary. Nixon asked Hardin to suggest a replacement, and the Secretary nominated three men: Butz, Palmby, and USDA Under Secretary J. Phil Campbell, a former Democratic commissioner of agriculture in Georgia who changed parties in 1968. Nixon chose Butz. The next day, Earl Butz took office with the declaration that $1 per bushel corn was not in the farmer's or the country's best interests, and he promised to do something about it. By the fall of 1974, corn was selling for close to $4 per bushel, and all-out production was the order of the day, something that Henry A. Wallace never even dreamed of. The outspoken Butz, who has a penchant for lecturing people about what a great bargain food prices are, has not been terribly popular with consumers, but he is generally well-liked by his farm constituents.

THE DEPARTMENT TODAY

Although USDA has 79,100 employees, only 11,250 are stationed in Washington. The others work in thousands of extension offices, county courthouses, experiment stations, research laboratories, meat and poultry inspection points, and other places throughout the world. Roughly a third of the department's employees are classified as professionals—economists, veterinarians, biologists, etc. Many of these are former farm boys, freed from farm work by the technological revolution in agriculture but anxious to retain their ties to food production and marketing.

USDA has about 18,200 women on the payroll, of whom 13,500 are clerical workers, 3,895 are administrative and technical, and just 730 are professionals. Several hundred women currently in dead-end secretarial jobs are being trained for technical and administrative slots formerly for men only. What's more, USDA is searching for talent among women students in the ag colleges—veterinarians, chemists, animal and crop scientists, analysts.

Since 1970, the total USDA work force has been inching down, reductions coming mostly in the field offices, not so much in the giant Washington headquarters, which is sprawled along Independence Avenue, south of the Mall and near the Smithsonian Institution.

Among the top agencies within the department, the Agricultural Marketing Service is best known for market news reporting, food-grading programs, and labeling standards. It also provides information to consumers on which foods will be in abundant supply or where shortages may pop up. The Agricultural Research Service is responsible for breakthroughs in sterilized insect control, meat-type hogs, dairy production gains, Marek's disease vaccine, and development of the Beltsville turkey. However, the trend in funding of ARS research has been down in recent years.

Farm programs, such as there are these days, are run by the most important operating agency in USDA, Agricultural Stabilization and Conservation Service, which has committees in about 2,900 counties throughout the U.S. Much of its recent work has been in crop disaster relief. The Animal and Plant Health Inspection Service, among other things, inspects millions of beef, pork, lamb, and poultry carcasses each year. It also can react quickly to outbreaks of animal diseases and slap on quarantines when necessary.

The Economic Research Service churns out hundreds of regular reports on the agricultural outlook, farm income and expenses, price and supply trends, and other matters of great importance to farmers and agribusiness. The USDA director of economics, Dr. Donald Paarlberg, has been gradually bringing ERS more into the mainstream of world economics, so that the agency is beginning to take a less parochial view of its responsibilities. It is now following economic trends overseas, foreign oil and political maneuvers, and the impact that these have on U.S. farmers and consumers.

The USDA Extension Service is a major information outreach agency, linked to programs at the state and county levels. It includes about 16,500 extension agents who help farmers with production and management advice. As suburban sprawl has gobbled many formerly rural counties in recent years, extension programs have adapted to include horticultural advice, home garden tips, and disseminating ways to control crabgrass and dandelions—a far cry from counseling farmers on how to hedge their soybeans or file tax forms.

Supply and marketing cooperatives run by producers are given a management hand from the Farmer Cooperative Service, which is a much more tranquil agency these days than when Orville L. Freeman was evangelizing for farmer bargaining power through cooperative action. Farmers Home Administration provides low-cost loans for farm purchase, construction, and improvements and for equipment and operating supplies. The Federal Crop Insurance Corporation provides insurance against unavoidable losses for most of the key farm crops.

The Food and Nutrition Service has mushroomed, right along with the food-aid programs which it runs within USDA. The Foreign Agricultural Service, which promotes exports of U.S. food and fiber and has offices around the world, is one of the new prima donna agencies within the government. Its administrator, David L. Hume, is making plans to promote sale of U.S. beef and pork to foreign markets in the years ahead. The Forest Service manages 187 million acres of forests and grasslands. There are rumblings that it will be moved completely over to the Interior Department or to a new Department of Natural Resources.

When meat processors don't pay farmers on time, or when locker plants short-weight consumer purchases, the complaints eventually go to the Packers and Stockyards Administration at USDA, a sleepy, old-line agency headed by Marvin L. McLain, who was an assistant secretary at USDA when Ezra Taft Benson was Secretary (1953–61).

The job of pumping new life into rural communities through sewage and water grants and trying to lure industry to small towns falls on the Rural Development Service. Present RDS officials have the good fortune of being in charge at a time when migration from farms has slowed to a trickle and when small towns and cities are actually growing faster than metropolitan areas—a phenomenon for which the USDA agency does not take credit.

Finally, the Statistical Reporting Service compiles the eagerly awaited monthly USDA Crop Production reports, based on thousands of reports and sample surveys. It is also responsible for major reports on grain stocks, vegetables and fruits, hogs, cattle, and poultry. The reports, kept under elaborate security until 3 P.M. on the scheduled release date, often have a big impact on the commodity markets.

LOBBIES LOOK TO WASHINGTON

Food and farm organizations make up one of the largest and most influential lobbies in Washington. Scores of food and agribusiness companies have their own men in town, and all of the major farm and commodity groups are represented.

The once-potent "farm bloc" in Congress, actually a coalition of midwestern Republicans and southern and southwestern Democrats, was at its peak in 1940, when the farm population was 30.5 million (23 percent of the U.S. population). The coalition then declined rapidly during and after World War II, as farmers and their sons and daughters were drawn to better-paying jobs in the cities. Farm population is now stabilizing at about 9.3 million (less than 5 percent of the U.S. population). While the farm bloc no longer exists, agriculture is getting more attention than ever in Congress and at the White House. The "farm problem" of the 1930s, 1940s, and 1950s has become the "food problem" of the 1970s and 1980s. U.S. food power is recognized as a trump card for balance-of-payments problems, as a powerful diplomatic tool, and as a contribution to world peace and security abroad.

Since 1960, there has been a steady shift of farm organizations and commodity trade groups to Washington from former headquarters in such places as Chicago, Kansas City, and St. Louis. This reflects the growing influence of the federal government on all aspects of food and agriculture, not merely major farm policy and trade questions but also complex Food and Drug Administration regulations, labeling requirements, food contamination problems, and similar matters.

As the government withdrew from farm program tinkering and efforts to preserve farming as a way of life, it dug deeper into the technical aspect of foods. Several Washington law firms specialize in federal food regulatory matters, much of their work involving the almost 2,000 food additives used by U.S. processors. Associations such as the Food and Drug Law Institute, National Agricultural Chemicals Association, and Animal Health Institute keep busy working on the highly technical matters of federal food regulation.

The most effective of the Washington food and farm groups, in terms of influencing regulations and legislation and having their voices heard, are the specialized commodity organizations, those which concentrate on milk, fertilizer, feed, feed grains, cattle, or chickens. They know the ins and outs of how government actions will affect their commodities, and they can draw on very specialized expertise from within their industry to deal with Washington. The general farm organizations have become too general, too watered down, and too slow-moving.

Right at the top among the specialized farm groups with the most clout in Washington is the American National Cattlemen's Association, a well-financed Denver-based organization which represents the nation's ranchers and feeders. ANCA has a record for getting things done on tax, meat import, and land-use issues. Its chief lobbyist is C. W. (Bill) McMillan, who believes that a Washington association lobbyist is really a quarterback, advising his client where and when and how to get things done, rallying support from members at the most opportune time, and "not troubling congressmen with matters until they are starting to think about them anyhow." ANCA's most notable success in recent years was in fighting off a beef price rollback in early 1973. Two days before the House was to act, ANCA organized a "fly-in" of feedlot operators to convince House members that a price rollback would mean a production cutback and even higher beef prices. ANCA also loses a few, such as a recent fight with the National Broiler Council on whether chicken should be allowed in hot dogs.

The National Cotton Council of America has its power enhanced by the fact that chairmen of the Senate and House agriculture committees have often been from the Cotton Belt. The council's top staff man is Albert Russell, Memphis-based—a man who has a way for making his opinions known in Washington. Macon Edwards heads up the Washington office. The most active group in fighting for higher dairy supports and for blocking foreign dairy product sales in the U.S. is the National Milk Producers Federation. The federation represents milk cooperatives, but it was not involved in the illegal campaign contributions made by some member co-ops, a point which NMPF executive vice president Patrick Healy wants to make sure that Congress understands. The American Meat Institute is an organization for packers and processors. Its top staff man, Richard E. Lyng, was until recently USDA's assistant secretary for consumer and marketing affairs, including meat inspection programs.

The various sugar groups in Washington have a wheeler-dealer reputation which is probably somewhat exaggerated (although the registered lobbyists for the old sugar quota countries were known for cutting corners). Until the Sugar Act expired, most of the sugar republics looking for a chunk of the U.S. import quotas retained high-priced Washington law firms. The American Sugar Cane League is represented by Horace Godfrey, who had been in charge of sugar and other agricultural programs as administrator of the Agricultural Stabilization and Conservation Service under President Johnson. The U.S. Cane Sugar Refiners' Association, headed by Irv Hoff, is one of the most influential commodity groups.

The Grocery Manufacturers of America speaks for food processors on such matters as labeling, fortification, and inspection requirements. It led the assault in 1974 on legislation to set up a separate federal agency for consumer advocacy. GMA's top hand is George Koch, formerly a lobbyist for Sears, Roebuck & Co. The National Association of Food Chains, the trade association for supermarkets, is one of the most active associations in Washington. Chief staff man is Clarence (Clancy) Adamy, a hard-driving and highly regarded association executive who often disputes USDA food price and margin figures. The National Agricultural Chemicals Association represents pesticide manufacturers. The president is Parke Brinkley, a former commissioner of agriculture for Virginia. The Animal Health Institute is supported by animal drug manufacturers and has been effective in quietly heading off FDA proposals which it thinks are too restrictive. Fred Holt, a former journalist (as are many Washington trade association officials), heads AHI.

The grain and feed industries have an impressive track record in influencing legislation and agency actions. The National Grain and Feed Association, headed by Alvin Oliver, and the American Feed Manufacturers Association, under the direction of Oakley M. Ray, are the two key associations. Companies such as Ralston Purina, Continental Grain, Cargill, Bunge, Cook Industries, and General Mills all have their own Washington offices. The activities of the company representatives have a big influence on the positions that the associations take.

In food regulatory matters, the National Canners Association president, Charles Carey, is a power. In recent years, NCA has led a loose coalition of food and agribusiness groups in opposing farm bargaining legislation promoted by the American Farm Bureau Federation.

The American Farm Bureau Federation with headquarters in Chicago is the biggest, most conservative, and most influential of the general farm organizations. The Farm Bureau favors disentanglement of agriculture from government, a freer hand for farmers to produce for the market, fewer controls and subsidies. Some of its members have been critical of the Farm Bureau recently for being too quiet in Washington, not flexing its muscles more often. One of the reasons that it hasn't been noisier is that its policies have been generally embraced by both the Nixon and the Ford administrations.

The leadership at USDA since 1969—Clifford Hardin, Earl Butz, Clarence Palmby, Carroll Brunthaver, Don Paarlberg, Clayton Yeutter—either have been Farm Bureau members or are closely allied to its philosophy. When he was House minority leader, Gerald Ford leaned heavily on the Farm Bureau for advice on agricultural matters and met regularly with Michigan Farm Bureau officials. This close relationship was strained in October 1974, when Ford stalled a wheat and corn sale to Russia and imposed prior approval requirements for grain exports. The Farm Bureau's top hand in Washington is Roger Fleming, secretary-treasurer, who has a major input into the organization's policymaking. The Farm Bureau is well organized and especially strong at the state and local levels. It is weakest on Capitol Hill, with a reputation for being too conservative and uncompromising.

The National Farmers Union is aligned politically on the other side of the fence. It is liberal, brash at times—siding with organized labor, consumer groups, and the Democrats much more often than with the Republicans. It has traditionally favored controlling agricultural production, federal farm supports, grain reserves, shields against corporate invasion of agriculture, and protection of farm laborers. NFU's chief lobbyist is Reuben Johnson. Farmers Union likes to organize farmer "fly-ins" to Washington, farmers and their wives calling on congressmen to press NFU policies.

National Farmers Organization, best known for its group marketing programs and for milk dumping and calf slaughtering, is represented in Washington by Charles Frazier, a former USDA employee who spends much of his time pushing legislation to reduce corporate inroads in agriculture.

The National Grange is the only general farm organization with its headquarters in Washington. It has its own building two blocks from the White House, on some of the most expensive real estate in the city, adjoining one of the new buildings of the Executive Office of the President. The Grange's impact on food-farm issues is minor because its membership is relatively small in the Corn Belt and chief livestock-producing areas. (Among people who work in the Lafayette Park area of Washington, the Grange is best known for growing corn and a few other plants each year on a three-foot strip of dirt between the sidewalk in front of its building and the street.)

Although the crusty old midwestern and southern farm bloc is just a memory, and mammoth farm programs have been picked apart and discarded, food is going to remain on center stage in Washington for years to come. The world will look to the U.S. to help cope with the hunger of a rising population.

There are sound reasons to believe that the U.S. agricultural plant will be able to take care of the American food needs in the years ahead—at a cost of less than 20 percent of family take-home pay. And the U.S. will also raise enough to continue exporting food—at least through the year 2000. Farm exports will continue to account for the output from about one in every four acres harvested in the U.S.—about two-thirds of the wheat production, two-thirds of the rice output, half the soybean crop, and a fifth of the corn sales. Roughly half of the $15 billion increase in realized net farm income in 1973 was the result of farm exports. The importance of exports to the agricultural economy will grow further in the final decades of this century. There is still room for improvement in yields per acre in the U.S. and also in developing countries overseas that look to Washington for help.

Over the long haul, years of serious surplus production will be rare. More common will be the periods when food supplies and food demand are in precarious balance or when the supply is far short of the demand. Experts agree that the importance of the U.S. in meeting world food needs is not temporary, a result of recent crop failures or devaluation of the dollar. Although the U.S. has only 6 percent of the world's population and less than 1 percent of the farm laborers, it will continue to be the leader in agricultural exports. A sixth or more of the value of world farm product trade originates from the U.S., year after year. World demand for U.S. food will keep growing long after effects of crop failures and economic turmoil in 1972–74 are stabilized.

Looking ahead, Washington's farm and food policies will be tuned to producing more food, not on devising Rube Goldberg-type ways to handle surpluses.

36 MONTHLY CHECKS FOR MILLIONS

Every month, government aid checks help support more than 74 million people in the United States. The beneficiaries of these checks are men, women and children—the aged, the disabled, the blind, pensioners, social security retirees, low-income families, students and recipients of other forms of government aid. About half the payments go for what is popularly called "welfare." The other half are for past services rendered (like pensions and social security payments) or to help people become productive in the future (education grants, job training, and so on).

This year the government will issue 750 million checks to individuals for one or another kind of personal support. You may argue whether such statistics are signs of progress or decay, but the fact is that well over a third of the American people receive regular financial support through government channels (not counting nearly five million people who work as federal employees or as members of the armed forces).

The annual government outlay for all these payments has been estimated at $138.3 billion for the fiscal year 1975, but by the time the final returns are in, the figure probably will be higher than that. A congressional study by the Joint Economic Committee has found that, between 1968 and 1974, the number of beneficiaries rose 50 percent, even before the surge of additional claims brought on by the recession of 1974–75. In the same period, the dollar went up 170 percent. Both inflation and recession have taken their toll, but much of the bigger bill traces to new programs. In the past ten years the federal government has added or increased job training allowances, grants to students, school lunch programs, medicare and medicaid, legal services for the poor, and other antipoverty programs. While some of the funding today is lean, the programs are there and the built-in escalation of cost will be permanent.

Although many of these programs do not fit a strict "welfare" definition, they are described by government as "income transfer programs," and they involve checks—checks by the millions. The "people programs" of assistance (whether for "need," disability, or retirement) now account for 45 percent of the federal budget, compared with 30 percent in 1968. And if the figures seem overwhelming, just remind yourself that the dollars flow out through at least twenty-one different channels, including the following programs:

Aid to families with dependent children (known as AFDC)	Old age and survivors insurance (under social security system)
Old age assistance	Disability insurance
Aid to the blind	Railroad retirement
Aid to the disabled	Civil service retirement
General assistance	Other federal employee retirement

Unemployment insurance
Workmen's compensation
Veterans' pensions
Veterans' compensation
National school lunch program
Food stamps

Food distribution
Public housing
Veterans' medical care
Medicare
Medicaid

The average yearly payment today is roughly $2,000 per recipient. Like all averages, of course, it conceals a wide range of differences. At one end of the scale, it may be the support for a welfare family headed by a single woman with dependent children. At the other, it may be the pension check for a retired top-level government executive. This average payment has risen from $476 in 1968. As recently as 1973 it was $1,300, compared with today's $2,000. The pace of the rise, fueled partly by inflation and partly by legislative increases in the programs, has started to raise some warning signals among thoughtful observers in Congress and the Executive Branch.

Since Washington is the focal point for policy underlying the government support programs, much of the rising controversy is heard here—on Capitol Hill, in research foundations, within the Social Security Administration, and throughout the offices of the Department of Health, Education and Welfare. It is within HEW that the government comes to grips with its people-help services.

HOW WE PAY THE COSTS

The foundation stone for federal social programs today is the Social Security system, created by act of Congress in 1935 and put into motion in 1937. In that first year, the tax was 1 percent each on employer and employee, based upon the first $3,000 of wages or salary. Today the rate is 5.85 percent on each (a total of 11.7 percent) on $14,100 of pay. What began as a trickle into the fund has enlarged into a river (and some fear may become a raging torrent).

The American people, in an effort to be generous with themselves, have been building a bigger and bigger edifice of support programs. The dispute these days no longer centers on whether such programs are warranted or desired. This was disposed of years ago. The question today is: How much can we afford? Financial experts and actuaries on Capitol Hill debate the question ad infinitum. Several years ago, Representative Wilbur Mills of Arkansas, then chairman of the powerful Ways and Means Committee, was restrained by some of his colleagues when he proposed increases in pay-out which were not sufficiently funded by the tax collection rates at the time. Even after cutting his initial proposals, he led the Congress in passage of the 20 percent increase, which became law in 1972.

Fundamentally, the question is how much the economy of the U.S. can carry. Whatever the financial arrangements, retirement benefits and other support programs for the nonworking populace are paid for out of the income of the working segment. The total production of goods and services will have to expand much faster in the future than it has in the past few years if it is to accommodate a still-growing population and also provide bigger pensions for more people. Men and women are retiring earlier and living longer. At the same time, the work week is being reduced and economic productivity is rising more slowly. The equation is falling short on one end. Younger people will find themselves working harder for those who will be collecting pensions. It is this thought which promotes the rising doubts about our ability to make good on the promises we have made to ourselves.

Some analysts forecast that the problem of higher pay-out costs will be met by letting inflation erode the real purchasing power of the monthly checks —by simple debasement of money. Others feel that the system will be shored up by millions of new workers coming into the labor market. It is true, of course, that more families now have two or more workers, and the contributions of these multiple-worker families could sweeten the kitty for a while, covering up the actuarial deficiencies that might still be present. However the figures are arranged, retirement benefits and other public social payments are a charge against the productive capacity of the nation. Future pensions will come out of future production, regardless of what today's operating statements look like. If all this seems a little vague or theoretical, apologies are extended. But the fact is that the answers to such questions carry with them the future security of millions of today's working men and women. Whether we can fulfill on our programs in years to come will depend on how much improvement we make in the productive capacity of our economy—so our social security in the final analysis will depend upon our economic strength, involving government policy on business, labor, and investment.

THE SOCIAL SECURITY UMBRELLA

Meanwhile, social security rolls along, providing retirement support for 27 million people, roughly one out of every eight in the country. No longer do high-incomers shun the checks. Chauffeur-driven Cadillacs drive up alongside battered Chevrolets to the social security office to let their owners fill out forms and records.

In addition, nearly all of the 23 million people who are sixty-five and over are covered by health insurance under medicare. Another 1.9 million disabled people under sixty-five have been covered by medicare. Social security officials say that 100 million people are now paying into the fund, counting employees and self-employed.

Unemployment compensation, which is now being paid to more than 6 million, is funded through employer payments, with the amounts varying from each employer, depending on the unemployment experience of the particular company or organization. Some unions, like the auto workers, have "supplemental unemployment benefits" (SUBs) which bring workers and their families enough extra income to sustain them during lay-off periods without drastic changes in spending patterns. In 1972, total U.S. unemployment benefits were $6.4 billion, and the 1975 figure will be much higher, due to added unemployment and higher rates of pay.

Social security retirement benefits, plus medicare and unemployment benefits, account for the largest amount of money that flows into and out of the assistance pipeline, but the largest amount of controversy surrounds other kinds of social aid—those for "the needy," "the poor," "the disadvantaged." The statistics are hard to unravel, because it is commonplace for one family or household to benefit from a number of different kinds of help: aid to dependent children, food stamps, disability pay, public housing, free school lunches, rent supplements, extra-early schooling, educational opportunity grants, and so on. If all the benefits were added together, a mother and four children in Portland, Oregon, theoretically could receive money or services worth $13,800 a year. Actually, such a case is unlikely, but more and more families—aided by up-to-date antipoverty legal staffs—are learning to put their benefits together and fashion a support package that provides for more than just "meat and potatoes."

When the Joint Economic Committee of the House and Senate issued its comprehensive study of public welfare in 1974, it concluded that "much of the information needed to evaluate the performance of our public welfare system has yet to be collected." On this most people agree, yet even in the absence of final and definitive data, a consensus is forming—among liberals, conservatives, and middle-of-the-roaders—that the welfare system needs overhauling.

NEW IDEAS ON WELFARE

One of the recent ironies in welfare reexamination is that the Nixon administration, which promised "leaner government institutions" and more self-reliance on the part of the poor, actually proposed a "Family Allowance Plan" (FAP) which would have provided a basic minimum income for all families. In earlier days, a Republican administration would have regarded such a plan as an inexcusable "handout." But the Nixon idea was to dissolve many of the individual programs for the poor, dismantle the administrative machinery, and let the low-income families operate in the open marketplace. In the face of a cool reception from Congress and a lack of push from the administration, the proposal slowly withered away.

Yet today, other plans are being proposed. The Ford administration, working along similar lines, leans toward an income supplement program that would replace the present welfare programs with a $22 billion "cash transfer" plan. The Ford plan would be keyed to work incentives, and government grants would be reduced as a family's income rose, somewhat in the manner of the "negative income tax" proposed by conservative economist Milton Friedman of Chicago in the early 1960s. If the Ford plan were adopted whole hog, it would do away with food stamps, supplementary security income, and aid to families with dependent children (AFDC).

Some welfare analysts, including Richard Nathan of the Brookings Institution, support the basic idea of an income guarantee but disagree with the actual amount proposed ($3,600) and also with the simultaneous abolition of the food programs. In his view, this would shortchange poor families and leave them worse off than they are now.

Whatever the outcome of the current debate, more and more students of welfare seem to be gravitating toward the all-cash approach. Some espouse it because they do not like the proliferation of federal bureaucracy. Some favor it because they think it would give the poor more freedom of choice. Both elements seem to think it would be less cumbersome—for recipients and the government. In any event, it is not likely that welfare costs will drop in the near future. Whether the long upward staircase will finally reach a landing and level off remains to be seen, but it does not seem likely within the present decade.

If anyone had gone to sleep in 1932 and awakened forty-three years later, he would hardly believe his eyes. Until the social changes of the mid-1930s came about, the federal government provided for the defense of the nation, ran the courts, supervised the antitrust laws, collected taxes, regulated interstate commerce, and subsidized a few major industries. But to most Americans in times past who read the preamble to the Constitution, the phrase "promote the general welfare" did not mean paying out billions of dollars to millions of individuals (except old soldiers, their widows, and offspring).

But now look. "The general welfare," in terms of direct payments, is embedded in the social consciousness and federal budget more deeply than anything else. Defense budgets fluctuate. Agricultural payments are trimmed. Railroad subsidies are out of fashion. And even the oil depletion allowance has fallen on evil times. But the level of public payments to individuals has had its sharpest rise within the past ten years. In 1964 federal outlays for social insurance, public aid, veterans' programs, and miscellaneous social-welfare programs (leaving out health-and-medical and education) cost $204 for every man, woman, and child in the population. (Note: This is *not* the average payment to recipients, but the average amount paid out per member of the population.) Ten years later, the figure was close to $650 per capita.

Measured in constant dollars—after making allowance for inflation—the "income maintenance" curve has been steadily upward in all categories—more steeply in public assistance, somewhat less so for social insurance, although the economic slowdown of the early Seventies and the recession of 1974–1975 tended to accelerate the curve. In 1964, for example, "public aid" payments on a per capita basis were $32. Ten years later, they were close to $140. Population growth and inflation both have contributed to the rise in welfare and related expenditures. But the per capita and deflated figures indicate that a rise in real payments has taken place despite inflation.

The number of persons receiving federal welfare payments annually has risen by 60 percent in the past ten years, when population was rising only 10 percent. The bulk of this increase has come in aid to families with dependent children, where the number of recipients rose 15 percent.

In the same ten years, the number of families eligible for such aid also nearly tripled, from just over a million in 1964 to about 3.2 million in 1974, while the number of dependent children in this category rose from about 3.2 million in 1964 to 7.8 million a decade later. A substantial but unknown number of these families were headed by only one adult.

Payments to veterans, their dependents, and survivors have risen substantially—from about $4 billion in 1964 to $6.8 billion ten years later. But the number of beneficiaries has remained virtually unchanged at about 3.2 million persons. In other words, the average payment rose from $1,250 to $2,125, an increase of some 70 percent.

You can interpret such figures in a number of ways, but the broad picture that emerges is one of a nation growing increasingly beneficent toward its citizens who are disabled—physically, mentally, socially, economically—and to those who have performed in the public service as civilian employees or uniformed veterans. Whatever method or system comes out of the present debate on welfare and social security reform, it is not likely that the U.S. will sharply alter the commitment out of which the present system grew. The policy of government-guaranteed support for more and more people has a strong consensus of U.S. public opinion behind it, but unless the American economy becomes more productive in the years ahead, U.S. citizens will find themselves splitting the pie into smaller and smaller pieces. In the end, welfare and social security will be worth only as much as economic productivity can make them.

37 MONITORING THE ENVIRONMENT

When Washington plunged into "the environment" some ten years ago, it got a lot more headaches than it bargained for. "The environment" turned out to be the one issue (or bundle of issues) that knows no definition, no boundaries, no limits of potential federal involvement.

Environmentalism is everything that affects the quality of physical life (and, by extension, the emotional and spiritual life) in America. It is far more than the concerns once grouped under the heading of "conservation," such as parks and forests, preservation of scenic beauty, and management of natural resources and wildlife. Today environmentalism covers everything from pure air to historic preservation; from clean water to birth control; from recycled beer cans to mass transit; from strip-mining regulation to ocean-dumping treaties; from zoning to protection of wild mustangs; from noise control to bans on dangerous pesticides; from inner-city playgrounds to weather modification.

At the start of the Seventies, it appeared that nothing would get in the way of the steamrolling national commitment to a cleaner environment. Then came the worldwide fuel crunch, and the need for new sources of fuel became a competitive national commitment that threatened progress in the environment. Every facet of the energy question involves tradeoffs and balances between these two commitments. For example, greater use of high-sulfur coal would lessen the nation's dependence on oil, but would increase air pollution. Exploration of the West's vast oil shale reserves would lessen dependence on foreign oil, but at what cost to the ecology of Rocky Mountain states? Auto emission standards improve air quality but hamper gas mileage. Offshore oil drilling unlocks much-needed reserves, but at a risk to shoreline ecology. And one of the major obstacles to increased electric generation by atomic energy is concern over potential dangers both to the environment and to human health. These are just a few of the many interlocking pieces in the energy-environment puzzle with which Washington deals.

Washington got into environmental problems in the first place because many of them are interstate problems that called for uniform federal standards. Furthermore, environmentalists have felt that Congress is more hospitable to environmental legislation than many state legislatures, which are closer to local business interests. When citizen concern over the environment came alive all over the nation during the Sixties, giving rise to vocal national movements, Washington was the obvious pressure point, for it had been involved in the issues ever since Theodore Roosevelt's days. In the matter of money, the federal government has always been able to get hold of large sums of taxes more easily than the states, so federal grants-in-aid became a convenient tool for environmental encouragement.

Responsibility for quality-of-life matters is dispersed throughout more federal departments, agencies, and committees than any other issue in Washington. At the top of the command chain is the Council of Environmental Quality (CEQ), a White House advisory body with little statutory responsibility but a lot of power when it wants to assert itself. The nuts-and-bolts task of overseeing the whole federal environmental crusade falls to the Environmental Protection Agency (EPA), created in late 1970 in a consolidation and reorganization of several existing agencies. Beneath the CEQ and the EPA there is a sprawling array of agencies each with a piece of the action. Some fifteen agencies are involved in something that could be called "environmental protection." Some eleven agencies attempt to improve man's understanding, description, and prediction of the natural surroundings. On a more particular level: six agencies in three Cabinet departments administer federal recreation areas, four agencies in two departments manage federally owned land, parts of three departments manage water resources. In the largest sense, every federal body has at least an indirect role in environmental protection, owing to the requirement that every major federal action be preceded by an "environmental impact statement." Some environmental agencies run at cross-purposes with each other. It is not surprising in Washington to find one agency trying to preserve the very swamp that another one would like to drain.

Plans to consolidate similar environmental functions into a new Cabinet department have been kicking around Washington for decades, ranging from Harold Ickes's New Deal–proposed Department of Conservation to the Nixon plan for a Department of Energy and Natural Resources. Except for the creation of the EPA and NOAA (the National Oceanic and Atmospheric Administration), none of these plans has gone anywhere, because federal agencies traditionally resist all efforts to diminish their independence by merger.

SHARED RESPONSIBILITY

The Executive Branch, of course, has no monopoly on environmental policymaking. Most of the rules and standards that these agencies execute were written (or at least roughed in) on Capitol Hill, where environmental jurisdiction is equally fragmented. Seven House committees (Appropriations, Agriculture, Government Operations, Interior and Insular Affairs, Interstate and Foreign Commerce, Merchant Marine and Fisheries, and Public Works) have environment subcommittees, as do five Senate committees (Appropriations, Agriculture and Forestry, Commerce, Interior and Insular Affairs, and Public Works). And the federal courts, especially the U.S. District Court and Court of Appeals for the District of Columbia, hear the pleadings of participants in the environmental struggle—citizen activists, businessmen, bureaucrats, scientists, and the new breed of environmental law specialists. The judicial decisions often have the effect of writing new laws ranging from auto emissions to the Alaska pipeline.

How much money does the federal government spend in environmental activities each year? It's largely a matter of definition. The Office of Management and Budget, which prepares the federal budget, puts the figure at about $7 billion for fiscal 1975, a little more than 2 percent of the $315 billion current federal budget. The bulk of this money—more than $4 billion in fiscal 1975—is distributed to state and local governments for the construction and modernization of sewage treatment facilities, the principal weapons in the fight against water pollution. Less than $1 billion is spent on air pollution, mostly on research and development to determine safe levels of various pollutants, devise monitoring systems and emergency plans, enforce federal standards, and provide technical assistance.

The rest of the environmental money is spread over the environmental divisions of such departments as Interior, Agriculture, Defense, and Commerce. Interior, which gets the lion's share, includes such old-line agencies as the Bureau of Land Management, whose 450 million acres in the Far West and Alaska amount to 20 percent of the entire U.S. land area; the Bureau of Outdoor Recreation; the National Park Service, which operates nearly 300 parks, historic sites, and monuments in 47 states, plus the District of Columbia, Puerto Rico, and the Virgin Islands (covering 29 million acres); and the Bureau of Sport Fisheries and Wildlife, which administers 95 hatcheries and 356 wildlife refuges containing some 31 million acres.

The principal environmental activity of the Department of Agriculture is the Forest Service (founded in 1905), which manages the nation's 187 million acres of national forest. This rich natural resource is operated under a plan called the Multiple Use Sustained Yield Act, which allows commercial lumbering and mineral mining to an extent (in the words of the federal budget) "that will best protect resources without impairing the productivity of the land," while providing recreation and wildlife protection at the same time. The Forest Service frequently incurs the wrath of conservationists who contend it is more interested in leasing federal lands to lumbermen than protecting natural life. The Soil Conservation Service (SCS), also in Agriculture, devises and implements soil and water management plans in agricultural areas. The SCS's goals of increasing cultivable land area by "channelizing" meandering streams have often been at odds with the rising "leave-it-alone" spirit of environmental protection.

Over at the Commerce Department is the National Oceanic and Atmospheric Administration (NOAA), a collection of eight previously separate federal agencies, including the Weather Service. NOAA engages in everything from weather prediction and modification experiments to coastal wetlands management, from deep-sea exploration to marine mammal protection. It also administers laws aimed at protecting whales and fur seals, whose danger of extinction has been a particularly fervent concern of environmentalists in recent years.

Other environmental projects are scattered all over the Washington bureaucracy. The Federal Aviation Administration and the National Aeronautics and Space Administration (NASA) have responsibility for the adverse effects of aviation, such as noise, pollution, and sonic booms. The Smithsonian Institution collects data on plants and animals for use in studying the effects of environmental change on natural life. The Federal Highway Administration of the Department of Transportation works on ways to minimize highway noise (including ways to make quieter diesel engines) and soil erosion due to road building. The Army Corps of Engineers administers the federal program under which dredged and fill materials may not be dumped into navigable waterways without a permit. The Interior Department's Bureau of Mines conducts research into methods of reducing environmental damage at strip-mining sites, and is also studying techniques for inexpensive conversion of coal to low-pollution fuel gas. The Department of Housing and Urban Development studies the impact of urbanization. And so it goes in hundreds of offices around Washington.

THE ROOTS OF CONCERN

In the United States, as in other developed parts of the world, the "environmental spirit" came over people only after they had achieved a high standard of living. In many younger nations still developing, environmental concerns tend to be viewed as luxuries that are secondary to creation of jobs and exploitation of natural resources. In nineteenth-century America, smoke billowing from factory chimneys was a sign of well-being. The nation's resources—including pure air and water—seemed to be a limitless bounty that needed no protection. This attitude extended well into the twentieth century, bucked only by the unpopular warnings of naturalists like Henry David Thoreau, the landscape architect and federal park crusader Frederick Law Olmstead, and Sierra Club founder John Muir.

Washington first entered the environmental picture during the Presidency of Theodore Roosevelt. In partnership with Forest Service Director Gifford Pinchot, he forged a new national policy of conservation and rational use of timber and mineral resources. As a great lover of the out-of-doors, Roosevelt withdrew some 234 million acres of public land from commercial bidding, creating many national forests, parks, and mineral reserves. He established the first national wildlife refuges, and in 1908 held the first White House conference on the environment. The "Rough Rider's" intent was merely to set aside chunks of natural territory, not to dictate to private citizens and businesses what they might or might not do to the environment in the course of conducting their private business affairs and managing their private property.

The depression accidentally gave the movement a shot in the arm. A decade of droughts in the West and Midwest underscored the folly of overgrazing, clear-cutting of forests, and other agricultural techniques that wasted precious soil and moisture. The most spectacular environmental project of the New Deal—the Civilian Conservation Corps—addressed crises in both natural and human resources. It employed hundreds of thousands of jobless young men, putting them to work planting millions of trees, revegetating range land, building ponds and fences for cattle, developing nature preserves, and improving recreational facilities in parks. The depression was also a period of widespread damming of rivers into reservoirs for water supply and electric generation. Decades later, dams would come under fire as antiecological, but during the depression they were seen as valuable federal projects to serve both the environment and the economy.

In the Forties and Fifties, it was back to business as usual on the quality-of-life front. The environment took a back seat to the war in Europe and the Pacific, followed by postwar economic recovery and the industrial boom of the Fifties, which spawned a prosperous middle-class consumer economy and spreading suburbia. But prosperity took its toll. Many rivers and lakes succumbed to biological deterioration from agricultural fertilizer runoffs, silt from construction sites, raw sewage, and industrial wastes. Wildlife suffered from accumulations of pesticides that had helped boost crop yields. The number of motor vehicles increased geometrically, fogging the skies of America's cities with a haze of auto exhaust.

By the early Sixties, the effects of zooming industrial growth were painfully evident to nearly everyone. Eyes were opened by such books as *The Quiet Crisis,* written in 1963 by Stewart Udall, Secretary of the Interior in the Kennedy and Johnson administrations, and Rachel Carson's *Silent Spring,* which attacked the dangers of certain pesticides. In 1967, the oil tanker *Torrey Canyon* went aground and collapsed off the southern coast of England, polluting hundreds of miles of beaches with 80,000 tons of crude oil. Closer to home, in 1969 a Union Oil Company well blew out in a federally owned oil field in the channel off Santa Barbara, California, coating the beaches and killing thousands of shore birds. Secretary of the Interior Walter J. Hickel, who had taken office just a few days before the Santa Barbara spill, observed that his authority to suspend drilling in such cases was based not on environmental considerations, but on the need to prevent the wasting of valuable oil. Hickel, who surprised many people by turning out to be a strong environmentalist, promptly ordered a review of federal oil and gas leasing regulations, with greater emphasis on ecological considerations.

AN AVALANCHE OF BILLS

Congress, which has a knack for spotting a fast-rising popular issue, wasted no time in translating citizen concern into legislation. In 1964 some 250 environmental bills were introduced in the Senate and House, a volume that would swell to an estimated 8,000 bills by 1970. Many of the bills were duplicative of others, and many were grandstanding gestures that had a negligible chance of consideration by any committee, let alone of passage. But out of the legislative outpouring of the Sixties and early Seventies came some major laws, such as the Wilderness Act, the Wild and Scenic Rivers Act, the landmark Clean Air Act Amendments of 1970 (which set auto emission standards), and the most costly environmental bill ever, the Federal Water Pollution Control Amendments, which authorized an expenditure of nearly $18 billion on waste-treatment construction over a three-year period.

The most important legislation passed in that hectic period was the National Environmental Policy Act (NEPA), adopted by Congress in 1969 and signed into law by President Nixon on January 1, 1970. NEPA put no environmental restrictions on any private individual or company, nor on any state or local government. It was aimed solely at the federal government itself, and was designed to make every major federal action responsive to environmental considerations. For the first time in history, every proposed highway, dam, office building, pipeline, power plant, airport, channel improvement, lease of mineral rights, or any other project that used federal funds or a federal permit would have to pass environmental muster *before* work commenced. The medium for all this was the so-called 102 process (from Section 102, requiring an "environmental impact statement").

NEPA was born after several years of congressional hearings, investigations, studies, prototype bills, squabbles over committee jurisdiction, and compromises both within and between the two chambers of Congress. Earlier traces of NEPA can be found in a seminal "Congressional White Paper on a National Policy for the Environment," developed by Senate Interior Committee Chairman Henry Jackson (D-Wash.) and former Representative Emilio Daddario (D-Conn.), whose House Subcommittee on Science, Research and Development had become an early champion of environmental improvement.

NEPA came closer to fruition when Jackson picked up and expanded a bill introduced previously by Senator Gaylord Nelson, a leading conservationist since his days as a Democratic governor of Wisconsin. Senator Edmund Muskie (D-Me.), a powerful advocate as chairman of the Public Works Subcommittee on Air and Water Pollution (now called the Subcommittee on Environment and Pollution), introduced a similar bill called the Environmental Quality Improvement Act, but Jackson's bill prevailed.

Meanwhile, over on the House side of Capitol Hill, NEPA was championed by Representative John Dingell (D-Mich.), who had transformed an obscure fisheries and wildlife subcommittee into an environmental stronghold. Dingell succeeded in keeping NEPA out of the jurisdiction of Representative Wayne Aspinall (D-Col.), the development-oriented House Interior Committee chairman who had kept the Wilderness Act bottled up in committee for eight years. So NEPA was passed by the House in a strange form, as an amendment to the Fish and Wildlife Act of 1946.

NEPA was immediately seized by environmental activists as their principal weapon to halt, delay, or modify federal projects that they deemed disastrous to the environment. Between 1970 and 1973, more than 400 lawsuits were filed charging violations of NEPA. Filing suit in federal courts throughout the nation, the environmental lobby won judgments that federal agencies had to file impact statements for projects that the agencies had originally thought to be of little consequence to the environment; that agencies had to redo impact statements that had been hastily drafted to justify, after the fact, a project already under way; that agencies had to demonstrate not merely that they had prepared impact statements, but had given them serious weight in their decisionmaking. In one particularly far-reaching decision, the U.S. Court of Appeals for the District of Columbia ruled in 1973 that the AEC had to prepare an impact statement on its research and development program on liquid metal fast breeder nuclear reactors. The AEC had argued that impact statements would be necessary only for the construction of particular reactors of this type. The court disagreed, ruling that a large R&D investment would tend to prejudice the AEC toward eventual adoption of the system and make later environmental review less meaningful.

The NEPA process has produced some notable changes in policy. It led to an AEC decision to suspend indefinitely plans to dispose of radioactive wastes in salt mines beneath Lyons, Kansas, and in bedrock along the Savannah River in Georgia. It led to the rejection of oil and gas leasing applications for an area near Steamboat Lake, Colorado. It caused the Soil Conservation Service to decrease the degree of stream channelizing at a watershed project in Alabama and Tennessee. The Army Corps of Engineers, the favorite target of environmental activists, estimated in 1973 that it had abandoned some 24 projects, delayed 44 for further analysis, and substantially altered 200 others —all due to NEPA. More significantly, tens of additional federal actions have probably been nipped in the bud within agencies, because of the probability of a NEPA struggle if they had been publicly proposed.

ENVIRONMENTAL WATCHDOGS

A by-product of the National Environmental Policy Act was the creation of the Council on Environmental Quality, a three-member panel commissioned to "formulate and recommend policies to promote the improvement of the quality of the environment." Its offices are located just across Lafayette Park from the White House, in a restored Victorian townhouse. Here the CEQ has a small staff that monitors environmental activities at all levels of government and in the private sector. From 1970 until 1973, it was chaired by Russell E. Train, a respected conservationist and former federal tax judge who is now head of the Environmental Protection Agency. Train was succeeded by Russell Peterson, a former governor of Delaware who had presided over the enactment of that state's tough curbs on coastal industrial development.

The CEQ's role in the federal environmental structure has been ambiguous at times. Occasionally it has acted as an independent arbiter, coming down hard on ecologically unsound proposals of its sister agencies in the bureaucracy. In this vein, Russell Train suggested in 1971 that the Corps of Engineers correct deficiencies in the impact statement for the controversial Tocks Island Dam, a proposal (still pending) for a flood control and water supply project on the upper Delaware River between Pennsylvania and New Jersey.

On other occasions the CEQ has acted as a confidential adviser to the White House on environmental matters, and has not always kept the public informed of recommendations that it has made to the President or the outcome of those recommendations. In 1972 the CEQ submitted to the White House a confidential draft of an executive order restricting the much-criticized timbering practice of clear-cutting. The White House was originally favorable to the recommendation, but decided to ask the chief of the Forest Service to get comments on the proposal from the wood products industry, via the National Forest Products Association. Within a week, the White House was flooded with protests from lumbermen and congressmen from timber states, and the proposed executive order was quietly left to die. The CEQ made no public protest against the coziness of the decision process. When the details became known later, environmentalists complained that the opportunity for participating in an important decision had been shared with business interests but not with the public at large.

There is nothing ambiguous about the far-ranging responsibilities of the EPA, the independent environmental superagency. Its creation brought together under one authority the water quality programs of the Interior Department, air quality and solid waste management programs of the Department of Health, Education and Welfare, pesticide jurisdiction from the Department of Agriculture, radiation regulation from the Atomic Energy Commission, and miscellaneous other scattered responsibilities. As the chief implementer of federal antipollution standards in all of these areas, the EPA administrator is often under fire from all sides—from trade associations that complain the standards are too strict and from the environmental lobby that often feels EPA bends over backwards to accommodate business. The first EPA administrator, William D. Ruckelshaus (late of the Justice Department), set a standard of vigor and candor that has been continued under Train's leadership there.

EPA's powers are broad. It can ban the use of pesticides whose toxicity lingers too long in the environment, an action taken against DDT in 1972. It sets the specific standards for allowable air and water pollution, and reviews the permits that states must issue to business and municipalities which discharge wastes into waterways. EPA can get a federal court order to close any facility that fails to meet its antipollution standards, as it did in 1974 with the Reserve Mining Company plant on Lake Superior. As watchdog of the 1970 Clean Air Amendments, EPA determines the degree of auto pollution permitted in auto exhaust and the deadlines for compliance. The administrator is also empowered to postpone a deadline, owing to such mitigating factors as technological barriers, potential employment dislocations, or fuel shortages. In the broadest application of its power, the EPA has drafted multifaceted air pollution plans for every large metropolitan area in the nation, calling for combinations of such tactics as reduced downtown parking, car pooling, better mass transit, and increased auto inspections. Some of the EPA's proposed programs—such as a stiff surcharge tax on downtown parking (essentially a "commuter tax") and reduced gasoline sales—have been greeted less than enthusiastically by many. After extensive public hearings, for example, EPA abandoned a 1973 draft proposal for Los Angeles that would have curtailed gasoline sales (and presumably auto use) by as much as 82 percent from May to October, the "smog season" in southern California.

Between 1971 and 1974 the federal environmental effort was severely hampered by stingy, strings-attached budgeting by the House Agriculture Appropriations Subcommittee, chaired by Representative Jamie L. Whitten (D-Miss.). Whitten, a thirty-five-year House veteran, is no fan of an energetic federal role in much of anything—except price supports for Delta cotton planters. He has consistently been a foe of environmental and consumer activism, and in 1966 his subcommittee staff authored a pro-pesticide book that was subsidized and promoted by several chemical companies. Yet for nearly four years his subcommittee passed judgment on the budgets of not only the Consumer Product Safety Commission and the Office of Consumer Affairs, but much of the federal environmental structure—the CEQ, EPA, and National Commission on Water Quality. Whitten has occasionally attached budgetary conditions that have the effect of negating an agency's statutory authority. The fiscal 1975 EPA appropriation, for example, prohibited the agency from spending its funds in such a way as to "reduce the supply or increase the cost of electricity to the consumer." This sweeping condition, if followed to the letter, would neutralize the EPA's air-quality program as it applies to coal-burning electric generation plants.

In early 1975, faced with a challenge to his chairmanship, Whitten voluntarily surrendered jurisdiction over consumer and environmental budgets to the Appropriations Subcommittee on HUD, Space Science, and Veterans, which covered these fields until 1971. Chaired by Representative Edward Boland (D-Mass.), the subcommittee is expected to be far more hospitable to conservation interests.

CITIZEN LOBBIES

Looking over the shoulder of the federal agencies and congressional committees is a phalanx of environmental action groups that form a kind of "environmental lobby." Several of the environmental groups active in Washington have very deep roots, such as the Sierra Club (1892), the National Audubon Society (1905), the National Parks and Conservation Association (1919), the Izaak Walton League (1922), the Wilderness Society (1935), and the National Wildlife Federation (1936). But environmental lobbying, as it is practiced today, dates only from the early 1950s, when a conservation coalition first used scientific studies to block construction of a dam in Colorado that would have inundated a section of Dinosaur National Monument. In 1954, in connection with that battle, the first environmental lobbyists registered with the House and Senate for the express purpose of influencing public policy. Barely two decades later, there were more than thirty such registered lobbyists working on Capitol Hill, backed up by office staffs totaling several hundred people.

The lobby in Washington mushroomed with passage of NEPA and the other detailed antipollution laws in the late Sixties and early Seventies. New organizations were founded that tended to be more militant than the older organizations. These focus largely on legislative and legal action, rather than supplying the traditional services to citizen members (conservation publications, outings, discussion groups, etc.). Organizations like the Environmental Defense Fund, the Natural Resources Defense Council, Friends of the Earth, Environmental Action, the Environmental Policy Center, Zero Population Growth, and others have plunged into litigation covering everything from pesticides, land use planning, and nuclear power to dams, clear-cutting, and auto emissions.

During the heady era following Earth Day in 1970, ecology groups multiplied like amoeba—spinning off, splintering, and merging with dizzying speed. The Environmental Policy Center, for example, gave birth to such specialized lobbies as the Coalition to Stop Strip Mining, the American Rivers Conservation Council, and the League of Conservation Voters (which rates, endorses, and raises money for pro-environment members of Congress). Those groups which exist largely on citizen contributions have had to be careful about political activity that might jeopardize their federal tax exemption. The venerable Sierra Club overstepped the fine line in 1966 when it bought full-page ads opposing a proposed federal dam across the Colorado River just below the Grand Canyon National Park. The IRS moved on the Sierra Club within days (much faster than normal), and the group lost its exemption.

The nature lobbyists win some battles (like the supersonic transport plane) and lose some others (like the Alaska pipeline), but on balance their record has been awesome, especially considering the greater financial resources and staffs of the industrial trade associations with whom they often joust in Congress. In the spring of 1973 the environmental lobby and the highway lobby were locked in battle over a House bill to use some funds from the Highway Trust Fund in support of mass transit. The members of the mammoth highway lobby (industries such as the road builders, rubber manufacturers, oil industry, and automakers) poured money and manpower into the contest. (A week before the vote, a delegation of 125 Georgia truckers, contractors, and motel owners visited Washington, entertained the entire Georgia congressional delegation at lunch, and then asked each legislator to stand and declare how he was going to vote.) The environmentalist Highway Action Coalition reported only $3,000 spent on its lobbying effort, but managed to convince a majority of the House that the time had come to beef up mass transit funding. In the final vote, the Highway Trust Fund was opened up for limited funding of mass transit.

There have been other successes, with more of them won through the courts than in Congress. The Environmental Defense Fund led the attack on DDT and the Cross-Florida Barge Canal. The Natural Resources Defense

Council was successful in assuring an ecological review of the oil leasing program in the Gulf of Mexico and the Soil Conservation Service's stream channelizing, and won a ban on DES, a cancer-inducing growth stimulant used to fatten cattle.

LEADERS ON THE HILL

The growing political clout of the nature lobby—coupled with the continued popularity of the issue with grass-roots voters—has not been lost on Congress, where it is difficult to find any member these days who doesn't boast of being a longtime environmentalist. Their consciousness of the issue was heightened by the 1972 defeat of two well-entrenched Coloradans who were not noted for their environmental concern: House Interior Committee Chairman Wayne Aspinall and Senator Gordon Allott, the ranking Republican on the Senate Interior Committee, who once described environmentalists as "moral exhibitionists or pastoral romantics." Many of the new self-professed friends of the environment on Capitol Hill merely vote the right way when an important bill comes up. The real champions are the representatives and senators who are in the thick of the battles from start to finish: the likes of Representatives Dingell; Henry Reuss of Wisconsin; Ken Hechler, the West Virginian who took on the strip-mining industry; Morris Udall of Arizona, chief sponsor of land-use planning legislation; the aforementioned Senators Jackson, Muskie, and Nelson, as well as Senators Philip Hart of Michigan, Lee Metcalf of Montana, and Clifford P. Case of New Jersey.

One of the obstacles to the development of a strong "environmental bloc" in Congress is the fact that conservation doesn't pour federal money into congressional districts the way "pork barrel" projects do—projects that alter the environment for man's economic benefit. Thus, the Corps of Engineers, the Bureau of Reclamation, the Tennessee Valley Authority, and the Soil Conservation Service tend to have stronger bases of support on the Hill than agencies whose mission it is to keep the natural environment in its natural state. When George Bush (later GOP national chairman and emissary to the People's Republic of China) was a freshman Texas congressman in 1967, he backed a group of constituents who objected to a Corps of Engineers proposal to destroy a stream called Buffalo Bayou by turning it into a drainage ditch as wide as a football field. He went before the Public Works Subcommittee of the House Appropriations Committee to respectfully decline his share of the "pork barrel." Following his testimony, a veteran congressman tapped Bush on the shoulder and said, "Son, if you want to stay here—and get anywhere here—don't keep money from going to your district."

THE WHITE HOUSE AND THE ENVIRONMENT

The Nixon record on environmental affairs was very mixed, with a tendency toward tempering ecological concern with economic pragmatism. The administration pushed for development of the supersonic transport plane, despite the environmental warnings, because it felt that such an innovation in air travel was inevitable and that the U.S. should not risk losing out to other nations. The Nixon team continually backed the trans-Alaska pipeline on the grounds that the environmental harm would be negligible compared to the benefit of tapping those oil reserves. But in a surprisingly bold move, President Nixon halted construction of the Cross-Florida Barge Canal (into which more than $50 million had already been invested), to forestall what he called "potentially serious environmental damage." But soon thereafter, he attended a ceremony initiating construction of the Tennessee-Tombigbee Waterway, a facsimile of the barge canal that environmentalists, scientists, and even the EPA had grave doubts about.

Early in his administration, President Nixon declared that "the 1970s absolutely must be the years when America pays its debt to the past by reclaiming the purity of its air, its water and our living environment. It is literally now or never." But when Congress started spelling out the size of this debt, the President balked at asking taxpayers to meet the whole bill. Congress authorized the spending of $18 billion for sewer construction between fiscal years 1973 and 1975, and the President responded with a veto, claiming the amount was inflationary and more than the cities and states could absorb in that period of time. Congress overrode the veto, and the President then directed the EPA to withhold some of the money. It was only after several cities sued in federal court that they received their full allotments.

Equally dismaying to environmentalists was President Nixon's 1974 performance on the so-called land-use bill, a measure that would have set general federal guidelines for land-use planning and offered funds to set up state and local land-use commissions. The President had previously declared such legislation to be the nation's "number one environmental priority." The bill was backed by Interior Secretary Rogers C. B. Morton and by EPA Administrator Train, who said the bill "would give new force to efforts already under way in a number of states and communities to give the citizens of this country a real say in determining the course and quality of our physical growth." But as the battle lines were drawn in Congress, the White House fell strangely silent on the issue. A massive lobbying effort—headed by the U.S. Chamber of Commerce and joined by associations of home builders, cattlemen, construction trade unions, and the American Farm Bureau Federation—sent the bill down to defeat in the House, 211–204. (The supporters of the bill put on no less an effort, backed by such groups as AFL–CIO, the major state, county, and municipal associations, the National Association of Realtors, and the leading environmental groups.) Nixon's reversal on the issue was seen by many observers to have little to do with environmental considerations, and a lot to do with his desire to mollify conservative supporters for his own protection on the impeachment issue.

When the Arab oil embargo put a squeeze on the U.S., the White House began beating a hasty retreat from earlier proclaimed environmental standards, some of which (like the Clean Air Act of 1970) the White House hadn't been very happy with in the first place. In the spring of 1974, a consortium of the Federal Energy Office, the Office of Management and Budget, and the White House Domestic Council proposed a batch of amendments that would have weakened the Clean Air Act. The proposals included exempting coal-fired power plants from certain pollution standards until the mid-1980s and banning state air quality standards that exceeded federal standards. Most significantly, the administration suggested that all federal energy projects—which could include everything from nuclear power plants and hydroelectric dams to oil shale mining and offshore drilling—be exempted from the environmental review now required under NEPA.

These proposals for loosening the standards were strongly opposed by the administration's top environmental officials, the CEQ's Peterson and the EPA's Train. Train stated emphatically, "I'm going to fight against them to the last wire, because I don't think they're necessary and I do think they'd do substantial harm." Train stood his ground, in the face of obvious hostility from the White House, and the proposals were substantially altered (including a backing off of the NEPA waiver for energy projects) before being sent up to Capitol Hill. In the end, Congress put together its own bill, called the Energy Supply and Environmental Coordination Act of 1974, which did relax air pollution standards, but not as much as the administration had asked. Among other things, the bill postponed for one year (plus an additional year at the discretion of the EPA) auto exhaust emission standards that were originally set for 1976 car models; postponed deadlines for limiting downtown parking in certain pollution-ridden cities; and encouraged conversion of power plants from oil to coal if it could be done with minimal harm to the surroundings. (In the spring of 1975, Train suggested postponing the auto exhaust goals until the 1980 model year; he confessed that the catalytic converter pushed so enthusiastically by the EPA probably poses a health threat all its own—the production of sulfur gases.)

President Ford has basically continued the policies of his predecessor, complicated by further worsening of the inflation and energy situations. He infuriated environmentalists by vetoing a bill that would have required reclamation of strip-mined land. The product of a long congressional fight and many compromises, the bill was anything but extreme. As a matter of fact, some fervent opponents of strip mining thought it was nearly worthless. But supporters of the bill, including EPA and the Interior Department, considered it to be a good first step. In vetoing the legislation, Ford said it would trim coal output at a time when the nation could not afford any decrease in supply. (But most experts, including those in the federal bureaucracy, had testified that the loss of coal would be negligible, if there were any loss at all.) In early 1975, Congress was hard at work on a new strip mining bill not much different from the original legislation, and the White House was silent on the prospect of a veto.

THE SCOREBOARD

How is Washington doing in its first decade of the environment crusade?

The record is mixed. Today's automobiles are individually emitting fewer pollutants than before federal controls went into effect, but these gains are offset by the constantly increasing number of cars on the road. Sewage treatment by municipalities and industry is being rapidly upgraded, but the volume of liquid wastes is also mounting in most urban areas. In 1973 there were still several thousand community sewer systems that were discharging effluent that had either no treatment whatsoever or very inadequate mechanical filtering. Billions of additional dollars (most contributed by Uncle Sam) must be spent before municipal and industrial polluters will be able to meet strict federal standards by the end of the Seventies.

Progress is being made in the managing of solid wastes (the fancy word for "trash"). Using private technology and EPA experimental grants, municipalities have built plants that recover metal, glass, and paper fiber for resale, and factories that convert trash into fuels (liquid, solid, and gaseous) that can be burned to generate electric power.

Washington, of course, is not in the environmental business alone. Some of the most forceful initiatives are being taken at state and local levels. Oregon and Vermont, for example, have put restrictions on the sale of goods in disposable containers, which waste virgin materials and energy as well as present a problem of disposal. Over the past two decades, Oregon passed the laws necessary to restore the once filthy Willamette River to unusual purity (with the help of some $30 million in federal sewage treatment grants). A number of state and local governments have put controls on the phosphate content of detergents sold in their jurisdictions, to minimize the risk of algae pollution of rivers and lakes. Before the federal government became heavily involved in environmental protection, states were reluctant to pass stiff curbs that might drive industries into other states that were more lax. But with federal standards being set nationally today, businesses have no place to hide, and states are freer to impose stricter guidelines of their own.

Many facets of the environment transcend national boundaries. Ocean dumping of wastes, safe handling of oil in supertankers, and limits on the killing of whales and seals have international dimensions requiring cooperation among all nations. Each year sees more activity in international forums, conferences, and informal consultations.

In America, as in most other nations of the world, the crusade is closely linked to efforts to limit population growth. It is dawning on many people that a sound environment in the future will require the industrial nations to slow down the frantic pace at which they are consuming the earth's resources. If total population continues to soar, environmental rules will have a hard time coping with the problem of numbers. Environmental improvement, either consciously or unwittingly, is the impulse behind much of the "no growth" spirit that pervades zoning decisions today. It is closely related to the decline in America's birth rate.

Environmentalism is one of those issues that is often obscured by emotional rhetoric which separates the populace into "good guys" and "bad guys." But the goals of more jobs and more production—now considered business rallying cries—have actually had broad support and the tacit approval of a consumption-oriented citizenry. Today, people say they care about the environment. But do they care enough to foot the staggering bill that will be presented in the form of taxes, or as a hidden pass-through expense in prices for things they buy, or—as is most likely—some of both?

Problems get attention when the necessity gets great enough. One thing that politicians are not fond of doing is getting ahead of their constituencies. Foresight is a commonly applauded virtue, but in political life an elected official who acts with too much foresight may wind up in the position of a drum major whose band has turned off two blocks back and left him marching alone up front.

Necessity is not only the mother of invention. It is also the cardinal principle of legislative action. Increasingly nowadays, American voters consider a modicum of environmental prudence to be a necessity. Perhaps the lesson is brought home in something less than heroic terms, but brought home it is: in bans on swimming and water skiing where the water is dangerously polluted; in a shortage of oysters on the half shell (for the same reason); in an increase in respiratory illness around big cities; in the loss of shade trees to auto exhaust; in silted harbors, murky days, and a scarcity of game fish in the old familiar creeks and nearby rivers.

If, as has been projected, the year 1999 will see 90 percent of the American people living on 10 percent of the land, and if pollution seems to be a problem today, think what it will be in that final year of the current century. It is this thought which led former President Nixon to suggest that the time for action is *now*. And it is this thought which has promoted environmental action in Washington.

But it will not be precipitate action, for ordinary citizens still cherish their jobs, and as recession took center stage in 1975, jobs gained a few notches on the priority scale, wage earners realizing that the jobs would be restored by investment in new technology, but that such investment would not rise until profits rose (and profits *will* only come out of the prices paid by the customers). So the environmental issue comes full cycle, back home to the consumer-and-taxpayer, which, after all, is where all costs come to rest.

After a pause for adjustment to new realities of the energy crunch and of higher fuel prices and technology costs, the environmental cleanup will resume. It will catch its second wind and become politically glamorous with *all* candidates. Ensuing Congresses will find themselves pledged to press for action—on both sides of the political aisle.

Issues of environment in subsequent political campaigns will not revolve around "whether" but simply "how soon," and "at what cost"—matters of speed and degree which, in the political atmosphere of Washington, can be resolved with some sweeping declarations of intent, some less grandiose legislative authorizations of power, and finally, some appropriations of money.

38 GOVERNMENT AND HEALTH

When the great debates were raging in Washington during the 1960s over medicare and medicaid, the American Medical Association fought the proposals on two grounds:
1. That they would lead directly to socialized medicine.
2. That the costs of medical service would increase sharply.

Now that the results are in, the AMA's score is: Wrong on Count 1. Right on Count 2 (for perhaps different reasons than it envisioned).

Americans spend more on health than any other people in the world. More per capita, more in total, more as a percentage of the gross national product. This is not to say that we are the healthiest. We are not. More than a dozen other countries have a better infant mortality record than the U.S. And these countries exceed us in female life expectancy. More than twenty-five other countries outstrip us in male life expectancy. In other departments there is both good news and bad news. The U.S.—largely with government research and public health aid—has lowered the death rate in most of the contagious diseases. The bad news is that several major killers—including diabetes, cirrhosis of the liver, and respiratory disease—have higher death rates than in 1950 and are still climbing. While the cancer death rate is trending down for women, it is at a record high for men and still rising. The death rate for heart disease is still mounting, too (although some health statisticians prefer to discount the rate, on the basis of the advanced age of many of its victims, and are now proclaiming a slight downturn in the age-adjusted rate).

So once again there is debate about a national health plan, and Washington is at the center of the storm. Meanwhile, federal spending for health continues to rise.

Before medicare and medicaid were enacted in 1965, federal spending for health care and research totaled $5 billion, which was less than 5 percent of the federal budget in that fiscal year. Today federal outlays are approximately $35 billion and account for nearly 12 percent of the budget. One out of every four dollars spent on health care in America comes out of federal coffers. And despite the Nixon administration's reputation for frugality, rising costs doubled federal health spending between 1969 and 1974.

Part of the reason for the spectacular surge in health spending is the growing realization by Americans that, in health, we have a long way to go. In terms of expertise and research, the U.S. ranks high, but the American life style still does not encourage the best of health habits. People of all income levels seem to eat the wrong meals, get too little exercise, live under too much tension, and overuse drugs, tobacco, and alcohol (despite the warnings of their doctors and the National Institutes of Health, funded by the federal government). And while top-flight medical attention is always available somewhere, it is not always there when you need it at a price you can afford.

This mix of facts induced the federal government, less than ten years ago, to start getting deeper into health care. The result was a medicare plan for the aged and a joint federal-state medicaid program for the poor. While these programs have helped narrow the "distribution gap," they did not deal directly with the average American family's problem of soaring costs of illness—either routine or catastrophic. And so Washington is getting into the act a second time around. To meet the problems of the average family, health planners in Washington are buzzing with ideas for a new broader role for Uncle Sam: national health insurance. As with medicare ten years ago, various plans have been proposed in Congress. Each has its special appeals, special advocates, and special opponents.

HEADQUARTERS IN WASHINGTON—HEW

Whatever new health insurance plan is adopted, one sure result is an expansion in the federal health establishment in Washington. The brain center of this establishment is the Department of Health, Education and Welfare, headquartered in a low, drab building on Independence Avenue at the foot of Capitol Hill. A grab-bag department whose mission is to protect the health and happiness of the American people, it oversees social services whose total price tag now exceeds that of every other department in the Cabinet—even the budget of the Department of Defense. Under its wing are such agencies as the Office of Education, National Institutes of Health, Social Security Administration, Food and Drug Administration, Public Health Service, Gallaudet College, and Howard University.

Among government agencies, HEW ranks fourth in employment. Its roster of 130,000 follows the Department of Defense (1 million-plus), the Postal Service, and the Veterans Administration. HEW's employees are spread all over the United States, in ten regional offices, nineteen Food and Drug Administration offices, and more than 1,000 offices of the Social Security Administration. They are also spread all over the Washington metropolitan area, with a concentration of 6,000 or so in the towering, privately owned Parklawn Building in suburban Rockville, Maryland. HEW likes to call itself the "people to people" department, and prides itself on the fact that 96¢ out of every dollar in the HEW budget is returned to individuals and public and private organizations in the form of benefits, grants, and contracts.

To grasp the immensity of the federal health effort, consider the fact that nearly 50 million people—about one-quarter of the national population—receive health care funded totally or in large part by Uncle Sam. By the end of fiscal 1975, 21.6 million aged people will be under medicare, administered by the Social Security Administration. Another 28 million low-income citizens will have their medical bills covered by medicaid. Under medicaid, the federal government provides matching funds to state governments, to cover 50 to 83 percent of the cost of the states' health assistance programs. The medicare and medicaid programs together account for well over half of all the federal government's health expenditures.

Concerned that government funds are frequently misspent on unneeded and low-quality health care, HEW pushed for creation of some sort of monitoring system. Federal dollars are now being used to set up a nationwide network of Professional Standards Review Organizations (PSROs), panels composed primarily of physicians (not federal employees) who will check on the medicare and medicaid performance of their peers. When a patient is treated at a hospital, the care he receives will be compared with the "normal treatment" for that ailment (length of stay, type of medication and surgery, etc.) as defined by the PSRO physicians. If the treatment costs far more than the norm, the government will not reimburse the physician for the excess. If the PSRO detects fraud, fines can be imposed. The PSRO concept continues to be very controversial within the medical profession. (As a matter of fact, in 1975 the AMA filed suit—its first ever against the federal government—to block implementation of the PSRO system, objecting primarily to the inclusion on some peer review boards of nonphysicians, such as health economists or hospital administrators.) Still, by the end of 1975, about 120 out of a national system of 182 PSROs are expected to be in operation.

Washington is heavily immersed in the business of underwriting the nation's medical schools. Nearly half of the annual revenue of these institutions is derived from federal grants for construction, education, and research. HEW is attempting to cut back on operational support of this type, preferring to assist individual students rather than institutions. It envisions a "national health service scholarship" program, under which about 2,000 students each year would have all their medical school costs covered, in exchange for a period of public service—at any level of government—after graduation. HEW also plans to channel scholarship funds toward students from disadvantaged backgrounds and students planning a career in "family medicine" (general practice).

Research spending (the bulk of the federal health program until the advent of medicare and medicaid in the mid-Sixties) continues to grow every year, but at a slightly slower rate than during the past twenty years. Cancer and heart-related research are now getting a lion's share of the biomedical research budget.

THE NATIONAL INSTITUTES OF HEALTH

About two-thirds of all U.S. health research funds are administered by the National Institutes of Health (NIH). A semiautonomous wing of HEW, NIH is composed of eleven separate institutes and another eight divisions, together employing some 10,000 people on a budget of $2 billion a year. Its home is a rolling, beautifully landscaped 300-acre campus in suburban Bethesda, Maryland, directly across the road from the famous Naval Medical Center, where Washington area naval personnel and veterans are treated. (The center is also the place where Richard Nixon used to be treated for minor illnesses when he was President, and where Mrs. Gerald Ford was operated on for breast cancer.) While most of the NIH research money is distributed in grants to thousands of nonfederal scientists around the nation, the Bethesda campus is the site of an extensive intramural federal research program. There NIH operates a 500-bed clinical center, where patients with rare diseases are given free treatment by research physicians studying those ailments.

In addition to NIH, Washington supports biomedical research in several other agencies, including the Department of Defense, the Atomic Energy Commission, and the Veterans Administration. Hardly any health problem known to man—including mental illness, overpopulation, and the process of aging—is untouched by research projects funded totally or partially by the federal government. More than 60 percent of the $3.5 billion spent each year on American biomedical research comes from Washington.

Since passage of the Hill-Burton Act after World War II, Washington has funneled billions of dollars into hospital construction throughout the United States. Federal funds helped pay for 470,000 additional beds in 10,000 hospitals and clinics. Ten years ago, Hill-Burton funds accounted for 13 percent of all expenditures for hospital construction in the nation, but this percentage has been dropping since then, to about 4 percent today. Supporters of the federal construction program now acknowledge that Hill-Burton may have succeeded too well, contributing to an oversupply of hospital space in many areas of the country. While some areas still have a shortage, the national hospital bed vacancy rate is a very high 27 percent. As a result, the Nixon administration tried to phase out the politically popular Hill-Burton program, encountering some resistance from Congress (which would like to keep the money flowing, but for hospital modernization rather than new construction).

In addition to financing health care, Uncle Sam is a direct provider of treatment to millions of Americans. The Department of Defense has over 200 hospitals and clinics for military personnel and dependents. The VA operates 17 hospitals, 82 nursing homes, and 212 outpatient clinics throughout the nation. HEW and the Bureau of Indian Affairs provide medical care and facilities funding for Indians and Alaska natives living on federal reservations. Merchant marine personnel are treated at eight Public Health Service hospitals and twenty-six clinics situated along the Atlantic, Pacific, and Gulf coasts. The number of PHS hospitals—which are badly outmoded—has dwindled from a high of 30, back when the American merchant marine was vigorous. Presidents Eisenhower, Kennedy, Johnson, and Nixon all proposed that the hospitals be shut down, but Congress resisted. Under President Ford, a commitment was finally made to modernize the PHS facilities, perhaps for use by the general communities surrounding them.

Finally, the government provides operating revenue to community-run health centers specializing in general care, birth control services, mental health, prenatal care, alcoholism, and drug abuse. In increasingly large amounts, the federal government is extending loans and grants to found nonfederal Health Maintenance Organizations (HMOs), the new concept in prepaid, group practice clinics.

RISE OF GOVERNMENT HEALTH POLICIES

Washington hasn't always been so deeply involved in the health business. Before the depression, health was caught up in the same rhetoric of self-reliance that characterized all public policy debates. Until FDR's New Deal, a majority of American voters elected national governments on the basis of how *little* they did, in a direct and personal way, to touch people's everyday lives. "Cleanliness is next to godliness," of course, so it was all right for Uncle Sam to fund public sanitation and control epidemics. It was also all right for the government to take a limited role in medical research and assistance to the extremely needy. But anything beyond that smacked of "socialized medicine"—something that might be fine for authoritarian societies in Europe, but not for America.

The depression changed all that. The New Deal's Federal Security Agency

(FSA) became a catchall for health programs, encompassing the embryonic National Institutes of Health, the social security program, and the Public Health Service. After World War II, President Truman proposed a national health insurance plan tied into social security. But that was an idea whose time had not yet come. The American Medical Association (AMA) saw red and collected a "war chest" of funds to lobby the Truman plan to death. Truman had no better luck trying to transform the FSA into a new Cabinet-level Department of Health, Education, and Social Security.

The federal health boom—marked by peaks and valleys, but with a definite upward trend—accelerated during the Eisenhower administration. Through the cooperative efforts of Senator Robert A. Taft, Sr. (R-Ohio), and the AMA, Congress and the new President approved a massive addition to the Cabinet—the Department of Health, Education and Welfare. The first HEW Secretary, Houston *Post* publisher Oveta Culp Hobby, was sworn in on April 11, 1953, barely three months after Ike's inaugural. As Congress and the Presidency empowered HEW to dispense more and more social services in the two decades after its founding, its budget soared into range of the nation's military expenditures. In 1973 the HEW budget ($82 billion) finally passed that of the Department of Defense ($75 billion).

SOME FRIENDS AND CHAMPIONS

The Fifties saw the growing power of forceful spokesmen for increased federal spending on health research. Senator Lister Hill (D-Ala.), father of the Hill-Burton hospital construction program in 1946, chaired the Senate Appropriations Health Subcommittee, and Representative John E. Fogarty (D-R.I.) championed health funding as chairman of the House counterpart. These legislators staged well-publicized hearings that featured an array of witnesses from the top echelons of medical research—polio vaccine discoverer Dr. Jonas Salk, heart surgeon Dr. Michael DeBakey, cardiologist (and Eisenhower's presidential physician) Dr. Paul D. White, and many others. Preeminent in the campaign for a national commitment to health research was Mrs. Mary Lasker of New York—multimillionaire businesswoman, widow of an advertising genius, and head of a foundation that supports research through grants and prestigious awards for achievement.

This "medical research lobby" prodded Congress into approving hefty boosts in federal research funds virtually every year. NIH was so inundated with money that it frequently returned a portion of its annual appropriation to the Treasury. Health funding was a politically appealing issue for congressmen, as long as it didn't raise the specter of "socialized medicine." During the Fifties and early Sixties, as health analyst Stephen Strickland has pointed out, "research remained one of the few areas in which a congressman could cast a vote for health," since the AMA blocked attempts to give Uncle Sam a role in the delivery of health care to the public at large.

Presidents Kennedy and Johnson propelled the federal government into many areas where it once dared not tread, and health care was one. During the Sixties, the administration and Congress produced an unprecedented flow of landmark health legislation. In 1963 Congress passed the Health Professions Education Act, making grants and loans available to schools that train medical and paramedical personnel. In the same year, it approved legislation to fund community mental health centers. In 1964 came the Surgeon General's report on the dangers of cigarette smoking. A year later, over the strenuous opposition of the AMA, Congress passed the nation's first health insurance programs, medicare and medicaid. Regional medical projects were funded, to demonstrate better techniques of research, teaching, and treatment of heart disease, cancer, and stroke.

CONFLICTS AND CHALLENGES

A few clouds began to hang over the federal health establishment in the late Sixties. First of all, the mounting cost of the war in Southeast Asia cut into federal funding of many research efforts, especially medical. Then in October 1967 a House Government Operations subcommittee chaired by Representative Lawrence H. Fountain (D-N.C.) issued a report charging NIH with, among other things, lax management and overly generous support of too many medical research projects, some of which were considered to be of dubious value. Some of the leaders who had kept medical research funds flowing for two decades departed the scene. Representative Fogarty died of a heart attack on the opening day of Congress in 1967. The following year, after forty-five years in Congress, Senator Hill retired. So did Dr. James Shannon, who had been the respected director of NIH since 1955 and had guided it through the boom years of rising appropriations. In fiscal 1969, Congress trimmed $20 million off the previously sacred budget of NIH.

President Nixon's first budget, for fiscal year 1970, proposed an NIH appropriation $35 million below the previous year. Scientists across the country began to fear that the Nixon years would be lean ones for medical research. Congress, however, was not acquiescent to these attempted economies. The House and Senate Appropriations Health Subcommittees, under the new leadership of Senator Warren Magnuson (D-Wash.) and Representative Daniel Flood (D-Pa.), pushed through a 1970 appropriation $56 million greater than the President had requested. The scenario was similar in 1971, when Congress gave NIH nearly $100 million more than was budgeted, and in 1972, when more than $140 million was added. Despite these boosts, however, the federal flow of medical research funds began to slow. No longer would the administration or Congress lavish money on medical research in the open-handed manner of the Fifties and Sixties.

Meanwhile, the cost of health care was soaring at an even greater rate than the rest of the inflation-ridden national economy. Among the factors responsible for this situation were medicare and medicaid. "The principal assumption that underlay the enactment of medicare and medicaid was that the health delivery system was in fine shape, and that all the old and sick needed to improve their health care was increased purchasing power," observed LeRoy G. Goldman, staff director of the Senate Labor and Public Welfare Subcommittee on Health, in the *National Journal*. "Well, the system couldn't cope with the increased demand, and the result has been inflation and higher prices."

One part of the crisis in medical costs is the wide variation in the price of prescription drugs that are therapeutically equivalent. To encourage the use of lower-priced versions of comparable medicines, HEW proposed in 1974 that federal reimbursements for medicare and medicaid patients be pegged to the lowest-priced brand of a given drug. (But if a physician certified that a higher-priced brand was essential for a given patient, the government would approve the higher reimbursement.) HEW's proposal—called the MAC regulation, for "maximum allowable cost"—came under fire from both the Pharmaceutical Manufacturers Association and the AMA. The AMA was livid over the possibility of government interference with the physician's judgment in prescribing drugs, and threatened in early 1975 to file suit if the proposed rule was implemented.

It became evident to everyone that the heavier demand stimulated by medicare and medicaid required a greater supply of medical and paramedical personnel. The product of this realization was the Comprehensive Health Manpower Act of 1971. In addition to grants to medical schools based on current enrollment, the law held out incentives for shortening curricula and enrolling additional medical, dental, and nursing students. The health manpower plan was proposed by the Nixon administration and was guided through legislative channels by two men who were emerging as Congress's chief champions of an active federal role in health policy: Representative Paul G. Rogers (D-Fla.), chairman of the House Commerce Subcommittee on Public Health and Environment, and Senator Edward M. Kennedy (D-Mass.), chairman of the Senate Labor and Welfare Subcommittee on Health.

PREPAID MEDICAL SERVICE THROUGH HMOS

Boosting the supply of medical personnel is one way to improve the delivery of health care. A more revolutionary approach—a genuine restructuring of the system—is represented by the concept of the Health Maintenance Organization (HMO). At an HMO, physicians with various specialties practice together. Their patients pay a fixed sum in advance, and the treatment they receive—including periodic checkups, immunizations, and prenatal care—stresses prevention of illness through early detection of problems. The HMO concept originated years ago in such prepaid, group-clinic programs as the Kaiser-Permanente plan in California. It was embraced by the Nixon administration and congressional leaders of both parties as a way to hold down medical costs and improve health care, especially in rural and inner-city areas where doctors are in short supply. A small amount of federal aid—about $29 million from 1971 to 1973—was distributed to help finance pilot HMOs, and the encouraging results have led to a major federal program. The House failed to approve the Senate-passed $5.2 billion HMO bill in 1972, but Senator Kennedy came back the following year with an $805 million version. This amount was eventually scaled down to win passage as the Health Maintenance Organization Act of 1973, which authorizes $375 million in federal aid over a five-year period.

In 1970 there were only 25 HMOs in the United States. By 1974, however, there were 128 in operation and another 292 in various stages of organization. HEW, which pushed the prepay concept unequivocally a few years ago, backed off slightly after objections from conservative segments of the AMA. Dr. Charles C. Edwards, who was then HEW assistant secretary for health, said in 1973, "It is not our intention to impose a single system of health care on anyone, but we intend to support a major effort to demonstrate the value of HMOs and allow HMOs to compete equally for the health dollar."

One medical leader who is very cautious about the HMO idea is Dr. Malcolm Todd, the 1974 president of the AMA and head of Physicians to Reelect the President in 1972. Commenting in 1973 on the reduction of federal funding for HMOs, Todd said he was glad to see a "slowdown on this thing," and added that his group had "used all the force we could bring to bear against this" [the more massive earlier proposals]. HMO theorist Dr. Paul M. Ellwood, Jr., belittles the idea that these prepaid group practices are the path to socialized medicine. Some HMOs are nonprofit clinics with salaried physicians, others are profit-making, but none is owned or operated by the federal government. "Doctors in HMOs are working for themselves, not the government," Dr. Ellwood noted in an interview in *Medical Economics*. "I don't expect all doctors to leave fee-for-service practice for HMOs," he says. "Active competition between the two systems will improve both, and help stave off the conversion of the health industry to a public utility status." Even Senator Kennedy is cautious in his optimism about the future role of this technique. He sees the new HMO program as an attempt to "introduce a modest degree of pluralism into what is otherwise a monolithic fee-for-service health care system." Fortunately, the government is watching the HMO experiment carefully, looking for possible flaws. A Senate investigation revealed in 1975 that an unreasonably high portion of the federal money paid to certain profit-making HMOs in California had gone into administrative expenses and profits, rather than health care for their patients.

THE CANCER RESEARCH BOOM

In the field of biomedical research, the Nixon administration favored a heroic "breakthrough" approach to finding cures for killing diseases, as evidenced by the privileged, semi-independent status accorded cancer research. In his State of the Union address in January 1971, President Nixon proclaimed, "The time has come in America when the same kind of concentrated effort that split the atom and took man to the moon should be turned toward conquering this dread disease." While the President originally intended that the cancer crusade be led by the National Cancer Institute at NIH, with substantially greater fundings, Senator Kennedy, Senator Jacob K. Javits (R-N.Y.), and others in the Senate proposed that the institute be absorbed by a new National Cancer Authority, separate from NIH and directly responsible to the President.

Despite widespread warnings that it would be unwise to isolate the cancer battle from other related biomedical research, President Nixon eventually endorsed the Senate bill and it passed with only one dissenting vote. But on the House side, Representative Rogers (called "Mr. Health" around Washington) was skeptical of separating the cancer program from the supervision of NIH. In a compromise conference with the Senate, he convinced their conferees to approve a bill leaving the program within the National Cancer Institute, but with increased funding and a direct line to the White House. President Nixon signed the bill on December 23, 1971. At the signing ceremony, he backed off from his earlier optimistic analogies to atomic research and the Apollo moon program, noting that "biomedical research is, of course, a notoriously uncertain enterprise." But he pledged that the cancer fight would never have to be stymied by a lack of federal funding or the "familiar dangers of bureaucracy and red tape."

The White House and Congress have kept their promise on cancer. From a 1970 figure of $180 million, cancer outlays grew to about $560 million by

1974, accounting for more than one-quarter of all federal expenditures on medical research. Not surprisingly, the special attention lavished on cancer has caused resentment in other parts of the medical research establishment. HEW's Dr. Charles Edwards said in 1973 that it was a "mistake" to have given the cancer crusade virtual carte blanche status, and warned that overly generous funding of cancer research could destroy the momentum of other health research programs. Acknowledging that diseases of the heart cause more deaths than cancer, HEW is beefing up the budget for research on heart, lung, and blood ailments. Funds for these research specialties reached the $300 million range in fiscal 1975.

FRICTION WITH THE WHITE HOUSE

During the last two years of the Nixon administration, NIH had strained relations with its superiors at HEW and the White House. The problem was not primarily budgetary, since the Nixon years had seen a half-billion-dollar growth in the NIH budget, breaking through the $2 billion mark. The problem stemmed from the administration's intrusions into an organization that for years has been given a free rein—too free, some would say—to conduct its affairs as it pleases. NIH resented interference from "downtown," meaning cost-conscious efficiency experts at HEW and the Office of Management and Budget (of which, incidentally, HEW Secretary Caspar W. Weinberger had previously been director).

In 1973, NIH Director Dr. Robert Q. Marston quit under fire from the administration. Among other things, Dr. Marston had fought the legislation giving special status to cancer research, criticized administration budget restraints, and supported the right of free speech of NIH personnel who opposed American policy in Southeast Asia. In a mordant departing speech, Marston offered the opinion that "creative people are to be valued more than organizational arrangements." Not long thereafter came the resignation of Dr. John F. Sherman, a twenty-one-year NIH stalwart who had been deputy director and then acting director after Dr. Marston's departure. Dr. Sherman said, "NIH's proud record of excellence, if not the very purpose of the organization, is threatened by the second Nixon administration." He said that "negative management" from HEW and OMB superiors "cast a pall of gloom and despair" over NIH, eroding the atmosphere of security that is necessary for creative research. While the agency's budget continues to rise, the number of personnel available to oversee its programs has been shrinking. The overall budget increase has not been spread evenly over the various divisions, and continuity of funding has occasionally been disrupted by anti-inflation impoundments of appropriations.

Beyond tangible management policies, some NIH personnel felt their work was just not appreciated by the Nixon team. They pointed out, for example, that in 1972 President Nixon telephoned Redskins quarterback Sonny Jurgensen in the hospital to wish him a swift recovery from an Achilles tendon injury on the football field. But the President couldn't take the trouble, they noted, to telephone a word of congratulation to Dr. Christian B. Anfinsen, the NIH chemist who had won a Nobel prize for chemistry a few weeks before the Jurgensen episode.

Morale continues to be low at NIH. Marston's successor, Robert S. Stone, resigned at the end of 1974—the second NIH director whose resignation was requested by HEW officials "downtown" in less than two years. NIH scientists protested the firings and complained that the Office of Management and Budget is starving basic research programs by putting so much money into dramatic "missions" like cancer research. (Some scientists referred bitterly to a "disease-of-the-month club" mentality on Capitol Hill.) HEW's Dr. Edwards (who resigned in 1975 to become an executive of a medical supply company) defended his administration and stated that NIH scientists have not been selective enough in their research and have not weeded out unproductive projects. "The scientific community has got to get its head out of the clouds and begin to live in the real world, where funds of all kinds are limited," he said.

One of the running debates in the federal health setup focuses on the appropriate balance between research done intramurally at NIH and research farmed out, by grant or contract, to universities and independent research centers. Most of the Institutes' research budget is distributed around the nation, and during one recent fiscal year as many as 67,000 scientists were at work on NIH-funded projects at 2,000 research centers. NIH-supported research, conducted internally and externally, has made the United States the world leader in health technology over the past twenty years. The work of more than forty American winners of Nobel prizes in physiology and medicine was supported by NIH grants. Three recent Nobel winners—Dr. Anfinsen, Marshall Nirenberg in 1968, and Julius Axelrod in 1970—did their digging as full-time NIH scientists. As health analyst Stephen Strickland has noted, the intramural programs have been a training ground for many scientists and medical administrators now employed at academic and research institutions around the nation. Some federal officials have opposed a major expansion of the intramural programs, Strickland adds, "because they thought the best way to secure popular support for biomedical science was to spread financial support around."

NATIONAL HEALTH INSURANCE—COMING SOON

A mammoth legislative struggle is now taking shape in the Washington health establishment—the biggest one since the passage of medicare and medicaid in the Sixties. The issue is national health insurance. Everyone seems resigned to eventual passage of some type of program, so each interest group wants to make sure the final bill is favorable to its particular constituency. There are several health insurance plans now pending before Congress, including versions promoted by the White House, AMA, organized labor, American Hospital Association, National Council of Senior Citizens, Health Insurance Association of America, and senators of such divergent ideologies as Edward M. Kennedy and Senate Finance Committee Chairman Russell Long (D-La.). Because the battle lines are not clearly drawn and several proposals share similar elements, the health insurance debate promises to be one of the most confusing ever.

One front-running proposal has enjoyed the support of both the HEW hierarchy and key members of the House Ways and Means Committee, which has primary jurisdiction over such legislation. Sometimes called the Mills-Schneebeli-Packwood bill, it was pushed by Representative Wilbur Mills when he was chairman of Ways and Means. It calls for a program that would retain modified forms of medicare and medicaid for the aged and the poor. The majority of the American people (all those not covered by one of the government assistance programs) would be covered by insurance provided by their employers. The insurance would be written by private insurance companies, with premium rates and minimum coverage regulated by state and federal governments. Each employer would pay 75 percent of the premiums for its employees and their families.

Under this plan, the citizen would go to the doctor or hospital of his choice for treatment. He would show his government-issued health credit card, and all billings would be made to the private insurance company that covers him. In each year, the employee would pay the first $150 of his own medical expenses (with a combined family deductible equaling some multiple of that). Above that, his insurance would cover 75 percent of the expenses up to $1,050 (or $1,500 for a family). Most importantly, the employee would be spared the financial crisis of a long and complicated illness, since his insurance would cover 100 percent of all costs exceeding $1,050 or $1,500.

Benefits under the Mills-Schneebeli-Packwood plan would be the same for everyone, and would include visits to physicians, stays in hospitals and nursing homes, prescription drugs, medical supplies and appliances, lab and X-ray services, birth control, and maternity care. The insurance would also cover special services for children, such as dental care, eyeglasses, and hearing aids.

Other health insurance plans on Capitol Hill are narrower in scope. The AMA's "medicredit" proposal, for example, would merely change the tax laws to allow individuals and/or employers to take tax credits for the cost of privately purchased health insurance. The credits would range from 10 percent, for the well-to-do, to 100 percent, for the poor. (In late 1974, the AMA leadership indicated they would be willing to compromise their medicredit plan in favor of an employer-financed proposal resembling the bill that HEW likes.) Other proposals, including a bill sponsored by Senator Long and Senator Abraham Ribicoff (D-Conn.), would have the federal government cover only the costs of catastrophic illnesses. Under the Long-Ribicoff bill, Uncle Sam would pick up the tab after sixty days in the hospital or $2,000 of medical bills.

The question of how much each program would cost depends, of course, on the amount of coverage in each plan. The plans differ in how the payments will be made. Will the employer pay most of the premium, eventually passing the cost on to the consumer in higher prices of goods and services? Will the citizen pay for his own insurance, perhaps with a tax credit? Will Uncle Sam provide insurance directly, with citizens and corporations footing the bill through income and payroll taxes? Then there is the issue of how to monitor costs and quality in health care. Should physicians on review committees look over the shoulders of their colleagues in the medical profession (as in the current Professional Standards Review Organizations)? Or should Uncle Sam impose strict performance requirements and cost controls? These are just a few of the questions with which Congress and the President must grapple before a compromise health insurance system can be forged.

Whatever version of national health insurance prevails, it can be expected to preserve the traditional supremacy of the private sector in the providing of health services. Senator Kennedy, in introducing his insurance plan in early 1974, said he hoped the federal government would not curtail in any way the "freedom of every physician and every patient to choose where and when he or she will give or receive health care."

GOVERNMENT HEALTH INVOLVEMENT—HERE TO STAY

The past decade has seen a spectacular growth and greening of the federal health establishment. On the thermometer that is most conspicuous in Washington—the scale of federal appropriations—health as a national issue has gone from lukewarm to fever hot. But the cost of health care seems to have risen just as rapidly, and so have the expectations and demands of the American people. As HEW Secretary Weinberger has been careful to note, "We must begin with the hard reality—whatever our preferences and desires—that our national resources are not unlimited, but finite; health care, as basically vital as it is, must compete for its share of those resources with other high priorities of federal concern." And Dr. Charles Edwards (who became a vocal critic of federal health policy after leaving the government) has warned that the nation's health delivery system is not yet prepared for the surge of demand that would follow the creation of national health insurance. The result would be another bout of serious inflation. In the face of such soaring costs, he warned, the government might be pressured by the public to become even more directly involved in the health industry.

The federal government's concern with the health of each individual can be plotted over the past sixty years as a path from marginal interest to deep involvement. The path is strewn with recurring, strangely similar calls to action, statements of crisis, and legislative proposals. It is with a sense of déjà vu that one reads today of Theodore Roosevelt's national health insurance plan in the Progressive party platform of 1912. Or the 1928 plea by Senator Matthew M. Neely for federal funds to find a cure for cancer. Or attempts—frequent throughout the Thirties and Forties—to institute health insurance for the poor and federal aid to medical education. In each era, the latest proposal to carry the government deeper into the health business was greeted by organized opposition as an unspeakably un-American notion. Yet after enactment, the vast majority of these programs were eventually accepted as social services that any concerned government ought to provide for its citizens. The odds are very good that today's legislative battles over health policy will produce still more programs that will, in time, be taken for granted by new Americans with new ideas about the proper role of government in their lives.

39 HOUSING HELPER

Housing, in one sense, is about as local as anything can be. You live in only one place at one time. Your house or apartment was probably put up by a builder based in your home area. Your city, county, or state sets construction standards, puts in roads, sees that water and sewer are there, provides schools, police, and fire protection.

That's all local. So housing is a local matter, isn't it?

Well, not really. These days housing in the U.S. is affected more and more by Washington, even though public housing has caused the federal bureaucracy to stub its toe with great pain and embarrassment, in full view of millions of its supporters and detractors. And when the housing construction industry sinks into despair—as it did during 1974—Washington is where the builders come to complain and cajole.

How can this be—this paradox of local control and national involvement? The answer lies in the programs by which the federal government for decades has insured and guaranteed mortgage loans through the FHA and VA. The answer lies, too, in the growing structure of federal standards, orders, and regulations with which homebuilders must contend.

Washington permeates every part of the housing industry, which is traditionally one of the most fiercely independent of all large industries in America. At the highest level, the Federal Reserve Board and the government's housing credit corporations regulate the amount of money available for new construction, rehabilitation, and individual mortgage loans. In the realm of construction standards, Washington is getting deeper and deeper into an area that was once the exclusive province of local government. The Federal Housing Administration (FHA) sets standards for the housing that it subsidizes and backs with mortgage insurance, and these guidelines have become something like a national building code, covering everything from insulation and wiring to flooring adhesives and modular units.

The Washington influence is strong, too, in the marketing of housing. Since the civil rights push of the Sixties, Washington has banned racial discrimination in the sale and rental of all housing. Since 1968, more than 8,000 complaints of unfair housing discrimination have been filed with the Department of Housing and Urban Development (HUD) and in federal courts. HUD has a team of investigators (too small for the size of the task, really) who look into complaints and attempt to mediate disputes to forestall court action.

Even real estate sales commissions have come under federal scrutiny, as the Justice Department Antitrust Division has attacked price fixing among members of multiple listing services. And don't forget federal environmental safety policies, which have had a profound effect on everything from methods of construction to site preparation to zoning. In several regions of the country (like the Washington, D.C., metropolitan area) local governments have aggravated housing shortages by prohibiting additional hookups to overloaded sewage treatment systems—responding, in large part, to stiffer federal water quality standards.

In the booming industry of recreational communities and vacation homes, HUD requires that companies engaging in interstate sales register with the government and make full disclosure of all relevant information to prospective buyers.

There are several special things about housing in America, and each one is the result of some action that has been taken—or not taken—in Washington. The U.S. has the world's highest percentage of homeownership (about 63 percent of all households), made possible by the FHA program providing long-term, low-interest, small-down-payment mortgage loans. But the U.S. is not a uniformly well-housed nation. Nearly 7 million American households have shelter that is considered inadequate—dilapidated, with faulty plumbing and heating or none at all. Some 700,000 households are classified "overcrowded." An additional 5.5 million households suffer from a burdensome housing cost: having to pay rent of more than 25 percent out of an income under $10,000. This adds up to more than 13 million households—20 percent of all American families—that are "ill-housed" by one of these standards.

The policymakers of Washington have long expressed concern about the feast-or-famine characteristics of housing in America, but their efforts to assist housing-deprived households have failed to solve the problem.

The major beneficiaries of federal housing programs are not the poor (who are overwhelmingly renters) but middle- and upper-middle-incomers, who tend to be homeowners. The homeowner's subsidy consists of substantial federal tax savings for deduction of mortgage interest payments and local property taxes, as well as the waiving of capital gains taxes on the sale of a residence if the money is reinvested in a comparably priced home. In 1972 more than 24 million taxpayers (generally the wealthiest one-third of all American taxpayers) took advantage of these indirect federal housing subsidies.

But Uncle Sam offers the renter no such windfall (although Congress in 1974 played with the idea of allowing renters to deduct $200 of rent each year, a very modest benefit aimed at low-incomers). Nor does Washington give direct housing assistance to more than a handful of the nation's poor. Of the 18 million households with incomes under $5,000 per year, about 94 percent receive no federal housing assistance whatsoever. Federally subsidized public housing has amounted to less than 2 percent of the nation's total shelter stock since public housing was conceived in the Thirties. And in recent years the amount of federal funds directly invested in low- and moderate-income housing (about $2.5 billion in 1972) has been dwarfed by the indirect subsidies given to homeowners annually through tax savings (about $10 billion in 1972).

For more than fifteen years, urban renewal has been one of the most talked about—and least acted upon—topics in Washington. The administrations of John Kennedy and Lyndon Johnson focused a lot of attention on urban housing problems, with personal visits to slum areas, dedications of urban parks, and lots of "urban talk." But relatively little money was put behind the talk. The Nixon administration, whose political attitudes and power base related more to the suburbs, considered the big cities merely an unpleasant chore to contend with, and the current condition of urban renewal testifies to this.

But the rural housing situation is worse, not even enjoying the lip-service interest paid to urban affairs. More bad housing is found scattered throughout rural America than in all the cities of the nation. For example, 60 percent of all the housing units occupied in 1970 by rural blacks (mostly in the South) lacked running water or sanitary systems, or both. Probably the worst living quarters in the nation are occupied by American Indians, the poorest minority group of all.

ROOTS IN THE DEPRESSION

While federal housing policies over the past four decades have not solved the housing problems of the poor, they have made America's middle- and upper-middle-income majority the best-housed in the world. As with so many government programs, Washington's concern for housing (in particular, encouraging homeownership) grew out of the crisis of the Great Depression. In the early Thirties, half of all home mortgages in America were in default. One of the reasons for this (beside the fact that income had plummeted) lay in the way mortgage loans were made in those days. Typically, the home-owner had to put down 50 percent of the cost of the house. His loan for the remainder was at a high interest rate, for a term of only one to ten years. His monthly payments covered only interest, with the principal payable in a lump when the note fell due. If the homeowner couldn't pay off the principal then, he would either refinance his home or default. There was no large-scale market for the buying and selling of mortgages.

Needless to say, this precarious structure was easily toppled by economic insecurity. The Roosevelt administration decided to completely overhaul the American system of home financing. The Federal Housing Administration, created in 1934, conceived the idea of government mortgage insurance to protect the lender against default (with the small premium paid by the borrower). The mortgages that the FHA insured carried manageable interest rates and twenty-year terms, and covered as much as 80 percent of the price of the house. To help idle capital find its way into the housing market, the New Dealers set up the Federal National Mortgage Association (called "Fannie Mae"), which could raise money by selling bond issues to the public, and then invest the proceeds by buying up existing mortgages so lenders could make new home loans. At the foundation of the new credit system was the Federal Home Loan Bank Board—a sort of Federal Reserve System for savings and loan institutions—that pumps federal money into mortgages when housing construction needs a lift.

These new organizations did not involve direct government subsidies, but were financial mechanisms to put some order in the housing market and boost the economy. The New Deal's first attempt to improve the housing of the poor came in 1937, with the birth of low-rent subsidized public housing. Setting a pattern that would persist for the next several decades, the government made contracts with local housing authorities to build apartment complexes. The housing authorities, typically, build the units with the proceeds of bond issues and administer them, and Uncle Sam helps pay the principal and interest on the bonds. But public housing of this type has never been a large part of the nation's total housing supply, averaging only about 30,000 units built per year since the program began.

At the end of World War II, Congress launched the enormous Veterans Administration housing program, a double-edged sword to do a favor for returning GIs and stimulate homebuilding in a nation starved for new shelter. Today the VA guarantees 60 percent (or up to $12,500) of the ex-service-man's mortgage against default. VA loans can cover as much as 100 percent of the price of the home, thereby requiring no down payment. Loans made under the FHA and VA programs have interest rate ceilings of 9.5 percent (although the one-half percent the FHA charges for mortgage insurance brings its effective interest rate to 10 percent).

The FHA and VA programs have been immensely successful. The FHA has backed more than 10 million mortgages and the VA has underwritten another 9 million, together accounting for more than $280 billion of home-owner loans. The government itself does not make individual mortgage loans. Instead it insures and guarantees loans made by private, profitmaking financial institutions. The nation's savings and loans and commercial banks, therefore, have always been very fond of the FHA and VA loan programs, because they are given the opportunity to make a little money with virtually no risk of a loss. Ever since the early Fifties, there have been proposals kicking around Congress to put Uncle Sam into the business of making mortgage loans directly, but private lending institutions have always seen to it that these bills get nowhere.

In almost every session since World War II, Congress has passed some sort of housing legislation, with many bills being omnibus bills containing a little something for everybody. One recent study of federal housing policy arrived at an estimate that there are forty-six separate housing programs that carry no federal subsidy and an additional twenty with subsidies. These include programs targeted at every conceivable segment of the population: the poor, the elderly, the handicapped, racial minorities, college students, rural residents, and veterans. Not a few top federal housing officials have been driven to distraction trying to keep track of all the programs under their personal jurisdiction.

CABINET STATUS FOR HOUSING

The government's housing programs were scattered around several departments until Congress created the Department of Housing and Urban Development in 1965. President Johnson's pick for the first HUD Secretary, urban affairs expert Robert Weaver, was also the first black ever appointed to a Cabinet position. HUD grew like Topsy during the late Sixties as Congress added layer upon layer of new federal programs to its existing responsibilities. Today it employs some 3,500 people in the Washington metropolitan area and an additional 11,500 people in ten regional offices, thirty-nine area offices, and thirty-eight insuring offices.

HUD's Washington office, appropriately, is a modern edifice in the redevelopment area of Southwest Washington, which was one of the District's worst slum areas until the middle 1950s. The HUD building, dog-bone in shape with exposed concrete surfaces, was designed by the famed architect Marcel Breuer and resembles the UNESCO building in Paris. HUD bigwigs have offices with panoramic views of the Potomac riverfront. (HUD is proud that its headquarters was built with a cost per square foot of $17, reportedly one of the lowest in the annals of extravagant federal office construction.)

There were only three HUD Secretaries between 1965 and the end of 1974, a rather low number compared to the rapid turnover in some other departments. Weaver was succeeded in 1969 by former auto executive and Michigan Governor George Romney, who tried to introduce assembly-line techniques to the homebuilding industry. His pet program was "Operation Breakthrough," a research and development experiment to speed up output and reduce costs through mass production of housing components (such as modular bathrooms and kitchens). The experiment, which accounted for the construction of some 3,000 units in nine cities, got very mixed reviews, and the consensus is that the glowing prospects for mass production were oversold by the program's creators.

When Romney resigned at the start of the second Nixon term (complaining privately that the administration didn't really care much about housing and urban affairs), he was replaced by James Lynn, a corporate lawyer from Cleveland who had been under Secretary of Commerce. Housing industry leaders were less than enthusiastic about Lynn's performance, charging that he was little more than an administrative caretaker. (But Lynn survived the Cabinet shake-up that followed Ford's ascent to the Presidency and was tapped for the important job of directing the Office of Management and Budget.) Many HUD career employees were distrustful of President Nixon, remembering that in 1971 he proposed shrinking HUD and merging it into a new Department of Community Development. Symptomatic of dissension in the ranks at HUD was the stormy resignation in 1974 of HUD Under Secretary Floyd Hyde, a respected former mayor (of Fresno, California) and director of the now moribund Model Cities program. Hyde criticized the Nixon team (and to a lesser extent Congress) for "indifference" to urban problems.

In early 1975 President Ford filled the HUD vacancy with another housing neophyte, Carla Anderson Hills, who had previously been assistant attorney general in charge of the Justice Department's Civil Division. While the housing industry complained about her total lack of experience in housing and urban affairs, no one denied that Mrs. Hills had excelled at every challenge she had faced in her career. Some housing partisans were even hoping that her open mind would make it easier for them to impress upon her their arguments for renewed federal action in housing.

The Nixon administration's heaviest burden in the housing field was the obligation of implementing a bundle of programs that it hadn't conceived and didn't particularly like—the subsidy programs passed by Congress in 1968. In that last year of the "Great Society," the Johnson White House and Capitol Hill made a commitment to encourage the construction or rehabilitation of 26 million housing units over the following ten years, with at least 6 million targeted at low- and middle-income people. This was a very tall order, considering that construction over the previous decade had averaged less than 1.5 million new units annually, of which fewer than 5 percent were built with some degree of federal subsidy.

The 1968 legislation put Uncle Sam into the business of subsidizing mortgage interest rates, and predictably, federal housing expenditures soared.

But so did the number of units constructed and "rehabbed" with federal money. During the first Nixon term, subsidy support was extended to an additional 1.6 million low- and moderate-income families—more than had been covered in the entire thirty-four previous years of federal housing involvement. In 1970 nearly 430,000 units of new subsidized housing were begun, a whopping 30 percent of the total 1.5 million starts that year.

The two big new programs of the 1968 act were interest-subsidy plans for rental units (called Section 236) and homeownership (Section 235). Under the 236 plan, private and nonprofit developers would conceive an apartment project and line up a loan with FHA mortgage insurance at the prevailing interest rate. The developer would pay 1 percent interest and the federal government would pay the difference. The apartments could be rented only to low- and moderate-income tenants at rents of no more than 25 percent of their income. The developer was officially limited to a 6 percent profit on his investment, but tax shelter opportunities often led to a much higher effective rate. Over the first several years of the 236 program, tenants had a median income of $5,300. About 76 percent of the tenants were white, and about 20 percent were Negro.

The Section 235 program was, like Section 236, an interest-subsidy program. Developers would build or rehabilitate individual houses (often clusters of townhouses in the suburbs or individual old rowhouses in center-city neighborhoods) and then sell to moderate-income families. (Most 235 buyers had incomes of about $6,500 in 1972.) The buyer arranged a regular FHA-insured mortgage (usually about $18,500) with a savings and loan institution, but he paid only 1 percent of the interest himself, with the federal government picking up the rest. As under the 236 rental program, a solid majority of the 235 purchasers were white (66 percent), while 22 percent were black and 11 percent Spanish-American.

HOUSING MORATORIUM

The details of these two subsidy programs are more or less irrelevant today, because the programs are in limbo, with drastically reduced funding. The Nixon administration, in January 1973, declared them a failure and suspended them indefinitely. The proclamation was controversial, because the 235 and 236 programs had both fervent advocates and critics. They were basically production-oriented programs, so the housing industry was enthusiastic about them. The critics maintained, however, that the dollars poured into those programs built structures of too high a quality for too few people (mostly lower middle class), while doing little to improve the severe housing deprivation of the real poor. Some critics also argued that the programs were full of juicy incentives for padded costs and outright fraud. In the 236 programs, the builder's profits, developer's tax write-offs, and the architect's and engineer's professional fees all depended on total project cost, so there was a built-in incentive to build bigger and better than necessary.

The 235 program was marred by a few unscrupulous real estate speculators who were able to bribe local FHA officials into preparing phony appraisals and approving FHA-insured mortgages for families that couldn't possibly keep up the monthly payments. Here's how the scheme worked: the speculator would buy a rundown house for very little money and make a few superficial repairs. A bribed FHA appraiser would put an inflated value on the property, and the speculator would sell it for a quick profit to an unsuspecting moderate-income buyer, who would have to make only a small down payment and start making monthly payments (principal and 1 percent interest) on his FHA-insured mortgage. The buyer would soon find, however, that the cosmetic repairs masked major flaws, which he wouldn't have enough money to repair. Unable to fix up the house (and often unable to maintain the monthly payments, besides), the buyer would abandon it, sticking the government for the amount of the mortgage and the burden of trying to sell a dilapidated house.

In this way, the FHA became the largest owner of slum housing in several cities around the country. (At the end of 1974, the government's nationwide inventory of single-family houses acquired through foreclosures numbered about 74,000, and they were costing Uncle Sam about $460,000 a day to maintain.) When the fraud came to light all over the nation, criminal convictions were won against many real estate operators and local FHA officials, although no one at HUD headquarters in Washington was ever accused of a role in the scandal.

The Nixon administration's disenchantment with existing housing programs covered not only 235 and 236, but also the venerable program of funding large apartment complexes for the poor and elderly (the conventional kind of "public housing," administered by local housing authorities). Today some 4,500 cities and towns have federally funded public housing, providing more than a million homes for 2.5 million people. In addition to paying the principal and interest on the housing authority bonds that built the complexes, the federal government has been chipping in some $300 million each year to cover operating deficits. Some public housing is very attractive, safe, and financially sound, especially the more recent projects. But much of it—in particular the drab, high-rise buildings of the Fifties—has become crime-infested shells. The classic example was the Pruitt-Igoe project in St. Louis: 33 eleven-story buildings (2,870 apartments), completed in 1956 and virtually abandoned by the early Seventies. In 1973 the project was declared a total loss and plans were made to demolish the entire group. It is highly unlikely that the federal government will spend any more money after fiscal 1976 to build public housing projects as we know them today.

A NEW APPROACH

The Nixon administration proposed replacing the construction-oriented programs with an expanded combination of housing allowances and leased housing—two concepts that had been kicking around in prototype programs for more than a decade. Instead of building housing especially for the poor and moderate-income sections of the population, why not put more money into their pockets so they can find what they need from the general stock of private housing? This would have the alleged benefit of dispersing the poor more evenly throughout a community and enabling them to live with greater dignity, without the stigma of being lumped in with other needy people. Under the administration's leased housing plan, a needy family would find its own apartment or rental house and pay a portion of the rent themselves (an amount equal to between 15 and 25 percent of their gross family income). The rest of their rent would be paid to the owner of the unit by the local housing authority, which would in turn be reimbursed by the federal government. Private landlords would assume the responsibility for maintaining the units.

The basic flaw of this plan, its critics contend, is the assumption that the housing supply will spontaneously expand to meet the greater demand generated by more money in the pockets of the poor. But in the tight money markets of today, housing starts and rehabilitations are down sharply. And in some areas, rental construction is being neglected in favor of condominium and single-family development, because apartment projects just aren't turning an adequate profit over and above soaring maintenance and utility expenses. During a credit pinch, as housing expert Morton Schussheim has noted, "simply to provide [low-income] families with more money for housing would lead to higher rents in many housing markets with little increase in the supply." Schussheim, like some other housing experts, feels that the allowance plan could be useful if enforcement of housing codes and laws against racial discrimination are improved, but it should be coupled with a continuation of federal production programs.

Defenders of the now-abandoned 235 and 236 programs maintain that accommodations for moderate-income families just wouldn't have been built over the past few years in the absence of strong federal inducements. They point out, too, that the FHA fraud scandal was really centered more in the nonsubsidized mortgage insurance programs than in the 235 program. As for foreclosure rates, the 21,000 foreclosures on 235 homes (as of the middle of 1974) represent less than 5 percent of the 440,000 units built or rehabilitated under the program since 1969—admittedly a higher foreclosure rate than in the general market, but not as high as the program's detractors would lead one to believe. Of the 3,700 apartment projects built under the 236 program, about 170 have either been foreclosed or had the mortgages assigned to the FHA.

In the 1974 Housing and Community Development Act, Congress provided just enough money for 235 and 236 to meet past commitments and then terminate both programs. The act puts emphasis on so-called Section 8 assistance—a modified form of the leased housing concept with a minimum of supervision by either the federal government or local housing authority. Uncle Sam will assist low-income families to rent housing from private landlords, who will own, operate and maintain the units, and collect the rent directly from their tenants.

HELP FOR THE CITIES

The last two letters of HUD's initials stand for "Urban Development," a federal activity that has meant different things in different eras. As conceived in the Housing Act of 1949 and implemented through the Fifties, urban development meant slum clearance: acquisition of private land by public renewal authorities, wholesale demolition, and subsequent reconstruction. The federal commitment in funds was minuscule, and the results were proportional. By the end of the Eisenhower administration, only 41 renewal projects in some 475 participating communities had been completed. In the first two years of the Kennedy administration, the pace picked up considerably. By 1963, some 1,000 communities—including virtually all cities of over 250,000 people—had urban renewal programs receiving some amount of federal assistance.

By the middle of the Sixties (as urban riots spread across America), it dawned on a lot of people that urban renewal had done little for the poor residents of the cities, and in fact had probably aggravated their plight. In many cities, more housing was demolished than was built anew. The relocated poor people couldn't afford the new apartments and townhouses, many of which were intended to bolster the urban tax base with high-salaried residents. In response to this problem, HUD in the late Sixties gave top priority to renewal projects with inexpensive housing and downplayed renewal of commercial districts. The Johnson administration, as a cornerstone of its Great Society package, conceived the Model Cities program.

Model Cities was not just a housing program, but a comprehensive urban improvement plan that recognized the interrelation of such factors as education, job training, recreation, health, crime prevention, and housing. About 60 percent of the Model Cities dollar has gone into social development programs rather than construction. Spending for the Model Cities program hit a peak of about $590 million in 1973. In 1974 the Nixon administration and Congress replaced it with general, no-strings-attached urban assistance, in the style of revenue sharing. Given the very limited funding (spread over some 100 cities) and the reluctance of some federal agencies to surrender control to Model Cities planners, the program's concrete success was hardly startling. Many observers credit it, however, with bringing an unprecedented number of grass-roots leaders into the urban planning process, and with pioneering better coordination of the many different pieces in the urban puzzle.

FINANCING HOUSING

Washington sees its principal mission in the housing field to be the stimulation of private construction, not primarily because people need more and better housing, but because the nation needs a healthy homebuilding industry to keep the economy rolling. Like the auto industry, homebuilding has a tremendous spillover effect on the rest of the economy. Homebuilding is very vulnerable to rising interest rates and tightening mortgage money. In times of extreme inflation, many people look for a higher yield on their savings than they can get from the "thrift institutions," whose rates are constrained by law (and, more practically, by the income they receive from their mortgages).

When the thrift institutions lose deposits, Washington is expected to boost the pool of mortgage money so that homebuilding and the whole economy don't suffer a decline. The instruments of this boost are the Federal Home Loan Bank System, which makes short- and long-term loans to savings and loan associations; Federal National Mortgage Association, since 1968 a private, government-sponsored corporation that makes mortgage money available by buying existing mortgages from mortgage companies, S&Ls, banks, life insurance companies, and other lenders; Government National Mortgage Association (called "Ginnie Mae"), a wholly government-owned corporation that operates like Fannie Mae in the realm of federally subsidized mortgages; and Federal Home Loan Mortgage Corporation ("Freddie Mac"), which buys mortgages from S&Ls and markets them in convenient packages to investors.

Each of these corporations operates in a slightly different way, filling a different need of the housing finance industry. What they have in common is their function as a conduit between private capital and the housing market. They tap this capital by selling bond issues, and the government's backing of the corporation gives its bond offerings a safety and public appeal enjoyed by few commercial issues.

Despite the efforts of these federal backstops, the housing industry over the past couple of years has had a hard time competing for capital with other investments. This is reflected in a steadily declining volume of housing starts: from a record 2.3 million in 1972 to 2.1 million in 1973 to a sickly 1.4 million during the inflation-wracked year of 1974.

Out of these lean times in the conventional housing industry has come a brash new star—the mobile home. Mobile home manufacturing soared by 80 percent between 1968 and 1972, and today approaches 600,000 new units per year. In 1972 mobile homes accounted for about 31 percent of all single-family new housing units. They are certainly second-best to conventional homeownership (having relatively short life expectancies, and price deprecia-tions that reflect this), but in many regions of the country mobile homes are about the only kind of housing that moderate-income families can afford to own. The FHA and VA have a hand in promoting mobile home ownership by offering mortgage insurance and loan guarantees. While the output of mobile homes continues to mount, they still comprise a very small portion (less than 5 percent) of the nation's total housing stock.

THE HOUSING LOBBY

The guardian angel of the housing industry is the National Association of Home Builders, one of the nation's largest trade associations, with some 75,000 members and a Washington-based staff of nearly 200. Its head-quarters is a large modern building (called the National Housing Center) at 15th and M Streets in downtown Washington. The industry that NAHB represents accounts for a big chunk of the gross national product ($45 billion worth of new residential construction in the peak year 1972). The homebuild-ing industry has traditionally been localized and fragmented among thousands of relatively small builders. Of the estimated 110,000 homebuilders in the nation, more than half probably produce fewer than 25 units of housing each year. But the industry is gradually becoming dominated by large builders, characterized by annual sales of more than $10 million, operations in several metropolitan areas simultaneously, and increasing reliance on mass-produc-tion techniques (everything from preformed roof trusses to entire rooms and sections of houses). By 1974, the nation's 650 largest homebuilders ac-counted for about one-third of all residential construction.

The enormity and geographic spread of the housing industry gives it an unusually strong voice on Capitol Hill, where virtually every member of Congress has a contingent of homebuilders and subcontractors in his district (or, at least, is acutely aware of the spillover effect of homebuilding on the whole economy of his district).

NAHB lobbies Congress and the executive branch on everything that could have some remote impact on their industry. In 1962, for example, it tried in vain to stall President Kennedy's executive order on equal housing opportu-nity for racial minority groups, claiming that open occupancy would cause new housing construction to plummet. (They were wrong: open-housing laws have had a negligible effect on housing starts, and have also had a negligible effect—due to inadequate enforcement—on patterns of segregation in housing.)

When the Johnson administration curtailed credit to put the brakes on inflation in 1966, housing starts fell by a startling 20 percent, and NAHB launched a major campaign for long-range federal housing production goals. The 1968 production programs—and the quantitative target of 26 million new or rebuilt housing units over the following decade—were conceived at a massive strategy conference convened by NAHB in the fall of 1967, attended by representatives from more than forty trade associations and public interest groups, congressmen, federal bureaucrats, and academicians.

The NAHB often lobbies in conjunction with other organizations that share its interest in a strong housing industry, such as the building trades unions, U.S. Savings and Loan League, National Forest Products Association, and associations of architects, real estate salesmen, engineers, and everyone else who makes his living from residential construction. During the housing slump of 1974, the NAHB and its associated organizations poured money into full-page newspaper ads urging the government to render all kinds of assistance. They sought looser credit from the Federal Reserve Board and "Fannie Mae" for home mortgages. They sought legislation to exempt from taxation the first $1,000 earned as interest on savings and loan accounts, the main source of home loans. They opposed, unsuccessfully, the issuance by commercial banks of high-interest notes that induced many depositors to withdraw their money from thrift institutions. The newspaper ads, of course, were just the visible tip of an enormous lobbying effort focused on Capitol Hill. But the builders' efforts seemed to have been canceled out by the general decay of the economy. Total housing starts for 1974 came to about 1.4 million units of single-family houses and apartments—down 35 percent from the previous year and down 43 percent from the record 2.3 million units in 1972.

WHERE NOW?

In recent years, advocates of better housing have looked enviously at the big-dollar federal budgets that resulted in putting men on the moon, building 42,500 miles of interstate highways, and (some years earlier) developing atomic energy. With understandable puzzlement, they have asked why a similar commitment has not been made to improving housing for the poor. Why hasn't housing assistance caught the voter's fancy?

Part of the answer lies with the 63 percent of Americans who hold title to their own homes. Their homeownership is the result of painstaking, month-by-month labor, saving, and paying-off-the-mortgage. They like to think they "made it on their own," despite the help they had from Uncle Sam—perhaps with a FHA or VA mortgage, certainly through homeowner tax deductions and the hidden mechanisms of the federal housing credit corporations. Most homeowners don't consider the kind of government help they've received to be subsidies, at least not comparable to direct housing payments to the poor. In any event, the homeowning majority (which is also the politically active majority) has indicated to their elected officials in Washington, either explicitly or merely by saying nothing, that federal housing assistance to the poor is not a pressing item on the agenda.

But housing standards in America have been escalated—by building codes, zoning, inflation, health standards, market demand, and other factors—to levels of quality that make homeownership unattainable by a quarter of the population. The poor will continue to be renters. And if they are to have decent rental housing, it must be subsidized until the poor can increase their purchasing power through education, training, and enforcement of equal opportunity hiring. The subsidy could be one to the builder as an interest subsidy, to the renter as a direct allowance, or one of a dozen other forms.

For the moment, Washington is uncertain about where it's heading in housing. Subsidy programs for the poor are being funded on a limited, tentative, trial-and-error basis. But the political pendulum might swing back again, and some future administration may turn toward the demands of low-income city dwellers and the rural poor. When this swing comes, Congress will be asked to increase its appropriations to build housing with government support. And when this happens, the Department of Housing and Urban Development will perk up. Morale in the HUD headquarters building will improve. Teletypes and photocopiers will buzz again with housing news, as Washington again pours out money for better shelter throughout the fifty states.

40 BATTLEGROUND OF TRANSPORTATION

Washington has been knee deep in the transportation business since the nation was founded.

In the early days of the Republic, the government financed the construction of national roads between the eastern seaboard and the western territories. In the middle of the nineteenth century, Washington gave away huge amounts of western land to spur the builders of railroads. The government has been in the vanguard, too, of technological research that has had a secondary effect on everything from nuclear ships to jet aircraft. (The government would have immersed itself in development of a supersonic transport plane, if a tenuous coalition of environmentalists and congressional cost cutters hadn't defeated it.)

Now, in the final quarter of the twentieth century, America has the most sprawling network of transportation in the world—hundreds of thousands of miles of highways, railroad track, navigable waterways, and airline routes. This system is the underpinning of economic and social life, for it is the means by which Americans move themselves and their goods for profit and pleasure. Sometimes it works with a smooth efficiency; sometimes it bogs down in frustrating irrationality. For better or for worse, it is the product of policies made—or not made—in Washington.

In fact, today the federal government exerts more direct control over transportation than it does over any other part of the economy. No other sector receives as wide an array of federal support, direct and hidden, as the transportation industries. Various highway taxes collected by Uncle Sam built and maintain the $70 billion, 42,500-mile Interstate Highway System. Public subsidies bolster most of the nation's regional airlines, enabling them to reach small isolated cities that could not otherwise support scheduled service. Washington picks up part of the tab for developing subways and commuter bus lines and subsidizes their operating deficits, too. Federal funds cover a portion of the cost of building and operating America's merchant marine. Washington finances the harbor and channel improvements upon which the barge industry relies. Washington subsidizes all passenger rail service, and has virtually (if temporarily) nationalized the bankrupt railroads of the Northeast, with a commitment in 1974 of some $2.2 billion in grants and guaranteed loans. Through the federal regulatory agencies, Washington passes judgment on the routes and fees charged by airlines, truckers, railroads, barges, and pipeline companies. This federal involvement is no small matter, since the transportation industries account for nearly 20 percent of the GNP.

Washington does not now have, and never has had, a coherent national transportation policy. About the closest thing to it has been the government's tacit, but distinct, preference for highways. In this Washington has been extremely responsive to not only the highway lobby but the wishes of the

American citizenry. The car is America's favorite mode of transportation, for everything from daily commuting to a trip across the country. (The rise of the automobile, of course, was made possible as much by increasing middle-class affluence as by Congress's commitment to more roads.) The growing dominance of the automobile has had tremendous impact on other modes of transportation (not to mention such things as housing, suburban growth, and the decay of the inner city). It led to the gradual deterioration of mass transit, which in most cities means bus systems. It also contributed to the decline of intercity rail service. Trains lost their cost advantage to cars years ago, and on some routes have nearly lost their time edge as well.

What passes for transportation policy is the mass of decisions—some dovetailing, some contradictory—made in congressional committees, executive agencies, and independent commissions all over Washington. It has been estimated that more than twenty separate government bodies focus on some facet of transportation. As in other policy areas, the industry and labor lobbies exert a powerful influence over the shape of transportation policy, especially in Congress. Committees on the Hill just don't have the staff expertise, manpower, and financial resources to cope with their responsibilities, so they rely on lobbyists for everything from drafting a bill to preparing the statistical rationale for it. The 1974 Northeast railroad aid legislation, for example, was drawn up by lawyers of the Union Pacific Railroad, which isn't one of the bankrupt companies, but which has a vital stake in the speedy recovery of Northeast lines to which it connects.

DEPARTMENT OF TRANSPORTATION

At the top of the federal transportation structure—in rank if not power—is the Department of Transportation. "Dee Oh Tee," as it is known around Washington, came into being on April 1, 1967, the product of an attempt to provide some sort of central approach to transportation planning. It consolidated several agencies that had been functioning on transportation matters for many years before DOT was even thought of. DOT employs more than 105,000 persons (38,000 of whom belong to the U.S. Coast Guard, one of DOT's subunits). The Washington staff totals 8,762 persons, and they are housed in three buildings in Southwest Washington's urban renewal area.

Existing under the DOT umbrella are the following agencies: Federal Aviation Administration, Coast Guard, Federal Highway Administration, National Highway Traffic Administration, Federal Railroad Administration, Urban Mass Transportation Administration, St. Lawrence Seaway Development Corp., National Transportation Safety Board, and the U.S. Railway Association. In addition to the individual agencies, there is an office of the secretary of transportation, employing some 2,200 people. President Nixon's first Transportation Secretary was John A. Volpe, a construction tycoon and former governor of Massachusetts who later served as ambassador to Italy. He was succeeded by Claude S. Brinegar, a scholarly, soft-spoken official who stayed in the post through the first few months of the Ford administration. A PhD economist and longtime executive of the Union Oil Company, Brinegar did not seem comfortable with the political maneuvering and in-fighting that is an essential part of the Washington scene. He was replaced in early 1975 by William T. Coleman, Jr., a black corporate lawyer from Philadelphia who has experience in transportation law (and deeper experience in civil rights).

As a member of the President's Cabinet, the Secretary of Transportation has the major job of proposing and coordinating transportation programs and policies. In fact, though, DOT has little control over the two major determinants of transportation policy—routing and pricing. The congressmen who created DOT made sure that the new baby did not take away too much power or authority from the grandfatherly and aging regulatory agencies that really rule the nation's surface, air, and water transportation—agencies like the Civil Aeronautics Board, the Interstate Commerce Commission, and the Federal Maritime Commission. DOT can only tell these agencies what it thinks they ought to do. And they don't treat DOT any differently from any other party who comes before them with suggestions on the proper course of action. DOT has encountered outright hostility from the old-line regulatory agencies for advocating less regulation and more competition between the various modes of transport. In dealing with Congress, DOT finds itself in the same position as any other Executive Branch department. It can only recommend and lobby for a piece of legislation. Final decisions—like how much to appropriate for mass transit or highways—are up to legislators.

The biggest of DOT's components is the Federal Aviation Administration (FAA), employing nearly 57,000 persons in locations all over the world. The FAA establishes and enforces safety rules for airports (such as antihijacking programs), airplanes, and pilots, both commercial and private. It also licenses pilots. The men on land who guide planes through America's air lanes are air controllers in the employ of the FAA. FAA also administers the airport trust fund—a kitty, derived from taxes paid by airport users, that helps finance airport improvements. The FAA has no say in the allocation of air routes or setting of fares, which are in the bailiwick of the CAB.

The year 1974 was a rough one for the FAA, which came under fire from Capitol Hill for lax air safety standards. A House report criticized the agency for dragging its feet in ordering McDonnell Douglas to redesign a DC-10 cargo door that it found to be faulty. The FAA finally did get around to issuing the order, but not until the malfunctioning door was blamed for a massively fatal crash near Paris, France. Then there was an uproar over an airliner crash near Dulles International Airport, a Washington area facility used by many congressmen. When the tragedy was found to have resulted from confusion about the plane's altitude, Congress told the FAA to order the installation of a ground-proximity warning system in every airliner.

Probably the most powerful unit in DOT is the Federal Highway Administration. The administration and its predecessors, which date back to the early 1800s, have always played a key role in our country's transportation system. It decides where federally funded roads will go, working in tandem with local planners. The highway administration is in charge of the $6 billion Highway Trust Fund, which has put up about 90 percent of the money used to build the Interstate Highway System over the past two decades. While Congress set the limit on how much money should be spent on the massive project, it was the highway administration's job to dole it out to localities. Now that the gigantic interstate system is almost completed, the administration will focus its attention on improving some 10,000 miles of roads that feed the interstate highways. The highway administration doesn't just build and plan roads. It is also in charge of a safety program for trucks that operate interstate, and it has control over Lady Bird Johnson's famed Highway

Beautification Program. As antihighway sentiment bubbled over in the late 1960s and early 1970s, the highway administration started to devote more attention to the safety of the roads built under its jurisdiction.

There is an agency at DOT that can properly say it was fathered by consumer advocate Ralph Nader. The National Highway Traffic Safety Administration came into being in 1966 when Congress, prodded and attacked by Nader, voted out an auto safety act. The 922 employees of the administration work on a variety of tasks, including safety standards that automakers must meet. The most famous, and to some the most notorious, of these was the interlocking seat belt device, which prevented a car from starting until the passengers belted up. (But Congress, in response to rising public annoyance, sidestepped the federal safety officials by passing a bill in 1974 outlawing the annoying interlocking seat belt devices.) The administration also develops model highway safety programs for state motor vehicle bureaus. But it has been reluctant to take away federal funds from states that refuse to adopt its standards, and that's one reason why there is a lack of national uniformity on auto safety standards.

The federal government first took formal note of mass transit in 1964, when, in an effort to aid several failing commuter train systems, it set up a mass transportation unit in its housing and urban development program. That unit was transferred to DOT in 1968 and given the formal name of the Urban Mass Transportation Administration. UMTA employs 400 persons, a strikingly small number when compared with the nearly 5,000 employees of the Federal Highway Administration. This is indicative of how our transportation policy has favored highways over mass transit. But UMTA's stock is beginning to go up, what with growing public concern about auto congestion, air pollution, soaring fuel costs, and the social dislocations caused by highway building, especially in urban and suburban areas. Mass Transit won a victory—more symbolic than financial—when Congress voted in 1973, for the first time, to allow limited Highway Trust Fund moneys (collected from taxes on such things as gasoline, motor oil, tires, tractor-trailer trucks, and automotive parts) to be used for mass transit projects to a limited degree.

The mass transportation unit is primarily a funding agency that helps localities come up with money to improve their mass transit system. Grants are made for the purchase of new buses and commuter trains. Grants are also made for demonstration projects that test new ideas in mass transit, such as bus express lanes on highways and "dial-a-ride," a cross between a bus line and a taxi service. Grants are used to further the training and education of mass transit executive and managerial personnel. July 1974 was a typical month for UMTA's financial assistance program. St. Louis got $12 million to help buy 240 new buses. Bloomington, Illinois, received $1.1 million to buy 20 buses and renovate a garage. Cumberland, Maryland, was given about $600,000 to buy the assets of a local private bus line that was failing. Philadelphia got $30 million to help start construction of a rail line that would link the downtown area of the city to the international airport outside it. Clearwater, Florida, obtained about $216,000 to buy four new buses and other equipment. Manchester, New Hampshire, received $20,000 to assist local planning officials in determining the transit needs in their area. Monroe, Louisiana, was given $15,000 to update data about its transportation system.

UMTA's capital grant program has helped accelerate the trend toward public takeover of failing, privately owned transit systems. There have been some striking successes in restoring the health of sick lines with the purchase of new rolling stock and the improvement of services. Some of the UMTA demonstration projects have paid off successfully with novel mass transit ideas. But some demonstration projects have not lived up to their ballyhoo. Take, for example, UMTA's "people mover" rail system being built in Morgantown, West Virginia, a town of some 29,000 people that happens to be in the district of Chairman Harley Staggers of the House Commerce Committee, which has a big say in transportation policy. Originally estimated to cost $13.5 million for a 2.2-mile elevated system, the problem-plagued project has now soared beyond $65 million. But even critics of the cost overrun concede that lessons learned from mistakes in the Morgantown project will save many millions of dollars in subsequent projects.

At the end of 1974, Congress and the White House took the first giant step toward the rejuvenation of American mass transit. They made a commitment to spend $11.8 billion on mass transit over the following six years. About $7.8 billion of that will go towards new equipment, and the remaining $4 billion will be spent on operating subsidies—the first ever to be paid by the federal government. Most of the money will be paid out to state and local governments to spend as they see fit. To get a sense of the significance of this commitment, keep in mind that a mere $3 billion had been spent on mass transit over the previous fourteen years of federal involvement.

One of the most independent members of the DOT family is the National Transportation Safety Board, a 300-employee body that acts as a detective to establish the causes of transportation accidents. Its probers cover all modes of transportation, even gas pipelines. The board's accident investigations give rise to specific recommendations on what other government agencies can do to prevent hazardous situations from turning into disasters. In 1973 the board made 271 safety suggestions, most of which were not acted upon. Therein lies the board's essential defect: its ideas are not binding on any other agency.

Fulfilling a role somewhat analogous to the FAA's is the Federal Railroad Administration, whose more than 1,400 employees concentrate on problems involving equipment and track maintenance and operating safety standards. (The crucial economic policies governing the nation's railroads—rates, routes, and the abandoning of unprofitable services—are set outside of DOT, at the ICC.) The unit's potential power over the railroads was amply demonstrated in mid-1974, when it ordered the Penn Central to close down a section of unsafe tracks and reroute trains while repairs were made. But the railroad administration shows this sort of toughness infrequently, and more often it protects rather than polices the industry.

The DOT structure also includes the venerable U.S. Coast Guard, established in 1790. The Coast Guard's wide range of maritime duties includes searches and rescues, marking the coasts to aid navigators in preventing accidents, inspection of small boats for safety violations, and drafting of many of the safety regulations that it enforces. The Guard is also supposed to help protect the marine environment. The newest part of DOT is the U.S. Railway Association, a nonprofit government corporation that will play a key role in reorganizing the ailing rail service of seventeen northeastern and midwestern states. Finally, there's the St. Lawrence Seaway Development Corporation, a government-owned company that administers, with Canada, the commercial waterway between the two countries' borders.

The independent regulatory agencies have a louder say about the nuts and bolts of transportation policy than the giant DOT. The granddaddy of them all is the Interstate Commerce Commission. Formed in 1887, it regulates all forms of surface transportation: railroads, trucks, household movers, freight forwarders, water carriers, bus lines, and even pipelines. The ICC decides who gets which route and how much they can charge their customers. It rules on mergers of carriers and regulates their issuance of stock. The agency was originally established to end the "destructive" competition between the railroad barons of the post-Civil War period and to curb the abuses of their monopoly power. But today it is often cited as the best example of the way in which a regulatory agency can successfully stifle the forces of free competition.

On a practical level, the most striking characteristic of the ICC is the amount of time it takes to do its work. Merger cases drag on for ten years at a time. Rulemaking cases never seem to progress. And enforcement investigations dawdle while consumers are being maltreated. The agency's 2,130 employees are often ridiculed by Washington newsmen, who jokingly accuse them of sleepwalking on the job.

Cries for abolition of the ICC have come from noted economists, from Senator William Proxmire (D-Wis.), and from Ralph Nader (who calls the agency the "Interstate Commerce Omission"). While not suggesting abolition, DOT and the Federal Trade Commission have both urged a trimming of the ICC's powers over rates and marketplace entry.

The ruler of the American airways is the Civil Aeronautics Board, established in 1938. The Board parcels out routes to airlines, approves or rejects air fares, grants subsidies to local service carriers that run a deficit, regulates relationships between airlines, investigates fraud by travel agents and tour organizers, and monitors citizen complaints about air service.

Much of the problem with the CAB's performance stems from its dual role as regulator and promoter of the air industry. It has traditionally shielded the scheduled carriers from the competition of charter airlines and competition among themselves (from carriers that would like to serve an existing route at substantially lower fares). Robert Timm, who took over the chairmanship of the board during the Nixon administration (but was demoted by Ford), has indicated that the CAB's top priority should be an improvement of the profit picture of the scheduled airlines, through higher fares and fewer flights. When Pan Am came begging for a $120 million-a-year subsidy (to cover losses incurred in competition with government-owned foreign carriers), it was not surprising that the CAB endorsed the proposal, while DOT, the White House, and much of Congress turned thumbs down.

The Federal Maritime Commission, an independent regulatory agency, was set up in 1961, but its ancestors date back to 1916. The commission regulates a broad spectrum of ocean shipping activity, including pacts between shipping conferences, ratemaking, and the operations of ocean freight forwarders and terminal operators. It protects American carriers against discriminatory practices by foreign governments, and retaliation is the name of the game when a U.S. line is treated unfavorably abroad. It also administers the various laws Congress has passed to shelter American shipping from foreign competition, such as the Jones Act of 1920, which requires that all goods shipped between U.S. ports be carried on U.S.-flag vessels. (This requirement substantially raises the cost of goods "imported" to Alaska and Hawaii from the U.S. mainland.) The FMC's 319 employees operate far from the public spotlight. In fact, the most publicity that the agency received in recent years came when its then chairman-designate, Helen D. Bentley, was heard cussing out a maritime officer over a ship's radio.

SHIPS AND TRAINS

Of greater significance to the American merchant marine is the federal Maritime Administration, a Commerce Department branch that doles out the government's subsidies for the construction and operation of U.S.-flag vessels. For decades the size of the U.S. merchant marine—in number of ships and percentage of world trade carried—has been declining, due to the much lower shipbuilding costs and sailors' wages in other countries. Through the Sixties, the government picked up roughly 40 percent of the cost of building some ten ships each year—an output of new vessels that wasn't even keeping pace with the scrapping of outmoded ships. In 1968 President Nixon made a campaign pledge to "restore the United States to the role of a first-rate maritime power," and within two years he and Congress made good on it. The Merchant Marine Act of 1970 has boosted the annual federal construction subsidy from about $100 million to more than $275 million, while continuing to pay operating subsidies of about $240 million each year. At the same time, the act seeks to reduce, over a period of years, the subsidy proportion of each project from 40 percent to 25 percent.

The 1970 goal of thirty new ships a year has not been met, but production is booming in American shipyards for the first time in years. The steady decline in the percentage of American trade tonnage carried in U.S. ships has recently leveled out. Particular emphasis is being put on the construction of bulk cargo ships, to carry liquefied natural gas, grain, and oil. (About 17 percent of the U.S. wheat sold to the Soviet Union in 1972 was shipped in American vessels.) American passenger ships, incidentally, are nearly an extinct species, driven out of existence by the speed and cheapness of air travel and lower wage costs of foreign oceanliners. In 1974 there were only two U.S.-flag passenger ships left.

Another endangered species is rail passenger service, which is now in the hands of Amtrak, a government operation that began in May 1971. Over the past few decades, train ridership and profits declined steadily. The railroads, which make their money primarily in hauling freight, put little money into passenger trains and simply let the equipment and service deteriorate. Most rail companies were happy to let Amtrak take the burden off their backs. Since the Amtrak takeover, rail service has improved slightly and ridership has steadily increased nationwide (with an exceptional surge during the gasoline shortage in the winter of 1973–74). But the whopping deficits continue, requiring Congress to contribute some $200 million each year.

DOT is urging Congress to allow Amtrak to abandon many of its especially unprofitable long-haul routes. The legislators are anxious to trim the Amtrak subsidy, but at the same time they are afraid of the political repercussions back home of cutting cities and states off the rail lines. Most observers feel that long-haul train service is on the way out. The future of passenger service lies in high-speed trains between large cities no more than a few hundred miles apart (like the popular Metroliner between Washington and New York, which could considerably shorten its current three-hour runs if the track were smoother and straighter).

What better example could there be of the fragmentation of the federal transportation structure than the existence of an influential transport agency in the Department of Defense? It's the Army Corps of Engineers, whose public works projects are even more important to the barge industry than the rate-setting functions of the ICC. Since 1824, the corps has improved the nation's waterways by dredging harbors and channels and building canals. The chief beneficiaries of these toll-free waterways are some 1,700 operators of tugboats and barges. The barge business is a large, but publicly little-known, segment of the transportation industry. There are about 25,500 miles of commercially navigable waters in the U.S., mostly east of the Mississippi River (compared to some 210,500 miles of railroads and 649,000 miles of paved roads nationwide). Barges carry about 15 percent of the nation's total domestic tonnage, specializing in such bulk commodities as coal, petroleum products, lumber, and sand and gravel.

POWER ON THE HILL

After all is said and done, the real formulator of transportation policy—incoherent though it may be—is Congress. The members of the House and Senate decide the relative funding of highways and mass transit. They decide how airports will be developed, and how much money to give the Corps of Engineers for channel improvement. They determine the future structure of rail service in the Northeast. They make end-runs around the "independent" regulatory agencies when a ruling is not to their liking. They veto auto safety features proposed by the National Highway Traffic Safety Administration. They decide whether to bail out a financially troubled airline.

Congress, of course, does not speak with one voice on transportation. Power is spread over several different committees, each in charge of a different mode of transportation. Some issues don't fall neatly into one jurisdiction or another. Former DOT Secretary John Volpe noted in dismay that the bill to open the Highway Trust Fund for mass transit had to pass through three committees in each chamber: the House committees on Public Works, Ways and Means, and Banking and Currency, plus the Senate committees on Public Works, Finance, and Banking, Housing, and Urban Affairs. Within each committee, of course, there are varying alignments of regional and commercial interests. Congressmen and senators vote according to the needs of their home areas. Those from predominantly rural states, where highways are the chief means of getting around, cannot be expected to feel the same about mass transit as the representatives of densely urban states.

Senator Jennings Randolph (D-W.Va.), chairman of the Senate Public Works Committee, was an executive of the American Road Builders Association for several years between a stint in the House and his election to the Senate. To him, better highways are invaluable to the economic health of his lightly settled home state. For a number of years the Transportation subcommittee of the House Public Works Committee was chaired by Chicago's Representative John Kluczynski (D-Ill.), who died in 1975. He had been an opponent of busting the Highway Trust Fund until 1973, when Mayor Richard J. Daley let him know that the Chicago Transit Authority could use an infusion of federal funds. Kluczynski was succeeded in the subcommittee chairmanship by Representative James Howard (D-N.J.). The steadily growing mass transit forces are led in the Senate by Senator Harrison A. Williams, Jr., a Democrat from the most urban state in the nation, New Jersey.

The same patterns of enlightened self-interest are seen in the making of congressional aviation policy, co..trolled by the Senate and House Commerce Committees. Senator Warren Magnuson (D-Wash.), chairman of the Senate unit, keeps in mind the interest of the Seattle-based Boeing Company, whose sales of 727 and 747 jumbojets are directly related to the health of the aviation industry. Senator Howard Cannon (D-Nev.), chairman of the Commerce Subcommittee on Aviation, pushes for an easing of restrictions on low-cost charter flights, which would benefit the convention and tourism business of Las Vegas. Similar considerations motivate Senator Daniel Inouye, the Hawaiian Democrat who chairs the subcommittee on Foreign Commerce and Tourism. The House Committee on Interstate and Foreign Commerce has jurisdiction over Amtrak, too. (Was it just a coincidence when Amtrak set up a Turbo Train run—long since discontinued—between Washington and Parkersburg, West Virginia, stopping in the tiny city of Keyser, the hometown of House Commerce Chairman Harley Staggers?) Senator Vance Hartke (D-Ind.), chairman of the Commerce Subcommittee on Surface Transportation, is hospitable to all the transportation interests, especially the railroads (whose trade association and unions have rewarded him handsomely in campaign contributions).

Transportation has not normally been a hot issue on the Hill, lacking "sex appeal" with the voters. There are signs, though, that citizen interest is picking up, especially as the subject becomes more entwined with such issues as the environment, energy policy, and the whole controversy over "growth" versus "no growth."

THE LOBBIES

Every time Congress, the Executive Branch, and the regulatory agencies make a policy, they get a lot of coaching from the transportation lobbies. The most powerful and multifaceted is the "road gang"—a loose coalition of trade associations interested in more and more highways. They range from the manufacturers of the raw materials that go into a road (cement, steel bars, sand, etc.) to the makers of automobiles. They include the oil companies, associations of state highways officials, rubber companies, and highway users (such as the American Automobile Association and the American Trucking Associations, which are sometimes at odds over issues such as the width of trucks). When fuel conservation became a popular issue, some members of the highway lobby tried to change their public image as a foe of mass transit. The Atlantic Richfield Oil Company, for example, bought full-page newspaper ads soliciting bright new transportation ideas from citizens.

The scheduled airlines are represented by the Air Transport Association, and their opposition, the charter lines, is championed by the National Air Carrier Association. The Association of American Railroads presents the case for its members, and the American Trucking Associations are the persuasive voice of that industry. The barge industry's American Waterways Operators has for years fended off attempts to institute federal users' fees on channels developed with government funds. The Shipbuilders Council of America and the Seafarers International Union were the force behind passage in 1974 of a bill requiring that 30 percent of all oil imported into the U.S. be carried in American tankers by 1977—a bill that was damned as inflationary by the White House, the oil companies, and the Federal Energy Administration. (President Ford vetoed it.) The commercial users of trains and trucks are represented in Washington, too. The Transportation Association of America carries the ball for big manufacturers who send their products from plant to market by rail and highways. The National Industrial Traffic League is the spokesman for shippers, the middlemen of commercial transportation.

Also potent on the lobbying scene are the unions of transportation workers, such as the Teamsters, Longshoremen, Air Line Pilots Association, United Transportation Union, and the Brotherhood of Airline and Railway Clerks. (The latter two unions inserted in the Northeast railroad bill a section that provides a federal allowance—equal to base pay and average overtime—to be paid to each laid-off worker until a new position can be found for him in the reorganized and merged railway system.) The power of the transportation unions is awesome, since nothing can cripple major parts of the economy more quickly than a strike. Congress can, and sometimes does, push through resolutions ordering striking workers back to work, but the political clout of the unions has prevented Congress from coming to grips with the matter through permanent legislation for dealing with strikes.

A LOOK AHEAD

The future of federal involvement in transportation varies from mode to mode. The government is beefing up its mass transit spending, but it is still peanuts compared to the money that is being poured into highway construction. (In fiscal 1975, federal highway spending dwarfed mass transit outlays by a margin of about 5 to 1.) In the rail sector, DOT will wage an unpopular fight for abandonment of unprofitable routes and rationalization of the spaghetti pattern of redundant tracks in the northeastern and north central states. Meanwhile, federal support for bankrupt railroads will be tantamount to nationalization. In aviation, the lean times of the Seventies brought an end to decades of expansion, in terms of both seat capacity and new routes. With the encouragement of the CAB and DOT, the airlines will probably continue to prune, or at least stabilize, their capacity. (In 1973, only about half of the seats on the average flight were occupied, but this rate began to rise as airlines trimmed their schedules in response to the rising cost of fuel.)

Deregulation—attempts to save the consumer money through increased competition among different modes—will be talked about more and more, but little will be done. The plain truth is that the various branches of transportation have grown comfortable with the current patterns of government-sanctioned market division and would like to keep it that way. The massive subsidies will continue, too. If they were cut back, the money would be made up in higher transportation costs for the users, including millions of consumers. Even if the amounts are the same, the relative invisibility of subsidies make them more attractive politically.

The question of subsidies always involves tradeoffs between costs and benefits. Should every city in America be accessible by air, even if the low volume of traffic creates losses that must be subsidized by higher fares on densely traveled routes? Is rail passenger service worth enough to justify its subsidy? Should the U.S., for reasons of national defense and prestige, keep building merchant ships that cost more to build and operate than foreign vessels? To what degree should use of automobiles (which consume about 30 percent of all the liquid petroleum used in America) be curtailed in the interests of saving fuel and easing urban congestion? Should Pan Am and TWA be subsidized so that Americans can fly to Europe on an American plane, even if government-owned foreign carriers will do it for less? Should the government regulators, through rate manipulation, channel long-haul freight traffic away from trucks and toward the more fuel-efficient railroads and water carriers? Will oil supplies continue to support private automobile commuting in which one person drives only himself?

There are no easy answers to these and other transportation puzzles. In the past, the approach has been piecemeal and pluralistic, with the dominant lobbies prevailing. There are few indications that things will be handled differently in the future, since the amalgam of interests that ultimately make national policy represents the needs and attitudes of consumers in all fifty states and the worldwide facts of life about fuel. These are often contradictory, so Washington will continue to be a battleground for transportation issues. Transportation policy, in the last analysis, will be "whatever is doable," and the political complex of Washington is where the nation will find out what that is.

41 THE POSTAL SERVICE

The U.S. Postal Service is one of the oldest and one of the newest operations that Washington oversees.

In 1789 the Post Office was established by the new United States government as one of its principal departments, exceeded in seniority only by the Departments of State, Treasury, War, and Justice.

In 1970 Congress voted to toss the Post Office out of the federal Cabinet hierarchy and established the Postal Service as a semiautonomous service corporation. The service started life in its new form on July 1, 1971.

The new Postal Service is insulated from the federal government by a board of governors which picks the management and has the full responsibility of hiring and firing the postmaster general. But the service is still under the watchful eye of Congress. Congress appropriates money for some of its public functions, and in the fiscal year 1974, $1.7 billion was supplied to the budget from public funds (over and above $9.6 billion collected from mail users). While this is still a substantial sum, it is less than the $2 billion provided by Congress in 1971—the last year of postal operations within the federal structure. One symbol of the changeover was the shift of the postal administrative offices from the massive stone headquarters building in the old Federal Triangle to a modernistic rose-colored building at L'Enfant Plaza in the heart of redeveloped Southwest Washington.

The Postal Service today employs 703,000 people, making it larger than any government department except Defense (which employs a million civilians). Even this number, however, is down from the 729,000 who were on its rolls in 1971, the last year of direct federal management. Most of the employees work under union contracts—the first labor contracts negotiated with the federal government through collective bargaining. These 703,000 people, with all their machines and trucks, mail bags and airplanes, handle more than 90 billion pieces of mail a year.

Whether anyone thinks postal service is good or bad probably depends on his experience within the past twenty-four hours. With such astronomical numbers of letters to be delivered, almost everyone is sure to have some horror stories to tell at the office or at the lunch table. As one postal official recently said: "If we achieve an accuracy rate of 99½ percent, that's almost superhuman, and yet even with that rate, we still make 450 million mistakes a year, which is enough to make most people mad more than once."

So, like the tax collector, the postmaster general is not the most popular man in town. But the new Postmaster General, Benjamin F. Bailar, seems determined to convince the public that their Postal Service is, indeed, giving them a good deal. Bailar has said that "there is no better bargain in the country" than U.S. mail service, and he cites figures to show that a 10¢ stamp costs the average American worker one minute and nine seconds of work, while comparable postage in Western Europe requires two minutes of work.

Bailar comes by such financial comparisons naturally. His first position in the Postal Service was as chief financial officer, to which he was recruited in 1972 by then Postmaster General Elmer T. Klassen. Bailar had been vice president for international operations of the American Can Company, of which Klassen had been president. Klassen persuaded him to come to Washington, and in the three years before he assumed the top job, he rose to become deputy postmaster general. He took over as postmaster general when Klassen resigned the post in February 1975. Now age forty, Bailar is one of the youngest men ever to hold the highest postal job.

Bailar's style, within the service and toward the public, is somewhat different from that of the man he succeeded. Klassen had become postmaster general directly out of private business, and at a time when the Postal Service was making a transition from a political to managerial orientation.

When he came into the public arena Klassen was known as a tough-minded operating man with an eye for efficiency. In his experience in the public glare, however, he found out that quasi-public officials did not have the same latitude and freedom that he was accustomed to in private business. Attempting to squeeze payroll costs, he cut back on hiring in March 1972, and ran smack into public wrath. Around Christmas time, in that year, large post offices throughout the country (New York, Chicago, Los Angeles) became glutted with piled-up undelivered mail and parcels. The pandemonium lasted for months, and Klassen vowed that he would not try that particular tactic again. Nevertheless, he did bring about the retirement or dismissal of thousands of middle-level postal experts, some of whose talents were sorely missed in the two years that followed. Only recently has the service succeeded in filling all the gaps and returning to a normal operating rhythm, and many of the sharpest attacks on postal performance reflect the near-chaos of those earlier pile-ups around the country.

Klassen succeeded Winton (Red) Blount, Nixon's last postmaster general and the last postmaster general in American history to be a member of the President's Cabinet. As a businessman in private life, Blount had believed in an independent postal service corporation, and as postmaster general he testified strongly in behalf of the new plan. Congress passed the legislation in 1970, a year and a half after Blount took office as postmaster general in January 1969. When the Postal Service began its life on July 1, 1971, he was its first head and served in that capacity until he turned the job over to Klassen on January 1, 1972. As successor to Klassen, Benjamin F. (for Franklin) Bailar became the second nonpolitical appointee to be postmaster general under the new corporate set-up, and the first to bear the name of Benjamin Franklin, who was postmaster general 200 years ago.

POSTAL POLITICS

The birth of the new postal corporation was not easy. The concept of a federal subsidiary cast adrift from the traditional political ties was frightening to many postmasters throughout the country and to the more than half million postal employees. On March 16, 1970, just four days after the House Post Office and Civil Service Committee recommended the new corporation, 152,000 postal employees went on strike. (It was not called a strike at that time, only a "stoppage.") The issues in contention involved wages, but also the whole reorganization plan for the postal service. It was finally agreed that a plan would be worked out jointly in negotiations between the department and the unions. This they did, and in April the negotiating parties agreed on a plan which President Nixon adopted as his proposal to Congress.

The major provisions were adopted by Congress and formed the basic standards for the corporation called the U.S. Postal Service, a wholly owned subsidiary of the United States government. The four basic provisions adopted provided the skeleton of the new corporation:

1. Removal of the postal operation from political domination, and the establishment of career promotions.

2. Financing authority under which the Postal Service could float its own bond issues.

3. Collective bargaining between management and employees.

4. Setting of postal rates by the corporation after recommendations from the Postal Rate Commission. (Congress, however, can still override the rate recommendations or the timetable for their adoption.) The service was instructed by Congress to avoid deficits, and to price each class of mail to cover its true costs.

While none of these standards seems particularly radical, they represented a sharp departure from the procedures in the U.S. Post Office in the past. Over the years, Post Office and politics had come to be almost synonymous, and the postmaster general in most administrations was understood to be the President's principal political patronage dispenser. James A. (Big Jim) Farley was Franklin D. Roosevelt's political mastermind. Arthur Summerfield had been Republican national chairman before he became President Eisenhower's first postmaster general. Larry O'Brien became Democratic national chairman after being postmaster general in the administration of President Lyndon Johnson.

Yet, gradually, the idea of an operations-minded postmaster general was growing on Presidents and people. President Truman had broken the ice by advancing Jesse Donaldson from administrative ranks within the department to become the top postmaster in 1947. President Kennedy appointed a lawyer and insurance executive, J. Edward Day, as postmaster general when he took office in 1961. President Nixon followed suit with a business executive when he appointed Winton Blount in 1969. By this time, with postal deficits mounting every year, the stage was set for cutting the umbilical cord and letting the Postal Service start living a life of its own.

The groundwork had been laid by a Commission on Postal Reorganization appointed by President Johnson in 1967 and headed by Frederick R. Kappel, former chairman of the board of the AT&T Company, the world's biggest private corporation. In 1968, the Kappel Commission recommended that the Post Office Department be converted into an independent government corporation. When the U.S. Postal Service went into business, Kappel was appointed by President Nixon to be one of the eleven members of the board of governors, and he was subsequently selected chairman.

THE VITAL STATISTICS

The U.S. Postal Service is the world's largest mail system. Its annual budget is $12 billion. Of this, $9.5 billion is payroll for the 703,000 people in its employ, and this payroll covers more people and dispenses more in wages and salaries than any other payroll in the country (public or private) except the Defense Department.

Its annual mail volume (more than 90 billion pieces) is almost half of all the mail in the world.

It operates 31,000 post offices. In addition, 350,000 mailboxes (or "postal receptacles") are open twenty-four hours a day in every location from main post offices to street corners and shopping centers.

It is one of the nation's biggest users of transportation service and purchases $767 million of air, rail, highway, and water transportation per year. In addition, it operates a fleet of 226,000 cars and trucks. Its rural letter carriers travel more than 2 million miles a day.

It occupies (either owns or rents) 154.5 million square feet of space in nearly 42,000 locations.

It issues 30 billion stamps every year.

Such statistics add up to one basic fact: the U.S. Postal Service is the biggest personal service business in the world.

How efficient is it? Most people would think it is too cumbersome and too costly. Postal officials agree that it should be more efficient, more automated, faster, and more predictable. Yet with the volume that it handles, it is something like the bear who walks on his hind legs. The question isn't so much whether he does it well. The wonder is that he does it at all.

WHO PAYS WHAT

The difficulty in trying to bring down the cost of different kinds of mail service is that the operation is still pretty much hand work—a "people business." It is still what the economists call "labor intensive." Machines play a part, but people do most of the processing. While machine scanning, sorting, and dispatching are on the rise—and the postal officials are pressing hard to get more efficiency from automation—the biggest part of the postal budget is still payroll. As the Postal Service tries to keep up with the rise of pay scales in other, more automated, technological industries, it boosts its own costs proportionately more than others.

In this respect the Postal Service is like a symphony orchestra or a college faculty, where productivity rises much more slowly than in the mass-production assembly-line operations. On the surface, it might appear that mail is easily adapted to assembly-line techniques. If letter writers would all use identical symbols, identical writing, identical size envelopes, and send them all to just a few easily identified addresses, automation could substitute for people and the cost of delivering the mail could be drastically reduced. The fact is, however, that mail originates at hundreds of thousands of different points and is delivered to hundreds of thousands of other points every day.

Large-scale mailers, however, do process their mail for easier delivery, using the guidelines set down by the Postal Service. Publishers with prearranged schedules bundle their periodicals and identify them with special symbols so that many bundles go straight through to their final zip-code destination without having to be opened or examined. Presorting and plain marking by mass mailers has been making rapid strides in recent years and promises even more speed in delivery in the future. But techniques like this are hard to apply to the individual letters that you and I send or receive.

These epistles, written with love in various degrees of hand scrawls, still must receive individual attention from postal employees at almost every point along the way.

There is a common myth that somehow we personal letter writers, putting a 10¢ stamp on our letters (and soon a 12¢ or 13¢ stamp) are paying the way for "business mail." What most people do not know is that businesses are the biggest users of first-class mail. Banks, insurance companies, public utilities, department stores, and other forms of corporate enterprise use more first-class mail than do individual letter writers. So the issue of relative costs is not between private users and business users. It is between various classes and types of business users: first class, second class, third class, fourth class. Cost accounting being what it is—difficult at best in a jumbled-up operation like mail handling—it is anyone's guess as to what classes of mail carry other classes of mail. There have been many attempts to sort out costs by type. Some of the studies have been by the Postal Service, some by users, some by third parties, and many of the studies end up contradicting one another.

PILES OF MAIL

First-class mail is by far the biggest category of mail handled, both in number of pieces and in revenue taken in. In fiscal year 1974, first-class mail accounted for 51.6 billion pieces out of the 90 billion total. At the 10¢ base rate, this accounted for well over $5 billion of income out of a total of more than $10 billion. The second-largest category in volume is third class, with more than 22.5 billion pieces, which carries circulars, brochures, direct-mail solicitations, and other business mail sent out in large quantities and pre-packaged by the mailer to eliminate extra sorting by postal employees. Second-class mail, for newspapers, magazines, and some other editorial matter, is next in volume, accounting for slightly less than 9 billion pieces. Second class carries a preferentially low rate on the reading matter portion, but the advertising within a publication carries a higher rate, so each publication has its own cost and price, and this may vary from issue to issue.

One of the greatest surprises for most people is the rate which third class (so-called junk mail) now pays. While it used to be sent for a penny or two, an average one-page solicitation letter, with a small folder and order card enclosed, now costs more than six cents to mail.

Perhaps the least successful of all postal services today is parcel post, and while other types of mail are growing every year, parcel post has been shrinking over the past several years, from 915 million pieces in 1972 to 890 million in 1973 and 859 million in 1974. There seems no question that private delivery services are eating steadily into the business of delivering packages, boxes, and other cartons, both within cities and from city to city. Postal officials admit that private carriers can probably do much of this business more economically, though they point out that the private carriers deal mainly with business firms that have an orderly pattern of pickup and delivery, so the service can be regularized.

Some of the biggest headaches for the Postal Service are in the biggest cities. The largest post offices in the country, ranked by income are: (1) New York, (2) Chicago, (3) Los Angeles, (4) Philadelphia, (5) Boston. The sixth in size of income is Washington. (In terms of mail volume, it ranks fourth. Its lower status in income results from the enormous amount of mail sent free by congressmen, senators, and the executive departments of the government. (This "free mail" is one of the reasons that Congress makes its annual appropriation to the postal budget.) Atlanta is seventh, Dallas is eighth, San Francisco is ninth, and Detroit, Michigan, is tenth.

The volume of business per post office also determines what "class" it receives as a designation. There are 5,407 first-class post offices, each one handling more than $93,000 of postal business. There are 7,477 second-class post offices, handling more than $18,500 worth apiece, and 12,233 third-class post offices (mainly in villages and small towns). In addition there are 5,883 fourth-class post offices owned and operated by the postmasters, 3,955 branches and stations manned by employees, and 5,959 contract and rural branch stations not manned by postal employees. Grand total: 31,000 post offices in the fifty states, plus the District of Columbia, Virgin Islands, Puerto Rico, Samoa, and other scattered sites.

Perhaps the most significant statistic of all is the number of businesses and families actually served, because each of these is a destination, an address, a place to which mail will—at some time or other—be delivered, and from which mail may be picked up. Postal statisticians say there are slightly more than 57 million families served on city routes, and another 12.5 million in the country, for a grand total of approximately 70 million families. With the 5 million businesses that are also serviced, mail can be delivered to any of 75 million addresses. It can also originate from the same 75 million. If it starts from any one of these points, it can be sent to any one of the other 74,999,999 points, so the statistical permutations and combinations of points of origin and destination are positively astronomical, boggling the mind of an average customer.

In an attempt to unravel the skein of destinations, the Post Office in 1963 instituted the zip code system, consisting of five digits representing major post offices and subdivisions, with the first left-hand digit representing the larger geographical area, the next two representing a metropolitan area or sectional center, and the last two representing a small town or a delivery unit within a metropolitan area. For business mailers, it became mandatory to sort by zip code for second- and third-class bulk mail on January 1, 1967, and the postal experts say zip code numbers are now being used on 95 percent of all categories of domestic mail, but not necessarily on 95 percent of all mail volume.

THE PEOPLE WHO DO THE WORK

Until the Postal Service began operating under its new charter in 1971, there were no women employees in certain special functional jobs, such as postal inspectors. Now the entire service is open to women and there are 126,000 women employed in the Postal Service. The traditional "mailman" may be a "mailperson." The hiring of more women was an innovation which came with the new corporate policies. It broke a mostly-male tradition which had been in existence since Benjamin Franklin was postmaster general in 1775, even before the nation had declared its independence. Nineteen women are now serving as postal inspectors.

Pay and working conditions are negotiated in bargaining sessions between the Service and four unions, three of which are AFL-CIO affiliates. The fourth, the National Rural Letter Carriers Association, is an independent union. Collective bargaining was set forth in the original Postal Reorganization Act as a standard operating procedure, and the law stipulated that the National Labor Relations Board be the ruling body in jurisdictional matters, just as it is for private corporations. The law also provides for compulsory arbitration as a final resort to head off a strike.

Since postmasters are no longer picked by political patronage, the newer breed of men and women in charge will rise through the ranks by merit ratings, in much the same way that military officers are promoted in the armed forces. Of the 30,288 postmasters now in the service, 12,800 have been appointed this way. While the severing of the political patronage bonds appeared to weaken congressmen's influence in their home districts, many of these same congressmen privately breathed sighs of relief when this "privilege" was taken away from them. They said (not for publication) that the disappointments of the rejected job seekers often outweighed any possible political gratitude from the few successful appointees.

Most people don't associate the Postal Service with any heroic deeds these days. Yet there is still some drama left, even in the age of mass processing, computer scanning, and zip code identification. Mail fraud is still a federal offense, and frequently a corporate bilking scheme that cannot be pinned down any other way shows up on the work agenda of U.S. postal experts. Perhaps the most celebrated recent case was that involving Clifford Irving, who claimed to have written the exclusive inside biography of Howard Hughes. Members of the Postal Inspection Service subsequently testified that letters supposedly written by Howard Hughes to Irving and the McGraw-Hill publishing company were actually written by Irving himself. The postal records show that during the fiscal year 1974, the service investigated 9,840 fraud cases, leading to 1,570 arrests and 1,394 convictions.

WHAT'S AHEAD

Looking back over the history of mail service, the noteworthy entries concern such things as the date when postage stamps were adopted (1847), when street letter boxes were first employed (1858), and the start-up of the Pony Express (1860). Compared with such soul-stirring events, it is hard to work up the same enthusiasm for later developments, such as the installation of the first optical scanner (1965), mandatory presorting by zip code for second and third class (1967), and the sale of the first U.S. Postal Service bonds (1972). Yet this latter series of improvements probably promises as much for better mail delivery than many more colorful innovations of the past. The bonds are the foundation of a sound financial structure. And a sound financial structure will enable the Postal Service to continue its progress toward optical scanning of zip codes and ordinary addresses. Until such techniques become the rule rather than the exception, mail processing will still be hand work, and our Postal Service will continue to struggle with the methods of the nineteenth century.

None of this is new or startling, but it is at the heart of improved service for the 75 million families and businesses that use the U.S. Postal Service. When the public was introduced to the independent postal corporation, it got more than its share of propaganda flak about a "new era" of automation, computer processing, electronic scanning, and Rube Goldberg ideas to speed mail to its destination without benefit of human hand or mortal eye. The hopes were oversold, and the expectations were overblown. Progress is coming, but it is coming in slow steps, even as the birth pangs of the new U.S. Postal Service gradually recede into the past. As the mail volume rises, so also will costs. The one thing that's sure is that it will cost the user of the mails more next year than it does today.

42 PATRON OF THE ARTS

In the downtown of a Michigan city, workmen have installed a massive steel sculpture by Alexander Calder. A thousand miles east of there, Eugene Ormandy is conducting a rehearsal of the Philadelphia Orchestra. In a poor mountain area of West Virginia, a troupe of actors is performing for youngsters on the makeshift stage of a 4H summer camp. In Washington, D.C., painter Leon Berkowitz is working on an abstract painting of blended, shimmering colors.

Three thousand miles away, a group of student filmmakers at the University of California (Berkeley) are completing a documentary film. A team of young painters in Fort Wayne, Indiana, have transformed the exterior walls of buildings in a blighted neighborhood into bold works of art. In New York City, fifty-two Harlem youths are taking lessons from a professional jazz drummer. In a small town in Montana, a local poet is introducing a classroom of fifth-graders to the joy of free-form poetic expression.

What these activities have in common—besides being evidence of the "culture boom" in America—is that they have all been supported, in varying degrees, by federal tax dollars.

The agent of this largess (which is still peanuts in a federal budget of $350 billion) is the National Endowment for the Arts (NEA). By Washington standards, the NEA is very small, with a staff of roughly one hundred. It doesn't even have a building of its own, but in 1974 shunted from a K Street office building (where it was muscled out by the staff of the Watergate special prosecutor) to new quarters at Columbia Plaza, across a freeway from the Kennedy Center for the Performing Arts. The endowment hopes to find a permanent roost in the magnificent old Post Office Building on Pennsylvania Avenue.

Befitting its youth, size, and mission, the NEA is a lively, imaginative organization, as approachable and free of bureaucratic inertia as any federal agency can be. Through its leadership, the federal government is embracing the arts with the enthusiasm of a repentant philistine. Starting with a paltry $2.5 million appropriation in 1965, Congress has increased the NEA budget virtually every year, sometimes exponentially, to a level of $75 million in fiscal 1975.

Uncle Sam, a johnny-come-lately to an arts scene long dominated by private foundations, is becoming the rich uncle of hundreds of cultural organizations throughout the nation. Museums, symphonies, dance troupes, opera and ballet companies, experimental theaters, small literary magazines, college departments of art, music, drama, and filmmaking—all of these have benefited from endowment matching grants, not to mention hundreds of outright grants to individuals in the arts. Applications for financial aid rose from 1,383 in 1970 to 14,000 in 1973. Individual grants of up to $10,000 a year are being made to painters, sculptors, choreographers, architects, musicians, craftsmen, city planners, poets, photographers, composers, filmmakers, and anyone else who can show a potential for excellence in any field falling within a loose definition of "the arts."

Under a program called Artists-in-Schools, more than 300 painters, printmakers, craftsmen, and sculptors are working with 175,000 students in more than 500 schools across the nation. Nearly 1,200 poets are visiting elementary and secondary schools under the same program, encouraging lyrical, uninhibited thoughts from young minds numbed by "Look, Jane. See Spot run."

The federal culture establishment is not a group of bureaucrats afraid of taking a chance on untried, high-risk projects. "The description of 'art' as a painting hanging on a museum wall or a performance of music or drama or dance on a stage," says NEA chairman Nancy Hanks, "is inadequate, to say the least." Recognizing the depth and breadth of the nation's ethnic roots, the endowment has encouraged the preservation of neglected forms of artistic expression among such groups as Indians, southern blacks, mountain people, and Spanish-speaking people.

THE DRIVING FORCE

The person most responsible for the robust health of the federal arts program is Chairman Hanks. When she was appointed in 1969 (taking over from the endowment's first chairman, Roger L. Stevens), the NEA was getting about $8.25 million from Congress. By 1971, the appropriation had increased to $15 million, and in the following year it doubled to $30 million. Her rapport with Congress (which is not noted for culture-mongering) is nothing short of remarkable. Art critic Jo Ann Lewis, writing in the *Washingtonian,* has called her "an administrative genius, a rare breed in the arts, where institutions usually have been run by artists, scholars and rich dilettantes, most of them inept administrators."

The endowment's deputy chairman is Michael Straight, a wealthy, England-educated man of many talents. His Georgetown mansion (owned previously by Jacqueline Kennedy, following the President's assassination) is often the scene of parties for and by the NEA staff. The staff is full of people with credentials resembling those of no other bureaucrats in Washington. For example, the head of the endowment's music program, Walter Anderson, is a professional pianist and former music professor. (The furnishings of his endowment office include a piano, on which he plays and composes during his workday.) The chief of the visual arts program, Brian O'Doherty, is a former physician and current art critic, author, and conceptual artist. (A couple of years ago, a show of his work at Washington's Corcoran Gallery included an electrocardiogram he had made of Marcel Duchamp's heartbeat.)

The endowment's overseers, at least officially, are members of the presidentially appointed National Council on the Arts. The council's better-known members, past and present, include film star Clint Eastwood, choreographer Jerome Robbins, painter Jamie Wyeth, jazz pianist Billy Taylor, furniture designer Charles Eames, dancers Judith Jamison and Edward Villella, actress Rosalind Russell, actor James Earl Jones, opera singers Beverly Sills and Robert Merrill, concert pianist Van Cliburn, the late jazz composer Duke

Ellington, and actor Gregory Peck. The council comes to Washington a few times a year for meetings and a glamorous party or two.

Until nine years ago, America relied on voluntary, private support of the arts. Most people felt that federal funding of the arts smacked of old-world monarchy extending patronage to fawning artists or new-world socialism commissioning works that glorify the state. Congress—especially the House —viewed the arts and humanities as a luxury for the effete. Considering how hard it was to convince Congress that millions of Americans had a physical need for better housing, health care, and diet, it isn't surprising that Congress balked for years at the concept of a national need for creative stimulation. How do you convince a congressman who knows only the "pork barrel" economics of public works projects that the intangible benefits of cultural expenditures in his community can hold their own against the tangible benefits of dams, harbor improvements, and military construction?

A START THAT FIZZLED

The first attempt at such persuasion was made nearly a hundred years ago by Samuel S. Cox, a congressman from New York who introduced in 1877 a bill to establish a federal "council on art matters." His bill got nowhere. In 1891 Congress passed legislation, which President Harrison signed into law, renaming a New York music school the National Conservatory of Music. However, the government was not about to part with any funds to aid the grandly named establishment. (The conservatory's only claim to fame was having Antonin Dvořák as its artistic director from 1892 to 1895, during which time he composed the *New World Symphony,* premiered by the New York Philharmonic Orchestra.)

The federal government's visible interest in the arts dates from such New Deal projects as the Federal Writers' Program and extensive commissioning of statuary and murals for post offices, train stations, government offices, and public monuments. But these programs of the Works Progress Administration had as their primary goal the employment of destitute artists, and as a secondary goal, the decorating of public buildings. Unlike the creative work funded by Uncle Sam today, all the depression projects were a form of pragmatic public relief, not a case of *ars gratia artis.* When the government commissions a work today, there are no strings attached, no requirement that the product serve some governmental purpose. While acknowledging the historical precedent of the New Deal projects, today's federal culture officials winced when former Representative H. R. Gross (R-Iowa) derided their efforts as a "latter-day WPA arts program."

The presence of notable art in Washington itself is of relatively recent origin. For more than 140 years the nation's capital had no federal collection of fine European and American art, nothing analogous to the Louvre in Paris or the National Gallery in London. Until the National Gallery of Art was opened in 1941, residents of Washington and tourists had to make do with the Corcoran Gallery, donated by Washington banker-philanthropist W. W. Corcoran and opened in 1871; the small (though innovative) Phillips Collection of modern art and its nineteenth-century roots, begun in 1918 by collector-critic Duncan Phillips; and the Freer Gallery of Art, a superb collection of Oriental art (with some excellent works by Whistler) that was opened to the public in 1923. The Freer was a federal institution from its opening, but the government barely lifted a finger to assist in its birth. It did donate a site on the Mall next to the Smithsonian, but the whole collection, as well as the building to house it, was paid for by Detroit freight car tycoon Charles Lang Freer.

Andrew Mellon, the Pittsburgh industrialist who had been Secretary of the Treasury under Harding, Coolidge, and Hoover, announced in the mid-Thirties his intention to donate to the nation his collection of priceless Old Masters, to be housed in a museum constructed at his expense. Then Mellon made good on his offer (to the tune of $15 million for the building alone) and modestly resisted efforts to name the museum after him. The government chipped in a 6½-acre site on the Mall at the foot of Capitol Hill. Today the National Gallery of Art (where the Mellon collection has been supplemented with major bequests from collectors like Joseph Widener, Samuel Kress, Chester Dale, and Lessing Rosenwald) is one of the world's great museums.

Gifts of art have sometimes been made under controversial circumstances. Mellon's offer to the government, for example, came during an IRS attempt to collect more than $1.3 million of alleged back taxes. Mellon denied underpayment and said he had merely forgotten to take a legal deduction for the value of paintings he had donated to his foundation, the A. W. Mellon Educational and Charitable Trust. He also maintained he had inadvertently neglected to make a public announcement that the foundation's paintings would someday be turned over to the nation. The IRS suspected that the national gallery plan was an expedient afterthought, but Mellon was exonerated and the nation was culturally richer for it.

A more recent philanthropic hassle erupted over the Joseph H. Hirshhorn modern art collection, which is now housed in a cylindrical concrete structure next to the Smithsonian Institution. Hirshhorn indicated in the middle Sixties that he would give his broad collection to the U.S. government if a museum for it were built on the Mall, at public expense, and named after him. Some congressmen were not enthusiastic about naming a building on the Mall after a uranium magnate and stock speculator whose career included a conviction for currency smuggling during World War II. Some arts officials feared that naming a public museum after one donor would discourage later gifts. And tinging the whole debate was an undercurrent of anti-Semitism, Hirshhorn being a Jewish immigrant from Latvia. But rather than lose the collection to one of several other interested parties (including Great Britain, Israel, and New York State), President Johnson and Smithsonian Secretary Dillon Ripley met Hirshhorn's terms (and convinced Congress to do likewise). The donor later contributed some personal funds to help meet construction cost overruns on the $17 million building. Opened in the fall of 1974, the magnificent Hirshhorn collection contains, incredibly, more than 6,000 items ranging from the late nineteenth century to the present day. It is particularly rich in sculpture, including nineteen by Rodin, fifty-five by Henry Moore, twenty-five by David Smith and eleven by Alexander Calder.

A NEW START

In 1951 President Truman asked the Commission on Fine Arts to study the possibility of an active role for the government in the encouragement and support of the arts. The report, completed in 1953 and delivered to President

Eisenhower, was packed with recommendations for action. All of them were ignored, except the call for a federal performing arts center in Washington, which was unique among the world's capitals in its lack of adequate facilities for opera, ballet, and symphony. In 1958 President Eisenhower signed the law establishing a National Cultural Center. But the project languished from a lack of federal funding, until the assassination of President Kennedy raised the possibility of building and naming the center as a cultural memorial to him, using both private and public money.

As it turned out, the Kennedy Center project was a major event in breaking the barrier of government resistance to support of the arts. In 1964, during the Johnson administration, Congress passed a second piece of legislation authorizing federal grants in support of construction of the center, and by a matching formula, the federal government ultimately contributed $23 million. Along with the donation of government land and other smaller amounts, the federal government's contribution came to a value of more than $30 million, or something in the neighborhood of 40 percent of the cost of building the center. Today the federal budget includes $1.5 million a year toward maintenance and upkeep, and the center is visited by thousands of people from every part of the world.

The John F. Kennedy Center for the Performing Arts (as it is formally known) is an appropriate tribute to the late President, because President Kennedy, more than any previous chief executive, made federal promotion of the arts and humanities a top-priority item. Part of Kennedy's impact was style—artists and intellectuals present for the inauguration, the elegant restoration of White House décor, and appearances at state dinners by renowned musicians (such as Pablo Casals and Igor Stravinsky). But there was also substance.

A year after taking office the young President asked August Heckscher, a well-to-do journalist and culture administrator, to submit a study of the government's role in the arts and humanities. Among the recommendations of the Heckscher report, delivered to the President in 1963, was the creation of a national arts and humanities foundation with the power to make federal grants to state arts councils and private cultural institutions. President Kennedy did not live to see any of these recommendations reach fruition, but President Lyndon Johnson took the first step by creating the new position of Special Assistant to the President on the Arts and filling it with Roger L. Stevens, the New York City real estate mogul and Broadway producer who had been board chairman of the proposed National Cultural Center since 1961.

Legislation creating a twenty-six-member National Council on the Arts, without federal funding, was passed by Congress in August 1964. Conservative House opponents of the arts council bill warned that, innocuous as it seemed, it was the arts establishment's foot in the door of the Treasury. Their predictions were sound. In the following session debate raged over legislation that would create a National Endowment for the Arts and a companion agency for the humanities, both having grantmaking powers.

When the bill was reported out of the House Education and Labor Committee, Representative Albert Quie (R-Minn.) issued a minority report, endorsed by five other members, charging that the bill would "create a federal czar over the arts." Opponents of the bill, led by then Representative H. R.

Gross, used every tactical weapon in the legislative arsenal to delay a final vote on the bill, extending the debate for several days. Gross proposed sarcastically that belly dancing be included among the enumerated arts that would be eligible for grants. The amendment was defeated, as were Gross's amendments to include baseball, squash, pinochle, and poker. The lengthy debate was marked by witty exchanges between Gross and Representative Frank Thompson, Jr. (D-N.J.), the acerbic-witted congressman who has consistently been the House's chief champion of federal support of the arts. When the dust settled, the House passed the bill 251–128.

Five days before Christmas, 1965, Vice President Humphrey presented to the American Ballet Theatre a check representing the first federal subsidy of the arts since the nation was born. The check had all the more significance because the recipient, a renowned dance company based in New York City, was teetering on the brink of financial collapse. "The Treasury of the United States had saved a national treasure," New York *Herald Tribune* dance critic Walter Terry wrote of the grant. Funding for the first year of the endowment's operation came to barely $2.5 million each for the arts and the humanities endowments.

The National Endowment for the Humanities, which receives the same amount of federal funding as the Endowment for the Arts, has a much lower profile than its sister organization. Besides funding academic research, the NEH (chaired by Ronald Berman) has supported such diverse programs as community discussion groups that meet regularly to talk about foreign policy, centers for study of the roots of Afro-American music, archaeological excavations in Nebraska, education of American Indians in South Dakota, and historical research focusing on a particular community's role in the American Revolution.

Achievements of the National Endowment for the Arts (NEA) were solid enough in the first few years to silence most of the congressional criticism. Many of the works conceived or produced under NEA subsidy—such as choreographer Alvin Ailey's *The River* and playwright Howard Sackler's *The Great White Hope*—dispelled fears that federal grants would be an artist's meal ticket for mediocre work.

Furthermore, the endowment developed its own built-in constituency and lobby, in the form of arts councils in all fifty states and the District of Columbia, American Samoa, Guam, the Virgin Islands, and Puerto Rico. About 20 percent of the NEA budget is passed through to the state councils directly, with each council receiving a $150,000 matching grant in 1974. When officials of these state and local agencies came to Washington and told a congressman that life in his district would be enriched by increased federal grants for the arts, they made believers of once skeptical critics. Senator Barry Goldwater (R-Ariz.), eschewing conservatism for pragmatism, became an enthusiast of the NEA when he saw the economic benefit of silversmithing instruction given to Hopi and Navajo youths at federally funded ethnic culture centers in his home state. "Stores are selling Navajo Indian jewelry at prices far above anything we dreamed of a few years ago," the senator said. (He may have missed the artistic point, but NEA officials weren't about to quibble.)

During the 1973 debate on the NEA appropriation, self-confessed "middlebrow" Representative Gerald Ford told his House colleagues that he was sorry he had opposed the National Endowments for the Arts and Humanities in the early days. He said he was converted to the path of enlightenment when officials of his home town, Grand Rapids, Michigan, told him they wanted federal assistance to purchase "a Calder." Ford said he didn't know what "a Calder" was at that time, and added (not giving his House colleagues much credit for cultural exposure), "I doubt if many people here do today." Ford went on to say that the completed sculpture, which cost $45,000, was "somewhat shocking to a lot of our people out home," and that he for one "did not really understand, and I do not today, what Mr. Calder was trying to tell us." But after all was said and done, the erstwhile philistine confessed, "I can assure the members that Calder, in the center of the city, in an urban redevelopment area, has really helped to regenerate a city." As President, Gerald Ford's new-found interest in the arts remains strong, encouraged by First Lady Betty Ford, who years ago studied modern dance with the pioneering Martha Graham.

SNIPING FROM THE HILL

Not all congressmen bowed down in praise before the advancing parade of federal arts funding. Former Representative William J. Scherle (R-Iowa) insisted that "culture should not be spoon-fed to an effete elite at the expense of the general public." When the soaring cost of the war in Southeast Asia was being used as an excuse to cut nonmilitary programs the late Representative Frank T. Bow (R-Ohio) warned the House that "we can't have guns and butter," and described the federal arts program as "guns with strawberry shortcake covered with whipped cream and a cherry on top."

The ranks of the arts supporters on Capitol Hill suffer minor defections when an occasional controversial NEA program comes under fire of the conservatives. There was a brief flap in 1970, for example, when an NEA-funded literary anthology paid $750 for a poem (by Aram Saroyan) consisting of the seven-letter word, "lighght." The merits of that particular work aside, some congressmen apparently wanted the NEA to hold its poets to a higher standard of words per dollar or, as they say in the parlance of military appropriations, "more bang for the buck."

In an appeal to this kind of benefit-cost mentality, Representative Frank Thompson commented in 1973 on the relative amounts of federal money spent on crime reduction and the arts. "I cannot say, of course, that any of the Arts Endowment programs or those in the humanities will have direct bearing on such matters as crime or drug abuse or any other infraction of society's laws or mores." But, the congressman went on to argue, "the mind of a child or teenager is less likely to become destructive, either to himself or to other people and their property, when it is actively involved in the expenditure of his or her own creative energy."

The most surprising and well-mounted (but in the end unsuccessful) attack on the federal arts establishment to date was Senator William Proxmire's attempt to limit the size of its fiscal 1974 funding increase. The liberal Democrat warned that if public funding surpasses and eventually replaces private arts funding, the nation will suffer from the "dead hand of government and the dead hand of censorship over art." Proxmire said that the genuine artistic geniuses of any era are rebels who don't want, or at least shouldn't want, a subsidy from Big Brother. "There is no way to promote excellence in the arts," Proxmire told the Senate, "by shoveling out the money; it will promote stale, sterile and second-rate art."

In a multipronged attack, in which he was virtually alone among his Senate colleagues, Proxmire complained that federal support for the arts is essentially an "upper-middle-class subsidy," since this socioeconomic stratum accounts for the vast majority of the performing and visual arts audiences as well as the reading public. He also criticized grants made to already well-established arts figures, such as a $1,000 grant for an essay by best-selling novelist-poet Robert Penn Warren and a payment to wealthy editor-author George Plimpton for work on a public television program.

But fears of mediocrity and subtle censorship, so far, have been largely unfounded. As the Washington *Post* has observed editorially, "contrary to earlier misgivings by conservatives and liberals alike that federal support of the arts might lead to federal control of the arts, the [arts] council has maintained a healthy and at times even scrappy independence." For example, after the 1973 Supreme Court ruling endorsing local, rather than national, standards for determining what is obscene, the National Council on the Arts formally urged local arts organizations to act as watchdogs against attempts to curtail artistic freedom in the name of decency.

When Senator James L. Buckley (Cons.-R-N.Y.) complained that the NEA-supported dance company of Eleo Pomare used allegedly anti-American material in a performance at the Kennedy Center, Nancy Hanks defended the dance company as "outstanding" and added firmly, "We may in no way interfere with the actual activities of the organizations" receiving federal funds. She had apparently chosen to forget an incident in 1970, when she put pressure on George Plimpton, the editor of an NEA-supported anthology, to delete a sexually graphic short story. When Plimpton balked, Miss Hanks decided to cut off funding for the whole project. In any event, this one episode of censorship has not been repeated. In fact, Erica Jong, the feminist poet-novelist, used an NEA grant for subsistence during the writing of her raunchy novel *Fear of Flying*. While the NEA certainly avoids interference with a grantee's ongoing work, it remains to be seen whether a grantee who perpetrated some sort of public outrage would get renewed funding for the following year. As Deputy Chairman Michael Straight has observed, "We can't be dictated to by Congress, but we can't forget that's where the money comes from."

RISK BUSINESS

The NEA has bent over backwards to take a chance on propositions that private philanthropy steers away from. Among the hundreds of programs that have received federal funding in recent years are the following, none of which could be considered conventional:

• the Otrabanda Company, a theatrical troupe that has traveled along the Mississippi River on a raft, giving performances in small shore communities;

• urban wall painting in Cincinnati, Ohio, Fort Wayne, Indiana, Boston, and other cities; works by young local painters;

• recruitment of architecture students at predominantly black North Carolina Agricultural and Technical State University;

• Artrain, an art exhibition in three Pullman cars, prepared by the Michigan Council on the Arts, which has toured Michigan and remote parts of the

Rocky Mountain states, bringing the visual arts to many people with no previous experience in viewing art.

The endowment doesn't neglect, of course, traditional arts organizations like classical ballet companies, municipal museums, symphony orchestras, and resident professional theater companies. Recipient institutions are found in the nation's largest cities, as well as in communities that are a long way from being hotbeds of culture. Grants have been made to the Guggenheim Museum and the Museum of Modern Art in New York and the Art Institute of Chicago, as well as the Honolulu Academy of Arts, the John and Mable Ringling Museum of Art in Sarasota, Florida, the Newark Museum Association, and the Historical Museum and Institute of Western Colorado, Grand Junction, Colorado. The New York Philharmonic, the Philadelphia Orchestra, and the Chicago Symphony have all received NEA support, as have the Erie (Pennsylvania) Philharmonic Society, the Shreveport (Louisiana) Symphony Orchestra, the Wichita (Kansas) Symphony Society, and the Anchorage (Alaska) Symphony Orchestra.

While encouraging experimental "street theater," the NEA has put money into such renowned professional companies as the Arena Stage (Washington, D.C.), the Tyrone Guthrie Theater (Minneapolis, Minnesota), and the New York Shakespeare Festival. Among the sixty dance companies that have toured the nation with NEA support in the past several years are such diverse troupes as the Martha Graham Dance Company, the American Ballet Theatre, the Inner City Repertory Dance Company, and the Merce Cunningham Company.

One arts organization—the American Film Institute (AFI), based at the Kennedy Center in Washington—has been the recipient each year of far more NEA funds than any other. It has received as much as $1.75 million—$1.1 million of which must be matched—from the NEA's congressional appropriation in a single year, more than ten times as much as the next largest conventional grant. (The only other NEA grant even approaching its gifts to the AFI was the $1 million matching offer made in 1974 to the venerable but financially unsound Metropolitan Opera Company of New York City.) Some people question whether the NEA should indefinitely cover so large a portion of its budget. The endowment has a policy of considering its funds as seed money to stimulate private, state, and local funding, and Miss Hanks says, "Our money is not life or death to anybody." Its relationship with the AFI appears to be a deviation from that policy. In 1974 an attempt was made on Capitol Hill to wean AFI away from the endowment, making it dependent upon Congress for an annual appropriation. The House, however, did not go along with the idea.

The AFI was begun in 1967, with an initial funding of about $4 million contributed equally by the NEA, the Ford Foundation, and the member corporations of the Motion Picture Association of America (whose rather meager funding in subsequent years has been a disappointment to the institute). The NEA funds are used for such scholarly and popular activities as preservation of fast-deteriorating old films (silents, documentaries, newsreels, early talkies), historical research, publication of film criticism, training of filmmakers, and exhibition of new and old films of uncommon quality. The institute is directed by George Stevens, Jr. (son of the late Hollywood producer-director), who formerly was in charge of filmmaking services at the

United States Information Agency. In 1973 the AFI was embroiled in a controversy over the last-minute cancellation of a showing of the Costa-Gavras film *State of Siege* in conjunction with the opening of its theater in the Kennedy Center. Many people—including several film directors who withdrew their films in protest—charged that the showing was canceled because the film is politically radical and was repugnant to the Nixon administration. Stevens insisted, however, that the showing was canceled because it would have been insensitive to show a film dealing with political assassination to an audience that included Senator Edward M. Kennedy (D-Mass.), brother of two assassinated leaders, and other members of the Kennedy family (to whom Stevens is personally close).

INDIVIDUAL GRANTS

In addition to supporting arts organizations, the NEA makes direct grants to individuals who have shown unusual creativity in the fields of choreography, poetry, the novel, playwriting, museum administration, musical composition and arranging (jazz, classical, folk/ethnic), libretto writing, painting, sculpture, art criticism, architecture, photography, crafts, and filmmaking. Unlike grants to arts organizations, which must be matched by other private or public funds, grants to individuals are made outright. The amounts of the awards vary, with a top fellowship of about $10,000 per year (for composers). The ceiling for painters, for example, is $7,500, and for writers it is $6,000. The standards are tough, and applications are reviewed by panels of experts in each field. While the vast majority of the NEA grant recipients are little-known artists for whose work there is scant commercial demand, substantial grants have also been given to numerous artists who have received critical acclaim, such as painter-sculptor Rockne Krebs and choreographers Alvin Ailey, Antony Tudor, Gerald Arpino, Paul Taylor, and Erick Hawkins.

The NEA has added a new dimension to its role as patron by becoming a watchdog over the federal government's own artistic endeavors, such as the design of federal buildings and urban renewal projects, the accessibility of federal museums with galleries to physically handicapped visitors, layout and graphics in government posters, stationery, and publications, even the design of postage stamps. Practicing what it preaches, the endowment has decorated its own offices with modern prints, posters, and gaily colored furniture by America's top designers (a far cry from the bureaucratic beige that predominates in most federal offices).

PRIVATE FUNDS STILL DOMINANT

Despite large increases in federal support of the arts during the Nixon administration, the United States lags far behind most European nations in per capita public expenditures for culture. The U.S. government spends less than 40¢ per citizen on the performing and visual arts, compared with Great Britain's $1.23, Israel's $1.34, Canada's $1.40, and West Germany's $2.80. Of course, the United States has a tradition of decentralized government, and adding state and local expenditures—more than $30 million—to the equation would give a more favorable comparison. More important, the United States still believes that private philanthropy to the arts and humanities, estimated to be about $2.5 billion annually, should be the cornerstone of support. Uncle Sam's spending on the arts and humanities since 1965 is still dwarfed by the combined outpourings of such giant foundations as Ford ($260 million since 1957), Rockefeller ($68 million), and Mellon ($43 million).

The NEA and NEH are being careful—through requirements that their grants be matched by other funds—to assure that a reliance on public money does not dry up philanthropic sources. "Federal money is not to replace private money, but to push it up," Miss Hanks has said. One particularly ingenious mechanism for this purpose is the NEA's "treasury fund," a receptacle for private donations, which are matched dollar for dollar by federal funds before being granted, again on a matching basis, to a cultural organization. The more than $16 million of private contributions made to the NEA by the close of fiscal 1973 has been quadrupled through the treasury fund, with $1 from the donor being matched with the NEA's $1, added to the grantee's matching $2.

As the price tag for federal arts promotion gets bigger and bigger, cracks may appear in the solidarity of support the programs enjoy today. The likes of former Representative John Hunt (R-N.J.) will continue to complain, as Hunt did in 1973, that increased arts funding takes money away from mental health programs that he deemed to be more therapeutic than the arts. "Do I have to go out in Central Park and meet some strange individual beating on tom-toms in order to get an inspiration?" Hunt asked on the House floor, adding, "We need programs good for all citizens, not just for people going around the park in tippy-toe shoes." But while Hunt and his cronies poked fun at ballet, which they apparently consider effeminate, the American dance audience—in communities of all different sizes and levels of sophistication— grew by more than 600 percent between 1965 and 1974. Museum attendance has soared to more than 600 million visits, and concert attendance has surpassed 12 million per year.

One might think that this burgeoning demand for culture would ease the financial pains of the arts, but the opposite is true. Ticket prices and museum admission charges fall short of soaring expenses. If the fine arts are booming, the pop arts are booming even more, with ticket prices pegged to give a handsome return to both performers and impresarios. But salaries in the fine arts remain woefully low, especially for dancers. (A dancer with the New York City Ballet in 1973 received a weekly base salary of about $150.) "The fine arts don't operate on the free enterprise system," observed Washington *Post* writer Henry Allen, "because not enough people give a big enough damn about them to pay what they cost."

Senator Proxmire has suggested that the federal subsidy should be limited, forcing relatively affluent culture consumers and the private patrons of art to "give a big enough damn," or else. Or else what? Let a fine orchestra or dance company go under? Let rising ticket prices shrink arts audiences until only the rich are left? The federal arts establishment and its friends on Capitol Hill are determined that this should not happen. They are determined that the U.S. government, as the head of a multilevel public and private partnership, will be the court of last resort for the beleaguered arts.

43 IMPORTED WEALTH
(AND SOME HOME GROWN)

Washington is the full-time or part-time home of an uncommonly large number of millionaires, near-millionaires, and multimillionaires. Washington is not unique in this, of course. Every city of comparable size has a resident plutocracy, but usually it is based on home-grown industrial fortunes accumulated around the turn of the century, long before the hefty income and inheritance taxes.

The special characteristic of the Big Money in Washington is that most of it wasn't made here. It was brought here by the people who made it and the people who inherited it. Washington, a city without manufacturing and mighty financial houses, became the home of money from Chicago, Akron, Pittsburgh, New York, Scranton, Carson City, Erie, Rochester, and a dozen other industrial, mining, and mercantile centers.

The owners of out-of-town fortunes began invading Washington in earnest toward the end of the last century, looking for the glamor and respectability of serving in government or merely hobnobbing with those who did. In the days when state legislatures selected senators, rich mine operators from the West—men like William Stewart and Francis Newlands of Nevada, George Hearst of California, Simon Guggenheim of Colorado, and William A. Clark of Montana—could easily arrange to be elected to the Senate, and a few of them increased their already immense fortunes through speculation in Washington real estate. The nouveau riche, spurned by the mellowed money of Boston and Philadelphia, found they could become social lions in egalitarian Washington.

Some of the most opulent embassies and clubs in Washington today are housed in buildings that were once the homes of these wealthy interlopers. Various members of the McCormick and Patterson families from Chicago (farm machinery and newspaper publishing) built mansions here, including one now used by the Brazilian Embassy on Massachusetts Avenue, and one now occupied by the Washington Club, a women's club on Dupont Circle. The gaudiest mansion of them all, now the Indonesian Embassy on Massachusetts Avenue, was built by silver-rich Thomas F. Walsh. His daughter Evalyn married the debonair Ned McLean, who had come originally from Cincinnati, where his family made its money in real estate and publishing. Evalyn McLean possessed the legendary Hope Diamond, now on exhibit at the Smithsonian Institution.

Perry Belmont, a New York congressman, ambassador to Spain, and son of the Rothschild's financial representative in America, built an extravagant townhouse on New Hampshire Avenue that is now the home of the Order of the Eastern Star. The headquarters of the Society of the Cincinnati, on Massachusetts Avenue near Dupont Circle, was the turn-of-the-century residence of Larz Anderson III, a wealthy American minister to Belgium and ambassador to Japan, whose wife had inherited a shipping fortune estimated at $17 million. Across the street from the Anderson House stands the Cosmos Club, a men's club that occupies a mansion built by Richard Townsend and his wife, who was an heiress to the Erie Railroad fortune. The Townsends' daughter Mathilde was married first to the blueblooded Senator Peter Goelet Gerry of Rhode Island, and later to wealthy diplomat Sumner Welles from New York, who divided his time between the Massachusetts Avenue house and his Maryland country estate, Oxon Hill.

The Turkish Embassy, along Rock Creek Park off Sheridan Circle, was built in 1915 by Edward Hamlin Everett, a bottling, beer, and oil magnate. The stately French Embassy on Kalorama Road was built by lead tycoon William W. Lawrence and bought soon thereafter by gold and diamond magnate John Hays Hammond. The Phillips Collection is located in the former home of the late Duncan Phillips, a pioneering modern art collector and an heir to the Jones & Laughlin steel fortune of Pittsburgh. Other notable Washington mansions were built by George Westinghouse, Mrs. George Pullman, Mrs. Marshall Field, members of the Hearst family, and the Leiter family of merchants and wheat speculators from Chicago.

The influx of big money to Washington continued into this century. The Foxhall Road palace of the ambassador of Belgium was built in 1931 by Raymond T. Baker, who had been a director of the mint and who was married successively to Bromo-Seltzer heiress Margaret Emerson and (at the time the house was built) Delphine Dodge of the automobile fortune. The historic townhouse at 1801 F Street N.W.—once the home of Chief Justice John Marshall—was bought in 1925 by Representative Robert Low Bacon, a wealthy New York congressman and son of a man who was a Secretary of State, ambassador to France, and partner in the financial house of J. P. Morgan. (His widow, Virginia Murray Bacon, scion of an old Virginia family, is still visible on the Washington social scene.) Mr. and Mrs. Robert Woods Bliss (she an heiress to the Castoria patent medicine fortune and he an ambassador to Argentina) bought the Dumbarton Oaks estate in George-town in 1920, and twenty years later gave it and their peerless collection of Byzantine and pre-Columbian art to Harvard University. Coleman Jennings, now in his eighties, still lives in his mansion in the Kalorama section. His fortune originated with his father, a mining engineer and partner of the aforementioned Mr. Hammond in South Africa.

And so it continues today. People who have made or inherited a mound of money keep coming to Washington for one reason or another. Some get elected to Congress, are appointed to high level government positions, or settle here after a stint overseas as an ambassador (a position often procured through a big donation to the victorious political party). Some come here to use Washington as a base for social climbing or making a name for themselves as patrons of the arts. Some come here just to enjoy the excitement of living in the nation's capital. The upper positions of the federal government have always attracted moneyed people. Many men and women who are successful in their chosen careers somehow manage to get themselves a federal position.

WEALTH IN GOVERNMENT

Former President Nixon showed a special preference for self-made men when he filled his administration's top positions: people like former Director of Management and Budget Roy Ash (a co-founder of the mammoth conglomerate Litton Industries); energy czar and Treasury Secretary William E. Simon (a former bond trader and youthful partner of the Salomon Brothers investment banking firm); former Postmaster General E. T. Klassen (who joined the American Can Company as a seventeen-year-old office boy and worked his way up to president); former Housing and Urban Development Secretary George Romney (onetime head of American Motors); and John A. Volpe (the heavy-construction magnate who went on to be governor of Massachusetts, Secretary of Transportation and ambassador to Italy).

Others of the men who served Nixon are inheritors. George Bush—onetime congressman, GOP national chairman, ambassador to the United Nations and President Ford's emissary to Communist China—showed unusual spunk in overcoming a privileged New England background (Andover and Yale) and moving to Texas, where he made it big in oil. Nixon's second Secretary of Commerce and President Ford's international trade negotiator, Frederick Dent, left the womb of the elite St. Paul's School and Yale and slipped into the presidency of his family's South Carolina textile company, Mayfair Mills. Prior to becoming a Maryland congressman, Secretary of Commerce Rogers C. B. Morton was president of his family's Kentucky flour and biscuit firm, Ballard and Ballard Company. Elliot Richardson, who until his resignation in the "Saturday Night Massacre" had been Nixon's jack-of-all-trades (Secretary of HEW, Defense, and Attorney General) and was appointed by Ford to be ambassador to England, inherited money from his mother, a member of the Shattuck family, prominent in Boston as lawyers and professors of medicine. Richardson's wife, the former Anne Hazard, is an heiress to a large and very old Rhode Island fortune based originally on textiles and later on railroads, caustic soda and coke. Secretary of the Navy J. William Middendorf II (who was also ambassador to the Netherlands) is a wealthy former investment banker (as well as art collector and composer of military marches).

President Ford hasn't appointed as many well-heeled people to top positions as Nixon did, but he more than compensated with the selection of Nelson Rockefeller as his Vice President. An heir to the billion-dollar Standard Oil fortune assembled by his grandfather, Rockefeller had been in and out of federal positions for years. Ever since the 1940s, he has maintained a large Washington home for use during his periodic visits.

In decades past, the Supreme Court was full of rich men. Today the only member with unusual wealth is Associate Justice Lewis F. Powell, Jr., a Richmond, Virginia, corporate lawyer who received a large holding of Sperry & Hutchinson stock from his father, whose family's furniture manufacturing company was absorbed by S&H some years ago.

Then there's Congress, where the poorest members are those who have only their $42,500-a-year salary to live on. But these are a minority in both chambers of Congress, where prosperous lawyers and businessmen abound, and most members have outside income from corporate directors' fees, speaking fees, dividends, interest, and payments from law firms in which they used to be active. A number of the southern members have extensive agricultural holdings. Senate Judiciary Committee Chairman James O. Eastland (D-Miss.) has received in recent years more than $150,000 per year in federal cotton subsidies for his family's 5,200-acre delta plantation. Senator Russell Long (D-La.), whose Finance Committee writes oil depletion laws, has considerable income from gas and oil, as do several other members from the South and Southwest.

As elsewhere in Washington, many of the fortunes sitting in the House and Senate were inherited. Included in this group are Representative Pierre S. du Pont IV, Republican from (naturally) Delaware; Representative H. J. Heinz III (R-Pa.), a grandson of the Pittsburgh pickle mogul; Senator Edward M. Kennedy (D-Mass.), son of financial wizard Joseph P. Kennedy; Senator Claiborne Pell (D-R.I.), a member of a socially distinguished New York family and husband of a great-granddaughter of the A&P food chain founder; Senator James L. Buckley (Cons.-R-N.Y.), son of a Connecticut oil producer; Senator Lloyd Bentsen (D-Tex.), a lawyer, financier and son of a Texas real estate operator with thousands of acres in the Rio Grande Valley; and Senator Bill Brock (R-Tenn.), whose family's Chattanooga candy company invented the chocolate-covered cherry. Representative Millicent Fenwick (R-N.J.), an elegant, pipe-smoking, onetime fashion model, author, and state legislator, inherited several million dollars from her mother, a member of New Jersey's illustrious Stevens family. As international shippers, landowners, and inventors since colonial times, the Stevenses created the world's first steam-driven ferryboat system (on the Hudson River in 1811), built America's first steam locomotive (part of an experimental railroad set up on the family estate in Hoboken in 1825), and endowed the Stevens Institute of Technology.

We mustn't forget Senator Robert Taft, Jr. (R-Ohio), from a Cincinnati family long prosperous in real estate and law; Senator Lowell P. Weicker, Jr. (R-Conn.), whose grandfather was a cofounder of the Squibb pharmaceutical company; and Senator Philip Hart (D-Mich.), whose wife is an heiress to the Briggs auto body fortune of Detroit (which once included the Detroit Tigers baseball team). Then there's Representative Richard Ottinger (D-N.Y.), whose forebears made a pile in plywood; Representative Williamson S. Stuckey, Jr. (D-Ga.), whose family's pecan shops (now owned by Pet Milk) are a fixture on southern highways; and Representative James T. Broyhill (R-N.C.), of the furniture company that bears his family's name.

Congress has some self-made millionaires, too. Senator Charles Percy (R-Ill.) worked his way up to the presidency of the Bell and Howell camera company before he was thirty years old. Representative James Scheuer (D-N.Y.) made a bundle developing moderate-income housing projects in several cities around the country (including Washington, where, in partnership with Roger L. Stevens, he built the first apartments in the Southwest redevelopment area). Numerous members of Congress were born rich and increased their wealth substantially through brains and hard work. Senator Stuart Symington (D-Mo.), for example, used his family's money to get control of and rescue a number of failing corporations (including the giant Emerson Electric Manufacturing Company of St. Louis) before turning to the political life.

Washington is full of rich people who held important government positions in previous years and can't resist spending a portion of their time in or near the capital city. This list would include W. Averell Harriman, fabulously wealthy heir to the Union Pacific Railroad fortune, financier, diplomat, and erstwhile star polo player; Wiley T. Buchanan, Jr., current ambassador to Austria, onetime ambassador to Luxembourg, chief of protocol, and Texas businessman whose wife is an heiress to the Dow Chemical fortune; Jefferson Patterson, a former ambassador and scion of John R. Patterson, the Dayton, Ohio, marketing genius who founded the National Cash Register Company (NCR) in 1884; Sol Linowitz, former board chairman of Xerox, ambassador to the Organization of American States, chairman of the Urban Coalition, and currently an international lawyer; Gordon Gray, chairman emeritus of the National Trust for Historic Preservation, former secretary of the army, broadcasting executive, and son of a former board chairman of R. J. Reynolds Tobacco Company; True Davis, a Missouri animal serum magnate, former ambassador to Switzerland, assistant secretary of the treasury and ex-president of the United Mine Workers' National Bank of Washington; and veteran diplomat David K. E. Bruce, whose father was a wealthy senator from Maryland (with banking and agricultural interests) and whose first wife was Ailsa Mellon, the daughter of Andrew Mellon.

In the same category of retired public servants is George McGhee, an independent oil producer, former ambassador to Germany, and son-in-law of Everette Lee De Golyer, a pioneering geologist who founded the Amerada oil company; Edward Foss Wilson, former board chairman of the Wilson meat packing company of Chicago and onetime assistant secretary of health, education and welfare; and former Federal Reserve Board Chairman William McChesney Martin, Jr., son of a prominent St. Louis banker-lawyer, owner of his own seat on the New York Stock Exchange at the age of twenty-five, and president of the exchange by the age of thirty-two. George W. Renchard, a retired diplomat who served most recently as ambassador to Burundi, has lived in Washington on-and-off throughout his foreign service career. (His wife, the former Stellita Stapleton, grew up in Washington, residing in the Massachusetts Avenue mansion that is now the Philippine Embassy. Her father was an Englishman with land holdings in Ecuador, and her mother's family was descended from the first territorial governor of Nebraska, where the Renchards still have extensive property.)

The wives of several former federal officials are descended from Charles Pratt, the nineteenth century oil pioneer who became a partner of Rockefeller in the Standard Oil trust: Mrs. Christian A. Herter, widow of the former Massachusetts governor and U.S. Secretary of State; Mrs. Robert H. Thayer, whose husband is an ex-assistant secretary of state and minister to Rumania; and Mrs. Paul H. Nitze, wife of a former Wall Street investment banker and longtime official at the departments of State and Defense. Mrs. Robert F. Kennedy, an heiress to the Skakel family's carbon and coke riches, never held public office, but she continues to be a magical force in the capital's social-political life. Sargent and Eunice Kennedy Shriver are active Washingtonians, too.

CULTURAL BENEFACTORS

The biggest inheritances lurking around the capital are owned not by political figures but by patrons and administrators of the arts. The largest fortune—dwarfing even Nelson Rockefeller's—is that of Paul Mellon: president of the National Gallery of Art, son of its chief benefactor (former

Treasury Secretary Andrew Mellon), art collector, sportsman (Rokeby Farms stables of Upperville, Virginia), philanthropist, and possessor of a centi-million-dollar fortune (based on Gulf Oil, Alcoa aluminum, Koppers coke, and numerous other manufacturing and banking firms). Marjorie Merriweather Post, until her death in 1973, was Washington's wealthiest female resident, with a fortune (derived from the General Foods Corporation) estimated conservatively at $200 million. A generous supporter of the National Symphony Orchestra, Mrs. Post gave to the nation her two principal homes, the 26-acre Hillwood, bordering Rock Creek Park in upper Northwest Washington, and the 17-acre Mar-A-Lago in Palm Beach, both of them complete with priceless art collections and maintenance endowments.

The director of the National Gallery of Art is young art historian J. Carter Brown, an heir to the multifaceted Brown fortune of Rhode Island. (He was formerly married to Constance Mellon Byers, an adopted daughter of the late Richard King Mellon of Pittsburgh.) The president of the National Trust for Historic Preservation is James Biddle, scion of the patrician Biddle banking family of Philadelphia and husband of the former Louisa du Pont Copeland. Mrs. Jouett Shouse, long active in politics and an heiress to the Filene department store fortune of Boston, donated her Wolf Trap Farm in suburban Virginia to the federal government for use as an open-air summer music center. Marjorie Phillips, widow of the late Duncan Phillips, still takes an active role in the Phillips Collection. S. Dillon Ripley II, the aristocratic head of the Smithsonian Institution, is a renowned ornithologist and descendant of a chairman of the Union Pacific Railroad Company.

The chairman of the John F. Kennedy Center for the Performing Arts is Roger L. Stevens, a former New York City real estate tycoon (once a part owner of the Empire State Building), Broadway producer (*West Side Story, Bus Stop, Cat on a Hot Tin Roof,* among other shows), and a leading Democratic fund raiser. The center's former general director is William McCormick Blair, Jr., an erstwhile Chicago lawyer, protégé of Adlai Stevenson, and former ambassador to Denmark and the Philippines. A leading figure in the center's fund raising is Mrs. Polk Guest, ex-wife of former Ambassador to Ireland Raymond Guest, who is an heir to the Phipps steel fortune. The director of the American Film Institute (housed within the center) is George C. Stevens, Jr., a film director whose wife is Guest's daughter Elizabeth. Washington arts philanthropist Henry Strong (head of the Hattie M. Strong Foundation) is a descendant of a Rochester, New York, buggy whip maker who in 1881 went into partnership with photography pioneer George Eastman and became the first president of Eastman Kodak.

PILLARS OF THE PRESS

A number of individuals in the Washington coterie of journalists, editors, and publishers are inheritors of varying amounts of wealth. Chief among these is Mrs. Katharine Graham, principal owner of the highly lucrative Washington *Post, Newsweek* magazine, and several broadcasting stations. Mrs. Graham inherited the *Post* from her father, the late Eugene Meyer, a Wall Street financier and assembler of the Allied Chemical Company who came to Washington during World War I to take the first of several government positions he held over the following two decades.

Michael Straight—deputy chairman of the National Endowment for the

Arts—is an heir to the Payne-Whitney fortune of New York (Standard Oil of New Jersey, J. P. Morgan, etc.), an author, onetime editor and co-owner of the *New Republic,* and a co-owner today of *Antiques* magazine. (Straight's wife is the former Nina Auchincloss Steers, a half-sister of Jacqueline Kennedy Onassis.) The *Washingtonian* magazine, which deals with all aspects of life in the nation's capital, was begun and is still partly owned by Laughlin Phillips, a former foreign service officer and son of Duncan and Marjorie Phillips. Philip Stern—an heir to the Rosenwald millions of Sears, Roebuck—is a modern art collector, philanthropist for liberal causes and author who specializes in advocacy of tax reform. The *Congressional Quarterly,* a weekly report on the activities of the House and Senate, was founded and nurtured here by Nelson Poynter, a newspaper editor and owner of the St. Petersburg, Florida, *Times.*

Affluent members of the working press corps here include Walter Ridder, capital correspondent for his family's chain of papers, which merged in 1974 with the Knight newspaper chain; Ben Welles, a former New York *Times* diplomatic correspondent and son of Sumner Welles; Joseph Medill Patterson Albright, Washington correspondent for the San Francisco *Chronicle* and a member of the eminent publishing family whose properties have included the Chicago *Tribune,* New York *Daily News* and *Newsday,* and the now-defunct Washington *Times-Herald;* and Peter Andrews, Washington correspondent and part-owner of the Buffalo *Courier-Express.* Nan Tucker McEvoy, whose family owns the San Francisco *Chronicle,* is best known in Washington as the founder of Preterm, a nonprofit clinic that offers abortions, vasectomies, and sex counseling. Finally, there's Ruth (Bazy) McCormick Tankersley, who once took an active role in her family's Chicago *Tribune* and Washington *Times-Herald,* but contents herself today with operating the nation's largest Arabian horse farm, located in rural Montgomery County, Maryland.

MISCELLANEOUS RICH

This survey of Washington's imported fortunes, by no means a definitive list, must also include such affluent residents as the Archbold and Hufty families, descendants of the Rockefeller partner who was the first president of Standard Oil of New Jersey. (John D. Archbold's Hillandale estate, on Reservoir Road west of Georgetown, covers more than 20 acres and carries the highest tax assessment of any private residence in Washington.) Captain Peter Belin, owner of the historic Georgetown house Evermay, is an heir to the Jermyn coal fortune of Scranton, Pennsylvania, and the riches of the du Ponts, with whom the Belins were associated—in business and through marriage—from early in the 1800s. Also living in Washington are Mr. and Mrs. Hugh D. Auchincloss, he a partner of the investment firm Thomson and McKinnon, Auchincloss Kohlmeyer Inc., she the mother of Mrs. Jacqueline Onassis; the Mars family (Forrest Mars, Sr. and Jr., and John F. Mars) of candy bar fame; W. Horton Schoellkopf, Jr., heir to a Buffalo, New York, banking and electric power fortune; and Barbara Marx Hubbard, daughter of toy tycoon Louis Marx, sister-in-law of Daniel Ellsberg of Pentagon Papers fame, and proprietor of the New Worlds Training Center, a futurist seminar program she runs out of her mansion next to Rock Creek Park, near Porter Street N.W.

Longtime Washingtonians Arthur W. Gardner and his sister Joan Gardner

(Mrs. A. Britton) Browne are grandchildren of the late John Wendell Anderson, a Detroit lawyer who bought 5 percent of the newly incorporated Ford Motor Company for $5,000 in 1903 and sold his interest for $12.5 million in 1915. Elinor Morse Ryan Brady (widow of the late Rear Admiral Parke H. Brady) is a descendant of telegraph inventor Samuel F. B. Morse and a granddaughter of Thomas Fortune Ryan, the turn-of-the-century Wall Street tycoon whose vast wealth ranged from streetcar systems and coal mines to tobacco companies and Congolese diamond mines (and once included a controlling interest in the Equitable Life Assurance Society).

Then there are Mr. and Mrs. John Logan (he a prominent trade association executive, she the former Polly Guggenheim, whose first husband was an heir to that family's copper mining millions), owners of the Firenze House estate along Rock Creek Park; Kimball Firestone, a grandson of tire magnate Harvey Firestone and Washington vice president of the family company; John W. Hanes, Jr., a partner in the investment firm of Wertheim and Co., a former State Department official, and member of the North Carolina hosiery and textile family; Kay Halle, an authoress and hostess whose family founded Halle Brothers department store in Cleveland, Ohio; Elwood Quesada, a developer of the L'Enfant Plaza office complex in Southwest, former Air Force general and husband of Kate Davis Pulitzer of the publishing family; and a smattering of folks with links to fortunes named Colgate, Lewisohn, Pillsbury, Willys, Fleischmann, Reynolds, and Astor.

HOMETOWN WEALTH

Notwithstanding the formidable array of wealth listed above, not *all* of the big money in Washington was imported. While Washington has always lacked heavy industry and manufacturing, it has nonetheless spawned some prosperous local businesses. Some of the home-grown fortunes in Washington today date from the middle of the nineteenth century. There are members of the Glover and Eustis families, descended from founders and early officials of the Riggs National Bank, Washington's largest. There are descendants of the families that owned the city's major department stores and retail houses—families like Jelleff, Hechinger, Hahn, Woodward, Lothrop, Kann, and Lansburgh. The city's oldest media dynasty is that of the *Star* newspaper and WMAL broadcasting, owned and operated for more than a century by the Noyes, Kauffmann, and Adams families and their offshoots, who in 1974 sold controlling interest to Texas financier Joe Allbritton (subject to approval by the Federal Communications Commission). The Grosvenor family, triple-generation editors of the *National Geographic* magazine, are scions of Alexander Graham Bell and Boston utilities promoter Gardiner Greene Hubbard, Bell's father-in-law and early financial backer. (Unfortunately for their descendants, Bell and Hubbard sold a controlling interest in their telephone system to a group of Boston bankers not long after its founding.)

The Heurich family made it big with Washington's most popular beer (now defunct) and later in local real estate. The Corby family started in baking and is now active in construction. The Willards owned the hotel bearing their name for more than 100 years, until it closed in the late Sixties. Local families that have done unusually well as owners of stockbrokerage houses include the Folgers, Flemings, Nolans, Ferrises, Joneses, Kreegers, Lemons and Johnstons. The late David Lawrence started out as a newspaper reporter and became a millionaire as editor-owner of the magazine *U.S. News and World Report*. And the late Merle Thorpe became comfortably fixed when he sold *Nation's Business* magazine to the U.S. Chamber of Commerce. (Pook's Hill, his former home in Bethesda, Md., became the residence of Crown Princess Martha of Norway during her World War II exile in the United States.)

Washington was the birthplace, and is still the headquarters, of the Marriott Corporation, a fast-food and hotel company with sales exceeding $640 million a year. Founder J. Willard Marriott—the son of a prosperous Utah sheep rancher and sugar beet farmer who took a beating in the depression—came to Washington in 1927 and opened a hole-in-the-wall restaurant downtown that sold A&W Root Beer, chili con carne and hot tamales. Today the multimillionaire Marriott, a political conservative, contributes handsomely to the GOP, gives about a tenth of his income to the Mormon church, and divides his time between a large home in the Wesley Heights section of the District, a cottage in New Hampshire and a 5,000-acre farm in Virginia. His son, J. Willard Marriott, Jr., now heads the family empire which operates some 1,000 eating establishments in D.C. and twenty-six states. A similar local success story is that of Government Employees Insurance Company (GEICO), a giant insurance firm that, contrary to the name, has no connection whatsoever with Uncle Sam or his employees. GEICO was a pioneer in insuring low-risk individuals (like clean-living federal bureaucrats) at low rates, and has branched out from auto insurance into many other kinds. The soaring value of GEICO stock made rich men of Leo Goodwin, Jr., Lorimer Davidson, and especially David Lloyd Kreeger, the recently retired GEICO board chairman and patron of Washington culture.

Among the newer local fortunes are those associated with the success of Giant Food Stores, a Middle Atlantic grocery chain with annual sales of about $500 million and a reputation for being a leader in consumer-oriented marketing. Giant is owned largely by the families of N. M. Cohen and the late Jacob Lehrman, and to a lesser extent by its president, Joseph Danzansky, the Washington lawyer who was so tenacious in his unsuccessful campaign to bring professional baseball back to Washington after the departure of the Senators. Milton Elsberg, Myron and Sylvan Gerber and their families have built their Drug Fair chain, an innovator in discount retailing, into a $200 million-a-year business.

D. F. Antonelli and Kingdon Gould founded PMI, a parking lot and real estate empire. Gould, who inherited a small sum from an estate dating back to nineteenth century "robber baron" Jay Gould, has served recently as U.S. ambassador to Luxembourg and to the Netherlands, after making six-figure contributions to the campaigns of Richard Nixon, including $100,000 in 1972. Aaron Goldman guided the Macke Company—vending machines and food concessions—into annual sales of some $180 million. George H. Olmsted, a retired major general in the Army Reserves, has used Washington as his headquarters for assembling a lucrative complex of firms in insurance, banking and manufacturing, capped by the International Bank and Financial General Bankshares. Ulysses (Blackie) Auger parlayed a humble short-order restaurant, begun after World War II, into a twelve-restaurant fleet, the flagship of which is the immensely popular Blackie's House of Beef. The bulk of his wealth, however, is the Washington real estate into which he invested his restaurant profits.

The high average affluence of Washington has always made it a good city for selling automobiles, and a number of families have made a lot of money with dealerships established decades ago. The Steuart brothers—L. P. and Guy—began selling the Ford Model T in 1916, and today their heirs sell Chryslers, Fords, Volvos, Mazdas, Saabs, Plymouths, and Datsuns (as well as operating cab companies, insurance agencies and the largest heating oil distributorship in Washington). Floyd Akers had a monopoly franchise for the sale of Cadillacs in the Washington area for decades, until his Capitol Cadillac and Suburban Cadillac empire was divided in the Sixties. Ourisman Chevrolet, begun in 1921 by Ben Ourisman and headed today by his son Mandell, is perhaps the nation's largest Chevy dealership. One of the largest Ford dealerships is the suburban Virginia company of John Koons, started in 1941. Koons and his sons now sell Chevrolets, Pontiacs, and Oldsmobiles, as well as Fords. Other old Washington auto fortunes include those of the Cherner (Ford), Pohanka (Olds), and Lustine (Chevy) families.

Many local fortunes—medium to very large—have been accumulated over the past forty years in construction and real estate, two economic activities that couldn't help but boom as the population of the Washington area increased almost geometrically. Preeminent among local developers was the late Morris Cafritz, a rags-to-riches figure who started out owning bowling alleys. His widow Gwen continues to be a leading hostess and benefactor of the arts, while his sons carry on the family business. (Cafritz, one of the city's most generous philanthropists, created in 1948 the $30 million Cafritz Foundation, which concentrates on local charities.) A comparably large fortune was amassed by Garfield Kass, who died in 1975 at the age of 85. In 1963 Kass sold most of his buildings and shopping centers (including the Seven Corners shopping center in suburban Virginia) to British interests for $38 million, while retaining most of his undeveloped land.

The population surge since World War II enriched many local builders, land developers and investors, among them Charles E. Smith, Sam Eig, the late George Hyman, Isadore Gudelsky, Carl Freeman, the Kettler brothers, Marshall Coyne, the Magazine brothers, Milton Polinger, the Miller brothers, the late Sam Bogley, Leo Bernstein, Floyd Davis, Richard Norair, Dermot Nee, Norman Bernstein, Oliver T. Carr, Jr., Wallace Holladay, the Howar brothers, and John Safer (one of Richard Nixon's biggest financial backers, through a 1972 political donation of $250,000). The highest flying of all the big Washington developers today is Abe Pollin, owner of the NBA Capital Bullets basketball team and the NHL Washington Capitals hockey team, and also developer, in 1973, of the $20 million Capital Centre sports and entertainment arena in suburban Largo, Maryland. One of the lowest-profile big Washington developers is Theodore Lerner, whose holdings include the Wheaton Plaza shopping center, Landover Mall, and Tysons Corner shopping center.

Some bigtime developers lost their shirts, too. Witness, for example, Jerry Wolman, former "wonder boy" developer and owner of the Philadelphia Eagles football team, who fell on hard times before making a partial comeback in the Seventies. Or the late Bernard Siegel, who made a pile in the grocery business and then overextended himself buying rural land in Montgomery County, Maryland. Or the Pomponio brothers, whose high-rise office buildings across the Potomac in Rosslyn, Virginia, gave Washington its first semblance of a skyline, but who eventually met with foreclosure and criminal suits during a temporary glut of office space.

Anyone who happened to own any amount of raw land in, and just beyond, the Washington suburbs during the boom of the Fifties and Sixties found himself sitting on a gold mine, with the possibility of a 1,000 percent gain per acre over the 1950 price. Among the many longtime landowners who benefited in a big way from the suburbanization of Washington were A. Smith Bowman, the distiller of Virginia Gentleman bourbon (the capital's "in" brand), whose 7,000-acre Sunset Hills Farm in Fairfax County became the nucleus of the new town of Reston, Virginia; and William W. Rapley, whose family owned the National Theatre, National Publishing Company, and a farm that became the site for the White Oak (Maryland) Naval Ordnance Lab (the profits on the sale of which bought Avenel Farm, a spread of more than 1,000 acres in suburban Potomac, Maryland).

THE "BETTER" ADDRESSES

If you would like to see where many rich people of Washington live (at least part of the year, anyway), just drive through Georgetown, the historic district of Northwest Washington between K and R Streets, from 27th to 36th Streets. Not all Georgetowners are rolling in money, of course. Many of the smaller houses and apartments in subdivided old mansions are rented by young professionals, students, secretaries, hippies, and others who value the Georgetown mystique. The big houses are the homes of such people as Averell Harriman, Kay Graham, Peter Belin, Gordon Gray, Hugh Auchincloss, Roger Stevens, H. J. Heinz III, Michael Straight, and Washington "cave dwellers" like Armistead Peter III, whose Tudor Place estate (on Q Street between 31st and 32nd) was built by his tobacco-exporting ancestors in 1815.

For sheer density of rich people, Georgetown is matched only by Kalorama, the neighborhood of embassies and private homes between Connecticut and Massachusetts Avenues north of Dupont Circle. There, along Embassy Row and certain blocks of Wyoming Avenue, Kalorama Road, Belmont Road, Tracy and Bancroft Places, S Street, 23rd and 24th Streets, you'll find residences owned by S. Dillon Ripley, journalist Ben Welles, art donor Joseph Hirshhorn, James Biddle, World Bank President Robert McNamara, and diplomat George W. Renchard (whose family occupies a stately house at 22nd and S that was once the nation's official diplomatic guest house, when President Truman lived at Blair House during the White House renovation from 1948 to 1952).

No single street in Washington can match the District's Foxhall Road in its number and architectural variety of elegant homes. Proceeding north from Reservoir Road, Foxhall Road goes past (on the left) the historic Uplands estate, once the residence of former Ambassador to Norway "Daisy" Harriman, and (on the right) the long, winding drive to the sylvan estate of Mrs. Parke H. Brady (whose relatives own Uplands). Next to Uplands is the residence of the German ambassador to the U.S. Farther up on the same side of the road is Mt. Vernon College, across from which is the relatively modest home of publisher Laughlin Phillips and the elegant white-columned house of his mother, Mrs. Duncan Phillips (complete with a photoelectric-light burglar alarm beaming across the driveway). Then Foxhall proceeds past (on the left) the Belgian ambassador's residence—a replica of an eighteenth century Parisian mansion—and across the road, the 1930s-style contemporary home of Mrs. Morris Cafritz, whose terrace affords an unparalleled view of the city's taller monuments. Next to the Cafritz house is the ten-foot-high concrete wall fronting the home of Mr. and Mrs. David Lloyd Kreeger. Built less than ten years ago from a design by Philip Johnson and Richard Foster, the strikingly modern house might someday be opened to the public as a museum of the Kreegers' collection of Impressionist, Post-Impressionist, and modern art. Farther up the road, on the opposite side, is the unmarked, unadorned entrance to Nelson Rockefeller's wooded, 16-acre property, whose rambling, country-style house is far from the road, hidden from public view.

Many of Washington's wealthy live in the Woodland Drive area, called home by the likes of True Davis, assorted du Ponts, William McChesney Martin, Jr., Senator Hugh Scott (R-Pa.), Jefferson Patterson, environmental chief Russell Train, lawyer Thomas G. Corcoran, and stockbroker-diplomat John Clifford Folger. Others live in the Forest Hills section of the District, and in Spring Valley or Wesley Heights. Some prefer luxury high-rise buildings like the Colonnade at 2801 New Mexico Avenue, the Foxhall near Ward Circle, or the Towers at 4201 Cathedral Avenue. The *ne plus ultra* cooperative complex, of course, is the Watergate, wherein resides a very mixed bag of prominent people, some wealthy, some merely powerful: Federal Reserve Chairman Arthur Burns, former Budget Director Roy Ash, gallery director J. Carter Brown, U.S. Circuit Court Judge David Bazelon, federal arts czar Nancy Hanks, Clare Boothe Luce, and such senators as Clifford Hansen, Stuart Symington, Jacob Javits, and Abraham Ribicoff.

The District is the preferred place of residence of most Washington plutocrats, but a few of them can be found in the Maryland suburbs of Bethesda and Chevy Chase. The "better" suburban addresses are McLean, Virginia (which is home to the Kennedys, Elliot Richardson—when he is not in London—William Simon and a host of others) and Potomac, Maryland. Potomac's most spectacular estate is Marwood, the gatehouse of which is visible on River Road about a mile beyond Potomac Village. The château-style mansion, overlooking the Potomac River, was occupied in the Thirties by then SEC Chairman Joseph P. Kennedy, and is now owned by Grady Gore, who amassed his fortune in Washington real estate.

So there is a sampling of the Big Money in Washington. Some of it is highly visible. Some of it lives in a low-key fashion that shuns the spotlight. Its owners are mobile, spending much of the year out of Washington (especially when hot, humid air settles over the city in the summer). Since so many of Washington's big fortunes are controlled by people whose hometown allegiances lie elsewhere, the local cultural, educational, and social service organizations have derived comparatively little benefit from this wealth.

The large fortunes that inhabit Washington are as distinctive a fixture here as the Washington Monument. The capital city, after all, has a facet which is dazzling and glittering. Some of the glitter is financed by Uncle Sam (through tax dollars). Some of the glamor is financed by embassies and corporations, with their lavish expense-account entertaining. The rest is provided, as a private public service, by the city's affluent minority.

44 SEEING THE SIGHTS

The odds are pretty good that you'll be coming to Washington sometime in the near future. Maybe next week, maybe next year. You might come by yourself, with your family, or with a few friends. Perhaps you'll visit as a tourist on vacation, perhaps for a business purpose. The visit may be your first or your twentieth, but sooner or later, you'll be coming to the nation's capital. When you do, you'll get a lot more out of your visit if you do some homework first, if you find out how Washington works, what goes on in the buildings you see through the cab windows, who those people are, scurrying along the sidewalks, and some background on how the capital got to look the way it does. That's what this book is all about, but no book can give you all the sounds and scenes and personal experiences that you want. You'll have to see for yourself.

When you do visit Washington, you will have plenty of company—probably more than you'd prefer. That's because the same things that attract you to Washington—the ceremonial splendor, the open green spaces of the Mall, the historical heritage, and the trappings of power—attract millions of other Americans and foreign visitors, too. The number of visitors mounts continually, and now totals about 20 million every year. Some 725,000 of these are registered delegates to more than 740 conventions (a "convention" being defined as any meeting that books at least 100 rooms at a hotel or motel in the Washington metropolitan area). A large number of the visitors are executives and lawyers who come to do business with the government. More often than not, they arrive by plane or train in the morning and leave for home at 6 P.M., scheduling no time for Washington social and cultural activities.

But the vast majority of the 20 million visitors are tourists, pure and simple. Their migration waxes and wanes according to the weather and their children's school schedules. The heavy influx begins in April, when the Japanese cherry trees, azaleas, and dogwoods bloom. It hits a peak with about 4.5 million visitors in June, then falls off to around 2 million during the hot, humid month of August, when Congress closes shop and half of the bureaucracy seems to desert the city for the beaches of New England or Rehoboth, Delaware, and Ocean City, Maryland. If you can't tolerate long lines and don't mind drab winter weather, come to Washington from November to February, when you'll have to contend with only a mere 50,000 other tourists each month. Or for a happy medium, try the crisp, sunny months of September and October, when the kids are back to school and the crowds fall from 800,000 to 200,000 before vanishing into winter.

Tourism is the most important nongovernmental activity in the Washington economy, so it is taken very seriously by the locals. National Park Service personnel dispense tourist information from kiosks all over Washington at major monuments. The Washington Area Convention and Visitors Bureau

(1129 20th Street N.W., between L and M Streets) is happy to deluge you with booklets and maps of all sorts and, like the Park Service, has a phone number you can call for recorded information on the day's events. (Check the D.C. phone book for the current numbers.) Most gas stations give away free maps marked with the locations, hours, and fees for all major sights.

Washington has been tardy in developing a central visitors' center—a first-stop information pavilion to give the tourist's subsequent ramblings some rational order and historical perspective—but the void will be filled by the time the Bicentennial begins in 1976. A National Visitors Center will be located in the old (but modernized) Union Station, just a few blocks from the Capitol. The center—which will include a parking garage and minibus and subway connections to downtown—has been designed to share the vaulted, turn-of-the-century building with a few remaining Amtrak trains. The highlight of the center's presentations will be a half-hour orientation film of history and current facts about Washington.

The newest aid to a meaningful Washington visit is the Public Citizen Visitors Center, created in 1974 by Ralph Nader. Located in a small storefront at 1200 15th Street, the center was born of Nader's disappointment that too many tourists leave the capital sated with monuments and droning tour spiels, but still very ignorant about the daily routine of government work. At his center, volunteers suggest a wide variety of off-the-beaten-track activities. Tourists are urged to go up to Capitol Hill to watch a congressional committee at work (and maybe meet their congressman), to attend a hearing before a regulatory commission on an issue of interest to them, to listen to House and Senate floor debate from the visitors' gallery (however dull such debate usually is), and to sample a few of the special events and tours that the center lists in a biweekly schedule of unusual activities.

BOOKS TO READ

Before you make your trip to Washington, look around your local bookshops for recently revised guidebooks. The most exhaustive guide to the public buildings, parks, statues, churches, and historic mansions is *Washington, D.C., A Guide to the Nation's Capital* (Hastings House, New York, 1968). Originally written during the depression by the WPA Federal Writers' Program and updated twice, its 500 pages are packed with an awesome array of details (much of it more than you need). It lacks nuts-and-bolts tourist information about getting around the city, lodging, restaurants, and night life, but is interesting for background. One of the better pocket-size books is the *New York Times Guide to the Nation's Capital* (Bantam, New York, 1968), which includes meaty and witty essays on federal institutions like the Supreme Court and Congress, as well as chapters on dining out and activities for children. Another good book is *The Washington Guidebook* by John and Katharine Walker (Metro Publishers Representatives, Washington, D.C., 1969). The Smithsonian Institution publishes a handsome fold-out pamphlet, entitled *Guide to the Nation's Capital,* available for 75¢ in the old Smithsonian building on the Mall and in all Smithsonian bookshops. The intangible character of the city is captured beautifully in *The Evidence of Washington* (Harper & Row, New York, 1966), an expensive "coffee table book" with photos by Evelyn Hofer and text by William Walton.

Later, after you get to Washington, you will find that any good bookstore is stocked with a dismaying array of specialty publications—walking tours of particular neighborhoods, books on historic homes, outdoor sculpture, architecture, art collections, and every other facet of Washington past and present. Each month's *Washingtonian* magazine, available at all newsstands, has a useful wrap-up of special cultural events, night life, and restaurants.

PLACES TO STAY

In preparation for your trip, be sure to make your room reservation well in advance. If you're coming at a peak period of the spring or summer, give yourself many weeks of lead time. The Washington metropolitan area has about 250 hotels and motels, with a total of about 31,000 rooms. They are nearly evenly divided between the District of Columbia and the suburbs (some of the "suburban" motels, like the enormous Marriott establishments in Rosslyn and Crystal City, Virginia, are in urban settings just across the Potomac River bridges from the District, barely ten minutes from downtown). The suburban motels tend to be more uniform in price, style, and modernity, while the District offers a broad range. The District has elegant old hotels like the Hay-Adams, Sheraton-Carlton, Mayflower, and Jefferson, as well as posh new ones like the Madison, Loew's L'Enfant Plaza, Washington Hilton, Georgetown Manor, and Embassy Row. The once dilapidated neighborhood north of Capitol Hill will soon be brightened by a new 900-room Hyatt Hotel, with the same splashy design gimmicks (glass-walled elevators, four-story lobbies, etc.) used in other Hyatt inns.

For the best advice on lodging in Washington, don't ask Washingtonians (who don't stay in their own city's hotels much), but ask friends and business colleagues who have been here recently. Tailor your choice to your particular needs. (If, for example, you have business with a government office in the suburbs—like the Bureau of Standards in Gaithersburg, Maryland—there's no point in staying downtown.) For status points with your friends back home, check into the luxurious Watergate Hotel, next to the office building where the Democrats' offices were bugged. (It's a favorite of star performers appearing at the nearby Kennedy Center.) Or take a room across the street at the nondescript Howard Johnson Motor Lodge, where the Watergate crew took a room to monitor the bugged phones. If you prefer to stay outside the downtown area but not in the suburbs, you might like the Shoreham Americana, a sprawling edifice perched along the woods of Rock Creek Park, at Connecticut Avenue and Calvert Street N.W., or the nearby Sheraton Park on Woodley Road. If you are watching your budget closely, look through the Washington tourist guides for the many moderate- and low-priced hotels in the District, some of which are near Union Station on Capitol Hill.

GETTING AROUND TOWN

If you stay in the suburbs, you are faced with either a stiff taxicab fare into the central sightseeing and government areas or the hassle of parking your car for the day. On-street parking is very restricted in the District during the workday, and commercial garages (there are no public ones) charge up to $4 a day, if you can even find one that isn't full by 9 A.M. Within the District, taxis are one of the best bargains in America. They have no meters, operating instead on a zone system. The way Congress drew the zones, one person can travel by cab from Capitol Hill to the White House, or virtually anywhere else downtown, for a mere 85¢. The publicly operated Metrobus system is convenient for daily commuting, but its intricacies are difficult for tourists to figure out during a brief stay. The same might be true of the Metro subway system, the first downtown sections of which are scheduled to be completed sometime in 1975.

The best innovation in tourist transportation in recent years is the Tourmobile, a continuous shuttle of minibuses that travel a twelve-stop circuit around the Mall, including most of the major sightseeing attractions. For a modest fee ($2 adults, $1 children under twelve), you can ride all day, getting on and off as you please, all the while enjoying a tour guide's spiel over the loudspeaker. (A separate tour goes to Arlington National Cemetery.) As in every major city, there are companies that conduct tours in full-size buses, and independent tour guides who take small groups around the city in everything from converted taxicabs to new black limousines. (Don't bother to be impressed by any D.C. limousine whose license plate carries the letter L in front of the number—it's just rented.) The independent, solo practitioners of the tour-guide industry stand around next to their cars at all the popular sights, advertising their services with raspy voices, hoping that the tourists walking by are getting just tired enough to be interested in a chauffeured tour. Every driver has his own distinctive tour banter, including obscure bits of information—historical and current, social and political, true and apocryphal —about every building and personality in town.

THE STREET SYSTEM

If you want to try negotiating the streets of Washington yourself, you had better learn how they are laid out. The street system is actually very orderly— once you get the hang of it. The District of Columbia is divided into four parts. The largest is Northwest (where the business, government, and social activities mainly take place). This is followed in size by Northeast, Southeast, and Southwest. At the center of the four parts is the Capitol building. North Capitol Street, radiating due north, divides Northwest from Northeast, and South Capitol Street divides Southwest from Southeast. The main east-west dividing lines are East Capitol Street (separating Northeast from Southeast) and the Mall (which separates Northwest from Southwest). All the east-west streets in the District are known by letters of the alphabet starting with A Street nearest the Capitol and moving on through the alphabet, with a few inexplicable omissions—no J Street, X, Y, or Z Street. And I Street is spelled Eye Street, so it won't be confused with First Street. When letters are exhausted, the alphabet continues with words of two syllables in alphabetic sequence (Adams, Bryant, Channing, etc.), followed by words of three syllables (Albemarle, Brandywine, Chesapeake, etc.). All the north-south streets are numbered, in each direction, east and west, from the Capitol. So most street addresses in Washington enable you to visualize the precise and relative locations of a building. An office building at 1729 H Street N.W., would be located northwest of the Capitol, between 17th and 18th Streets, about eight blocks north of the Mall.

Much to the consternation of some visitors, however, the orderly grid pattern is thrown into confusion by Pierre L'Enfant's network of diagonal avenues, which range across the city, crossing each other at squares and traffic circles (usually decorated with a massive equestrian statue of some general).

Whether or not you ever figure out the avenues—named for states of the union—you'll nonetheless find them useful as the shortest distance between two points (if you happen to take the right one). As a general rule, avoid the system of freeways and parkways (Rock Creek Parkway, Whitehurst Freeway, Southwest Freeway, etc.). A boon to savvy Washingtonians, they can be a nightmare to visitors. As for the infamous traffic circles: always yield to cars already in the circle, and don't stop once you're into the flow (except, of course, for a traffic signal).

SEEING THE SIGHTS

The first fact about sightseeing in Washington is that you won't be able to see it all in one visit. There are longtime Washingtonians who go sightseeing in their own hometown week after week without seeing everything. If you have taken tours at the White House, Mount Vernon, and the Capitol, ridden the elevator up the Washington Monument, or stood at the foot of the statues of Jefferson and Lincoln, you have already suffered "museum feet" and surveyed some of the great vistas. Maybe you have seen the magnificent works at the National Gallery of Art and the Phillips Collection. Maybe you've stood gazing at the Census Clock at the Commerce Department, watching the American population grow, adjusted each second for births, deaths, and immigration. You may have seen the dinosaurs and anthropology displays at the Museum of Natural History, visited Ford's Theatre, or quietly stood at the Arlington Cemetery graves of President John F. Kennedy and his brother Robert.

But if it has been a few years since your last visit, you have some catching up to do. There's the John F. Kennedy Center for the Performing Arts—a dazzling white marble, red-upholstered box perched along the Potomac, west of the downtown area. But don't just take the guided tour, with its recitation of which nations donated which chandelier, tapestry, or sculpture to help build the center. Stroll down the Hall of States and the Hall of Nations and read the billboards of current and coming attractions. Then step up to the box office window of the Concert Hall, Eisenhower Theater, Opera House, or American Film Institute and buy tickets for the next performances. That's what the Kennedy Center is—a place to enjoy symphony, choral music, dance, films, classic drama, contemporary theater, and the pop arts.

On another tack, you can take a cab out to the National Zoo and try to catch a glimpse of the two giant pandas that were given to the United States after President Nixon's ice-breaking trip to China in 1972. You may have to wait in line, and when you finally get to the front of it, the black and white pandas might be asleep, out of view in their sumptuous Oriental-modern enclosure. But when Hsing-Hsing (male) and Ling-Ling (female) are in a playful mood, their antics are worth the wait. And while you're at the zoo, go visit the giant bird cage.

Back downtown and across from the White House is Lafayette Park. The area was spruced up a few years ago by the renovation of the onetime home of the Corcoran Gallery of Art into the Renwick Gallery. Its 1853 French Second Empire structure is at the corner of Pennsylvania Avenue and 17th Street. Renamed after its architect, James Renwick (who also did the Smithsonian "castle"), its interior restored to the original Victorian splendor, the gallery focuses on distinctive design in American crafts and manufacturing.

Exhibits there have covered the furniture of Frank Lloyd Wright, American quilts, Shaker furniture, art glass, food preparation utensils, and many other things.

If you haven't been to Washington within the past two years, you will hardly recognize the areas along the Mall near the Capitol. Cleared at last of dreary "temporary" buildings from the Second World War, tennis courts, and dull structures like the old Armed Forces Medical Museum (moved to Walter Reed Hospital in upper Northwest), the new Mall is a showcase of bold modern architecture. The newest must-see attraction is the Joseph H. Hirshhorn Museum and Sculpture Garden, located next to the Smithsonian. Designed by Gordon Bunshaft of Skidmore, Owings and Merrill, the museum is a windowless, doughnut-shaped concrete cylinder on piers, reminiscent of the gun turret of the USS Monitor ironclad. The 6,000-piece collection it houses was assembled rather indiscriminately, but it manages to include many masterpieces of contemporary American painting and modern sculpture from all over the world. Immediately east of the Hirshhorn is the new Air and Space Museum, designed by the St. Louis firm of Hellmuth, Obata and Kassabaum. There, inside a towering enclosure with glass walls and ceilings, will stand (and hang from cables) airplanes, missiles, and space vehicles from every period in the history of manned flight.

Across the Mall from the Air and Space Museum is the new annex to the National Gallery of Art, funded (like the main building) with large gifts from the Mellon family. Designed by I. M. Pei and Partners as an interaction of triangular and trapezoidal shapes, the building will exhibit some of the National Gallery's more modern art. Flanking a new, fan-shaped reflecting pool at the base of Capitol Hill are two new office buildings: one, for the Department of Labor, a rather lackluster bureaucratic box; the other, for HEW, a work by Marcel Breuer and Associates, architects of the HUD headquarters building in the Southwest redevelopment area.

SOME SPECIAL PLACES

Now, if you want a change of pace, here are a few suggestions of unusual sights in the Washington area—some of them well known, some obscure. Most of them do not require a major investment of time, so keep them in mind if you're here for a day of business meetings and find that you have an unscheduled hour or so. In no particular order, they are:

Folger Shakespeare Library (201 East Capitol Street, two blocks east of the Capitol). The building's neoclassical exterior opens into a hushed Elizabethan world of dark wood paneling, tile floors, and vaulted ceilings. Founded by Standard Oil millionaire Henry Clay Folger, the library is probably the world's greatest collection of Shakespeareana and other materials from the seventeenth century. Locked away in underground safes for perusal by scholars are rare first-quarto editions of Shakespeare's plays and 79 of the world's 250 known copies of the first-folio editions. Also on the premises, but not on view, is one of Queen Elizabeth I's corsets. The public display area features many items related to the playwright's career, as well as exhibits focusing on aspects of life in his times—such as music, astronomy, military techniques, and marital customs. The library has a small theater—used by an excellent drama company—patterned after an open-air, courtyard stage like the long-gone Globe Theatre in London.

Theodore Roosevelt Island (in the Potomac River, accessible by causeway from Virginia via the George Washington Parkway). Called Analostan or Mason's Island in the late-eighteenth and nineteenth centuries, when the distinguished Mason family of Virginia owned a manor house and plantation there, the island today is the only national park in an urban setting. Once cultivated, the land is now a densely forested bit of wilderness, traversed by simple paths. At the center of the island is a memorial to Theodore Roosevelt. While the shrine itself is strangely formal, the island is gloriously natural and serene.

Museum of African Art (316 A Street N.E., on Capitol Hill). Housed in a Victorian townhouse that black abolitionist Frederick Douglass occupied during the 1870s, the museum has a threefold mission—to show the influence of African art on the development of modern Western art, through such revolutionaries as Picasso, Modigliani, and Klee; to display traditional African arts and crafts, such as tribal religious symbols, drums, apparel, and weaponry; and to display contemporary art by black Americans and Africans.

Chesapeake and Ohio Canal (Georgetown, south of M Street N.W.). Where else can you find, inside a modern American city, a genuine nineteenth-century canal, complete with water, functioning locks, and a well-worn towpath, flanked by quaint townhouses and old brick warehouses? Beginning in Washington in 1828, the 185-mile C&O was excavated parallel to the Potomac River, reaching Cumberland, Maryland, in 1850. Never really competitive with the railroad, the canal boats continued to carry grain, coal, and other goods until 1924.

U.S. Naval Observatory (Massachusetts Avenue, southeast of the intersection with Wisconsin Avenue N.W.). In addition to a mighty array of telescopes, the observatory has atomic clocks, accurate to a millionth of a second per day, that determine the standard time by which America sets its watches. Self-correcting and monitored by a control panel like something out of Houston Space Control, the clocks are in vaults that are carefully insulated from noise vibration. The old mansion on the property, once the home of the chief of naval operations, is now the official vice presidential residence. Tours at 2 P.M., Monday through Friday. Nighttime tours a few evenings a month, by appointment.

Freer Gallery of Art (on the Mall, west of the old Smithsonian). Perhaps the finest collection of Oriental art in the world, the Freer also contains a notable group of paintings by James McNeill Whistler. The tranquil Asian art is raucously upstaged by the infamous Peacock Room, a blue-green-gold dining room that Whistler designed for a turn-of-the-century London industrialist. On the walls of the room are paintings of two peacocks—one of them, representing Art, is resplendently regal, while the other, representing Wealth, is a vulgar roustabout with a mantle of coins.

Washington Cathedral (Wisconsin Avenue at Massachusetts Avenue). Don't miss an opportunity to witness construction of what is the world's newest (and perhaps last) great Gothic cathedral. Using medieval building principles, with an assist from modern tools like power cranes, the Episcopal Church has been at work on the cathedral since 1908. Among the illustrious Americans buried in its crypts are President Woodrow Wilson and Admiral George Dewey.

Library of Congress (Capitol Hill, immediately east of the Capitol). With more than 72 million items—books, maps, manuscripts, recordings, photos, art prints, and technical reports—the Library is far and away the largest in the world. Be sure to see the Gutenberg Bible, printed in Germany about 1455 by the inventor of movable-type printing (and one of the only three perfect vellum copies in the world). On display in the Whittall Pavilion are five stringed instruments made in the early eighteenth century by the legendary Stradivarius. Stored in special air-conditioned cases, they are occasionally exercised in concerts at the Library by visiting string quartets.

Islamic Center (2551 Massachusetts Avenue N.W., along Embassy Row). Commonly called "the Mosque," this exotic Arabian structure is the spiritual center for Moslems throughout the Washington area. Its tall, slender minaret is a familiar landmark, rising high above the trees of neighboring Rock Creek Park.

Old Pension Office (5th and G Streets N.W.). Built in 1883 as a memorial to the Union forces of the Civil War, this gigantic barn-of-a-building has a clerestory hall that's 100 feet tall and covers 30,000 square feet (about 60 percent the size of a football field). The roof is supported by eight Corinthian columns, each made of 55,000 separate bricks. Decades ago, the great hall was the scene of the inaugural balls of five Presidents. Around the exterior of the building is a bas-relief frieze depicting branches of the Union Army in action.

Franciscan Monastery (14th and Quincy Streets N.E., near Catholic University and the National Shrine of the Immaculate Conception). Beneath the Byzantine-style church are dark passageways fashioned after the catacombs of Rome, in which the early Christians sought refuge from pagan persecution. The Grotto of Bethlehem is a hypothetical reproduction of the birthplace of Jesus. Around the grounds, resplendent in the spring and summer, are reproductions of the Grotto of Lourdes in the Pyrenees and the Garden of Gethsemane in Jerusalem.

Frederick Douglass House (14th and W Streets S.E., across South Capitol Street Bridge from the rest of the District). Situated on a large estate with a commanding view of downtown Washington, this restored Victorian house was the last home of Frederick Douglass (1817–1895), an escaped slave who became a world-famous antislavery orator and newspaper editor. After the Civil War, he held a number of public and diplomatic posts, including minister to Haiti. He bought his Anacostia estate in 1889, largely with the proceeds of a long and lucrative lecturing career. (While you are in this part of town, stop at the Anacostia Neighborhood Museum, a Smithsonian project in a converted movie theater, with displays on the historical development of the Anacostia section of the District.)

Dumbarton Oaks (3101 R Street N.W.). Dominating the territory of upper Georgetown, this 27-acre estate of manicured gardens surrounding an early nineteenth-century mansion was once the home of Mr. and Mrs. Robert Woods Bliss, beneficiaries of the Castoria patent medicine fortune. Now owned by Harvard University, Dumbarton houses an art collection whose eminence in Byzantine and early Christian art is comparable to that of the Freer in Oriental art. A choice collection of pre-Columbian art is displayed in an adjoining pavilion, built in 1963 from a design by Philip Johnson, consisting of nine interlocking, domed glass cylinders. (The estate is also famous as the scene of the 1944 discussions between the Allies on a world organization, later named the United Nations.)

Anderson House (2118 Massachusetts Avenue N.W., west of Dupont Circle). Like many embassies and private clubs in Washington, this opulent mansion was once a private residence. Built in 1905 by Ambassador and Mrs. Larz Anderson, both inheritors of vast wealth who brought their bundle to the nation's capital, it is today the headquarters of the Society of the Cincinnati, a patriotic-social organization of descendants of Revolutionary War officers. A stroll through the splendor of Anderson House is a reasonable substitute for a visit to an embassy, most of which are not normally open to the public.

National Collection of Fine Arts, National Portrait Gallery (8th and G Streets N.W.). Both museums are located in the Old Patent Office, a treasure of Greek Revival architecture built between 1837 and 1867. The NCFA is an exciting mélange of everything from nineteenth-century Romantic (Hudson River School, Indian paintings by George Catlin, and dark, mystic canvases of Ryder and Blakelock) to the most avant-garde of contemporary painting, prints, and sculpture. The portrait gallery houses hundreds of portraits of prominent figures in American history, including Peter Hurd's excellent likeness of the late Lyndon B. Johnson, which the President pronounced to be the "ugliest thing I've ever seen."

Octagon House (corner of New York Avenue and 18th Street N.W., two blocks west of the White House). If you could visit only one historic house in Washington, it should be this 1800 Federal masterpiece of Dr. William Thornton, the physician who designed the original Capitol. Built for Colonel John Tayloe, a wealthy Virginia planter, the three-story brick house was the first mansion built downtown in the new City of Washington. President Madison lived there in 1814 and 1815, while the gutted White House was being repaired after it was burned by the British. Owned since 1902 by the American Institute of Architects, the handsome restored house is not really octagonal, but six-sided with a semicircular bay in front.

Needless to say, these suggested sights are a random group, and only a sampling of what can be seen. Flipping the pages of any good D.C. guidebook will bring to mind tens of others—ones to suit every taste, ranging from the Explorers Hall of the National Geographic Society to the Woodrow Wilson House, Decatur House, Textile Museum, Wax Museum, and aquarium in the basement of the Commerce Department.

Visitors with a special interest in modern architecture could fashion a special circuit of their own, including such outstanding buildings as the Arena Stage, at 6th and M Streets S.W. (designed by Harry Weese); Canal Square, 31st Street near M, N.W. (Arthur Cotton Moore); the Watergate complex, along the Potomac at Virginia Avenue N.W. (Luigi Moretti); Dulles International Airport, near Chantilly, Virginia (Eero Saarinen); Martin Luther King, Jr., Memorial Library, 901 G Street N.W. (the office of Mies van der Rohe); Euram Building, Dupont Circle (Hartman and Cox); Longfellow Building, at Connecticut and Rhode Island Avenues N.W. (William Lescaze); Danish Embassy, 3200 Whitehaven Street N.W. (Wilhelm Lauritzen); Metro Operations Control Center, 5th Street between F and G Streets (Keyes, Lethbridge and Condon); Georgetown University Library, 37th and Prospect Streets (John Carl Warnecke and Associates); Florence Hollis Hand Chapel of Mount Vernon College, W Street N.W., west of Foxhall Road (Hartman and Cox); German Embassy, 4645 Reservoir Road, N.W. (Egon Eiermann); Brazilian Embassy, 3006 Massachusetts Avenue N.W. (Olavo Regis de Oliveira); Brewood Building, 1147 20th Street N.W. (Wilkes and Faulkner); and the Third Church of Christ, Scientist and Christian Science Monitor building, 16th and Eye streets N.W. (I. M. Pei and Partners).

While Washingtonians seem to have a penchant for bland colonial reproduction houses, the city and suburbs have some examples of imaginative residential design by such fine local architects as Hugh N. Jacobsen, Grosvenor Chapman, Arthur Keyes, Charles B. Goodman, and Winthrop Faulkner. Indispensable for architectural touring is the AIA's *A Guide to the Architecture of Washington, D.C.* (McGraw-Hill, 1974.)

Since everyone back home is going to ask you whether you visited the Watergate, why disappoint them? For the easiest memento, have someone take a snapshot of you standing under the large letters "Watergate 600" at the entrance of the office building at 600 New Hampshire Avenue N.W., which houses, among other tenants, the offices of the Swedish Embassy and an annex of the Japanese Embassy. (This isn't the building where the Democrats were burglarized, but the "Watergate" letters are clearer, so it's the most popular posing spot.) Have a drink at the Watergate Terrace Restaurant and keep the cocktail napkin. Buy a necktie with the house label of Watergate Men's Wear, or buy a bottle of house-brand whiskey at Watergate Liquors.

Since so many people wonder where the name "Watergate" came from, here is the story of its origin: originally spelled "Water Gate," the phrase refers to a set of forty broad granite steps, forming a terrace that slopes down to the Potomac, next to the Memorial Bridge and the Lincoln Memorial. Completed in the early Thirties, about the time the bridge was finished, the steps were intended to be a symbolic, ceremonial entry to Washington by water, hence a "water gate." For decades, the steps were seats for the thousands of Washingtonians and tourists who attended free summer concerts there, given for years by the National Symphony from a floating orchestra shell and, more recently, by military bands from an enclosure on the shore. In the summer of 1973, however, the noise of low-flying planes approaching National Airport drove most of the open-air concerts away, to the refuge of the Jefferson Memorial steps.

Back when Foggy Bottom (the historic nickname of that neighborhood of the District) was a slum area of old warehouses, gas tanks, and dilapidated homes, the only other thing named "Watergate" was a river-view restaurant famed for its popovers. Then came modern construction. Down went the decrepit (but charming) old buildings, like the towering Heurich Brewery, and up went the People's Life Insurance Building, the Watergate complex, the Howard Johnson Motor Lodge, the Columbia Plaza apartments, and the Kennedy Center. The Watergate buildings, incidentally, are owned by an Italian company in which the Vatican had a controlling interest until it sold its stock in 1969.

AFTER DARK

As for night life in Washington, it is not the nation's finest, but it's not dead either. If it's highbrow entertainment you seek, and you're visiting any time except summer, you can buy tickets to a performance by the National Symphony, the Opera Society of Washington, the Arena Stage, the D.C. Black Repertory Company, or the Folger Theatre Group. Or take in a pre- or post-Broadway play at the venerable National Theatre or Ford's Theatre, both downtown. Or check the amusement pages of the papers to see what out-of-town troupes are performing at the Kennedy Center. On a Sunday afternoon, you can go to the free concert at the Phillips Collection, or at 7 P.M., the free performance of the National Gallery Orchestra (except in summer). If you're visiting in the summer, consider a trip to the outdoor concerts, opera, and ballet at Wolf Trap Farm or the Merriweather Post Pavilion (in nearby Virginia and Maryland, respectively).

For pop entertainment, check to see who's on stage at the Cellar Door, a Georgetown spot that is renowned as a showcase for national talent in folk rock, hip humor, blues, and electric bluegrass. Or consider Etcetera, a downtown jazz and blues nightclub. Or the Blue Room of the Shoreham Americana or Mr. Henry's Upstairs on Capitol Hill. Or Blues Alley, a Georgetown jazz club that really *is* located down an alley. For the best in up-to-the-moment political comedy, see Mark Russell's show in the Marquee Lounge of the Shoreham Americana.

Owing to the large diplomatic population of Washington, the city offers as wide a variety of good international cuisine as any city in the nation (except New York, Chicago, and San Francisco). All the popular cooking styles are well represented: southern Italian, Cantonese Chinese, Mexican, and of course French. There are also restaurants where you can find the food of Hungary (Csiko's); Spain (El Bodegon, Los Gitanos, El Tio Pepe, and others); Greece (the Astor in D.C., and Taverna Cretekou in Alexandria, Virginia); India (Gaylord's, Taj Mahal, Apana); northern Italy (Cantina d'Italia, Tiberio, Mama Regina Ristorante in Silver Spring, Maryland); Cuba and the Caribbean (Omega, El Caribe, Junkanoo, and others); northern China (Empress, China Gate in Alexandria, Virginia, and Peking); Switzerland (the Swiss Chalet); Japan (Mikado, Tokyo, Japan Inn, and others); and the Middle East (Mama Ayesha's Calvert Café, Iron Gate Inn, Arabian Night, and Rudy's in McLean, Virginia).

There are also a few good seafood restaurants—stretching from the plain, bustling Crisfield in Silver Spring, Maryland, to the posh, quiet Sea Catch at the Fairfax Hotel in the District—but not as many as one would expect, given Washington's proximity to the rich waters of the Chesapeake Bay. You can get a good steak-and-potatoes meal just about anywhere, and some restaurants—like Le Steak, the Publick House, and the Palm—specialize in steak. Washington also has a fair number of regular American bars, the most interesting of which is the Old Ebbitt Grill on F Street downtown. The bar, chandeliers, paneling, and mementos at the Ebbitt are more than 100 years old, and were moved to their present site in the 1920s, when the original Ebbitt House at 14th and F Streets was leveled to build the National Press Building. Among the most popular restaurants for tourists are those atop the tall buildings of Rosslyn, Virginia, offering panoramic nighttime views of the lighted monuments across the Potomac in the District. These restaurants include Regina d'Italia, La Bella Vista, and the Chaparral.

As for cost, plan on spending at least $10 a person for a good dinner in Washington. At the ritzy places—including such French spots as Sans Souci, Rive Gauche, Le Bagatelle, Jockey Club, Jean-Pierre, Company Inkwell, Chez

Camille, Le Provençal, La Niçoise, and La Toque d'Argent—consider your-self lucky to escape for $25 a person. While nearly all of the area's best restaurants are in the District, the suburbs now boast several top-flight places. For some help in selecting a restaurant to suit your tastes and pocketbook, consult the current issue of the *Washingtonian* magazine, which carries descriptions of a representative sampling each month. For budget-priced places (including many excellent international eateries), look for a paperback copy of the Washington, D.C., *Underground Gourmet,* by Judith and Milton Viorst.

Like many would-be visitors to Washington, you might be wondering if this is a "safe city." At this time, it is no more or less safe than other cities of comparable size. The District's crime rates—lower in several categories than many smaller cities'—tend to get more national attention and press coverage because this is the nation's capital and because some people expect it to be a Shangri-La. In terms of the numbers of policemen visible in the public areas of the city, Washington is one of the best-patrolled urban areas in America. As in most other cities, street crime is concentrated in low-income residential areas far from the tourist sights, so there is no need for tourists to scurry back to suburban motels at sundown. Exercising the same precautions you would in any other American city at night, you can enjoy the night life of Washing-ton with a minimal risk of trouble.

But it is not the night life that attracts visitors to Washington. It is that special mixture of history, scenery, monuments, and politics that makes the nation's capital a magnet for millions. Even the statues in the parks reflect the mixture. There are, of course, the customary patriots and soldiers—some from Revolutionary War days (foreign generals Lafayette, Kosciusko, and von Steuben, not to mention Washington), some from the Civil War (Sheri-dan, Thomas, Logan), and even an admiral (Farragut) with spyglass. Some are foreigners, like Irish patriot Robert Emmet (at 24th and Massachusetts Avenue N.W.), the Ukrainian poet Taras Shevchenko (at 22nd and P Streets N.W.), and the South American liberator Simón Bolívar (at Constitution Avenue and 18th Street N.W.). Some are political philosophers, like the Englishman Edmund Burke, who spoke for the American colonies, and some are labor leaders, like Samuel Gompers. Some are symbolic, like Freedom atop the Capitol, and some are gilded horses (at the Memorial Bridge, gifts from Italy). And there are the other gifts, like the carillon from the Nether-lands, the cherry trees from Japan, and the Kennedy Center chandeliers from Sweden.

Behind each of these is a story, but on your first visit you will be too tired or hurried to find it out. Another day you will come back, stop for a moment, and reflect. Maybe you won't even get around to it on your second visit. But you will be back many times, with your children or their children. And every time you come, Washington will be somewhat the same, but also somewhat different—like the nation of which it is the capital, forever unfinished.

45 CAPITAL OF THE FUTURE

What will Washington be like in the year 2000?

As a capital city, it will be a massive metropolitan region of 5 million people linked by a 98-mile Metro subway system—extending into the Maryland and Virginia suburbs. There still will be no high-rise buildings towering over national monuments, but the city will be ringed with business districts in the suburbs, with office buildings twenty-four to thirty-six stories tall.

Pennsylvania Avenue will be a newly refurbished ceremonial route. Modern pedestrian esplanades will border it on the north, opposite the Federal Triangle. The Mall, full of buildings constructed in the 1960s and 1970s, will be about as it is now. Washington will still be a city of green and gray—a mixture of grassy parks and marble buildings—more traditional than modern. Some people will live closer to the city center—on Capitol Hill, in Southwest, Southeast, and the near Northwest—reversing the mid-century outward trend.

The White House will look just as it does now, but the Presidency will be more powerful and foreign affairs will occupy more of the President's time. As a nation among nations, operating in collaboration with others, the U.S. will require its chief executive to be a foreign policy expert even more in the twenty-first century than he was in the twentieth.

For energy purposes, Washington will direct that most fuels be produced or mined within the fifty states, except that uranium will come from abroad to fuel nearly 1,000 atomic power plants (less than 150 today). Governmental experiments will be approaching breakthroughs on practical applications for hydrogen fusion and capture of direct solar rays for electric power.

The Department of the Interior will be renamed the Department of Natural Resources, and the scattered consumer offices of the federal government will be drawn together into a Department of Consumer Affairs. The Department of Agriculture will still be known by its old name (despite numerous attempts to transform it into a Department of Food and Fiber).

Low-income American families will be on an "income maintenance plan" (IMP) that will put a floor under the amount of money that each family has available to spend. A national health insurance plan will operate through private insurers, but federal standards will be so uniform that private insurers will be little more than "contract operators."

Railroads will again connect the major cities for passenger traffic as well as freight, and high-speed commuter trains will cover the distance between New York and Washington in two hours (at an average speed of 110 miles an hour). Air travel will be the norm for longer distances, but luxurious over-the-road buses will be equipped with special lounges, reading cubicles, and new luxuries for the white-collar traveler.

Cable television will revolutionize the pattern of shopping, enabling many consumers to do all their ordering without leaving the house. By electronic inquiry and request, shoppers will be presented with displays of clothing, foods, appliances, books, and household necessities. Ordering will be by telephone or preprinted order blanks (like laundry lists). Billing will be by computer printout, rendered biweekly, or simply deducted automatically from the customer's bank account.

The cable hookup will also serve for emergency calls to the fire and police departments (and the Federal Communications Commission will be busy sorting out the priorities for use of the house-to-house cables for education, entertainment, and service).

The general educational system will be much as it is today, except that higher proportions of the school population will be in the lower and intermediate grades, with college enrollments leveled out in percentages (as a result of lower birth rate in the 1970s and 1980s). Federal aid to higher education will be making a comeback, after a dry spell, and nearly every private college or university (including the Ivy League institutions) will receive some per-student subsidy in addition to research grants and support payments for teaching assistants.

The exploration of outer space will be picking up again, in cooperative efforts of the nations of the world under the aegis of the U.N. Scientists will be searching for clues to more efficient uses and sources of power, hoping to unlock the secrets of the huge magnetic force of the universe so as to harness it for driving the simple machines of man.

The world food problem will not be solved, but in the twenty-five years between 1975 and 2000, new varieties of corn, wheat, sorghum, rice, and other cereal grains will be developed for arid climates and the humid tropics, and balanced economies will be in vogue—in contrast to the high reliance on industrialization which characterized the early and mid-twentieth century.

More educated people will be performing service tasks, but they will be aided by machinery that will take the jobs out of the old-fashioned category of "manual labor." Garbage pickup will be almost fully containerized and automated. Reusable cartons will replace throwaways. Recycling service centers will be standard in many communities. In other cities and suburban counties, regular weekly pickups will be arranged for reusable materials, as part of the tax-paid service.

Prepackaged foods will command even more of the daily grocery bill as families become smaller—on average—and more single people will maintain a ménage of one. Group living, in various forms, however, will be making a comeback, and the divorce rate, after rising sharply in the 1970s and 1980s, will be leveling off and starting to trend downward. (Some children of the Eighties and Nineties will conclude that their parents were slightly kooky, "way back then.")

The U.S. population, after a slow-up in its growth rate through the 1970s and 1980s, will stabilize, then start to grow again through immigration. The complexion of the average American will be darker, as a larger proportion of the populace will trace their ancestry to Africa, Asia, and the Latin countries.

The English language will be firmly established throughout the world as the language of diplomacy, international trade, conferences, and tourism. It will continue to be the second language taught in Soviet Russia, China, India, Africa, and South America.

Washington will strengthen its position as an international capital, and the International Monetary Fund and World Bank will be even more important in international currency and lending operations. A world currency will be under serious discussion, based on a combination of gold and "paper gold." It will embody some principles of the U.S. Federal Reserve System, with long-term stabilizing loans grafted on.

Europe will still be disunited, but the European Market will be a reality and political understanding will gradually flow from economic collaboration.

Automobiles will be petroleum-powered, but the grades of gasoline will be different, and engines will be more economical. Cars will be smaller, and prices will be higher. A few electric-powered vehicles will be seen in the cities, especially for delivery vans to make short runs and operate close to home base.

Men's clothing will trend toward the "Nehru jacket" which made an abortive appearance on the scene in the 1960s. "Unisex" styles will be popular, but the women's lib movement of the 1970s will be old-fashioned, having won its point (as the women's suffrage movement phased out after passage of the Nineteenth Amendment).

A two-bedroom apartment in most cities will rent for $500 a month (New York excluded, where the rate will be higher). The average three-bedroom suburban home, newly constructed, will sell for $95,000. A Vega-size General Motors car, called "the Capsule," will retail for $7,000. It will still be powered by an internal combustion piston engine, with four cylinders, high-compression, with antiemission equipment that will require unleaded gasoline. Gasoline will cost $2.25 a gallon, including $1.75 in federal and state taxes.

Median family income for the U.S. will be $22,000. Social security taxes will be 14 percent (7 percent employer, 7 percent employee) up to $24,000 of gross income.

The federal government will have import quotas on petroleum and export quotas on food to protect the balance of payments and the grocery bill, even though prices of food and fuel will be more than double what they are today.

Beef at the supermarket will cost $4 a pound for flank steak, $6 a pound for cube steaks, $8 a pound for sirloin. Milk will be $1 a quart, middle-grade bread 75¢ a loaf. Men's top-grade shoes will range from $105 to $130 a pair. A three-pound box of laundry detergent will cost $2.89 (on a weekend special). Men's suits will be priced from $210 to $380, but fewer men will wear them to the office, preferring casual clothes instead.

The year 2000 will be election year for the One-Hundred-Seventh Congress. (It is the ninety-fourth today.) And it will be a presidential election year, too, to elect the nation's forty-fourth (if each President between now and then serves one term). If any President is assassinated, dies in office, is incapacitated, or resigns, the number will be higher. If someone serves two terms, the number will be lower.

Republicans and Democrats will still be the major power groups, but a third party will be on the scene, making a strong appeal to older voters—retirees and the white-collar middle class—who will represent the largest aggregate in the voting public.

Out of nine contenders for the presidential nomination in 2000, three will be women. All will be over forty-five years of age, and two will be in their middle sixties. Life expectancy of the American population by then will have risen to seventy, and anyone in his sixties, in good health, will have a reasonable expectation of living to age seventy-eight. Members of the post-World-War II population explosion (now in their middle twenties) will be in their fifties, and the "youth culture" of the 1960s will be the topic of nostalgic books on "how it used to be" back in the 1960s when Woodstock and *Hair* and frontal nudity shocked the nation's parents.

Mass transit in the major metropolitan centers will be heavily subsidized from tax revenues, even though fares will be more than $1 a ride in Washington and San Francisco, and around 85¢ in other cities.

The labor force will total 120 million people—approximately 45 percent of the population.

The U.S. population will be 260 million—more than a quarter of a billion—making the U.S. the world's fourth-largest nation in population, behind China, India, and the Soviet Union. Its growth will be slower than it was in the 1960s, with the gain averaging around a million people a year from a combination of births, deaths, and immigration. Family size will be growing again, as children born in the 1970s to small-family units hark back to "the good old days" and begin to emulate their grandparents of the 1940s and 1950s whose families were larger.

The U.S., still a major world power, will share its potency with the Arab Confederation, a Union of African Nations, China, the Soviet Union, and the European Community, which will still be squabbling, but will cooperate on major matters. Latin America will remain a collection of individualistic nations. India will continue to suffer from economic problems, but will be making progress in the production of food. Australia and Canada will be growing slowly but steadily, balancing industry, agriculture and population. Japan, pressured by high prices for raw materials and a demanding labor force, will be turning to the Soviet Union in political and economic alliances.

The world will avoid atomic war, but there will be times when big-power confrontation will be perilously close. Tensions will continue over the Middle East, the Mediterranean, and issues involving the oceans. Friction will persist between China and the Soviet Union.

The United Nations veto power will be trimmed, and one issue for U.N. debate will be control of the Arctic and Antarctic—for world peace, weather control, and mineral exploitation. Underwater explorations of the ocean bottoms will be undertaken on a large scale, and the jurisdiction over undersea resources will be a source of disagreement among nations.

The Soviet Union will be developing its Siberian oil and gas reserves, and the U.S. will be drawing much of its domestic oil from the Alaskan North Slope. Offshore pumping will be going full tilt in the North Sea and along the coasts of Southeast Asia, Africa, and South America. New discoveries will be coming to light in the Amazon Valley and Central Africa.

Washington will be dealing with more and more nations headed by Socialist political leaders. A series of energy crunches, inflationary crises, and raw materials problems will have toppled established governments, creating conditions conducive to tight central dictation over economic life. International trade will be subject to rising controls.

In the U.S. Congress average committee members will have more say in the selection of their chairmen from among the members. Several new joint committees of the Senate and House will be added to the existing joint committees on economics and the budget, but the two houses will continue to work individually with strong traditions of institutional rivalry.

Women will occupy a conspicuous number of Cabinet, Senate, and House positions, but a majority of public officials will be men. The average age of political figures will be higher than it is today.

Two-thirds of the population will live on one-third of the land. And 90 percent of the total population will live on 10 percent of the land—mainly in urban centers and metropolitan regions. Even more than it is now, the voting public will be an urban public and political power will center in the big city areas.

What will the political issues be in the year 2000?

Personal rights to privacy (after a long period of putting everything out in the open).

Economic opportunity (a perennial on the American scene, ever since the first colony at Jamestown).

Education for all. After a brief period of disillusionment and dissatisfaction with the system of higher education, the U.S. public will turn to the job of making higher education fit the needs of the twenty-first century, with more continuing education, new combinations of interprofessional training, and innovative work-study arrangements for people of all ages.

More opportunities for the retired to do useful work. When the burden of paying for retirement programs finally sinks into the consciousness of the working population, new schemes will be advanced to make use of the wasted talents and skills of older people—in paying jobs, part-time employment, and public service work. Finally it will dawn on the voting public that social security payments, retirement benefits, and private pension plans all come out of the paychecks of the working populace. New arrangements to use the services of the idle elderly will help level out the rise in social security taxes, increase national production, and at the same time provide happier lives for the older generation.

These issues will be handled by Congress in much the same way that issues are handled today—slowly, haphazardly, with much delay, with a certain amount of backing and filling, and without any sudden definitive action. Political habits do not change quickly, not even over the span of one generation. The "new politics" of the 1972 McGovern campaign—with emphasis on open decisions, wide participation, and maximum minority representation—will be more or less standard by the year 2000, but the pattern will not be entirely new, having made gradual inroads each year along the way. Closed committee sessions will be almost a thing of the past in Congress, but even now they are increasingly rare. Private deliberations and consultations will still take place behind closed doors.

Congress itself will be better staffed to do its job than it is today. But constituencies will be larger, by more than 15 percent, and the volume of work will be increased even more, as government programs penetrate deeper into people's lives.

Washington will be an even greater focal point of daily economic and political decisions. Despite the fiscal efforts of the federal government toward revenue sharing and decentralizing of services, decisionmaking will continue to flow to the center. As in other nations of the world, the United States government will become a national government rather than a collection of states, which it started out to be. Programs will increasingly resemble the unemployment benefit system—with the federal government setting the standards and the states doing the work.

Over this kind of system, Washington will preside—drawing on the opinions and attitudes of 260 million people, dispensing laws and regulations in accordance with what it hears from the home precincts. It may not be much different from what it is today, but there will be a lot more of it.

INDEX OF NAMES

Abdesselam, M., 254
Abdul-Jabbar, Kareem, 311
Abel, I. W., 385
Abelson, Philip H., 416
Abourezk, James, 140
Abplanalp, Robert, 61, 63, 67
Abzug, Bella, 274, 368
Acheson, Dean, 172, 233
Acheson, Mrs. Dean, 118
Adams, Sherman, 6, 182, 424
Adams family, 531
Adamy, Clarence (Clancy), 447
Addison family, 118
Adler family, 120
Agger, Carolyn E., 281
Aggrey, O. Rudolph, 302
Agnew, Spiro, 19, 116, 122, 130, 138, 166, 178, 192, 261
Agronsky, Martin, 266
Aiken, George, 69, 442
Aiken, Lola, 278
Ailes, Roger, 165
Ailes, Stephen, 98, 194, 395
Ailey, Alvin, 518, 522
Akers, Floyd, 533
Albert, Carl, 43–44, 140, 149
Albright, Joseph M. P., 530
Alexander, Clifford, Jr., 303, 309, 324
Alexander, Herbert E., 163
Alfaro, Ricardo J., 119
Ali, M. Hossain, 251
Alioto, Joseph, 372
Allbritton, Joe, 531
Allen, George, 71
Allen, Helen Greenwood, 283
Allen, Henry, 523
Allen, James, 139, 156
Allen, James E., Jr., 402
Allen, Paul, 314
Allende, Salvador, 51, 233, 255
Allott, Gordon, 465
Alphand, Hervé, 248
Alsop, Joseph, 110, 115, 121, 264
Alsop, Stewart, 117
Amitay, Morris, 254
Ancker-Johnson, Betsy, 276
Andersen, H. Carl, 185
Anderson, Clinton, 442–443
Anderson, George W., 220
Anderson, Gwen, 275
Anderson, Jack, 152, 183, 210, 259, 260, 270
Anderson, John, 149
Anderson, John Wendell, 531
Anderson, Marian, 318
Anderson, William, 370
Andrews, Peter, 530
Anfinsen, Dr. Christian B., 478, 479
Angelo, Bonnie, 280
Annenberg, Walter H., 188, 237
Annunzio, Frank, 288
Ansberry, Louise, 115
Antonelli, D. F., 532
Arbenz-Guzmán, Jacobo, 232
Archbold, John D., 115, 530
Archbold family, 119, 530
Armstrong, Anne, 275

Arnold, Thurman, 193–194, 202
Arpino, Gerald, 522
Ash, Roy, 39, 294, 333, 334, 341, 342, 430, 526, 535
Ashurst, Henry Fountain, 6
Aspin, Les, 225
Aspinall, Wayne, 461, 465
Atkinson, Dr. Lewis, 310
Auchincloss, Hugh D., 530, 534
Aug, Stephen, 205
Auger, Ulysses (Blackie), 532–533
Austern, H. Thomas, 197, 395
Axelrod, Julius, 479

Bacon, Robert Low, 525
Bacon, Mrs. Robert Low, 110, 114, 525
Bagge, Carl, 394
Bailar, Benjamin F., 54, 505–506
Bailey, Douglas, 164
Bailey, Mildred C., 276
Bailey, Pearl, 92, 307
Baker, Donald I., 429
Baker, Robert G. (Bobby), 182–183
Baker, Russell, 270
Ball, George, 230
Banuelos, Romana Acosta, 276
Banzhaf, John, 201
Baraka, Imamu (LeRoi Jones), 306
Baring, George R. S., 247
Barkan, Alexander, 381
Barksdale, Marie, 312
Barnard, Francie, 142
Barry, Mr. and Mrs. Marion, Jr., 303
Bass, Mike, 315
Bass, Ross, 208
Baus, Herbert M., 165
Baylor, Elgin, 308
Bazelon, David, 170, 535
Beale, Betty, 7, 104, 280
Beall, J. Glenn, 215
Beam, Jacob, 238
Beard, Dita, 210, 270, 282
Beard, Edward, 141
Beatty, Warren, 92
Beck, Dave, 388
Becker, Arthur M., 195
Becker, Ralph, 253
Bedell, Catherine, 276
Behn, Sally A., 283
Belafonte, Harry, 317
Belin, Capt. Peter, 530, 534
Bell, Terrel H. (Ted), 402
Bellmon, Henry, 155
Belote, Melissa, 102, 286
Benson, Ezra Taft, 443, 445
Bentley, Helen Delich, 276, 500
Bentsen, Lloyd, 527
Ben-Veniste, Richard, 192
Berger, Marilyn, 280
Berkowitz, Leon, 513
Berliner family, 120
Berman, Dr. Edgar, 284

Berman, Ronald, 518
Bernhard, Berl, 327
Bernstein, Carl, 259, 264
Bernstein, Leo, 533
Bernstein, Norman, 533
Berry, Paul, 313
Best, Judah, 192
Bethune, Mary McLeod, 105
Bickley, Cynthia, 285
Biddle, Mr. and Mrs. James, 111, 529, 534
Biemiller, Andrew, 207, 379
Bigelow, K K, 209
Biggs, Verlon, 315
Bing, Dave, 308
Bingham, Robert W., 157
Bittman, William, 192, 193
Black, Shirley Temple, 275, 307
Blackmun, Harry A., 48, 174
Blair, William McCormick, Jr., 529
Blair family, 119
Blanton, Thomas, 184
Bliss, Ray, 67
Blount, Winton (Red), 6, 506, 507
Boggs, Corinne, 274
Boggs, Hale, 44, 183, 274, 396
Bogley, Sam, 534
Bohlen, Charles (Chip), 238
Bok, Derek, 33
Boland, Edward, 44, 463
Bolen, David B., 302
Bolling, Richard, 150, 282
Bond, Julian, 303
Bonner, Walter, 192
Booker, Simeon, 313
Bork, Robert H., 168
Boston, Bernie, 313
Bourne, Dr. Blanche, 310
Bow, Frank T., 519
Bowie family, 119
Bowles, Chester, 230
Bowman, A. Smith, 534
Boyle, Tony, 388
Brademas, John, 278
Braden, Tom, 115, 264
Bradlee, Ben, 267
Brady, Adm. and Mrs. Parke H., 531, 534
Brailsford, Larry, 312
Brannan, Charles F., 443
Brasco, Frank J., 186
Breeskin, Adelyn D., 285
Brennan, Peter, 342, 382–383
Brennan, William J., Jr., 46–47, 171, 172
Breuer, Marcel, 485
Brewster, Daniel, 171, 185
Brezhnev, Leonid, 252
Bridges, Styles, 182
Briggs, Ellis, 237
Brimmer, Andrew, 301
Brinegar, Claude S., 495
Brinkley, David, 77, 264
Brinkley, Parke, 447
Brock, William, 164, 527
Broder, David, 269
Brooke, Edward W., 156, 164, 302, 306
Brooks, Mary, 276

Brown, Claude, 306
Brown, Constance Mellon Byers, 56, 529
Brown, George Scratchley, 41
Brown, Jim, 77
Brown, J. (John) Carter, 55–56, 72, 116, 529, 535
Brown, John Nicholas, 55
Brown, Larry, 7, 314
Brown, Ronald, 304
Brown, Sterling A., 305, 306
Brown, Tyrone, 309
Brown, Virginia Mae, 276
Browne, Joan Gardner, 530–531
Browne family, 119
Broyhill, James T., 527
Broyhill, Joel, 107
Bruce, Blanche K., 305
Bruce, David K. E., 116, 237, 528
Brunel, David, 163
Brunthaver, Carroll, 441, 448
Bryant, Charles I., 310
Bryant, Robert E., 310
Bryant, William B., 306, 309
Buchanan, Pat, 265
Buchanan, Roy, 92
Buchanan, Wiley T., 111, 528
Buchen, Philip, 13, 21, 22, 37–38
Buchwald, Art, 72, 257, 270
Buckley, James L., 145, 160, 374, 417, 520, 527
Buckley, William F., Jr., 269
Bullins, Ed, 78
Bullock, Dr. Samuel, 310
Bumpers, Dale, 166
Bunche, Ralph, 305
Bundy, McGeorge, 230
Bunker, Ellsworth, 275
Bunshaft, Gordon, 541
Bunyan, Maureen, 313
Burch, Dean, 261, 429
Burger, Warren E., 45–46, 48, 171, 172, 173, 174, 175
Burke, Edmund, 547
Burke, James, 214
Burling, Edward, 197
Burling, Mrs. Poe, 115
Burns, Arthur F., 50, 333, 334, 335, 341, 342, 535
Burrell, Berkeley, 313
Burris, Carol, 282
Burros, Marian, 281
Burton, Phillip, 138, 149
Burwell, Dr. Hartford, 310
Bush, George, 465, 526
Butterfield, Alexander, 128, 129
Butz, Earl Lauer, 32–33, 440, 441, 442, 443–444, 448
Byrd, Harry, 145, 244
Byrd, Robert C., 42–43, 149
Byrd, Titus, 42
Byrnes, John, 11

Caddell, Patrick, 165
Cadieux, Marcel, 245
Cafritz, Mr. and Mrs. Bill, 116
Cafritz, Gwen, 7, 113, 114, 116, 286, 533, 535
Cafritz, Morris, 533
Cahn, Jean Camper, 283, 308
Cain, James M., 92
Cain, Richard H., 310
Calder, Alexander, 513, 516, 519
Calhoun, John, 302
Campbell, J. Phil, 443
Cannon, Howard, 428, 502

Cannon, James M., 17
Cantacuzene, Princess Julia Grant, 6
Caplin, Mortimer, 195
Carey, Charles, 447
Carmichael, Stokely, 59, 306
Carnegie, Andrew, 416
Carpenter, Liz, 204, 283
Carpenter, Rene, 281
Carper, Elsie, 280
Carr, Austin, 308
Carr, Oliver T., Jr., 533
Carson, Rachel, 460
Carswell, G. Harrold, 42, 162, 169
Carter, Chester C., 312
Carter, Jimmy, 165
Carter, Tim Lee, 141
Carter, W. Beverly, Jr., 302
Carusi family, 119
Casals, Pablo, 517
Case, Clifford P., 187, 278, 380, 465
Casey, William J., 424
Cash, Johnny, 112
Cassady, Jack, 92
Cassell, Charles, 303
Catto, Henry, Jr., 112
Caudle, T. Lamar, 180
Celler, Emanuel, 382
Chambliss, Dr. Harriette C., 310
Chandler, William, 316
Chapman, Groxvenor, 545
Charles, Mrs. Robert H., 120
Chatel, Millicent, 283
Chatham, Patricia F., 114, 115
Chavez, Cesar, 388
Cheek, James E., 122, 308
Chenier, Phil, 315
Chennault, Anna, 115–116
Cherner family, 533
Cheshire, Maxine, 104, 182, 259, 280
Chewning family, 119
Childs, Marquis, 121, 264
Chiles, Lawton, 157
Chisholm, Shirley, 274, 278, 282
Choate, Robert, 289–290
Chotiner, Murray, 66
Christian, George, 26
Chung, Connie, 281
Clagett family, 118, 119
Clapper, Raymond, 35
Clark, C. Warfield, 310
Clark, Dr. Charles H., 310
Clark, Dr. John F. J., 310
Clark, Roy, 100
Clark, Tom, 201
Clark, William A., 524
Clarke, David A., 107
Claybrook, Joan, 282
Clements, Earle, 208
Cliburn, Van, 514
Clifford, Clark, 194, 195, 204, 254
Clifton, Bill, 100
Cline, Patsy, 100
Cobb, Dr. W. Montague, 309
Cohen, Barbara Stubbs, 280
Cohen, Ben, 201
Cohen, N. M., 532
Cohen, Vincent, 309
Colby, William Egan, 50–51, 223, 368
Cole, Earl F., 179
Coleman, William Thaddeus, Jr., 35–36, 172, 301–302, 495
Collins, Tom, 165

Colson, Charles, 192, 215
Compton, Ann, 281
Conable, Barber, 149
Conger, Clement, 25
Connally, John, 56, 63, 178, 180, 194
Connelly, Matthew J., 180
Connor, John, 6
Contee family, 118
Cook, G. Bradford, 134
Cook, Mercer, 306
Cooke, Eileen D., 408
Cooke, Jack Kent, 101
Cooley, Harold, 210
Coolidge, Calvin, 85, 339
Cooper, John Sherman, 116, 237
Cooper, Peggy, 285, 314
Coopersmith, Esther, 118
Corby family, 531
Corcoran, Thomas G., 172, 194, 199, 201, 395, 535
Cornely, Dr. Paul, 309
Cors, Allan D., 209
Cotton, Norris, 182
Countryman, Vern, 368
Cousteau, Jacques-Yves, 416
Cowan, James R., 302
Cox, Archibald, 168, 191, 262, 275
Cox, Edward Finch, 295
Crane, Margery A., 280
Crawford, H. R., 302
Cronkite, Walter, 262, 264, 265
Cummings, Samuel, 98
Curley, James M., 185
Custis, George Washington Parke, 317
Custis family, 119
Cutler, Lloyd, 194, 395

Daddario, Emilio, 418, 460
Daley, Richard J., 502
Dantley, Adrian, 308
Danzansky, Joseph, 98, 532
Danziger, Joan, 285
Darden, Orlando, 312
Darlington family, 119
Darneille family, 119
Dash, Sam, 192
Davidge family, 119
Davidson, Lorimer, 532
Davies, Joseph E., 115, 157, 286
Davies, Roger, 239
Davis, Benjamin O., Jr., 302
Davis, Floyd, 533
Davis, Gene, 102, 285
Davis, Karen, 284
Davis, L. Berkley, 209
Davis, Ossie, 306
Davis, R. Hilton (Dixie), 209
Davis, Shelby, 188
Davis, True, 116, 528, 535
Davison, Frederic E., 308
Dawes, Charles G., 339
Day, J. Edward, 194, 507
Dayan, Moshe, 241
Dean, Jimmy, 100
Dean, John, III, 122, 178, 191, 192
DeBakey, Dr. Michael, 474
de Besche, Hubert, 249
Deer, Ada, 282
Dees, Morris, 165
DeFunis, Marco, 176, 330, 400
Delaney family, 102
Delisle, Paul, 257
Dell family, 102

Dellums, Ronald V., 225, 302
Dempsey, Jack, 50
Denison, Jane, 280
Dennard, Cleveland L., 308
Denney, Alice, 285
Denniston, Lyle, 173
Dent, Frederick, 342, 526
DePreist, James, 314
de Roulet, Vincent, 188
Devron, Howard, 78
Dewey, Thomas E., 12, 49, 158
Dickens, Charles, 81
Dickerson, Nancy, 281
Dickson, Paul, 414, 415
Diggs, Charles C., 302
Dingell, John, 461, 465
Dirksen, Everett, 13, 15, 42,
   43, 152, 324
Doar, John, 192
Dobrivir, William, 201
Dobrynin, Anatoly, 246, 249
Dodd, Thomas, 179, 184, 185
Dole, Robert, 11, 131
Donaldson, Jesse, 507
Donovan, Eileen R., 275
Dorati, Antal, 71, 102
Dorrance, Nesta, 285
Douglas, Cathy, 46, 282
Douglas, Helen Gahagan, 64
Douglas, Paul, 292, 293
Douglas, William O., 14, 16,
   46, 75, 123, 171, 172, 174,
   185, 282
Douglass, Frederick, 304, 314,
   316, 542, 543
Dowdy, John, 186
Drew, Dr. Charles, 305, 306,
   309
Drew, Elizabeth, 280
Drew, Lenore, 307
Dubridge, Lee, 419
Dubrow, Evelyn, 282
Duerk, Alene B., 277
Duffey, Joe, 164
Dugas, Julian, 303
Dulles, Allen, 223, 233
Dulles, John Foster, 233
Duncan, Charles T., 303, 309
Duncan, Todd, 305, 309, 314
Dunlap, Lillian, 276
Dunlap, Louise C., 282
Dunlop, John Thomas, 33–34,
   383
Dunlop family, 118
du Pont, Pierre S., IV, 527

Eagleton, Thomas, 98, 261, 270
Eastin, Maurice, 351
Eastland, James, 156, 527
Eastwood, Clint, 514
Eaton, Rev. David H., 311
Eberle, William D., 395
Eckhardt, Bob, 149
Eckstine, Billy, 92, 307
Edelson, Mary Beth, 285
Edwards, Dr. Charles E., 476,
   478, 479, 481
Edwards, Edwin, 274
Edwards, Macon, 447
Eftis, Naomi, 284
Ehrlichman, John, 18, 122,
   148, 191, 282
Eig, Sam, 533
Eisenhower, Dwight D., 18, 19,
   24, 26, 27, 36, 42, 49, 50, 62,
   65, 86, 116, 144, 145, 158,
   181, 182, 229, 276, 418, 424
Eisenhower, Mamie, 115
Elder, Lee, 308
Ford, John, 13

Ellington, Edward Kennedy
   (Duke), 92, 307, 514–515
Elliott, Cass, 92
Ellsberg, Daniel, 414, 530
Ellsworth, Dorothy, 282
Ellwood, Dr. Paul M., Jr., 477
Elsberg, Milton, 532
Elson, Rev. Dr. Edward L. R.,
   143
Engman, Lewis A., 295, 425
Epps, Dr. Charles, 310
Epps, Dr. Roselyn, 284, 310
Ersham, Henrietta, 285
Ertegun, Ahmet, 248–249
Ervin, Sam, 155, 369
Estes, Billy Sol, 185
Eustis family, 119, 531
Evans, John R., 205
Evans, Rowland, Jr., 115, 264
Everett, Edward Hamlin, 525

Farkas, Ruth L., 188, 275
Farley, James A., 507
Farmer, James, 301
Faulkner, Winthrop, 545
Fauntroy, Walter E., 59, 98,
   107, 302, 303, 306, 311
Feggans, Ed, 312, 316
Feldman, Mike, 194
Felton, Rebecca L., 274
Fendrick, Barbara, 285
Fenoaltea, Sergio, 249
Fenwick, Millicent, 527
Ferguson, Dr. Angella, 310
Ferguson, C. Clyde, 302
Ferris family, 531
Fichandler, Zelda, 284
Fields, Daisy, 282, 287
Finch, Robert, 62, 135
Firestone, Kimball, 209, 531
Firestone, Leonard, 188
Fisher, Joseph L., 107
Fitzgerald, A. Ernest, 128–129,
   135
Fitzgerald, Ella, 307
Fitzgerald, William, 312
Fitzsimmons, Frank, 342, 388
Flanigan, Peter, 232
Flather family, 119
Fleischer, Sophie, 114
Fleming, Peter, 192
Fleming family, 531
Flemming, Arthur S., 327
Fletcher, James, 277
Flood, Daniel, 475
Fogarty, John E., 474, 475
Foggie, Samuel L., 312
Foley, Edward, 194
Foley, Thomas S., 138, 442
Folger, Bitsy, 116
Folger, Henry Clay, 541
Folger, John Clifford, 535
Folger, Lee, 116
Folger family, 531
Forbes, Mary Lou Werner, 280
Ford, Dick, 12
Ford, Elizabeth Bloomer
   (Betty), 13, 25, 26, 286–287,
   472, 519
Ford, Gerald R., 10–19, 22, 23,
   24, 25, 28, 29, 33, 36, 37, 38,
   45, 46, 63, 65, 77, 103, 105,
   138, 139, 148, 149, 156, 163,
   167, 168, 230, 231, 262, 275,
   276, 298, 301, 333, 334, 341–
   342, 343, 375, 379, 419, 431,
   433, 435, 449, 518–519
Ford, Henry, II, 112, 292–293
Ford, Jim, 12
Ellender, Allen, 274

Ford, Michael, 13–14
Ford, Steven, 13, 72
Ford, Susan, 13
Ford, Tom, 12
Fortas, Abe, 43, 169, 171, 179,
   185, 202, 281
Fortune, Sandra, 314
Foster, Bob, 308
Foster, Richard, 535
Fountain, Lawrence H., 475
Foxe, Fanne, 138
Franco, Francisco, 212
Frandsen, Julius, 266
Frankfurter, Felix, 35, 46, 49,
   171, 202
Franklin, Barbara, 276
Franklin, John Hope, 305
Fraser, Arvonne, 282
Fraser, Donald, 282
Frawley, Patrick J., Jr., 184
Frazer, Susan, 285
Frazier, Charles, 448
Frazier, E. Franklin, 305, 306
Freeman, John, 247
Freeman, Orville L., 443, 445
Freer, Mr. and Mrs. Robin, 111
Frenkil, Victor H., 183
Frenzel, Bill, 159
Friedersdorf, Max, 22
Friedman, Milton, 50, 335,
   356, 453
Friedman, Milton A., 19, 22
Fryklund, Richard, 258
Fulbright, J. William, 166, 194,
   231, 238, 265, 414
Funderburk, Dr. William, 309,
   317
Furness, Betty, 292

Gabor, Eva, 6
Galbraith, John Kenneth, 334,
   335, 356
Gallagher, Cornelius E., 186,
   372
Gallagher, Thomas J., Jr., 180
Gardner, Arthur W., 530–531
Gardner, John W., 163, 201,
   212
Garfield, James A., 83, 181
Garland, Allen H., 352
Garment, Leonard, 39
Garner, Erroll, 77
Garner, John N., 149
Garrecht, Claire M., 277
Garrett, Ray, Jr., 134
Garth, David, 165
Gay, Connie B., 100
Gaye, Marvin, 92, 308
Gelb, Leslie, 418
Gerber, Myron, 532
Gerber, Sylvan, 532
Gereau, Mary C., 282
Gesell, Gerhard, 171
Gewirz family, 120
Gibson, Andrew E., 435
Gibson, James O., 304
Gilliam, Dorothy, 313
Gilliam, Sam, 285, 314
Glaser, Vera, 280
Glasmann, Jay W., 211
Glennan, T. Keith, 404
Glover family, 119, 531
Gobel, George, 45
Godfrey, Arthur, 92
Godwin, Mills, 38
Goeltz family, 102
Goldberg, Arthur, 28, 171, 382
Goldfine, Bernard, 182, 424
Goldman, Aaron, 532
Goldman, LeRoy G., 475

Goldman family, 120
Goldwater, Barry, 42, 44, 49, 148, 158, 165, 518
Goldwater, Barry, Jr., 373
Goodell, Charles, 15, 342
Goodman, Charles B., 545
Goodwin, Leo, Jr., 532
Gordon, Kermit, 418
Gore, Albert, 164, 208
Gore, Grady, 535
Gore, Louise, 118
Gorman, Mike, 212
Gorrell, Edgar S., 427
Gould, Kingdon, 157, 188, 532
Goulden, Joseph C., 198
Grace, Bishop C. M., 307
Graham, Bruce M., 344
Graham, Gordon, 313
Graham, Katharine, 115, 123, 267, 280, 529, 534
Graham, Martha, 287, 519
Graham, Philip L., 172
Grammer, Billy, 100
Grant, Jim, 282
Grant, Ulysses S., 6, 104, 179, 180, 181
Granton, Fannie, 314
Gray, Gordon, 528, 534
Gray, Kenneth, 141
Gray, L. Patrick, 51
Gray, Robert, 204
Green, Constance, 300
Green, Edith, 277–278
Green, June L., 282
Green, William, 376, 388
Greene, Cornelius, 308
Greenfield, Meg, 280
Greenspan, Alan, 16, 39–40, 334
Griffin, Robert P., 10, 43, 149
Griffiths, Martha, 277, 278, 326
Griswold, Erwin, 168
Gross, H. R., 515, 517–518
Gross, Laura Merriam Curtis, 114, 206
Gross, Nelson, 164
Grosvenor family, 531
Gude, Gilbert, 107
Gudelsky, Isadore, 533
Guest, Mrs. Polk, 285, 529
Guest, Raymond, 529
Guggenheim, Charles, 164
Gullatee, Dr. Alyce, 310
Gurney, Edward J., 186

Hagans, Theodore R., Jr., 313, 316
Hagerty, Jim, 26
Haggard, Merle, 112
Hagner family, 119
Hahn, Gilbert, Jr., 115, 122, 201
Hahn family, 120, 531
Haig, Alexander, 18, 36
Haile Selassie, 248
Halberstam, David, 260
Haldeman, H. R. (Bob), 6, 18, 122, 128–129, 148, 192
Halle, Kay, 531
Halleck, Charles, 15
Halperin, Morton, 418
Halpern, Seymour, 185
Halsey, W. F., 37
Halusa, Arno, 246
Hamilton, Alexander, 80, 180
Hamilton, George, IV, 100
Hamilton family, 119
Hammer, Armand, 116
Handler, Philip, 415
Hanes, John W., Jr., 531
Hanford, Elizabeth, 276

Hanks, Nancy, 55, 285, 514, 520, 521, 523, 535
Hansen, Clifford, 7, 535
Hansen, Julia Butler, 277, 278
Hardin, Clifford M., 443, 448
Harding, Dr. Fann, 282
Harding, Warren G., 85, 110, 179, 181–182, 339
Hardy, Willie, 303
Harlow, Bryce, 18, 209
Harps, William S., 313
Harriman, Averell, 28, 116, 527–528, 534
Harris, Fred R., 282
Harris, Herbert E., 107
Harris, LaDonna, 282
Harris, Louis, 164
Harris, Patricia, 281, 309
Harris, Ruth Bates, 277
Harris, Samuel E., 312
Harrison, Benjamin, 515
Hart, Peter D., 164
Hart, Philip, 164, 292, 432, 465, 527
Hartke, Vance, 165, 205, 502
Hartmann, Robert, 15, 19, 21, 22, 37, 110, 148
Haslem, Jane, 285
Hastie, William H., 305, 306, 309
Hatcher, Andrew, 301
Hathaway, Stanley K., 32
Hawkins, Erick, 522
Hawn, Goldie, 92
Hayes, Elvin, 315
Hayes, Helen, 92
Hayes, Rutherford B., 84, 178
Haynsworth, Clement F., Jr., 42, 43, 169
Hays, Wayne, 138
Hayward, J. C., 313
Haywood, Claire, 314
Hearst, Patty, 169
Hebert, F. Edward, 138, 225
Hechinger family, 120, 531
Hechler, Ken, 465
Heckscher, August, 517
Height, Dorothy, 304
Heinz, H. J., III, 527, 534
Held, Barbara, 283
Heller, Walter, 334
Helms, Jesse, 141
Helms, Richard, 223
Hemenway, Russell, 163
Henderson, Frances, 278
Hersh, Seymour, 223, 259, 260
Herter, Mrs. Christian A., 528
Hetzel, Mrs. Kurt, 120
Heurich family, 531
Hewitt, Frankie, 284
Hickel, Walter J., 460
Hill, Lister, 474, 475
Hillman, Sidney, 375
Hills, Carla Anderson, 34–35, 275, 486
Hills, Roderick M., 35
Himmelfarb family, 120
Hinton, Dr. David, 310
Hirshhorn, Joseph, 122, 516, 534
Hiss, Alger, 61, 64, 172, 372
Hobbs, Claude, 209
Hobby, Oveta Culp, 275, 401, 474
Hobson, Julius, 303
Hodgson, James, 382
Hoff, Irv, 447
Hoffa, James, 184, 192, 194, 372, 380, 385, 388
Hoffman, Edwin, 98

Hogan, Larry, 107
Holifield, Chet, 278
Holifield, Vernice, 278
Holladay, Wallace, 533
Hollinshead, Dr. Ariel C., 284
Holm, Jeanne, 276
Holt, Fred, 447
Holt, Marjorie, 107
Holton, Linwood, 194
Holtzman, Elizabeth, 382
Hooks, Benjamin L., 302
Hooks, Robert, 78, 314
Hoover, Herbert, 85, 86, 158, 169, 336, 337, 345
Hoover, Ike, 24
Hoover, J. Edgar, 169, 259, 370
Hope, Bob, 112
Hope, Cliff, 442
Horowitz, Arlene, 278
Horsky, Charles, 197, 198
Houston, Ken, 315
Howar, Barbara, 116, 286
Howar brothers, 533
Howard, James, 502
Howard, Warren, 313
Howrey, Edward F., 195
Hubbard, Barbara Marx, 530
Hubbard, Gardiner Greene, 531
Hufty family, 530
Hughes, Harold E., 115
Hughes, Howard, 511
Huidekoper family, 119
Hume, David L., 445
Humes, John, 188
Humphrey, George, 62
Humphrey, Hubert, 113, 157, 158, 164, 182, 189, 518
Hundley, Mary, 317
Hundley, William, 192
Hunt, E. Howard, 192, 193
Hunt, James V., 182
Hunt, John, 523
Hurd, Peter, 544
Hyde, Floyd, 486
Hyman, George, 533

Ickes, Harold, 457
Ignatius, Paul, 395
Ikard, Frank, 207, 394
Inouye, Daniel, 502
Irving, Clifford, 511
Isham, Sheila, 285

Jackson, Bob, 201
Jackson, Rev. E. Franklin, 311
Jackson, Henry, 150, 164, 165, 189, 230, 378, 460–461, 465
Jackson, Robert, 172
Jackson, Samuel C., 309
Jacobsen, Hugh N., 545
Jagerson, Todd, 328
James, Daniel (Chappie), 302
Jamison, Judith, 514
Jarman, John, 139
Javits, Jacob K., 380, 477, 535
Jaworski, Leon, 187, 191
Jefferson, Roy, 315
Jefferson, Thomas, 65
Jelleff family, 531
Jenkins, Alfred, 238
Jenkins, Elaine B., 312
Jenkins, Howard, Jr., 302, 312
Jenner, Albert, 191
Jennings, Coleman, 525
Jerould, Leslie, 282
Jeru-Ahmed, Hassan, 311
Johnson, Andrew, 2, 137, 185
Johnson, J. Bennett, 274
Johnson, Lady Bird, 204, 283, 286, 496

Johnson, Louis, 314
Johnson, Luci Baines, 96
Johnson, Lynda, 25
Johnson, Lyndon B., 6, 8, 16,
    18, 23, 24, 26, 36, 42, 54, 56,
    60, 64, 65, 88, 96, 103, 112,
    116, 148, 153, 156, 158, 161,
    162, 169, 182, 183, 194, 229,
    271, 276, 283, 292, 309, 414,
    474, 544
Johnson, Nicholas, 424
Johnson, Philip, 535, 543
Johnson, Reuben, 448
Johnston family, 532
Jolson, Al, 92
Jones, Doris, 314
Jones, Dr. Frank, 310
Jones, Dr. George, 310
Jones, James Earl, 514
Jones, Jerry, 22, 23
Jones, Judy, 284
Jones, K. C., 315
Jones, Mary Gardner, 276
Jones family, 531
Jong, Erica, 55, 520
Jordan, B. Everett, 183
Jordan, Barbara, 274
Joynt, Mr. and Mrs. Howard,
    116
Jurgensen, Sonny, 7, 123, 478
Just, Ward, 269

Kalb, Marvin, 265
Kalish, James, 416
Kalmbach, Herbert W., 187,
    192
Kann family, 531
Kappel, Frederick R., 507
Kass, Garfield, 533
Katzenbach, Nicholas, 6
Kauffmann family, 531
Kaufmann family, 120
Kaukonen, Jorma, 92
Kauper, Thomas E., 429
Kearney, John P., 352
Keating, Kenneth, 237
Kefauver, Estes, 291
Kelley, Clarence M., 51–52,
    169, 372
Kemp, Jack, 141
Kendall, Donald, 61, 66, 112
Kenen, I. L. (Si), 254
Kennan, George, 238
Kennedy, Caroline, 27
Kennedy, Edward M., 7, 43,
    104, 156, 164, 189, 240, 428,
    476, 477, 479, 480, 522, 527
Kennedy, Ethel, 115, 528
Kennedy, John F., 8, 16, 18,
    23, 24, 26, 27, 36, 44, 47, 58,
    64, 88, 103, 112, 116, 156,
    164, 220, 226, 229, 231, 273,
    283, 291, 292, 309, 402, 418,
    474
Kennedy, Joseph P., 46, 47,
    527, 535
Kennedy, Robert F., 18, 46, 88,
    115, 121, 158, 168, 188, 192
Keppel, Francis, 402
Kessler, Gladys, 281
Kessler, Ron, 370
Kettler brothers, 533
Keyes, Arthur, 545
Keynes, John Maynard, 337
Khrushchev, Nikita, 64
Kilberg, Barbara, 282
Kilmer, Billy, 7
Kilpatrick, James J., 264, 266,
    269
Kimelman, Henry L., 122

Kinard, John, 314
King, Leslie, 12
King, Martin Luther, Jr., 59,
    60, 88–89, 188, 271, 299,
    318, 369
King family, 120
Kintner, Earl, 194
Kiplinger, W. M., 62
Kirkland, Lane, 385–386
Kirkpatrick, Miles W., 295
Kissinger, Henry, 1, 7, 21, 29–
    30, 39, 72, 121, 139, 220,
    227, 230, 231, 233, 234–235,
    370, 371
Kissinger, Nancy Maginnes, 30
Kittrell, Flemmie P., 306
Klassen, Elmer (Ted), 54, 506,
    526
Kleberg, Robert J., Jr., 112
Klein, Herb, 66
Kleindienst, Richard, 49, 180,
    192, 254
Kluczynski, John, 502
Knauer, Virginia Harrington,
    40–41, 276, 294, 351
Knauer, Wilhelm, 40
Knight, Frances G., 276
Knight, Jennie Lea, 285
Knoblauch, Christine, 285
Knudsen, William, 136
Koch, Edward, 373
Koch, George W., 394, 447
Kohler, Foy, 238
Kohlmeier, Louis M., Jr., 423
Koons, John, 533
Kosciusko-Morizet, Jacques,
    246
Kraemer, F. G. (Fritz), 29
Kraft, John F., 164
Kraft, Joseph, 264, 269
Krag, Jens Otto, 246
Krause, E. J., 352
Krebs, Rockne, 285, 522
Kreeger, David Lloyd, 7, 116,
    121, 122, 532, 535
Kreeger family, 531
Krettek, Germaine, 408
Kushner, Lawrence, 296
Kyl, John, 208

Lafontant, Jewel, 277
LaHay, Wauhillau, 280
Laird, Melvin, 11, 15, 17, 18,
    63, 221, 230, 270
Laise, Carol, 275
Lammerding, Nancy, 25
Landers, Ann, 111
Lane, Thomas J., 185
Lansburgh family, 120, 531
Larkin, Robert D., 132
Larrabee, Don, 268
Lasker, Mary, 212, 474
Latch, Rev. Edward G., 143
Lavine, Dr. Thelma, 283
Lawrence, David, 532
Lawson, Belford, 122, 309
Lawson, Marjorie, 122, 281,
    309
Laylin, John G., 200
Ledbetter, Rev. Theodore S.,
    311
Lee, Charles W., 406
Lee, Julia M., 283
Lee family, 119
Lees, Michelle, 285
Leffall, LaSalle D., 307, 309
Legare family, 119
Lehrman, Jacob, 532
Leiter family, 119
Lemon family, 531

Lerner, Theodore, 533
LeRoy, David, 15–16
Levi, Edward Hirsch, 31–32,
    168
Lewine, Frances, 280
Lewis, Anthony, 173
Lewis, Colston A., 302
Lewis, Jo Ann, 514
Lewis, John L., 146, 376
Liddy, G. Gordon, 191
Lincoln, Abraham, 82, 102,
    284, 299, 442
Linder, Robert D., 23
Lindh, Patricia, 276
Lindsay, John, 58
Linowitz, Sol, 98, 200, 528
Lisagor, Peter, 263, 266
Livingston, Jane, 285
Loeb, William, 280
Logan, John, 115, 531
Logan, Polly Guggenheim, 111,
    114, 115, 286, 531
Logan, Rayford W., 305
Long, Edward, 184, 185, 372
Long, Russell, 149, 150, 187,
    479, 480, 527
Longworth, Alice Roosevelt,
    110, 286
Longworth, Nicholas, 286
Loory, Stuart, 259
Loridan, Walter, 246
Lothrop family, 119, 531
Louis, Arthur M., 104
Louis, Morris, 102, 285
Love, Ed, 314
Luce, Clare Boothe, 155, 535
Luchs family, 120
Lucy, Bill, 303
Lustine family, 533
Luttrell family, 119
Lyng, Richard E., 395, 447
Lynn, James T., 38, 334, 486

MacArthur, Douglas, 34, 67, 86
Mackall family, 118
Mackin, Catherine, 281
MacLaine, Shirley, 92
MacLeish, Rod, 266
Magazine brothers, 533
Magnuson, Warren, 150, 288,
    404, 475, 502
Magruder, Jeb, 122
Magruder family, 119
Mahon, George, 149, 225
Malatesta, Peter, 116
Malcolm X, 302
Malone, Mike, 314
Manasco, Carter, 208
Mandel, Marvin, 164
Mann, Dr. Marion, 309
Mansfield, Michael J. (Mike),
    41–42, 69, 148, 162, 230
Marchetti, Victor, 223
Marilley, Jane E., 283
Marino, Bishop Eugene A., 311
Markley, Rod, 209
Marks, John, 223
Marks, Leonard, 195
Marland, Sidney P., Jr., 402
Marriott, J. Willard, 532
Mariott, J. Willard, Jr., 532
Mars family, 530
Marsh, Jean, 248
Marsh, John O., Jr., 21, 22,
    38–39, 148
Marshall, Dr. C. Herbert, Jr.,
    310
Marshall, George C., 218, 233

Marshall, George Preston, 315
Marshall, Thurgood, 47–48,
171, 172, 306, 309
Marson, Mike, 315
Marston, Dr. Robert Q., 478
Martin, William McChesney,
Jr., 528, 535
Martindale, Steve, 116
Marttila, John, 165
Marx, Louis, 530
Mason, K. R., 352
Mathe, Carmen, 285
Mathias, Bob, 141
Mathias, Charles, 185
Matney, Bill, 313
Matthews, Burnita Shelton, 282
Mayer, Louis B., 211
Maynard, Robert, 313
Mazique, Dr. Edward, 310, 317
Mazique, Marguerite, 317
McCarran, Pat, 146
McCarthy, Eugene, 160
McCarthy, Joseph, 46, 184,
233, 238
McClellan, John, 150, 225
McClendon, Sarah, 280
McCormack, John, 43, 44, 183,
203
McCormick, Col. and Mrs.
Robert R., 7
McCracken, Paul, 335, 342
McDonald, John, 181
McDonald, Larry, 141
McElroy, Neil, 116
McEvoy, Nan Tucker, 284, 530
McFall, John, 149
McGee, Gale, 7, 118
McGhee, George, 98, 528
McGinniss, Joe, 163
McGovern, George, 56, 59,
107, 122, 156, 164, 165, 261,
277, 378, 379
McGrory, Mary, 269, 280
McGuire, R. Grayson, 312
McIntire, Carl, 89
McKinley, William, 84
McKneally. Martin, 185
McLain, Marvin L., 445
McLaughlin, Marya, 281
McLean, Evalyn Walsh, 114,
273, 524
McLinton, Harold, 315
McMillan, C. W. (Bill), 446
McMillan, John, 107
McMurtry, Larry, 74, 92
McNair family, 102
McNamara, Robert S., 57–58,
111, 218, 219, 225, 255, 258,
534
Meany, George, 34, 67, 342,
375, 376–379, 380, 383, 385,
388
Mein, Gordon, 239
Meisch, Adrien, 245–246
Mellon, Paul, 528–529
Merriam, William, 206, 210
Merrill, Robert, 514
Merthan, Lawrence, 204
Mesta, Perle, 114
Metcalf, Lee, 465
Metzenbaum, Howard, 157, 164
Meyer, Eugene, III, 121
Micciche, S. J., 173
Middendorf, J. William, II,
188, 526
Mikva, Abner, 369
Milford, Dale, 141
Miller, Arnold, 385, 388
Miller, Arthur R., 361

Miller, Dale, 116, 204
Miller, Herbert (Jack), 192
Miller, Scooter, 116
Miller, W. M. (Fish Bait), 143
Miller brothers, 533
Milliken, William G., 38
Mills, Wilbur, 138, 149, 166,
341, 451, 479
Mineta, Norman, 140
Minnelli, Liza, 247
Minow, Newton, 423
Mitchell, B. Doyle, 312
Mitchell, Bobby, 315
Mitchell, Clarence, 16, 304
Mitchell, Clarence, Jr., 304
Mitchell, Jesse H., 312
Mitchell, John, 63, 162, 168,
174, 180, 191, 192, 424
Mitchell, Juanita Jackson, 304
Mitchell, Martha, 280
Mitchell, Parren, 304
Mizell, Wilmer (Vinegar
Bend), 141
Mobutu, Sese Seko, 182
Moella, Patricia, 285
Mollenhoff, Clark, 191, 371
Molloy, James T., 143
Monroney, Mike, 208
Moore, Rev. Douglas, 303
Moore, G. Curtis, 239
Moore, Rev. Jerry A., Jr., 311
Moore, Thomas Gale, 426
Moorer, Thomas H., 371
Moos, Malcolm, 19
Moran family, 119
Morgan, Thomas E., 141
Morris, Mrs. George Maurice,
116
Morrison, Jim, 92
Morse, Wayne, 145, 406
Morton, Jelly Roll, 307
Morton, Rogers Clark Ballard,
17, 33, 434, 466, 526
Morton, Thruston, 32
Moss, Frank E., 288
Mossadegh, Mohammed, 232
Moyers, Bill, 26
Muhammad, Elijah, 311
Mul-Key, Herb, 315
Murphy, Betty Southard, 276
Murphy, Ed, 313
Murphy, Frank, 202
Murphy, George, 184, 185, 208
Muskie, Edmund, 150, 164,
335, 461, 465
Muskie, Jane, 280

Nabrit, James, Jr., 305
Nader, Ralph, 163, 194, 201,
203, 211, 213, 250, 288, 289,
292, 293, 298, 380, 393, 424,
428, 497, 537
Napolitan, Joseph, 164, 166
Natcher, William, 302
Nathan, Raymond, 351
Nathan, Richard, 453
Neal, James F., 192
Nee, Dermot, 533
Neely, Matthew M., 481
Neff, Francine I., 276
Nelson, Charles, 302
Nelson, Gaylord, 461, 465
Nessen, Ronald Harold (Ron),
17, 22, 26, 27, 40, 72, 262
Newman, Constance, 276, 302
Nimitz, Chester W., 37
Nirenberg, Marshall, 479
Nitze, Mrs. Paul H., 528
Nixon, Pat, 182, 286

Nixon, Richard, 2, 10, 12, 15,
18, 19, 22, 23, 24, 26, 27, 33,
36, 50, 60, 61–64, 105, 107,
111, 122, 131, 147, 148, 153,
155, 156, 158, 161, 163, 165,
167, 168, 169, 173, 178, 188,
191, 212, 231, 259, 260–261,
262, 268, 276, 294, 337, 338,
419, 430, 433, 443, 475, 477
Noel, Cleo A., Jr., 239
Nolan family, 531
Noland, Kenneth, 102, 285
Norair, Richard, 533
Nordlinger family, 120
North, Kerry, 208
Novak, Robert, 264
Noyes family, 119, 531
Nugent, Pat, 96
Nye, Gerald P., 6

O'Brien, Larry, 161, 507
O'Doherty, Brian, 514
Okun, Arthur, 334, 418
Oliver, Alvin, 447
Olmsted, George H., 532
Onassis, Jacqueline Bouvier
Kennedy, 88, 115, 273, 286,
514, 530
O'Neill, Thomas Philip, Jr.
(Tip), 44, 149
Orfila, Alejandro, 116
Orlans, Harold, 420
Ormandy, Eugene, 513
Orme family, 119
Ortona, Egidio, 246, 249
Orwell, George, 373
Osborne, John, 269
Ottinger, Richard, 157, 527
Ourisman, Florenz, 157
Ourisman, Mandell, 533
Owens, Angela, 313
Owens, Brig, 315
Owens, Hugh F., 205
Owens, Dr. Nolan, 310

Paarlberg, Dr. Donald, 444, 448
Pace, Frank, 339
Packard, David, 6, 112
Packard, Jean, 279
Palmby, Clarence D., 440, 443,
448
Park, Tongsun, 117, 206
Parker, Barrington, 309
Parkinson, Kenneth, 192
Pastore, John, 7
Patman, Wright, 138
Patterson, Jefferson, 528, 535
Payne, Frederick G., 182
Pearson, Drew, 210
Pechman, Joseph, 418
Peck, Gregory, 515
Pell, Claiborne, 527
Percy, Charles, 164, 527
Perkins, Frances, 275
Perkins, J. Carter, 209
Peter, Armistead, III, 534
Peter family, 118
Peterson, Esther, 283, 292
Peterson, Peter, 232
Peterson, Phyllis, 283
Peterson, Russell, 462, 467
Phillips, Channing, 310
Phillips, Duncan, 515, 525,
529, 530
Phillips, John, 92
Phillips, Laughlin, 530, 534
Pierce, Roxanne, 286
Pike, Otis, 225
Pinker, Irene, 282
Pinkett, Flaxie, 283, 312

Pinkett, John, 283, 312
Pipkin, James, 209
Pittman, Portia Washington, 317
Pitts, Cornelius C., 313
Plaza, Galo, 246
Plimpton, George, 520
Poage, W. R., 138
Podell, Bertram L., 186
Pohanka family, 533
Pollack, Irving M., 134
Pollin, Abe, 101, 533
Pomare, Eleo, 520
Pomponio brothers, 534
Porter, Katherine Anne, 92–93, 281
Porter, Paul, 202
Post, Marjorie Merriweather, 110, 114, 157, 273, 285–286, 529
Powell, Adam Clayton, 14, 167, 184, 185, 310
Powell, John H., Jr., 302
Powell, Lewis F., Jr., 49, 171, 526
Powers, Francis Gary, 260
Poynter, Nelson, 530
Price, Melvin, 138, 225
Proxmire, William, 14, 35, 70, 150, 499, 519–520, 523
Prudhomme, Dr. Charles, 310
Purcell, Graham, 208
Pyle, Christopher, 269

Quayle, Oliver, III, 164
Quesada, Mr. and Mrs. Elwood, 531
Quie, Albert, 517
Quinn, Arthur L., 253
Quinn, Arthur Lee, 253–254
Quinn, Sally, 280

Rabb, Max, 18, 26
Radford, Charles E., 371
Radin, Rhea, 283
Ramey, Dr. Estelle, 284
Ramsbotham, Sir Peter, 247
Rand, Ayn, 39, 40
Randolph, A. Philip, 87
Randolph, Carol, 313
Randolph, Jennings, 150, 501
Rangel, Charles, 184, 302
Rankin, Jeannette, 273–274
Rapley, William W., 534
Raspberry, William, 313
Rather, Dan, 265
Rauh, Joseph L., Jr., 14, 16, 172, 201
Rawls, Nancy V., 275
Ray, Dixy Lee, 53–54, 275, 437
Ray, Oakley M., 447
Reagan, Ronald, 34
Reasoner, Harry, 264
Rebozo, Charles G. (Bebe), 61, 63, 67, 112, 178, 261
Reedy, George, 26
Rees, Dr. Albert, 334
Reese, Matt. 164
Rehnquist, William H., 48–49, 135, 171, 172
Reich, Charles, 172
Reid, Charlotte T., 276
Reid, Herbert O., 309
Reinecke, Ed, 178
Reinhardt, John E., 302
Renchard, Mr. and Mrs. George W., 528, 534
Reno, Don, 100

Reston, James, 121, 148, 259, 264
Reuss, Henry, 138, 465
Reuther, Walter, 380, 381, 385, 388
Reynolds, Frank, 264
Rhodes, John Jacob, 44–45, 149
Rhyne, Charles, 192
Ribicoff, Abraham, 77, 150, 254, 297, 480, 535
Rice, Emmett J., 313
Rice, Theron J., 209
Rich family, 119
Richardson, Elliot, 35, 168, 172, 372, 526, 535
Richey, Charles, 171
Riddell, Mrs. Richard J., 284
Ridder, Walter, 530
Riegle, Don, 163
Riggs family, 119
Riley, Joseph H., 98
Ripley, S. (Sidney) Dillon, II, 54–55, 516, 529, 534
Rivlin, Alice M., 143, 278
Robb, Chuck, 25
Robbins, Jerome, 514
Robbins, Dr. Mary Louise, 284
Robbins, Routh, 283
Roberts, Ellen, 280
Robinson, Dr. Alvin, 310, 315–316
Robinson, Aubrey, 309
Robinson, Jacqueline, 315
Robinson, Max, 313
Robinson, Spottswood, III, 306, 309
Rockefeller, Nelson Aldrich, 10, 17, 28–29, 42, 55, 276, 526, 528, 535
Rodino, Peter, 137, 382
Rogers, Paul G., 476, 477
Rogers, Walter E., 395
Rogers, William P., 62, 66, 98, 200, 230, 233
Rogers, Willie Mae, 294
Rolark, Calvin, 313
Romney, George, 38, 155, 486, 526
Roncallo, Angelo D., 186
Roosevelt, Ann M., 282
Roosevelt, Eleanor, 273, 286
Roosevelt, Franklin D., 6, 18, 25, 26, 27, 46, 47, 63, 65, 67, 86, 87, 103, 144, 158, 222, 286, 322, 337–338, 340
Roosevelt, Theodore, 81, 84, 110, 435, 459, 481, 542
Roosevelt family, 119
Rosenberg, Julius and Ethel, 372
Rosenthal, Benjamin S., 297
Ross, Nellie Tayloe, 6
Ross, William B., 165
Rostow, Walt, 6, 230
Roudebush, Richard. 165, 208
Roundtree, Dovey. 281
Rovere, Richard, 269
Rowan, Carl, 264, 266, 301, 313
Rowe, James H., 194
Rowse, Arthur, 290
Ruckelshaus, Jill, 274
Ruckelshaus, William D., 168, 274, 462
Ruder, William, 351
Rumsfeld, Donald, 21, 22, 36–37, 148
Rush, Kenneth, 334
Rusk, Dean, 230
Russell, Albert, 447

Russell, Fred J., 188
Russell, Mark, 546
Russell, Richard, 152
Russell, Rosalind, 514
Russell, Wendell, 308
Rust family, 119
Ryan, Joan, 281

Sack, Leo, 157
Sackler, Howard, 518
Sadat, Anwar, 72
Safer, John, 533
Safire, William, 269
St. Clair, James D., 191
Salah, Abdullah, 246
Salinger, Pierre, 26
Salk, Dr. Jonas, 474
Samuels, Howard, 164
Samuelson, Paul, 340–341
Sandler, Dr. Bernice, 282
Sanford, Enid, 285
Saroyan, Aram, 519
Sarro, Ron, 280
Sasscer family, 119
Saul family, 119
Saunders, Charles B., Jr., 409–410
Sawhill, John, 52, 435
Saxbe, William, 31, 372
Saxe, Ruth M., 282
Scammon, Richard M., 164
Scherle, William J., 519
Scheuer, James, 527
Schlafly, Phyllis, 282
Schlesinger, Arthur, Jr., 402
Schlesinger, James Rodney, 30–31, 41, 51, 53, 217–218, 219, 223, 275
Schnyder, Felix, 246, 249
Schoellkopf, W. Horton, Jr., 530
Schoeneman, George J., 180
Schorr, Daniel, 261
Schroeder, Patricia, 225
Schultze, Charles L., 418
Schussheim, Morton, 489
Schweitzer, Pierre-Paul. 255
Scott, Hugh, 42, 148, 535
Scott, Dr. Roland, 310
Scott, Stanley S., 302
Scouten, Rex, 24
Scudder, Dr. John, 306
Seaborg, Dr. Glenn, 437
Seamans, Robert, 435
Seeger, Pete, 92
Seidman, L. William, 16, 22, 38, 110, 334, 342
Semmes family, 119
Sevareid, Eric, 77, 121, 265
Sevilla-Sacasa, Guillermo, 6, 76, 247, 248
Shabazz, Rev. Lonnie, 311
Shackleton, Polly, 107
Shaffer, Charles, 192
Shaller, Herman I., 135
Shanahan, Eileen, 280
Shanker, Albert, 385, 386, 406
Shannon, Dr. James, 475
Shapiro, David, 192
Shapp, Milton, 164
Shaw, Bernard, 313
Shaw, Carolyn Hagner, 122, 123
Sheehan, Neil, 261
Shepard, Adm. and Mrs. Tazewell, 116
Sherman, Dr. John F., 478
Sherrill, Robert, 269
Shields, Mark, 164

Shippen, Mrs. Lloyd Parker, 120
Short, Bob, 101
Shouse, Mrs. Jouett, 285, 529
Shriver, Eunice Kennedy, 528
Shriver, Sargent, 118, 528
Shultz, George P., 30, 34, 52, 131, 270, 333, 342, 375, 382, 383
Sibour, Jules Henri de, 119
Sidey, Hugh, 264, 266
Siegel, Bernard, 533–534
Sikes, Robert L. F., 225
Silard, John, 201
Sills, Beverly, 514
Simmons, Jeanne B., 132
Simon, Norton, 157
Simon, William E., 16, 22, 30, 334, 342, 343, 434, 526, 535
Simpson, Richard, 431
Sinatra, Frank, 112, 116
Sirica, John J., 49–50, 171
Sisco, Jean, 283
Sisco, Joseph J., 283
Sistrunk, Manny, 315
Sizemore, Barbara A., 278–279, 309
Slack, Carstens, 209
Slichter, Sumner, 340
Smathers, George, 207–208
Smith, C. Arnholt, 61
Smith, Charles E., 533
Smith, Chloethiel Woodard, 283
Smith, Howard K., 77, 265
Smith, Kate, 92
Smith, Margaret Chase, 274
Smith, Mary Louise, 56–57, 161, 277
Solomon, Harold, 102
Spain, Jayne B., 276
Sparkman, John, 116, 150, 231
Spellman, Gladys N., 107
Sprizzo, John, 192
Squier, Robert D., 164
Staats, Elmer Boyd, 53
Staggers, Harley, 498, 502
Stahl, Leslie, 281
Stans, Maurice, 66, 122, 180, 192, 424
Starke, George, 315
Stassen, Harold, 45
Steele, Robert, 141
Stein, Herbert, 275, 333, 335, 342, 418
Stein, Jacob, 192
Steinhilder, August C., 408
Stennis, John, 106, 150, 184, 225
Stephenson, Malvina, 280
Stern, Philip, 251, 530
Sterrett family, 119
Steuart, Guy and L. P., 533
Stevens, George C., Jr., 521–522, 529
Stevens, Jacob W., 132
Stevens, Roger L., 111, 514, 517, 527, 529, 539
Stevenson, Ad'ai, 158, 247, 378
Stevenson, Adlai, III, 155, 369
Stever, H. Guyford, 419
Stewart, Potter, 47, 171, 174, 175
Stock, Robert L., 133
Stoessel, Walter, 238
Stokes, Louis, 302
Stone, Robert S., 478
Stone, W. Clement, 61, 112, 157
Stovall, Lou, 314

Straight, Michael, 514, 520, 529–530, 534
Strauss, Robert S., 56, 161, 378
Stravinsky, Igor, 517
Strickland, Stephen, 474, 479
Strong, Henry, 529
Stroud, Kandy, 280
Strout, Richard (TRB), 269
Stuckey, Williamson S., Jr., 527
Sturtevant family, 119
Sukarno, 232
Sullivan, Leonor K., 277, 288
Sulzberger, Arthur Ochs, 121
Summerfield, Arthur, 507
Sundlun, Bruce, 11
Sundlun family, 120
Surrey, Stanley, 211
Surrey, Walter, 253
Sweig, Martin, 183, 203
Symington, J. Fife, 187
Symington, James, 141
Symington, Stuart, 225, 527, 535
Syphax, Dr. Burke, 309
Syphax, William T. (Tommy), 312, 317
Szulc, Tad, 261

Taft, Robert A., 47, 148, 165, 474
Taft, Robert, Jr., 155, 527
Talmadge, Herman, 150
Tankersley, Ruth (Bazy) M., 530
Taylor, Billy, 308, 514
Taylor, Charley, 315
Taylor, Grace, 283
Taylor, Hobart, 200
Taylor, Hobart, Jr., 122, 309
Taylor, Paul, 522
Taylor, Thomas K., 206
Teeter, Robert M., 164
Teeters, Nancy, 284
terHorst, Jerald F., 17, 38, 40, 262
Terry, Walter, 518
Thayer, Mrs. Robert H., 528
Theis, Paul, 22
Thomas, Alma, 285, 314
Thomas, Charles, 367
Thomas, Fred, 313
Thomas, Helen, 280
Thomas, Lowell, 40
Thomas, Stanley B., Jr., 302
Thompson, Frank, Jr., 71, 518
Thompson, John, 315
Thompson, Llewellyn (Tommy), 238
Thorpe, Merle, 532
Thrower, Randolph, 194
Thurmond, Strom, 145, 231
Tillmon, Johnnie, 304
Timm, Robert D. 205–206, 499
Tobriner family, 120
Todd, Dr. Malcolm, 476–477
Todman, Terence, 302
Toomer, Jean, 307
Townes, Dr. Eva, 310
Train, Russell E., 52, 76, 462, 466, 467, 535
Train family, 119
Travell, Dr. Janet G., 283
Treleaven, Harry, 165
Trotter, Virginia Y., 276, 401
Truitt, Anne, 285
Truman, Bess, 115, 182, 286
Truman, Harry S, 12, 18, 24, 26, 27, 87, 103, 144, 146, 156, 158, 180, 182, 194, 229, 231, 340, 418

Truscott, Nancy, 281
Tucker, Sterling, 59–60, 303
Tudor, Antony, 522
Turner, Carl C., 179
Turner, Jim, 289
Tussing, Arlon, 436
Tydings, Joseph, 214–215

Udall, Morris, 465
Udall, Stewart, 460
Ulasewicz, Tony, 193
Ullman, Al, 149
Unseld, Wes, 315

Valenti, Jack, 395
Vance, Jim, 313
Vandenberg, Arthur, 13
Van Landingham, Marian, 285
Vaughan, Harry, 182
Verrett, Jacqueline, 135
Vesco, Robert, 180, 424
Viguerie, Richard A., 164
Villella, Edward, 514
Vinson, Fred M., 47, 172, 182
Viorst, Judith, 281, 547
Viorst, Milton, 281, 547
Voight, Margaret, 114
Volner, Jill Wine, 192, 281
Voloshen, Nathan M., 183, 203
Volpe, John, 237, 495, 501, 526
von Hoffman, Nicholas, 269

Waddy, Joseph, 309
Walker, Arthur, 132
Walker, Harold, 313
Walker, John, 56, 537
Walker, John T., 311
Walker, Katharine, 537
Walker, William N., 23
Wallace, George, 164
Wallace, Henry A., 442, 444
Wallace, Henry Cantwell, 442
Walsh, Julia M., 283
Walsh, Thomas F., 524
Walter, Francis E., 146
Walters, Barbara, 280
Warnke, Paul C., 194, 417
Warnock, William, 246
Warren, Earl, 171, 173, 174, 175, 185, 321
Warren, George F., 339–340
Warren, Robert Penn, 520
Washington, Bennetta B., 59, 276
Washington, Bill, 313
Washington, George, 80
Washington, Martha, 317
Washington, Walter E., 7, 8, 58–59, 75, 107, 122, 276, 303, 306, 311
Washington family, 119
Watson, Arthur K., 188
Watson, Barbara M., 275
Watson, Dr. Pearl, 310
Wattenberg, Ben, 164
Weaver, Robert, 301, 306, 485
Weaver, Warren, Jr., 173, 191
Weicker, Lowell P., Jr., 527
Weidenfeld, Sheila Rabb, 26
Weinberger, Caspar W., 34, 295, 478, 481
Weinstein, Allen, 372
Weinstein, Bernice, 285
Weintz, Walter, 165
Welles, Ben, 530, 534
Welsing, Dr. Frances, 284, 310
Wentworth, Hazel, 284
Westerman, Sylvia, 281
Westwood, Jean, 161, 277
Wexler, Anne, 165

Whalley, J. Irving, 179, 186
Wheeler, Burton K., 6
White, Byron R., 47, 171, 172, 174, 175, 262, 401
White, F. Clifton, 165
White, George M., 143
White, Dr. Jack, 307, 310
White, Kevin, 164
White, Marjorie E., 280
White, Dr. Paul D., 474
White, Theodore H., 117
Whitehead, Clay, 429, 431
Whitman, Ann C., 276
Whitman, Marina von N., 275
Whitten, Jamie L., 139, 463
Whitten, Les, 270
Whyte, William G., 17, 209, 342
Wickard, Claude R., 442
Wicker, Dr. Henry, 310
Wicker, Tom, 264, 269
Wild, Claude C., Jr., 210
Wilkins, Beriah, 98
Wilkins family, 119
Wilkowski, Jean M., 275
Will, George F., 269
Willard, Beatrice, 276
Willard family, 119, 531
Williams, Dr. Daniel Hale, 306
Williams, Dr. E. Y., 310
Williams, Edward Bennett, 101, 194

Williams, G. Mennen (Soapy), 43
Williams, Harrison A., Jr., 150, 502
Williams, Lorraine, 284
Williams, Bishop Smallwood E., 311
Williams, Mr. and Mrs. Wesley S., Jr., 309
Willkie, Wendell, 13, 49
Willoughby, Dr. and Mrs. Winston Churchill, 122, 317
Wilner family, 120
Wilson, Edward Foss, 528
Wilson, Ernest, Jr., 316
Wilson, John, 303
Wilson, John J., 191, 192
Wilson, Woodrow, 6, 84
Winchester, Lucy, 117
Winslow, Gail H., 283
Winter-Berger, Robert N., 11
Wirtz, Willard, 382
Wise, Helen D., 409
Witteveen, Hendrikus Johannes, 57, 255
Wolf, Warner, 78
Wolf family, 120
Wolfson, Louis E., 179
Wolman, Jerry, 533
Woodcock, Leonard, 15, 381, 385, 388

Woods, Rose Mary, 192, 204, 286
Woodson, Carter, 305
Woodward, Bob, 40, 259, 264
Woodward family, 531
Woodworth, Laurence N., 143
Wooldridge, William O., 179
Wouk, Herman, 92, 121
Wray, Link, 92
Wright, Helen P., 284
Wright, J. Skelly, 284
Wright, Rosemary, 285
Wurf, Jerry, 385, 386
Wyeth, Jamie, 514

Yablonski, Jock, 388
Yankelovich, Daniel, 164
Yeldell, Joseph, 303
Yeutter, Clayton, 448
Yolton, Guy, 164
Young, E. Merl, 182
Young, Jefferson Banks, 302

Zacharias, Ellis, 222
Zahedi, Ardeshir, 117, 247
Zarb, Frank Gustav, 52, 434
Zicarelli, Joseph, 186
Ziegler, Ron, 26, 40, 261, 262
Zlotnick, Mr. and Mrs. Sidney, 116, 122

INDEX OF SUBJECTS

ABC network, 265, 281, 313
Acacia Mutual Life Insurance Co., 98
ACTION, 135, 232
AFL-CIO, 67, 213, 374, 379–389, 466; COPE, 207, 381–383
Agency for International Development, 51, 239, 247, 256
Agricultural Adjustment Administration, 440, 442
Agriculture Department, 86, 126, 232, 253, 290, 344–345, 358, 413, 428, 440, 441–442, 443, 444, 445; Graduate School, 401
Air and Space Museum, 55
Air California, 427
Air Line Pilots union, 376, 392, 503
Air Transport Association, 391, 395, 427, 502
Alibi Club, 119
Allegheny Airlines, 97
Amalgamated Clothing Workers union, 292
American Airlines, 210, 427
American Apparel Manufacturers Association, 396
American Arbitration Association, 166
American Association for the Advancement of Science, 417
American Association of Community Junior Colleges, 407
American Association of Political Consultants, 164, 165
American Association of Retired Persons, 5, 323

American Association of School Administrators, 5, 409
American Association of State Colleges and Universities, 407
American Automobile Association, 5, 204, 502
American Ballet Theater, 518, 521
American Bankers Association, 391, 397
American Bar Association, 68, 116, 184, 295, 391
American Battle Monuments Commission, 126, 232
American Civil Liberties Union, 109, 212, 323, 372
American Council on Education, 407
American Dental Association, 383
American Dry Milk Institute, 393
American Enterprise Institute, 417
American Farm Bureau Federation, 443, 447, 448, 466
American Federation of Teachers, 385, 386, 406, 407
American Feed Manufacturers Association, 447
American Film Institute, 100, 521
American Horse Council, 208
American Hospital Association, 213, 393, 479
American Hot Dip Galvanizers Association, 392

American Institute of Architects, 143, 392, 544, 545
American Insurance Association, 297
American Israel Public Affairs Committee, 254
American Library Association, 408
American Meat Institute, 395, 447
American Medical Association, 393, 470, 472, 474, 480; AMPAC, 207, 213, 215
American National Cattlemen's Association, 446
American Petroleum Institute, 204, 207, 213, 394
American Retail Federation, 283
American Rivers Conservation Council, 464
American Road Builders Association, 204, 501
Americans for Constitutional Action, 206, 212
Americans for Democratic Action, 14, 212
American Society of Composers, Authors and Publishers, 5
American Stock Exchange, 283
American Sugar Cane League, 447
American Textile Manufacturers Institute, 393, 396
American Trucking Associations, 204, 391, 502, 503
American Waterways Operators, 503

Amtrak, 500–501, 502
Anchorage Symphony Orchestra, 521
Animal Health Institute, 446, 447
Apple Pie, 78
Architecture, contemporary, 544–545
Arena Stage, 102, 284, 521
Arent, Fox, Kintner, Plotkin and Kahn, 194
Army Corps of Engineers, 458, 461, 501
Army-McCarthy hearings, 191
Army Museum of Pathology, 89
Arnold and Porter, 193, 253, 281, 303, 309
Arthur D. Little, Inc., 413
Asbestos Workers Union, 376
Ashland Oil Co., 210
Associated Press, 260, 266, 280
Association Executives Club, 391
Association of American Colleges, 407
Association of American College Women, 282
Association of American Railroads, 208, 395, 502
Association of American Universities, 407
Association of Independent Colleges and Schools, 407
Association of Women in Science, 282
AT&T, 313, 327, 429, 430
Atlantic Records, 249
Atlantic Richfield Oil Co., 502
Atomic Energy Commission, 31, 53, 217–218, 275, 412, 429, 435, 437, 461
Australian Meat Board, 107
Aviation Consumer Action Project, 206, 211
Avignone Frères caterers, 117

Bachelors and Spinsters Ball, 120
Back Alley Theater, 284
Bagatelle restaurant, 73
Bailey, Deardourff and Eyre, 164
Ballard and Ballard, 32
Baltimore *Sun*, 17, 276
Baring Brothers, 247
Battelle Memorial Institute, 414
Bay of Pigs affair, 18, 223, 260
Berlin, Roisman and Kessler, 281
Big V supermarkets, 312
Birdseye Co., 286
Black Caucus, 11, 65, 163, 302
Blackman's Development Center, 311
Black Muslims, 311
Black United Fund, 303
Blair House, 27, 87
BLK Group, 312
Board of Trade, 98, 304
Boeing Co., 276, 502
Bogan and Freeland, 195
Bolling plan, 150
Bonus marchers, 85–86
Booked Up, 74
Braniff Airways, 205, 210
Braun's caterers, 117
Bretton Woods, 7, 250

Brookings Institution, 74, 99, 278, 284, 411, 418, 420
Brotherhood of Railway, Airline and Steamship Clerks, 282, 503
Browne, Beveridge, DeGrandi, and Kline, 195
Brown v. *Board of Education of Topeka*, 36, 48, 174, 309, 399
Brunswick Corp., 37
Bryant and Bryant, 310
Budget Bureau, 31, 53, 217, 339, 373, 418
Buckley Amendment, 373–374
Bureau of Economic Analysis, 343
Bureau of Engraving and Printing, 86
Bureau of Indian Affairs, 278, 473
Bureau of Labor Statistics, 343, 363
Bureau of Land Management, 458
Bureau of Mines, 458–459
Bureau of Narcotics and Dangerous Drugs, 232
Bureau of National Affairs, 268
Bureau of Outdoor Recreation, 458
Bureau of Reclamation, 465
Bureau of Sport Fisheries and Wildlife, 458
Burke-Hartke bill, 200, 214, 381
Burning Tree Club, 45, 74, 119, 121, 209
Business Service Centers, 349, 350

Cabinet members, 29–36
Campaign funding legislation, 61
Capital Centre, 77, 100, 101
Capitals hockey team, 101
Capitol Cab cooperative, 312
Capitol City Liquor Co., 312
Capitol Hill Club, 161
Caplin and Drysdale, 195
Carborundum Co., 37
Carl Byoir and Associates, 297
Carlton Club, 209
Carnation Corp., 210
Carnegie Institution, 99, 411, 416–417
Carpet and Rug Institute, 204
Carter Barron Amphitheatre, 100
Cast Iron Soil Pipe Institute, 392
Cave dwellers, 118–120
CBS network, 262, 265, 280, 281, 313
Cellar Door, 123
Census Bureau, 72, 125, 343, 363–365, 370
Center for Law and Social Policy, 201
Center for the Study of Responsive Law, 293
Central Intelligence Agency, 50–51, 124, 126, 218, 220, 222–223, 230, 232, 233, 260, 368
Changing Times, 97, 280, 290
Charles Town race track, 101
"Checkers" episode, 181

Cherry Blossom Festival, 85, 87
Chevy Chase Club, 53, 110, 119, 120, 121
Chicago Symphony Orchestra, 521
Chrysler Corp., 200
Citizens Communications Center, 201
Citizens' Research Foundation, 163
City Tavern, 111, 119
Civil Aeronautics Board, 71, 186, 195, 205, 232, 253, 289, 421, 427–428, 429, 430, 496, 499
Civilian Conservation Corps, 459
Civil Rights Commission, 126, 302, 323, 326, 327, 331
Civil Service Commission, 125, 126, 274, 276, 277, 323, 326, 367, 369
Clayton Act, 421
Clean Air Act, 170, 460, 466
Clean-Rite Maintenance Co., 312
Cleveland Browns, 281
Clifford, Warnke, Glass, McIlwain and Finney, 194, 197
Clyde's, 79, 123
Coalition for a Democratic Majority, 118
Coalition to Stop Strip Mining, 464
Coast Guard, 495, 498; Spars, 277
Cohn and Marks, 195
Colgate-Palmolive Co., 394
Colleges, Washington area, 99
Columbia Country Club, 119
Commerce Department, 85, 198, 232, 345, 352, 413, 435
Commission on Fine Arts, 516
Commission on Postal Reorganization, 507
Committee for Economic Development, 437
Committee for Full Funding of Economic Programs, 405–406, 408
Committee for National Health Insurance, 213
Committee on the Right of Privacy, 37
Committee to Reelect the President, 66, 127, 158, 159, 161, 178, 187, 189, 211, 212, 261, 424
Common Cause, 159, 163, 164, 201, 203, 211–212, 282
Communications Workers union, 376, 379
Community Development Department, HUD, 486
Comsat General Corp., 97
Conference for Women in the Visual Arts, 285
Congress, 137–140. *See also* House Committees; Joint Committees; Senate Committees
and the arts, 519–520; blacks in, 302–303; blocs and parties, 144–145; corruption in, 183–185; decision-making, 145–147; and economy, 336–337; and environment, 465; and foreign

Congress (*Continued*)
policy, 230–231; friends of
business in, 352–353; housekeeping, 143–144; houses of,
150–152; leaders, 41–45,
148–150; and Pentagon,
224–225; and President,
147–148; profile, 140–141;
setting, 152–153; staffs, 141–
143; and transportation, 501–
502; women in, 277–279
Congressional Budget Office,
143, 278
Congressional Directory, 12
Congressional Quarterly, 97,
530
Congressional Record, 34, 75,
79, 184, 250
Congress Watch, 250, 282
Construction Industry Stabili-
zation Committee, 33–34
Consultants, political, 163–
166
Consumer Bill of Rights, 291
Consumer Federation of
America, 289, 293
Consumer Price Index, 343
Consumer Product Safety
Commission, 170, 276, 294,
296, 302, 350, 351, 428, 431
Consumer Protection Agency,
139, 154, 294, 297, 298
Consumers' Research, 291
Consumers Union, 289, 291
Continental Grain, 447
Continental Oil Co., 54, 209
Control Data Corp., 199
Cook Industries, 447
Corcoran, Foley, Youngman
and Rowe, 194
Corcoran Gallery of Art, 72,
89, 103, 117, 285, 515
Corning Glass Works, 209,
327
Cosmos Club, 53, 59, 76, 110,
119, 525
Cost of Living Council, 34,
36, 394
Coudert Brothers, 200
Council of Better Business
Bureaus, 297
Council of Economic Advisers,
16–17, 21, 39, 50, 275, 345,
426
Council of European and
Japanese National Ship-
owners Associations, 253
Council on Environmental
Quality, 53, 276, 457, 461–
462
Country Gentlemen, 100
Courtesy Associates, 283
Covington and Burling, 193,
197, 198, 200, 201, 253,
309, 395, 427
Cox, Langford and Brown,
194, 200, 253
Crazy Horse night club, 78
Crop Reporting Board, 344
Cross-Florida Barge Canal,
464, 465–466
Current Population Survey, 363
Cushman, Darby and Cush-
man, 195
Customs Bureau, 370
Customs Court, 170

Daniels and Houlihan, 253
Danzansky, Borkland, Margolis
and Adler, 195

Dart Drug, 98
Daughters of the American
Revolution, 318
D.C. Black Repertory Com-
pany, 78, 299, 314
D.C. Board of Higher Educa-
tion, 312
D.C. City Council, 107
D.C. Department of Human
Resources, 284
D.C. Registry of Women
Artists, 285
D.C. Repertory Dance Com-
pany, 314
D.C. Striders, 102
D.C. Teachers College, 308
Defense Department, 126, 135,
194, 199, 216–217, 218, 231–
232, 358, 359, 367, 369, 414,
473
Defense Intelligence Agency,
222
Defense Property Disposal
Service, 350
Defense Supply Agency, 350
Defense Systems Acquisition
Review Council, 224
DeFunis case, 176, 330, 400
Delaware Park race track, 101
Delegation of European Com-
munities, 246
Democratic National Com-
mittee, 56, 158, 161, 277,
379
Dilworth, Paxson, Kalish, Levy
and Coleman, 36
Dinosaur National Monument,
464
Diplomats soccer team, 101
Domestic Council, 282, 295,
466
Doors (rock group), 92
Dow Jones, 268, 269
Drug Enforcement Administra-
tion. 168
Drug Fair, 98, 532
Du Pont Co., 193

Economic Policy Board, 22,
334
Economic Research Service,
444
Eddie Leonard Sandwich Shop,
79
Education Commission of the
States, 403
El Caribe, 78
Elections Research Center,
164
Energy Research and Develop-
ment Administration, 17,
434–435, 437
Energy Resources Council,
434, 438
Environmental Action Founda-
tion, 213, 464
Environmental Defense Fund,
464
Environmental Policy Center,
213, 282, 464
Environmental Protection
Agency, 52, 53, 170, 351,
412, 457, 462, 467
Equal Employment Opportun-
ity Commission, 303, 324–
325, 326, 327, 384
Equity Funding Corp., 38
Erie Philharmonic Society,
521

European Economic Com-
munity, 253
Evans and Novak, 206, 257
Evergreen Review, 16, 46
Executive Protective Service,
79
Export-Import Bank, 52, 230,
232, 239, 256, 309

Fair Campaign Practices Com-
mittee, 166
Fairchild Industries, 97–98
Family Assistance Plan, 453
Farmer and Ewing, 195
Farmer Cooperative Service,
445
Farmers Home Administration,
445
Federal Aviation Administra-
tion, 372, 458, 495, 496
Federal Bureau of Investiga-
tion, 51, 89, 127, 130, 168–
169, 366, 369–370, 372
Federal City Club, 121
Federal City Council, 98
Federal Communications Com-
mission, 195, 261, 276, 297,
302, 372, 421, 423, 424, 426,
429, 430
Federal Contract Research
Centers, 414, 415
Federal Crop Insurance Corp.,
445
Federal Deposit Insurance
Corp., 428
Federal Energy Administra-
tion, 17, 52, 232, 434, 435,
437, 466, 503
Federal Highway Administra-
tion, 458, 495, 497
Federal Home Loan Bank
Board, 336, 425, 428, 484
Federal Home Loan Mortgage
Corp., 490
Federal Housing Administra-
tion, 180, 370, 482, 484, 485,
488
Federal Loyalty Security Pro-
gram, 371–372
Federally Employed Women,
282
Federal Maritime Commission,
126, 274, 424, 429, 430, 496,
499
Federal National Mortgage
Association, 484, 490
Federal Power Commission,
195, 297
Federal Register, 351, 374
Federal Railroad Administra-
tion, 495, 498
Federal Reserve Board, 50,
301, 345, 428, 492
Federal Security Agency, 473–
474
Federal-State Reports, 290
Federal Trade Commission,
8, 34, 85, 170, 194, 195, 276,
293, 294–296, 297, 364, 394,
396, 421, 422–423, 424, 425,
499
Federal Wage System, 129
Federal Writers' Program, 515
Federation of Organizations
for Professional Women, 282
Fendrick Gallery, 285
Ferris and Co., 283
Firemen and Oilers Union, 376
Firestone Co., 98, 209
Fivers, the, 120

Fletcher, Heald, Rowell, Kenehan and Hildreth, 195
Florida Atlantic Lines, 186
Flying Tiger Line, 116
Folger, Nolan, Fleming and Douglas, 116
Food and Drug Administration, 71, 132, 289, 291, 297, 394, 412, 415, 428
Food and Drug Law Institute, 446
Food and Nutrition Service, 445
Food for Freedom, 443
Food for Peace Program, 239
Ford Foundation, 415, 417, 418, 437, 521
Ford Motor Co., 37, 58, 98, 209, 255, 298, 327
Ford's Theatre, 102, 284
Foreign Agricultural Service, 445
Foreign Service, 127, 130, 275
Forest Service, 442, 445, 458
Franklin Institute, 416
Freedmen's Hospital, 304, 306, 309
Freer Gallery of Art, 515–516, 542
Fried, Frank, Harris, Shriver and Kampelman, 281, 309
Friends of the Earth, 213, 282, 464

Gadsby and Hannah, 253
Galland, Kharasch, Calkins and Brown, 195, 253
Gallaudet College, 75, 99, 401
Garfinckel, Brooks Brothers, Miller and Rhoads, 98
Garfinckel's 73, 97
General Accounting Office, 53, 326, 416
General Electric Co., 209, 224
General Foods Corp., 273
General Learning Corp., 402
General Mills, Inc., 298, 447
General Motors Corp., 98, 136, 194, 292, 327
General Services Administration, 25, 71, 126–127, 133, 350
Geological Survey, 412
Geophysical Laboratory, 416
George Town Club, 110, 117, 206
Georgetown University, 70, 99, 192, 284, 305, 417
George Washington University, 99, 201, 283, 284, 310
Giant Food, 98, 283, 292, 532
G.I. Bill, 399, 401
Ginsburg, Feldman and Bress, 194
Goodyear Tire & Rubber Co., 210
Government Employees Insurance Co., 98, 532
Government National Mortgage Association, 490
Government Printing Office, 72, 79, 105, 348–349
"Green Book," 122–123
Greenwood's Transfer and Storage Co., 283, 312
Gridiron Club, 280
Grocery Manufacturers of America, 298, 394, 447
Gross national product, 345
Guards, The, 77

Guggenheim Museum, 521
Gulf of Tonkin incident, 414
Gulf Oil Corp., 210
Gutenberg Bible, 105, 543

Hale and Dorr, 191
Hale Observatories, 416
Hanafi Moslems, 311
Hatch Act, 134
Hayden Stone, 52
Head Start, 398, 401
Health, Education and Welfare Department, 73, 95, 125, 126, 132, 276, 278, 294, 301, 302, 336, 343–344, 370, 373, 413, 414, 415, 441, 471–472; Education Division, 401–402; MAC regulation, 476, 478; Office of Civil Rights, 325, 331
Health Insurance Association of America, 479
Health Maintenance Organizations, 473, 476–477
Health Research Group, 211
Heart and Lung Institute, 282
Hecht's, 97, 98
Henri Gallery, 285
Highway Safety Act, 292
Highway Trust Fund, 464, 496, 497, 501, 502
Hill and Knowlton, 73, 204, 283
Hill-Burton Act, 473
Hirshhorn Museum, 55, 76, 89, 516
Hogan and Hartson, 50, 193, 194, 253, 309
Honolulu Academy of Arts, 521
Hot line (Washington-Moscow), 76, 226
House Committees: Administration, 139; Agriculture, 138, 210, 442; Appropriations, 16, 149, 225, 278, Health Subcommittee, 475; Armed Services, 138, 208, 225; Banking and Currency, 138, 277, 501, Subcommittee on Consumer Affairs, 288; Commerce, 502, Subcommittee on Public Health and Environment, 476; District, 107, 302, Appropriations Subcommittee, 107, 302; Education and Labor, 71, 277, 408, 517–518; Foreign Affairs, 141; Government Operations, 278; Internal Security, 138, 371–372; Interstate and Foreign Commerce, 262, 502; Judiciary, 14, 107, 149, 169, 191, 192; Merchant Marine and Fisheries, 277; Monopoly, 31; Post Office and Civil Service, 506; Public Works, 501–502; Rules, 146; Special Subcommittee on Education, 287; Steering and Policy, 138; Ways and Means, 11, 138, 149, 231, 278, 479, 501
House Democratic Caucus, 138, 149, 154
House Democratic Study Group, 149, 162–163
House Republican Conference, 15, 37, 149

House Republican Policy Committee, 44, 149
Housing and Urban Development Department, 88, 89, 95, 127, 180, 258, 302, 309, 343, 370, 415, 416, 482, 485-487
Howard, Poe and Bastian, 281
Howard University, 58, 59, 69, 72, 84, 99, 121, 284, 299, 302, 304, 305–307, 308, 401; Hospital, 309; Law School, 281, 305, 308; Medical School, 284, 309, 310
Howrey, Simon, Baker and Murchison, 195
Hudson Institute, 414

IBM Corp., 6, 97, 430
Immigration and Naturalization Service, 168, 232
Impeachment: of Samuel Chase, 180, 185; of Johnson, 2–3, 185; lobby, 213; and Watergate, 63
Independent Natural Gas Association of America, 395
Indian Claims Board, 129
Indians (drama), 102
Inner City Repertory Dance Co., 521
Institute for Defense Analyses, 414
Institute for Policy Studies, 417
Insurance Workers union, 376
Inter-American Development Bank, 96, 243
Inter-American Tropical Tuna Commission, 245
Interarms, 98
Interior Department, 86, 195, 208, 278, 284, 412, 435, 443
Internal Revenue Service, 85, 180, 188, 195, 350, 358–359, 365–366, 371, 518
International Bank, 98, 532
International Club, 247
International Development Association, 255
International Institute of Sex Identities, 282
International Labor Organization, 245
International Ladies' Garment Workers Union, 282
International Monetary Fund, 4, 6–7, 57, 72, 76, 96, 243, 250, 254–255
International Snowmobile Manufacturers Association, 396
Interstate Commerce Commission, 73, 195, 276, 289, 421, 425–426, 428, 429, 432, 496, 499
ITT Corp., 98, 178, 180, 205, 206, 210, 270, 282, 430
Ivins, Phillips and Barker, 195
Izaak Walton League, 3, 463

Jacob's Ladder, 285
Japan Air Lines, 253
Jefferson Airplane, 92
Jefferson Memorial, 86
Jefferson Place Gallery, 285
Jockey Club restaurant, 118, 247
John Birch Society, 141
John R. Pinkett, Inc., 312
Joint Chiefs of Staff, 220–222, 226

Joint Committees: on Atomic Energy, 150; Economic, 278, 453; on Internal Revenue Taxation, 143

Jones, Day, Reavis and Pogue, 71, 194, 195

Justice Department, 31, 49, 85, 157, 167–168, 192, 215, 232, 254, 309, 325, 365, 422, 429, 430, 432

Kaiser-Permanente health care plan, 476

Kann's, 97

Kefauver-Harris amendments, 290

Kennedy Center for the Performing Arts, 55, 76, 89, 99, 100, 102, 285, 513, 517

Kennedy Stadium, 101

Kimberly-Clark Corp., 298

Kiplinger Washington Letter, 62, 97, 156, 269

Kirlin, Campbell and Keating, 195

Kominers, Fort, Schlefer and Boyer, 195

Koteen and Burt, 77

Ku Klux Klan, 42, 85

Labor Department, 85, 276–277, 325–326, 329–330, 336, 343, 413

Landrum-Griffin Act, 10, 43, 380

Laurel Race Course, 101, 118

Law Enforcement Assistance Administration, 168, 366, 391, 412, 416

Lawson and Lawson, 309

Leadership Conference on Civil Rights, 323

League of Conservation Voters, 213, 464

League of Women Voters, 163, 282

Lee, Toomey and Kent, 195

Leva, Hawes, Symington, Martin and Oppenheimer, 194–195

Lewis & Thos. Saltz, 103

Library of Congress, 86, 99, 105, 284, 306, 307, 543; Congressional Research Service, 73, 153; Coolidge Auditorium, 75; James Madison Library, 89, 153

Lincoln Memorial, 85, 299, 300

Lobbies and lobbying, 203–206; ambassadorial, 252–254; costs and contributions, 206–207; education, 405–410; environment, 213, 463–465; food and farm organizations, 445-449; housing, 491–492; impeachment, 213; labor union, 381–383; medical research, 474; public interest. 211–212; special issue, 210–211, 212–213; transportation, 502–503

Lockheed Aircraft Corp., 224

Loew's Inc., 211

Longshoremen's union, 503

Loomis Sayles and Co., 283

Lord & Taylor, 97

Los Angeles Lakers, 101

Los Angeles *Times,* 15, 17, 37, 259, 267

Lost and Found night club, 78

LTV, Inc., 430

Luck caterers, 117

Lufthansa, 253

Machinists union, 376, 379

Macke Co., 532

Madame Paul's, 123

Madison Square Garden, 101

Maine State Society, 92

Mamas and Papas, 92

Manhattan Laundry and Dry Cleaning, 312

Maritime Administration, 500

Market Opinion Research Co., 164

Marriott Corp., 97

Marshall Field, 53

Marshall Plan, 418

Martha Graham Dance Company, 521

Martin Marietta Corp., 98, 209

Marx Brothers, 101

Maryland Arrows, 101

Mayer, Brown and Platt, 195

Mayo Clinic, 48

McCarran-Walter Immigration Act, 146

McClellan Committee. 380

McDonnell Douglas Corp., 496

McGraw-Hill, 268, 511

McGuire's funeral homes, 312

Mellon (A. W.) Educational and Charitable Trust, 516

Merce Cunningham Company, 521

Metro (subway), 89, 105

Metropolitan Club, 53, 73, 119, 121, 197, 198, 209

Microwave Communications, Inc., 98

Millers' National Federation, 393

Mills-Schneebeli-Packwood bill, 479, 480

MIRVs, 227–228

Mitre Corp., 414

Mr. Henry's, 308

Model Cities program, 486, 490

Monterey, aircraft carrier, 13

Montgomery Ward Co., 298

Morgan, Lewis and Bockius, 195

Morin, Dickstein and Shapiro, 192

Motion Picture Association of America, 395, 521

Motor Vehicles Manufacturers Association, 204, 395

Mudge, Rose, Guthrie and Alexander, 62, 67, 192, 195

Muhammad's Mosque No. 4, 77, 311

Munger, Tolles, Hills and Rickershauser, 35

Museum of African Art, 123, 299, 314

Museum of Modern Art, 521

Nader's Raiders, 293

Nathan's restaurant, 79, 116

National Academy of Sciences, 99, 415–416, 419

National Aeronautics and Space Administration, 277, 412, 458

National Agricultural Chemicals Association, 446, 447

National Air Carrier Association, 502

National Airlines, 427

National Archives, 85, 427

National Assessment of Education Progress, 399, 403

National Association for Mental Health, 284

National Association for the Advancement of Colored People, 16, 48, 58, 212, 304; Legal and Educational Defense Fund, 36, 48, 277, 307

National Association of Counties, 212

National Association of Food Chains, 447

National Association of Home Builders, 323, 392, 491–492

National Association of Manufacturers, 211, 298, 392, 394

National Association of Margarine Manufacturers, 392

National Association of Metal Name Plate Manufacturers, 392

National Association of Realtors, 466

National Association of State Universities and Land-Grant Colleges, 407

National Association of Trade and Technical Schools, 407

National Association of Women Lawyers, 35

National Audio-Visual Association, 408

National Audubon Society, 463

National Ballet, 102, 103, 284, 285

National Bankers Association, 313

National Bank of Washington, 116, 313

National Broiler Council, 446

National Bureau of Economic Research, 50

National Bureau of Standards, 25, 74, 125–126, 296, 413

National Cancer Authority, 477

National Cancer Institute, 477

National Canners Association, 391, 395, 447

National Citizens' Committee for Broadcasting, 424

National Coal Association, 208, 395

National Collection of Fine Arts, 89, 285

National Commission on Water Quality, 463

National Committee for an Effective Congress, 163

National Conservatory of Music, 515

National Consumers League, 289, 290, 292, 293

National Cotton Council of America, 393, 396, 447

National Council of Jewish Women, 278

National Council of Negro Women, 304

National Council of Senior Citizens, 213, 479

National Council on the Arts, 514, 517
National Education Association, 386, 403, 406, 407
National Electrical Contractors Association, 327
National Endowment for the Arts, 55, 89, 285, 513, 518–519, 521, 522
National Endowment for the Humanities, 518
National Environmental Policy Act, 460–461, 466–467
National Farmers Organization, 448
National Farmers Union, 442, 448
National Federation of Business and Professional Women's Clubs, 164
National Football League Players Association, 376
National Forest Products Association, 462, 492
National Gallery of Art, 55, 72, 515, 516
National Geodetic Survey, 412
National Geographic, 97, 531
National Geographic Society, 416
National Grain and Feed Association, 447
National Grange, 448
National Highway Traffic Safety Administration, 495, 497, 501
National Home Study Council, 407
National Horse Show, 101
National Ice Cream Mix Association, 391
National Industrial Traffic League, 503
National Information Center on Political Finance, 163
National Institute for Community Development, 312
National Institute of Education, 404
National Institutes of Health, 99, 212, 307, 413, 472–473, 475, 478, 479
National Journal, 97, 268, 475
National Labor Relations Board, 50, 170, 276, 297, 302, 312, 375, 383–384, 421, 511
National Lawyers Club, 73
National League of Cities, 212
National Marine and Fisheries Service, 413
National Mediation Board, 384
National Military Command Center, 226
National Military Intelligence Center, 226
National Milk Producers Federation, 447
National Observer, 97, 269
National Oceanic and Atmospheric Administration, 457, 458
National Oceanic Survey, 25
National Organization for Women, 3, 213, 282, 323
National Parks and Conservation Association, 463
National Park Service, 23, 24–25, 458

National Planning Association, 417
National Portrait Gallery, 89
National Press Club, 73, 257, 279, 280
National Recovery Administration, 393
National Rifle Association, 203, 204, 214, 392
National Right to Life Committee, 323
National Rural Letter Carrier Association, 510–511
National School Boards Association, 405, 408
National Science Foundation, 414, 419
National Security Agency, 133, 222
National Security Council, 21, 219, 220, 229–230
National Shrine of the Immaculate Conception, 96
National Soft Drink Association, 392, 396
National Student Association, 407
National Student Lobby, 407
National Symphony Orchestra, 7, 71, 99, 102, 285, 529
National Transportation Safety Board, 495, 498
National Treasury Employees Union, 282
National Trust for Historic Preservation, 114, 529
National Turkey Federation, 392
National Urban Coalition, 304
National Welfare Rights Organization, 213, 304
National Wildlife Federation, 463
National Zoological Park, 55, 118
Nation's Business, 97, 268, 532
Natural Resources Defense Council, 201, 464–465
Naval Medical Center, 473
Naval Observatory, 79, 413
NBC network, 264, 280, 281, 313
Neighborhoods, Washington, 94–95
Neiman-Marcus, 97
Nellum, A. L., and Associates, 312
Newark Museum Association, 521
New Deal, 86, 421, 439, 442, 515
New Republic, 97, 269
Newspaper Guild, 376
New Statesman, 247
Newsweek, 97, 269, 280
New York City Ballet, 523
New York Philharmonic Orchestra, 515, 521
New York Shakespeare Festival, 521
New York Stock Exchange, 205, 425, 429
New York Times, 17, 26, 51, 69, 148, 173, 175, 191, 213, 223, 259, 260, 261, 264, 267, 280; *Magazine,* 269
1925 F Street Club, 109, 119
North American Aviation, 132

North Atlantic Treaty Organization, 36, 217
Northern Virginia Aquatic Club, 102

Occidental Petroleum Co., 208
Occupational Safety and Health Administration, 350–351, 391
Office of Consumer Affairs, 276, 294, 297
Office of Defense Mobilization, 55
Office of Economic Opportunity, 21, 36, 88, 135, 415, 416
Office of Education, 401–402, 413, 415
Office of Federal Contract Compliance, 325–326
Office of Management and Budget, 21, 23, 39, 52, 130, 131, 137, 217, 232, 278, 295, 338–339, 466, 478, 479
Office of Price Administration, 62
Office of Production Management, 136
Office of Science and Technology, 418–419
Office of Strategic Services, 50, 54, 223
Office of Technology Assessment, 137, 418
Ofield Dukes and Associates, 313
Omega restaurant, 78
One America Inc., 312
116 Club, 73, 206
Opera Society of Washington, 103
Opinion Research Corp., 165
Organization of American States, 98, 246
Organization of Petroleum Exporting Countries, 230–231, 436
Otrabanda Co., 520
Overseas Private Investment Corporations, 256

Pacific Southwest airlines, 427
Packers and Stockyards Administration, 445
Panama Canal Co., 129
Pan American Union, 78
Pan American World Airways, 205, 329, 499, 504
Papert, Koenig, and Lois, 165
Parvin Foundation, 16
Passport Office, 276
Pattern Makers union, 376
Patton, Boggs, Blow, Verrill, Brand and May, 195, 396
Patuxent Naval Air Station, 132
Peace Corps, 88, 232
Peanut Butter Manufacturers and Nut Salters Association, 391
Penn Central Railroad, 498
Pentagon, 69, 76, 124, 132, 133. *See also* Defense Department, 216–222, 414; chain of command, 226–228; and Congress, 224–225; intelligence gathering, 222–224
Pentagon Papers, 171, 175, 261, 267, 414

Peoples Drug Stores, 98
Peoples Life Insurance Co., 98
Pharmaceutical Manufacturers Association, 204, 395, 476
Philadelphia Orchestra, 513, 521
Philadelphia Plan, 330
Philippine Air Lines, 253
Phillips Collection, 74, 515, 525, 529
Phillips Petroleum Co., 209, 210
Pier Nine, 78
Pierson, Ball and Dowd, 195
Pimlico race track, 101
Plus One, 78
Poor People's March, 60, 89
Postal Inspection Service, 511
Postal Reorganization Act, 294, 511
Postal Service, 95, 126, 134, 505–512; information sharing, 370–371
Post Pavilion, 100
Postum Cereal Co., 285
Potomac Institute, 304, 417
Poultry and Egg Institute, 391
Prather, Levenberg, Seeger and Doolittle, 195
Pratt Institute, 307
President, 10–11; biographical facts, 11–16; and Congress, 147–148; corruption, 181–183
President's Committee on Consumer Interest, 294
President's Science Advisory Committee, 418, 419
Preterm clinic, 284, 530
Pride, Inc., 60, 303
Prince George's County Council, 107
Procter & Gamble, 116, 209
Project Hope, 117
Project Independence, 435
Public Citizen, Inc., 163, 211, 293; Visitors Center, 537
Public Health Service, 473

Quantas, 253
Quaker Oats Co., 298
Quality Inns, 98

Ralston Purina Co., 33, 443, 447
Rand Corp., 31, 33, 217, 414, 416
Rapp, Collins, Stone and Adler, 165
RCA Corp., 98
Reconstruction Finance Corp., 182, 336
Recording Industry Association, 208
Renwick Gallery, 89
Republican Congressional Committee, 16
Republican National Committee, 56, 67, 161, 162, 275, 277
Republic Corp., 35
Reserve Mining Co., 463
Resources for the Future, 411, 417
Restaurants, D.C. area, 546–547
Retail Clerks Union, 376
Reynolds (R. J.) Tobacco Co., 157

Rhodesian Information Office, 244
Ridgewell's Caterers, 75, 117
Ringling Bros. and Barnum & Bailey Circus, 98
Ringling Museum of Art, 521
Ripon Society, 162
Rockefeller Brothers Fund, 55
Rogers and Wells, 200, 253
Roper Organization, 164
Rosecroft race track, 101
Rubber Manufacturers Association, 204
Rubber Workers union, 376
Rural Development Service, 445
Rural Electrification Administration, 442

Sade and Co., 283
St. Lawrence Seaway Development Corp., 495, 498–499
St. Louis *Post-Dispatch,* 267
St. Matthew's Cathedral, 111
St. Vitus Dance, 120
Saks Fifth Avenue, 97
Salary Reform Act, 130
Salomon Brothers, 30
Salt Institute, 392
Sam Harris Associates, 312
Sans Souci restaurant, 72, 123
Schuyler, Birch, Swindler, McKie, and Beckett, 195
Scott Paper Co., 394
Sea Catch restaurant, 103
Seafarers International Union, 157, 503
Seagram distilling company, 312
Sears, Roebuck & Co., 298, 327, 447
Secret Service, 369
Securities and Exchange Commission, 134, 170, 205, 210, 421, 424, 425, 428, 429
Securities Investor Protection Act, 294
Seldom Scene, 100
Senate Committees: Agriculture, 150, 210; Appropriations, 150, Health Subcommittee, 474, 475; Armed Services, 150, 208, 225; Banking, Housing and Urban Affairs, 35, 150, 397, 501; Budget, 150; Commerce, 150, 502, Subcommittee on Consumer Affairs, 288, Subcommittee on Surface Transportation, 502; District, 98, 107, Appropriations Subcommittee, 107; Ethics, 184; Finance, 150, 231, 501; Foreign and Tourism Subcommittee, 502; Foreign Relations, 150, 231, 258, 414; Interior, 150, 436, 460; Judiciary, 150, 169; Labor and Public Welfare, 150, 408, Subcommittee on Health, 475, 476; Public Works, 150, 501; Rules, 14; Subcommittee on Environment and Pollution, 461
Senatorial Campaign Committee, 162
Sharon, Pierson, Semmes, Crolius and Finley, 195
Shell Oil Co., 209
Shenandoah Downs, 101

Sheraton-Carlton Hotel, 121, 198, 209
Sherman Antitrust Act, 421
Shipbuilders Council of America, 503
Sholls Colonial Cafeteria, 72
Show Palace, 78
Shreveport Symphony Orchestra, 521
Sierra Club, 213, 459, 463, 464
Singer Co., 276
Small Business Administration, 351
Smithsonian Institution, 54, 78, 82, 97, 117, 413, 529
Social Security Administration, 343–344, 365, 373, 401, 413, 451, 452
Soil Bank Plan, 443
Soil Conservation Service, 458, 461, 465
Southern Christian Leadership Conference, 59
Southern Railway, 98, 426
Sports, 101–102
Sports International, 102
Sputnik, 416, 418
SST (plane), 415, 419
Standard Oil Co. of California, 329
Stanford Research Institute, 414, 416
State, County and Municipal Workers union, 379, 385, 386
State Department, 25, 69, 79, 222, 233–237, 253, 367; Operations Center, 240–241
State Farm Mutual Automobile Insurance Co., 297
Steptoe and Johnson, 194, 395
Stern Community Law Firm, 201
Stern Family Fund, 201
Stitt, Hemmendinger and Kennedy, 253
Stokely-Van Camp, 33
Stoneman Family, 100
Strategic Arms Limitation Talks, 227–228
Student Loan Marketing Association, 391
Student Nonviolent Coordinating Committee, 303
Subversive Activities Control Board, 261
Subversives lists, 368, 369–370
Sugar Act, 447
Sulgrave Club, 110, 119, 120
Supreme Court, 75, 167, 169, 172–176, 309; justices, 45–49, 171–172
Surrey, Karasik and Morse, 253
Susquehanna River Basin Commission, 126
Sutherland, Asbill and Brennan, 194
Swann case, 176, 331
Swindell-Dressler, 200
Swissair, 253

Taft-Hartley Act, 2, 145, 380
Tariff Commission, 5, 247, 253, 276, 302, 352
Taylor's caterers, 117
Teamsters Union, 386, 388, 503
Teapot Dome scandals, 84–85, 177, 179, 181–182

Tennessee-Tombigbee Waterway, 466
Texaco, Inc., 98, 209
Texas State Society, 92
Thalidomide scandal, 291–292
Theodore Roosevelt Island, 102
3M Corp., 210
Tidal Basin scandal, 138, 149
Time, 67, 262, 269, 280
Timonium race track, 101
Tire Retreading Institute, 392
Tocks Island Dam, 462
Torpedo Factory Art Center, 285
Torrey Canyon, oil tanker, 460
Townsend-Greenspan and Co., 39
Transportation, 105–106, 494–495, 499–503
Transportation Association, 503
Transportation Department, 88, 344, 414, 431, 458, 495–499; National Driver Register, 366
Trans World Airways, 205, 206, 504
Treasury Department, 126, 211, 232, 416, 431, 439

UNESCO, 57
Unemployment compensation, 452
Union Oil Co., 460
Union Pacific Railroad, 54, 495
United Aircraft, 205, 206
United Auto Workers, 15, 327, 376, 379, 381, 388
United Farm Workers, 388
United Mine Workers, 116, 375–376, 385, 388
United Nations, 36, 239, 281, 305, 309
United Press International, 260, 266, 280
Urban Institute, 415
U.S. Beet Sugar Association, 210, 396
U.S. Brewers Association, 391, 395
U.S. Cane Sugar Refiners Association, 210, 396, 447
U.S. Chamber of Commerce, 209, 296–297, 391, 392, 466
U.S. Conference of Mayors, 212
U.S. Information Agency, 195, 301
U.S. News and World Report, 97, 532
U.S. Patent Office, 306
U.S. Railway Association, 495

U.S. Savings and Loan League, 492
U.S. Steel Corp., 17, 37, 98, 209
United Steelworkers, 375, 376
United Transportation Union, 503
University Club, 38
Urban League, 60, 212, 303, 304, 323
Urban Mass Transporation Administration, 495, 497–498

Verner, Liipfert, Bernhard and McPherson, 195
Veterans Administration, 126, 130, 165, 208, 368, 472, 473, 485
Veterans of Foreign Wars, 72
Vietnam Veterans Against the War, 89
VISTA, 88, 276
Voice of America, 74

Wagner Act, 2, 375
Wall Street Journal, 17, 70, 208, 265, 267, 268
Waltz Group, 120
Warren Commission, 16
Washington *Afro-American*, 263
Washington Bullets, 101, 313
Washington Cathedral, 96, 121, 542
Washington Club, 524
Washington Debutante Ball, 120
Washington Golf and Country Club, 79
Washingtonian, 269, 514, 530, 538, 547
Washington International Horse Show, 101
Washington Monthly, 97, 269, 369
Washington Monument, 83–84
Washington Opportunities for Women, 282–283
Washington *Post*, 17, 45, 68, 74, 75, 79, 98, 104, 111, 121, 172, 175, 194, 259, 261, 263, 264, 267, 269, 280, 281
Washington Post Co., 97
Washington Press Club, 279
Washington Redskins, 7, 99, 101, 194
Washington Representatives Group, 209
Washington Senators, 101
Washington Society of Investment Analysts, 283
Washington *Star*, 7, 17, 70, 104, 111, 173, 263, 267, 269, 280, 281, 531

Washington Technical Institute, 307, 308
Washington Theater Club, 103, 284
Washington Women Art Professionals, 285
Watergate: and lawyers, 191–193; and news corps, 261–263; and Nixon, 61–68; and political corruption, 177–179
Welfare, income supplement program, 453
Western Airlines, 205
Westinghouse Corp., 209
West Virginia, battleship, 268
White House Correspondents Association, 280
White House Council on International Economic Policy, 232
White Motors Co., 200
Wichita Symphony Society, 521
Wild and Scenic Rivers Act, 460
Wilderness Act, 460, 461
Wilderness Society, 463
Williams, Connolly and Califano, 194
Wilmer, Cutler and Pickering, 194, 395
Wolf Trap Farm, 100, 285, 529
Women's Air Force, 277
Women's Army Corps, 276
Women's Caucus, 277
Women's Equity Action League, 282
Women's Lobby, 213, 282, 323
Woodmont Country Club, 120, 121
Woodward & Lothrop, 73, 97, 98, 283
Wool Bureau, 396
Workshops for Careers in the Arts, 285
Works Progress Administration, 515
World Bank, 4, 7, 57, 58, 72, 96, 105, 239, 243, 247, 250, 253, 254, 255
World Food Conference, 439

Xerox Corp., 98, 200

Young Americans for Freedom, 162
Young Republican National Federation, 162

Zenith Corp., 298
Zero Population Growth, 464

AH/PS   EG/WS   M

KIPLINGER